Lecture Notes in Computer Science 15952

Founding Editors

Gerhard Goos
Juris Hartmanis

Editorial Board Members

Elisa Bertino, *Purdue University, West Lafayette, IN, USA*
Wen Gao, *Peking University, Beijing, China*
Bernhard Steffen, *TU Dortmund University, Dortmund, Germany*
Moti Yung, *Columbia University, New York, NY, USA*

The series Lecture Notes in Computer Science (LNCS), including its subseries Lecture Notes in Artificial Intelligence (LNAI) and Lecture Notes in Bioinformatics (LNBI), has established itself as a medium for the publication of new developments in computer science and information technology research, teaching, and education.

LNCS enjoys close cooperation with the computer science R & D community, the series counts many renowned academics among its volume editors and paper authors, and collaborates with prestigious societies. Its mission is to serve this international community by providing an invaluable service, mainly focused on the publication of conference and workshop proceedings and postproceedings. LNCS commenced publication in 1973.

Matthieu Rivain · Pascal Sasdrich
Editors

Constructive Approaches for Security Analysis and Design of Embedded Systems

First International Conference, CASCADE 2025
Saint-Etienne, France, April 2–4, 2025
Proceedings

Editors
Matthieu Rivain 📷
CryptoExperts
Paris, France

Pascal Sasdrich 📷
Ruhr University Bochum
Bochum, Germany

ISSN 0302-9743　　　　　　ISSN 1611-3349　(electronic)
Lecture Notes in Computer Science
ISBN 978-3-032-01404-7　　ISBN 978-3-032-01405-4　(eBook)
https://doi.org/10.1007/978-3-032-01405-4

© The Editor(s) (if applicable) and The Author(s), under exclusive license to Springer Nature Switzerland AG 2026

This work is subject to copyright. All rights are solely and exclusively licensed by the Publisher, whether the whole or part of the material is concerned, specifically the rights of translation, reprinting, reuse of illustrations, recitation, broadcasting, reproduction on microfilms or in any other physical way, and transmission or information storage and retrieval, electronic adaptation, computer software, or by similar or dissimilar methodology now known or hereafter developed.
The use of general descriptive names, registered names, trademarks, service marks, etc. in this publication does not imply, even in the absence of a specific statement, that such names are exempt from the relevant protective laws and regulations and therefore free for general use.
The publisher, the authors and the editors are safe to assume that the advice and information in this book are believed to be true and accurate at the date of publication. Neither the publisher nor the authors or the editors give a warranty, expressed or implied, with respect to the material contained herein or for any errors or omissions that may have been made. The publisher remains neutral with regard to jurisdictional claims in published maps and institutional affiliations.

This Springer imprint is published by the registered company Springer Nature Switzerland AG
The registered company address is: Gewerbestrasse 11, 6330 Cham, Switzerland

If disposing of this product, please recycle the paper.

Preface

CASCADE is a new conference, a merger of two well-established events: CARDIS and COSADE. Since 1994, CARDIS has served as the venue for experts from academia, industry, and standardization bodies to discuss advances in the security of smart cards and embedded applications, addressing challenges in areas such as banking, telecommunications, e-passports, and the Internet of Things (IoT). Since 2010, COSADE has provided an international platform focused on side-channel analysis and implementation attacks, secure and efficient hardware/software designs, resilient architectures, and practical evaluation methods. CASCADE unites the legacies of both conferences to foster research and exchange on cryptographic implementations and embedded security. It welcomes contributions from both academia and industry, with a special emphasis on supporting European PhD students through constructive feedback, local engagement, and opportunities to connect with real-world industrial challenges. This first edition of CASCADE was held in Saint-Étienne, France, from April 2 to 4, 2025. It was organized by Université Jean Monnet and took place on the premises of Télécom Saint-Étienne.

CASCADE 2025 adopted a two-phase review process, with the first cycle spanning from submission on October 1, 2024, to notification on November 29, 2024, and the second cycle from December 17, 2024, to February 22, 2025. Each submission was evaluated through a double-blind review, where both authors and reviewers remained anonymous. Each paper received four independent reviews, ensuring a broad and balanced assessment. In line with the IACR policy on conflicts of interest, reviewers did not evaluate papers where recent collaborations or institutional affiliations could bias judgment.

For its first edition, CASCADE received a total of 51 submissions – 17 in the first cycle and 34 in the second. The Program Committee consisted of 36 members, who were supported by 9 external reviewers, producing a total of 197 reviews. Each committee member reviewed between one and two papers during the first cycle, and between three and four in the second. Out of the 51 submissions, 24 papers were accepted – 6 from the first cycle and 18 from the second – which are included in these proceedings and were presented at the conference. This corresponds to an overall acceptance rate of 47.1%, with individual acceptance rates of 35.3% and 52.9% for the first and second cycles, respectively. When necessary, papers underwent a conditional acceptance process, with minor revisions overseen by a Program Committee member acting as shepherd. We would like to sincerely thank the Program Committee members and external reviewers for their time and dedication in reviewing, discussing, and, when needed, shepherding the submissions.

In addition to the presentation of the accepted papers, the CASCADE 2025 program featured three invited talks. Ileana Buhan gave a talk on "Detecting and Mitigating Side-Channel Leaks in Software Implementation: Challenges, Automation, and Tools". Thomas Prest gave a talk on "Masking-Friendly Lattice Schemes and Lattice-Friendly

Masking Schemes". And Chitchanok Chuengsatiansup gave a talk on "CryptOpt: Verified Compilation with Randomized Program Search for Cryptographic Primitives". We warmly thank all three speakers for accepting our invitation and contributing to the conference program.

CASCADE 2025 received financial support from ALPhANOV, Brightsight, CEA Leti, CryptoExperts, eShard, Google, Idemia, Infineon, NewAE, PEPR Cybersécurité, PEPR Quantique, PQShield, Qualcomm, Saint-Étienne Métropole, Siemens, Thales, and Université Jean Monnet. We extend our sincere thanks to our sponsors for their generous contribution to the success of the event.

We would like to thank the General Chairs, Pierre-Louis Cayrel, Brice Colombier, and Vincent Grosso, for their dedicated efforts in organizing a smooth and successful event. Our gratitude also goes to the Steering Committee, Jean-Luc Danger, Vincent Grosso, Thomas Pöppelmann, Werner Schindler, and François-Xavier Standaert, for their trust, guidance, and support in shaping the technical program of this first edition of CASCADE.

May 2025

Matthieu Rivain
Pascal Sasdrich

Organization

General Chair

Pierre-Louis Cayrel   UJM Saint-Étienne, France
Brice Colombier   UJM Saint-Étienne, France
Vincent Grosso   CNRS and UJM Saint-Étienne, France

Program Committee Chairs

Matthieu Rivain   CryptoExperts, France
Pascal Sasdrich   Ruhr-Universität Bochum, Germany

Steering Committee

Jean-Luc Danger   Télécom ParisTech, France
Vincent Grosso   CNRS, France
Thomas Pöppelmann   Infineon Technologies AG, Germany
Werner Schindler   Bundesamt für Sicherheit in der Informationstechnik, Germany
François-Xavier Standaert   UCLouvain, Belgium

Program Committee

Anita Aghaie   Siemens AG, Germany
Melissa Azouaoui   NXP Semiconductors, Germany
Josep Balasch   KU Leuven, Belgium
Julien Béguinot   Télécom ParisTech, France
Sonia Belaïd   CryptoExperts, France
Shivam Bhasin   NTU, Singapore
Olivier Bronchain   NXP Semiconductors, Belgium
Gaëtan Cassiers   UCLouvain, Belgium
Durba Chatterjee   Radboud University, Germany
Elke De Mulder   Google, USA
Viktor Fischer   UJM Saint-Etienne, France
Benedikt Gierlichs   KU Leuven, Belgium

Marc Gourjon   NXP, Germany
Patrick Haddad   Rambus, France
Karine Heydemann   Thales DIS, France
Elif Bilge Kavun   University of Passau, Germany
Ben Marshall   PQShield, UK
Thorben Moos   UCLouvain, Belgium
Nicolai Müller   Ruhr-University Bochum, Germany
Svetla Nikova   KU Leuven, Belgium
Colin O'Flynn   Dalhousie University, Canada
Maximilian Orlt   TU Darmstadt, Germany
Ilia Polian   University of Stuttgart, Germany
Robert Primas   Intel Labs, Austria
Jan Richter-Brockmann   Ruhr-University Bochum, Germany
Thomas Roche   NinjaLab, France
Mélissa Rossi   ANSSI, France
Markku-Juhani O. Saarinen Tampere University, Finland
Patrick Schaumont   Worcester Polytechnic Institute, USA
François-Xavier Standaert UCLouvain, Belgium
Petr Svenda   Masaryk University, Czech Republic
Abdul Rahman Taleb   ANSSI, France
Aleksei Udovenko   University of Luxembourg, Luxembourg
Srinivas Vivek   IIIT Bangalore, India
Gabriel Zaid   Thales ITSEF, France
Rina Zeitoun   IDEMIA, France

Additional Reviewers

Jonas Bertels
Alexandre Berzati
Alex Charlès
Jan-Pieter D'Anvers
Victor Lomné
Jean-Pierre Thibault
Kathrin Wirschem
Lennert Wouters
Liang Zhao

Contents

Attacks on Post-quantum Cryptography

Simple Power Analysis Assisted Chosen Cipher-Text Attack on ML-KEM 3
  Alexandre Berzati, Andersson Calle Viera, Maya Chartouny, and David Vigilant

A Horizontal Attack on the Codes and Restricted Objects Signature
Scheme (CROSS) 27
  Jonas Schupp and Georg Sigl

Improvement of Side-Channel Attacks on Mitaka 45
  Vladimir Sarde and Nicolas Debande

Message-Recovery Horizontal Correlation Attack on *Classic McEliece* 67
  Brice Colombier, Vincent Grosso, Pierre-Louis Cayrel, and Vlad-Florin Drăgoi

Breaking HuFu with 0 Leakage: A Side-Channel Analysis 93
  Julien Devevey, Morgane Guerreau, Thomas Legavre, Ange Martinelli, and Thomas Ricosset

Securing Post-quantum Cryptography

X2X: Low-Randomness and High-Throughput A2B and B2A Conversions
for $d + 1$ Shares in Hardware 119
  Quinten Norga, Jan-Pieter D'Anvers, Suparna Kundu, and Ingrid Verbauwhede

Area Efficient Polynomial Arithmetic Accelerator for Post-quantum
Digital Signatures and KEMs 159
  Dina Kamel and François-Xavier Standaert

Efficient Error Detection Methods for the Number Theoretic Transforms
in Lattice-Based Algorithms 185
  Mohamed Abdelmonem, Lukas Holzbaur, Håvard Raddum, and Alexander Zeh

A Fault-Resistant NTT by Polynomial Evaluation and Interpolation:
Application to ML-KEM and ML-DSA 211
  Sven Bauer, Fabrizio De Santis, Kristjane Koleci, and Anita Aghaie

Homomorphic Encryption and White-Box Cryptography

Hybrid Homomorphic Encryption Resistance to Side-Channel Attacks 235
    Pierugo Pace, Hervé Pelletier, and Serge Vaudenay

White-Box Implementation Techniques for the HFE Family 261
    Pierre Galissant and Louis Goubin

Attacks on Symmetric Cryptography

The Dangerous Message/Key Swap in HMAC 291
    Antoine Wurcker and David Marçais

Practical Second-Order CPA Attack on ASCON with Proper Selection
Function 311
    Viet Sang Nguyen, Vincent Grosso, and Pierre-Louis Cayrel

Side-Channel Attacks

On the Success Rate of Simple Side-Channel Attacks Against Masking
with Unlimited Attack Traces 343
    Aymeric Hiltenbrand, Julien Eynard, and Romain Poussier

A Comparison of Graph-Inference Side-Channel Attacks Against SKINNY 367
    Stian Husum, Håvard Raddum, and Martijn Stam

Physical Security

Robust and Reliable PUF Protocol Exploiting Non-monotonic
Quantization and Neyman-Pearson Lemma 387
    *Neelam Nasir, Julien Béguinot, Wei Cheng, Ulrich Kühne,
    and Jean-Luc Danger*

Towards Package Opening Detection at Power-up by Monitoring Thermal
Dissipation 410
    *Julien Toulemont, Geoffrey Chancel, Frédérick Mailly,
    Philippe Maurine, and Pascal Nouet*

Partial Key Overwrite Attacks in Microcontrollers: A Survey 429
    Pcy Sluys, Lennert Wouters, Benedikt Gierlichs, and Ingrid Verbauwhede

RISC-V

Combined Masking and Shuffling for Side-Channel Secure Ascon
on RISC-V 451
   Linus Mainka and Kostas Papagiannopoulos

A Hardware Design Methodology to Prevent Microarchitectural Transition
Leakages 478
   Mathieu Escouteloup and Vincent Migliore

Machine Learning

Taking AI-Based Side-Channel Attacks to a New Dimension 505
   Lucas David Meier, Felipe Valencia, Cristian-Alexandru Botocan,
   and Damian Vizár

Avenger Ensemble: Genetic Algorithm-Driven Ensemble Selection
for Deep Learning-Based Side-Channel Analysis 532
   Zhao Minghui and Trevor Yap

Improving Leakage Exploitability in Horizontal Side Channel Attacks
Through Anomaly Mitigation with Unsupervised Neural Networks 554
   Gauthier Cler, Sebastien Ordas, and Philippe Maurine

Profiling Side-Channel Attack on HQC Polynomial Multiplication Using
Machine Learning Methods 580
   Tomáš Rabas, Jiří Buček, Vincent Grosso, Karolína Zenknerová,
   and Róbert Lórencz

Author Index 603

Attacks on Post-quantum Cryptography

Simple Power Analysis Assisted Chosen Cipher-Text Attack on ML-KEM

Alexandre Berzati[1], Andersson Calle Viera[1,2], Maya Chartouny[1,3(✉)], and David Vigilant[1]

[1] Thales DIS, Pont-Audemer, France
{alexandre.berzati,andersson.calle-viera,maya.saab-chartouni,
david.vigilant}@thalesgroup.com
[2] Sorbonne Université, CNRS, Inria, LIP6, 75005 Paris, France
[3] Université Paris-Saclay, UVSQ, CNRS, Laboratoire de mathématiques de Versailles, 78000 Versailles, France

Abstract. Recent work proposed by Bernstein *et al.* (from EPRINT 2024) identified two timing attacks, KyberSlash1 and KyberSlash2, targeting ML-KEM decryption and encryption algorithms, respectively, enabling efficient recovery of secret keys. To mitigate these vulnerabilities, correctives were promptly applied across implementations. In this paper, we demonstrate a very simple side-channel-assisted power analysis attack on the patched implementations of ML-KEM. Our result showed that original timing leakage can be shifted to power consumption leakage that can be exploited on specific data. We performed a practical validation of this attack on both the standard and a shuffled implementations of ML-KEM on a Cortex-M4 platform, confirming its effectiveness. Our approach enables the recovery of the ML-KEM secret key in just 30 s for the standard implementation, and approximately 3 h for the shuffled implementation, achieving a 100% success rate in both cases.

Keywords: ML-KEM · Kyber · Lattice-based cryptography · Post-quantum cryptography · Side-channel attacks · Simple power analysis

1 Introduction

Quantum computers represent a major threat to current cryptographic systems. Assuming that powerful enough computers will be available in the future, conventional public key algorithms such as RSA [RSA78] and Diffie-Hellman key exchange [DH76] can be broken by Shor's [Sho94] quantum algorithm. This has led to the development of post-quantum cryptography, which aims to create quantum-resistant algorithms. The National Institute of Standards and Technology (NIST) has standardized four post-quantum cryptography (PQC) algorithms. In the key encapsulation method (KEM) category, ML-KEM [NIS23], derived from Kyber [SAB+22], has been selected as the primary algorithm by the NIST. Its security is based on the module learning with errors problem (MLWE) [LS15].

Side-channel attacks (SCA) exploit the physical implementation of cryptographic systems, such as power consumption, electromagnetic emanation, or timing information to infer secrets. In a recent work [BBB+24], Bernstein et al. reported two timing attacks on ML-KEM named "KyberSlash1" and "KyberSlash2". The first variant targets the division step in the decryption (K-PKE.Decrypt, Algorithm 1), which directly reveals information about the secret key. The second variant targets the division operation in the encryption (K-PKE.Encrypt, Algorithm 1), leaking details about the ciphertext and enabling the construction of a plaintext-checking oracle during decapsulation, allowing key recovery. The results demonstrated that the secret keys could be recovered within a few hours using KyberSlash1 and a few minutes using KyberSlash2. In response to these vulnerabilities, the reference implementation of ML-KEM was quickly updated to counter the KyberSlash attacks. Then, a majority of other open-source implementations integrated the patch as well. Even if the reference implementation is not expected to thwart side-channel analysis other than timing, we show in this paper that these modifications enable a simple side-channel-assisted power analysis attack. The attack presented here remains really practical and achieves full key recovery in approximately 30 s.

Our Contribution. In this article, we will present new results. In fact,

- We analyzed the implementation of a part of the ML-KEM decapsulation procedure following the KyberSlash attacks and confirmed that it results in data-dependent leakage that can be exploited.
- We did a practical demonstration of a chosen ciphertext attack, assisted by simple power analysis, on ML-KEM versions 512, 768, and 1024.
- We also present a detailed attack strategy for a shuffled version of ML-KEM, and its practical demonstration.
- Detailed notebooks are provided. They outline the end-to-end attack that can be reproduced. We also provided a dataset of messages for those who do not have the equipment to perform trace acquisitions for the attack.
- Finally, we showcase how a simple modification to the code of the sensitive function can effectively reduce the leakage without introducing any overhead.

2 Background Information

2.1 Notation

For α an even integer (resp. odd), we define $r' := r \mod^{\pm} \alpha$ the unique $-\frac{\alpha}{2} < r' \leq \frac{\alpha}{2}$ (resp. $-\frac{\alpha-1}{2} \leq r' \leq \frac{\alpha-1}{2}$) such that $r' = r \mod \alpha$.

Let us define a polynomial ring $R = \mathbb{Z}[X]/(X^n + 1)$ with n a power of 2 and $R_q = \mathbb{Z}_q[X]/(X^n + 1)$. We also define R_q^k the module of rank k whose elements are polynomials from R_q.

Polynomials from R_q are denoted by lowercase letters, e.g., $v \in R_q$. We denote matrices and vectors with bold uppercase letters and bold lowercase letters, e.g., $\mathbf{A} \in R_q^{k \times k}$ and $\mathbf{u} \in R_q^k$. Unless otherwise stated, vectors are represented columnwise. Given a matrix $\mathbf{A}$ (resp. a vector $\mathbf{u}$), we denote by $\mathbf{A}^T$ (resp. $\mathbf{u}^T$) its transpose. We denote $\hat{f}$ the NTT representation of f.
For $i \in [0, k[$, the i-th polynomial of a vector $\mathbf{u} \in R_q^k$ will be denoted by $\mathbf{u}_i$.
For $j \in [0, n[$, the j-th coefficient of a polynomial $v \in R_q$ will be denoted by $v[j]$.
$\lceil \cdot \rfloor$ denotes the function that rounds to the nearest integer.

2.2 ML-KEM

ML-KEM [NIS23] is a post-quantum key encapsulation mechanism currently being standardized by NIST. It is derived from CRYSTALS-Kyber [SAB+22], which was selected at the end of the third round of the NIST competition. This scheme is based on lattice cryptography, with its security relying on the difficulty of solving the module learning with errors (MLWE) problem [LS15]. ML-KEM offers three security levels: ML-KEM-512 (corresponding to NIST security level 1), ML-KEM-768 (level 3), and ML-KEM-1024 (level 5).

Compress and Decompress. ML-KEM uses several mechanisms to compress and decompress the size of ciphertexts. The same methods are used to map bits elements to coefficients from $\mathbb{Z}_q$ which allow to recover a message bit even after small noise is added to it. Conversely, we can also map elements from $\mathbb{Z}_q$ to bits using the same methods. Let us describe how they work.
$\mathtt{Compress}_d$ lossily compresses an element from $\mathbb{Z}_q$ to $\mathbb{Z}_{2^d}$ with $2^d < q$:

$$\mathtt{Compress}_d : \mathbb{Z}_q \longrightarrow \mathbb{Z}_{2^d}$$
$$x \longmapsto \left\lceil \frac{2^d}{q} \cdot x \right\rfloor \mod 2^d.$$

$\mathtt{Decompress}_d$ takes an element in $\mathbb{Z}_{2^d}$ and maps it to an element in $\mathbb{Z}_q$.

$$\mathtt{Decompress}_d : \mathbb{Z}_{2^d} \longrightarrow \mathbb{Z}_q$$
$$y \longmapsto \left\lceil \frac{q}{2^d} \cdot y \right\rfloor.$$

Algorithm 1 outlines a simplified view of the key-generation, encryption, and decryption processes of the internal public key encryption algorithm (PKE). SampleA is the function generating a uniformly random matrix $\hat{\mathbf{A}}$ in the NTT domain. SampleB samples coefficients from the centered binomial distribution.

KeyGen. In the KeyGen process, an LWE instance $(\hat{\mathbf{A}}, \hat{\mathbf{t}} = \hat{\mathbf{A}} \cdot \hat{\mathbf{s}} + \hat{\mathbf{e}} \mod q)$ is computed, where $\hat{\mathbf{A}}$ is uniformly generated using a seed ρ, the secret $\hat{\mathbf{s}}$ and the error $\hat{\mathbf{e}}$ are sampled from the same centered binomial distribution. The public key consists of $(\rho, \hat{\mathbf{t}})$, while the secret key is $\hat{\mathbf{s}}$.

Encryption. To encrypt a message m, a vector $\mathbf{y}$ and errors $\mathbf{e}_1$ and e_2 are generated, all drawn from a centered binomial distribution. Two LWE instances are then constructed, which (up to some details) are represented as $(\mathbf{A}^T \mathbf{y} + \mathbf{e}_1, \mathbf{t}^T \mathbf{y} + e_2)$. Next, μ is computed as $\lceil \frac{q}{2} m \rfloor$ and added to the right-hand side of the pair. Finally, the resulting pair $(\mathbf{u}, v)$ is compressed into $(\mathbf{c}_1, c_2)$.

Algorithm 1. K-PKE

1: **K-PKE.KeyGen**(d)
2: $\quad (\rho, \sigma) \leftarrow G(d \| k)$
3: $\quad \hat{\mathbf{A}} \leftarrow \texttt{SampleA}(\rho)$
4: $\quad \mathbf{s} \leftarrow \texttt{SampleB}(\sigma, coins_0)$
5: $\quad \mathbf{e} \leftarrow \texttt{SampleB}(\sigma, coins_1)$
6: $\quad \hat{\mathbf{s}} \leftarrow \text{NTT}(\mathbf{s})$
7: $\quad \hat{\mathbf{e}} \leftarrow \text{NTT}(\mathbf{e})$
8: $\quad \hat{\mathbf{t}} \leftarrow \hat{\mathbf{A}} \circ \hat{\mathbf{s}} + \hat{\mathbf{e}}$
9: **return** $\left(\text{ek}_{\text{PKE}} = (\hat{\mathbf{t}} \| \rho), \text{dk}_{\text{PKE}} = (\hat{\mathbf{s}}) \right)$

10: **K-PKE.Encrypt**$(\text{ek}_{\text{PKE}}, m, r)$
11: $\quad \hat{\mathbf{A}} \leftarrow \texttt{ExpandA}(\rho)$
12: $\quad \mathbf{y} \leftarrow \texttt{SampleB}(r, coins_2)$
13: $\quad \mathbf{e}_1 \leftarrow \texttt{SampleB}(r, coins_3)$
14: $\quad e_2 \leftarrow \texttt{SampleB}(r, coins_4)$
15: $\quad \hat{\mathbf{y}} \leftarrow \text{NTT}(\mathbf{y})$
16: $\quad \mathbf{u} \leftarrow \text{NTT}^{-1}(\hat{\mathbf{A}}^T \circ \hat{\mathbf{y}}) + \mathbf{e}_1$
17: $\quad \mu \leftarrow \texttt{Decompress}_1(\texttt{ByteDecode}_1(m)) = \lceil \frac{q}{2} m \rfloor$
18: $\quad v \leftarrow \text{NTT}^{-1}(\hat{\mathbf{t}}^T \circ \hat{\mathbf{y}}) + e_2 + \mu$
19: $\quad \mathbf{c}_1 \leftarrow \texttt{Compress}_{d_u}(\mathbf{u})$
20: $\quad c_2 \leftarrow \texttt{Compress}_{d_v}(v)$
21: **return** $\mathbf{c} = (\mathbf{c}_1 \| c_2)$

22: **K-PKE.Decrypt**$(\text{dk}_{\text{PKE}}, \mathbf{c})$
23: $\quad \mathbf{u}' \leftarrow \texttt{Decompress}_{d_u}(\mathbf{c}_1)$
24: $\quad v' \leftarrow \texttt{Decompress}_{d_v}(c_2)$
25: $\quad w \leftarrow v' - \text{NTT}^{-1}(\hat{\mathbf{s}}^T \circ \text{NTT}(\mathbf{u}'))$
26: $\quad m \leftarrow \texttt{Compress}_1(w)$
27: **return** m

Decryption. To decrypt, the values $(\mathbf{u}', v')$ are first recovered from $(\mathbf{c}_1, c_2)$, with $\Delta_{\mathbf{u}} = \mathbf{u}' - \mathbf{u}$ and $\Delta_v = v' - v$ representing the differences between the received and original values. The decryption procedure then computes $w = v' - s^T \mathbf{u}'$, serving as an approximation of the message polynomial. Specifically, we have:

$$\begin{aligned}
w &= v' - \mathbf{s}^T \mathbf{u}' \\
&= v + \Delta_v - \mathbf{s}^T (\mathbf{u} + \Delta_\mathbf{u}) \\
&= \mathbf{t}^T \mathbf{y} + e_2 + \mu + \Delta_v - \mathbf{s}^T (\mathbf{A}^T \mathbf{y} + \mathbf{e}_1 + \Delta_\mathbf{u}) \\
&= (\mathbf{As} + \mathbf{e})^T \mathbf{y} + e_2 + \mu + \Delta_v - \mathbf{s}^T (\mathbf{A}^T \mathbf{y} + \mathbf{e}_1 + \Delta_\mathbf{u}) \\
&= \mu + \left(\mathbf{e}^T \mathbf{y} + e_2 + \Delta_v - \mathbf{s}^T \mathbf{e}_1 - \mathbf{s}^T \Delta_\mathbf{u} \right) \\
&= \left\lceil \frac{q}{2} m \right\rfloor + \varepsilon
\end{aligned} \tag{1}$$

where $\varepsilon = \mathbf{e}^T \mathbf{y} + e_2 + \Delta_v - \mathbf{s}^T \mathbf{e}_1 - \mathbf{s}^T \Delta_\mathbf{u}$ is the noise. The approximate polynomial w is decoded into the message m, one bit at a time using the function $\texttt{Compress}_1$. Informally, it can be described as follows: if a given coefficient of the polynomial $w[i]$ is within the range $[q/4, 3q/4[$, then $m_i = 1$; otherwise, $m_i = 0$.

KEM. The CPA-secure PKE is converted into a CCA-secure KEM using the well-known Fujisaki-Okamoto (FO) transformation [FO99] and is described in Algorithm 2.

Algorithm 2. ML-KEM

1: **procedure ML-KEM.KeyGen**(d,z)
2:     $(\text{ek}_{\text{PKE}}, \text{dk}_{\text{PKE}}) \leftarrow \texttt{K-PKE.KeyGen}(d)$
3:     $\text{ek} \leftarrow \text{ek}_{\text{PKE}}$
4:     $\text{dk} \leftarrow (\text{dk}_{\text{PKE}} \parallel \text{ek} \parallel H(\text{ek}) \parallel z)$
5: **return** (ek, dk)

6: **procedure ML-KEM.Encaps**(ek,m)
7:     $(K, r) \leftarrow G(m \parallel H(\text{ek}))$
8:     $\mathbf{c} \leftarrow \texttt{K-PKE.Encrypt}(\text{ek}, m, r)$
9: **return** $(K, \mathbf{c})$

10: **procedure ML-KEM.Decaps**(dk,$\mathbf{c}$)
11:     $m' \leftarrow \texttt{K-PKE.Decrypt}(\text{dk}_{\text{PKE}}, \mathbf{c})$
12:     $(K', r') \leftarrow \texttt{SHA3}(m' \parallel h)$
13:     $\bar{K} \leftarrow \texttt{SHAKE256}(z \parallel \mathbf{c})$
14:     $\mathbf{c}' \leftarrow \texttt{K-PKE.Encrypt}(\text{ek}_{\text{PKE}}, m', r')$
15:     **if** $\mathbf{c} \neq \mathbf{c}'$ **then**
16:         $K' \leftarrow \bar{K}$
17: **return** K'

2.3 Simple Power Analysis

Side-channel attacks exploit unintended information emitted from devices activity, such as timing, electromagnetic (EM) emissions, or power consumption, to infer secret information. One of the most accessible forms of SCA, and certainly the most visually intuitive, is Simple Power Analysis (SPA). SPA leverages distinct fluctuations in power consumption, or EM traces to differentiate the operations performed by a device. Compared to other types of SCA, an SPA requires minimal equipment, is relatively little invasive, and can necessitate only a few traces to perform the attack. When dealing with cryptographic operations SPA focuses on analyzing the traces of a device to extract information about secret data.

A well-known example of SPA is the attack on the square-and-multiply algorithm, commonly used in modular exponentiation. This algorithm's sequence of squaring (bit to 0 and bit to 1) and conditional multiplication (only bit to 1) reveals patterns in the power traces depending on the bit values of the exponent. By observing these power variations, an attacker can deduce the entire secret exponent bit by bit.

Such an example demonstrates that even the simplest SCA can be remarkably powerful in recovering secret information. In the following, we will show how to use an SPA to recover the full secret ML-KEM secret key with only three traces.

2.4 Prior Work

CCA Assisted with SCA. The FO transform offers guaranteed security against chosen-ciphertext attacks (CCA). However, for real-life implementations, an attacker can access side-channel information during the process, which can be used as a distinguisher to mount hybrid SCA assisted CCA. Without loss of generality, we will explain the general methodology when applied to ML-KEM-512, but the type of attack applies to the other two security levels as well.

Let us recall that the secret key vector $\mathbf{s} \in R_q^k$ is of the form:

$$\forall i \in [0, k[,\ \mathbf{s}_i = \mathbf{s}_i[0]X^0 + \mathbf{s}_i[1]X^1 + \cdots + \mathbf{s}_i[n-1]X^{n-1}.$$

For ML-KEM-512, we have $\eta_1 = 3$, so $\forall j \in [0, n[,\ \mathbf{s}_i[j] \in [-3, 3]$.

The ciphertext is of the form $c = (c_1, c_2)$ and in the decryption procedure we have $\mathbf{u}' = \text{Decompress}_{d_u}(c_1) \in R_q^k$ and $v' = \text{Decompress}_{d_v}(c_2) \in R_q$ where:

$$\forall i \in [0, k[,\ \mathbf{u}'_i = \mathbf{u}'_i[0]X^0 + \mathbf{u}'_i[1]X^1 + \cdots + \mathbf{u}'_i[n-1]X^{n-1},\ \text{and}$$

$$v' = v'[0]X^0 + \cdots + v'[n-1]X^{n-1}.$$

For ML-KEM-512, we have $k = 2$, i.e., $\mathbf{s} = (\mathbf{s}_0, \mathbf{s}_1)$ and $\mathbf{u}' = (\mathbf{u}'_0, \mathbf{u}'_1)$.

In the decryption procedure inside the decapsulation, we compute:

$$w = v' - \mathbf{s}^T \mathbf{u}'. \qquad (2)$$

Let us denote by $V \in \mathbb{Z}_q$ and $U \in \mathbb{Z}_q$ two carefully chosen values[1] such that $\mathbf{u}' = (UX^0, 0)$ and $v' = VX^0 + \cdots + VX^{n-1}$.

Figure 1a shows a visualization of the computation of w for a normal ciphertext while Fig. 1b shows the same computation for a chosen ciphertext.

---

[1] U is chosen to scale the possible values of $\mathbf{s}$ just enough to be at the border $\frac{q}{4}$ or $\frac{3 \times q}{4}$. Then, adding different V allows us to distinguish the correct value.

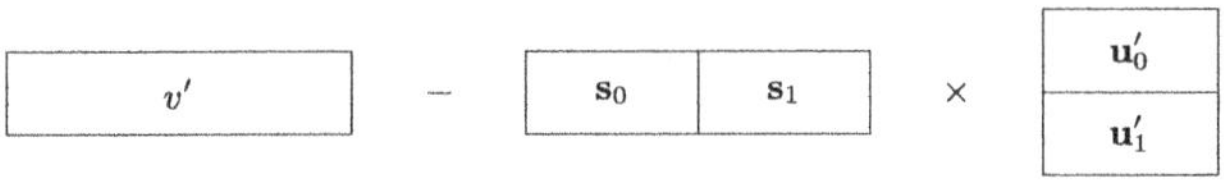

(a) A normal valid ciphertext.

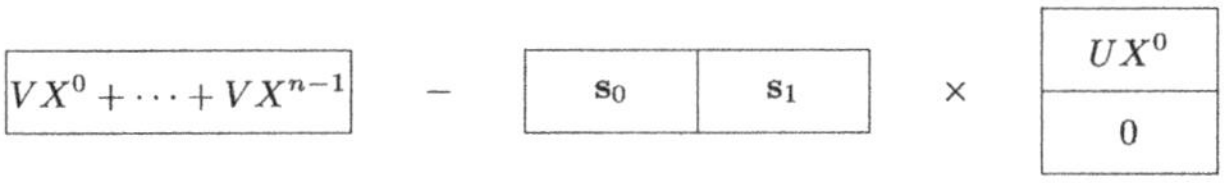

(b) A crafted ciphertext.

Fig. 1. Decryption equation computed when different type of ciphertext are used.

For the second case, which typically corresponds to some type of ciphertext chosen by an attacker, we can further develop equation (2) as follows:

$$\begin{aligned} w = v' - \mathbf{s}^T \mathbf{u}' &= VX^0 + \cdots + VX^{n-1} - \mathbf{s}_0 \times UX^0 \\ &= VX^0 + \cdots + VX^{n-1} - \left(U\mathbf{s}_0[0]X^0 + \cdots + U\mathbf{s}_0[n-1]X^{n-1}\right) \\ &= (V - U\mathbf{s}_0[0])X^0 + \cdots + (V - U\mathbf{s}_0[n-1])X^{n-1}. \end{aligned} \tag{3}$$

After decoding this quantity onto the message bits, each coefficient can only take one of two values, 0 or 1, depending on the values of the message polynomial. More precisely, for $j \in [0, n[$, the message coefficient $w[j] = V - U\mathbf{s}_0[j]$ is decoded into the message bit $m[j] = \text{Compress}_1(w[j])$. Based on its possible values, we are able to infer two conditions on the coefficients of the secret polynomial $\mathbf{s}_0$:

- If $m[j] = 1$ we know that $(V - U\mathbf{s}_0[j]) \in [q/4, 3q/4[$.
- If $m[j] = 0$ we know that $(V - U\mathbf{s}_0[j]) \in [0, q/4[\cup[3q/4, q[$.

Thus, the knowledge of the value of the bit $m[j]$ for different tuples U, V can be used as a binary distinguisher for the possible values of $\mathbf{s}_0[j] \in [-3, 3]$. For successive carefully chosen ciphertext, this method allows to recover the entire secret key. Different variants of this attack exist in the literature [BDH+19, QCZ+21, XPR+22, RBRC22, SCZ+23, RRD+23, TUX+23, RRCB20]. The main difference being the number of bits of the message that can be recovered per query to the decapsulation procedure and the operation targeted by the attack.

KyberSlash. In a recent work [BBB+24], Bernstein et al. proposed a timing attack on ML-KEM. The core idea is to exploit non constant time divisions on certain platforms. They proposed two variants, "KyberSlash1" and "KyberSlash2".

The first variant targets the division step in the decryption (K-PKE.Decrypt 1):

```
t = (((t << 1) + KYBER_Q/2)/KYBER_Q) & 1;
```

Since t can be a coefficient of the message m, leakage on this value can be exploited by an attacker to gain sensitive information. By crafting specific ciphertexts, this variable execution time can be used to recover the entire secret key.

The second variant targets the division step in the encryption (K-PKE.Encrypt 1):

```
t[j] = ((((uint16_t)u << 4) + KYBER_Q/2)/KYBER_Q) & 15;
```

For this attack, timing leakages reveal details about the ciphertext and enable the construction of a plaintext-checking oracle during decapsulation, allowing full key recovery.

The results demonstrated that the secret keys could be recovered reliably within a few hours using KyberSlash1 and a few minutes using KyberSlash2. To counter this attack, dedicated modifications were made to the reference implementation of the ML-KEM. However, as we will show later, these modifications enable a simple side-channel attack assisted with chosen ciphertext attack.

3 New Theoretical Leakage

In this section, we highlight a new potential leakage arising from the new implementation of the polynomial compression in the decryption after "KyberSlash1". We briefly start by explaining the differences between the specification of the compression routine and its implementation. Then, we present the post-"KyberSlash1" implementation, followed by an analysis of the newly generated leakage.

3.1 Difference Between Specification and Implementation

The ML-KEM specification, Algorithm 2, uses a generic compression function as defined in Sect. 2.2. From an algorithmic perspective, this allows to set parameters d_u, d_v, and 1 to compress **u**, v, and the message polynomial w, respectively. However, in practice, the implementation separates these cases into: polyvec_compress for compressing the vector **u**, poly_compress for compressing the polynomial v, and, poly_tomsg for compressing the message polynomial w. Furthermore, rounding is performed on coefficients in $]-1664, 1664]$, meaning:

- $m[j] = 1$ if $w[j] \in \,]-1664, -832[\, \cup\, [832, 1664[$.
- $m[j] = 0$ if $w[j] \in [-832, 832[$.

In the next section, we will focus on the poly_tomsg implementation to describe the new attack path.

3.2 Post-KyberSlash poly_tomsg Implementation

The KyberSlash attacks [BBB+24] led the authors of the reference implementation to release a patched version[2] which became the new standard across multiple

---

[2] https://github.com/pq-crystals/kyber/commit/bc8e640727b5178eb1c65867d6ba65 99b3ad88e5.

```c
1  void poly_tomsg(uint8_t msg[KYBER_INDCPA_MSGBYTES],
2                  const poly *a){
3    unsigned int i,j;
4    uint32_t t;
5    for(i=0;i<KYBER_N/8;i++) {
6      msg[i] = 0;
7      for(j=0;j<8;j++) {
8        t  = a->coeffs[8*i+j];
9        t <<= 1;
10       t += 1665;
11       t *= 80635;
12       t >>= 28;
13       t &= 1;
14       msg[i] |= t << j;
15     }
16   }
17 }
```

Fig. 2. C Code of the new poly_tomsg implementation.

implementations such as [KSSW22,KPR+,BDK+,KLJJ]. Figure 2 presents the updated implementation of the poly_tomsg function.

One of the modifications addressed the critical division by q, which on some platforms, was not constant-time and therefore vulnerable to timing attacks, as highlighted in "KyberSlash1". To resolve this, the updated implementation adopts an approach inspired by Barrett reduction, i.e., approximating the division by q using a precomputed constant. Specifically, for a given a, the division $\frac{a}{q}$ is approximated by computing $\frac{(a \times x)}{2^s}$, where $x = \left\lceil \frac{2^s}{q} \right\rceil$. If $\frac{x}{2^s}$ is a sufficiently accurate approximation of $\frac{1}{q}$, the results remain identical. This method offers two significant advantages. First, it avoids the need to normalize values back to the positive range $\mathbb{Z}_q$. Second, it replaces costly and potentially insecure division operations with efficient multiplications and bit-shifts, which are constant-time and thus secure.

In the patched ML-KEM implementation, the authors chose $s = 28$ resulting in $x = \left\lceil \frac{2^{28}}{q} \right\rceil = 80635$, as shown line 13 of Fig. 2.

3.3 Newly Generated Leakage

Our analysis started by observing that from Fig. 2, the decoding of the message involves a lot of arithmetic operations involving signed and unsigned data. Since q is relatively small, we decided to enumerate, for all the possible values of a message, the Hamming Weights (HW) resulting from each C step of poly_tomsg. This result is illustrated in Fig. 3.

First, we observe two distinct classes of HW based on whether the coefficient is negative or positive, which is expected due to the two's complement

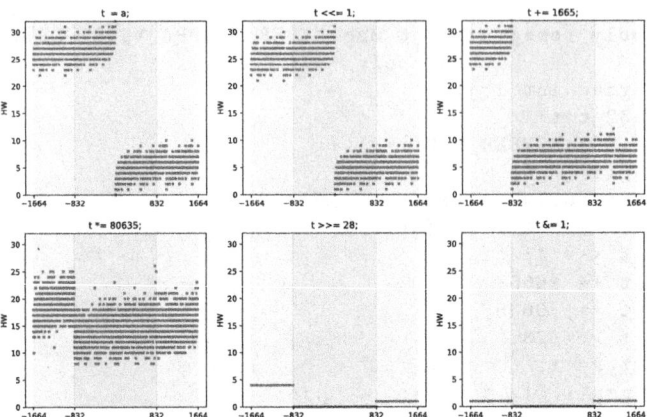

Fig. 3. HW evolution given the steps of the `poly_tomsg` function, (■: coefficients rounded to 0, □: coefficients rounded to 1).

representation of negative values. Then, shifting right by 1 doesn't produce significative change in the HW. Next, when 1665 is added to the coefficient, a noticeable difference in HW is visible between negative coefficients in the range of $]-1664, -832[$ and all the remaining coefficients. After multiplying each coefficient by 80635, a slight difference remains visible between these two classes. Finally, extracting the bit 28 also produces difference in HW which is expected since we want to recover a bit sign from coefficients rounded to 0 and 1.

In the following, we have chosen to focus the analysis on negative messages since it allows to exhibit two classes with strong difference in HW. The first class contains coefficients of the message in the range $[-832, 0[$ and the second class contains coefficients in the range $]-1664, -832[$.

Figure 4 illustrates the effect of shifting by 1 and adding 1665 on the coefficient t for the first class. Similarly, Fig. 5 shows this effect for the second class.

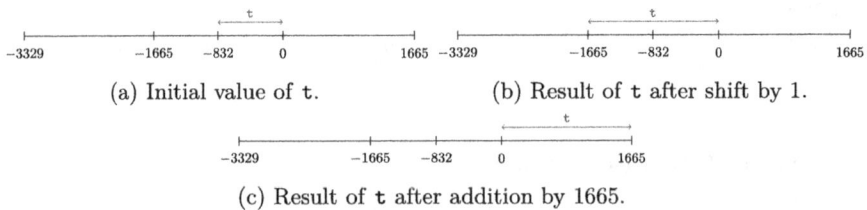

Fig. 4. Representation of steps in lines 11 and 12 from Fig. 2 for $t \in [-832, 0[$.

For the first case, the coefficients initially in the $[-832, 0[$ are transformed into positive values within the range $]0, 1664[$ at the end of the addition by 1665. However, for the second case, after the addition, the coefficients in the range

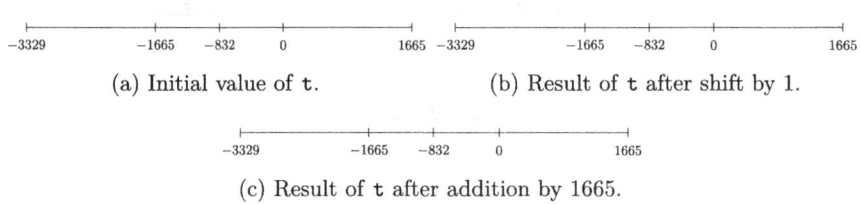

Fig. 5. Representation of steps in lines 11 and 12 from Fig. 2 for $t \in\,]-1664, -832[$.

$]-1664, -832[$ are transformed into negative values within the range $]-1664, 0[$.

Consequently, the clear HW difference between the two classes is explained because in the first class the negative coefficients become positive and in the second class the negative coefficients remain negative. This clear difference in HW from negative values rounded to 0 and rounded to 1 could potentially be observable on side channel traces, where either power consumption or electromagnetic emissions are directly linked to the HW of values.

This work builds upon the idea presented by Tosun et al. [TMS24], who first investigated leakage vulnerabilities arising from central reduction operations in lattice-based cryptographic schemes. Specifically, they exploit the differences in Hamming weight between coefficients in the range $\left[-\frac{q}{2}, 0\right[$ and those in the range $\left[0, \frac{q}{2}\right]$, which produces two distinct classes of coefficients. We extend this observation on a specific implementation. We highlight the leakage amplification caused by the transition from negative values in the range $\left[-\frac{q}{2}, 0\right[$ into a positive value in the range $\left[0, \frac{q}{2}\right]$ over a single instruction. As we will see in the sequel, this unique targeting leads to a simple and efficient attack.

4 Exploiting the New Leakage

Having established a clear HW difference between the two classes, in Sect. 4.3 we first perform a t-test to confirm the difference between negative coefficients rounded to 0 and negative coefficients rounded to 1. We then demonstrate its practical exploitation on the poly_tomsg function. As seen in Sect. 2.4, side-channel information can be used as an oracle to mount hybrid SCA assisted CCA targeting the decapsulation procedure.

4.1 Experimental Setup

The evaluation was done on a ChipWhisperer-Lite 32-bit [OC14], with an STM32F3 micro-controller. We chose this target as it is often used in academic research targeting embedded systems. We used the ChipWhisperer built-in FPGA to perform the acquisition of the power consumption traces at 4 samples per cycle. We targeted the C reference implementation from [BDK+] as it is the default one that serves as a base layer for most of the other implementations. We compiled the ML-KEM-512 version using gcc-arm cross-compiler arm-none-eabi-gcc 12.2.1, with the option -Os. The trace analysis and statistical testing is done in Python, using the "numpy" [HMvdW+20] and "scipy" [VGO+20] packages. All the materials used to capture and process the traces, as well as the complete attack, will soon be available as Jupyter notebooks.

4.2 Identifying Operation

The first step is to precisely identify the location where the 256 coefficients are processed within the `poly_tomsg` function. In a non-profiled setting, detecting clear repeating patterns in the power consumption trace is helpful for building an attack as straightforward as possible.

In Fig. 6a, we can observe the same repeating pattern occurring 32 times, each one spanning around 500 samples. Those patterns should correspond to the `for` loop line 5 of the C code in Fig. 2. Figure 6b corresponds to a zoomed view on the first 510 samples. We can see repeating patterns, specifically 8 of them, which have been highlighted for better visibility. Looking at the C code in Fig. 2 allows to identify those patterns to the second `for` loop line 7.

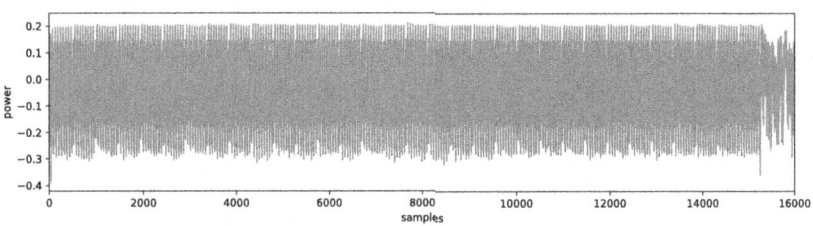

(a) 10 traces for complete `poly_tomsg` execution on 16000 samples.

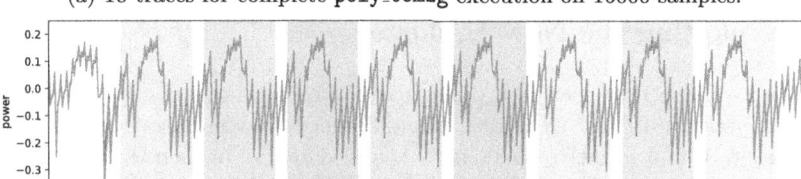

(b) 10 traces for `poly_tomsg` execution zoomed on the 8 first coefficients.

Fig. 6. 10 power consumption traces for random inputs of `poly_tomsg`.

Each of the identified colored patterns correspond to the execution of the assembly code snippet shown in Fig. 7.

According to our analysis in Sect. 3.3, the instructions that should provide side-channel information should be the `addw` and perhaps the `muls`. Prior work

```
 1 ...
 2 ldrsh.w  r3, [r4], #2           ; t = a->coeffs[8*i+j];
 3 ldrb.w   ip, [r0]
 4 lsls     r3, r3, #1             ; t <<= 1;
 5 addw     r3, r3, #1665          ; t += 1665;
 6 muls     r3, r7                 ; t *= 80635;
 7 ubfx     r3, r3, #28, #1        ; t >>= 28; and t &= 1;
 8 lsls     r3, r1
 9 adds     r1, #1
10 orr.w    r3, r3, ip
11 cmp      r1, #8
12 strb     r3, [r0, #0]
13 ...
```

Fig. 7. Assembly code on Cortex-M4.

often exploits the leakage produced from the right shift by 28 but in our case due to the the compiler optimization flag -Os, this shift and the next and are actually merged into an ubfx instruction. The direct extraction of the bit 28 could result in less visible leakage in this case. Having clearly identified the targeted operation, we can now start the attack.

4.3 Building Reference Means

In all the rest, we consider $i \in [0, k[$ and $j \in [0, n[$. Following our previous notations, during the decapsulation algorithm, within the poly_tomsg, we compute $w = v' - \mathbf{s}^T \mathbf{u}'$ as described in Eq. 3.

Our objective is to determine two sets of U and V coefficients such that $w_j = V - U\mathbf{s}_i[j]$ is negative and has a specific rounding regardless of the value of the secret in $[\![-\eta_1, \eta_1]\!]$. For the first set we want all the message's coefficients to be rounded to 0, which we will refer to as $\mathcal{D}_0$. For the other set, we want all the message's coefficients to be rounded to 1 and it will be denoted by $\mathcal{D}_1$.

For $\mathcal{D}_0$, we set V as the center of the interval $[-832, 0[$, i.e., $V = -416$. For U, we must select a value that ensures w_i remains within $[-832, 0[$ regardless of the secret's value. Therefore, we choose U such that $-832 < -416 + \mathbf{s}_i[j]U < 0$, i.e., $|U| < 416 \cdot \frac{1}{\eta_1}$. For our attack we restrict the values to $0 < U < 416 \cdot \frac{1}{\eta_1}$.

Similarly, for $\mathcal{D}_1$, we set $V = -1248$ as the center of the interval $]-1664, -832[$, and we also choose U such that $0 < U < 416 \cdot \frac{1}{\eta_1}$.

Note that the chosen values of U and V for $\mathcal{D}_0$ and $\mathcal{D}_1$ correspond to their decompressed forms. However, the compressed representations of U and V must be sent to the decapsulation algorithm, where they will be decompressed to match the specified values. In other words, we are looking for a y such that:

$$0 < \text{Decompress}_{d_u}(y) = U < 416 \cdot \frac{1}{\eta_1}.$$

Table 1 summarizes the possible ciphertexts to build $\mathcal{D}_0$ and $\mathcal{D}_1$ depending on the security version of ML-KEM.

Table 1. Ciphertexts used for the attack on ML-KEM.

	$\mathcal{D}_0$		$\mathcal{D}_1$	
	U max	V	U max	V
ML-KEM-512	137	−416	137	−1248
ML-KEM-768	205	−416	205	−1248
ML-KEM-1024	206	−416	206	−1248

Based on Table 1, for ML-KEM-512, we have $137 = \mathtt{Decompress}_{10}(42)$; for ML-KEM-768, we have $205 = \mathtt{Decompress}_{10}(63)$; and for ML-KEM-1024, we have $206 = \mathtt{Decompress}_{11}(127)$.

T-test Between Values. To determine if there is a difference between the class $\mathcal{D}_0$ and $\mathcal{D}_1$ we performed a *specific t-test* as specified in [GJJR11,SM15]. We collected 42 power consumption traces on the ChipWhisperer for both classes. Figure 8 represents 10 traces among the 42 for each class, together with the corresponding t-test result.

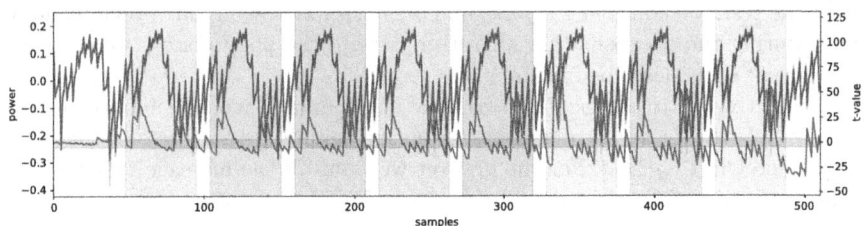

Fig. 8. 10 traces for each class and t-test (■: coefficients from $\mathcal{D}_0$, □: coefficients from $\mathcal{D}_1$, ■: t-test result).

Here, we can see that each pattern shows a significant t-value at the beginning and at the end of each window, indicating potentially exploitable leakage.

Figure 9 highlights the 57 samples corresponding to the 256 coefficients from the `poly_tomsg` function, superposed in the same figure. In addition to the t-test results, this confirms clear differences between the traces of coefficients from $\mathcal{D}_0$ and coefficients from $\mathcal{D}_1$, specifically between the samples 5 and 12.

Therefore, for each dataset we compute the mean between the samples 5 and 12, denoted as $\mathcal{M}_0$ and $\mathcal{M}_1$. These respective means will be used as references to test for coefficients rounded to 0 and for coefficients rounded to 1 respectively.

```
 1 ...
 2 ldrsh.w  r3, [r4], #2         ; t = a->coeffs[8*i+j];
 3 ldrb.w   ip, [r0]
 4 lsls     r3, r3, #1           ; t <<= 1;
 5 addw     r3, r3, #1665        ; t += 1665;
 6 muls     r3, r7               ; t *= 80635;
 7 ubfx     r3, r3, #28, #1      ; t >>= 28; and t &= 1;
 8 lsls     r3, r1
 9 adds     r1, #1
10 orr.w    r3, r3, ip
11 cmp      r1, #8
12 strb     r3, [r0, #0]
13 ...
```

Fig. 7. Assembly code on Cortex-M4.

often exploits the leakage produced from the right shift by 28 but in our case due to the the compiler optimization flag -Os, this shift and the next and are actually merged into an ubfx instruction. The direct extraction of the bit 28 could result in less visible leakage in this case. Having clearly identified the targeted operation, we can now start the attack.

4.3 Building Reference Means

In all the rest, we consider $i \in [0, k[$ and $j \in [0, n[$. Following our previous notations, during the decapsulation algorithm, within the poly_tomsg, we compute $w = v' - \mathbf{s}^T \mathbf{u}'$ as described in Eq. 3.

Our objective is to determine two sets of U and V coefficients such that $w_j = V - U\mathbf{s}_i[j]$ is negative and has a specific rounding regardless of the value of the secret in $[\![-\eta_1, \eta_1]\!]$. For the first set we want all the message's coefficients to be rounded to 0, which we will refer to as $\mathcal{D}_0$. For the other set, we want all the message's coefficients to be rounded to 1 and it will be denoted by $\mathcal{D}_1$.

For $\mathcal{D}_0$, we set V as the center of the interval $[-832, 0[$, i.e., $V = -416$. For U, we must select a value that ensures w_i remains within $[-832, 0[$ regardless of the secret's value. Therefore, we choose U such that $-832 < -416 + \mathbf{s}_i[j]U < 0$, i.e., $|U| < 416 \cdot \frac{1}{\eta_1}$. For our attack we restrict the values to $0 < U < 416 \cdot \frac{1}{\eta_1}$.

Similarly, for $\mathcal{D}_1$, we set $V = -1248$ as the center of the interval $]-1664, -832[$, and we also choose U such that $0 < U < 416 \cdot \frac{1}{\eta_1}$.

Note that the chosen values of U and V for $\mathcal{D}_0$ and $\mathcal{D}_1$ correspond to their decompressed forms. However, the compressed representations of U and V must be sent to the decapsulation algorithm, where they will be decompressed to match the specified values. In other words, we are looking for a y such that:

$$0 < \mathtt{Decompress}_{d_u}(y) = U < 416 \cdot \frac{1}{\eta_1}.$$

Table 1 summarizes the possible ciphertexts to build $\mathcal{D}_0$ and $\mathcal{D}_1$ depending on the security version of ML-KEM.

Table 1. Ciphertexts used for the attack on ML-KEM.

	$\mathcal{D}_0$		$\mathcal{D}_1$	
	U max	V	U max	V
ML-KEM-512	137	−416	137	−1248
ML-KEM-768	205	−416	205	−1248
ML-KEM-1024	206	−416	206	−1248

Based on Table 1, for ML-KEM-512, we have $137 = \texttt{Decompress}_{10}(42)$; for ML-KEM-768, we have $205 = \texttt{Decompress}_{10}(63)$; and for ML-KEM-1024, we have $206 = \texttt{Decompress}_{11}(127)$.

T-test Between Values. To determine if there is a difference between the class $\mathcal{D}_0$ and $\mathcal{D}_1$ we performed a *specific t-test* as specified in [GJJR11,SM15]. We collected 42 power consumption traces on the ChipWhisperer for both classes. Figure 8 represents 10 traces among the 42 for each class, together with the corresponding t-test result.

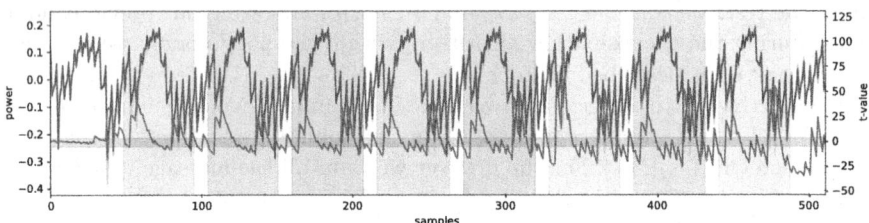

Fig. 8. 10 traces for each class and t-test (■: coefficients from $\mathcal{D}_0$, □: coefficients from $\mathcal{D}_1$, ■: t-test result).

Here, we can see that each pattern shows a significant t-value at the beginning and at the end of each window, indicating potentially exploitable leakage.

Figure 9 highlights the 57 samples corresponding to the 256 coefficients from the poly_tomsg function, superposed in the same figure. In addition to the t-test results, this confirms clear differences between the traces of coefficients from $\mathcal{D}_0$ and coefficients from $\mathcal{D}_1$, specifically between the samples 5 and 12.

Therefore, for each dataset we compute the mean between the samples 5 and 12, denoted as $\mathcal{M}_0$ and $\mathcal{M}_1$. These respective means will be used as references to test for coefficients rounded to 0 and for coefficients rounded to 1 respectively.

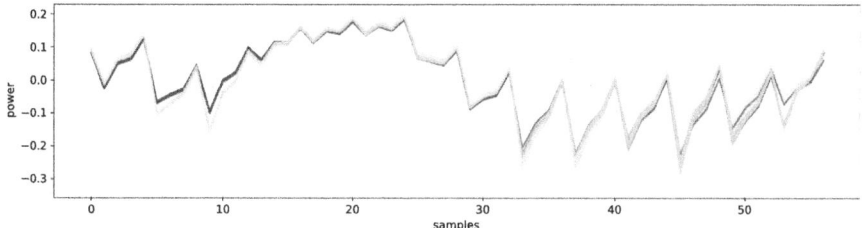

Fig. 9. Samples of the 256 coefficients of poly_tomsg superposed (■: coefficients from $\mathcal{D}_0$, □: coefficients from $\mathcal{D}_1$).

4.4 Recovering the Secret Key

With the reference means $\mathcal{M}_0$ and $\mathcal{M}_1$ established for the datasets $\mathcal{D}_0$ and $\mathcal{D}_1$, respectively, we can now exploit crafted ciphertexts to determine whether each coefficient of the message will be rounded to 0 or 1. This distinguisher provides direct information on the secret key. In fact, we can adaptively select malicious ciphertexts to partition the set of possible values of the secret key coefficient. Accumulating a sufficient number of these queries allows to recover the exact secret key coefficient.

Choice of U and V. We need to find malicious ciphertexts that provide information on the secret key. To achieve this, we use the strategy from [RRD+23] and adapt it to our use case. Note that, as we have seen on Fig. 9, we can distinguish between negative coefficients rounded to 0 and negative coefficients rounded to 1.

Figure 10 and Fig. 14 depicts the successive queries exploiting this difference, depending on the level of ML-KEM targeted, the attack step and the rounded values previously detected.

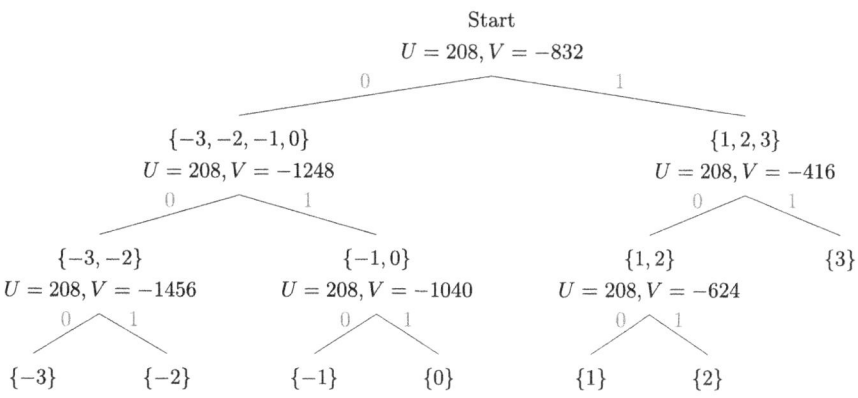

Fig. 10. Query tree for ML-KEM-512 with $\eta_1 = 3$.

For instance, in the case of ML-KEM-512, at the beginning of the attack we know that $s_j[i] \in \{-3, -2, -1, 0, 1, 2, 3\}$. We start by sending the crafted ciphertext corresponding to $U = 208$ and $V = -832$ to the decapsulation procedure. Then, in the decapsulation we compute $w[i] = V - Us_j[i] = -832 - 208s_j[i]$. If $s_j[i] \in \{-3, -2, -1, 0\}$ then $-832 \leq w[i] < 0$ and therefore will be rounded to 0. If $s_j[i] \in \{1, 2, 3\}$ then $-1664 < w[i] < -832$ and therefore will be rounded to 1. So now we have partitioned the possible values of $s_j[i]$ depending on the result given from our distinguisher. We continue in the same manner until we have only one possibility for the secret coefficient targeted. We can repeat this procedure until we find all the coefficients of the secret key. In practice, since the coefficients are independent and because the coefficient U stays the same throughout the whole process, we can recover all 256 coefficients of the secret in parallel by taking $v = V + VX^1 + \ldots + VX^{n-1}$, as detailed in Eq. 3.

4.5 Attack Validation

We compute the euclidean distance with respect to $\mathcal{M}_0$ and $\mathcal{M}_1$ and we choose the minimal value as a metric to determine whether a new trace corresponds to a coefficient rounded to 0 or to 1.

Number of Traces. To construct the means, we can perform $\text{Decompress}_{d_u}(416 \cdot \frac{1}{\eta_1})$ possible queries for each dataset, $\mathcal{D}_0$ and $\mathcal{D}_1$. For instance, for ML-KEM-512, it takes around 4 minutes on our setup to collect the traces for each dataset. After that, since we are targeting the 256 coefficients of the secret key in parallel, we will use the windows from the 256 coefficients per query resulting in $256 \times \text{Decompress}_{d_u}(416 \cdot \frac{1}{\eta_1})$ sub-traces to construct each mean.

Moreover, we need 3 traces to recover all the 256 coefficients of a polynomial of the secret key,. Therefore, we need $3 \times k$ traces to recover the entire secret key. For instance, for ML-KEM-512, it takes around 30s on our setup.

Success Rate. To assess the performance of our attack, we decided to test it on the 10 first keys of the KAT files for each security level of ML-KEM. We have found a 100% success rate each time. Table 2 summarizes the attack performance for each security level of ML-KEM.

Table 2. Summary of our results.

	Nb of traces $\mathcal{M}_0$	Nb of traces $\mathcal{M}_1$	Nb of attack traces	Success rate
ML-KEM-512	42	42	6	100%
ML-KEM-768	63	63	9	100%
ML-KEM-1024	127	127	12	100%

5 Application to Shuffled Implementation of `poly_tomsg`

Shuffling is a simple and low cost countermeasure that increases the number of traces required to perform a side-channel attack. Practical implementations often use the Fisher-Yates algorithm [Dur64] which is an efficient and robust method to create a random permutation.

5.1 Adapting the Attack Strategy

Figure 15 shows a proof of concept implementation of a shuffled `poly_tomsg` function using the Fisher-Yates algorithm to produce a permutation denoted `index`. This permutation is used as the index of the polynomial a being compressed. Even though the order in which we store the message bits is random, we can still exploit the same leakage as before by making some adjustments to our attack. However, in this scenario, we can no longer perform the attack in parallel due to the shuffling and so each coefficient must be targeted individually.

The attack proceeds as before, by first constructing the reference means $\mathcal{M}_0$ and $\mathcal{M}_1$, as detailed in Subsect. 4.3. For each coefficient of the secret key, the attacker performs queries to recover its value. This time, initial values U and V are sent to the decapsulation algorithm to count the total number of coefficients rounded to 1, establishing a baseline reference denoted $\mathcal{N}_0$. The attacker then modifies U and V, repeats the query, and observes the updated count 1 denoted $\mathcal{N}_1$. Based on these results, the attacker can compare $\mathcal{N}_0$ and $\mathcal{N}_1$ and determine the current position in the corresponding attack tree Fig. 11 for ML-KEM-512 or

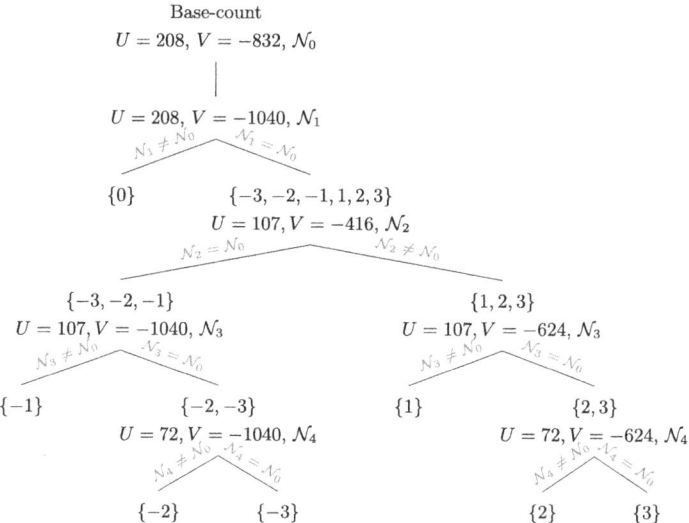

Fig. 11. Query tree for ML-KEM-512 with $\eta_1 = 3$, $\mathcal{N}_i$ denotes the number of coefficients of w rounded to 1.

Fig. 16 for the other security level. At each step, this allows to refine the possible values of the secret coefficient and allows to select the next U and V values to send with a new query. This process is iterated until a leaf is reached and only one possible secret coefficient is left. An attacker has to repeat this search for all the $256 \times k$ coefficients, to recover the secret key.

Figure 11 and Fig. 16 depict the successive queries to perform to recover one secret coefficient depending on the ML-KEM security level targeted, the attack step and the rounded values previously detected.

5.2 Attack Validation

Again, we compute the euclidean distance with respect to $\mathcal{M}_0$ and $\mathcal{M}_1$ and we choose the minimal value to determine wether a new trace corresponds to a coefficient rounded to 0 or to 1.

Number of Traces. Following the same procedure described in Sect. 4.5, we will also need $\texttt{Decompress}_{d_u}(416 \cdot \frac{1}{\eta_1})$ traces to construct the means. However, to recover the entire secret key, we need at most 5 queries per coefficient of each polynomials. Therefore, we need at most $5 \times 256 \times k$ queries for ML-KEM-512 and at most $4 \times 256 \times k$ queries for ML-KEM-768 and ML-KEM-1024, to recover the entire secret key. However, in practice the number of queries is significantly reduced since the most frequently occurring value in the secret key is 0, which only needs 2 queries for each security level of ML-KEM. In practice, for ML-KEM-512, it took around 2 hours and 30 minutes on oursetup to recover the secret key.

Success Rate. To assess the performance of our attack, we decided to test it on the first key of the KAT files for each security level of ML-KEM. We guessed the entire secret key each time with no error. Table 3 summarizes the attack performance for each security level of ML-KEM.

Table 3. Summary of our results on the shuffled version.

	Nb of traces $\mathcal{M}_0$	Nb of traces $\mathcal{M}_1$	Nb of attack traces (worst case)	Success rate
ML-KEM-512	42	42	2 560	100%
ML-KEM-768	63	63	3 072	100%
ML-KEM-1024	127	127	4 096	100%

6 Reducing the Leakage Without Overhead (for Cortex M4)

From our observation of Fig. 2, one main source of leakage comes from the sign change involved by the addition at line 12. One simple way to minimize it is to invert order of the addition and multiplication (respectively lines 12 and 13) so that the multiplication spreads on the most significant bits and reduces the impact of the sign change due to the addition. We intuited that this simple switch could lead to a more gradual differentiation between the two datasets, $\mathcal{D}_0$ and $\mathcal{D}_1$, rather than the abrupt change currently observed.

Figure 12 provides a visual representation of how this modification affects the evolution of the HW across all potential values of a message coefficient.

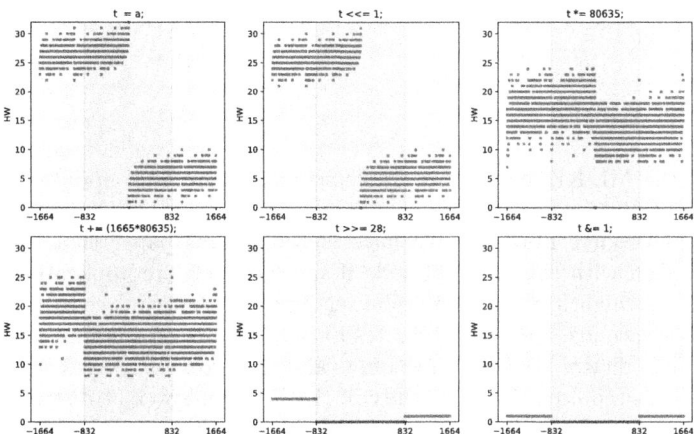

Fig. 12. Coefficient's HW evolution given the computation steps , (■: coefficients rounded to 0, □: coefficients rounded to 1).

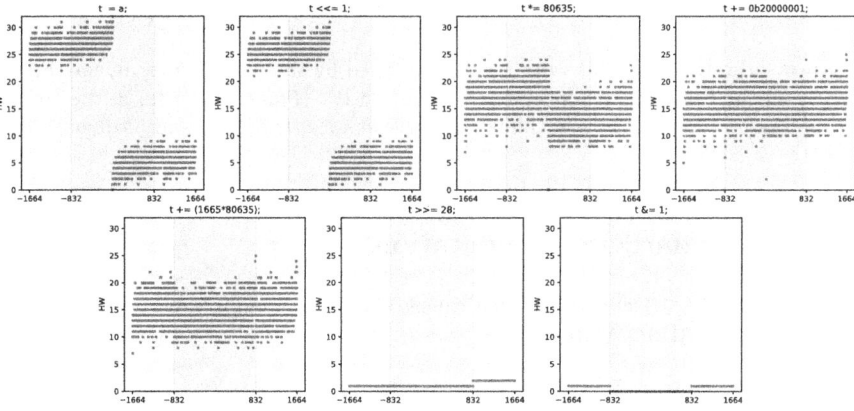

Fig. 13. HW evolution given the steps of the poly_tomsg function, (■: coefficients rounded to 0, □: coefficients rounded to 1).

The difference between the two datasets has been reduced but it is important to note that this trick is not ultimate. Some remaining slight difference still exists and might be enough to mount an SCA. To ensure formal resistance to SCA, only a rigorous masked implementation must be used. When considering the low cost proposed countermeasure, the bit we want to extract, encoding the rounding of the coefficient, is located at the position 28. This positioning leaves us with sufficient space to introduce a constant to change the HW of the value, either into the three most significant bits or into some of the least significant bits, as long as this modification does not cause an overflow (carry) or an underflow (borrow) (Fig. 13).

7 Conclusion

Recently, the ML-KEM reference implementation has been updated to thwart the KyberSlash threat, and this source code has been rapidly integrated into various open-source libraries. We have shown in this paper that special care must be taken with this piece of code if side channels are applicable. We have presented a straightforward Simple Power Analysis that can recover the private key in a few seconds, and a few minutes in the presence of shuffling. We describe a simple and efficient strategy since only valid ciphertext is needed, and no clone open device is required. From a study of the Hamming weight distributions, we have highlighted the origin of the leakage. We exploit a sign change during the instruction flow within the KyberSlash updated code. The advantage is that if the right dedicated ciphertexts are used, averaging classes can be realized without knowing the device's private key. We showed that a simple adjustment to the source code can significantly reduce this leakage, all while maintaining efficiency with zero overhead. However, the proposed low-cost update does not, in theory, completely defeat side-channel analysis. A rigorous masked implementation must be used to achieve formal resistance when side channels are applicable.

Acknowledgements. This work has been funded by the French government (France 2030) and the European union - Next Generation EU (France Relance) in the context of the Resque project. We also thank the reviewers for their time and feedback.

A Other Security Levels Query Tree for Attack on Standard Implementation

Figure 14 details all the successive queries used to mount our attack on ML-KEM-768 and ML-KEM-1024.

B Shuffled Implementation of `poly_tomsg`

We give in Fig. 15 the shuffled implementation of the `poly_tomsg` that we targeted in Sect. 5.

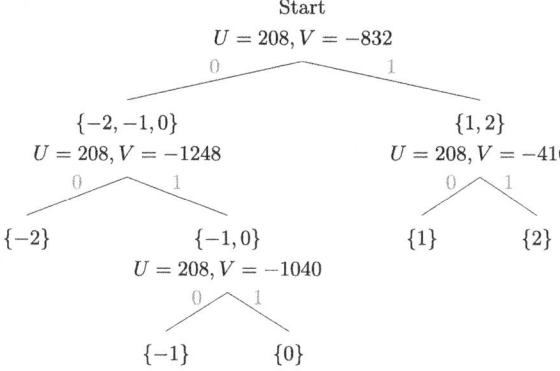

Fig. 14. Query tree for ML-KEM-768 and ML-KEM-1024 with $\eta_1 = 2$.

```
1  static uint8_t index[KYBER_N] = {0, 1, ..., 254, 255}
2
3  void shufflepoly_tomsg(uint8_t msg[KYBER_INDCPA_MSGBYTES],
4                        const poly *a){
5    unsigned int i,j;
6    uint32_t t;
7    unsigned int temp, random_index, s_i, s_j;
8    for(i = KYBER_N - 1; i>=1; --i) {
9      randombytes(&random_index, 1);
10     random_index = random_index%(i + 1);
11     temp = index[i];
12     index[i] = index[random_index];
13     index[random_index] = temp;
14   }
15   for(i = 0; i < KYBER_INDCPA_MSGBYTES; i++){
16     msg[i] = 0;
17   }
18   for(i=0;i<KYBER_N/8;i++) {
19     for(j=0;j<8;j++) {
20       temp = index[8*i+j];
21       s_i = temp>>3;
22       s_j = temp&0x7;
23       t   = a->coeffs[temp];
24       t <<= 1;
25       t += 1665;
26       t *= 80635;
27       t >>= 28;
28       t &= 1;
29       msg[s_i] |= t << s_j;
30     }
31   }
32 }
```

Fig. 15. C Code of the shuffled poly_tomsg implementation.

C Other Security Levels Query Tree for Attack on Shuffled Implementation

Figure 16 details all the successive queries used to mount our attack on the shuffled versions of ML-KEM-768 and ML-KEM-1024.

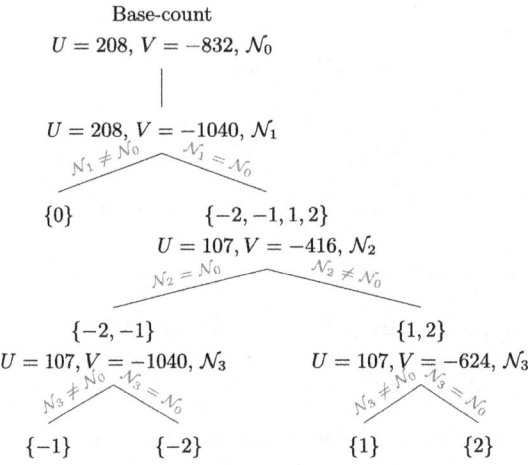

Fig. 16. Query tree for ML-KEM-768 and ML-KEM-1024 with $\eta_1 = 2$, $\mathcal{N}_i$ denotes the number of coefficients of w rounded to 1.

References

[BBB+24] Bernstein, D.J., et al.: Kyberslash: exploiting secret-dependent division timings in kyber implementations. IACR Cryptol. ePrint Arch., 1049 (2024)

[BDH+19] Băetu, C., Durak, F.B., Huguenin-Dumittan, L., Talayhan, A., Vaudenay, S.: Misuse attacks on post-quantum cryptosystems. In: Ishai, Y., Rijmen, V. (eds.) EUROCRYPT 2019. LNCS, vol. 11477, pp. 747–776. Springer, Cham (2019). https://doi.org/10.1007/978-3-030-17656-3_26

[BDK+] Bos, J., et al.: Kyber official implementation. https://github.com/pq-crystals/kyber

[DH76] Diffie, W., Hellman, M.E.: New directions in cryptography. IEEE Trans. Inf. Theory **22**(6), 644–654 (1976)

[Dur64] Durstenfeld, R.: Algorithm 235: random permutation. Commun. ACM **7**(7), 420 (1964)

[FO99] Fujisaki, E., Okamoto, T.: Secure integration of asymmetric and symmetric encryption schemes. In: Wiener, M. (ed.) CRYPTO 1999. LNCS, vol. 1666, pp. 537–554. Springer, Heidelberg (1999). https://doi.org/10.1007/3-540-48405-1_34

[GJJR11] Goodwill, G., Jun, B., Jaffe, J., Rohatgi, P.: A testing methodology for side channel resistance validation. In: NIST Non-Invasive Attack Testing Workshop, National Institute of Standards and Technology (2011)

[HMvdW+20] Harris, C.R., et al.: Array programming with NumPy. Nature **585**(7825), 357–362 (2020)

[KLJJ] Kannwischer, M.J., Lim, T., Jones, R., Jones, N.: MLKEM-C-EMBEDDED optimized for embedded microcontrollers. https://github.com/pq-code-package/mlkem-c-embedded

[KPR+] Kannwischer, M.J., Petri, R., Rijneveld, J., Schwabe, P., Stoffelen, K.: PQM4: post-quantum crypto library for the ARM Cortex-M4. https://github.com/mupq/pqm4

[KSSW22] Kannwischer, M.J., Schwabe, P., Stebila, D., Wiggers, T.: Improving software quality in cryptography standardization projects. In: IEEE European Symposium on Security and Privacy, EuroS&P 2022 - Workshops, Genoa, Italy, 6–10 June 2022, pp. 19–30. IEEE Computer Society, Los Alamitos (2022)

[LS15] Langlois, A., Stehlé, D.: Worst-case to average-case reductions for module lattices. Des. Codes Crypt. **75**(3), 565–599 (2015)

[NIS23] NIST. FIPS 203: Module-lattice-based key-encapsulation mechanism standard. Federal Inf. Process. Stds. (NIST FIPS), National Institute of Standards and Technology, Gaithersburg, MD (2023). https://nvlpubs.nist.gov/nistpubs/FIPS/NIST.FIPS.203.pdf

[OC14] O'Flynn, C., Chen, Z.D.: ChipWhisperer: an open-source platform for hardware embedded security research. In: Prouff, E. (ed.) COSADE 2014. LNCS, vol. 8622, pp. 243–260. Springer, Cham (2014). https://doi.org/10.1007/978-3-319-10175-0_17

[QCZ+21] Qin, Y., Cheng, C., Zhang, X., Pan, Y., Hu, L., Ding, J.: A systematic approach and analysis of key mismatch attacks on lattice-based NIST candidate KEMs. In: Tibouchi, M., Wang, H. (eds.) ASIACRYPT 2021. LNCS, vol. 13093, pp. 92–121. Springer, Cham (2021). https://doi.org/10.1007/978-3-030-92068-5_4

[RBRC22] Ravi, P., Bhasin, S., Roy, S.S., Chattopadhyay, A.: On exploiting message leakage in (few) nist pqc candidates for practical message recovery attacks. IEEE Trans. Inf. Forensics Secur. **17**, 684–699 (2022)

[RRCB20] Ravi, P., Roy, S.S., Chattopadhyay, A., Bhasin, S.: Generic side-channel attacks on CCA-secure lattice-based PKE and KEMs. IACR Trans. Cryptogr. Hardw. Embed. Syst. **2020**(3), 307–335 (2020)

[RRD+23] Rajendran, G., Ravi, P., D'Anvers, J.-P., Bhasin, S., Chattopadhyay, A.: Pushing the limits of generic side-channel attacks on LWE-based KEMs - parallel PC oracle attacks on Kyber KEM and beyond. IACR Trans. Cryptogr. Hardw. Embed. Syst. **2023**(2), 418–446 (2023)

[RSA78] Rivest, R.L., Shamir, A., Adleman, L.M.: A method for obtaining digital signatures and public-key cryptosystems. Commun. ACM **21**(2), 120–126 (1978)

[SAB+22] Schwabe, P., et al.: CRYSTALS-KYBER. Technical report, National Institute of Standards and Technology (2022). https://csrc.nist.gov/Projects/post-quantum-cryptography/selected-algorithms-2022

[SCZ+23] Shen, M., Cheng, C., Zhang, X., Guo, Q., Jiang, T.: Find the bad apples: an efficient method for perfect key recovery under imperfect SCA oracles - a case study of Kyber. IACR Trans. Cryptogr. Hardw. Embed. Syst. **2023**(1), 89–112 (2023)

[Sho94] Shor, P.W.: Algorithms for quantum computation: Discrete logarithms and factoring. In: 35th Annual Symposium on Foundations of Computer Science, Santa Fe, NM, USA, 20–22 November 1994, pp. 124–134. IEEE Computer Society Press (1994)

[SM15] Schneider, T., Moradi, A.: Leakage assessment methodology. In: Güneysu, T., Handschuh, H. (eds.) CHES 2015. LNCS, vol. 9293, pp. 495–513. Springer, Heidelberg (2015). https://doi.org/10.1007/978-3-662-48324-4_25

[TMS24] Tosun, T., Moradi, A., Savas, E.: Exploiting the central reduction in lattice-based cryptography. IEEE Access **12**, 166814–166833 (2024)

[TUX+23] Tanaka, Y., Ueno, R., Xagawa, K., Ito, A., Takahashi, J., Homma, N.: Multiple-valued plaintext-checking side-channel attacks on post-quantum KEMs. IACR Trans. Cryptogr. Hardw. Embed. Syst. **2023**(3), 473–503 (2023)

[VGO+20] Virtanen, P., et al.: SciPy 1.0: fundamental algorithms for scientific computing in Python. Nat. Methods **17**(3), 261–272 (2020)

[XPR+22] Xu, Z., Pemberton, O., Roy, S.S., Oswald, D., Yao, W., Zheng, Z.: Magnifying side-channel leakage of lattice-based cryptosystems with chosen ciphertexts: the case study of kyber. IEEE Trans. Comput. **71**(9), 2163–2176 (2021)

A Horizontal Attack on the Codes and Restricted Objects Signature Scheme (CROSS)

Jonas Schupp[1]() and Georg Sigl[1,2]()

[1] TUM School of Computation, Information and Technology, Technical University of Munich, Munich, Germany
{jonas.schupp,sigl}@tum.de
[2] Fraunhofer Institute for Applied and Integrated Security (AISEC), Garching, Germany

Abstract. CROSS is a post-quantum secure digital signature scheme submitted to NIST's Call for Additional Signatures which was recently selected for round 2. It features signature and key sizes in the range of SLH-DSA while providing a substantially faster signing operation. Within this work, we provide the first passive side-channel attack on the scheme. The attack recovers the secret key from all except one parameter sets and security levels from a single power trace while requiring at maximum two power traces for the R-SDP(G) 1 Fast instance. To successfully mount the attack, we show how to recover the secret key from side-channel information gained from the syndrome computation in CROSS' identification protocol. We furthermore show how the hypothesis space for the attack can be restricted using information from the published signature.

Keywords: Post-Quantum Cryptography · Side-Channel · Horizontal Attack

1 Introduction

Given the possible insecurity of classic asymmetric cryptography in the presence of a quantum computer being capable of running Shor's Algorithm [10], the National Institute of Standardization (NIST) started a competition to find quantum secure replacements in 2016 [7]. In July 2022, NIST selected the algorithms Crystals-KYBER as Key Encapsulation Mechanism as well as Crystals-Dilithium and Falcon as signature algorithms [2]. All of these algorithms, apart from the already selected SPHINCS+/SLH-DSA [1] and a yet to be chosen Key Encapsulation Mechanism, are based on structured lattices. This led to an additional call by NIST asking specifically for signature schemes based on different mathematical problems. There are several advantages of having schemes based on different problems available. On one hand, this allows for alternatives in case there is a breakthrough in cryptanalysis for one of the problems being used and on the other hand it allows for schemes with specific advantages, e.g. small signatures or low computational requirements to be used for specific applications. Of the 40 submissions accepted by NIST in June 2023, they selected 14 to advance to round 2 [3]. One of these is the Codes and Restricted Objects Signature Scheme (CROSS). It is a promising candidate as it offers reasonable signature and key sizes which are in the range of SPHINCS+ but offers significantly faster signing and key generation routines according to [3].

NIST also asked for research in side-channel resistance of the new schemes as side-channel attacks are an eminent threat for cryptographic implementations, especially on embedded devices. As there is to the best of our knowledge no research on the passive side-channel resistance of CROSS so far, we propose the first horizontal attack on this signature scheme requiring only a single power trace for all except one of the parameter sets and at maximum two traces for the R-SDP(G) 1 Fast parameter set.

Related Work. While we are not aware of any passive attacks published on CROSS, the attack strategy we follow is similar to the one introduced by Clavier et al. in [8] and used by Bauer et al. in [5] for ECC implementations. Their work was furthermore inspired by the work of Walter in [11]. We furthermore rely on the concept of Correlation Power Analysis (CPA) as introduced by Brier et al. in [6] and use Hamming Weights as our leakage model.

Contribution. In this work, we present the first power side-channel attack on CROSS which requires a trace of a single signature generation for all except one of the parameter sets and at maximum two traces for the R-SDP(G) 1 Fast parameter set. The attack works with the outlined performance against all security levels and optimization corners. Our target is the latest reference implementation of the scheme as available on the submission team's webpage.[1] Please note that while the attack targets the latest version available for Round 1 of the NIST competition (Version 1.2) it is directly and without modification applicable to the Round 2 version of the scheme. The only thing to be taken into consideration is the altered notation. The attack leads to full recovery of a representation of the secret key which can be used to sign arbitrary messages. Our attack target is the syndrome computation in each round of the identification protocol underlying CROSS which is essentially a matrix-vector multiplication. Instead of computing the full matrix vector product, part of the multiplication where the upper vector entries are multiplied with an identity matrix is implemented by priming the result vector with these values. This forces us to implement our attack in several stages as we can build hypothesis on the upper part of the vector before recovering the lower part. First, we target the intermediate results of the multiplication with a horizontal correlation based attack which allows us to recover most of the respective coefficients under attack. Second, we target the intermediate results of the addition of the multiplication results which

---

[1] https://www.cross-crypto.com/CROSS_submission_package_v1.2.zip.

we can now compute based on the first attack's result to attack the remaining coefficients. Additionally, we outline how to recover the secret key of the scheme from the ephemeral secret sampled in each execution of the identification scheme using the information recovered with our attack. We also show how to recombine the information gained in several rounds of the protocol. Furthermore, we explain how to reduce the number of required key hypothesis based on the special structure of the restricted syndrome decoding problem. Finally, we show the practicality of our attack with traces measured on ChipWhisperer's CW308 platform using an STM32F303 microcontroller.

Organization. The remainder of this work is structured as follows: Within chapter two, we outline CROSS with emphasis on the parts which are necessary for the attack. In chapter three, we explain the necessary stages to mount a successful attack on the algorithm. Finally, in chapter four, we show experimental results from measurements on a microcontroller and demonstrate the feasibility of the attack.

2 Introduction to CROSS

In the following, we provide an overview of CROSS according to the latest version of its specification [4]. The scheme is based on the hardness of the Restricted Syndrome Decoding Problem (R-SDP) which can be seen as a variant of the syndrome decoding problem. Additionally, it features a second variant based on the Restricted Syndrome Decoding Problem in a Subgroup (R-SDP(G)). It is constructed using the Fiat-Shamir transform to make an interactive Zero-Knowledge Identification protocol non interactive. The scheme has relatively small signatures and keys, at least compared to other code-based schemes, while showing competitive performance when it comes to computational complexity. On a high level perspective, the scheme is constructed from a Zero-Knowledge Identification protocol which is executed for t rounds and explained in the following section.

Table 1 shows the parameters for all instantiations of the scheme with p and z being the moduli for the respective finite fields the coefficients in the scheme are sampled from. The codewords of the random linear code used in the scheme have length n and dimension k while the number of rounds is defined as t and the fixed weight of the second challenge is w. In the next sections, we provide a high level overview of the main functions of the scheme while omitting details which are not relevant for this work.

Notation. We here define the notation we use throughout this work. For any uncovered notation we refer to [4] as we omit any notation used in the pseudocode of the signing operation in case it is irrelevant for the attack. Matrices are represented by uppercase letters $\mathbf{A}$ while vectors are indicated as lowercase letters $\mathbf{v}$. The identity matrix of size m is denoted as $\mathbf{I}_m$. Any representations of length n vectors in $\mathbb{F}_z$ are denoted by lowercase bold Greek letters, e.g. $\boldsymbol{\eta}$.

Table 1. Parameter choices, keypair and signature sizes recommended for both CROSS-R-SDP and CROSS-R-SDP(G), assuming NIST security categories 1, 3, and 5, respectively.

Algorithm and Security Category	Optim. Corner	p	z	n	k	m	t	w	Pri. Key Size (B)	Pub. Key Size (B)	Signature Size (B)
CROSS-R-SDP 1	fast	127	7	127	76		163	85	32	77	19152
	balanced	127	7	127	76		252	212	32	77	12912
	small	127	7	127	76		960	938	32	77	10080
CROSS-R-SDP 3	fast	127	7	187	111		245	127	48	115	42682
	balanced	127	7	187	111		398	340	48	115	28222
	small	127	7	187	111		945	907	48	115	23642
CROSS-R-SDP 5	fast	127	7	251	150		327	169	64	153	76298
	balanced	127	7	251	150		507	427	64	153	51056
	small	127	7	251	150		968	912	64	153	43592
CROSS-R-SDP(G) 1	fast	509	127	55	36	25	153	79	32	54	12472
	balanced	509	127	55	36	25	243	206	32	54	9236
	small	509	127	55	36	25	871	850	32	54	7956
CROSS-R-SDP(G) 3	fast	509	127	79	48	40	230	123	48	83	27404
	balanced	509	127	79	48	40	255	176	48	83	23380
	small	509	127	79	48	40	949	914	48	83	18188
CROSS-R-SDP(G) 5	fast	509	127	106	69	48	306	157	64	106	48938
	balanced	509	127	106	69	48	356	257	64	106	40134
	small	509	127	106	69	48	996	945	64	106	32742

2.1 The CROSS-ID Protocol

The Zero-Knowledge protocol used in CROSS is built upon a 5-pass protocol, typically consisting of a commitment sent by the prover to the verifier, and a pair of a challenge and a response sent from the verifier to the prover and back which is repeated twice with different messages. Depending on the values of the two challenges, the prover provides different responses in order to prove its knowledge of the secret error vector η (resp. ζ for R-SDP(G)) without actually revealing it. Within this work, we however only focus on the computation of the commitment which depends on the secret key and on a subset of rounds, namely on those where second binary challenge is 1. In order to compute the commitments one first needs to sample an ephemeral secret η' as well as a vector $\mathbf{u}'$ uniform in $\mathbb{F}_p$. These can then be used to compute the transformation σ in $\mathbb{F}_z$ which maps η' to η and can similarly be used to map $\mathbf{u}'$ to $\mathbf{u}$. With $\mathbf{u}$, one can then compute the syndrome $\tilde{\mathbf{s}}$. Next, a hash of the syndrome $\tilde{\mathbf{s}}$ and the map σ on one hand as well as of the Seed used to sample η' and $\mathbf{u}'$ on the other hand is published. Depending on the challenges provided by the verifier one then computes a response based on the syndrome and the first challenge and finally reveals either the seed used to sample η' and $\mathbf{u}'$ in case the second binary challenge is 1 or a computed value $\mathbf{y}$ and the map σ which maps η' to η and $\mathbf{u}'$ to $\mathbf{u}$.

2.2 Key Generation

The key generation has a keypair consisting of a public and a secret key as output. The secret key consists of a seed used to sample the error vector η (resp. ζ). The public key contains a seed used to sample the parity check matrix $\mathbf{H}$ as well as the syndrome $\mathbf{s}$ of η computed through $\mathbf{H}$. To reduce the key sizes, neither η nor $\mathbf{H}$ are saved directly but both are only stored as their respective seeds. For R-SDP(G) the error vector η is computed from ζ using the generator matrix $\mathbf{M}_G$ which is also part of the public key. We refer to [4] for a more detailed description as well as for the corresponding pseudocode.

2.3 Signature Generation

Within the signature generation algorithm, the secret key and the message to be signed are taken as input to compute the respective signature. Please note that the public key can be recomputed from the secret key as the public key's seed is derived from the private key's seed. After expanding the matrix $\mathbf{H}$ as well as the error vector η, a seed and a salt is drawn from the system's TRNG and expanded for each round using a binary tree structure. These seeds are then used in the CROSS-ID protocol described above and finally the responses to be published are packed to form the actual signature. The pseudocode of the signature generation is shown in Algorithm 1 where line 2 refers to the expansion of the key material, the commitments are computed and packed in lines 3–17 and the challenges and responses are calculated in 18–31. The signature is finally packed in lines 32–42. Within this algorithm orange highlights operations carried out only for the RSDP-(G) parameter sets while green is used for parts only computed for RSDP.

2.4 Signature Verification

In the signature verification, one of the two following actions is executed based on the corresponding value of the second challenge. Either the values η' and $\mathbf{u}'$ are sampled based on the published seed or the map σ is used to recompute $\tilde{\mathbf{s}}$ in combination with $\mathbf{y}$. Finally it is checked whether these values match the ones computed during signature generation via hash comparison and subsequently a decision about the correctness of the signature is made.

Algorithm 1: SIGN(pri, Msg), taken from [4]

Data: λ: security parameter,
$g \in \mathbb{F}_p^*$: generator of a subgroup $\mathbb{E}$ of $\mathbb{F}_p^*$ with cardinality z
$\mathbb{E}^n$: restricted subgroup
$\mathbf{M}_G$: $m \times n$ matrix of $\mathbb{Z}_z$ elements, employed to generate vectors
$\eta \in G \subset \mathbb{E}^n$
t: number of iterations of the ZKID protocol
$\mathcal{B}_w^t$: set of all binary strings with length w and Hamming weight t
c: a fixed constant, equal to the number of nodes in the seed tree
dsc: a fixed constant, greater than t employed to obtain domain separation

Input: pri: private key constituted of $\text{Seed}_{\text{sk}} \in \{0,1\}^{2\lambda}$
Msg: message to be signed $\text{Msg} \in \{0,1\}^*$

Output: Signature Signature

1 **Begin**

    // Key material expansion

2     $\eta, \zeta, \mathbf{H}, \mathbf{M}_G \leftarrow \text{EXPANDPRIVATESEED}(\text{Seed}_{\text{sk}})$
    $\eta, \mathbf{H} \leftarrow \text{EXPANDPRIVATESEED}(\text{Seed}_{\text{sk}})$

    // Computation of commitments

3     $\text{Mseed} \xleftarrow{\$} \{0,1\}^\lambda$, $\text{Salt} \xleftarrow{\$} \{0,1\}^{2\lambda}$
4     $(\text{Seed}[0], \ldots, \text{Seed}[t-1]) \leftarrow \text{SEEDTREELEAVES}(\text{Mseed}, \text{Salt})$
5   **for** $i \leftarrow 0$ **to** $t-1$ **do**
6         $\zeta', u_i' \leftarrow \text{CSPRNG}(\text{Seed}[i] \| \text{Salt} \| i+c,)$
        $\delta_i \leftarrow \zeta - \zeta'$
        $\eta_i' \leftarrow \zeta' \mathbf{M}_G$
        $\eta_i', u_i' \leftarrow \text{CSPRNG}(\text{Seed}[i] \| \text{Salt} \| i+c,)$
7         $\sigma_i \leftarrow \eta - \eta_i'$
8   **for** $j \leftarrow 0$ **to** $n-1$ **do**
9             $v[j] \leftarrow g^{\sigma_i[j]}$
10   **end**
11         $u \leftarrow v \star u_i'$ // $\star$ is component-wise product
12         $\tilde{s} \leftarrow u \mathbf{H}^\top$
13         $\text{cmt}_0[i] \leftarrow \text{HASH}(\tilde{s} \| \delta_i \| \text{Salt} \| i + c + \text{dsc})$
        $\text{cmt}_0[i] \leftarrow \text{HASH}(\tilde{s} \| \sigma_i \| \text{Salt} \| i + c + \text{dsc})$
14         $\text{cmt}_1[i] \leftarrow \text{HASH}(\text{Seed}[i] \| \text{Salt} \| i + c + \text{dsc})$
15   **end**
16     $d_0 \leftarrow \text{MERKLEROOT}(\text{cmt}_0[0], \ldots, \text{cmt}_0[t-1])$
17     $d_1 \leftarrow \text{HASH}(\text{cmt}_1[0] \| \ldots \| \text{cmt}_1[t-1])$
18     $d_{01} \leftarrow \text{HASH}(d_0 \| d_1)$

```
18
            // First challenge vector extraction
19          $d_m \leftarrow \text{Hash}(\text{Msg})$
20          $d_\beta \leftarrow \text{Hash}(d_m || d_{01} || \text{Salt})$
21          $\text{beta} \leftarrow \text{CSPRNG}(d_\beta, (\mathbb{F}_p^*)^t)$
            // Computation of first round of responses
22          for $i \leftarrow 0$ to $t - 1$ do
23              for $j \leftarrow 0$ to $n - 1$ do
24                  $\mathbf{e}'_i[j] \leftarrow g^{\boldsymbol{\eta}'_i[j]}$
25              end
26              $\mathbf{y}_i \leftarrow \mathbf{u}'_i + \text{beta}[i]\mathbf{e}'_i$
27          end
            // Second challenge vector extraction
28          $d_b \leftarrow \text{Hash}(\mathbf{y}_0 || \ldots || \mathbf{y}_{t-1} || d_\beta)$
29          $\mathbf{b} \leftarrow \text{CSPRNG}(d_b, \mathcal{B}^t_{(w)})$
            // Computation of second round of responses
30          $\text{MerkleProofs} \leftarrow \text{MerkleProof}((\text{cmt}_0[0], \ldots, \text{cmt}_0[t-1]), \mathbf{b})$
31          $\text{SeedPath} \leftarrow \text{SeedTreePaths}(\text{Mseed}, \mathbf{b})$
            // Signature composition
32          $\text{rsp}_0 \leftarrow (\mathbb{F}_p^n \times \mathbb{F}_z^m)^{t-w}$ ¦ $\text{rsp}_0 \leftarrow (\mathbb{F}_p^n \times \mathbb{F}_z^n)^{t-w}$
33          $\text{rsp}_1 \leftarrow (\{0,1\}^{2\lambda})^{t-w}$ // empty array
34          $j \leftarrow 0$
35          for $i \leftarrow 0$ to $t - 1$ do
36              if ($\mathbf{b}[i] = 0$) then
                    // $\text{cmt}_0[i]$ is recomputed by the verifier, $\text{cmt}_1[i]$ must be
                    sent
37                  $\text{rsp}_0[j] \leftarrow (\mathbf{y}_i, \delta_i)$ ¦ $\text{rsp}_0[j] \leftarrow (\mathbf{y}_i, \sigma_i)$
38                  $\text{rsp}_1[j] \leftarrow \text{cmt}_1[i]$
39                  $j \leftarrow j + 1$
40              end
41          end
42          $\text{Signature} \leftarrow \text{Salt} || d_{01} || d_b || \text{MerkleProofs} || \text{SeedPath} || \text{rsp}_0 || \text{rsp}_1$
            // all Signature components are encoded as binary strings
43          return Signature
44 end
```

3 Attack Strategy

As discussed above, the secret key of CROSS consists only of a seed of 2λ length. Within this work we do not target that seed directly but instead the error vector $\boldsymbol{\eta}$ (resp. $\boldsymbol{\zeta}$ in the case of R-SDP((G))) which is the only secret material sampled from the seed and therefore corresponds to full secret key recovery. As visible in Algorithm 1, the only operation in the algorithm where $\boldsymbol{\eta}$ is used directly is to compute the map σ in line 7. This line represents the transformation between the longterm secret $\boldsymbol{\eta}$ and the ephemeral secret $\boldsymbol{\eta}'$ which is sampled uniform at random in $\mathbb{F}_z^n$ for every round of the zero-knowledge protocol. Depending on the corresponding bit of the second challenge, either the seed used to sample $\boldsymbol{\eta}'$ (and $\mathbf{u}'$) or the map σ is published. For this attack, we focus on the w of t fraction of rounds where the seed gets published and we can therefore obtain $\mathbf{u}'$ and $\boldsymbol{\eta}'$. One can furthermore notice that the correspondence between $\mathbf{u}$ and $\mathbf{u}'$ is derived from the same map as the transformation between $\boldsymbol{\eta}$ and $\boldsymbol{\eta}'$. A recovery of a pair of $\mathbf{u}$ and $\mathbf{u}'$ can therefore be used to recover $\boldsymbol{\eta}$ from $\boldsymbol{\eta}'$.

Recovering η_i from a Pair of Values u_i and u_i'. Given a pair of u_i and u_i' this can be achieved by recovering the map v_i from the pair, looking up the precomputed value of σ_i for the corresponding entry in $\mathbf{v}$ based on a Look-Up Table and recomputing η_i from the map σ_i and η_i' as visible on the following lines.

$$v_i = (u_i \cdot u_i'^{-1}) \mod p$$
$$\sigma_i \Leftarrow v_i$$
$$\eta_i = (\eta_i' \cdot \sigma_i) \mod z$$

Component-Wise Transformation. It is furthermore worth noticing that the transformation σ and therefore also v is defined component-wise, allowing us to recover $\boldsymbol{\eta}$ element by element from any pair of $\mathbf{u}$ and $\mathbf{u}'$. This allows us to gain information on a limited number of coefficients of $\mathbf{u}$ per round and to combine this information later on to learn the longterm secret $\boldsymbol{\eta}$. In the case of R-SDP(G) we can then use $\boldsymbol{\eta}$ to recover $\boldsymbol{\zeta}$ directly as $\boldsymbol{\eta} \leftarrow \boldsymbol{\zeta} \mathbf{M}_G$ which allows us to recover $\boldsymbol{\zeta}$ directly as part of $\boldsymbol{\eta}$.

$$\boldsymbol{\zeta} = [\eta_{n-m}; ...; \eta_n]$$

Reducing the Hypothesis Space. Another aspect that simplifies the attack here is the way the coefficients of $\mathbf{u}$ are computed. We recall here that $\mathbf{u}'$ is sampled uniform at random from $\mathbb{F}_p^n$ while the map $\mathbf{v}$ is a representation of the map $\sigma \in \mathbb{F}_z^n$. Therefore σ can take only $|z|$ possible values for each entry which leads to the same limitation for $\mathbf{v}$ and thus requires us to consider only $|z|$ hypotheses for each entry in $\mathbf{u}$. These can be computed by taking all possible values of each entry in $\mathbf{v}$ into account and computing the resulting values $\mathbf{u}$ given that $\mathbf{u}'$ is published as part of the signature.

With this approach, we only need an exploitable operation in the code to recover a coefficient of $\mathbf{u}$ in a round where $\mathbf{u}'$ is published as part of the signature. Such a spot exists via the syndrome computation where $\mathbf{u}$ gets multiplied with the parity check matrix $\mathbf{H}$ which is part of the public key to obtain the syndrome y. While the (restricted) syndrome decoding problem itself is computationally hard, its intermediate results can still be used in an implementation attack in case they are accessible via a side-channel. Within the next sections, we outline how we can extract the entire secret key representation $\boldsymbol{\eta}$ from this syndrome computation using only a single trace for all parameter sets except one and at maximum two traces for R-SDP(G) 1 Fast.

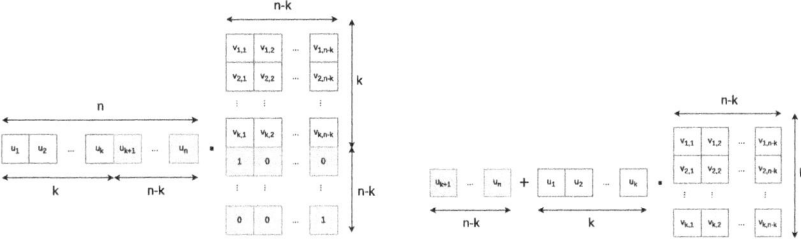

Fig. 1. Illustration of the matrix-vector multiplication used in the syndrome computation and how the multiplication with the identity matrix is substituted

3.1 Prerequisites

The operation we target with our attack is essentially a matrix vector multiplication in $\mathbb{F}_p$ with $p = 127$ for R-SDP and $p = 509$ for R-SDP(G). While the operands in this multiplication are actually of that size and bitwidth, we want to recall here that our hypothesis space is limited by the way the values of the vector are sampled which leaves us only $z = 7$ hypotheses per entry in $\mathbf{u}$ for the R-SDP parameter sets and $z = 127$ hypotheses per entry for the R-SDP(G) instances. As the systematic part of the parity check matrix $\mathbf{H}$ is just an identity matrix of dimension $(n-k) \times (n-k)$, this part of the multiplication is usually omitted and replaced by copying the corresponding $(n-k)$ values of $\mathbf{u}$ as initialization values into the result vector $\tilde{\mathbf{s}}$ before the multiplication results are accumulated as sketched in Eq. (1). This leaves us with the pseudocode as shown in Algorithm 2 which we also visualize in Fig. 1. Here one can see that after copying the upper part of $\mathbf{u}$ to $\tilde{\mathbf{s}}$ we are left with $(n-k) \times k$ multiplications, subsequent additions to the corresponding entry in $\tilde{\mathbf{s}}$ and finally reductions which form the entire matrix vector multiplication. To mount our attack, we need to capture each of these operations for a single matrix-vector multiplication as the vector $\mathbf{u}$ changes for each multiplication.

$$\tilde{6s} = \mathbf{u}\mathbf{H}^\top \tag{1}$$

$$\tilde{6s} = \mathbf{u}\left[\mathbf{V}_{tr}\mathbf{I}_{n-k}\right]^\top \tag{2}$$

$$(s_1, ..., s_{n-k}) = (u_1, ..., u_n) \begin{pmatrix} v_{tr,1,1} & \cdots & v_{tr,1,n-k} \\ v_{tr,2,1} & \cdots & v_{tr,2,n-k} \\ \cdots & \cdots & \cdots \\ v_{tr,k,1} & \cdots & v_{tr,k,n-k} \\ 1 & \cdots & 0 \\ 0 & \cdots & 0 \\ \cdots & \cdots & \cdots \\ 0 & \cdots & 1 \end{pmatrix} \tag{3}$$

$$(s_1, ..., s_{n-k}) = (u_{k+1}, ..., u_n) + (u_1, ..., u_k) \begin{pmatrix} v_{tr,1,1} & \cdots & v_{tr,1,n-k} \\ v_{tr,2,1} & \cdots & v_{tr,2,n-k} \\ \cdots & \cdots & \cdots \\ v_{tr,k,1} & \cdots & v_{tr,k,n-k} \end{pmatrix} \tag{4}$$

Algorithm 2: Syndrome Computation

1 **for** $i \leftarrow 1$ **to** $n - k$ **do**
2     $\tilde{s}_i = u_{k+i}$
3 **end**
4 **for** $i \leftarrow 1$ **to** k **do**
5   **for** $j \leftarrow 1$ **to** $n - k$ **do**
6        $s_i = (s_i + u_i \cdot v_{tr,i,j}) \mod p$
7   **end**
8 **end**

3.2 CPA on the Syndrome Computation to Recover the Lower k Entries of u

To mount the attack, we can now compute hypotheses on the intermediate results of the multiplications in line 6 of Algorithm 2 and run a CPA-style attack on the corresponding $n-k$ samples per coefficient in **u**. We illustrate this attack strategy in Fig. 2 where we try to attack the red value via the intermediate results of its multiplications with the yellow elements of the public matrix. As discussed above, this leaves us with z possible values for an entry in **u** and, as $\mathbf{V}_{tr}$ is part of the public key, we can compute hypotheses on the (unreduced) multiplication results using a Hamming Weight Leakage Model. The necessary samples here all belong to one iteration of the outer loop in Algorithm 2 and consist of one full execution of the inner loop, meaning that we need the first $n-k$ subtraces to attack the first

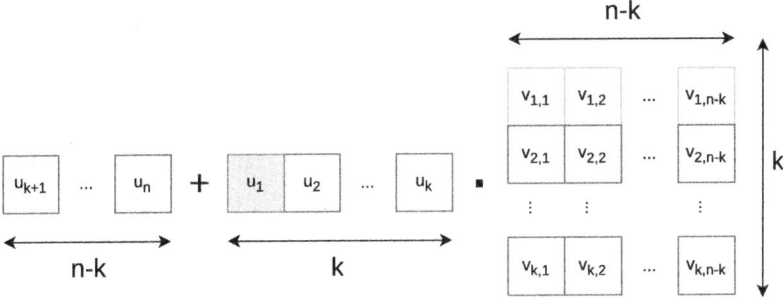

Fig. 2. Illustration of the attack path for the CPA-Style attack on the lower k entries of **u** resp. η

coefficient in **u**. Please note that the number of attack points here is relatively limited as e.g. for RSDP-1 we only have 51 samples per coefficient and e.g. for RSDP(G)-1 we even only have 19 samples. Under the assumption of Hamming Weight Leakage, we can not expect to obtain unique results per coefficient here as there is usually more than one possible hypothesis leading to the same sequence of hamming weights. However, we can discard non-unique samples or putting it differently, samples where more than one coefficient correlates within a certain threshold of the most likely hypothesis. As we also got more than one chance to recover each entry in **u** as there are w (which is at minimum 79 for RSDP(G)-1) rounds where **u**′ gets published, we can safely discard these ambiguous results and can still recover most of the entries in **u** successfully as shown below. As we essentially have w attack results per coefficient in **u**, though we discard those which are not distinct, we also apply a majority voting based strategy to further reduce the number of incorrectly recovered coefficients. To summarize this leaves us with a horizontal DPA for each of the k first coefficients of **u** for w rounds. In the case of R-SDP, a recovery of the k entries in different vectors **u** equal to a recovery of this part of the secret key error vector η. In the case of R-SDP(G), we need the upper m entries of η which form the secret key ζ. This attack result is nevertheless necessary as it is prerequisite to attack the upper part of η.

3.3 CPA on the Syndrome Computation to Recover the Upper $n - k$ Entries of u

In order to successfully attack the second part of the coefficients in **u** one first needs to recover a significant part of **u** successfully using the strategy described in Sect. 3.2. Once this is done, one can now compute new hypotheses along the other axis of the parity check matrix respectively the calculations corresponding to this dimension. We illustrate our approach in Fig. 3 where we attack the red value via hypotheses we compute on the reduced addition results. We can compute these hypotheses because we can calculate the multiplication results of the yellow column of the matrix with the vector **u** based on the results of the

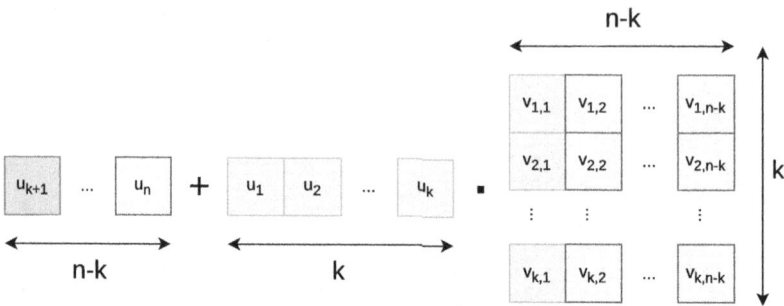

Fig. 3. Illustration of the attack path for the CPA-Style attack on the upper $n-k$ entries of **u** resp. η

first attack stage. Putting it differently, to attack the entry u_{k+1} we need the traces $1, (n-k)+1, 2\cdot(n-k)+1, ..., k*(n-k)+1$. This yields k subtraces per coefficient to be attacked in **u** and therefore, as $k > (n-k)$ for all parameter sets, a more reliable attack, simply due to the larger number traces available. As we compute our hypotheses here based on the results of the addition as described in line 6 Algorithm 2, we need to know the first k entries in **u** to precompute the results of the respective multiplications successfully such that the only unknown input is the entry of **u** copied into the respective position in $\tilde{\mathbf{s}}$ in the first place and accumulated in all subsequent iterations.

4 Results

To assess the feasibility and efficiency of the attacks described above, we first evaluate them on simulated traces before performing the attack on an actual implementation on an ARM Cortex-M4 based microcontroller as described below. Please note that throughout the results section, we usually talk about recovery of values in η which always refer to an attack on the corresponding value in **u** and subsequent recovery via $\mathbf{u}'$ and η'.

Results Based on Simulated Hamming Weight Leakages. In this stage, we compute upon the following expectations which can be assumed to be applicable to a microcontroller implementation in general. First, we expect noisy Hamming Weight Leakage from all results which are written back into a register at some point during the execution of the algorithm. This is e.g. experimentally confirmed for load and store operations in [9]. As we first only want to assess the theoretical feasibility of the attack, we assume this leakage to be noise free as we try to reproduce our results with real measurements anyways. More concretely, we therefore expect leakage from the following (intermediate) results of the syndrome computation:

– The unreduced result of one multiplication $u_i \cdot v_{tr,i,j}$

– The reduced result of one addition $(s_i + u_i \cdot v_{tr,i,j}) \mod p$

The artificial traces we build from these expectation consist of two sample points per atomic operation, one being the Hamming Weight of the unreduced result of one multiplication as outlined above and one being the Hamming Weight of the reduced addition result. While this model is an oversimplification it is device independent and sufficient to assess whether an attack is feasible in an ideal scenario with the leakages described above. We discuss below how well these expectations match reality, for now, we assume them to correct.

Results Based on Measurements. We perform our attack on a ChipWhisperer CW308 board as platform with an 32-bit STM32F303RCT7 microcontroller running at 10 MHz. As measurement oscilloscope we use a Picoscope 6402D with a sampling rate of 2.5 Gs/s measuring the power consumption of our device via a shunt resistor and a DC-Block with 20 MHz cutoff frequency. We use arm-none-eabi-gcc in version 13.2.1 for all experiments in this work. On the implementation side, we had to make some adaptions to the reference implementation due to the limited SRAM size of the victim board. Our targeted implementation therefore currently only contains the side-channel relevant functions as well as the functions necessary to compute its inputs. Regarding the expected leakage points above, we can confirm that we can exploit leakage from all mentioned intermediate results though the practicability heavily depends on the chosen parameter set. Concretely, there is less leakage for R-SDP(G) which we mainly attribute to the lower number of subtraces per attack and the larger coefficients as $p = 509$. To get distinct results for R-SDP(G) we therefore also have to narrow down which part of the trace we were actually attacking. For R-SDP we take the trace of all operations within a loop iteration while for R-SDP(G) we undertake some further refinement steps. Here, we use a Signal-to-Noise calculation to determine where information about the public matrix entries is visible in the trace. In a second step, we then only use the intervals following the points where information about these entries is present as the public matrix entries are one operand of the multiplication, indicating that the desired value should be computed at some point afterwards.

4.1 Result of a Single CPA

The smallest unit of the attack strategy described above is one CPA with a Hamming Weight based hypothesis on either the multiplication or subsequent addition result along either a row or a column of the public matrix with an element of the vector under attack. In the simulated setting, we get distinct results in between 20% and 70% of the attacks depending on the parameter set. We show a sample of the to be expected correlation coefficients in Fig. 4 for R-SDP 1 Fast as well as in Fig. 5 for R-SDP(G) 1 Fast. Both plots show an example for a coefficient where we get a distinct result, i.e. there is exactly one maximum correlation, as well as a sample where more than one hypothesis yields a similarly high correlation, as mentioned above, we discard such samples.

We furthermore choose a threshold of 80% of the maximum correlation which needs to be the maximum magnitude for the second highest value to consider the highest one distinct. This threshold is visualized by the red lines in the above mentioned figures. While this threshold was initially chosen based on simulated results, we observed that it seems to also work well for real traces of the R-SDP parameter sets. For the R-SDP(G) parameter sets, we had to increase the threshold to 95% for the first attack stage described below as the limited number of attack traces per CPA does not yield such high differences in the correlation coefficient. Please note that this approach discards several correct but not sufficiently distinct results but leaves us with an acceptable ratio of correct choices for the subsequent attack steps.

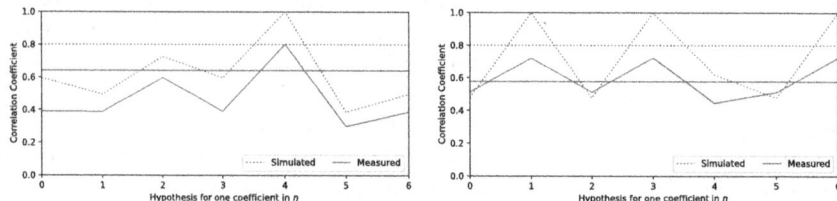

Fig. 4. Simulated and measured correlation coefficient for two coefficients in η for the R-SDP 1 Fast instance of which one yields a distinct and one a not distinct result. The decision boundary of 80% of the maximum magnitude is marked as red line (Color figure online)

4.2 Attack on the First k Entries of η

After obtaining distinct results of several CPAs for each of the lower k entries of η from several rounds of CROSS' identification protocol, we now employ a majority voting based strategy the recover a single coefficient from a set of distinct CPA results. Here we first calculate the corresponding entry in η for a result as discussed in Sect. 3 and then accumulate these results for each possible value

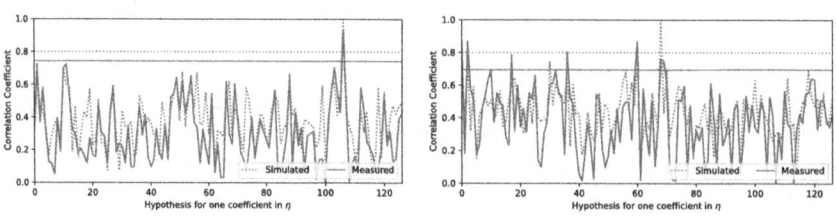

Fig. 5. Simulated and measured correlation coefficient for two coefficients in η for the R-SDP(G) 1 Fast instance of which one yields a distinct and one a not distinct result. The decision boundary of 80% of the maximum magnitude is marked as red line (Color figure online)

for this entry in η which leaves us with a distinct result for this entry. We also choose here to only consider results which are at least recovered twice to further reduce the number of errors in the result. To visualize this approach, we plotted the number of recovered entries in η as well as the number of distinct CPA results against the number of attacked rounds from a single signature generation in Fig. 6 for R-SDP 1 Fast and in Fig. 7 for R-SDP(G) 1 Fast. As visible in Fig. 6, we recover all k lower entries for R-SDP 1 Fast within less than 30 attackable rounds thus leaving 55 rounds headroom to either decrease the necessary measurement length within one signature generation or to recover results in a noisier setting from a single signing operation. We furthermore want to point out that the attacks work despite a significant number of incorrect distinct results which are indicated by the dashed lines. In the case of R-SDP(G) 1 Fast, as shown in Fig. 7 we fail to recover all lower k values in η in the measured setting while this should in theory be feasible as illustrated by the dotted red line reaching $k = 36$ within the rounds contained in one signature. This result is partially due to the fact that we only have 19 subtraces per CPA as well as larger values as $p = 509$ in this case. Here we need additional results from further signing operations to successfully recover all lower k entries. To give an overview over all results for this first attack stage, we refer to Table 2 where we summarize the number of distinct hypothesis we gain per round of the ID-Protocol, the fraction of correct hypothesis of those, as well as the resulting number of rounds of the ID-Protocol required to recover the lower k entries of η.

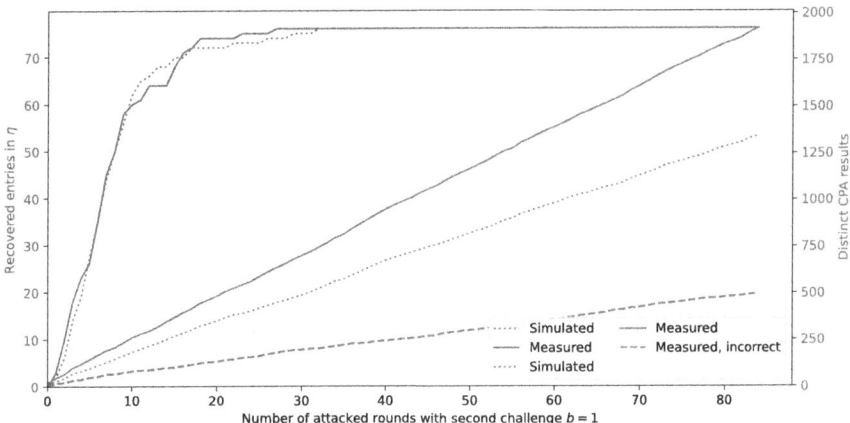

Fig. 6. Number of coefficients in η recovered per round of the ID-Protocol for R-SDP 1 Fast

4.3 Attack on the Upper $n - k$ Entries of η

As discussed in Sect. 3, we rely on the lower k entries of η to successfully compute hypotheses on the upper part, requiring us to successfully recover the lower part

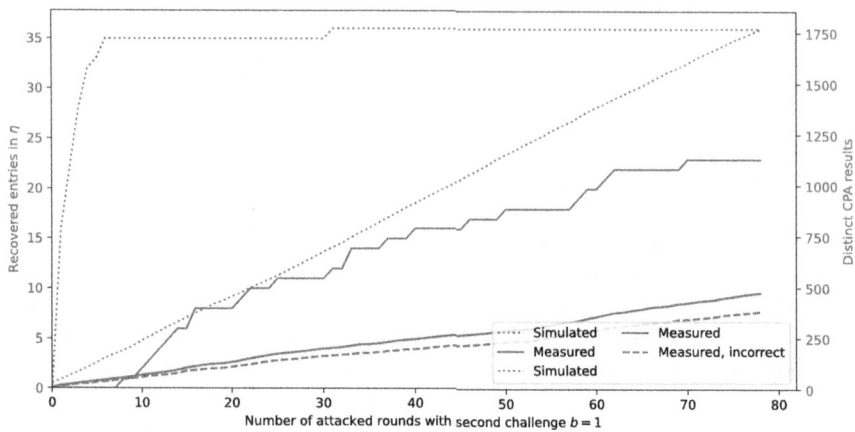

Fig. 7. Number of coefficients in η recovered per round of the ID-Protocol for R-SDP(G) 1 Fast

Table 2. Number of Rounds of the ID-Protocol necessary to recover the lower k entries in η as well as number of distinct CPA results and correctness rates of these results

Algorithm and Security Category	Distinct CPA results/round	Frac. of correct CPA results	# rounds for lower k rec.
CROSS-R-SDP 1	23	74%	27
CROSS-R-SDP 3	31	81%	59
CROSS-R-SDP 5	42	83%	76
CROSS-R-SDP(G) 1	27	13%	158
CROSS-R-SDP(G) 3	32	29%	123
CROSS-R-SDP(G) 5	31	43%	157

Table 3. Number of Rounds of the ID-Protocol necessary to recover the upper $n - k$ entries in η as well as number of distinct CPA results and correctness rates of these results

Algorithm and Security Category	Distinct CPA results/round	Frac. of correct CPA results	# rounds for upper $n - k$ rec.
CROSS-R-SDP 1	50	99%	3
CROSS-R-SDP 3	74	99.8%	3
CROSS-R-SDP 5	99	99.9%	3
CROSS-R-SDP(G) 1	9.8	79%	3
CROSS-R-SDP(G) 3	18	80%	3
CROSS-R-SDP(G) 5	25	82%	3

of η first. We refer to Table 3 for the measured results for this attack stage, leading to successful recovery of the upper $n-k$ entries in η in all cases. Please note that the results here are significantly better than they were for the first attack stage allowing us to recover most of the upper $n-k$ values in a single attack round. In order to ensure that each value is actually recovered correctly, we utilize a second and a third round leading us to distinct results in our majority voting approach. Please note that one can easily use the remaining rounds from one signature generation to boost the results significance as they had to be measured for the first stage of the attack anyways. In the case of R-SDP(G), our target value ζ is equal to the upper m entries in η, meaning that a full recovery of η is also a full recovery of ζ.

4.4 Result Summary

As discussed above, we can recover all entries in η in the case of R-SDP using a limited number of rounds of the identification protocol from a single signature generation. In the case of R-SDP(G), we need at maximum two signature generations for RSDP(G) 1 Fast and also only a single signature generation for all other parameter sets to recover all entries in ζ.

5 Conclusion

In this work we present the first horizontal side-channel attack on CROSS. The attack is built upon the well established concept of horizontal attacks and exploits leakage from the syndrome computation inside CROSS' identification protocol which is executed several times in one signature generation allowing us to mount a separate attack on each computation. Only a single trace of a signature generation is required for a successful attack on all except one of the parameter sets of CROSS while we require at maximum two traces for a successful attack on the R-SDP(G) 1 Fast instance. The next natural step for this work is to consider different countermeasures usable to prevent this approach which for example include shuffling of the execution order of operations during a syndrome computation as well as masking of the syndrome computation's inputs. Another approach interesting for future work might be to improve the attack further as we currently discard a significant amount of samples because we rather focus on keeping the number of incorrect recoveries low but also leave the information of all discarded attack results unused.

Acknowledgments. The authors acknowledge the finanical support by the Federal Ministry of Education and Research of Germany in the project "PoQ-KIKI", project identification number 16KIS2065.

References

1. Stateless hash-based digital signature standard. National Institute of Standards and Technology, NIST FIPS PUB 205, U.S. Department of Commerce (2024). https://doi.org/10.6028/nist.fips.205
2. Alagic, G., et al.: Status report on the third round of the nist post-quantum cryptography standardization process. Technical Report (2022). https://doi.org/10.6028/nist.ir.8413
3. Alagic, G., et al.: Status report on the first round of the additional digital signature schemes for the nist post-quantum cryptography standardization process. Technical Report (2024). https://doi.org/10.6028/nist.ir.8528
4. Baldi, M., et al.: CROSS Documentation (2024). https://web.archive.org/web/20250122122245/. http://www.cross-crypto.com/CROSS_Specification_v1.2.pdf. Accessed 22 Jan 2025
5. Bauer, A., Jaulmes, E., Prouff, E., Reinhard, J.-R., Wild, J.: Horizontal collision correlation attack on elliptic curves. Cryptogr. Commun. **7**(1), 91–119 (2014). https://doi.org/10.1007/s12095-014-0111-8
6. Brier, E., Clavier, C., Olivier, F.: Correlation power analysis with a leakage model. In: Joye, M., Quisquater, J.-J. (eds.) CHES 2004. LNCS, vol. 3156, pp. 16–29. Springer, Heidelberg (2004). https://doi.org/10.1007/978-3-540-28632-5_2
7. Chen, L., et al.: Report on post-quantum cryptography. Technical report (2016). https://doi.org/10.6028/nist.ir.8105
8. Clavier, C., Feix, B., Gagnerot, G., Roussellet, M., Verneuil, V.: Horizontal correlation analysis on exponentiation. In: Soriano, M., Qing, S., López, J. (eds.) ICICS 2010. LNCS, vol. 6476, pp. 46–61. Springer, Heidelberg (2010). https://doi.org/10.1007/978-3-642-17650-0_5
9. Kannwischer, M.J., Pessl, P., Primas, R.: Single-trace attacks on keccak. IACR Trans. Cryptogr. Hardw. Embed. Syst. **2020**(3), 243–268 (2020). https://doi.org/10.13154/tches.v2020.i3.243-268. https://tches.iacr.org/index.php/TCHES/article/view/8590
10. Shor, P.: Algorithms for quantum computation: discrete logarithms and factoring. In: Proceedings 35th Annual Symposium on Foundations of Computer Science, pp. 124–134 (1994). https://doi.org/10.1109/SFCS.1994.365700
11. Walter, C.D.: Sliding windows succumbs to big mac attack. In: Koç, Ç.K., Naccache, D., Paar, C. (eds.) CHES 2001. LNCS, vol. 2162, pp. 286–299. Springer, Heidelberg (2001). https://doi.org/10.1007/3-540-44709-1_24

Improvement of Side-Channel Attacks on Mitaka

Vladimir Sarde[1,2](✉) and Nicolas Debande[1](✉)

[1] Cryptography and Security Group, IDEMIA Secure Transactions, Pessac, France
{vladimir.sarde,nicolas.debande}@idemia.com
[2] Laboratoire de Mathématiques de Versailles, UVSQ, CNRS, Université Paris-Saclay, 78035 Versailles, France

Abstract. Mitaka is a variant of Falcon, which is one of the three post-quantum signature schemes selected by the NIST for standardization. Introduced in 2021, Mitaka offers a simpler, parallelizable, and maskable version of Falcon. Our article focuses on its physical security, and our results are threefold. Firstly, we enhance a known profiled side-channel attack on an unprotected Mitaka implementation by a factor of 512. Secondly, we analyze the masked implementation of Mitaka described in the reference article, which incorporates a different sampler and a protective gadget. We expose the first side-channel flaw on this sampler. This flaw enables to break the masked implementation with a first-order side-channel attack. In this scenario, the key can be recovered using only three times more traces compared to the attack on the unprotected implementation. Finally, we discuss and recommend new countermeasures to mitigate these attacks.

Keywords: Post-quantum cryptography · Signature scheme · Mitaka · Side-channel analysis · Lattice

1 Introduction

The current asymmetric cryptographic schemes rely on the complexity of hard mathematical problems such as the computation of discrete logarithms or factorization. However, the development of quantum computers presents a security issue for these schemes as such computers have the potential to efficiently compute solutions to these mathematical problems. To address this risk, research on post-quantum cryptographic algorithms has intensified. The National Institute of Standards and Technology (NIST) is currently conducting a post-quantum cryptography standardization project to select and normalize some of these schemes. In the signature scheme category, three algorithms have already been selected and are in the drafting phase: Falcon [11], Dilithium [5] and SPHINCS$^+$ [3].

In this paper, our focus is on Mitaka [9], a variant of Falcon known for its simpler implementation. Both schemes follow the *hash and sign* paradigm and are based on the concept introduced in [13]. In this paradigm, the signature of a message is a point in a specific lattice, close to the hash of this message. For security purposes, these protocols use Gaussian samplers to randomize the selected lattice point. This aspect is the only one that differs between Falcon and Mitaka. Falcon follows the *GPV framework* [12] optimized in [7], a fast yet complex sampler that can be challenging to implement accurately. On the other hand, Mitaka follows the framework developed by Ducas and Prest in [6], known as the *Hybrid Sampler*, which benefits from the same complexity while offering a simpler implementation, easy parallelization, and greater adaptability. The simplicity of Mitaka also allows several optimizations, making it a very compelling alternative for embedded systems. Firstly, Mitaka requires less computation than Falcon, drastically reduces the memory size of the orthogonal basis which is an important contributor to Falcon's memory consumption, and avoids the use of floating-point arithmetic [9]. These aspects are crucial for resource-constrained devices, such as smart cards, where implementing post-quantum standards presents a significant challenge. Secondly, Mitaka is easier to safeguard against side-channel attacks. The original article presents a masking scheme [9, Sect. 7], and in particular, a way to mask the sampler, which is recognized to be the most sensitive part of these protocols. This presents a significant advantage over Falcon, which is sensitive to various side-channel attacks, as those exposed in [2,14–16,21].

Among the previously mentioned side-channel attacks, the one introduced by Guerreau et al. in [14] on Falcon is particularly noteworthy. Recently, Zhang et al. improved this work in [21], significantly reducing the number of required traces from around 10^6 to 50,000. This enhancement makes the attack one of the most critical threats to Falcon within the current state of the art. Additionally, Zhang et al. have extended this approach to Mitaka, successfully retrieving the secret key with around $2 \cdot 10^6$ traces. The increased difficulty in attacking Mitaka arises from the hybrid sampler's operation, which significantly deteriorates the correlation between side-channel observations and the corresponding signatures. Consequently, extracting the key from Mitaka requires a significantly larger number of traces compared to the same attack on Falcon. Moreover, it is important to highlight that this attack targets an unmasked implementation of Mitaka. To the best of our knowledge, there have not been any practical attacks on the protected one. Nevertheless, it is worth mentioning that Prest in [20] has identified a theoretical flaw in the masking scheme related to the sampler when dealing with high-order masked implementations. Although this flaw remains theoretical, it compromises the security proof of the masking scheme.

Our Contributions. In this study, we significantly enhance the side-channel attack outlined in [21], targeting the unmasked implementation of Mitaka. Our improvement stems from the fact that the number of exploitable leakage points is not just one, as previously believed, but rather 512. This arises from the specific structure of Mitaka's hybrid sampler. Consequently, an attacker can construct their templates of equal quality and exploit the leakage with the same efficiency, all while reducing the number of generated signatures by a factor of 512. Furthermore, we delve into the analysis of the masking scheme proposed for Mitaka in the original article [9]. It was previously acknowledged in [20] that this scheme has a theoretical flaw in its sampler when handling high-order masked implementations. Here, we expose a new side-channel leakage in the one-dimensional sampler, recommended as a subroutine for this protected implementation. Leveraging this newfound leakage and the previous attack, we are able to exploit the theoretical vulnerability in a low-order masked context. Our study demonstrates that this masking scheme is susceptible to real-world first-order analysis, regardless of the order of protection. Subsequently, we showcase a successful first-order profiled attack against a first-order masked implementation. Finally, we propose several countermeasures to mitigate these attacks.

Roadmap. In Sect. 2, we lay out the notations used throughout the paper, recall the context, and previous fundamental results. Section 3 delves into the side-channel attack introduced in [14] and its enhancement presented in [21], targeting both Falcon and Mitaka. We describe our improvements for this attack in Sect. 4. Following this, Sect. 5 provides an analysis of the initially proposed masking scheme and of its corresponding sampler. The aforementioned attack is then adapted to this protected implementation. In Sect. 6, we present the experimental outcomes of these attacks, while Sect. 7 discusses potential countermeasures to safeguard Mitaka. Finally, we draw our conclusions in Sect. 8.

2 Preliminaries and Notations

2.1 Linear Algebra and Lattice

We use bold lowercase letters for vectors and bold uppercase letters for matrices. For a matrix $\mathbf{B}$, we note $\mathbf{b}_i$, the (i+1)-th column of $\mathbf{B}$. Vectors are considered as column vectors, we denote the transpose of a vector $\mathbf{v}$ by $\mathbf{v}^T$.

A lattice $\mathcal{L}$ of rank k is a discrete additive subgroup of $\mathbb{R}^l$, such that the vector subspace spanned by $\mathcal{L}$ is isomorphic to $\mathbb{R}^k$, with $k \leq l$. A lattice $\mathcal{L}$ spanned by a basis $\mathbf{B}$ is noted $\mathcal{L}(\mathbf{B})$. Several hard problems are known for lattices. The Mitaka scheme signs by solving a random instance of the *approximate closest vector problem*, named $ApproxCVP_\gamma$: given a basis $\mathbf{B}$ of a lattice $\mathcal{L} \subset \mathbb{R}^l$, and a point $y \in \mathbb{R}^l$, it is difficult to find $x \in \mathcal{L}$ such that $||x - y|| \leq \gamma$ for a fixed $\gamma \in \mathbb{R}$.

2.2 Template and Masking

The power consumption of a computing device is linked to the Hamming weight of the processed variables, a result of its physical structure. An attacker can exploit this property to perform template attacks, which involve two main phases. In the first phase, the attacker builds power consumption models for specific values of an intermediate variable using a device with a known secret key. In the second phase, the attacker matches a power trace from the target device with its templates to estimate the intermediate variable value.

There are several methods to protect an algorithm from these side-channel attacks. One of the most effective countermeasures is to mask the manipulated sensitive variables with random values. This breaks the correlation between the variable and the power consumption as the mask is unknown to the attacker. In this paper, we will focus on arithmetic masking. An arithmetic mask of degree $t \in \mathbb{Z}$ on a variable a is a set of $t+1$ shares $\left(a^{(i)}\right)_{0 \leq i \leq t}$ such that $a = \sum_{i=0}^{t} a^{(i)}$ and any subset of $l \leq t$ shares is independent of the secret a. For readability, we will note $\left(a^{(i)}\right)_{0 \leq i \leq t} := [\![a]\!]$.

2.3 NTRU

Mitaka is defined over NTRU modules. Let $\mathcal{K}$ be the cyclotomic field defined by $\mathcal{K} = \mathbb{Q}(\zeta_n) \simeq \mathbb{Q}[x]/(x^n+1)$ with n a power of two and ζ_n a $2n$-th primitive root of 1. In this paper, we use $n = 512$, as our analysis focus on MITAKA-512. The ring of algebraic integers of $\mathcal{K}$ is $\mathcal{R} = \mathbb{Z}[\zeta_n] \simeq \mathbb{Z}[x]/(x^n+1)$. In this scheme, a secret key consists of two polynomials $f, g \in \mathcal{R}$ such that f is invertible modulo q, where $q \in \mathbb{N}$. In practice, f and g have small coefficients. From these two polynomials, one can calculate $F, G \in \mathcal{R}$ such that $fG - gF = q$. The public key is defined by $h = f^{-1}g \pmod{q}$ and the NTRU module associated to h is $\mathcal{L}_{\text{NTRU}} = \{(u, v) \in \mathcal{R}^2 : uh - v = 0 \pmod{q}\}$. A public basis of $\mathcal{L}_{\text{NTRU}}$ is $\{(1, h), (0, q)\}$, and a secret one is $\{(f, g), (F, G)\}$. We will note these bases by:

$$\mathbf{B}_p = \begin{pmatrix} 1 & 0 \\ h & q \end{pmatrix} \text{ and } \mathbf{B}_s = \begin{pmatrix} f & F \\ g & G \end{pmatrix}.$$

The NTRU module $\mathcal{L}_{\text{NTRU}}$ is often seen as a lattice by associating a polynomial $h = \sum_{i=0}^{n-1} h_i x^i$ to a $n \times n$ matrix $M_h = [h, xh, ..., x^{n-1}h]$ where the jth column corresponds to the coefficients of the polynomial $x^{j-1}h = \sum_{i=0}^{n-1} h_i x^i x^{j-1} \in \mathcal{R}$. Notice that multiplying these matrix is equivalent to multiplying polynomials in $\mathcal{R}$. In Mitaka, this equivalence leads to a $2n$-dimensional NTRU lattice, with a secret basis composed of small vectors.

2.4 Orthogonalization

Let $\mathbf{u}, \mathbf{v} \in \mathbb{R}^n$ and $\mathbf{B}$ a basis of $\mathbb{R}^n$. We define $\langle \mathbf{u}, \mathbf{v} \rangle = \sum_{i=0}^{n-1} u_i v_i$ as the inner product. To compute the orthogonal basis associated to $\mathbf{B}$ with respect to the inner product, we use the GramSchmidt process.

The NTRU module is a free $\mathcal{R}$-module of rank 2 in $\mathcal{K}^2$. Write $\mathbf{x}, \mathbf{y} \in \mathcal{K}^2$ by $\mathbf{x} = (x_0, x_1)$ and $\mathbf{y} = (y_0, y_1)$. There exists a natural $\mathcal{K}$-bilinear form over $\mathcal{K}^2$ defined by $\langle \mathbf{x}, \mathbf{y} \rangle_\mathcal{K} := x_0^* y_0 + x_1^* y_1 \in \mathcal{K}$, with $*$ representing multiplication in the field $\mathcal{K}$. From this bilinear form, we can deduce a notion of orthogonality with respect to the module structure. To construct the orthogonal in this context, we just apply the Gram-Schmidt process. Thus, for $\mathbf{b}_0, \mathbf{b}_1 \in \mathcal{K}^2$ two linear independent vectors, we obtain: $\widetilde{\mathbf{b}_0} := \mathbf{b}_0, \widetilde{\mathbf{b}_1} := \mathbf{b}_1 - \langle \mathbf{b}_1, \widetilde{\mathbf{b}_0} \rangle_\mathcal{K} / \langle \widetilde{\mathbf{b}_0}, \widetilde{\mathbf{b}_0} \rangle_\mathcal{K} \cdot \widetilde{\mathbf{b}_0}$.

In this article, we use the following notations. We write $\mathbf{B} = \{\mathbf{b}_0, \mathbf{b}_1, \ldots, \mathbf{b}_{2n-1}\}$ the basis of the lattice, $\mathbf{B}^\mathcal{K} = \{\mathbf{b}_0^\mathcal{K}, \mathbf{b}_1^\mathcal{K}\}$ the same basis seen as polynomials, $\widetilde{\mathbf{B}} = \{\widetilde{\mathbf{b}_0}, \widetilde{\mathbf{b}_1}, \ldots, \widetilde{\mathbf{b}_{2n-1}}\}$ the orthogonalized basis with respect to the lattice structure (i.e. with respect to $\langle . , . \rangle$), $\mathbf{H}^{\mathcal{K}} = \{\mathbf{h}_0^{\mathcal{K}}, \mathbf{h}_1^{\mathcal{K}}\}$ the orthogonalized basis with respect to the free $\mathcal{R}$-module structure (i.e. with respect to $\langle . , . \rangle_{\mathcal{K}}$), and $\mathbf{H} = (\mathbf{h}_i)_{i \in [0, 2n)}$ the vectors of the basis $H^{\mathcal{K}}$ seen in the lattice structure. Notice that, by construction, $\mathbf{h}_i = \mathbf{b}_i$ if $i \leq n$ as $\mathbf{h}_0^{\mathcal{K}} = \mathbf{b}_0^{\mathcal{K}}$.

2.5 Gaussian Distributions

The Gaussian function with center $\mathbf{c} \in \mathbb{R}^m$ and standard deviation $\sigma \in \mathbb{R}$ is defined by the function $\rho_{\sigma,\mathbf{c}}(\mathbf{x}) = \exp\left(-\frac{\|\mathbf{x}-\mathbf{c}\|^2}{2\sigma^2}\right)$. From this definition, we can construct a Gaussian distribution of density $D_{\sigma,\mathbf{c}}(\mathbf{x}) = \frac{\rho_{\sigma,\mathbf{c}}(\mathbf{x})}{(2\pi\sigma^2)^{m/2}}$. We can extend this definition to a full-rank lattice $\mathcal{L}$. Note $\rho_{\sigma,\mathbf{c}}(\mathcal{L}) := \sum_{x \in \mathcal{L}} \rho_{\sigma,c}(x)$. The discrete Gaussian distribution over $\mathcal{L}$, with center $\mathbf{c}$ and standard deviation $\sigma \in \mathbb{R}$, is defined by the probability function $D_{\mathcal{L},\sigma,\mathbf{c}}(\mathbf{v}) = \frac{\rho_{\sigma,\mathbf{c}}(\mathbf{v})}{\rho_{\sigma,\mathbf{c}}(\mathcal{L})}$.

In this article, we are especially interested in the integer Gaussian $D_{\mathbb{Z},\sigma,c}$ with $c \in \mathbb{R}$. Finally, notice that the case $c \in [0, 1)$ is enough to study as $D_{\mathbb{Z},\sigma,c} = l + D_{\mathbb{Z},\sigma,c-l}$ for all $l \in \mathbb{Z}$.

2.6 Mitaka and the Gaussian Samplers

In this part, we briefly outline the Mitaka scheme [9]. This protocol is based on the concept of *hash and sign* in a lattice. Let $\mathcal{L}$ be our NTRU lattice in $\mathbb{R}^{2n}$. Concretely, to sign a message $\mathbf{m}$, one hashes it with a salt r to a random point $\mathbf{c}$ in $\mathbb{R}^{2n}$ that is a priori not in $\mathcal{L}$. Then the signer solves the ApproxCVP, using the secret basis composed of small vectors of $\mathcal{L}$, to find $\mathbf{z} \in \mathcal{L}$ close to $\mathbf{c}$. Note that the public key is composed of long vectors of $\mathcal{L}$ from which it is hard to compute a solution. The signature is finally defined as $\mathbf{s} = \mathbf{c} - \mathbf{z}$. An observer can verify the signature by checking the resolution of ApproxCVP, i.e., by confirming that z belongs to $\mathcal{L}$ and that $\|\mathbf{s}\| < \gamma$ for a public parameter γ.

Many variants of the *hash and sign* strategy have been proposed: [9,11–13]. The main difference between all these schemes is the way they implement the resolution of ApproxCVP. This resolution, with the knowledge of a good basis, often relies on two algorithms: *Babai's Rounding* and *Babai's Nearest Plane*. Let $\mathbf{B}$ be our private basis of $\mathcal{L}$ and $\mathbf{c}$ be a point in $\mathbb{R}^{2n}$, these algorithms aim at finding a point $\mathbf{z} \in \mathcal{L}(\mathbf{B})$ as close as possible to $\mathbf{c}$. Both are explained in detail and illustrated in [19, Sect. 2.2]. The idea of Babai's Rounding is as follows: one calculates the coordinates of $\mathbf{c}$ in $\mathbf{B}$, seen as a basis of $\mathbb{R}^{2n}$, and then rounds every coordinate c_i to the closest integer. The point $\mathbf{z}$ resulting is in $\mathcal{L}$ as it is an integer combination of vectors of $\mathbf{B}$.

On the other hand, the idea of Babai's Nearest Plane is to construct $\mathbf{z}$ by successively projecting orthogonally $\mathbf{c}$. One starts by projecting $\mathbf{c}$ on $\widetilde{\mathbf{b}_{2n-1}}$, rounds the result to an integer z_{2n-1}, and subtracts $z_{2n-1}\widetilde{\mathbf{b}_{2n-1}}$ to $\mathbf{c}$. The newly obtained $\mathbf{c}$ is in the hyperplane spanned by $\{\widetilde{\mathbf{b}_{2n-2}}, \widetilde{\mathbf{b}_{2n-3}}, \ldots, \widetilde{\mathbf{b}_0}\}$ modulo the rounding. The process is then iterated with $2n - 2, 2n - 3, \ldots, 0$. At the end, one can compute $\mathbf{z} = \sum_{i=0}^{2n-1} z_i \mathbf{b}_i \in \mathcal{L}$ close to $\mathbf{c}$.

Without any randomization, a signature based on these two previous algorithms follows a distribution that depends on the geometry of the secret basis. This is explained in detail and well illustrated in [19, Sect. 2.4, 2.5]. To counteract this flaw, a Gaussian noise is added during the rounding to ensure that the signature follows a public Gaussian distribution which does not depend on the secret basis. Concretely, instead of straightly rounding the coefficients in $\mathbb{Z}$ to calculate the z_i, an integer following a Gaussian distribution $D_{\mathbb{Z},\sigma}$ centered in the float value is sampled.

Therefore, the security of these schemes relies on the capacity to precisely and securely simulate the distribution $D_{\mathbb{Z},\sigma,x}$, with $x \in [0,1)$. Note that when Babai's Rounding algorithm is used, a continuous Gaussian D_σ is first subtracted before performing the randomize rounding to prevent a bias on the covariance of the Gaussian over $\mathcal{L}$ [18]. These algorithms solving the ApproxCVP while including a randomization are called samplers.

The randomization of Babai's Nearest Plane was first used as a sampler, named *KGPV sampler*, in [12] and is written in Algorithm 1. Note that Falcon uses an improvement of this sampler, named *Fast Fourier Nearest Plane*, described in [7]. However, the ideas of our study apply the same way in both cases.

The Mitaka's sampler is a mix between the ideas of Babai's Nearest Plane and Babai's Rounding, and is called the *Hybrid Sampler*. The structure of this sampler, introduced in [6], follows the framework of the KGPV sampler but at the ring level, i.e., in $\mathcal{R}$. The projections are computed in $\mathcal{K}$ with $\langle .,.\rangle_\mathcal{K}$. The randomization is accomplished at the ring level in two steps, as in the randomized Babai's Rounding algorithm. First, a continuous Gaussian is subtracted from the projection, a polynomial in $\mathcal{K}$, and then every coefficient of this polynomial is rounded by a discrete Gaussian distribution over $\mathbb{Z}$. Eventually, the obtained polynomial corresponds to a z_i in Algorithm 1. As $\mathbf{c} \in \mathcal{K}^2$, only two projections, and thus iterations, are needed. Note that the pseudocode is available in [9, Alg. 3].

Algorithm 1: KGPV Sampler.

Input : An orthogonal basis $\widetilde{\mathbf{B}}$ of $\mathbf{B}$, a center $\mathbf{c}$, and a standard deviation σ.
Output: A point $\mathbf{z} \in \mathcal{L}(\mathbf{B})$ following a distribution close to $D_{\mathcal{L}(\mathbf{B}),\sigma,\mathbf{c}}$.

1   $\mathbf{z} \leftarrow 0$
2   **for** $i \leftarrow 2n-1$ **to** 0 :
3       $c_i \leftarrow \langle \mathbf{c}, \widetilde{\mathbf{b}}_i \rangle / \|\widetilde{\mathbf{b}}_i\|^2$
4       $\sigma_i \leftarrow \sigma / \|\widetilde{\mathbf{b}}_i\|$
5       $z_i \leftarrow \texttt{SamplerZ}(\sigma_i, c_i - \lfloor c_i \rfloor) + \lfloor c_i \rfloor$
6       $\mathbf{c} \leftarrow \mathbf{c} - z_i \mathbf{b}_i$
7       $\mathbf{z} \leftarrow \mathbf{z} + z_i \mathbf{b}_i$
8   **return z**

2.7 Generation of a Discrete Gaussian Distribution

Both Mitaka and Falcon need a subroutine to generate a discrete Gaussian distribution over $\mathbb{Z}$, i.e., $D_{\mathbb{Z},\sigma,c}$ with c in $[0,1)$. Note that here, c corresponds to the decimal part of c_i the projection of $\mathbf{c}$ on $\widetilde{\mathbf{b}_i}$, as in Algorithm 1. This subroutine is really challenging to implement for two reasons. Firstly, the sampler has to generate a Gaussian distribution for which the center and the standard deviation are dynamic, i.e., dependent on the point and the key. Secondly, the sampler is a key target for side-channel attacks. The most efficient and secure way is to use the *SamplerZ*, from [11, Sect. 3.9.3][1], described in Algorithm 2. It is a three-step algorithm that takes as input the targeted center $c \in [0,1)$ and a standard deviation σ. Firstly, a table based sampler, named *BaseSampler*, is called to generate z^+ following a discrete half-Gaussian distribution centered on 0 and with a constant standard deviation. Secondly, a random bit b is sampled to compute $z = b + (2b-1)z^+$. It can be seen as the sign of the random variable. The integer z thus follows a bimodal Gaussian distribution. Thirdly, a rejection sampling is applied to obtain the targeted distribution. Note that z, the output of the SamplerZ, is used to compute z_i in Algorithm 1 a coordinate of $\mathbf{z}$ in the basis $\mathbf{B}$.

Algorithm 2: SamplerZ.

Input : A center $c \in [0,1)$, a standard deviation $\sigma \in [\sigma_{\min}, \sigma_{\max}]$.
Output: An integer $\mathbf{z}$ following a distribution close to $D_{\mathbb{Z},\sigma,c}$.

1 $z^+ \leftarrow$ BaseSampler()
2 $b \xleftarrow{\$} \{0,1\}$
3 $z \leftarrow b + (2b-1)z^+$
4 $x \leftarrow -\frac{(z-c)^2}{2\sigma^2} + \frac{(z^+)^2}{2\sigma_{\max}^2}$
5 $p \leftarrow \frac{\sigma_{\min}}{\sigma} \cdot \exp(x)$
6 **return** z with probability p, otherwise restart

---

3 Previous Work

In 2022, Guerreau et al. introduced in [14] a new template attack [4] on Falcon. This attack was then improved by Zhang et al. [21] the following year. As described before, Mitaka's sampler works partly the same way as Falcon's one, but at the ring level. Thus, the authors of [21] proposed applying the same attack to Mitaka, ignoring the continuous Gaussian noise subtracted in the randomized Babai's Rounding algorithm. In this section, we outline this attack without considering the continuous Gaussian noise for more generality and simplicity.

---
[1] Refer also to the Specifications v1.0 Sect. 4.4 for more details.

3.1 Attack Overview

Let us write the signature in the orthogonal basis as $\mathbf{s} = \mathbf{c} - \mathbf{z} = \sum_{i=0}^{2n-1} y_i \widetilde{\mathbf{b}}_i$. The authors suggested using side-channel observations to gather information on y_0, which we will denote as the offset on the vector $\widetilde{\mathbf{b}}_0$. This way, an attacker could be able to classify signatures into two sets according to the value of y_0. In each of these sets, the distribution of the signatures is biased in the direction of $\widetilde{\mathbf{b}}_0$. The attacker can then approximate the direction of $\widetilde{\mathbf{b}}_0$ thanks to a statistical metric. Additionally, the norm of $\widetilde{\mathbf{b}}_0$ is also estimated. Since $\widetilde{\mathbf{b}}_0 = \mathbf{b}_0$ by construction of the orthogonal basis, it is possible to recover the exact $\mathbf{b}_0$ through an exhaustive search. This leads to knowledge of the whole secret basis as $\mathbf{b}_0 = (f\ g)$, from which F and G can be computed, thereby reconstructing the secret key.

Exploited Leakages. Firstly, it is worth recalling that having knowledge of z_i computed by the sampler is essentially the same as knowing the offset y_i, with the center $c \in [0,1]$ of the Gaussian being the only differing factor. Indeed, at the $(2n-i)^{\text{th}}$ iteration, with $2n > i \geq 0$, the projection of $\mathbf{c} - \sum_{l=i+1}^{2n-1} z_l \mathbf{b}_l$ is calculated on the vector $\widetilde{\mathbf{b}}_i$, then the SamplerZ adds a Gaussian deviation to this projection to obtain the coefficient of $\mathbf{b}_i$. At this time, the coefficient of $\widetilde{\mathbf{b}}_i$ in the signature is exactly the offset coming from the Gaussian of center c produced by the SamplerZ. Then, the next iterations do not have any impact on this coefficient because we are handling $\mathbf{b}_j$ with $j < i$, yet $\mathbf{b}_j$ is orthogonal to $\widetilde{\mathbf{b}}_i$ when $j < i$.

The attack outlined in [14] and improved in [21] takes advantages of a side-channel flaw called half Gaussian leakage to identify signatures such that y_0 is in $(-1, 1]$. Furthermore, in [21], the authors exposed a second side-channel flaw to obtain information on z_0: the sign leakage. In this study, we focus to this second leakage as it yields better results in the context of Mitaka. The targeted part in both the KGPV sampler and the Hybrid Sampler is the rounding with a discrete Gaussian distribution over $\mathbb{Z}$. The idea is to recover through template analyzes the bit b, which defines the sign of the offset produced by the SamplerZ. This bit is manipulated three times for different calculations in lines 2, 3 and 4 in Algorithm 2. Depending on the b value, some variables flip sign, leading to important variations of Hamming weight and on power consumption.

Approximation of $\mathbf{b}_0$'s Direction. According to the sign drawn during the computation of z_0, and thus the sign of the offset y_0, the signatures are separated into two sets. Both sets can be put together by multiplying signatures with the minus sign by -1. From that classification, an attacker can compute an approximation, noted $\mathbf{b}_0^{raw}$, of the direction of $\mathbf{b}_0$. The authors of [21] proposed to use the first statistical moment, i.e., the expectation, to recover a multiple of $\mathbf{b}_0$. Indeed, the expectation for our selection of signatures is zero in every direction, as the distribution is Gaussian, except in the one of $\widetilde{\mathbf{b}}_0$. The more considered signatures, the more accurate the approximation is.

Approximation of b_0's Norm. By construction, each coefficient of $\mathbf{b}_0 = (f\ g)$ is an integer sampled from $D_{\mathbb{Z},\sigma,0}$ with $\sigma_0 = 1.17\sqrt{q/2n}$. Thus, the norm can be approximated by $\|\mathbf{b}_0\| \approx \sqrt{\sum_0^{2n-1} \sigma_0^2} = 1.17\sqrt{q}$. Then, one adjusts $\mathbf{b}_0^{raw}$ with this estimated norm, leading to a new vector named $\mathbf{b}_0^{adj}$. Eventually, all the coefficients of $\mathbf{b}_0^{adj}$ are rounded off to give the final approximation $\mathbf{b}_0^{int} = (f^{int}\ g^{int})^T$.

Exhaustive Search. Eventually, an exhaustive search to recover $\mathbf{b}_0$ is performed independently on f^{int} and g^{int}. For every tried polynomial f^{int} (resp. g^{int}), g^{int} (resp. f^{int}) can be computed thanks to h. This allows for splitting the research in two and provides a verification criterion.

Let $\mathbf{e} = \mathbf{b}_0^{int} - \mathbf{b}_0$ be the error on $\mathbf{b}_0^{int}$. To make the exhaustive search practical, the strategy is to gather enough traces such that $\|\mathbf{e}\|_\infty \le 1$ and $\|\mathbf{e}\|_1 \le 7$. In practice, the limiting criterion is the second one. Hence, it is enough for an attacker to try every f^{int} and g^{int} with 3 errors of weight 1. This guarantees a total recovery of $\mathbf{b}_0$ in approximately 30 min. In Sect. 6, we provide an estimate of the number of traces required to achieve $\|\mathbf{e}\|_1 \le 7$ in practical scenarios.

3.2 Practical Considerations

The authors of [21] obtained an accuracy of 100% on an ARM Cortex-M4 STM32F407IGT6 microprocessor for the sign classification, by using measured power consumption as side-channel information. In these conditions, they are able to recover the secret key with 170 000 traces on Falcon using this leakage. However, the continuous Gaussian noise disturbs the approximation of the $\mathbf{b}_0$'s direction by deteriorating the correlation between side-channel observations and the corresponding signatures. This increases significantly the number of required traces, leading to a key recovery with around $2 \cdot 10^6$ traces on Mitaka.

Note that the simultaneous exploitation of both half-Gaussian and sign leakage leads to secret key recovery with 45 000 traces for Falcon and $1.8 \cdot 10^6$ traces for Mitaka.

4 New Improvements of the Attack on Mitaka

In this section, we describe improvements of the previous attack on Mitaka to significantly decrease the number of needed traces.

4.1 Norm Estimation

As a first improvement, we propose to enhance the adjustment $\mathbf{b}_0^{adj}$ of $\mathbf{b}_0^{raw}$. In [21], Zhang et al. proposed adjusting $\mathbf{b}_0^{raw}$ by trying different norms in $\{1.17\sqrt{q}, 1.17\sqrt{q}-1, \ldots, 1.17\sqrt{q}-10\}$. We suggest taking the problem in an other way, by adjusting the norm of $\mathbf{b}_0^{adj}$ such that it minimizes $||\mathbf{b}_0^{adj} - \mathbf{b}_0^{int}||_1$ while keeping $||\mathbf{b}_0^{adj}|| \approx 1.17\sqrt{q}$. The idea is that if our estimate of the norm is accurate, we expect that the coefficients of $\mathbf{b}_0^{adj}$ will closely approximate the integer to which they will be rounded off. In our tests, we showed that this improves our estimation of the norm. Hence, it allows the attacker to find a better approximation of $\mathbf{b}_0^{int}$ and thus reduce the number of traces required to obtain an error norm $||\mathbf{e}||_1 \leq 7$. This also allows for avoiding the trials of all norm possibilities until a success is obtained.

Note that the exhaustive search from $\mathbf{b}_0^{int}$ to $\mathbf{b}_0$ can also be improved by prioritizing changes to coefficients further from an integer.

4.2 Multiplying the Points of Interest

The second contribution of this article is to notice that, in the context of Mitaka, the attack can be performed on 512 calls of the SamplerZ. Indeed, the previous attacks were only using the call that calculates the coefficient of $\mathbf{b}_0$. In Falcon, the projections and offsets are computed on the orthogonal basis $\widetilde{\mathbf{B}}$. Thus, the exploitation of the same leakage from another SamplerZ call would approximate another $\widetilde{\mathbf{b}}_i$, which is complicated to use to recover information on $\mathbf{B}$. Conversely, in Mitaka the sampling follows the basis $\mathbf{H}^{\mathcal{K}}$ on which, because of the Gram-Schmidt procedure, the first polynomial is $\mathbf{h}_0^{\mathcal{K}} = \mathbf{b}_0^{\mathcal{K}}$. Thus, the basis of the lattice associated to $\mathbf{H}^{\mathcal{K}}$, noted $\mathbf{H}$, has the same 512 first vectors as the secret basis $\mathbf{B}$. Therefore, by construction, any $\mathbf{h}_i = \mathbf{b}_i = (x^i f \; x^i g)^T$ with polynomial multiplications in $\mathcal{R} \simeq \mathbb{Z}[x]/(x^n + 1)$. In other words, every approximation of $\mathbf{h}_i = \mathbf{b}_i$ is actually an approximation of $\mathbf{b}_0$ with re-ordered coefficients.

Thus, in the context of Mitaka, the 512 calls to BaseSampler leak exploitable information. Moreover, these 512 calls produce leakages that are independent of each other. Indeed, each call to BaseSampler uses fresh data and generates a new random number. The physical noise of different side-channel observations is also often assumed to be independent. To summarize, an attacker could try to approximate all $(\mathbf{b}_i)_{i \in [\![0,511]\!]}$, realign them to get 512 independent approximations of $\mathbf{b}_0$, and finally average them to obtain a noise-free $\mathbf{b}_0^{raw}$. The key recovery is then performed with the exact same method and we expect to obtain the key from 512 times fewer signatures. This means a complete key recovery with 4500 traces instead of 2.25 million.

Note that a gain of factor 512 can thus also be achieved on the number of traces needed to build the templates. Indeed, one can build a template set by gathering the $512 \times N$ segments from N signature computations.

Nevertheless, in practice, an additional difficulty appears compared to the previous attack: the attacker needs to identify the 512 correct points of interest in a power trace. Indeed, the SamplerZ is called 512 times, one per coordinate, and each call generates potentially several rejected samplings before one is accepted. In the previous state of the art, it was accepted that one could locate the right call of BaseSampler, corresponding to the accepted sampling z_0. In our context, each call to the SamplerZ is easily identified on a power trace. Then, to distinguish the accepted samplings from the rejected ones, we can analyze the reference implementation of Mitaka in C [8]. In the SamplerZ, if a sampling is rejected, we restart an iteration of the sampler procedure immediately. On the other hand, if the sampling is accepted, we get out of the call, increment a counter, recover the next coefficient in the structure, come back to the SamplerZ, compute a floor value and finally start the same loop as before. We stress that all these operations will make differences in the power trace, giving criteria to differentiate the status of the sampling.

4.3 Template Construction

In Sect. 3.2, we mentioned the impact of the continuous Gaussian noise to exploit the signatures in a key recovery. Additionally, this noise also impacts the creation of the templates. Indeed, during the building phase, the signatures should be labeled according to the sign of the discrete offset, drawn in the SamplerZ, in order to create a training set for the template analysis. However, from the knowledge of the key and the signature, the attacker can only compute the final offset y_i, which is the sum between the discrete offset and the continuous offset. Consequently, the continuous offset can add errors in the labeling, thus reducing the quality of the templates.

To mitigate the influence of this noise, an attacker could select, for the training, signatures such that $y_i > l$ (resp. $y_i < l$) with $l \in \mathbb{R}^+$ (resp. $l \in \mathbb{R}^-$) a wisely chosen threshold. The larger l is, the higher the probability that the sign drawn and the sign of y_i matches. On the other hand, the larger l is, the smaller the number of signatures selected for the construction of the templates. This trade-off is discussed in Sect. 6.3.

5 Attack Against Mitaka Masked Implementation

In the original article introducing Mitaka [9], the authors initially proposed and proved an efficient masking scheme for this algorithm. This reliable security against side-channel attacks is one of the main advantages of Mitaka over Falcon. The construction was proven in the t-SNI model introduced in [1]. Quickly, this proof was broken theoretically by Prest in [20]. In this section we will present this masking scheme, its weakness, and a practical attack on masked Mitaka.

5.1 The Masking Scheme

We are interested in the portion of the masking scheme related to the sampling of $D_{\mathbb{Z},r,c}$, usually performed by the SamplerZ. This is operated by the *Gauss Share-by-Share* algorithm, described in Algorithm 3 which allows to generate a masked variable $[\![z]\!]$ following a Gaussian distribution $D_{\mathbb{Z},r,c}$. More precisely, Gauss Share-by-Share takes as input a masked center $[\![c]\!] =: (c^{(i)})_{i \in [\![0,t]\!]}$, and an unmasked standard deviation r. For the i-th share $c^{(i)}$, it generates the distribution $D_{1/B \cdot \mathbb{Z}, r/\sqrt{t+1}, c^{(i)}}$ such that the sum of all the shares gives

Algorithm 3: Gauss Share-by-Share.

Input : A center $[\![c]\!]$ arithmetically masked with degree t, an unmasked standard deviation r.
Output: A masked $[\![z]\!]$ such that z follows a distribution close to $D_{\mathbb{Z},c,r}$.

1 $B \leftarrow \lceil \sqrt{2(t+1)} \rceil$
2 **for** $i \leftarrow 0$ **to** t :
3 $\quad\mid\quad z^{(i)} \leftarrow D_{1/B\cdot\mathbb{Z}, c^{(i)}, r/\sqrt{t+1}}$
4 **if** $z \notin \mathbb{Z}$ // To check in a secure way
5 $\quad\mid\quad$ restart to step 2
6 **return** $[\![z]\!] = (z^{(0)}, \ldots, z^{(t)})$

$\sum D_{1/B\cdot\mathbb{Z}, r/\sqrt{t+1}, c^{(i)}} = D_{1/B\cdot\mathbb{Z}, r, c}$ with $B := \lceil\sqrt{2(t+1)}\rceil$. To guarantee an output in $\mathbb{Z}$, and not in $1/B \cdot \mathbb{Z}$, an additional rejection sampling is used.

Quickly after the presentation of Mitaka, Prest [20] highlighted a flaw in the proof of the initially proposed masking scheme. He also described a theoretical attack that targets the masked implementation of the sampler in the t-probing model. His attack uses the fact that the differences between the shares $c^{(i)}$ of the input and the shares $z^{(i)}$ of the output are Gaussian and not uniform. That implies that if an attacker has information on the difference between some shares, she has information on the whole difference $c - z$ because the unknown part, resulting of the others shares, is 0 on average. This allows an attack of degree l on an implementation with a masking scheme of degree $t > l$, with $t \geq 4$.

5.2 Another Sampler

The generation of $D_{\mathbb{Z},r,c}$ is directly accomplished by the SamplerZ in the unmasked version. In the masked version, one has to generate $D_{1/B\cdot\mathbb{Z}, r/\sqrt{t+1}, c^{(i)}}$. To do so, the authors of Mitaka [9] chose a table-based approach, following the technique introduced by Micciancio and Walter [17]. This sampler allows for efficient sampling from Gaussian discrete distributions with varying centers and standard deviations. The part of the sampler dedicated to the generation of a discrete Gaussian with varying center $c \in [0,1]$ is referred to SamplerC and is detailed in Algorithm 4. The main advantage of this algorithm is that it only requires base samplers with constant parameters. These last samplers are much easier to optimize and can be used to precompute samples in offline mode. Different approaches can be used to implement these subroutines of SamplerC, depending on the time and memory performance sought. In our study, we will rather consider the Knuth-Yao's implementation as a subroutine, even if that has only a low impact on our work.

The idea behind the SamplerC is rather simple. It takes as input the binary decomposition of the center $c = b_1...b_k \in 2^{-k}\mathbb{Z}$ with k digits of precision and randomizes-round it digit by digit with a discrete Gaussian. The first recursion computes g_k with the base sampler $D_{b_k + 2\mathbb{Z}, r_0}$. Hence, c and $2^{-k}g_k$ have the same last bit and therefore $c - 2^{-k}g_k \in 2^{-k+1}\mathbb{Z}$. Thus at the end of all recursions, the

Algorithm 4: SamplerC.

Input: A center c in $2^{-k}\mathbb{Z}$, a base sampler noted SamplerB for $D_{c'+2\mathbb{Z},r_0}$ with fix r_0 and $c' = 0$ or 1.
Output: A real g following a distribution close to $D_{c+\mathbb{Z},r}$.

1 **if** $k=0$
2   return 0
3 $g \leftarrow 2^{-k} \cdot$ SamplerB$(2^k c)$
4 **return** $g+$ SamplerC$(c - g)$ // $c - g \in 2^{-k+1}\mathbb{Z}$

---

output g is such that $c - g$ is in $\mathbb{Z}$. By construction, g follows $D_{c+\mathbb{Z},r}$ and hence $c - g$ follows $D_{\mathbb{Z},r,c}$ as required. Notice that one can reduce the recursion depth by taking a center c in base $b > 2$. However, this requires storing b base samplers and their samples. Since memory is the first limiting criterion in a constrained device, we consider $b = 2$ in our analysis, which has little impact on our study.

5.3 Different Sampler, Same Leaks

In the masked version of Mitaka, the SamplerC is used as a subroutine of Gauss Share-By-Share, which splits the computation of the Gaussian deviation into $t + 1$ parts. However, in this subsection, we consider the hypothetical situation where the SamplerC is used directly by the Hybrid Sampler, as in the unmasked implementation. This allows us to better visualize the similarities between the leakages of the SamplerZ and the ones of the SamplerC. In this case, the coefficients of the polynomials $\mathbf{z}_i$ in $\mathcal{K}$, with $i \in \{0,1\}$, used in the Hybrid Sampler are computed by taking $c - g$ with c the coefficients of the projection of $\mathbf{c}$ on $\mathbf{h}_i^\mathcal{K}$ and g the output of the SamplerC centered in c. Therefore, the sign of g directly provides the sign of the offset y, as defined in Sect. 3. Indeed, $g \in \{c, c+1, c+2, \ldots\}$ implies a positive offset, as $\mathbf{s} = \mathbf{c} - \mathbf{z}$, and conversely $g \in \{c-1, c-2, \ldots\}$ implies a negative offset. Hence, an attacker is able to recover the same information as previously by targeting the sign of g. On the other hand, notice that the SamplerC computes $g \sim D_{c+\mathbb{Z},r}$ by adding g_i whose size grows geometrically. Thus, the rough value of g is mainly determined by g_1 the result of the last call to the base sampler. Hence, an attacker can recover information on the sign of g observing only the sign of g_1. This relation is discussed in Sect. 5.4.

In the technique of [17], the base sampler computations are carried out offline. Thus, this part can be computed in batch and be stored in a secure way. However, the sampled value g_1 is still loaded, bitshifted and added. These several manipulations can be exploited by an attacker to construct her templates similarly to the previous case. Indeed, g_1 being small, negative and positive values have significantly different Hamming weights. Thus, as in the previous attack introduced in Sect. 3, one can build templates on the sign of g_1 that can be used to construct a bias set of signatures with respect to the sign. This leads to a similar attack as before.

Remark 1. The SamplerC computes $g \sim D_{c+\mathbb{Z},r}$ and the result following $D_{\mathbb{Z},r,c}$ is recovered by calculating $c - g$. This last subtraction could also lead to an important side-channel leakage, as sign variations occur depending on the result. This leakage could give perfect information on the sign. However, this leakage really depends on the implementation and on the analyzed device, so we do not consider it to retain a more general point of view.

5.4 Building the Templates

The attack adapted for SamplerC can be slightly modified to use the weakness of the masking scheme. In Gauss Share-By-Share, a distribution $D_{1/B\cdot\mathbb{Z},r/\sqrt{t+1},c^{(i)}}$ is computed for each share $c^{(i)}$ of the masked center $[\![c]\!]$. For an attacker willing to perform the same attack as before, the main difficulty comes from the creation of the templates. During the building phase, the attacker has, by hypothesis, access to the key and so can compute the offset y_0 applied in the direction of b_0. On the other hand, she can only observe shares of z_0 through side-channel observations. Let us assume that the attacker focuses on the sign of this offset. An ideal masking scheme should make the observation of one share independent of y_0. The attacker would thus be forced to combine the $t+1$ observations of all shares to retrieve an exploitable dependence and build her templates. This leads to an exponential growth in computing complexity and in the needed number of traces. Moreover, the combination of several observations is always technically challenging in practice.

Let us analyze the situation for an attacker trying to build a template to recover the sign of the value sampled for a given share in the specific case of $t = 1$, i.e., two shares in total. Let us assume, without loss of generality, that the attacker builds the template that aims at identifying a positive offset for the first share, noted $z^{(0)}$. As presented in Sect. 5.1, this masking scheme has a theoretical flaw in its conception. The discrete offset is the sum of all the shares, with the property that the sum of any subset of shares is 0 on average. Therefore each output of the SamplerC, called share by share, is directly correlated to the sign of the discrete offset y_i for a given coordinate. The attacker can thus use the sign of y_0 to isolate the signatures with positive first share in order to create her templates. Yet, this attack is hampered by different factors: the partiality of the leak, i.e., $\mathbb{P}(\text{sign}(g_1)|\text{sign}(g))$, the masking scheme, i.e., $\mathbb{P}(\text{sign}(z^{(0)})|\text{sign}(z))$, and the continuous Gaussian noise evoked in Sect. 2.6, i.e., $\mathbb{P}(\text{sign}(y)|\text{sign}(z))$. We show here, that these different bias do not prevent the construction. The partiality of the leak is estimated at 0.83 empirically by testing different combinations of centers and standard deviations that could occur in the context of Mitaka, ten thousand times each. The continuous Gaussian adds a level of noise whose intensity depends on the key. Thereafter, we will ignore this latter theoretically, as it is 0 on average, but consider it in every practical experimentation. Finally, the masking scheme decomposes the sampling into two shares, thus the couple of signs associated to a given couple of shares can take four values: $\{+,+\}_{0.25}, \{+,-\}_{0.25}, \{-,+\}_{0.25}$ and $\{-,-\}_{0.25}$, where the subscript 0.25 indicates the probability of each pair. However, if y_0, computed from the key by the attacker, is positive, then the distribution of the possible realizations becomes biased: $\{+,+\}_{0.50}$, $\{+,-\}_{0.25}$, $\{-,+\}_{0.25}$ and $\{-,-\}_0$. Indeed, the case $\{-,-\}$ leads always to a negative y, modulo the continuous Gaussian noise, as half of the mixed sign. From these observations, we can roughly assess an estimation of the rate of correct classification by $75\% \times 83\% + 25\% \times 17\% = 66.5\%$.

Furthermore, an attacker can also select signatures such that $y_0 > l$ with $l \in \mathbb{R}^+$, a wisely chosen threshold as explained in Sect. 4.3. This has a twofold impact. First, it reduces the proportion of small offset for a given share and thus reduces the partiality of the leak. Secondly, it enhances the bias in the masking scheme, as it reduces the proportion of shares with opposite signs in favor of shares with two same signs. In conclusion, an attacker is more likely to correctly label her side-channel observations than to mislabel them. Therefore, she has the ability to construct templates in a first-order manner and recover the key, despite the presence of masks. The experimental results are presented in Sect. 6.3.

Note that a similar analysis can be conducted for any degree of masking t, but the described bias decreases as t increases. Table 1 shows the probability estimation of correct labeling according to t. This rate gives only a rough idea, as is computed without considering the continuous offset.

Table 1. Probability of correct labeling g_1 knowing y depending on masking order t.

t	0	1	2	3	4	5	6
Probability	0.83	0.665	0.632	0.612	0.599	0.586	0.579

5.5 Exploiting the Templates

Once the templates are built, an attacker can try to recover the sign of every share computed by the SamplerC for a given execution of Gauss Share-by-Share during the matching phase. With this information, she can approximate the sign of the discrete offset generated and thus realize the same attack as in the case of the unmasked implementation. The success of this attack will depend, as before, on the partiality of the leak and the continuous Gaussian noise. The masking scheme no longer hinders the attack, as the templates are applied to each share. Nevertheless, a new parameter to consider for the attacker is the templates accuracy, noted a. It corresponds to $\mathbb{P}(\text{sign}(g_1)|L)$, with L the power trace and g_1 related to the specific targeted share.

Let us analyze here again the specific case of masked Mitaka with $t = 1$. The attacker aims at inferring the sign of the total offset z based on her template results regarding the sign of g_1 of each share. Concretely, if the observed sampling corresponds to $\{+,+\}$ (resp. $\{-,-\}$), the templates label the signature positively (resp. negatively). On the other hand, if the observed sampling has mixed signs, i.e. $\{-,+\}$ or $\{+,-\}$, the signature is discarded as no information is provided on the final sign. Recall that the leak gives only partial information, accurate at 83%, on the sign of one share. Let us now compute the theoretical success rate of the attack, depending on a. For each share independently, we have a probability a to detect the actual sign of g_1 and then a probability of 0.83 that this sign matches the sign of g. Thus, the probability of correctly predicting a $\{+,+\}$ (resp. a $\{-,-\}$) is estimated by $(a \times 0.83)^2$. However, in this context, we can show that the success rate of the classification of the sign of the total offset z using the strategy described above is actually equal to $0.83a + 0.17(1-a)$. This arises from the symmetry of the situation and the fact that a mixed sign introduced by error has 1 chance over 2 of resulting in a final offset matching the predicted one. Experimental results corresponding to this masking scenario with degree $t = 1$ are available Sect. 6.2.

To conclude the description of this attack, we should also notice that the improvements discussed in Sect. 4.2 are relevant in a masked context too. Indeed, it is still possible to distinguish the rejected samplings from the accepted ones. However, it is worth noting that the masking scheme's initial computation of a sampling over $1/B \cdot \mathbb{Z}$ rather than $\mathbb{Z}$ introduces an additional level of rejection. Yet, if the masked sampling is rejected, the iteration restarts immediately. Conversely, if it is accepted, i.e., if it lies in $\mathbb{Z}$, the algorithm exits the Gauss Share-by-Share function, increments the counter, and performs $t + 1$ floating divisions to compute the next masked center. Thus, we expect to also distinguish rejections from acceptances at this level in a power trace. Therefore, this improvement enables us to reduce by a factor 512 the number of needed traces both to compute the templates during the building phase and to recover the key in the matching phase. This allows an attacker to be more selective in the traces used for construction, i.e., by using a larger l, leading to a very efficient attack.

6 Experimental Results

Our experiences on the unmasked implementation of Mitaka are based on the official implementation available in [8]. However, as far as we know, there is no public masked implementation of Mitaka. Thus, the corresponding experiments are based on our implementation of this scheme, following the description and pseudocode available in the original article [9, Sect. 7 and Annex I]. In the same manner, we use our own implementation for the SamplerC following the framework of [17]. In both masked and unmasked cases, we target the 512 points of interest as described in Sect. 4.2, which significantly reduces the required number of traces. Moreover, we apply the enhanced norm estimation from Sect. 4.1. Although having a minor impact on the trace count compared to the first improvement, it enables precise estimation of $\mathbf{b_0}$'s norm and allows one to skip the exhaustive search over multiple norm possibilities as seen in previous attacks.

6.1 On Naive Mitaka

In our context, signatures were generated using the official Mitaka implementation [8]. This process allowed us to export the exact intermediate variables.

We then simulated the template analysis, i.e. the labeling phase by deliberately falsifying some intermediate variables to match the desired classification rate.

Note that in the naive setup, the classification rate is equal to the template accuracy a introduced in Sect. 5.5. This accuracy depends on the noise level of the environment and the quality of the measurements. Our results are depicted in Fig. 1. It shows the weight of the error $\mathbf{e}$ as a function of the averaged number of traces used. Each curve is labeled with the corresponding classification success rate. These attacks exploit the sign leakage, except for the blue curve with pentagon markers which combines sign leakage and half Gaussian leakage, both with perfect classification, as defined in [21]. While the half Gaussian leakage is irrelevant in a masked context, it provides a useful comparison for unmasked scenarios. However, as the half Gaussian leakage does not enhance the attack's efficiency, we focused on the sign leakage to test various classification accuracies, i.e. different success rates for correct signature labeling. In [14,21], the authors were able to construct such templates with a success rate of 1. The corresponding comparison curve in our graph is the green one with star markers. Notably, we achieved similar results to those presented in the original article but with 500 times fewer traces. Therefore, thanks to the proposed improvement, the required number of traces dropped significantly, from 2.2 million to only 4,500.

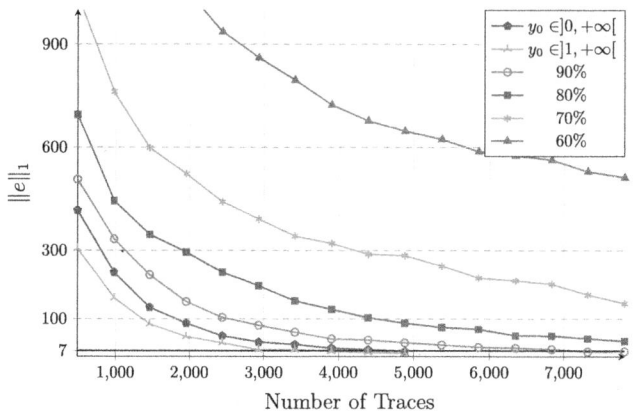

Fig. 1. Result of the improved attack on a naive implementation.

6.2 On Masked Mitaka

In the following, our experimental results correspond to the case of masked Mitaka with $t = 1$. We generated the signatures and the corresponding intermediate values from our own implementation, assuming that the sign of the targeted value is, as previously, recovered from side-channel with a given success rate. In our context, the targeted value is g_1, as defined in Sect. 5.3, independently in each share of the discrete Gaussian offset.

As in Sect. 5.5, we will note a the accuracy of the templates. The experimental results of the attacks are described in Fig. 2, which represents the weight of the error $\mathbf{e}$ as a function of the number of traces. The curves correspond to the results obtained for different levels of accuracy for the templates, varying from $a = 1$ in dark blue with pentagon markers to $a = 0.60$ in a noisier or in a more protected environment, in red with triangle markers. We add the curve corresponding to the perfect classification computed from the key in dotted green for comparison purposes. Our results take into account the continuous Gaussian noise, as we simulate the leakage after this noise was added. In the same manner, our implementation is subject to every actual bias and thus concretely describes an attacker's real configuration. Finally, note that the graph shows the number of generated traces, but only half of them are used, as mixed signs are discarded.

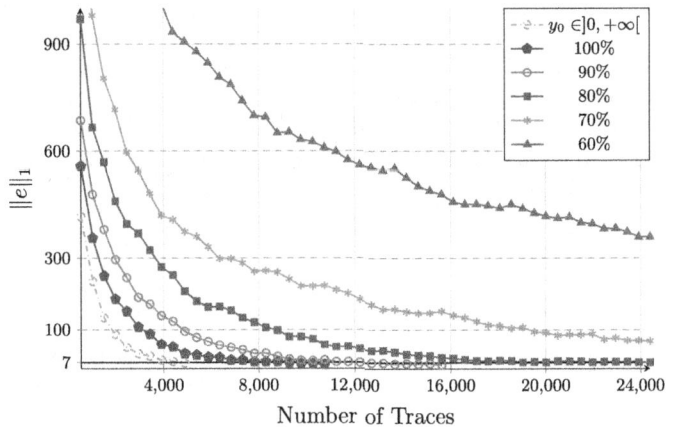

Fig. 2. Result of the improved attack on a masked implementation. (Color figure online)

We notice that we obtain a graph that depicts curves that are very similar to the ones from Fig. 1. Actually, the masking scheme can just be visualized as noise, as it increases the number of signatures mislabeled. This protection disturbs the attack but does not prevent it. Even with a lot of noise, implying a global classification of poor quality, the average of the signatures tends toward $\mathbf{b_0}$. With medium-quality templates, achieving an 80% success rate in labeling, an attacker can approach $\mathbf{b_0}$ with around 17 500 signatures generated. This is depicted by the purple curve with squares. However, the number of traces required for the attack may become prohibitive as template quality decreases.

6.3 Influence of the Threshold

In Sect. 5.4, we studied the template construction in the context of $t = 1$. We computed the theoretical success rate but did not consider the continuous Gaussian noise. Moreover, we suggested that the described bias can be enhanced by the choice of a threshold $l \in \mathbb{R}^+$. Therefore we present experimental results here, considering all factors. We obtain Table 2 for varying values of l, considering the leakage on the ith coordinate. The second line corresponds to the proportion of signatures that are kept for the templates' construction, i.e., such that the global offset $|y_i| > l$. The third line (resp. fourth line) corresponds to the average proportion of positive (resp. negative) first share when $|y_i| > l$. Each result is expressed as a percentage and represents an average of ten thousand tests conducted with various centers and standard deviations. Note that in this case, these two parameters do not seem to have an impact on the result.

Table 2. Influence of l in labeling during the building phase.

Value of $l \in \mathbb{R}^+$	0	1	2	3	4	5
Proportion of selected traces	100	72.6	48.3	29.6	16.4	8.0
Proportion of correctly labeled positive offset	65.8	68.0	70.1	74.7	76.8	78.6
Proportion of correctly labeled negative offset	53.2	56.5	60.3	62.5	65.6	68.5

We notice a gap between the classification of the negative and positive cases. This is explained by a small asymmetry when the last iteration of the SamplerC takes as input the bit $c' = 0$ and when the base sampler, computing $D_{c'+2\mathbb{Z}, r_0}$, outputs 0. In this situation, the offset produced by g_1 is null. The Hamming weight in this context corresponds to a positive offset. Therefore, this neutral offset is classified as positive, making this class a little more represented. Indeed, as an attacker knows only the total offset during the building phase, the number of traces labeled positively is fixed. Thus, adding more representatives of this class increases the percentage of success. Note that an attacker could use this fact to construct a better-quality template for the positive offset. She could then use it to label as positive the 50% of traces with the highest similarity score and label the rest as negative. Alternatively, she could achieve a satisfactory classification of the positive cases and only retain traces labeled $\{+, +\}$ in the matching phase. This doubles the number of traces to generate, but it can be worthy if the quality of both templates is unbalanced.

These results and remarks ensure that a trade-off can be obtained to guarantee that the construction of the templates is carried out on a biased set.

7 Countermeasures

To protect Mitaka against these attacks, several countermeasures can be considered. In [21], the authors suggested reducing the signal-to-noise ratio (SNR) thanks to two implementation tips. The first one aims at limiting the variation of the Hamming weight. For example, one can encode the sign on $\{1, 2\}$ instead of $\{0, 1\}$. The second approach involves computing all possible scenarios during execution. For instance, one can calculate all computations for both positive and negative signs and then select results consistent with what was drawn. This avoids signal differences that depend on sensitive choices. Their results show that these countermeasures do not completely prevent the leakage, but by reducing the SNR, they increase the number of traces required for the attack.

However, these protections do not take into account a stronger attack, such as the one presented in Sect. 4.2. An interesting countermeasure could be to shuffle the loop that calls the SamplerZ. Indeed, the order does not impact the sampling because the same operation is computed independently on each of the 512 coefficients. We suggest implementing this shuffling similarly to a Random Start Index (RSI), using a unique random XOR with the list of indices. This makes the countermeasure almost free in terms of computation.

This countermeasure forces the attacker to attack "on average." During the construction of the templates, they can no longer assign the calculated sign for y_i to the corresponding segment in the trace. Their best approach is to focus on traces where the number of positive or negative signs is significantly greater than the expected value. As a result, the probability of each sample having this sign increases on average. This methodology is much less effective because, when combined with other biases, the correct classification rate for training the template becomes very low. Additionally, this prevents the use of a threshold l (see Sect. 5.4) that could have strengthened this bias. Finally, the Bienaymé-Chebyshev inequality shows that the required number of traces to find one that deviates sufficiently from the mean to be exploitable quickly becomes very large. Indeed, the sign distribution follows a uniform probability law of $1/2$, so an attacker wishing to keep traces with 70% positive or negative signs will only retain about 1% of the generated traces. In this case, they will achieve a bias in each sampling of at most 56% (see Table 2).

An easy and inexpensive countermeasure that could complement the shuffling would be to implement the code around SamplerZ in constant time so that an accepted offset is no longer distinguishable from a rejected one in side-channel observations. In this scenario, an attacker would have to guess the accepted sampling from the rejected ones based only on the expected value of the rejection. As the difficulty of predicting the exact position of the accepted sampling depends on the targeted vector, a trade-off can be made between the number of targeted vectors (ranging from 1 to 512) and the accuracy in guessing the accepted sampling. This leads to an increase in the number of traces and noise. The exact acceptance ratio of the SamplerZ depends on the parameters, but we can roughly approximate it as 2, to give a concrete idea of the countermeasure. Thus, the noise is also multiplied by the same factor.

8 Conclusion

Falcon, currently drafted by NIST, could present challenges for embedded systems due to its complexity, especially regarding memory usage. In contrast, Mitaka offers a relevant alternative, sharing the same underlying paradigm as Falcon but with a simpler design. Recent advancements, especially the ANTRAG trapdoor generation discussed in [10], confirm Mitaka's potential. However, although initially thought to be more resilient to side-channel attacks, our study reveals vulnerabilities in its structure.

In this article, we significantly enhanced a previously known attack by tailoring it to Mitaka's specifications, resulting in a drastic reduction in the required number of traces. Moreover, we analysed the suggested masking scheme for Mitaka and exposed a novel side-channel weakness. We leveraged this vulnerability using a similar approach to the one used in the unprotected settings, targeting a first-order masked implementation of Mitaka and successfully recovering the key despite the protection. Finally, we suggest countermeasures to prevent this attack. Rather inexpensive, theses protections can be easily implemented.

Nevertheless, in a broader context, the advancements outlined in this article provide a framework for attacks targeting Mitaka's Gaussian sampler, as they expose a significant vulnerability in the functioning of the Hybrid Sampler. These insights could potentially be leveraged to exploit other side-channel leakages, posing a significant challenge to the practical security of Mitaka.

Acknowledgments. We thank the reviewers for their insightful comments.

References

1. Barthe, G., et al.: Strong non-interference and type-directed higher-order masking. In: ACM CCS, pp. 116–129 (2016)
2. Bauer, S., Santis, F.D.: A differential fault attack against deterministic falcon signatures. Cryptology ePrint Archive 422 (2023)
3. Bernstein, D., Hülsing, A., Kölbl, S., Niederhagen, R., Rijneveld, J., Schwabe, P.: The sphincs+ signature framework. In: ACM CCS, pp. 2129–2146 (2019)
4. Chari, S., Rao, J.R., Rohatgi, P.: Template attacks. In: Kaliski, B.S., Koç, K., Paar, C. (eds.) CHES 2002. LNCS, vol. 2523, pp. 13–28. Springer, Heidelberg (2003). https://doi.org/10.1007/3-540-36400-5_3
5. Ducas, L., et al.: CRYSTALS-dilithium: a lattice-based digital signature scheme. TCHES **2018**(1), 238–268 (2018)
6. Ducas, L., Prest, T.: A hybrid gaussian sampler for lattices over rings. Cryptology ePrint Archive, 660 (2015)
7. Ducas, L., Prest, T.: Fast Fourier orthogonalization. In: ACM ISSAC, pp. 191–198 (2016)
8. Espitau, T.: Supporting code for Mitaka signature (2022). https://github.com/espitau/Mitaka-EC22/tree/main
9. Espitau, T., et al.: MITAKA: a simpler, parallelizable, maskable variant of falcon. In: Dunkelman, O., Dziembowski, S. (eds.) EUROCRYPT 2022. LNCS, vol. 13277, pp. 222–253. Springer, Cham (2022). https://doi.org/10.1007/978-3-031-07082-2_9
10. Espitau, T., Nguyen, T.T.Q., Sun, C., Tibouchi, M., Wallet, A.: Antrag: annular NTRU trapdoor generation. Cryptology ePrint Archive (2023)
11. Fouque, P.A., et al.: Falcon: Fast-Fourier lattice-based compact signatures over NTRU, specification v1. 2. In: NIST Post-Quantum Cryptography Standardization Round, vol. 3 (2020)
12. Gentry, C., Peikert, C., Vaikuntanathan, V.: Trapdoors for hard lattices and new cryptographic constructions. In: SToC, pp. 197–206. ACM (2008)

13. Goldreich, O., Goldwasser, S., Halevi, S.: Public-key cryptosystems from lattice reduction problems. In: Kaliski, B.S. (ed.) CRYPTO 1997. LNCS, vol. 1294, pp. 112–131. Springer, Heidelberg (1997). https://doi.org/10.1007/BFb0052231
14. Guerreau, M., Martinelli, A., Ricosset, T., Rossi, M.: The hidden parallelepiped is back again: power analysis attacks on falcon. TCHES **2022**(3), 141–164 (2022)
15. Karabulut, E., Aysu, A.: FALCON down: breaking FALCON post-quantum signature scheme through side-channel attacks. In: ACM IEEE Design Automation Conference, pp. 691–696 (2021)
16. McCarthy, S., Howe, J., Smyth, N., Brannigan, S., O'Neill, M.: BEARZ attack FALCON: implementation attacks with countermeasures on the FALCON signature scheme. In: SECRYPT, pp. 61–71. SciTePress (2019)
17. Micciancio, D., Walter, M.: Gaussian sampling over the integers: efficient, generic, constant-time. In: Katz, J., Shacham, H. (eds.) CRYPTO 2017. LNCS, vol. 10402, pp. 455–485. Springer, Cham (2017). https://doi.org/10.1007/978-3-319-63715-0_16
18. Peikert, C.: An efficient and parallel Gaussian sampler for lattices. In: Rabin, T. (ed.) CRYPTO 2010. LNCS, vol. 6223, pp. 80–97. Springer, Heidelberg (2010). https://doi.org/10.1007/978-3-642-14623-7_5
19. Prest, T.: Gaussian sampling in lattice-based cryptography. Ph.D. thesis, École Normale Supérieure, Paris, France (2015). https://tel.archives-ouvertes.fr/tel-01245066
20. Prest, T.: A key-recovery attack against Mitaka in the t-probing model. In: Boldyreva, A., Kolesnikov, V. (eds.) PKC. LNCS, vol. 13940, pp. 205–220. Springer, Cham (2023). https://doi.org/10.1007/978-3-031-31368-4_8
21. Zhang, S., Lin, X., Yu, Y., Wang, W.: Improved power analysis attacks on falcon. In: Hazay, C., Stam, M. (eds.) EUROCRYPT 2023. LNCS, vol. 14007, pp. 565–595. Springer, Cham (2023). https://doi.org/10.1007/978-3-031-30634-1_19

Message-Recovery Horizontal Correlation Attack on *Classic McEliece*

Brice Colombier[1]([✉]) [iD], Vincent Grosso[1] [iD], Pierre-Louis Cayrel[1] [iD], and Vlad-Florin Drăgoi[2,3] [iD]

[1] Université Jean Monnet Saint-Etienne, CNRS, Institut d Optique Graduate School, Laboratoire Hubert Curien UMR 5516, 42023 Saint-Etienne, France
{b.colombier,vincent.grosso,pierre.louis.cayrel}@univ-st-etienne.fr
[2] Faculty of Exact Sciences, Aurel Vlaicu University, Arad, Romania
vlad.dragoi@uav.ro
[3] LITIS, University of Rouen Normandie, Saint-Etienne du Rouvray, France

Abstract. As the technical feasibility of a quantum computer becomes more and more likely, post-quantum cryptography algorithms are receiving particular attention in recent years. Among them, code-based cryptosystems were first considered unsuited for hardware and embedded software implementations because of their very large key sizes. However, recent work has shown that such implementations are practical, which also makes them susceptible to physical attacks. In this article, we propose a horizontal correlation attack on the *Classic McEliece* cryptosystem, more precisely on the matrix-vector multiplication over $\mathbb{F}_2$ that computes the shared key in the encapsulation process. The attack is applicable in the broader context of Niederreiter-like code-based cryptosystems and is independent of the code structure, *i.e.* it does not need to exploit any particular structure in the parity check matrix. Instead, we take advantage of the constant time property of the matrix-vector multiplication over $\mathbb{F}_2$. We extend the feasibility of the basic attack by leveraging information-set decoding methods and carry it out successfully on the reference embedded software implementation. Interestingly, we highlight that implementation choices, like the word size or the compilation options, play a crucial role in the attack success, and even contradict the theoretical analysis.

Keywords: Post-quantum cryptography · Side-channel attacks · Classic McEliece

1 Introduction

There is almost no day without a *Quantum Computing* breaking news. During the last five years the evolution of quantum technologies went from creating and improving qubits, investigating both quantitative as well as qualitative aspects [26,36,44], to practical simulated models of connecting qubits into quantum networks [25,43], all in a common goal of achieving a scalable quantum computer. From private companies to public organizations/governments announcing new quantum computing and security acts, all converge to this major technology challenge. The US Public Law No. 117–260 from 2022, also known as the *Quantum Computing Cybersecurity Preparedness Act* encourages the migration of information technology systems to quantum-resistant cryptography. Also, the European Union Agency for Cybersecurity urges all private data sensitive technologies to adopt quantum resistant cryptographic solutions [7].

The post-quantum cryptography standardization process initiated by NIST in 2016 aims at standardizing cryptography algorithms whose security is not threatened by the existence of a quantum computer of sufficient capacity. Two categories of algorithms are considered, namely digital signatures and key encapsulation mechanisms (KEMs). One KEM proposal under consideration in the fourth round of the standardization process is the *Classic McEliece* cryptosystem which is based on error-correcting codes [1] and its security relies on the hardness of the binary syndrome decoding problem.

While the first rounds of the standardization process focused on performing cryptanalysis of the algorithms, NIST explicitly stated that time has now come for more hardware implementations, and in particular side-channel resistant implementations. In this regard, it is of prime importance to evaluate the susceptibility of the implementations of these algorithms to physical attacks in general and to side-channel attacks in particular. It is also one of the main tracks followed by the NIST PQC seminar,[1] where the side-channel analysis topic is recurrent [37,39].

Even before being considered a strong candidate in the post-quantum cryptography race, code-based cryptosystems were subject to side-channel attacks [2,12,13,22,31]. The first round of the NIST post-quantum standardization process ended with the last documentation updates on June 12th, 2019. It was that moment that triggered even more specific side-channel attacks, *i.e.* oriented towards the *Classic McEliece* KEM. In a series of articles, either the security of session key or of the private key was successfully broken [11,19,20,24].

In this work, we focus on the core operation of the encapsulation process in the *Classic McEliece* cryptosystem, namely the matrix-vector multiplication over $\mathbb{F}_2$ between the public-key, *i.e.* the parity-check matrix of the error-correcting code, and a random vector of fixed, low Hamming weight. This operation has been targeted before by physical attacks, for instance by laser fault injection [11] or a profiled side-channel attack [17]. In both of these works, the value of the integer syndrome is exploited to recover the secret error vector. This breaks the security of the KEM and allows to recover the shared key, since the secret error vector is used as seed to derive the shared secret key.

Conversely here, we recover the secret error vector by performing an *unprofiled* horizontal correlation attack on the matrix-vector multiplication over $\mathbb{F}_2$. This attack directly relies on the constant-time property of the implementation of the matrix-vector multiplication. We show that a correlation exists between the columns of the parity-check matrix and the Hamming distance leakage dur-

---

[1] https://csrc.nist.gov/Projects/post-quantum-cryptography/workshops-and-timeline/pqc-seminars.

ing the execution. This allows to identify which columns of the parity-check matrix are involved in the syndrome computation and reveals the positions of the errors in the secret error vector.

Contributions

This article makes the following contributions:

- We propose the first unprofiled attack on the *Classic McEliece* cryptosystem. This attack uses a single side-channel trace and allows to recover the shared secret key of the KEM. Since it targets the matrix-vector multiplication step, it is applicable to any Niederreiter-like cryptosystem,
- We evaluate the attack success with respect to important implementation choices, namely the size of the words used for the implementation of the matrix-vector multiplication over $\mathbb{F}_2$ and the optimization options passed to the compiler. In particular, we highlight a discrepancy between the success rate of the attack in a simulated setting and the observations made on real side-channel traces.

Organization

This article is organized as follows. Section 2 presents the *Classic McEliece* cryptosystem before reviewing existing side-channel attacks that apply against it. Section 3 describes the proposed horizontal correlation side-channel attack. Section 4 provides experimental results, both with simulated and real side-channel traces, for various parameters. In Sect. 5, we discuss the influence of the implementation choices on the attack success rate, before concluding in Sect. 6.

2 Related Work

2.1 Notations

The following notations are used in this article. Sets are written as calligraphic uppercase letters, for example $\mathcal{S}$. Matrices are written in uppercase bold letters, for example $\mathbf{M}$. Vectors are written in lowercase bold letters, for example $\mathbf{v}$. The identity matrix of size n is written as $\mathbf{I}_n$. The jth column of a matrix $\mathbf{M}$ is written as $\mathbf{M}_{[:,j]}$. The entry on the jth column of the ith row of a matrix $\mathbf{M}$ is written as $\mathbf{M}_{[i,j]}$. The ith entry of a vector $\mathbf{v}$ is written as $\mathbf{v}_i$. The Hamming weight of a binary vector $\mathbf{v}$, *i.e.* the number of non-zero coordinates, is written as $\text{HW}(\mathbf{v})$. The Hamming distance between two vectors $\mathbf{u}$ and $\mathbf{v}$ is written as $\text{HD}(\mathbf{u}, \mathbf{v})$. The bitwise logical AND between two vectors $\mathbf{u}$ and $\mathbf{v}$ is written as $\mathbf{u} \wedge \mathbf{v}$ and the logical exclusive-OR is written as $\mathbf{u} \oplus \mathbf{v}$.

2.2 The *Classic McEliece* Cryptosystem

The *Classic McEliece* cryptosystem is a candidate to the NIST post-quantum cryptography standardization process [1]. After going through the first three rounds, it has been selected as a fourth round candidate on July 5th, 2022. As a KEM, its role is to allow for secure transfer of a shared secret key. It is split into three functions: key generation, encapsulation and decapsulation. During key generation, a public key $\mathbf{H}_{\text{pub}} = (\mathbf{I}_{n-k}|\mathbf{T})$ and its associate private key $\mathbf{G}_{\text{priv}}$ are generated. The encapsulation mechanism take as input the public key and outputs the shared secret key $\mathbf{k}$ that will be used in the next exchange and an encapsulated value $\mathbf{s}$ sent to the second party. The second party runs the decapsulation using its private key $\mathbf{G}_{\text{priv}}$ and the encapsulated message $\mathbf{s}$ to derive the shared secret key $\mathbf{k}$. We focus on the encapsulation step here.

***Classic McEliece* Encapsulation.** We target the encapsulation function of the *Classic McEliece* cryptosystem, described in Algorithm 1 and more precisely the ENCODE subroutine, shown on line 3 in Algorithm 1 and detailed in Algorithm 2. The specific operation we target with the proposed attack is the matrix-vector multiplication over $\mathbb{F}_2$ between the parity-check matrix and the random error vector. This operation is essentially the encryption step of the Niederreiter cryptosystem [32]. In this setting, a message is first encoded into a constant-weight vector before being multiplied by the parity-check matrix of a binary Goppa code. The security of this construct relies on the $\mathcal{NP}$-hardness of the binary syndrome decoding problem [6]: knowing $\mathbf{H}_{\text{pub}}$ and $\mathbf{s}$, recovering $\mathbf{e}$ is hard.

Algorithm 1. *Classic McEliece* encapsulation [1]

1: **function** ENCAPS($\mathbf{T}$)
2:    Draw a random vector $\mathbf{e} \in \mathbb{F}_2^n$ with $\text{HW}(\mathbf{e}) = t$.
3:    Compute $\mathbf{c} \leftarrow$ ENCODE($\mathbf{e}, \mathbf{T}$)
4:    Compute $\mathbf{k} \leftarrow \mathsf{H}(1 \,\|\, \mathbf{e} \,\|\, \mathbf{c})$ ▷ session key (shared secret)
5:    **return** $(\mathbf{c}, \mathbf{k})$

Algorithm 2. *Classic McEliece* encoding subroutine [1]

1: **function** ENCODE($\mathbf{e}, \mathbf{T}$)
2:    Define $\mathbf{H}_{\text{pub}} \leftarrow (\mathbf{I}_{n-k}|\mathbf{T})$
3:    Compute $\mathbf{s} \leftarrow \mathbf{H}_{\text{pub}} . \mathbf{e}$
4:    **return** $\mathbf{s}$

Embedded Software Implementations. For years, embedded software implementations of the Niederreiter cryptosystem were deemed impractical because of the high memory requirements for the public key storage. The first implementation on an 8-bit microcontroller was done by Heyse in 2010 [21], but with relatively low-security parameters: $n = 2048$, $k = 1751$ and $t = 27$. These values must be compared with the ones of the *Classic McEliece* submission provided in Table 1, that lead to even larger keys. Implementation challenges of code-based cryptosystems on embedded platforms are discussed in [9].

The selection of *Classic McEliece* as a candidate for the last rounds of the NIST post-quantum cryptography standardization process sparked a renewed interest for embedded software implementations. In [38], the public key is not stored but retrieved from the private key, following a streaming approach which had been described before in [42]. However, with the memory capacity of embedded devices increasing continuously, it was only a matter of time before the public key could be fully stored in the Flash memory. This happened in 2021, when Chen and Chou proposed an implementation of the *Classic McEliece* cryptosystem on an ARM Cortex-M4 target, along with many other optimizations [14].

2.3 Side-Channel Attacks

Side-channel attacks exploit the information leakage that occurs when an algorithm is being executed on a physical device. Profiled attacks require access to an open device for a preliminary training step, during which the attacker can freely set the secret values and perform side-channel measurements. A classifier is trained with this data and used to attack a closed device and recover the secret values. Conversely, an *unprofiled* attack does not require a training step, and is therefore more readily applicable. Well-known examples of unprofiled attacks are the differential power analysis (DPA) [23] and the correlation power analysis (CPA) [10].

Horizontal Attacks. A horizontal attack, as published by Walter [45] originally, consists in observing several intermediate values inside a single side-channel trace to extract secret information from it. This is in contrast with vertical attacks, of which the DPA and the CPA are examples, where a single intermediate value is repeatedly observed over several side-channel traces.

In [45], a DPA-style attack on the modular exponentiation algorithm used in the RSA cryptosystem is carried out, allowing the attacker to recover the secret exponent. This attack was later improved by Clavier *et al.* [16]. By using correlation, authors were able to distinguish a squaring from a multiplication by identifying if intermediate values were involved in a computation or not. We follow a similar approach in this article, essentially identifying which columns of the parity-check matrix are involved in the computation.

Side-Channel Attacks on the Niederreiter/*Classic McEliece* Cryptosystems. We focus here on side-channel attacks that aim at recovering the

Table 1. *Classic McEliece* parameters

Parameters set	348864	460896	6688128	8192128
n	3488	4608	6688	8192
m	12	13	13	13
t	64	96	128	128
$k = n - mt$	2720	3360	5024	6528
$n - k = mt$	768	1248	1664	1664

secret message in the Niederreiter cryptosystem or equivalently the secret random vector in the *Classic McEliece* cryptosystem. It is straightforward to see that if one is capable of recovering the secret random vector **e**, then the encapsulation step is effectively deterministic and broken. As a consequence, the attacker has access to the shared secret key, since all other operations are deterministic and the $\mathbf{H}_{\text{pub}}$ matrix is public.

In [24], authors attack the constant-time Berlekamp-Massey decoding algorithm used in the decapsulation step. This is done on the reference hardware implementation of *Classic McEliece*. They adapt the attack from [40] and identify error positions by repeatedly adding columns of the parity-check matrix to the syndrome, determining which ones correspond to a decoding failure. While the iterative chunking strategy they propose reduces the number of queries, the number of side-channel traces needed ranges from 334 to 654 for the *Classic McEliece* parameters. In contrast, the attack we propose succeeds with a single side-channel trace.

The approach followed in [17] is entirely different and targets the encapsulation step instead, in particular the matrix-vector multiplication over $\mathbb{F}_2$ used for the syndrome computation. It consists in deriving an integer syndrome from side-channel measurements, instead of the binary syndrome. Although this integer syndrome might be slightly incorrect in some positions, because of noise in the side-channel measurements and errors in the integer syndrome derivation, it is usually enough to recover the error positions using a distinguisher based on the dot product. This attack has the advantage of requiring a single side-channel measurement in the attack phase. However, being in the profiled attack setting, an open device is still required for the profiling phase. An improvement of the attack resistance to noise in the profiled setting was recently published by Grosso *et al.* [19] thanks to a t-test based attack method.

In [13], a horizontal attack is mounted not on the Niederreiter cryptosystem but on the McEliece cryptosystem, specifically on its variant that uses quasi-cyclic moderate-density parity-check (QC-MDPC) codes. This horizontal attack does not attack the syndrome computation but the key rotation, which is inherent to the quasi-cyclic property. Since the attack targets a hardware implementation, the registers which are overwritten during the key rotation step have a very distinctive leakage, which can be exploited to recover the key. Conversely, the attack we propose is more general since it does not exploit the structure of the matrix.

Guo et al. proposed a profiled key-recovery attack on the *Classic McEliece* cryptosystem [20]. Targetting the decapsulation step, it recovers the private key using between 300 and 800 side-channel traces. Since it targets the private key, i.e. the long-term secret, it is definitely a more serious threat than message-recovery attacks, which recover the shared secret key, i.e. the short-term secret. However, their attack requires specifically crafted ciphertexts, which correspond to single-bit error vectors. Arguably, these very specific error patterns could be easily detected during the decapsulation step and a countermeasure based on an early abort could prevent the attack.

It is worth noting that other post-quantum cryptosystems, based on lattices for instance, have been the target of horizontal side-channel attacks as well, as already highlighted in previous works [3,4].

In this work, we target the syndrome computation in the encapsulation step, but propose an *unprofiled* attack instead. Therefore, before outlining the attack procedure, we describe how the syndrome computation is usually implemented.

2.4 Software Implementations of the Syndrome Computation

The target operation of the proposed attack is the syndrome computation, which is a matrix-vector multiplication over $\mathbb{F}_2$, as given in Equation (1). This operation is the second step of the encoding routine in the encapsulation process (see line 3 in Algorithm 2), which is called after a uniform random constant-weight vector **e** has been drawn.

$$\mathbf{s} = \mathbf{H}_{\text{pub}}.\mathbf{e} \qquad (1)$$

Schoolbook Implementation. The matrix-vector multiplication over $\mathbb{F}_2$ is implemented in software by iterating over the matrix rows and columns and performing a logical AND operation between the matrix and the vector entries, while accumulating the result on the syndrome entry by a logical XOR operation. We refer to this matrix-vector multiplication method as the *schoolbook* method. This is described in Algorithm 3, where an $(n-k) \times n$ matrix **M** is multiplied by an n-bit vector **v** to obtain an $(n-k)$-bit syndrome **s**.

Algorithm 3. Schoolbook matrix-vector multiplication over $\mathbb{F}_2$.

1: **function** MAT_VEC_MULT_SCHOOLBOOK(**M**, **v**)
2:     **for** $r \leftarrow 0$ to $(n-k-1)$ **do**
3:         $\mathbf{s}_r \leftarrow 0$ ▷ Initialisation
4:         **for** $c \leftarrow 0$ to $(n-1)$ **do**
5:             $\mathbf{s}_r \leftarrow \mathbf{s}_r \oplus (\mathbf{M}_{[r,c]} \wedge \mathbf{v}_c)$ ▷ Multiply and add
6:     **return s**

However, for memory efficiency reasons, the schoolbook version of the matrix-vector multiplication algorithm described in Algorithm 3 is rarely used in actual implementations. This assumes that the vector and matrix entries, which are binary, are stored as they are, each occupying a full word. To avoid occupying a full word to store only one bit, matrix row and vector entries are usually packed into words.

Packed Implementation. In the *packed* implementation, a vector **b** of size w is used to accumulate, by a logical XOR operation, the result of the logical AND operation between the matrix entry and the vector entry, which are both words. In this manner, the XOR and AND operations are bitsliced, and a total of w bits are processed in parallel. We refer to w as the word width. Then, this word is repeatedly shifted and XORed over itself, to perform a logical XOR operation between all its bits. Then, the least-significant bit, on which the result has been accumulated, is extracted. Eventually, this bit is packed into a syndrome word by shifting it by an amount between 0 and $w-1$ and performing a logical OR operation with the previously stored word.

We refer to this matrix-vector multiplication over $\mathbb{F}_2$ method as the *packed* method, where bits are packed into w-bit wide words. This is described in Algorithm 4, where an $(n-k) \times \frac{n}{w}$ matrix **M** is multiplied by a vector **v** of size $\frac{n}{w}$ to obtain an syndrome **s** of size $\frac{n-k}{w}$. This method is used in the reference implementation of the *Classic McEliece* cryptosystem submitted to the NIST PQC standardization process [1] with $w = 8$. Conversely, in the additional vectorized reference implementation, the value which is used is $w = 64$. The optimized implementation by Chen and Chou [14] uses $w = 32$ this time. Given the variety of the word widths used in these packed implementations, it is important to evaluate how it affects the attack success. This will be experimentally highlighted and discussed in the next sections.

Algorithm 4. Packed matrix-vector multiplication over $\mathbb{F}_2$.

1: **function** MAT_VEC_MULT_PACKED(**M**, **v**, w)
2:     **for** $r \leftarrow 0$ to $\left(\frac{n-k}{w} - 1\right)$ **do**
3:         $\mathbf{s}_r \leftarrow \mathbf{0}$ ▷ Initialization
4:     **for** $r \leftarrow 0$ to $(n-k-1)$ **do**
5:         $\mathbf{b} \leftarrow \mathbf{0}$
6:         **for** $c \leftarrow 0$ to $\left(\frac{n}{w} - 1\right)$ **do**
7:             $\mathbf{b} \leftarrow \mathbf{b} \oplus (\mathbf{M}_{[r,c]} \land \mathbf{v}_c)$ ▷ Multiply and add
8:         $i \leftarrow \frac{w}{2}$
9:         **while** $i > 0$ **do**
10:            $\mathbf{b} \leftarrow \mathbf{b} \oplus (\mathbf{b} \verb|>>| i)$ ▷ Exclusive-OR folding
11:             $i \leftarrow \frac{i}{2}$
12:         $\mathbf{b} \leftarrow \mathbf{b} \land 1$ ▷ LSB extraction
13:         $\mathbf{s}_{r/w} \leftarrow \mathbf{s}_{r/w} \lor (\mathbf{b} \verb|<<| (r \bmod w))$ ▷ Bit packing
14:     **return s**

As a side note, the schoolbook method shown in Algorithm 3 may be seen as a special case of the packed method of Algorithm 4 with $w = 1$.

3 Horizontal Correlation Attack on the Matrix-Vector Multiplication

The section describes the proposed horizontal correlation attack on the *Classic McEliece* cryptosystem.

3.1 Attacker Model

We place ourselves in the framework of physical attacks, where an attacker has a physical access to the device. Therefore, the attacker can measure physical quantities such as power consumption or electromagnetic radiations while the device is running. In addition, we assume that the device under attack raises a reliable trigger signal before the encapsulation. This last constraint could be relaxed, considering the regular patterns followed by the power consumption of the device while the matrix-vector multiplication over $\mathbb{F}_2$ is being performed, as shown in the next subsection.

We also assume that the attacker knows the public key $\mathbf{H}_{\mathrm{pub}}$ and the syndrome $\mathbf{s}$, which are public, and aims at recovering the secret error vector $\mathbf{e}$ of Hamming weight t. Scenarios where the public key is generated on demand from the private key are out of scope, since the proposed attack targets the encapsulation step. Therefore, we assume that the public key is known to the attacker, and that she does not need to rely on specific techniques to obtain it. The value of t is a parameter of the cryptosystem and is assumed to be publicly known too. Even though the value of $\mathbf{s}$ is not necessary in the basic version of the attack, it is needed to carry out information-set decoding, as detailed in Subsect. 3.4.

Being in the *unprofiled* attack setting, the attacker model we rely on is rather weak. In particular, we do not assume that the attacker owns a copy of the device on which he can perform a preliminary profiling step.

3.2 Side-Channel Trace Acquisition and Reshaping

After implementing Algorithm 4 in C, we performed power consumption sidechannel measurements on the device running it. Experimental parameters are detailed in Sect. 4. An example side-channel trace of the power consumption of the microcontroller, while the matrix-vector multiplication over $\mathbb{F}_2$ is performed, is shown in Fig. 1.

Since NIST explicitly requires the implementations submitted to the PQC standardization process to be constant-time, the side-channel trace is very regular and patterns can easily be spotted in it. This is visible in Fig. 1, where a side-channel trace of the multiplication between a 32×64 matrix and a 64-bit vector is shown. One can easily see that a pattern is repeated 32 times, corresponding to the multiplication of the 32 matrix rows with the error vector.

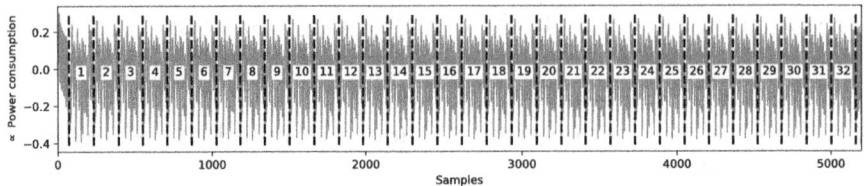

Fig. 1. Side-channel trace of the matrix-vector multiplication over $\mathbb{F}_2$ for $n = 64$ showing the $n - k = 32$ blocks.

Precise identification of this pattern's length is done by observing peaks in the auto-correlation of the side-channel trace.

Therefore, after performing the acquisition of the raw side-channel trace $\mathcal{T}_{\text{raw}}$ of length n_{samples} as depicted in Fig. 1, it is reshaped into a matrix $\mathcal{T}_{\text{reshaped}}$. The process is a simpler version of the one presented in [17]. Each row of this matrix contains the side-channel leakage associated with the multiplication of one matrix row with the error vector. Therefore, there are $(n - k)$ rows in $\mathcal{T}_{\text{reshaped}}$. The number of columns in $\mathcal{T}_{\text{reshaped}}$ is approximately $\frac{n_{\text{samples}}}{n-k}$, given that a few samples at the beginning and the end of $\mathcal{T}_{\text{raw}}$ do not correspond to the matrix-vector multiplication.

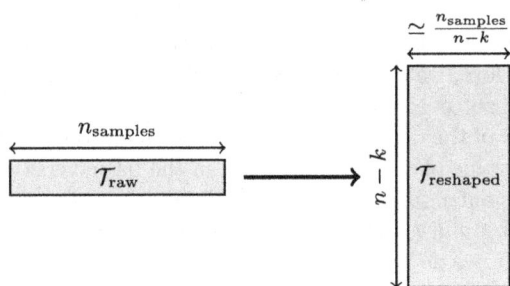

Fig. 2. Reshaping step applied on the raw trace (adapted from [17])

3.3 Horizontal Correlation Attack

The next step consists in performing a horizontal correlation attack between the columns of the parity-check matrix and sub-traces corresponding to the multiplication of one matrix row with the error vector. These sub-traces are easily identified due to the constant-time property of the matrix-vector multiplication over $\mathbb{F}_2$, as it will be shown in the Sect. 4. This defines a correlation matrix **C** of n rows and as many columns as the number of samples in the sub-traces. An entry of the correlation matrix **C** stores the value of the Pearson correlation coefficient, estimated using Eq. (2), between a column of the parity-check matrix and a column of the reshaped side-channel trace.

$$\rho(\mathbf{x},\mathbf{y}) = \frac{\sum_{i=1}^{N}(\mathbf{x}_i - \bar{\mathbf{x}})\cdot(\mathbf{y}_i - \bar{\mathbf{y}})}{\sqrt{\sum_{i=1}^{N}(\mathbf{x}_i - \bar{\mathbf{x}})^2}\sqrt{\sum_{i=1}^{N}(\mathbf{y}_i - \bar{\mathbf{y}})^2}} \quad \text{with} \quad \bar{\mathbf{x}} = \frac{1}{N}\sum_{i=1}^{N}\mathbf{x}_i \quad (2)$$

Formally, the value of each entry of the correlation matrix $\mathbf{C}$ is given in Eq. (3), where ρ stands for the Pearson correlation coefficient.

$$\mathbf{C}_{[i,j]} = \rho(\mathbf{H}_{\text{pub}[:,i]}, \mathcal{T}_{\text{reshaped}[:,j]}) \quad (3)$$

From there, the positions of the errors in the secret error vector are derived. This is done by keeping only the maximum value for every row of $\mathcal{C}$ and sorting them according to the maximum absolute value of the correlation coefficient. This process effectively sorts the columns of the parity-check matrix according to the probability that they are involved in the syndrome computation. Therefore, it reveals the secret error vector **e**.

The intuition behind this attack path is that every bit of the error vector, no matter the width w, will have a contribution to the side-channel leakage if it meets a 1 in the associated matrix column. The asymmetry of the logical AND operation is crucial here: the side-channel leakage associated with matrix columns which are aligned with a zero in the error vector will be essentially random. Conversely, side-channel leakage associated with matrix columns which are aligned with a one in the error vector will follow the changes of values in the matrix columns.

An illustration of the proposed attack on a toy example is shown in Fig. 3, with parameters $n = 8$, $k = 4$, $t = 3$ and $w = 2$.

The correlation between the columns of the reshaped side-channel trace and the matrix columns is computed to build the correlation matrix $\mathbf{C}$ in step ①. The maximum of the absolute values is computed for every column is computed in step ② and the permutation P that sorts the resulting vector is obtained in step ③. Finally, the permutation P is inverted and P^{-1} is applied to a vector made of t ones and $n - t$ zeroes to recover the secret error vector **e** in step ④.

The "n/a" entries in the $\mathbf{C}$ matrix denotes correlation values which cannot be computed because of the constant Hamming distance side-channel leakage for the last **b** computation, implying a zero variance. In reality, the side-channel leakage is always noisy and prevents such cases from happening.

3.4 Information-Set Decoding

Although the previous section suggested that the attack works by identifying the t matrix columns for which the absolute value of the correlation coefficient

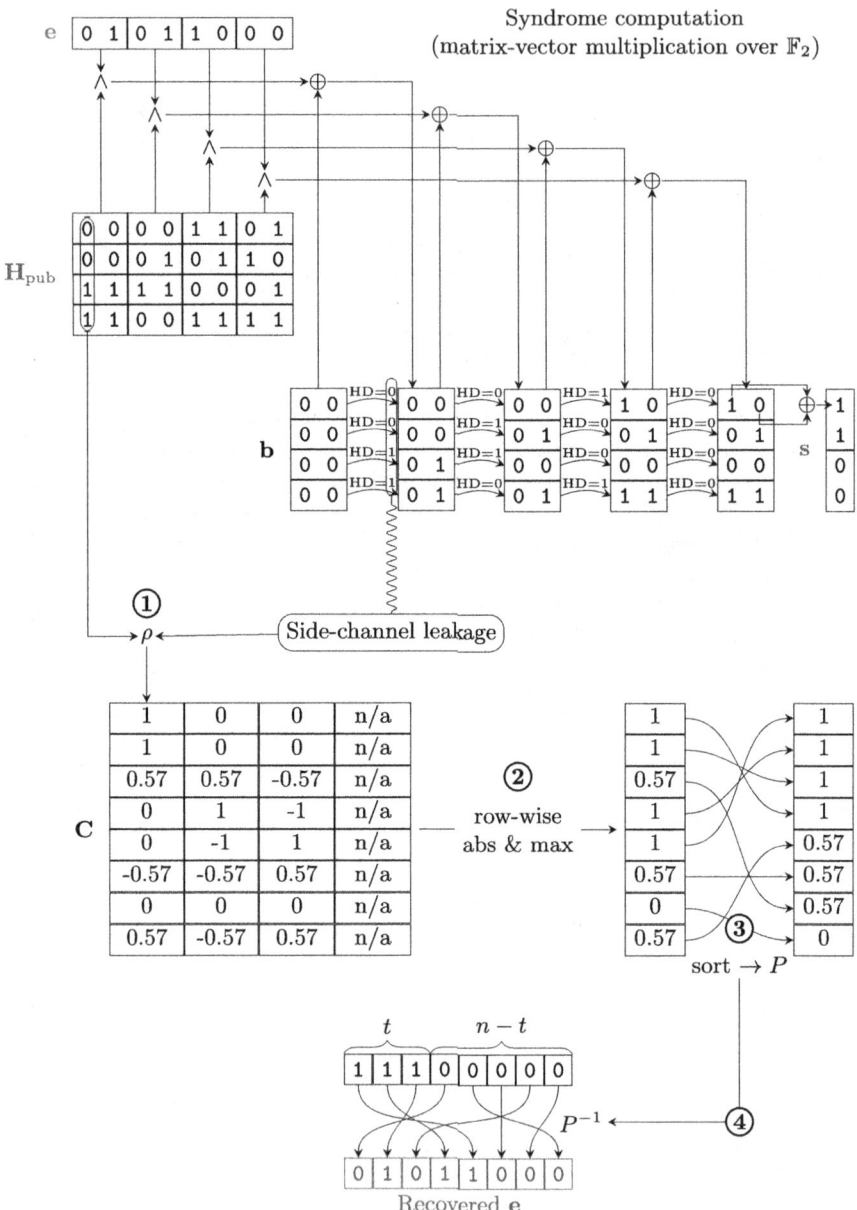

Fig. 3. Overview of the proposed horizontal attack on a toy example with parameters $n = 8$, $k = 4$, $t = 3$ and $w = 2$.

is the greatest, it is in fact sufficient to have those columns belong to the first $n - k$ ones, which are called the *information set*, instead of the first t columns strictly, like it was the case for the toy example in Fig. 3. First proposed by Prange [35], the information-set decoding strategy leverages linear algebra to decode more efficiently. The use of this strategy was already proposed in the context of physical attacks, to significantly improve the attack success rate [17, 20, 24].

Further improvements to the information-set decoding method may be used as well, to improve the success rate of this strategy [18, 27, 28, 41] [5, 29]. With these improvements, up to δ ones might be missing from the information set, as opposed to the Prange setting for which $\delta = 0$. These methods have an exponential time complexity with respect to the n parameter of the cryptosystem. Therefore, their running time quickly becomes prohibitive. However, they may still be used in a realistic setting up to $\delta = 3$. This is the value we keep for the experiments in the next section.

4 Experimental Results

4.1 Simulated Trace

In order to precisely control the signal-to-noise ratio (SNR) and observe its influence on the success rate of the proposed attack, we first experiment with a simulated trace. This trace is generated by considering both a Hamming weight and a Hamming distance leakage model. We did not investigate more advanced side-channel leakage simulators, like ELMO [30], since they are too device-specific. We do this at every step of Algorithm 4 where the **b** intermediate value is updated. Therefore, the Hamming weight leakage model is simulated by storing HW(**b**), and the Hamming distance leakage model by storing the Hamming distance between **b** and its previous value, denoted as HD(**b**, **b**⁻). The inputs **M** and **v** of the algorithm are chosen at random with HW(**v**) = t. Both the Hamming weight and the Hamming distance leakage are normalized, to contribute equally to the overall information leakage.

The number of ones found in the first $n - k$ positions of the error vector after sorting according to the absolute value of the correlation coefficient is shown in Fig. 4. Additionally, we plot the $[t - \delta; t]$ band in green for $\delta = 3$ as justified above. If the number of ones in the first $n - k$ positions of the vector is higher than $t - \delta$, then the correct error vector can be recovered using the information-set decoding strategy outlined above. The thick black line at the bottom of the plots shows the number of ones found in the first $n - k$ positions when choosing the error vector randomly.

The experiment is run 25 times for each set (n, k, t, SNR) of parameters, and the number of ones is averaged. As expected, the higher the SNR, the easier it is to identify which columns of the parity check matrix contributed to the syndrome computation.

Two other observations can be made. First, the wider the word, the lower the success rate. This is because the contribution of a single bit to the overall

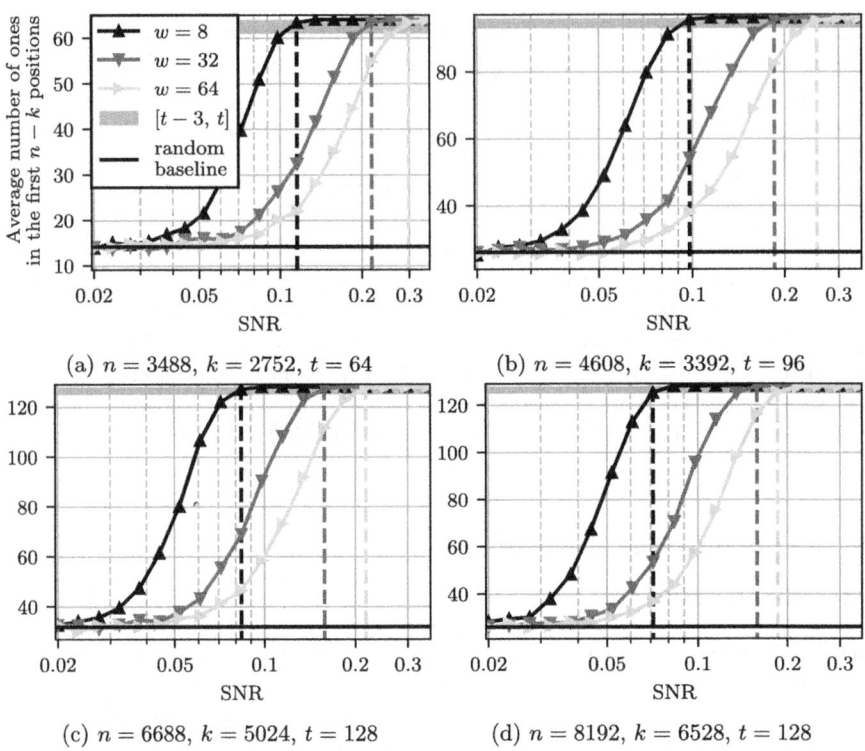

Fig. 4. Average number of ones in the first $n-k$ positions of the error vector for several SNR values for the *Classic McEliece* parameters.

correlation coefficient is less visible for large words. Therefore, the success rate of the attack is the highest for $w = 8$ and the lowest for $w = 64$. Second, the larger the cryptographic parameters, the higher the success rate. This is explained by the fact that the error vector is used $n - k$ times in the syndrome computation. Therefore, the number of samples used in the computation of the correlation coefficient is higher for large cryptographic parameters. Therefore, the success rate of the attack is the highest for $n = 8192$ and the lowest for $n = 3488$.

4.2 Real Trace

All the experiments are performed with the ChipWhisperer platform [33]. The target microcontroller embeds an ARM Cortex-M4 core, which is the embedded software target recommended by NIST for the PQC standardization process.[2] The ARM Cortex-M4 core has thirteen 32-bit registers. Therefore, one could argue that its "native" word width is $w = 32$.

---

[2] https://groups.google.com/a/list.nist.gov/g/pqc-forum/c/cJxMq0_90gU.

Unfortunately, the particular microcontroller we used embeds only 256 kB of Flash memory. Therefore, the public key associated with even the smallest *Classic McEliece* parameters does not fit in, since around 331 kB would be needed to store it ($\frac{n \times m \times t}{8} = \frac{3488 \times 12 \times 64}{8} = 331\,008$).

Consequently, we must scale the cryptosystem parameters accordingly. To accommodate this constraint while keeping the parameters choice unbiased, we selected two parameters sets from the Decoding challenge webpage:[3] $(n, k, t) = (640, 512, 13)$ and $(1600, 1280, 30)$.

For each parameter set, we perform the experiments for three different word widths w: 8, 32 and 64. We extracted the relevant `syndrome` function from the NIST reference implementation. Since it uses $w = 8$ natively, we simply made two variations for $w = 32$ and $w = 64$.

Additionally, we also explore the different optimization levels available when compiling the source code for the target microcontroller: `-O0`, `-O1`, `-O2`, `-O3` and `-Os`. The first one, `-O0`, corresponds to no optimization at all. This setting is commonly used when aiming at constant-time implementations, to prevent the compiler from optimizing the loops and ruining the developer's efforts. Settings ranging from `-O1` to `-O3` correspond to various optimization efforts, `-O3` being the highest, providing the best performance. Finally, `-Os` aims at minimizing the code storage footprint in memory.

The number of clock cycles required for the multiplication of one matrix row with the error vector for the two sets of parameters are given in Table 2. As expected, both the word width and the optimization level have a strong influence on these numbers.

Table 2. Number of clock cycles for the multiplication of a matrix row by the error vector

Word width	Optimization level					Word width	Optimization level				
	-O0	-O1	-O2	-O3	-Os		-O0	-O1	-O2	-O3	-Os
$w = 8$	3120	829	741	222	741	$w = 8$	7080	1830	1821	476	1821
$w = 32$	889	229	222	226	200	$w = 32$	1939	528	522	528	470
$w = 64$	743	206	194	153	194	$w = 64$	1463	456	443	443	419
(a) $n = 640, k = 512, t = 13$						(b) $n = 1600, k = 1280, t = 30$					

The experimental results obtained for the two parameters sets are shown in Fig. 5. Each experiment was repeated 200 times to provide sufficient statistical significance for the box plots.

Several observations can be made regarding these experimental results. First of all, for a given word width w, the optimization level used for the compilation has a strong impact on the success rate of the attack, except for $w = 64$ for which this impact is lower. For example, for $w = 32$, the only successful attack

---
[3] https://decodingchallenge.org/goppa.

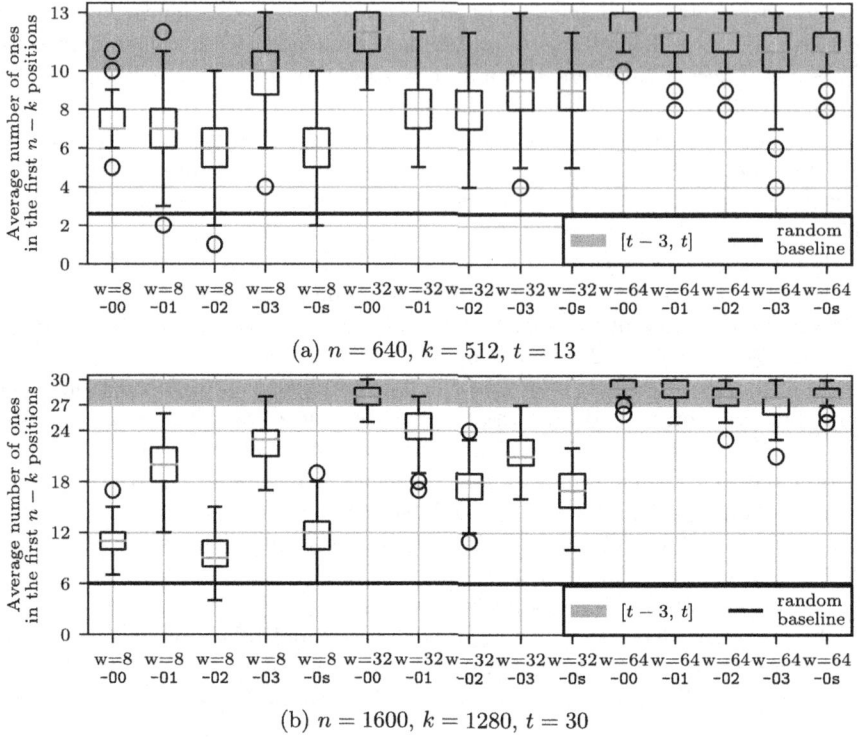

Fig. 5. Number of ones in the first $n - k$ positions of the error vector for several word widths and compilation options for the Decoding challenge parameters.

is the one performed on the program which was compiled with the -O0 option. However, this is not always the case and, contrarily to the intuition, the highest success rate is not always obtained for -O0. For example for $w = 8$, this is for the -O3 optimization level that the success rate is the highest. Overall, there is no clear relation between the optimization level and the attack success rate, but it does have an impact on it.

The second observation, which again is counterintuitive and contradicts the simulation results presented in the previous subsection, is that the wider the word, the higher the success rate. For $w = 64$, no matter the optimization level, there are always more than $t - 3$ ones in the first $n - k$ positions of the error vector, therefore allowing for a full recovery using the information-set decoding strategy. This observation is hard to explain without a better understanding of the internal architecture of the processor. Some possible causes are examined in the next section.

5 Discussion on the Attack Success

As highlighted in the previous section, while the attack is indeed successful in several settings, its success rate seems to depend heavily on implementation choices: the word width and the optimization level. Moreover, the attack as it is described relies on a specific leakage model: the Hamming distance leakage model. The objective of this section is to take a closer look at the effect of these settings and the conditions that make the attack successful.

5.1 A Closer Look at the Assembly

The attack success rate depends on the word width used for the implementation of the matrix-vector multiplication over $\mathbb{F}_2$ as well as the optimization level. Changing these parameters has an effect on machine code generated by the compiler. The influence of these parameters is examined below. We want to emphasize that, at the moment, we are not able to provide quantitative results about the exact role of every instruction in the observed side-channel leakage, especially with respect to the leakage model. Therefore, we restrict our analysis to a qualitative approach, highlighting the differences between the generated codes. Future works could focus on developing a complete assembly implementation of the target operation, in order to fully understand where the side-channel leakage might come from and to eliminate it.

As a preliminary step, it is important to note that the target microcontroller has 32-bit registers. Therefore, its "native" word width is 32 bits and we can expect implementations that use this width to be compiled in a more straightforward manner.

For ease of reading, the generated assembly codes are grouped together in Appendix A.

w = 8 When the word width is $w = 8$, then the processor must handle data which is smaller than its native register size. This is illustrated in Listings 1 to 3, where the generated codes are shown for different optimization levels. These are grouped if identical for different optimization levels.

As expected, with the lowest optimization effort -O0, the code is rather simple (see Listing 1). One should note that load and store instructions explicitly work with *bytes*, hence the b suffix (ldrb and strb). For higher optimization levels, the increment of the row and columns indices are embedded in the instruction, shortening the code but still matching precisely with the algorithm. Finally, for the highest optimization level -O3, the compiler determines that memory accesses can be grouped and loads words of 32 bits directly, hence the ldr.w variant shown in Fig. 3.

The differences between the generated codes depending on the optimization level might explain why the attack success varies so much between them for $w = 8$, as shown on the left-hand side of Fig. 5b.

w = 32 When the word width is $w = 32$, then the processor handles data which is of its native register size. Therefore, the generated code is more consistent across optimization levels, as shown in Listings 4 to 6. This might explain why the success rate of the attack for $w = 32$ seems more consistent, as shown in the center of Fig. 5b. However, there is no apparent reason why the attack only succeeds for the -O0 optimization level and not for the others.

We chose to not include the generated code for the -O3 optimization level. Indeed, it is different depending on the chosen n value. For $n = 640$, the inner for loop, found at line 6 in Algorithm 4, is fully unrolled. This is not the case for the larger value $n = 1600$, for which the generated code is very similar to the one obtained with optimization levels -O2 and -Os, shown in Listing 6.

w = 64 When the word width is $w = 64$, then the processor must handle data which is larger than its native register size. As such, when loading data, either a load double ldrd instruction or two distinct load ldr.w instructions are used. We denote those as step 1/2 in Listings 7 to 10. Some other instructions might be inserted between the two steps to better fill up the pipeline. Again, we do not include the code generated for the -O3 optimization level because of inconsistent loop unrolling depending on the value of n. Besides this difference, the code is the same as for $w = 32$. Therefore, similarly to the conclusion we drew for $w = 32$, it is hard to find a reason why the attack is almost always successful for $w = 64$.

5.2 Leakage Assessment

To try to better understand the differences of success rate depending on the word width and optimization levels, we conducted a leakage assessment on the side-channel traces. We used a rather common ANOVA (ANalysis Of VAriance) F-test, also referred to as NICV [8], which is a ratio between the inter-class and intra-class variances, where classes are intermediate values of the syndrome computation after application of a leakage model. We consider both the Hamming weight and Hamming distance leakage models in this analysis.

We perform the F-test on side-channel traces obtained with $n = 1600$ and $k = 1280$. Since we consider intermediate values of $\mathbf{b}$, this leaves us with a population of size of $\frac{(n-k) \times n}{w}$. For the largest value of $w = 64$ this is a population of 8000, which is statistically relevant considering the number of classes at hand. Instead of plotting the values of the F statistic for all samples, we keep only the maximum for a given set of parameters. In addition, we normalize it since what we are interested in is a comparison between values for a given leakage model.

Results are shown in Fig. 6. For the Hamming weight leakage model, in Fig. 6a, the highest F statistic values are systematically obtained for the lowest level of optimization -O0. Intuitively, this can be explained because the code is less condensed than for higher levels of optimization, allowing to better observe the Hamming weight values through the power consumption. The F statistic values are much lower for higher optimization levels. Nevertheless, even though the F statistic is very high for $w = 8$ and the -O0 optimization level, the attack does not succeed in this case, as shown in Fig. 5. Therefore, it confirms the intuition that the attack is not possible with the Hamming weight leakage model.

For the Hamming distance leakage model, in Fig. 6b, which is the one being exploited by the proposed attack, the variations observed for the different parameters almost follow the success rates from Fig. 5. This is a confirmation that the leakage model being exploited experimentally is really the Hamming distance leakage model.

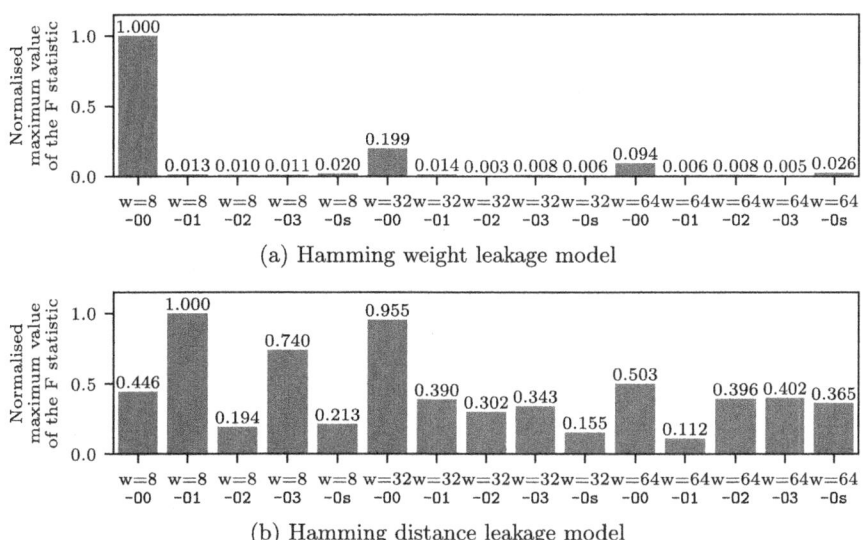

Fig. 6. Maximum value of the F statistic for several word widths and compilation options and two leakage models.

5.3 Dependency on the Hamming Distance Leakage Model

The attack path is better explained using a Hamming distance leakage model, directly illustrating the transitions from 0 to 1 or from 1 to 0 when updating the **b** value, as shown in line 7 of Algorithm 4. A Hamming weight leakage model would not allow to follow the proposed attack path, since, for a Hamming distance of 1, the Hamming weight might either increase or decrease, which makes it useless when computing the correlation.

Nevertheless, when implementing and compiling the line 7 of Algorithm 4, it is unavoidable that several machine code instructions are generated. In particular, the logical AND between the matrix entry and the error vector entry is computed *first*, before being accumulated on **b** by a logical XOR *later*. As a consequence, a Hamming weight leakage model on this intermediate value, storing the logical AND between the matrix entry and the error vector entry, could be leveraged for the attack as well. This is formalized in Eq. (4) after the definition of the Hamming distance.

$$\mathrm{HD}(\mathbf{b}, \mathbf{b}^-) = \mathrm{HD}(\mathbf{b}^- \oplus \mathbf{H}_{\mathrm{pub}[i,j]} \wedge \mathbf{e}_j, \mathbf{b}^-) = \mathrm{HW}(\mathbf{H}_{\mathrm{pub}[i,j]} \wedge \mathbf{e}_j) \quad (4)$$

Another related issue with the Hamming weight or Hamming distance leakage models is the so-called "double-cancellation" phenomenon [17,19]. It happens when two bits of the intermediate value $\mathbf{b}$ are flipped in opposite directions. While this is visible on the Hamming distance, this is hidden when considering only the Hamming weights. However, it requires two ones to be in the same word of width w in $\mathbf{e}$, which is quite rare and not an issue for the proposed correlation-based attack.

5.4 Hardware Implementations

While the experimental results provided show the attack success on a microcontroller, there is a strong possibility that the same attack path could be exploited for hardware implementations too. Indeed, the method of splitting the public-key matrix $\mathbf{H}_{\mathrm{pub}}$ and the error vector $\mathbf{e}$ in words of width w was also chosen in the FPGA implementation of *Classic McEliece* [15]. Consequently, the Hamming distance between intermediate values stored in the flip-flops of the digital design could be retrieved by side-channel analysis, and the same attack would apply. The Hamming distance model is usually very applicable when performing power or electromagnetic analysis of FPGA and ASIC implementations [4,34]. As a side note, a mixture of a Hamming weight and Hamming distance leakage was already exploited in a similar attack on the QC-MDPC McEliece cryptosystem in [13].

6 Conclusion

This article introduces the first unprofiled attack on the post-quantum cryptosystem *Classic McEliece*. Exploiting the constant-time property of the matrix-vector multiplication over $\mathbb{F}_2$ used in the encapsulation, the proposed horizontal correlation attack recovers the secret error vector $\mathbf{e}$, and therefore the KEM shared secret key, from a single side-channel trace.

We highlighted how implementation choices, namely the word width used for the bitsliced operations and the optimization level passed to the compiler, have a strong impact on the attack success rate. Using a leakage assessment methodology and disassembling the generated code, we tried to explain the success rate variations.

As next steps, it is worth investigating the feasibility of the attack on a different architecture, like RISC-V, or on a hardware target, like an FPGA. Another interesting aspect could be to better exploit the Hamming weight leakage, since it is very strong for the -O0 optimization level. Combining both the Hamming weight and the Hamming distance leakages could also lead to more powerful attacks.

Acknowledgements. This work received funding from the France 2030 program, managed by the French National Research Agency under grant agreement No. ANR-22-PETQ-0008 PQ-TLS.

A Assembly Codes for Different Optimization Levels and Word Widths

All the assembly codes shown below were obtained with the `arm-none-eabi-gcc` compiler, version 9.2.1 20191025. Annotations are by the authors and follow the notations used in the article.

Listing 1. $w = 8$, optimization level -O0

```
ldrb  r2, [r3, #0]      // Load byte e_j
...
ldrb  r3, [r3, #0]      // Load byte H_pub[i,j]
ands  r3, r2            // H_pub[i,j] ∧ e_j
uxtb  r2, r3            // Unsigned extend byte
ldrb  r3, [r7, #31]     // Load byte b
eors  r3, r2            // b = b ⊕ H_pub[i,j] ∧ e_j
strb  r3, [r7, #31]     // Store byte b
```

Listing 2. $w = 8$, optimization levels -O1, -O2 and -Os

```
ldrb.w  r3, [r2, #1]!   // Load byte H_pub[i,j]
ldrb.w  lr, [ip, #1]!   // Load byte e_j
and.w   r3, r3, lr      // H_pub[i,j] ∧ e_j
eors    r1, r3          // b = b ⊕ H_pub[i,j] ∧ e_j
```

Listing 3. $w = 8$, optimization level -O3

```
ldr.w  r4, [r2], #4   // Load 4 bytes H_pub[i,j], H_pub[i,j+1], H_pub[i,j+2] and H_pub[i,j+3]
ldr.w  r3, [r0], #4   // Load 4 bytes e_j, e_j+1, e_j+2 and e_j+3
...
and.w  r3, r3, r4     // H_pub[i,j] ∧ e_j, H_pub[i,j+1] ∧ e_j+1, H_pub[i,j+2] ∧ e_j+2
                      // and H_pub[i,j+3] ∧ e_j+3
eor.w  r1, r1, r3     // b_j = b_j ⊕ H_pub[i,j] ∧ e_j, b_j+1 = b_j+1 ⊕ H_pub[i,j+1] ∧ e_j+1
                      // b_j+2 = b_j+2 ⊕ H_pub[i,j+2] ∧ e_j+2 and b_j+3 = b_j+3 ⊕ H_pub[i,j+3] ∧ e_j+3
```

Listing 4. $w = 32$, optimization level -O0

```
ldr   r2, [r3, #0]     // Load e_j
...
ldr   r3, [r3, #0]     // Load H_pub[i,j]
ands  r3, r2           // H_pub[i,j] ∧ e_j
ldr   r2, [r7, #36]    // Load b
eors  r3, r2           // b = b ⊕ H_pub[i,j] ∧ e_j
str   r3, [r7, #36]    // Store b
```

Listing 5. $w = 32$, optimization level -O1

```
ldr.w r3, [r2, #4]!    // Load H_pub[i,j];
ldr.w r5, [r7, #4]!    // Load e_j;
ands  r3, r5           // H_pub[i,j] ∧ e_j
eors  r1, r3           // b = b ⊕ H_pub[i,j] ∧ e_j
```

Listing 6. $w = 32$, optimization levels -O2 and -Os

```
ldr.w r4, [r2], #4     // Load H_pub[i,j];
ldr.w r3, [r0], #4     // Load e_j;
...
and.w r3, r3, r4       // H_pub[i,j] ∧ e_j
eor.w r1, r1, r3       // b = b ⊕ H_pub[i,j] ∧ e_j
```

Listing 7. $w = 64$, optimization level -O0

```
ldrd  r0, r1, [r3]         // Load H_pub[i,j] in 2 registers
...
ldrd  r2, r3, [r3]         // Load e_j in 2 registers
and.w r5, r0, r2           // H_pub[i,j] ∧ e_j (step 1)
and.w r6, r1, r3           // H_pub[i,j] ∧ e_j (step 2)
ldrd  r2, r3, [r7, #112]   // Load b in 2 registers
eor.w r1, r2, r5           // b = b ⊕ H_pub[i,j] ∧ e_j (step 1)
str   r1, [r7, #56]        // Store b (step 1)
eors  r3, r6               // b = b ⊕ H_pub[i,j] ∧ e_j (step 2)
str   r3, [r7, #60]        // Store b (step 2)
```

Listing 8. $w = 64$, optimization level -O1

```
ldr.w r1, [r3, #8]!    // Load H_pub[i,j] (step 1)
ldr   r2, [r3, #4]     // Load e_j (step 1)
ldr.w r7, [r4, #8]!    // Load H_pub[i,j] (step 2)
ands  r1, r7           // H_pub[i,j] ∧ e_j (step 1)
ldr   r7, [r4, #4]     // Load e_j (step 2)
ands  r2, r7           // H_pub[i,j] ∧ e_j (step 2)
eor.w ip, r1, ip       // b = b ⊕ H_pub[i,j] ∧ e_j (step 1)
eors  r0, r2           // b = b ⊕ H_pub[i,j] ∧ e_j (step 2)
```

Listing 9. $w = 64$, optimization level -O2

```
ldr.w  r1, [r3, #8]!    // Load H_pub[i,j] (step 1)
ldr.w  r6, [r4, #8]!    // Load e_j (step 1)
ldr    r2, [r3, #4]     // Load H_pub[i,j] (step 2)
ands   r1, r6           // H_pub[i,j] ∧ e_j (step 1)
ldr    r6, [r4, #4]     // Load e_j (step 2)
...
and.w  r2, r2, r6       // H_pub[i,j] ∧ e_j (step 2)
eor.w  r5, r5, r1       // b = b ⊕ H_pub[i,j] ∧ e_j (step 1)
eor.w  r0, r0, r2       // b = b ⊕ H_pub[i,j] ∧ e_j (step 2)
```

Listing 10. $w = 64$, optimization level -Os

```
ldr.w  fp, [r4, #8]!    // Load H_pub[i,j] (step 1)
ldrd   sl, r1, [r8]     // Load e_j in 2 registers
ldr    r7, [r4, #4]     // Load H_pub[i,j] (step 2)
and.w  sl, sl, fp       // H_pub[i,j] ∧ e_j (step 1)
ands   r1, r7           // H_pub[i,j] ∧ e_j (step 2)
...
eor.w  r0, sl, r0       // b = b ⊕ H_pub[i,j] ∧ e_j (step 1)
eor.w  r3, r3, r1       // b = b ⊕ H_pub[i,j] ∧ e_j (step 2)
```

References

1. Albrecht, M.R., et al.: Classic McEliece: conservative code-based cryptography: cryptosystem specification. Technical report, National Institute of Standards and Technology (2022)
2. Avanzi, R., Hoerder, S., Page, D., Tunstall, M.: Side-channel attacks on the McEliece and Niederreiter public-key cryptosystems. J. Cryptogr. Eng. **1**(4), 271–281 (2011)
3. Aydin, F., Aysu, A., Tiwari, M., Gerstlauer, A., Orshansky, M.: Horizontal side-channel vulnerabilities of post-quantum key exchange and encapsulation protocols. ACM Trans. Embed. Comput. Syst. **20**(6), 110:1–110:22 (2021)
4. Aysu, A., Tobah, Y., Tiwari, M., Gerstlauer, A., Orshansky, M.: Horizontal side-channel vulnerabilities of post-quantum key exchange protocols. In: IEEE International Symposium on Hardware Oriented Security and Trust, pp. 81–88. IEEE Computer Society, Washington (2018)
5. Becker, A., Joux, A., May, A., Meurer, A.: Decoding random binary linear codes in $2^{n/20}$: How $1 + 1 = 0$ improves information set decoding. In: Pointcheval, D., Johansson, T. (eds.) Annual International Conference on the Theory and Applications of Cryptographic Techniques. Lecture Notes in Computer Science, vol. 7237, pp. 520–536. Springer, Cambridge, UK (Apr 2012)
6. Berlekamp, E.R., McEliece, R.J., van Tilborg, H.C.A.: On the inherent intractability of certain coding problems (corresp.). IEEE Trans. Inf. Theory **24**(3), 384–386 (1978)

7. Beullens, W., et al.: Post-quantum cryptography: current state and quantum mitigation. Publications Office of the European Union (2022). https://doi.org/10.2824/92307
8. Bhasin, S., Danger, J., Guilley, S., Najm, Z.: NICV: normalized inter-class variance for detection of side-channel leakage. IACR Cryptology ePrint Archive p. 717 (2013)
9. Biasi, F.P., Barreto, P.S.L.M., Misoczki, R., Ruggiero, W.V.: Scaling efficient code-based cryptosystems for embedded platforms. J. Cryptogr. Eng. **4**(2), 123–134 (2014). https://doi.org/10.1007/s13389-014-0070-1
10. Brier, E., Clavier, C., Olivier, F.: Correlation power analysis with a leakage model. In: Joye, M., Quisquater, J.-J. (eds.) CHES 2004. LNCS, vol. 3156, pp. 16–29. Springer, Heidelberg (2004). https://doi.org/10.1007/978-3-540-28632-5_2
11. Cayrel, P.-L., Colombier, B., Drăgoi, V.-F., Menu, A., Bossuet, L.: Message-recovery laser fault injection attack on the *Classic McEliece* cryptosystem. In: Canteaut, A., Standaert, F.-X. (eds.) EUROCRYPT 2021. LNCS, vol. 12697, pp. 438–467. Springer, Cham (2021). https://doi.org/10.1007/978-3-030-77886-6_15
12. Cayrel, P.L., Dusart, P.: McEliece/Niederreiter PKC: sensitivity to fault injection. In: International Conference on Future Information Technology, Busan, South Korea (2010)
13. Chen, C., Eisenbarth, T., Maurich, I., Steinwandt, R.: Horizontal and vertical side channel analysis of a McEliece cryptosystem. IEEE Trans. Inf. Forensics Secur. **11**(6), 1093–1105 (2016)
14. Chen, M., Chou, T.: Classic McEliece on the ARM Cortex-M4. IACR Trans. Cryptogr. Hardw. Embed. Syst. **2021**(3), 125–148 (2021)
15. Chen, P., et al.: Complete and improved FPGA implementation of Classic McEliece. IACR Trans. Cryptogr. Hardw. Embed. Syst. **2022**(3), 71–113 (2022)
16. Clavier, C., Feix, B., Gagnerot, G., Roussellet, M., Verneuil, V.: Horizontal correlation analysis on exponentiation. In: Soriano, M., Qing, S., López, J. (eds.) ICICS 2010. LNCS, vol. 6476, pp. 46–61. Springer, Heidelberg (2010). https://doi.org/10.1007/978-3-642-17650-0_5
17. Colombier, B., Dragoi, V.F., Cayrel, P.L., Grosso, V.: Profiled side-channel attack on cryptosystems based on the binary syndrome decoding problem. IEEE Trans. Inf. Forensics Secur. **17**, 3407–3420 (2022). https://doi.org/10.1109/TIFS.2022.3198277
18. Dumer, I.: On minimum distance decoding of linear codes. In: Joint Soviet-Swedish International Workshop on Information Theory, Moscow, Russia, pp. 50–52 (1991)
19. Grosso, V., Cayrel, P.L., Colombier, B., Dragoi, V.F.: Punctured syndrome decoding problem - efficient side-channel attacks against classic mceliece. In: Kavun, E.B., Pehl, M. (eds.) International Workshop on Constructive Side-Channel Analysis and Secure Design. Lecture Notes in Computer Science, vol. 13979, pp. 170–192. Springer, Munich (2023). https://doi.org/10.1007/978-3-031-29497-6_9
20. Guo, Q., Johansson, A., Johansson, T.: A key-recovery side-channel attack on Classic McEliece implementations. IACR Trans. Cryptogr. Hardw. Embed. Syst. **2022**(4), 800–827 (2022)
21. Heyse, S.: Low-reiter: niederreiter encryption scheme for embedded microcontrollers. In: Sendrier, N. (ed.) PQCrypto 2010. LNCS, vol. 6061, pp. 165–181. Springer, Heidelberg (2010). https://doi.org/10.1007/978-3-642-12929-2_13
22. Heyse, S., Moradi, A., Paar, C.: Practical power analysis attacks on software implementations of McEliece. In: Sendrier, N. (ed.) PQCrypto 2010. LNCS, vol. 6061, pp. 108–125. Springer, Heidelberg (2010). https://doi.org/10.1007/978-3-642-12929-2_9

23. Kocher, P., Jaffe, J., Jun, B.: Differential power analysis. In: Wiener, M. (ed.) CRYPTO 1999. LNCS, vol. 1666, pp. 388–397. Springer, Heidelberg (1999). https://doi.org/10.1007/3-540-48405-1_25
24. Lahr, N., Niederhagen, R., Petri, R., Samardjiska, S.: Side channel information set decoding using iterative chunking. In: Moriai, S., Wang, H. (eds.) ASIACRYPT 2020. LNCS, vol. 12491, pp. 881–910. Springer, Cham (2020). https://doi.org/10.1007/978-3-030-64837-4_29
25. LaRacuente, N., Smith, K.N., Imany, P., Silverman, K.L., Chong, F.T.: Modeling short-range microwave networks to scale superconducting quantum computation (2023)
26. Larsen, M.V., Guo, X., Breum, C.R., Neergaard-Nielsen, J.S., Andersen, U.L.: Deterministic multi-mode gates on a scalable photonic quantum computing platform. Nat. Phys. **17**(9), 1018–1023 (2021)
27. Lee, P.J., Brickell, E.F.: An observation on the security of McEliece's public-key cryptosystem. In: Barstow, D., et al. (eds.) EUROCRYPT 1988. LNCS, vol. 330, pp. 275–280. Springer, Heidelberg (1988). https://doi.org/10.1007/3-540-45961-8_25
28. May, A., Meurer, A., Thomae, E.: Decoding random linear codes in $\widetilde{\mathcal{O}}(2^{0.054n})$. In: Lee, D.H., Wang, X. (eds.) International Conference on the Theory and Application of Cryptology and Information Security. Lecture Notes in Computer Science, vol. 7073, pp. 107–124. Springer, Seoul (2011)
29. May, A., Ozerov, I.: On computing nearest neighbors with applications to decoding of binary linear codes. In: Oswald, E., Fischlin, M. (eds.) EUROCRYPT 2015. LNCS, vol. 9056, pp. 203–228. Springer, Heidelberg (2015). https://doi.org/10.1007/978-3-662-46800-5_9
30. McCann, D., Oswald, E., Whitnall, C.: Towards practical tools for side channel aware software engineering: 'grey box' modelling for instruction leakages. In: Kirda, E., Ristenpart, T. (eds.) USENIX Security Symposium, pp. 199–216. USENIX Association, Vancouver (2017)
31. Molter, H.G., Stöttinger, M., Shoufan, A., Strenzke, F.: A simple power analysis attack on a mceliece cryptoprocessor. J. Cryptogr. Eng. **1**(1), 29–36 (2011). https://doi.org/10.1007/s13389-011-0001-3
32. Niederreiter, H.: Knapsack-type cryptosystems and algebraic coding theory. Prob. Control Inf. Theory **15**(2), 159–166 (1986)
33. O'Flynn, C., Chen, Z.D.: ChipWhisperer: an open-source platform for hardware embedded security research. In: Prouff, E. (ed.) COSADE 2014. LNCS, vol. 8622, pp. 243–260. Springer, Cham (2014). https://doi.org/10.1007/978-3-319-10175-0_17
34. Peeters, E., Standaert, F., Quisquater, J.: Power and electromagnetic analysis: improved model, consequences and comparisons. Integration **40**(1), 52–60 (2007)
35. Prange, E.: The use of information sets in decoding cyclic codes. IRE Trans. Inf. Theory **8**(5), 5–9 (1962)
36. Preskill, J.: Quantum computing in the nisq era and beyond. Quantum **2**, 79 (2018)
37. Ravi, P., Chattopadhyay, A., D'Anvers, J.P., Baksi, A.: Side-channel and fault-injection attacks over lattice-based post-quantum schemes (kyber, dilithium): survey and new results. Cryptology ePrint Archive, Paper 2022/737 (2022). https://eprint.iacr.org/2022/737
38. Roth, J., Karatsiolis, E., Krämer, J.: Classic McEliece implementation with low memory footprint. In: Liardet, P.-Y., Mentens, N. (eds.) CARDIS 2020. LNCS, vol. 12609, pp. 34–49. Springer, Cham (2021). https://doi.org/10.1007/978-3-030-68487-7_3

39. Saarinen, M.J.O.: Wip: applicability of iso standard side-channel leakage tests to nist post-quantum cryptography. In: 2022 IEEE International Symposium on Hardware Oriented Security and Trust (HOST), pp. 69–72 (2022). https://doi.org/10.1109/HOST54066.2022.9839849
40. Shoufan, A., Strenzke, F., Molter, H.G., Stöttinger, M.: A timing attack against patterson algorithm in the McEliece PKC. In: Lee, D., Hong, S. (eds.) ICISC 2009. LNCS, vol. 5984, pp. 161–175. Springer, Heidelberg (2010). https://doi.org/10.1007/978-3-642-14423-3_12
41. Stern, J.: A method for finding codewords of small weight. In: Cohen, G., Wolfmann, J. (eds.) Coding Theory 1988. LNCS, vol. 388, pp. 106–113. Springer, Heidelberg (1989). https://doi.org/10.1007/BFb0019850
42. Strenzke, F.: Solutions for the storage problem of McEliece public and private keys on memory-constrained platforms. In: Gollmann, D., Freiling, F.C. (eds.) ISC 2012. LNCS, vol. 7483, pp. 120–135. Springer, Heidelberg (2012). https://doi.org/10.1007/978-3-642-33383-5_8
43. Sundaresan, N., Lauer, I., Pritchett, E., Magesan, E., Jurcevic, P., Gambetta, J.M.: Reducing unitary and spectator errors in cross resonance with optimized rotary echoes. PRX Quant. **1**(2) (2020). https://doi.org/10.1103/prxquantum.1.020318
44. Takeda, S., Furusawa, A.: Toward large-scale fault-tolerant universal photonic quantum computing. APL Photon. **4**(6), 060902 (2019)
45. Walter, C.D.: Sliding windows succumbs to big mac attack. In: Koç, Ç.K., Naccache, D., Paar, C. (eds.) CHES 2001. LNCS, vol. 2162, pp. 286–299. Springer, Heidelberg (2001). https://doi.org/10.1007/3-540-44709-1_24

Breaking HuFu with 0 Leakage
A Side-Channel Analysis

Julien Devevey[1(✉)], Morgane Guerreau[2], Thomas Legavre[1,3,4], Ange Martinelli[1], and Thomas Ricosset[3]

[1] ANSSI, Paris, France
{julien.devevey,ange.martinelli}@ssi.gouv.fr
[2] CryptoNext Security, Paris, France
morgane.guerreau@cryptonext-security.com
[3] Thales, Gennevilliers, France
{thomas.legavre,thomas.ricosset}@thalesgroup.com
[4] Sorbonne Université, CNRS, LIP6, Paris, France

Abstract. HuFu is an unstructured lattice-based signature scheme proposed during the NIST PQC standardization process. In this work, we present a side-channel analysis of HuFu's reference implementation.

We first exploit the multiplications involving its two main secret matrices, recovering approximately half of their entries through a non-profiled power analysis with a few hundred traces. Using these coefficients, we reduce the dimension of the underlying LWE problem, enabling full secret key recovery with calls to a small block-sized BKZ.

To mitigate this attack, we propose a countermeasure that replaces sensitive computations involving a secret matrix with equivalent operations derived solely from public elements, eliminating approximately half of the identified leakage and rendering the attack unfeasible.

Finally, we perform a non-profiled power analysis targeting HuFu's Gaussian sampling procedure, recovering around 75% of the remaining secret matrix's entries in a few hundred traces. While full key recovery remains computationally intensive, we demonstrate that partial knowledge of the secret significantly improves the efficiency of signature forgery.

1 Introduction

Unstructured Lattices vs. Structured Lattices. Lattice-based cryptography has become a cornerstone of post-quantum cryptography, offering strong protection against both classical and quantum adversaries. Its security is rooted in the hardness of well-studied mathematical problems, such as the Short Integer Solution (SIS) [Ajt96] and Learning With Errors (LWE) [Reg05] problems, which remain difficult even for quantum computers.

Algebraic variants of these problems allow for more efficient implementations and shorter key sizes in cryptographic primitives like Key Exchange Mechanisms (KEMs) and signature schemes. Notable examples include the standardized ML-KEM [NIS24b] and ML-DSA [NIS24a]. However, these structured variants introduce additional algebraic properties that can be exploited by adversaries. For example, attacks on Ideal-SVP provide improvements over generic attacks [CDW17,PHS19,BR20,BLNR22]. While no comparable attacks have been identified for "Module" variants, a direct reduction from generic problems has not been established.

In contrast, primitives based on unstructured lattices, though less efficient and compact, provide more conservative security guarantees. Studying these unstructured schemes provides valuable insight into the trade-offs between structured and unstructured lattices, offering a clearer understanding of their respective strengths and vulnerabilities.

Side-Channel Analysis. In both its structured and unstructured variants, lattice-based cryptography is often technical to implement and manipulates a lot of secret dependent variables. These variables are a perfect target for side-channel attacks (*SCA*), which exploit information leakages through physical data captured during the execution of the algorithm on a device. Nowadays it is the main threat to cryptographic algorithms and should be taken into account in the design phase of any modern algorithm. Indeed, while generic protections against SCA exist, they come at a non-negligible cost, which could most of the time be lowered by carefully choosing the operations performed by the algorithm. However, while being devastating on most implementations, exploiting leakage information to mount an effective cryptanalysis is often not straightforward.

The HuFu Signature Scheme. In this work, we propose to further explore SCA against unstructured schemes by targeting HuFu. The HuFu [YJL+23] signature scheme is a concrete instance of the GPV [GPV08] hash-and-sign framework, built upon the MP12 [MP12] trapdoor construction and the Peikert Gaussian sampler [Pei10]. It was a candidate in the first round of the additional signature track of the NIST PQC standardization process. Its security relies on the hardness of unstructured lattice problems, which makes it a more conservative choice security-wise compared to schemes like the NIST-standardized ML-DSA, which rely on module lattice problems. The MP12 trapdoor construction facilitates the creation of lattices with a *good* basis (serving as the secret key) and a *bad* basis (serving as the public key). The Peikert sampler then utilizes the good basis to efficiently generate Gaussian samples from the lattice, ensuring these points lie relatively close to any specified target point in the ambient space.

Although HuFu is a signature scheme, its underlying building blocks and their implementation have applications that extend well beyond digital signatures. The MP12 trapdoor construction forms the backbone of advanced cryptographic schemes, such as identity-based encryption as demonstrated in [ABB10], group signatures [dPLS18], anonymous credentials [JRS23], blind signatures [JS24]. On the other hand, the Peikert Gaussian sampler serves as a fundamental component in a wide variety of trapdoor-based lattice applications. Consequently, analyzing the side-channel vulnerabilities of HuFu offers valuable insights into the broader field of lattice-based cryptography.

HuFu was submitted to NIST's additional round of signature schemes but was cut from the competition from Round 2 onward. Issues about the signature encoding were raised[1] but quickly patched by the HuFu team.

Related Works. With the NIST standardization process coming to an end, significant attention has been given to implementation issues in lattice-based cryptography. Similar to this work, sign and zero values are common targets in horizontal attacks, as seen in [GMRR22, ZLYW23, LZY+25] for Falcon, in [KAA21, BVC+23] for ML-DSA, in [BVCV24] for ML-KEM, and in [GR24] for the more recent Hawk scheme. Exploiting such partial knowledge requires an additional cryptanalysis step, and a generic framework for evaluating the remaining strength of cryptosystems in the presence of side-channel *hints* was introduced in [DDGR20] and later improved in [DGHK23, MN23]. However, side-channel attacks on lattice-based schemes typically leverage their algebraic structure, making them difficult to extend to unstructured lattices. Nonetheless, such attacks on unstructured lattice schemes, though less common, do exist, notably against FrodoKEM [KH18, BFM+18].

1.1 Contributions

Our contributions consist of two attack paths (key recovery and signature forgery) involving side-channel analysis and lattice reduction. These attacks are illustrated in Fig. 1 and can be summarized as follows[2]:

Side-Channel Analysis of HuFu. We present in Sect. 3 a non-profiled power analysis attack on the HuFu signature scheme. This attack targets the multiplications between the secret matrices $\mathbf{S}$, $\mathbf{E}$, and the ephemeral vector $\mathbf{z}$. Using this method, we successfully recover almost all coefficients in $\mathbf{S}$ and $\mathbf{E}$ that are equal to 0.

Key Recovery. By leveraging the recovered zero coefficients in both $\mathbf{S}$ and $\mathbf{E}$, we achieve full secret key recovery in Sect. 4. Each column of $\mathbf{S}$ corresponds to a secret vector $\mathbf{s}$ in an LWE instance of the form $\hat{\mathbf{A}}\mathbf{s} + \mathbf{e}$, where $\mathbf{e}$ is the corresponding column of $\mathbf{E}$. By mapping known coefficients in $\mathbf{s}$ or $\mathbf{e}$ to lower-dimensional hyperplanes containing the LWE solution, we iteratively intersect the ambient lattice with these hyperplanes. This reduces the dimension of the unknown part of $\mathbf{s}$ until it becomes solvable via lattice reduction.

Partial Countermeasure and Enhanced SCA. We propose in Sect. 5 a simple countermeasure to eliminate leakage from the secret matrix $\mathbf{E}$. Consequently, we only have partial information about $\mathbf{S}$, preventing us from reproducing the initial attack that relied on coefficients from both $\mathbf{S}$ and $\mathbf{E}$. In response, we develop a deeper side-channel attack targeting the ephemeral vector $\mathbf{z}$, enabling us to recover additional coefficients in $\mathbf{S}$.

---

[1] https://groups.google.com/a/list.nist.gov/g/pqc-forum/c/Hq-wRFDbIaU/m/iLZctTiLAgAJ.
[2] All our code is available here: https://github.com/mB64s53wFvP7637M/KF7ns9y5bf.

Signature Forgery. Using the previous key recovery attack to reconstruct a subset of the columns of $\mathbf{S}$, we demonstrate in Sect. 6 how this knowledge weakens the forgery security of the scheme, up to a breaking point.

Broader Applicability. Although our attacks are demonstrated on HuFu, the side-channel techniques apply to any matrix-vector multiplication implemented similarly to the HuFu reference code, where the matrix is a long-term secret with many zero entries and the vector is a (Gaussian) ephemeral secret. This is particularly relevant in lattice-based constructions using the [MP12] strategy (e.g., [DM14,CGM19,YJW23]) to sample Gaussian (inhomogeneous) SIS solutions for a public matrix $\mathbf{A}$. Specifically, this applies when leveraging a trapdoor for $\Lambda^\perp(\mathbf{G}) := \{\mathbf{z} \in \mathbb{Z}^m \mid \mathbf{G}\mathbf{z} = \mathbf{0}\}$, where $\mathbf{G} = \mathbf{A}[\begin{smallmatrix}\mathbf{R}\\\mathbf{I}\end{smallmatrix}]$ for a small entries long-term secret matrix $\mathbf{R}$, by sampling a Gaussian $\mathbf{z}$ from $\Lambda^\perp(\mathbf{G})$ and computing $\mathbf{x} = [\begin{smallmatrix}\mathbf{R}\\\mathbf{I}\end{smallmatrix}]\mathbf{z} + \mathbf{p}$, with $\mathbf{p}$ ensuring a spherical Gaussian distribution on $\Lambda^\perp(\mathbf{A})$.

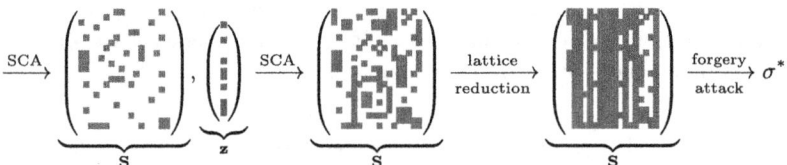

(a) Successful full key recovery attack leveraging recovered coefficients of $\mathbf{S}$ and $\mathbf{E}$ (in red) via SCA, followed by completion using lattice reduction.

(b) Successful forgery attack leveraging recovered coefficients of $\mathbf{S}$ (in red) via SCA, even when coefficients of $\mathbf{E}$ remain unrecovered. Blue entries in $\mathbf{z}$ represent coefficients whose signs are identified through SCA.

Fig. 1. Our two attack scenarios: key recovery (a) and signature forgery (b).

2 Preliminaries

Matrices are denoted by bold uppercase letters (e.g., $\mathbf{A}$), while vectors are represented by bold lowercase letters (e.g., $\mathbf{x}$). For a vector $\mathbf{x}$, let x_i denote its i-th component. For a matrix $\mathbf{A}$, let $A_{i,j}$ refer to the entry in the i-th row and j-th column. The notation $\mathbf{0}^{m \times n}$ represents the $m \times n$ zero matrix, and $\mathbf{0}^m$ denotes the m-dimensional zero vector.

In this work, all modular reductions are centered. Namely, the modular reduction $\cdot \bmod p$ maps $\mathbb{Z}$ to the interval $[-\frac{p}{2}, \frac{p}{2}) \cap \mathbb{Z}$. For any $x \in \mathbb{R}$, let $\lceil x \rfloor$ denote the nearest integer to x, with this notation extended component-wise to vectors. Note that for any $x \in \mathbb{Z}$ and $p \in \mathbb{N}$, $\lceil x/p \rfloor = (x - (x \bmod p))/p$.

A lattice $\Lambda \subset \mathbb{R}^n$ is defined as a discrete subgroup of $\mathbb{R}^n$. Its covolume $\text{Vol}(\Lambda)$ is the norm of the determinant of any of its bases. The n-dimensional Gaussian function $\rho : \mathbb{R}^n \to (0, 1]$ is given by $\rho(\mathbf{x}) := \exp(-\pi \|\mathbf{x}\|^2)$. For a positive definite matrix $\mathbf{\Sigma} = \mathbf{B}\mathbf{B}^t$, we can apply the invertible linear transformation $\mathbf{B}$ to define a Gaussian function $\rho_{\mathbf{\Sigma}}(\mathbf{x}) := \rho(\mathbf{B}^{-1}\mathbf{x}) = \exp(-\pi \mathbf{x}^t \mathbf{\Sigma}^{-1} \mathbf{x})$. For any $\mathbf{c} \in \text{span}(\mathbf{\Sigma})$, the Gaussian function centered at $\mathbf{c}$ with parameter $\mathbf{\Sigma}$ is defined as $\rho_{\mathbf{\Sigma}, \mathbf{c}}(\mathbf{x}) := \rho_{\mathbf{\Sigma}}(\mathbf{x} - \mathbf{c})$. The discrete Gaussian distribution centered at $\mathbf{c}$ with parameter $\mathbf{\Sigma}$ over a lattice Λ has probability mass function $D_{\Lambda, \mathbf{\Sigma}, \mathbf{c}}(\mathbf{x}) := \frac{\rho_{\mathbf{\Sigma}, \mathbf{c}}(\mathbf{x})}{\rho_{\mathbf{\Sigma}, \mathbf{c}}(\Lambda)}$ for all $\mathbf{x} \in \Lambda$, where $\rho_{\mathbf{\Sigma}, \mathbf{c}}(\Lambda) = \sum_{\mathbf{x} \in \Lambda} \rho_{\mathbf{\Sigma}, \mathbf{c}}(\mathbf{x})$. Similarly, the discrete Gaussian distribution on a lattice coset $\Lambda + \mathbf{v}$, where $\mathbf{v} \in \text{span}(\Lambda)$, is defined as $D_{\Lambda + \mathbf{v}, \mathbf{\Sigma}, \mathbf{c}}(\mathbf{x}) := \frac{\rho_{\mathbf{\Sigma}, \mathbf{c}}(\mathbf{x})}{\rho_{\mathbf{\Sigma}, \mathbf{c}}(\Lambda + \mathbf{v})}$ for all $\mathbf{x} \in \Lambda + \mathbf{v}$. For any positive $\varepsilon > 0$, the smoothing parameter $\eta_\varepsilon(\Lambda)$ is the smallest $s > 0$ such that $\rho(s \cdot \Lambda^*) \leq 1 + \varepsilon$, where $\Lambda^* := \{\mathbf{x} \in \text{span}(\Lambda) \mid \langle \mathbf{x}, \Lambda \rangle \subseteq \mathbb{Z}\}$ is the dual lattice of Λ.

For any set S, we use the notation $U(S)$ for the uniform distribution over S. We let B_1 be the centered binomial distribution with parameter 1, i.e. the distribution with mass probability $p(-1) = p(1) = 1/4$ and $p(0) = 1/2$. We let $X \hookleftarrow_\$ P$ denote that the random variable X follows the distribution P.

2.1 Learning With Errors

Problem Description. The *Learning With Errors* (LWE) problem involves recovering a secret vector $\mathbf{s} \in \mathbb{Z}_Q^n$ given a matrix $\mathbf{A} \in \mathbb{Z}_Q^{m \times n}$ and a vector $\mathbf{b} \in \mathbb{Z}_Q^m$, satisfying the relation $\mathbf{b} = \mathbf{A}\mathbf{s} + \mathbf{e} \bmod Q$, where $\mathbf{e} \in \mathbb{Z}_Q^m$ is a short error vector with entries sampled independently from an error distribution χ. While in its original formulation [Reg05], the secret vector is assumed to be uniformly sampled at random, it is usually sampled from the error distribution, as [ACPS09] proved that this was not weakening the problem.

BKZ. To find a short vector in a d-dimensional lattice Λ, one typically uses the BKZ algorithm [SE94], which is parameterized by its block size β. BKZ with block size $d > \beta > 50$ finds a vector $\mathbf{v} \in \Lambda$ such that:

$$\|\mathbf{v}\| \leq \delta_\beta^d \cdot \text{Vol}(\Lambda)^{1/d} \quad \text{and} \quad \delta_\beta \approx \left(\frac{(\pi \beta)^{1/\beta} \beta}{2\pi e}\right)^{1/(2(\beta-1))}.$$

Estimating the cost of BKZ with block size β is not a trivial task. The Core-SVP methodology considers that its cost is essentially the one of the β-dimensional SVP oracle that is used in BKZ and overlooks the polynomial overheads of the algorithm. Currently, the best classical algorithm known to solve SVP in dimension β was designed in [BDGL16] and has bit-cost 0.292β.

On the more practical side, the number of core-hours from G6K [ADH+19] are a good indicator of the cost of BKZ, as it holds records in high-dimension (i.e. up to 120) SVP-solving.

Primal Attack. Attacking an LWE instance typically involves two primary strategies: the *dual attack*, which involves solving a *Short Integer Solution* (SIS) instance, and the *primal attack*. The latter [ADPS16] is the most fundamental approach to solving the LWE problem. It interprets the LWE instance as a *Bounded Distance Decoding* (BDD) instance, where the goal is to find the closest vector to **b** in the lattice:

$$\Lambda_Q = \{\mathbf{y} \in \mathbb{Z}^m : \mathbf{y} = \mathbf{As} \bmod Q, \mathbf{s} \in \mathbb{Z}^n\}.$$

When the secret is sampled from the same distribution as the error, this approach is reduced to solving the *unique Shortest Vector Problem* (uSVP) instance defined on the following Q-ary lattice of dimension $m + n + 1$:

$$\mathcal{L}_{\text{LWE}} = \begin{pmatrix} Q\mathbf{I}_m & -\mathbf{A} & \mathbf{b} \\ 0 & \mathbf{I}_n & 0 \\ 0 & 0 & 1 \end{pmatrix} \cdot \mathbb{Z}^{m+n+1},$$

using Kannan's embedding [Kan87] with an embedding factor of 1. This lattice has covolume Q^m and contains a remarkably short vector **u** with norm:

$$\|\mathbf{u}\| = \sqrt{\|\mathbf{e}\|^2 + \|\mathbf{s}\|^2 + 1}.$$

In the case of the primal attack, it was shown [ADPS16] that it succeeds when the block size β is such that for some non-negative integer $\ell \leq m$:

$$\sqrt{\frac{3\beta}{4(\ell+n+1)}} \|\mathbf{s}, \mathbf{e}, 1\| \cdot \leq \delta_\beta^{2\beta-(\ell+n+1)-1} \cdot Q^{\ell/(\ell+n+1)},$$

where the $\sqrt{3/4}$ is a conservative choice, as estimated per [Duc18].

Approximate-CVP. For any matrix $\mathbf{A} \in \mathbb{Z}_Q^{m \times 2m+n}$ and vector $\mathbf{u} \in \mathbb{Z}_Q^m$, the nearest-colattice algorithm [EK20] finds a vector **x** such that $\mathbf{Ax} = \mathbf{u} \bmod Q$ and $\|x\| \leq B_\beta$ by calling BKZ with block size β, where:

$$B_\beta = \min_{k \leq m+n} \left(\delta_\beta^{2m+n-k} \cdot Q^{m/(2m+n-k)} \right).$$

2.2 HuFu

The HuFu signature scheme was introduced in [YJL+23] and is based on the Hash-and-Sign paradigm. This consists for lattice-based signatures in exhibiting a preimage by the trapdoored public matrix **A** of the target $H(\mu) = \mathbf{u} \in \mathbb{Z}_Q^m$ as a signature for the message μ. The shorter the preimage is, the better the security, as there are less admissible preimages.

However, the distribution of the preimage is critical, as bad choices may leak the signing key, i.e. the trapdoor stored in $\mathbf{A}$. Here, HUFU relies on the approximate preimage sampling technique from [YJW23].

Algorithms for key generation, signature and verification and HUFU-1 parameters are recalled in Fig. 2. Since our analysis does not target the BlockCholesky algorithm or the compression and encoding steps, we omit their description here. For complete explanations, we refer readers to the original HUFU specification [YJL+23].

Going into more details, the HUFU signature scheme is parameterized by modulus $Q = pq$, where p is a large power of 2 and q is a small power of 2. The key generation algorithm generates m plain LWE samples $\hat{\mathbf{A}}\mathbf{S} + \mathbf{E} \bmod Q$ with secret and noise coefficients each sampled from B_1. The final public matrix $\mathbf{A}$ is $(\mathbf{Id}_m | \hat{\mathbf{A}} | p\mathbf{Id}_m - \hat{\mathbf{A}}\mathbf{S} - \mathbf{E})$.

KeyGen(1^λ)

1: $\hat{\mathbf{A}} \leftarrow_\$ \mathbb{Z}_Q^{m \times n}$
2: **repeat**
3: $\quad (\mathbf{S}, \mathbf{E}) \leftarrow_\$ B_1^{n \times m} \times B_1^{m \times m}$
4: $\quad \Sigma_\mathbf{p} \leftarrow \sigma^2 \mathbf{I}_{n+2m} - \bar{r}^2 \cdot \begin{bmatrix} \mathbf{E} \\ \mathbf{S} \\ \mathbf{I}_m \end{bmatrix} \cdot \begin{bmatrix} \mathbf{E}^t & \mathbf{S}^t & \mathbf{I}_m \end{bmatrix}$
5: **until** $\Sigma_\mathbf{p} - \bar{r}^2 \mathbf{I}_{n+2m}$ is positive definite
6: $\mathbf{B} \leftarrow p\mathbf{I}_m - (\hat{\mathbf{A}}\mathbf{S} + \mathbf{E}) \bmod Q$
7: $\mathbf{C} \leftarrow \mathsf{BlockCholesky}(\Sigma_\mathbf{p} - \bar{r}^2 \mathbf{I}_{n+2m})$
8: **return** $\mathsf{vk} = (\hat{\mathbf{A}}, \mathbf{B})$, $\mathsf{sk} = (\mathbf{E}, \mathbf{S}, \mathbf{C})$

Verify(vk, μ, σ)

1: $\mathbf{u} \leftarrow H(\mu, \mathsf{salt})$
2: $\mathbf{x}_0' \leftarrow \mathbf{u} - \hat{\mathbf{A}}\mathbf{x}_1 - \mathbf{B}\mathbf{x}_2 \bmod Q$
3: **if** $\|(\mathbf{x}_0', \mathbf{x}_1, \mathbf{x}_2)\| \leq B$
4: $\quad$ Accept
5: **else**
6: $\quad$ Reject

Sign(sk, μ)

1: $\mathbf{A} \leftarrow [\mathbf{I}_m \ \hat{\mathbf{A}} \ \mathbf{B}]$
2: $\mathbf{p} \leftarrow \mathsf{SampleP}(\mathsf{sk})$
3: $(\mathbf{p}_0, \mathbf{p}_1, \mathbf{p}_2) \leftarrow \mathbf{p}$
4: $\mathbf{c} \leftarrow \mathbf{A}\mathbf{p} \bmod Q$
5: $\mathsf{salt} \leftarrow_\$ \{0, 1\}^{320}$
6: $\mathbf{u} \leftarrow H(\mu, \mathsf{salt})$
7: $\mathbf{v} \leftarrow \mathbf{u} - \mathbf{c} \bmod Q$
8: $\mathbf{e} \leftarrow \mathbf{v} \bmod p$
9: $\mathbf{v}' \leftarrow (\mathbf{v} - \mathbf{e})/p$
10: **for** $i = 1, \ldots, m$
11: $\quad z_i \leftarrow q \cdot \mathsf{SampleZ}_d(v_i'/q)$
12: $\mathbf{x}_0 \leftarrow \mathbf{E}\mathbf{z} + \mathbf{p}_0$
13: $\mathbf{x}_1 \leftarrow \mathbf{S}\mathbf{z} + \mathbf{p}_1$
14: $\mathbf{x}_2 \leftarrow \mathbf{z} + \mathbf{p}_2$
15: **if** $\|(\mathbf{x}_0 + \mathbf{e}, \mathbf{x}_1, \mathbf{x}_2)\| > B$
16: $\quad$ **goto** 2
17: **return** $\sigma = (\mathsf{salt}, \mathbf{x}_1, \mathbf{x}_2)$

Fig. 2. Simplified pseudocode of HUFU. HUFU-1 uses $(m, n) = (736, 848)$, $(p, q) = (2^{12}, 2^4)$ and $B = 62521$.

A HUFU signature is a preimage of $p\mathbf{v}' = p\lfloor \mathbf{u}/p \rfloor$, where $\mathbf{u} \in \mathbb{Z}_Q^m$ is the target: as $\mathbf{A}$ contains the identity matrix, this is equivalent to sampling a somewhat larger preimage of $\mathbf{u}$. This is achieved by choosing a short element $\mathbf{z} \in q\mathbb{Z}^m + \mathbf{v}'$. The signature is then $(\mathbf{E}\mathbf{z}, \mathbf{S}\mathbf{z}, \mathbf{z})$, which is still short and is a preimage of $\mathbf{v}'$. The first coordinate $\mathbf{E}\mathbf{z}$ is omitted from the signature, as it can be reconstructed as $\mathbf{u} - \hat{\mathbf{A}}(\mathbf{S}\mathbf{z}) - \mathbf{B}\mathbf{z}$. As it stands this signature leaks the secret matrices $\mathbf{S}$ and $\mathbf{E}$.

To solve this issue, the signer starts by sampling $\mathbf{p}$, and updates the target to $\mathbf{v} = \mathbf{u} - \mathbf{A}\mathbf{p} \bmod Q$. The signature is $(\mathbf{E}\mathbf{z}, \mathbf{S}\mathbf{z}, \mathbf{z}) + \mathbf{p}$, which is indeed a short preimage by $\mathbf{A}$ of $\mathbf{u}$. Once again, the first m coordinates are erased as they can be approximately recovered by the verifier.

A careful choice of the distributions of $\mathbf{z}$ and $\mathbf{p}$ makes it so that the final distribution of the signature is independent of the secret. This choice is the discrete Gaussian distribution: let $D_{q\mathbb{Z}^m+\mathbf{v}',r}$ be the output distribution of $(q \cdot \mathsf{SampleZ}_d(v'_i/q))_i$ and $D_{\mathbb{Z}^{2m+n},\boldsymbol{\Sigma}_p}$ be the output distribution of SampleP for some $r > 0$ and some positive-definite matrix $\boldsymbol{\Sigma}_p$. Conditioned on $\bar{r} > q\eta_\varepsilon(\mathbb{Z})$, the distribution of the signature is ε-close to a discrete Gaussian distribution centered around 0 with covariance matrix: $\boldsymbol{\Sigma} = \boldsymbol{\Sigma}_p + r^2 \mathbf{S}_0^\top \mathbf{S}_0 = \sigma^2 \mathbf{Id}_{2m+n}$, where $\mathbf{S}_0 = (\mathbf{E}^\top, \mathbf{S}^\top, \mathbf{Id}_m)$ and by choosing $\boldsymbol{\Sigma}_p$ accordingly.

The following result is a well-known fact, but we include a brief proof for completeness in Sect. A:

Lemma 2.1. *Let Q be a power of 2 and $m < n$ be integers, and let $\hat{\mathbf{A}} \leftarrow\$ U(\mathbb{Z}_Q^{m \times n})$. For $0 \leq k_2 < n$ and $0 < k_1 < n - k_2$, any k_1-row and $(n - k_2)$-column submatrix of $\hat{\mathbf{A}}$ contains an invertible submatrix $\hat{\mathbf{A}}_{sub} \in \mathbb{Z}_Q^{k_1 \times k_1}$ with probability:*

$$p_{k_1} = \prod_{i=1}^{k_1} \left(1 - 2^{i-1-(n-k_2)}\right).$$

3 Exploiting 0 Leakage

The goal of this section is to recover partial information via side-channel analysis on the private matrices $\mathbf{S}$ and $\mathbf{E}$, which we exploit in a key recovery and a signature forgery in the following sections. Namely we look for the location of the coefficients whose value is equal to zero, which we dub the "0 leakage".

Targeted Operations. We target the multiplications $\mathbf{E} \cdot \mathbf{z}$ and $\mathbf{S} \cdot \mathbf{z}$ at Lines 12 and 13 of the signature procedure described in Fig. 2. $\mathbf{S}$ and $\mathbf{E}$ are long-term secrets while $\mathbf{z}$ is an ephemeral secret vector. Hence, we are not in a classical setting for a DPA, as none of the operands is known by the attacker. From a side-channel point of view, the operations involving either $\mathbf{S}$ or $\mathbf{E}$ are similar and we will only describe the recovery of $\mathbf{S}$ for conciseness. The targeted C code is shown in Listing 1, taken from the official HuFu submission package.

Experimental Setup. The power traces have been recorded with a ChipWhisperer Lite with STM32F303 target (ARM Cortex M4). Due to limitations of our acquisition device, we executed the `mat_mul` code with matrices of smaller dimensions 8×8. However, we expect the attack to behave similarly in higher dimensions, as the traces will have identical patterns and point of leakages, and will only be longer with more individual multiplications involved. To validate the feasibility of our attack, we generated 100 datasets of 1500 power traces each. After performing the attack on each dataset separately, we aggregated the results of the 6400 coefficients on Fig. 8.

```
void mat_mul(int16_t *C, int16_t *A, int16_t *B, int l1,
    int l2, int l3)
{
  for (int i = 0; i < l1; ++i)
    for (int j = 0; j < l3; ++j)
    {
      mat_element(C, l3, i, j) = 0;
      for (int k = 0; k < l2; ++k)
        mat_element(C, l3, i, j) += mat_element(A, l2, i,
    k) * mat_element(B, l3, k, j);
    }
}
```

Listing 1. Reference C code of matrix-vector multiplication.

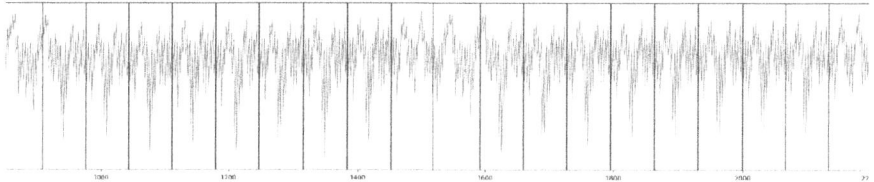

Fig. 3. Extract of power consumption during Listing 1 execution for l2 = 8.

Overview. The multiplication between $\mathbf{S}$ and $\mathbf{z}$ consists in $n \cdot m$ multiplications and additions of single coefficients $S_{i,j}$ and z_j. Figure 3 shows an extract of the power consumption during the multiplication between $\mathbf{S}$ and $\mathbf{z}$. The red line separates two multiplications between lines of $\mathbf{S}$ and $\mathbf{z}$, while the blue lines separate multiplications between single coefficients $S_{i,j}$ and z_i.

We exploit in our attack that $\mathbf{S}$ is ternary, i.e. the only possible values for its coefficients are $\{-1, 0, 1\}$. Consequently, multiplication between $S_{i,j}$ and z_i for some i, j can only result in three different cases:

1. 0, setting the Hamming weight to 0.
2. z_i, keeping the Hamming weight identical.
3. $-z_i$, greatly changing the Hamming weight.

We expect to see the above classification in the power consumption. In particular, $S_{i,j} = 0$ will always result in a Hamming weight of 0. For a non-zero $S_{i,j}$, we expect to see the power traces split into two groups, depending on the sign of $S_{i,j} \cdot z_i$. Those assumptions are confirmed by experimental analysis, as shown in Fig. 4a and Fig. 4b: a difference can be noted between samples 420–425 and samples 350–355. As we have no way to distinguish between the Cases 2 and 3, we focus on identifying only the Case 1 corresponding to $S_{i,j} = 0$.

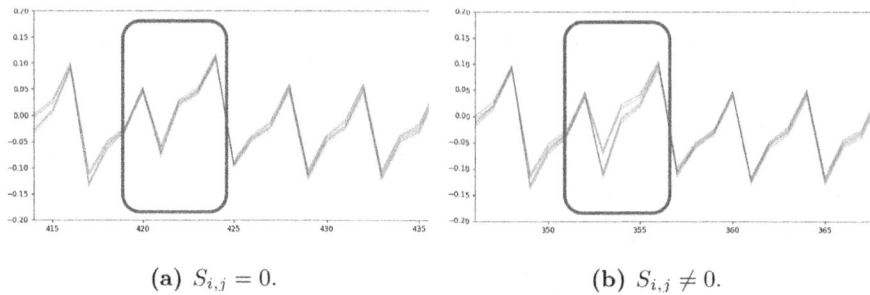

Fig. 4. Power consumption during the computation of $S_{i,j} \cdot z_i$.

Practical Attack. The goal is to determine whether the power traces at the selected points of interest are forming one or two clusters. To this end, we use the Kernel Density Estimator (KDE) from the Python package `sickit-learn`. To improve accuracy, we separated the power traces into 10 subsets and performed a majority voting to determine the final classification. Since we are only interested in finding the zero coefficients, we can choose conservative parameters for our KDE to drastically decrease the number of false positives.

Results. An extract of the results is shown on Table 1 (full results will be discussed in Sect. 5.3). From as few as 200 power traces, we are able to recover more than 90% of the $S_{i,j} = 0$. However, we must increase the number of traces to at least 600 to avoid any false positives, at which point we also get an accuracy of 97%. The results do not get much better with an increasing number of traces, and they remain steady around 98% up to 1500 power traces. By extension, we can also recover the same proportion of the $E_{i,j} = 0$.

Table 1. Percentage of $S_{i,j} = 0$ successfully recovered.

Number of traces	Recovered $S_{i,j} = 0$	False positives
200	93.4%	0.12%
600	97.9%	0%
1500	98.5%	0%

4 Key Completion via Lattice Reduction

In this section, we exploit the side-channel information from Sect. 3 to recover the secret matrix $\mathbf{S}$. We focus on individual LWE instances $\hat{\mathbf{A}}\mathbf{s} + \mathbf{e} = \mathbf{b} \bmod Q$, each corresponding to a single column of the matrices $\mathbf{S}$, $\mathbf{E}$, and $p\mathbf{I}_m - \mathbf{B}$, as defined in Sect. 2.2 and target them separately. The challenge of leveraging partial information about the error or secret in LWE has been explored through various methods, as discussed in [DDGR20,DGHK23], and [MN23]. In this work, we focus on the approach proposed in [MN23], which offers a framework particularly well-suited to tackling the specific challenges present in our context.

4.1 Partial Knowledge of the Secret

By utilizing side-channel information, we gain access to certain entries of $\mathbf{S}$. Building on this partial knowledge, we aim to recover individual columns $\mathbf{s}$ of $\mathbf{S}$, paving the way for a (partial) key recovery attack. To achieve this, we replace the k known coefficients of $\mathbf{s}$ in the LWE system, thereby reducing the number of unknowns by k.

Let $\tilde{\mathbf{s}}$ represent the partially known vector $\mathbf{s}$, defined as:

$$\tilde{s}_i = \begin{cases} s_i & \text{if the } i\text{-th component is known}, \\ 0 & \text{otherwise}. \end{cases}$$

Note that, in the context of Sect. 3, $\tilde{\mathbf{s}}$ is an all-zero vector due to the specific leakage model considered. However, we later consider cases where some nonzero s_i are known. Substituting $\tilde{\mathbf{s}}$ into the LWE relation gives:

$$\hat{\mathbf{A}}\mathbf{s} + \mathbf{e} = \mathbf{b} \bmod Q \iff \hat{\mathbf{A}}(\mathbf{s} - \tilde{\mathbf{s}}) + \mathbf{e} = \mathbf{b} - \hat{\mathbf{A}}\tilde{\mathbf{s}} \bmod Q.$$

Assume that k coordinates of $\mathbf{s}$ have been leaked. This simplifies the original LWE instance by removing corresponding columns and entries, leading to the reduced instance $(\mathbf{A}', \mathbf{s}', \mathbf{e}, \mathbf{b}')$, where:

- $\mathbf{A}'$ is derived by removing the k columns from $\hat{\mathbf{A}}$,
- $\mathbf{s}'$ consists of the remaining coordinates of $\mathbf{s} - \tilde{\mathbf{s}}$ after excluding the k-$\mathbf{0}$, and
- $\mathbf{b}'$ is $\mathbf{b} - \hat{\mathbf{A}}\tilde{\mathbf{s}}$.

This modification decreases the lattice problem's dimension by k, thereby weakening its security. However, relying solely on this method requires knowledge of a significant portion of $\mathbf{s}$ to render the attack practical (e.g., reducing dimensions below 200). Considering that the LWE error $\mathbf{e}$ also leaks information, a natural question emerges: *Can we further reduce the LWE instance dimension by exploiting partial knowledge of $\mathbf{e}$ alongside $\mathbf{s}$?*

4.2 Partial Knowledge of the Error

Knowing a coefficient of the error vector $\mathbf{e}$ reduces the dimension of the LWE solution by one, similar to knowing a coefficient of the secret vector $\mathbf{s}$. The core idea is that knowing one coordinate of $\mathbf{e}$ allows us to derive a linear combination of the components of $\mathbf{s}$. Specifically:

$$b_i - e_i = \sum_j \hat{a}_{i,j} \cdot s_j \bmod Q.$$

Since $\hat{\mathbf{A}}$ is sampled uniformly, its rows form a linearly independent generating system with high probability. Consequently, this relation reduces the dimension of the system induced by the LWE instance by one. More generally, knowing k such relations reduces the dimension by k.

Assuming that the first k coordinates of $\mathbf{e}$ are known (possibly after reordering), the LWE equation can be reformulated as:

$$(\hat{\mathbf{A}} \mid \mathbf{b}) \cdot (\mathbf{s}^\top, -1)^\top = (-\mathbf{e}_1, -\mathbf{e}_2)^\top \bmod Q,$$

where $\mathbf{e}_1 = (e_1, \ldots, e_k)$ and $\mathbf{e}_2 = (e_{k+1}, \ldots, e_m)$. Given that $\hat{\mathbf{A}}$, $\mathbf{b}$, and $\mathbf{s}$ can be decomposed (possibly after permuting columns) as:

$$(\hat{\mathbf{A}} \mid \mathbf{b}) = \begin{pmatrix} \mathbf{A}_1 & \mathbf{A}_2 & \mathbf{b}_1 \\ \mathbf{A}_3 & \mathbf{A}_4 & \mathbf{b}_2 \end{pmatrix}, \text{ and } \mathbf{s} = (\mathbf{s}_1 \mid \mathbf{s}_2)^\top,$$

where $\mathbf{A}_1 \in \mathbb{Z}_Q^{k \times k}$ is invertible with overwhelming probability, see Lemma 2.1. We can apply Gaussian elimination to the first k rows, transforming the system to the equivalent form:

$$\begin{pmatrix} \mathbf{I}_k & \mathbf{A}_1^{-1}\mathbf{A}_2 & \mathbf{A}_1^{-1}(\mathbf{b}_1 - \mathbf{e}_1) \\ \mathbf{A}_3 & \mathbf{A}_4 & -\mathbf{b}_2 \end{pmatrix} \cdot (\mathbf{s}_1 \mid \mathbf{s}_2 \mid -1)^\top = (\mathbf{0}^k, -\mathbf{e}_2)^\top \bmod Q.$$

By applying additional row operations to eliminate $\mathbf{A}_3$, the system simplifies to:

$$\begin{pmatrix} \mathbf{I}_k & \mathbf{A}_1^{-1}\mathbf{A}_2 & \mathbf{A}_1^{-1}(\mathbf{b}_1 - \mathbf{e}_1) \\ \mathbf{0}^{(m-k) \times k} & \bar{\mathbf{A}} & \bar{\mathbf{b}} \end{pmatrix} \cdot (\mathbf{s}_1 \mid \mathbf{s}_2 \mid -1)^\top = (\mathbf{0}^k, -\mathbf{e}_2)^\top \bmod Q,$$

where:

$$\bar{\mathbf{A}} = \mathbf{A}_4 - \mathbf{A}_3 \mathbf{A}_1^{-1} \mathbf{A}_2, \text{ and } \bar{\mathbf{b}} = \mathbf{A}_3 \mathbf{A}_1^{-1}(\mathbf{e}_1 - \mathbf{b}_1) - \mathbf{b}_2.$$

The values of $\mathbf{s}_1$ can be determined from the first k equations, leading to a new LWE instance with reduced dimension $(n-k)$ and parameters $(\bar{\mathbf{A}}, \mathbf{s}_2, \mathbf{e}_2, \bar{\mathbf{b}})$. Notably, both methods of exploiting known coordinates of $\mathbf{s}$ and $\mathbf{e}$ are specific instances of incorporating mod-Q hints, as outlined in [MN23].

4.3 Combining Insights from Secret and Error

We assume that $0 \leq k_1 \leq n$ coordinates of the secret vector $\mathbf{s}$ and $0 \leq k_2 \leq m$ coordinates of the error vector $\mathbf{e}$ are known. For the system's dimension to be reduced by exactly $k_1 + k_2$, the linear combinations defining the leakage on $\mathbf{s}$ must remain linearly independent.

Let $\hat{\mathbf{A}}_{\text{sub}} \in \mathbb{Z}_Q^{k_2 \times n}$ represent the submatrix corresponding to the leaked coordinates of $\mathbf{e}$. If $\hat{\mathbf{A}}_{\text{sub}}$ maintains rank k_1 after excluding k_2 columns related to the leaked coordinates of $\mathbf{s}$, the resulting LWE instance will have the desired reduced dimension. This condition holds with high probability, as shown in Lemma 2.1.

For the general case $0 \leq k_2 < m$ and $0 \leq k_1 < n - k_2$, we refer to Fig. 5, generated using the `leaky-estimator` from [DDGR20], to determine the BKZ block size needed to recover an entire column of $\mathbf{S}$.

When $k_1 + k_2 \geq n$, lattice reduction becomes unnecessary. Gaussian elimination can recover the secret, with the caveat that $\mathbb{Z}_Q$ is not a field.

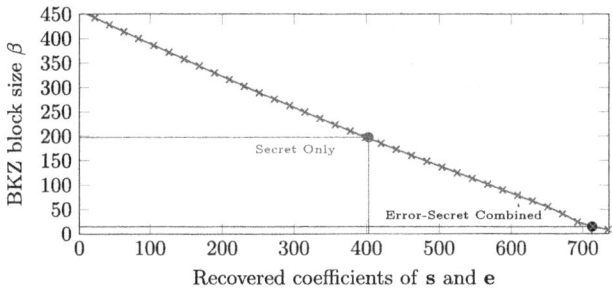

Fig. 5. Estimated evolution of the BKZ block size β as a function of the number of recovered coefficients of **s** and **e** for HuFu-1 with $(n, Q, \chi) = (848, 2^{16}, B_1)$.

4.4 Key Recovery with 0 Leakage

In HUFU, the LWE secrets and errors $(\mathbf{S}, \mathbf{E})$ are independently and identically distributed according to a centered binomial distribution with parameter 1. Therefore, on average, each column **s** of **S** contains $n/2$ zeros, and each column **e** of **E** contains $m/2$ zeros. By the law of large numbers, for large n and m, this is the case for all considered samples.

Secret Only. Based on Table 1, recovering more than 95% of the zeros in **S** with 100% accuracy requires 600 power traces. For HUFU-1, this is approximately 400 coefficients per column of **S**. Completing the remaining coefficients necessitates BKZ with a block size around 200. Consequently, recovering the full HUFU secret key would require over 2^{77} operations, making the attack unfeasible.

Error-Secret Combined. However, Recall that the attack in Sect. 3 applies to **E** as well. By exploiting leakage from both **S** and **E**, we can recover approximately $0.95 \cdot (n+m)/2$ coefficients per LWE instance, compared to $0.95 \cdot n/2$ when using **S** alone.

Using the same number of power traces for HUFU-1, this approach yields approximately 740 coefficients of $(\mathbf{s}, \mathbf{e})$. Consequently, the required BKZ block size reduces to 10, lowering the time complexity for full key recovery to roughly 2^{25}, which is computationally feasible within a reasonable time frame.

5 Trading 0 Leakage on E for More-than-0 Leakage on S

While devastating, the combined attack from Sect. 4 requires knowledge on both **S** and **E**. We now show how to get rid of the leakage on **E**.

5.1 First Countermeasure: Preventing the Leakage on E

We note that the computation $\mathbf{x}_0 = \mathbf{E}\mathbf{z} + \mathbf{p}_0$ is only ever useful to compute the norm of $(\mathbf{x}_0 + \mathbf{e}, \mathbf{x}_1, \mathbf{x}_2)$. However, the vector $\mathbf{x}_0 + \mathbf{e}$ can also be expressed as

$$\mathbf{u} - \hat{\mathbf{A}}\mathbf{x}_1 - \mathbf{B}\mathbf{x}_2.$$

Computing it this way prevents leakage on **E** here. Note that the computation of $\mathbf{x}_0$ is only there to ensure correctness and is not sensitive, as rejected signatures do not reveal any information on the private key.

Performance Cost. The countermeasure involves an additional matrix-vector multiplication and additional vector addition. We noticed an overhead in signature generation of around 5% in terms of CPU cycles on Intel architecture.

If we apply this simple countermeasure, an attacker is not able to recover information on the private matrix **E** anymore. As shown in Sect. 4.4, a lattice reduction with only the zero-coefficients of **S** is likely to be too costly. Hence, the goal of this section is to perform a deeper side-channel analysis to recover more information on **S**. We do so in two steps.

1. Target the Gaussian sampler to gain information on the sampled vector **z**.
2. Use this additional information to distinguish between the $S_{i,j} = \pm 1$.

5.2 Side-Channel Analysis of the Gaussian Sampler

Contrary to the CDT samplers of similar schemes Falcon and Hawk that have been analyzed in [GMRR22,ZLYW23,GR24], the distribution table of the HUFU sampler is designed to sample both negative and positive integers. This means that, for a sample of value 0, the inner counter will have been incremented during half of the table traversal, whereas it would not have been incremented at all in more traditional samplers. As the noise on the power traces grows bigger during the execution, recovering the z_i that are close to 0 without profiling proves much more challenging in this sampler than in the ones listed earlier. For this reason, we will not target the table traversal but rather the lines 15 and 2 in Listing 2.

```
int c = center;
c = (c > 8) * (16 - 2 * c) + c;
z = 0;
for (u = 0; u < TABLE_LEN; u += 3)
{
    uint32_t w0, w1, w2, cc;
    w0 = dist0[c][u + 2];
    w1 = dist0[c][u + 1];
    w2 = dist0[c][u + 0];
    cc = (v0 - w0) >> 31;
    cc = (v1 - w1 - cc) >> 31;
    cc = (v2 - w2 - cc) >> 31;
    z += (int)cc;
}
return (center > 8) * (27 - 2 * z) + z - 13;
```

Listing 2. Extract of the RCDT sampler used in the online phase.

Sign Recovery. The last operation executed at Line 15 is the subtraction between an intermediary value and 13. This is done to center the Gaussian sampler around 0 and output a sample in $[-12, 12]$. Let:

$$z_{\mathrm{CDT}} = (27 - 2 \cdot z) + z - 13 = 14 - z$$

be the final value outputted by the sampler. If the result of the final subtraction is negative, i.e. $z_{\mathrm{CDT}} < 0$, it induces a spike in power consumption as shown on Figue 6c, that is visible with bare-eyes and is detected with a simple threshold.

Identifying Zeros. The multiplication step (center > 8) * (27 - 2 * z) shows a similar leakage. However, it only reveals the sign of 27 - 2 * z if center is greater than 8. Otherwise, the intermediary result targeted here will be 0 independently of the value of z. We then know when $27 - 2z < 0$, i.e. $z > 13$. From last paragraph, we also know when $z_{\mathrm{CDT}} \geq 0$, i.e. $z \leq 14$. Hence, we isolate the case $z = 14$, i.e. $z_{\mathrm{CDT}} = 0$. We thus identify the z_{CDT} that are zero when center is greater than 8, which happens with probability 0.5.

Leakage on center. Now we need to gain information on the center variable. As shown on Fig. 6a, power consumption reveals whether the intermediary result $16 - 2 \cdot c$ at Line 2 is negative, implying that center is greater than 8. A simple threshold can be used to separate the power traces into two groups.

Results. We generated a dataset of 100,000 executions of the sampler. We were able to recover with 100% accuracy:

- for each execution, if z_{CDT} is negative or not,
- for each execution, whether center is greater than 8,
- for executions where center > 8, if z_{CDT} is 0.

The final value z_i is computed as $z_i = Q \cdot z_{\mathrm{CDT}} - c$ with $c < Q$. Thus, while $z_{\mathrm{CDT}} < 0 \implies z_i < 0$, the converse is not true. We discard any z_{CDT} such that $z_{\mathrm{CDT}} \geq 0 \wedge c \leq 8$ as the sign of the corresponding z_i cannot be determined with certainty. Experimentally, we can keep around 63% of the z_i. Note that when we cannot determine the sign of some z_i, we do not discard the complete power trace as there may be other interesting values in the vector **z**. We simply ignore this particular index i.

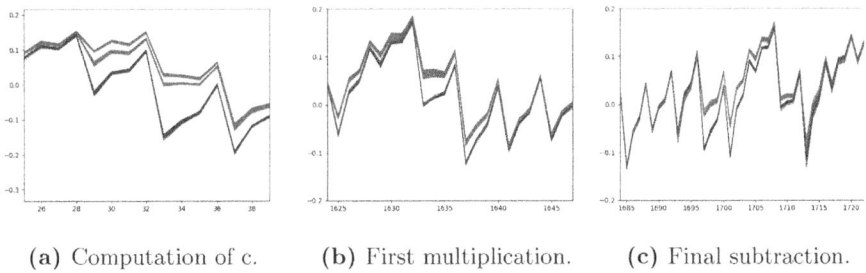

(a) Computation of c.   (b) First multiplication.   (c) Final subtraction.

Fig. 6. Power traces corresponding to negative (resp. non-negative) intermediary results are shown in blue (resp. red). (Color figure online)

5.3 Recovering the Sign of $S_{i,j}$

With the knowledge of the sign of z_i, we can further analyze the power traces from Sect. 3 to distinguish between the 1 and -1 coefficients of **S**. As described in Sect. 3, the power traces can be split into two groups when $S_{i,j}$ is non-zero. Those two groups depends on the sign of $S_{i,j} \cdot z_i$, hence on the sign of z_i for a fixed $S_{i,j}$. The power traces can thus be grouped depending on the sign of z_i.

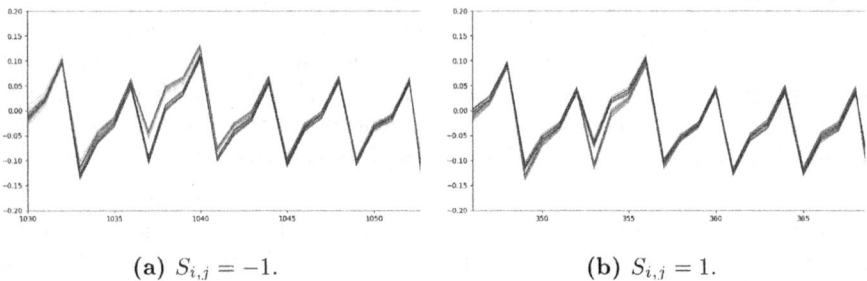

(a) $S_{i,j} = -1$. (b) $S_{i,j} = 1$.

Fig. 7. Power traces in red (resp. blue) correspond to $z_i < 0$ (resp. $z_i > 0$). (Color figure online)

As we can see on Fig. 7a and Fig. 7b, the relative position of those two groups is inverted depending on the value of $S_{i,j}$: if $S_{i,j} = -1$, the power traces corresponding to $z_i < 0$ will be positioned above the power traces corresponding to $z_i > 0$, and conversely for the $S_{i,j} = 1$.

Note that the special case where $z_i = 0$ is a blind spot of the classification detailed in Sect. 3. Indeed, the Hamming weight of the result will be set to 0 whatever the value of $S_{i,j}$. Thus, such z_i will not help us distinguish between ± 1 and may even induce some errors. However, this happens only when $z_{\mathrm{CDT}} = 0$ and $c \leq 8$. Since we already decided to discard the values $z_{\mathrm{CDT}} \geq 0 \wedge c \leq 8$, there are no $z_i = 0$ in our dataset.

5.4 Results

Figure 8 shows the percentage of recovered coefficients depending on the number of traces. The results concerning the zero coefficients have already been discussed in Sect. 3. If we consider all coefficients, it is possible to recover a high amount of coefficients with a low number of traces, but this may lead to false positives. As our attacks based on lattice reduction do not tolerate any false positives, we increase the number of traces up to 1500. Results for lower number of traces are only displayed to encourage future works regarding false positives tolerance. Besides, recall that to distinguish between the coefficients $S_{i,j} \in \{-1, 1\}$ we need additional information on the sign of z_i as detailed in Sect. 5.3, and we can only get this information for 63% of the z_i as explained in Sect. 5.2. The results shown on Fig. 8 take this into account.

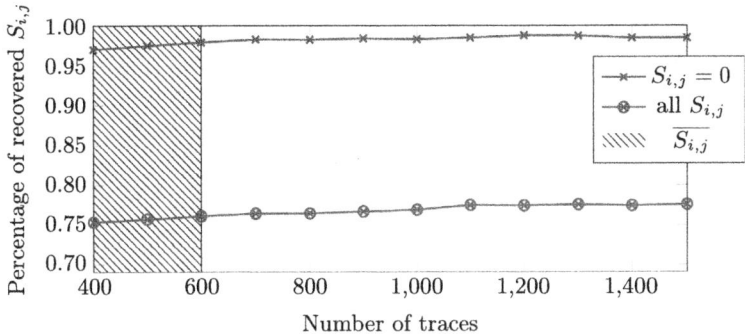

Fig. 8. Percentage of recovered $S_{i,j}$ equal to zero in blue and all the $S_{i,j}$ in red. Dashed area show where false positives $\overline{S_{i,j}}$ are found. (Color figure online)

Overall, with 1500 power traces, we retrieve without any false positive:

- more than 95% of the $S_{i,j} = 0$ with no additional information (Sect. 3),
- around 75% of all the $S_{i,j}$ with prior information on the sign of z_i (here).

6 Forging with Partial Knowledge of S

We combine the results from Sect. 5 with the attack from Sect. 4.1, and assume that d columns of $\mathbf{S}$ out of m were recovered this way. We exhibit in this section a strategy to forge a signature for a diminished cost using this knowledge.

Assuming that the first d columns $\mathbf{S}_1$ of $\mathbf{S}$ are known, up to reordering, let:

$$\mathbf{A} = (\mathbf{Id}_m|\hat{\mathbf{A}}|\mathbf{B}) = \begin{pmatrix} \mathbf{Id}_d & \mathbf{0}^{d\times m-d} & \hat{\mathbf{A}}^{high} & \mathbf{B}_1^{high} & \mathbf{B}_2^{high} \\ \mathbf{0}^{m-d\times d} & \mathbf{Id}_{m-d} & \hat{\mathbf{A}}^{low} & \mathbf{B}_1^{low} & \mathbf{B}_2^{low} \end{pmatrix},$$

where $\mathbf{B}_1^{high} \in \mathbb{Z}_Q^{d\times d}$, $\mathbf{B}_1^{low} \in \mathbb{Z}_Q^{m-d\times d}$, $\mathbf{B}_2^{high} \in \mathbb{Z}_Q^{d\times m-d}$ and $\mathbf{B}_2^{low} \in \mathbb{Z}_Q^{m-d\times m-d}$. We also let $\mathbf{B}_i^\top = ((\mathbf{B}_i^{high})^\top|(\mathbf{B}_i^{low})^\top)$ for $i \in \{1, 2\}$.

6.1 Partial Forgery Using $\mathbf{S}_1$

We first forge in the case where the $m-d$ last coefficients of the target are all 0s.

Lemma 6.1. *Let p, q, m, n, d be integers and $Q = pq$. Let $\mathbf{u} \in \mathbb{Z}_Q^d \times \{0^{m-d}\}$. Let $\mathbf{v} = \lceil \mathbf{u}/p \rceil \in \mathbb{Z}^d \times \{0^{m-d}\}$. Then $(\mathbf{x}_1^*, \mathbf{x}_2^*) = ((\mathbf{S}_1|\mathbf{0}^{n\times m-d})\mathbf{v}, \mathbf{v})$ is a valid HuFu signature for any μ such that $H(\mu) = \mathbf{u}$.*

Proof. Verification computes $\mathbf{x}_0^* = \mathbf{u} - \hat{\mathbf{A}}\mathbf{x}_1^* - \mathbf{B}\mathbf{x}_2^* = (\mathbf{u} \bmod p) + (\mathbf{E}_1|\mathbf{0}^{m\times m-d})\mathbf{v}$. Moreover $\|\mathbf{x}_0^*, \mathbf{x}_1^*, \mathbf{x}_2^*\| \leq B$ as we essentially set $\mathbf{p} = 0^{2m+n}$ and chose a short vector in $q\mathbb{Z}^m + \mathbf{v}'$, using notations from Sect. 2.2. □

6.2 Complete Forgery via Lattice Reduction

In practice, the probability of finding a $\mathbf{u} \in \mathbb{Z}_Q^m$ satisfying the above constraint is $1/Q^{m-d}$. Instead, we take any target $\mathbf{u} \in \mathbb{Z}_Q^m$, ignore its first d coordinates and find a suitable preimage of it for the last $m - d$ rows of $\mathbf{A}$.

Forgery. Let $H(\mu) = \mathbf{u} = (\mathbf{u}_1^\top | \mathbf{u}_2^\top)^\top$, with $\mathbf{u}_1 \in \mathbb{Z}_Q^d$ and $\|\mathbf{y}\| \leq B_{\mathbf{y}}$ with:

$$(\mathbf{Id}_{m-d} | \hat{\mathbf{A}}^{low} | \mathbf{B}_1^{low} | \mathbf{B}_2^{low}) \cdot \mathbf{y} = \mathbf{y}_0 + \hat{\mathbf{A}}^{low} \mathbf{y}_1 + \mathbf{B}_1^{low} \mathbf{y}_2 + \mathbf{B}_2^{low} \mathbf{y}_3 = \mathbf{u}_2 \bmod Q,$$

for some $B_{\mathbf{y}} > 0$ set later. We let $\mathbf{u}_1' = \mathbf{u}_1 - (\hat{\mathbf{A}}^{high} | \mathbf{B}_1^{high} | \mathbf{B}_2^{high}) \mathbf{y}$. At this point, our target is $\mathbf{u}'^\top = (\mathbf{u}_1'^\top | \mathbf{0}^{1 \times (m-d)})$. Let us now consider the forgery vector $(\mathbf{x}_1', \mathbf{x}_2')$ obtained with Lemma 6.1. The final forgery is:

$$\mathbf{x}_1 = (\mathbf{x}_1' + \mathbf{y}_1) \quad \text{and} \quad \mathbf{x}_2 = \begin{pmatrix} \mathbf{x}_2' + \mathbf{y}_2 \\ \mathbf{y}_3 \end{pmatrix}.$$

Verification. The verification algorithm recovers:

$$\mathbf{x}_0 = \mathbf{u} - \hat{\mathbf{A}} \mathbf{x}_1 - \mathbf{B} \mathbf{x}_2$$
$$= \begin{pmatrix} (\mathbf{u}_1' \bmod p) + \mathbf{E}_1 \lceil \mathbf{u}_1'/p \rfloor \\ \mathbf{y}_0 \end{pmatrix} = \begin{pmatrix} \mathbf{x}_0' \\ \mathbf{y}_0 \end{pmatrix}.$$

It then checks the norm of $(\mathbf{x}_0^\top, \mathbf{x}_1^\top, \mathbf{x}_2^\top)$, which is at most $\|(\mathbf{x}_0', \mathbf{x}_1', \mathbf{x}_2')\| + \|\mathbf{y}\|$ and must be $\leq B$. This last constraint drives the choice of $B_{\mathbf{y}}$. In practice, we empirically estimated $\|(\mathbf{x}_0', \mathbf{x}_1', \mathbf{x}_2')\|$ to derive $B_{\mathbf{y}}$.

6.3 Cost of Forging as a Function of d

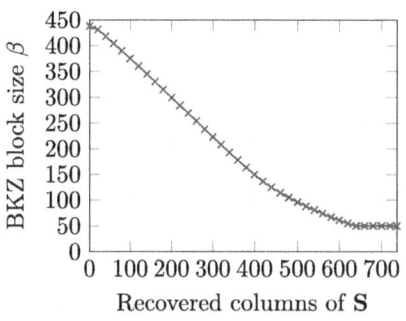

Fig. 9. Evolution of the block size to forge a signature.

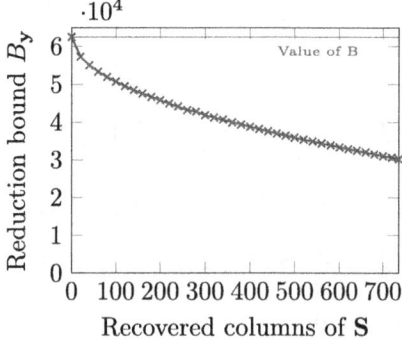

Fig. 10. $B_{\mathbf{y}}$ as a function of the number d of recovered columns of $\mathbf{S}$.

The cost of lattice reduction is estimated following the methodology outlined in the original HuFu submission. Specifically, we rely on the nearest colattice algorithm to determine the required BKZ block size and then estimate the associated computational cost using the Core-SVP model. Figure 9 illustrates the estimated BKZ block size for HuFu-1. The bound B_y is derived by performing a hundred forgeries for each value of d from Sect. 6.1 and computing the average norm of the resulting vector $(\mathbf{x}'_0, \mathbf{x}'_1, \mathbf{x}'_2)$ as a function of d as shown in Fig. 10.

6.4 Combining Key Recovery and Forgery

We try to estimate the total cost of running both the key recovery and the forgery attack. The combination of the two is parameterized by the amount d of columns recovered by the key recovery and used by the forgery attack. We estimate the cost of the combination as $\max(\log_2(d) + 0.292\beta_{kr}, 0.292\beta_{forge}(d))$, where β_{kr} is the block size necessary to recover a column given 75% of its coordinates as estimated via Sect. 4.1 and $\beta_{forge}(d)$ is the block size necessary to forge given d columns of $\mathbf{S}$ as estimated in Fig. 9. We present in Fig. 11a the evolution of the estimation of the total cost as a function of d when the amount of recovered coefficients is about 75%.

Then, we optimize over d and show in Fig. 11b the cost of the attack as a function of recovered coefficients per column. Of particular interests are the 50% and 75% threshold, as they correspond to the 0-only and all coefficients SCA attacks on $\mathbf{S}$. In the former case, the attack costs at least 62 bits, while in the latter, the attack cost is down to 29 bits.

We challenge our hypothesis that leaked coefficients are evenly distributed among all columns. In the case of the 75% recovered coefficients, we only need that there exist 500 columns whose at least 75% of their coefficients are recovered to run the attack with the claimed bit-cost. Running estimations with proba_estimates.py, it turned out to be the case every time.

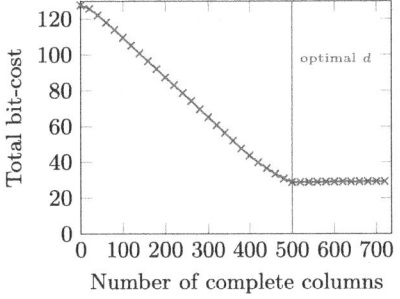
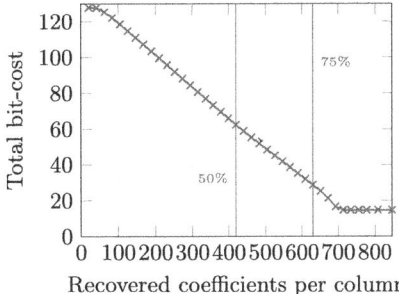

(a) ... as a function of the number of recovered columns when 75% of the coefficients of $\mathbf{S}$ are known.

(b) ... as a function of the amount of recovered coefficients per column during the side-channel step.

Fig. 11. Total estimated bit-cost of key-recovery and forgery.

7 Discussion

Combined Attack on Unstructured Lattices. Although our results target an unprotected implementation, they highlight an important insight: the absence of structure does not mitigate combined attacks (also known as partial key exposure attacks). Furthermore, full key recovery during the side-channel step is not necessary for a successful attack.

Further Countermeasures. The side-channel attack described in Sect. 3 and Sect. 5 relies heavily on the ternary nature of the matrices **S** and **E**. For this reason, increasing the standard deviation of the distribution used for the key generation could offer protection against such attacks. Alternatively, arithmetic masking, proven in the ISW [ISW03] model, is a reliable countermeasure, widely used in lattice-based cryptography [BBE+18,BGR+21,dPKPR24]. Regarding the vector **z**, masking Gaussian samplers remains a complex and performance-intensive task. In our attack, exploiting **z** is only effective when combined with information about **S**, so protecting **S** alone is sufficient to thwart our approach.

Future Works. Due to similarities with Falcon, HuFu may be vulnerable to Hidden Parallelepiped Attacks that rely solely on **z**. However, such attacks have only been performed on structured lattices. Extending them to unstructured lattices may present additional challenges.

Acknowledgements. We thank the anonymous reviewers for their useful remarks that helped improve the quality of this paper. This work has been partially supported by the European Union - Next Generation EU through the France Relance program and by the French government through the France 2030 program under the project RESQUE. This work has been further supported by the French Agence Nationale de la Recherche through the France 2030 program under grant agreement N. ANR-22-PETQ-0008 PQ-TLS.

A Proof of Lemma 2.1

Proof (of Lemma 2.1). Since Q is a power of 2, invertibility modulo Q is equivalent to invertibility modulo 2. Therefore, wlog we work modulo 2.

Consider $k_1 < n - k_2$ and let $\{\mathbf{a}_1, \ldots, \mathbf{a}_{k_1+1}\}$ be random vectors in $\mathbb{Z}_2^{n-k_2}$. For $\{\mathbf{a}_1, \ldots, \mathbf{a}_{k_1+1}\}$ to be linearly independent, two conditions must hold:

1. $\{\mathbf{a}_1, \ldots, \mathbf{a}_{k_1}\}$ are linearly independent (event $\mathcal{A}_{k_1}$).
2. $\mathbf{a}_{k_1+1} \notin \mathrm{span}(\mathbf{a}_1, \ldots, \mathbf{a}_{k_1})$ (event $\mathcal{B}_{k_1}$).

Let p_{k_1} denote the probability that $\{\mathbf{a}_1, \ldots, \mathbf{a}_{k_1}\}$ are linearly independent. Thus:

$$p_{k_1+1} = p_{k_1} \cdot \Pr[\mathcal{B}_{k_1} \mid \mathcal{A}_{k_1}] = p_{k_1} \cdot \left(1 - 2^{k_1 - (n-k_2)}\right).$$

Starting with $p_1 = 1 - 2^{-(n-k_2)}$, the result follows by induction. □

References

[ABB10] Agrawal, S., Boneh, D., Boyen, X.: Efficient lattice (H)IBE in the standard model. In: Gilbert, H. (ed.) EUROCRYPT 2010. LNCS, vol. 6110, pp. 553–572. Springer, Heidelberg (2010). https://doi.org/10.1007/978-3-642-13190-5_28

[ACPS09] Applebaum, B., Cash, D., Peikert, C., Sahai, A.: Fast cryptographic primitives and circular-secure encryption based on hard learning problems. In: Halevi, S. (ed.) CRYPTO 2009. LNCS, vol. 5677, pp. 595–618. Springer, Heidelberg (2009). https://doi.org/10.1007/978-3-642-03356-8_35

[ADH+19] Albrecht, M.R., Ducas, L., Herold, G., Kirshanova, E., Postlethwaite, E.W., Stevens, M.: The general sieve kernel and new records in lattice reduction. In: Ishai, Y., Rijmen, V. (eds.) EUROCRYPT 2019, Part II. LNCS, vol. 11477, pp. 717–746. Springer, Cham (2019). https://doi.org/10.1007/978-3-030-17656-3_25

[ADPS16] Alkim, E., Ducas, L., Pöppelmann, T., Schwabe, P.: Post-quantum key exchange - a new hope. In: Holz, T., Savage, S. (eds.) USENIX Security 2016, pp. 327–343. USENIX Association (2016)

[Ajt96] Ajtai, M.: Generating hard instances of lattice problems (extended abstract). In: 28th ACM STOC, pp. 99–108. ACM Press (1996). https://doi.org/10.1145/237814.237838

[BBE+18] Barthe, G., et al.: Masking the GLP lattice-based signature scheme at any order. In: Nielsen, J.B., Rijmen, V. (eds.) EUROCRYPT 2018. LNCS, vol. 10821, pp. 354–384. Springer, Cham (2018). https://doi.org/10.1007/978-3-319-78375-8_12

[BDGL16] Becker, A., Ducas, L., Gama, N., Laarhoven, T.: New directions in nearest neighbor searching with applications to lattice sieving. In: Krauthgamer, R. (ed.) 27th SODA, pp. 10–24. ACM-SIAM (2016). https://doi.org/10.1137/1.9781611974331.ch2

[BFM+18] Bos, J.W., Friedberger, S., Martinoli, M., Oswald, E., Stam, M:. Assessing the feasibility of single trace power analysis of Frodo. In: SAC. LNCS, vol. 11349, pp. 216–234. Springer, Cham (2018). https://doi.org/10.1007/978-3-030-10970-7_10

[BGR+21] Bos, J.W., Gourjon, M., Renes, J., Schneider, T., van Vredendaal, C.: Masking Kyber: first- and higher-order implementations. IACR TCHES, 2021(4), 173–214 (2021). https://tches.iacr.org/index.php/TCHES/article/view/9064, https://doi.org/10.46586/tches.v2021.i4.173-214

[BLNR22] Bernard, O., Lesavourey, A., Nguyen, T.-H., Roux-Langlois, A.: Log-S-unit lattices using explicit stickelberger generators to solve approx ideal-SVP. In: Agrawal, S., Lin, D. (eds.) ASIACRYPT 2022, Part III, LNCS, vol. 13793, pp. 677–708. Springer, Cham (2022). https://doi.org/10.1007/978-3-031-22969-5_23

[BR20] Bernard, O., Roux-Langlois, A.: Twisted-PHS: using the product formula to solve approx-SVP in ideal lattices. In: Moriai, S., Wang, H. (eds.) ASIACRYPT 2020, Part II. LNCS, vol. 12492, pp. 349–380. Springer, Cham (2020). https://doi.org/10.1007/978-3-030-64834-3_12

[BVC+23] Berzati, A., Viera, A.C., Chartouny, M., Madec, S., Vergnaud, D., Vigilant, D.: Exploiting intermediate value leakage in Dilithium: a template-based approach. IACR TCHES **2023**(4), 188–210 (2023). https://doi.org/10.46586/tches.v2023.i4.188-210

[BVCV24] Berzati, A., Viera, A.C., Chartouny, M., Vigilant, D.: Simple power analysis assisted chosen cipher-text attack on ML-KEM. Cryptology ePrint Archive, Paper 2024/2051 (2024). https://eprint.iacr.org/2024/2051

[CDW17] Cramer, R., Ducas, L., Wesolowski, B.: Short stickelberger class relations and application to ideal-SVP. In: Coron, J.-S., Nielsen, J.B. (eds.) EUROCRYPT 2017, Part I. LNCS, vol. 10210, pp. 324–348. Springer, Cham (2017). https://doi.org/10.1007/978-3-319-56620-7_12

[CGM19] Chen, Y., Genise, N., Mukherjee, P.: Approximate trapdoors for lattices and smaller hash-and-sign signatures. In: Galbraith, S.D., Moriai, S. (eds.) ASIACRYPT 2019. LNCS, vol. 11923, pp. 3–32. Springer, Cham (2019). https://doi.org/10.1007/978-3-030-34618-8_1

[DDGR20] Dachman-Soled, D., Ducas, L., Gong, H., Rossi, M.: LWE with side information: attacks and concrete security estimation. In: Micciancio, D., Ristenpart, T. (eds.) CRYPTO 2020, Part II. LNCS, vol. 12171, pp. 329–358. Springer, Cham (2020). https://doi.org/10.1007/978-3-030-56880-1_12

[DGHK23] Dachman-Soled, D., Gong, H., Hanson, T., Kippen, H.: Revisiting security estimation for LWE with hints from a geometric perspective. In: Handschuh, H., Lysyanskaya, A. (eds.) CRYPTO 2023, Part V. LNCS, vol. 14085, pp. 748–781. Springer, Cham (2023). https://doi.org/10.1007/978-3-031-38554-4_24

[DM14] Ducas, L., Micciancio, D.: Improved short lattice signatures in the standard model. In: Garay, J.A., Gennaro, R. (eds.) CRYPTO 2014, Part I. LNCS, vol. 8616, pp. 335–352. Springer, Heidelberg (2014). https://doi.org/10.1007/978-3-662-44371-2_19

[dPKPR24] del Pino, R., Katsumata, S., Prest, T., Rossi, M.: Raccoon: a masking-friendly signature proven in the probing model. In: Reyzin, L., Stebila, D. (eds.) CRYPTO 2024, Part I. LNCS, vol. 14920, pp. 409–444. Springer, Cham (2024). https://doi.org/10.1007/978-3-031-68376-3_13

[dPLS18] del Pino, R., Lyubashevsky, V., Seiler, G.: Lattice-based group signatures and zero-knowledge proofs of automorphism stability. In: Lie, D., Mannan, M., Backes, M., Wang, X. (eds.) ACM CCS 2018, pp. 574–591. ACM Press (2018). https://doi.org/10.1145/3243734.3243852

[Duc18] Ducas, L.: Shortest vector from lattice sieving: a few dimensions for free. In: Nielsen, J.B., Rijmen, V. (eds.) EUROCRYPT 2018, Part I. LNCS, vol. 10820, pp. 125–145. Springer, Cham (2018). https://doi.org/10.1007/978-3-319-78381-9_5

[EK20] Espitau, T., Kirchner, P.: The nearest-colattice algorithm: time-approximation tradeoff for approx-CVP. Open Book Series **4**(1), 251–266 (2020)

[GMRR22] Guerreau, M., Martinelli, A., Ricosset, T., Rossi, M.: The hidden parallelepiped is back again: power analysis attacks on falcon. IACR TCHES **2022**(3), 141–164 (2022). https://doi.org/10.46586/tches.v2022.i3.141-164

[GPV08] Gentry, C., Peikert, C., Vaikuntanathan, V.: Trapdoors for hard lattices and new cryptographic constructions. In: Ladner, R.E., Dwork, C. (eds.) 40th ACM STOC, pp. 197–206. ACM Press (2008). https://doi.org/10.1145/1374376.1374407

[GR24] Guerreau, M., Rossi, M.: A not so discrete sampler: power analysis attacks on HAWK signature scheme. IACR Trans. Cryptogr. Hardw. Embed. Syst. **2024**(4), 156–178 (2024). https://doi.org/10.46586/tches.v2024.i4.156-178

[ISW03] Ishai, Y., Sahai, A., Wagner, D.: Private circuits: securing hardware against probing attacks. In: Boneh, D. (ed.) CRYPTO 2003. LNCS, vol. 2729, pp. 463–481. Springer, Heidelberg (2003). https://doi.org/10.1007/978-3-540-45146-4_27

[JRS23] Jeudy, C., Roux-Langlois, A., Sanders, O.: Lattice signature with efficient protocols, application to anonymous credentials. In: Handschuh, H., Lysyanskaya, A. (eds.)CRYPTO 2023, Part II. LNCS, vol. 14082, pp. 351–383. Springer, Cham (2023). https://doi.org/10.1007/978-3-031-38545-2_12

[JS24] Jeudy, C., Sanders, O.: Improved Lattice Blind Signatures from Recycled Entropy. Cryptology ePrint Archive, Report 2024/1289 (2024). https://eprint.iacr.org/2024/1289

[KAA21] Karabulut, E., Alkim, E., Aysu, A.: Single-trace side-channel attacks on ω-small polynomial sampling: with applications to NTRU, NTRU prime, and CRYSTALS-DILITHIUM. In: HOST, pp. 35–45. IEEE (2021)

[Kan87] Kannan, R.: Minkowski's convex body theorem and integer programming. Math. Oper. Res. **12**(3), 415–440 (1987)

[KH18] Kim, S., Hong, S.: Single trace analysis on constant time CDT sampler and its countermeasure. Appl. Sci. **8**(10) (2018). https://www.mdpi.com/2076-3417/8/10/1809, https://doi.org/10.3390/app8101809

[LZY+25] Lin, X., et al.: Thorough Power Analysis on Falcon Gaussian Samplers and Practical Countermeasure. Cryptology ePrint Archive, Paper 2025/351 (2025). https://eprint.iacr.org/2025/351

[MN23] May, A., Nowakowski, J.: Too Many hints - when LLL breaks LWE. In: Guo, J., Steinfeld, R. (eds.) ASIACRYPT 2023, Part IV. LNCS, vol. 14441, pp. 106–137. Springer, Singapore (2023). https://doi.org/10.1007/978-981-99-8730-6_4

[MP12] Micciancio, D., Peikert, C.: Trapdoors for lattices: simpler, tighter, faster, smaller. In: Pointcheval, D., Johansson, T. (eds.) EUROCRYPT 2012. LNCS, vol. 7237, pp. 700–718. Springer, Heidelberg (2012). https://doi.org/10.1007/978-3-642-29011-4_41

[NIS24a] NIST. Module-Lattice-Based Digital Signature Standard. Federal Information Processing Standards Publication, NIST FIPS 204 (2024). https://doi.org/10.6028/NIST.FIPS.204

[NIS24b] NIST. Module-Lattice-Based Key-Encapsulation Mechanism Standard. Federal Information Processing Standards Publication, NIST FIPS 203 (2024). https://doi.org/10.6028/NIST.FIPS.203

[Pei10] Peikert, C.: An efficient and parallel gaussian sampler for lattices. In: Rabin, T. (ed.) CRYPTO 2010. LNCS, vol. 6223, pp. 80–97. Springer, Heidelberg (2010). https://doi.org/10.1007/978-3-642-14623-7_5

[PHS19] Pellet-Mary, A., Hanrot, G., Stehlé, D.: Approx-SVP in ideal lattices with pre-processing. In: Ishai, Y., Rijmen, V. (eds.) EUROCRYPT 2019, Part II. LNCS, vol. 11477, pp. 685–716. Springer, Cham (2019). https://doi.org/10.1007/978-3-030-17656-3_24

[Reg05] Regev, O.: On lattices, learning with errors, random linear codes, and cryptography. In: Gabow, H.N., Fagin, R. (eds.) 37th ACM STOC, pp. 84–93. ACM Press (2005). https://doi.org/10.1145/1060590.1060603

[SE94] Schnorr, C.P., Euchner, M.: Lattice basis reduction: improved practical algorithms and solving subset sum problems. Mathematical Programming (1994)

[YJL+23] Yu, Y., et al.: HuFu: hash-and-sign signatures from powerful gadgets (2023). https://csrc.nist.gov/csrc/media/Projects/pqc-dig-sig/documents/round-1/spec-files/HuFu-spec-web.pdf

[YJW23] Yu, Y., Jia, H., Wang, X.: Compact lattice gadget and its applications to hash-and-sign signatures. In: Handschuh, H., Lysyanskaya, A. (eds.) CRYPTO 2023, Part V. LNCS, vol. 14085, pp. 390–420. Springer, Cham (2023). https://doi.org/10.1007/978-3-031-38554-4_13

[ZLYW23] Zhang, S., Lin, X., Yu, Y., Wang, W.: Improved power analysis attacks on falcon. In: Hazay, C., Stam, M. (eds.) EUROCRYPT 2023, Part IV. LNCS, vol. 14007, pp. 565–595. Springer, Cham (2023). https://doi.org/10.1007/978-3-031-30634-1_19

Securing Post-quantum Cryptography

X2X: Low-Randomness and High-Throughput A2B and B2A Conversions for $d+1$ Shares in Hardware

Quinten Norga[✉], Jan-Pieter D'Anvers, Suparna Kundu, and Ingrid Verbauwhede

COSIC, KU Leuven, Leuven, Belgium
{quinten.norga,jan-pieter.danvers,suparna.kundu,
ingrid.verbauwhede}@esat.kuleuven.be

Abstract. The conversion between arithmetic and Boolean masking representations (A2B & B2A) is a crucial component for side-channel resistant implementations of lattice-based (post-quantum) cryptography. In this paper, we first propose novel d-order algorithms for the secure addition (SecADDChain$_q$) and B2A (B2X2A). Our secure adder is well-suited for repeated ('chained') executions, achieved through an improved method for repeated masked modular reduction. The optimized B2X2A gadget removes a full secure addition compared to state-of-the-art B2A approaches, by relying on the X2B operation. This component directly converts a simultaneously Boolean and arithmetically shared variable to $d+1$ Boolean shares. This approach reduces the required amount of SecADDs to $2d$, of which $2 \cdot \lceil \log_2(d) \rceil$ are max-order.

Secondly, we develop both a first- and high-order masked, unified hardware implementation that can compute both A2B & B2A conversions for power-of-two (p) and prime (q) moduli. Compared to state-of-the-art (high-throughput) hardware implementations that only support A2B$_p$, we reduce area utilization for a second-order implementation by 45% up to 60% and fresh randomness up to 62%, while supporting all four types of additive mask conversions. Our first-order design only requires 1,133/2,170 [LUT/FF] on Kintex-7 FPGAs.

Our proposed algorithms are proven secure in the d-probing model and their implementations are validated via practical lab analysis using the TVLA methodology. We experimentally show that our masked implementation is hardened against first- and second-order univariate and multivariate power-based side-channel attacks using 100 million traces, for each mode of operation.

Keywords: PQC · Hardware · Masking · Side-Channel Analysis

1 Introduction

The security of currently deployed public key cryptographic algorithms is typically based on the integer factorization or elliptic curve discrete logarithm problem. The threat of large-scale quantum computers is ever-increasing, potentially leaving current algorithms and their implementations vulnerable to potential quantum attacks [61] in the (near) future. The term 'Post-Quantum Cryptography' (PQC) encompasses all alternative cryptographic algorithms, that can resist these attacks and are soon to replace vulnerable algorithms and their implementations.

The National Institute of Standards and Technology (NIST) has recognized the need for replacing the existing public-key standards. It launched an initial PQC standardization effort in 2016 [52] and is continuing with an additional Digital Signature (DS) competition, launched in 2023 [54]. Noticeably, lattice-based schemes and their promising security and performance features, are popular candidates for both competitions. The final Kyber [50] and Dilithium [49] standards were published in Summer 2024, while seven out of 40 accepted submissions for the PQC DS competition (Round 1) are lattice-based [54]. One of the challenges for the deployment of new post-quantum schemes is protection against (physical) side-channel attacks.

Side-Channel Analysis (SCA) attacks aim at extracting sensitive information from electronic devices performing security-critical applications, by observing the physical characteristics of the calculations. First discovered and published by Kocher [38] in 1996, many types of physical behavior exist and can be abused by adversaries: execution time, instantaneous power consumption [39] or Electromagnetic (EM) radiation [29]. The security and confidentiality of a cryptographic implementation can be completely broken if its physical characteristics correlate to a secret key, typically called (side-channel) *leakage*. Many insecure implementations, including of lattice-based schemes, have been successfully attacked using side channels [22,35,55,56,63]. Therefore, protection against SCA attacks is a critical factor for the security of a physical device and remains an open challenge in academia and industry.

Masking is an algorithmic and well-studied approach for protecting cryptographic hardware or software implementations against (passive) EM or power side-channel attacks. Following the concept of secret sharing by Shamir et al. [60], a sensitive variable x is split into $(d+1)$ uniform random shares $(x^{\{i\}})$ for achieving security order d. Each of the shares separately is independent to the secret and only if an adversary combines information of all $d+1$ shares, it can learn something about the original secret x. The masking countermeasure [32,33,37,51,57] is popular because it can provide physical security through formal security and adversary models.

Masking the operations of lattice-based crypto schemes requires a mix of both Boolean and arithmetic mask representations. More precisely, polynomial multiplication and addition are preferably performed on arithmetic shares, whereas hashing (Keccak) inherently is a bitwise operation and thus prefers Boolean masking. Hence, there is a need for converting between both sharing types: from arithmetic to Boolean (A2B) and Boolean to arithmetic (B2A). These conversions are costly, even more so at higher protection orders, and are one of the major bottlenecks in masked implementations.

Related Work. Masking techniques have been applied to lattice-based cryptography in other work, mostly targeting software implementations. This includes PQC candidates Dilithium [45], Saber [6,20,27,41], Kyber [7,9,27,36] and NTRU [21,40]. A first-order A2B conversion was originally proposed by Goubin in [31], with Coron et al. proposing higher-order conversions [16,17] for power-of-two moduli. They propose to construct the A2B conversion from the Secure Addition (SecADD) operation, which can be seen as an arithmetic addition of two Boolean shared variables.

However, most lattice-based schemes (incl. Kyber and Dilithium) operate on polynomials with coefficients modulo a prime integer q. A secure addition modulo a prime integer q (SecADD$_q$) can be constructed from a regular SecADD and additional explicit modular reduction. This expensive procedure typically involves a combination of additional SecADD's and Secure Multiplexers (SecMUX). Techniques for the A2B$_q$/B2A$_q$ operation have been proposed by Barthe et al. [5] and in [59]. An alternate approach for A2B$_q$/B2A$_q$ was proposed in [9,45], where first a modulus conversion from a prime integer (q) to a power-of-two one (p) is performed after which the masked operations are performed.

More recently, table-based approaches have received more attention as they are becoming viable for high-order conversions [20,25,62], yet not as efficient as computational approaches. These techniques are out-of-scope for this work.

Contribution. We propose improvements from the algorithmic level down to the circuit level, applicable to arbitrary protection orders.

- State-of-the-art SecADD$_q$ strategies require 3 × SecADD or 2 × SecADD and a SecMUX. We propose a novel gadget, SecADDChain$_q$, which utilizes *interleaved modular reduction* and can be efficiently chained for repeated executions, requiring 2 × SecADD at all protection orders (Sect. 3).
- B2A conversions are typically computed by combining an A2B operation with expensive *pre-and post-processing stages*. Our B2X2A gadget consists of a simplified post-processing stage (without SecADD) and the novel X2B, which directly converts a mix of arithmetic and Boolean shares to an equivalent Boolean sharing (Sect. 3). By operating on a mix of arithmetic and Boolean shares, $d+1$ Boolean shares are directly computed instead of through an A2B and a d-order SecADD. Compared to state-of-the-art techniques, our approach requires 2 or 3 fewer SecADDs at second protection order and 2 up to 4 fewer SecADD operations at third order.
- Through *careful, manual masking* of all operations, we significantly reduce the masking overhead (area, latency, randomness). Our SecADD implementation requires 50% fewer random bits and clock cycles by not relying on universally composable gadgets, but is paired with an increased verification cost (Sect. 4 and 5). Additionally, we show that *half-cycle datapaths* can reduce the total execution time of highly non-linear, masked operations from 36% to 42% ($d = 1$) and 42% to 47% ($d = 2$).
- The side-channel resistance of our implementation is formally proven and experimentally verified in our Security Evaluations Lab using the Test Vector Leakage Assessment (TVLA) methodology (Sect. 5).

– Our RTL source code is made publicly available at https://github.com/KULeuven-COSIC/X2X.

Our unified, streaming hardware architecture can be *dynamically* configured to perform any type of mask conversion: $\text{A2B}_{2^k}/\text{A2B}_q/\text{B2A}_{2^k}/\text{B2A}_q$. Our work is directly applicable to any lattice-based PQC scheme, we specifically target Kyber parameters in our unified implementation. To the best of our knowledge, our design strategy results in the lowest overhead cost (latency, fresh randomness and area) compared to the current state-of-the-art.

2 Background and Preliminaries

2.1 Notation

A bit position (index) is indicated by the subscript, with the LSB at bit 0 (x_0) and MSB at position $k-1$ (x_{k-1}) for k-bit data words. For power-of-two moduli (2^p), $k = p$; for prime moduli q, the word width is $k = \lceil \log_2(q) \rceil$. All operations and units/costs are expressed in terms of k-bit data words/shares, unless explicitly specified. Rounding up to the next integer is denoted by $\lceil \cdot \rceil$.

2.2 Arithmetic, Boolean and Composite Sharing

At protection order d, a secret value $x \in \mathbb{F}_k^n$ is arithmetically masked by converting it into $d+1$ shares $x^{\{0:d\}}$, such that $x = \sum_{i=0}^{d} x^{\{i\}}$ modulo a predefined integer q. For Boolean masking, the sharing of a secret value x can be reconstructed as $x = \bigoplus_{i=0}^{d} x^{\{i\}}$. A negation (SecNOT) ($\sim$) on Boolean shared data is equivalent to performing binary invert on a single share. Throughout this work, all sharing is considered uniformly random.

We introduce the term *composite* sharing for secret values that consist of a combination of arithmetic and Boolean shares. $x^{\{a,b\}}$ corresponds to a secret value x consisting of a arithmetic shares, each shared as b Boolean shares. Or alternatively: $x = \sum_{i=1}^{a}(\bigoplus_{j=1}^{b} x^{\{i,j\}})$ with a (total) masking order $d = (a*b)-1$. Note that Boolean masking can be seen as a special form of composite masking where all $d+1$ Boolean shares belong to the same arithmetic share ($a = 1, b = d+1$). An arithmetically shared variable consists of $d+1$ arithmetic shares ($a = d+1, b = 1$).

2.3 (Extended) d-Probing Model

The most prominent and well-studied adversary and security model, the Ishai, Sahai, and Wagner (ISW) d-probing model [37], aims at capturing the capabilities of real-world adversaries. In such a context, the adversary can probe and observe up to d wires (intermediate values) of an ideal (glitch-less) circuit performing sensitive operations. In this model, a (masked) circuit is d^{th}-order probing secure if and only if the information gained from d (noise-free and instantaneous) probes does not reveal any information of any secret variable.

However, the discrepancy between theoretical and practical security has been shown to be problematic in the case of the original ISW d-probing model. This has resulted in the compromised security of theoretically secure designs and implementations [43,48]. An extended (and more robust) security model that captures different physical effects (naturally) present in digital logic circuits (CMOS) and hardware, was proposed by Faust et al. in [26]. It introduces glitch-extended [43,44], transition-extended [2,15] and coupling-extended probes [23], and incorporate such (natural) physical defects as part of the adversarial model.

2.4 Masking: A Side-Channel Leakage Countermeasure

By introducing masking countermeasures, an attacker can only obtain information about any sensitive value if they have access to all shares at once, while an incomplete set of shares results in strictly random information.

Following the Domain-Oriented Masking (DOM) scheme [33], d-order secure masked circuits are achieved by splitting sensitive variables into $d + 1$ (independent) shares. 'Manually' creating a complex d-probing secure circuit, consisting of multiple such secure (DOM) gates, requires careful analysis. Several security notions for composability have been proposed: Non-Interference (NI) [3] and Strong Non-Interference (SNI) [4] in the presence of glitches (and transitions) in hardware.

Definition 1 (t-Non-Interference [4]). *A gadget with one output sharing and m_i input sharings is t-Non-Interferent (t-NI) if any set of at most t_1 probes on its internal wires and t_2 probes on wires from its output sharings such that $t_1 + t_2 \leq t$ can be simulated with $t_1 + t_2$ shares of each of its m_i input sharings.*

Definition 2 (t-Strong-Non-Interference [4]). *A gadget with one output sharing and m_i input sharings is t-Strong Non-Interferent (t-SNI) if any set of at most t_1 probes on its internal wires and t_2 probes on wires from its output sharings such that $t_1 + t_2 \leq t$ can be simulated with t_1 shares of each of its m_i input sharings.*

A different approach is based on 'trivial composability' and the security notion of Probe-Isolating Non-Interference (PINI) [10]: HPC gadgets [14], which are derived from the DOM scheme. Introduced by Cassiers et al., the proposed gadgets can be instantiated at arbitrary protection orders and trivially combined into a larger circuit. In general, trivial composability and its low verification cost and guaranteed d-probing security comes at a high (overhead) cost, due to being overly conservative in applying certain countermeasures.

We target 'optimized composition' in the d-probing model in this work using glitch-robust (DOM) gates and avoiding transitional leakage through a fully pipelined design. As a result, the overhead introduced when masking A2B/B2A operations, is significantly reduced compared to strictly using (PINI) HPC gadgets. This manual analysis and algorithmic masking of operations results in a lower overhead, but requires a higher verification cost and can be error-prone in the case of larger and more complex circuits [46].

2.5 Masking Lattice-Based PQC: ML-KEM

Figure 1 illustrates the impact of different mask domains and the need for switching between both during several sub-operations for Kyber (or ML-KEM). The decryption procedure requires performing Boolean operations, like binomial sampling and hashing. The re-encryption stage requires performing polynomial multiplication, which is an arithmetic operation, after which a masked comparison is performed in the Boolean domain. Note again, these conversions are extremely costly and result in being (one of) the main contributor(s) of run time latency. For the pseudocode of the full algorithms of all (future) PQC standards, we refer to the initial/final NIST FIPS standards [53].

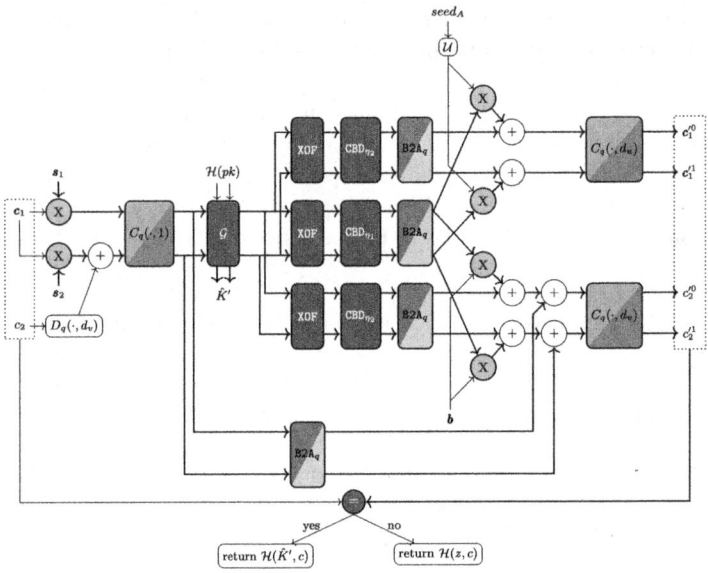

Fig. 1. The masked Decapsulation procedure for ML-KEM (FIPS 203). Operations that require Boolean masking are highlighted in blue, operations that prefer arithmetic masking are highlighted in yellow. Mask conversions are required to convert between these representations. [27] (Color figure online)

3 Optimized Secure Gadgets for Mask Conversions

The following section follows a bottom-up approach. Firstly, we optimize the secure addition (SecADD$_q$) by focusing on the masked modular reduction, requiring strictly 2 × SecADDs in total, even when chained repeatedly. Our strategy can be directly applied for arbitrary moduli q and arbitrary protection orders d, including Kyber ($q = 3329$) and Dilithium ($q = 8380417$).

Secondly, we propose a novel B2A gadget: B2X2A. We introduce a new primitive X2B, which operates on composite shares and eliminates a full secure addition from the post-processing stage, reducing the latency and randomness requirements at all protection orders. Compared to the A2B, which operates on an arithmetically shared variable, the X2B gadget can convert a mix of arithmetic and Boolean shares to $d+1$ boolean shares. The composability of all proposed gadgets is proven secure in the d-probing model and tested in TVLA setting. Table 1 gives an overview of all the gadgets used throughout this work, including a short description of their functionality and assumed security properties, on which we rely for proving their security in larger compositions.

Table 1. Overview of used gadgets in this work, with $t = d + 1$ shares. All gadgets operate on full (k-bit) data words, unless explicitly stated.

Algorithm	Description	Security	Reference
SecXOR	Masked logical XOR	t-NI	Algorithm 6
SecNOT	Masked Boolean negation	t-NI	Algorithm 7
SecAND	Masked logical AND	t-NI	[33] & Algorithm 8
SecOR	Masked logical OR	t-NI	Algorithm 9
SecREF	Strong refresh of Boolean masking	t-SNI	[4,14] & Algorithm 11
SecEXP	Doubling/Expanding of Boolean shares	t-NI	[17] & Algorithm 10
SecADD	Arithmetic addition of Boolean shares	t-NI	[5] & Appendix 4.1
FullXOR	Refresh and combine Boolean shares	t-NI	[5] & Algorithm 13
SecAddChain$_q$	Arithmetic addition mod (prime) q of Boolean shares	t-NI	Algorithm 2
A2B	Arithmetic to Boolean mask conversion	t-NI	[16] & Algorithm 3
X2B	Composite to Boolean mask conversion	t-NI	Algorithm 4
B2X2A	Boolean to arithmetic mask conversion	t-NI	Algorithm 5

3.1 Secure Addition (SecADD)

The secure addition is equivalent to performing an arithmetic addition ($s = x+y$ mod q) in the Boolean domain (Eq. 1). As we will demonstrate, it serves as the primary building block for higher-order mask conversions.

$$s^{\{0:d\}} = x^{\{0:d\}} + y^{\{0:d\}} \bmod q = \bigoplus_{i=0}^{d} x^{\{i\}} + \bigoplus_{i=0}^{d} y^{\{i\}} \bmod q \quad (1)$$

For power-of-two moduli ($p = 2^k$), the modular reduction is taken care of implicitly during computation. However, prime moduli (q) require explicit (masked) modular reduction. We show that our d-order SecADDChain$_q$ gadget outperforms state-of-the-art approaches when performing multiple secure additions in succession (which is the case in mask conversions). We first highlight two (costly) approaches from literature, which rely on an additional SecMUX or SecADD to complete the masked modular reduction.

SecMUX-Based Modular Reduction. Barthe et al. [5] introduced a simple, yet costly method for performing the SecADD$_q$ at arbitrary protection orders. It requires calculating both $s = x + y$ and $s' = x + y - q$ securely, one of which will be in range $[0, q)$. A costly SecMUX (Eq. 2) securely selects the desired shared data (s or s') that lies in the $[0 : q - 1]$ interval, based on the carry bits c (index $k - 1$).

$$\text{SecMUX}(s^{\{0:d\}}, s'^{\{0:d\}}, c_k^{\{0:d\}}) = \text{SecXOR}(\text{SecAND}(s, c), \text{SecAND}(s', \text{SecNOT}(c))) \quad (2)$$

SecADD-Based Modular Reduction. Subsequently, Fritzmann et al. [27] introduced a method for performing a first-order SecADD$_q$, which does not involve a SecMUX gadget and which we extend to arbitrary protection orders. By preprocessing the input data, which requires access to the initial masking of either input y (or x), the SecMUX operation can be removed.

In practice, we need one of the inputs to be in range $[-q, 0)$. This can be achieved by subtracting q from one of the inputs before it is shared: $y' = y - q$. The first SecADD operates on y' and x (or y and x') and computes $z = x + y'$ (Algorithm 1, Line 1). Next, a correction term c' is constructed and is added to this intermediate result z, ensuring that the result of the second SecADD $s = z + c' = x + y - q(+q)$ lies in $[0, q)$ (Line 4).

Algorithm 1. SecADD$_q$ (without SecMUX) (extended from [27])

Input Parameter : q ▷ q is prime
Input Data : $x^{\{0:d\}}$ and $y'^{\{0:d\}} = y^{\{0:d\}} + (2^k - q)$ ▷ Initial masking.
Output Data : $s^{\{0:d\}}$ such that $s = x + y \bmod q$

1: $z^{\{0:d\}} \leftarrow \text{SecADD}(x^{\{0:d\}}, y'^{\{0:d\}})$
2: $c_0^{\{0:d\}} \leftarrow z^{\{0:d\}} \gg (k - 1)$ ▷ Carry bit (share-wise).
3: $c'^{\{0:d\}} \leftarrow c^{\{0:d\}} \cdot q$ ▷ Share-wise.
4: $s^{\{0:d\}} \leftarrow \text{SecADD}(z^{\{0:d\}}, c'^{\{0:d\}})$

Note that the modular reduction and the construction of c' now is a linear (e.g. mask-friendly) operation, except for the secure additions themselves and can be generalized for $d + 1$ shares. There is no longer any need to explicitly select the correct result, using a SecMUX.

The main issue with this method arises when one of the Boolean masked inputs is not in range $[-q, 0)$. This is the case if the output of a SecADD$_q$ operation, in range $[0, q)$, is directly used as the input for another SecADD$_q$, as is the case during an A2B (and B2A) conversion. To subtract q from a Boolean masked variable, an additional secure addition with $(2^k - q)$ is required, as proposed in [11] (Algorithm 11). As a result, a full SecADD$_q$ now requires three SecADDs, which is costly in the context of mask conversions. More details are provided in Table 2.

Algorithm 2. SecADDChain$_q$ [t–NI]

Input Parameter : q	▷ q is prime
Input Data : $x^{\{0:d\}}$ and $y'^{\{0:d\}} = y^{\{0:d\}} + (2^k - q)$	▷ Initial masking.
Output Data 1 : $s^{\{0:d\}}$ such that $s = x + y \bmod q$	
Output Data 2 : $s'^{\{0:d\}}$ such that $s' = s + (2^k - q)$	

1: $z^{\{0:d\}} \leftarrow \text{SecADD}(x^{\{0:d\}}, y'^{\{0:d\}})$
2: $cc_0^{\{0:d\}} \leftarrow z^{\{0:d\}} \gg (k-1)$ ▷ Carry bit.
3: $cc_0^{\{0:d\}} \leftarrow \text{SecREF}(cc_0^{\{0:d\}})$ ▷ 1-bit
4: **if** final SecADD$_q$ **then**
5: $\quad c^{\{0:d\}} \leftarrow cc^{\{0:d\}} \cdot q$ ▷ Share-wise.
6: $\quad s^{\{0:d\}} \leftarrow \text{SecADD}(z^{\{0:d\}}, c^{\{0:d\}})$ ▷ in $[0:q)$
7: **else**
8: $\quad c'^{\{0:d\}} \leftarrow \text{SecNOT}(cc^{\{0:d\}}) \cdot (-q)$ ▷ Share-wise.
9: $\quad s'^{\{0:d\}} \leftarrow \text{SecADD}(z^{\{0:d\}}, c'^{\{0:d\}})$ ▷ in $[-q:0)$
10: **end if**

Interleaved Modular Reduction for Chained SecADDs. We propose the SecADDChain$_q$ gadget (Algorithm 2), which requires only two SecADD operations and is specifically useful in the context of chained additions, as is typically the case for A2B and B2A conversions. To achieve efficient chaining of SecADD$_q$ we provide two possible outputs: one is calculated if the SecADD$_q$ is one of many subsequent secure additions that need to be calculated, or the other if it is the final one in the chain.

For the algorithm in the previous section, if the secure addition is the final operation, the goal is to calculate $s = x + y$ which lies in $[0, q)$ with x and y consisting of $d+1$ Boolean shares. As described above, this can be achieved using strictly two SecADDs (Algorithm 1 & Algorithm 2, Line 6) if one of the inputs is pre-processed: $y' = y - q$.

If another SecADD$_q$ needs to be performed subsequently, the result of the operation needs to be pre-processed (by subtracting q) as it is one of the inputs of the next SecADD$_q$. Instead of doing this explicitly, our novel gadget SecADDChain$_q$ allows for this to be computed directly. The result will now be $s' = s + (2^k - q)$ (Algorithm 2, Line 9), which lies in $[-q, 0)$, allowing for the output to be used directly as an input for the next SecADD$_q$.

More specifically, first $z = x + y' (= x + y - q)$ is calculated. Using this intermediate result z, a different correction term c' is constructed in Line 8: $c' = (\sim z_{k-1}) \cdot (-q)$. This term is eventually added together with the intermediate result, in order to obtain the final result: $s' = z + c'$. Intuitively, if the intermediate result lies in $[-q, 0)$, the unshared correction term should be zero. If positive, $-q$ should be added back to the intermediate result in order to ensure the final result (s') lies in $[-q, 0)$. This is achieved by using the Boolean inverse of the carry bits (z_{k-1}) as a share-wise select signal for a multiplexer. If an uneven amount of carry bits are one, the unshared value is negative and an even amount of shares in c' is set to $-q$. As a result, the unshared c' is equal to zero, which is desired.

This extension allows for multiple secure additions to be directly chained in succession, without the need for repeated and explicit pre-processing of one of the inputs and thus strictly requiring two SecADDs. Such a thing is useful for

A2B$_q$/B2A$_q$ conversions, as the masked modular reduction is interleaved during successive operations. The only time when access to the initial masking is required is one of the inputs, y, of the very first secure addition of which many are performed in succession. The input is corrected with $-q$ before the initial sharing, so that $\bigoplus_{i=0}^{d} y'^{\{i\}} = y - q$. If not possible, a one-time pre-processing using the SecADD is required.

d-Probing Security: We show that the SecADDChain$_q$ gadget is correct and prove it to be $t-$NI, considering the leakage effects from Sect. 2.3 in Appendix A.

3.2 B2A

A method for converting $d+1$ Boolean shares to $d+1$ arithmetic shares (mod 2^k) was introduced in [17] and extended for arbitrary moduli q in [5]. Generally speaking, the B2A conversion is equivalent to an A2B operation with additional (costly) pre- and post-processing stages. We make several modifications to this procedure and propose a more efficient B2A conversion routine in Algorithm 5: B2X2A. It relies on the conversion (e.g., addition) of composite sharing to Boolean sharing through the X2B, to remove an additional secure addition in the post-processing. Correctness and security proofs are also provided. We conclude by comparing the overhead of published work and our methods.

X2B (and A2B). A B2A operations requires adding a $d+1$ Boolean shared variable with a $d+1$ arithmetically shared one (with one zero share). Traditionally, this is solved by first converting the second value to a $d+1$ Boolean shared variable using an A2B. Secondly, both Boolean shared variables can be securely added together (SecADD). Instead, we propose the X2B primitive, which is a variant of the A2B proposed in [17] but operates on a (specific) *composite* sharing $z^{\{0:d\}}$ (Eq. 3) and obtains an equivalent $d+1$ Boolean sharing. It directly adds arithmetic and Boolean shared variables together using secure additions that operate on different levels of Boolean sharing, exploiting the structure of the B2A operands. As we will demonstrate in the next section, this approach is more efficient for B2A operations compared to the state-of-the-art, where all secure additions and conversions operate on strictly identical share counts.

As described in Eq. 3, the input of X2B consists of a specific mix of arithmetic and Boolean sharing: all $d+1$ shares of $z^{\{0:d\}}$ are arithmetically shared, but one share $z^{\{0\}}$ consists in turn of a number of Boolean shares ($2d+1$ shares in total):

$$z^{\{0:d\}} = z^{\{0,0:d\}} + z^{\{1:d\}} = \bigoplus_{i=0}^{d} z^{\{0,i\}} + \sum_{j=1}^{d} z^{\{j\}} \tag{3}$$

The full X2B algorithm (and a comparison with the A2B) are shown in Algorithms 3 & 4. All terms are added using a tree-like structure ([17], Algorithm 4 & [59], Algorithm 3). In each layer, the first two terms are added using a

d-order SecADD or SecADDChain$_q$, the other terms using minimal share count. The Boolean share count of each arithmetic share $z^{\{j\}}$ ($2 \leq j \leq d$) is doubled before the arithmetic share count is halved by securely adding them together, using a $t-$NI SecADD. This process is repeated, as in the A2B operation.

Algorithm 3. A2B [t-NI]

Input Parameter: modulus m (q or p)
Input Data: An arithmetic sharing $z^{\{0:d\}}$ of coefficient z
Output Data: A Boolean sharing $B^{\{0:d\}}$ such that $\bigoplus_{i=0}^{d} B = z \bmod m$

1: **if** d=0 **then**
2:     **return** $B^{\{0\}} \leftarrow z^{\{0\}}$
3: **end if**
4: $x^{\{0:\lfloor(d+1)/2\rfloor-1\}} \leftarrow$ A2B($z^{\{0:\lfloor(d+1)/2\rfloor-1\}}$)
5: $x^{\{0:d\}} \leftarrow$ SecEXP($x^{\{0:\lfloor(d+1)/2\rfloor-1\}}$)
6: $y^{\{0:\lceil(d+1)/2\rceil-1\}} \leftarrow$ A2B($z^{\{\lfloor(d+1)/2\rfloor:d\}}$)
7: $y^{\{0:d\}} \leftarrow$ SecEXP($y^{\{0:\lceil(d+1)/2\rceil-1\}}$)
8: **return** $B^{\{0:d\}} \leftarrow$ SecADD$_m$($x^{\{0:d\}}, y^{\{0:d\}}$)

Algorithm 4. X2B [t-NI]

Input Parameter: modulus m (q or p)
Input Data: A *composite* sharing $z^{\{0,d\}}$ as in Eq. 3 of coefficient z
Output Data: A Boolean sharing $B^{\{0:d\}}$ such that $\bigoplus_{i=0}^{d} B = z \bmod m$

1: **if** d=0 **then**
2:     **return** $B^{\{0,0:d\}} \leftarrow z^{\{0,0:d\}}$
3: **end if**
4: $x^{\{0:\lfloor(d+1)/2\rfloor-1\}} \leftarrow$ A2B($z^{\{0:\lfloor(d+1)/2\rfloor-1\}}$)
5: **if** $d \geq 3$ **then**
6:     $x^{\{0:d\}} \leftarrow$ SecEXP($x^{\{0:\lfloor(d+1)/2\rfloor-1\}}$)
7: **else**
8:     $x^{\{0:d\}} \leftarrow x^{\{0:\lfloor(d+1)/2\rfloor-1\}}$
9: **end if**
10: $y^{\{0:\lceil(d+1)/2\rceil-1\}} \leftarrow$ A2B($z^{\{\lfloor(d+1)/2\rfloor:d\}}$)
11: $y^{\{0:d\}} \leftarrow$ SecEXP($y^{\{0:\lceil(d+1)/2\rceil-1\}}$)
12: **return** $B^{\{0:d\}} \leftarrow$ SecADD$_m$($x^{\{0:d\}}, y^{\{0:d\}}$)

In each step, the first element consists of $d+1$ shares, the second is expanded to $d+1$ shares, and the remaining terms double their Boolean share count using the $t-$NI SecEXP (Expand) gadget. Eventually, we obtain an equivalent representation of $z^{\{0:d\}}$ consisting of $d+1$ Boolean shares. Notice that for $d = 1, 2$ the X2B is equivalent to state-of-the-art A2B methods [16,17], and for higher orders is slightly more expensive due to non-minimal share count.

d-**Probing Security**: We show that the X2B gadget is $t-$NI, considering the leakage effects from Sect. 2.3 in Appendix B.

B2X2A. The goal of the B2A operation is to convert $d + 1$ Boolean shares $B^{\{0:d\}}$ to $d + 1$ arithmetic shares $A^{\{0:d\}}$. The first d output shares are newly sampled, random shares: $A^{\{0:d-1\}} = R_A^{\{0:d-1\}}$. The final output share $A^{\{d\}}$ is computed as $B - R_A$, using the d previously sampled random, arithmetic shares $R_A^{\{0:d-1\}}$. In the following sections, we will denote with superscript-free variables (e.g. R_A) the unshared value: $R_A = \sum_{i=0}^{d-1} R_A^{\{i\}} \bmod q$.

In other published work, $R_A^{\{0:d-1\}}$ is first converted to the Boolean domain (using an A2B), resulting in $R_B^{\{0:d\}}$: $\bigoplus_{i=0}^{d} R_B^{\{i\}} = \sum_{i=0}^{d-1} -R_A^{\{i\}} \bmod q$. Next, $B + R_B$ is computed using a secure addition, as both are Boolean shared operands. In total, a full A2B and ($d-$order) SecADD are required.

Our B2X2A gadget combines the A2B conversion and SecADD in a single operation: the X2B input $z^{\{1:d\}}$ is equal to $R_A^{\{0:d-1\}}$ and $z^{\{0\}}$ to $\sim B$. Note that B

consist of $d+1$ Boolean shares which means that z is compositely shared, consisting of d arithmetic shares and one Boolean sharing. The X2B is required to convert the compositely shared input, equal to $R_A + (\sim B) = R_A - B - 1$, to a Boolean sharing. As opposed to other work [5,17,27], all inversions are performed as negations in the Boolean domain[1]. The SecNOT performed on the X2B output, to obtain the desired result $B - R_A$, requires the Boolean inversion of only a single share ($\mathcal{O}(1)$) instead of a share-wise effort ($\mathcal{O}(d)$) in the case of negation on arithmetic shares. In the final step of post-processing, $d+1$ Boolean shares are securely combined using the FullXOR gadget [9,17,19], to obtain the final output share: $A^{\{d\}} = \bigoplus_{i=0}^{d} (B - R_A)^{\{0:d\}}$.

Algorithm 5. B2X2A [t–NI]

Input Parameter/Data : q ▷ $q = 2^n$ ($n = 1..k$) or prime
Input Data : $B^{\{0:d\}}$
Output Data : $A^{\{0:d\}}$ such that $\bigoplus_{i=0}^{d} B^{\{i\}} = \sum_{i=0}^{d} A^{\{i\}} \bmod q$

1: $A^{\{0:d-1\}}, R_A^{\{0:d-1\}} \leftarrow \text{Rand}([0:q-1])$
2: **if** q is prime **then**   ▷ Modify initial masking for SecADD$_q$.
3:      **for** $i = 0, 2 ... d - 2$ **do**
4:          $z^{\{i+1\}} \leftarrow R_A^{\{i\}}$
5:          $z^{\{i+2\}} \leftarrow R_A^{\{i+1\}} - q$ ▷ $-q$ correction.
6:      **end for**
7: **else**
8:      $z^{\{1:d\}} \leftarrow R_A^{\{0:d-1\}}$
9: **end if**
10: $z^{\{0,0:d\}} \leftarrow \text{SecNOT}(B^{\{0:d\}})$ ▷ $z = R_A - B - 1$
11: $y'^{\{0:d\}} \leftarrow \text{X2B}(z^{\{0:d\}})$
12: $y^{\{0:d\}} \leftarrow \text{SecNOT}(y'^{\{0:d\}})$ ▷ $y = -z - 1 = B - R_A$
13: $A^{\{d\}} \leftarrow \text{FullXOR}(y^{\{0:d\}})$ ▷ $A^{\{d\}} = y$, [17]

Cost: This approach is an improvement over the state-of-the-art, as $B - R_A$ is directly computed during the X2B as the inputs consist of different amounts of Boolean shares, and thus one does not need to perform the explicit secure addition during post-processing, on two inputs which now consist of $d+1$ Boolean shares. In the original method one needs to compute one A2B and one secure addition, while our improved method requires only the X2B operation. The X2B operation has the same computational cost as A2B for first and second security order, and only slightly higher than A2B for higher orders. When $d \geq 3$, minimal share count is no longer achieved, as a d−order secure adder is required in non-final layers of the tree. The total amount SecADDs is reduced in all cases, for high orders an additional max-order secure addition is required. For first-order implementations, only two SecADDs are required, for second order one-third of secure additions is removed, etc. For prime moduli, we give a comparison in Table 2. In all cases we obtain a more efficient end result, especially for practical masking orders.

---

[1] $\sim x = -(x+1)$.

Table 2. Detailed B2A$_q$ operation cost comparison ($d + 1$ shares, k-bit words). Max-order SecADD operations are explicitly listed, as their cost is relatively high compared to low-order operations.

	Order	# SecADD				Total	# SecMUX				Total
		1	2	3	d		1	2	3	d	
[5]	1	4				4	2				2
	2	2	4			6	1	2			3
	3	4		4		8	2		2		4
	d				4	$2(d+1)$				2	$2d+1$
[27]	1	2				2					
[11]	1	2				2					
	2	2	5			7					
	3	4	0	6		10					
	d				5 or 6[a]	$3d$ or $3d+1$[a]					
B2X2A (Algorithm 5)	1	2				2					
	2	2	2			4					
	3	2	0	4		6					
	d				$2 \cdot \lceil \log_2(d) \rceil$	**2d**					

[a] For *complete* or *incomplete* tree-structure.

d-**Probing Security:** We show that the B2X2A gadget is correct and prove it to be t−NI, considering the leakage effects from Sect. 2.3 in Appendix C.

4 High-Throughput and Low-Randomness Mask Conversions in Hardware

In this section, we first introduce our strategy and novel techniques for implementing the proposed secure gadgets and then demonstrate how a ($d+1$ share) A2B & B2A for prime and power-of-two moduli can be combined in a unified and compact accelerator in hardware: X2X. Our implementation follows a streaming approach, in which data flows through the entire pipelined (and unrolled) circuit, ensures all logic is maximally active, high throughput is achieved and transitional leakage in memory elements is avoided. We provide the SystemVerilog source code for all our designs, which we experimentally verify to be first- and high-order secure in the next section.

4.1 SecADD$_p$ and SecADD$_q$

A masked ripple-carry adder was proposed by Coron et al. [17], and more hardware-focused parallel prefix-type adders in [1,13]. We propose a Brent-Kung adder architecture [8] because it is more area-efficient than a Kogge-Stone or Schlansky architecture, at the cost of an increased latency yet high throughput. In general, our masking strategy relies on (selectively) combining share-wise gadgets (XOR, NOT...), t-NI (DOM-indep AND) and t-SNI refresh gadgets to ensure composability. A full description of SecADD$_{BK}$ and a security proof are given in Appendix D.

Our fully unrolled and pipelined implementation can compute the secure addition for power-of-two and prime moduli (see SecADDChain$_q$), on the same hardware by setting the appropriate control signals and using dynamic reconfiguration. Two SecADDs are instantiated, which are chained when the modulus is prime, computing either s or $s' = s - q$. Alternatively, for the secure addition modulo a power-of-two integer, we propose using both SecADDs in parallel instead of one being idle in this mode. Throughput is doubled in this mode, as two shared data words (x_1, y_1 and x_2, y_2) can be accepted each clock cycle.

Masking Techniques. We now illustrate the difference between masking techniques in hardware on the (Brent-Kung) SecADD operation (Table 3). We take into account two factors: implementation cost (or masking overhead) and verification cost (formal and/or experimental). Firstly, masking a Brent-Kung adder using HPC1 gadgets results in low verification cost. As they are PINI secure, they can be freely composed into a larger circuit. However, due to its (implicit) refreshing stage, both randomness cost and latency are high. Secondly, a t-NI SecADD can be constructed using DOM AND gates and explicit t-SNI refresh gadgets (see Appendix D). We formally prove its security and observe that the masking overhead is reduced, as expected. Thirdly, we include the overhead for a t-probing secure implementation, which we show in Sect. 5 results in a practically secure circuit and does not require any refresh gadgets, reducing the implementation cost even further.

Table 3. Comparison of first-order masking techniques of a Brent-Kung SecADD ($k = 13$).

Masking Technique	RND [bits]	Latency [cycles]	Verification
HPC1 (PINI)	228	18	Low
DOM + SecREF (t−NI)	176	11	High
DOM (t-probing)	114	9	High

In conclusion, the SecADD operation is a crucial operation in mask conversions, thus optimizing its masking overhead is critical. Our design has minimal implementation cost and is practically secure, yet has a higher verification cost compared to implementations that rely on universally composable gadgets. The security of the larger gadget is formally proven and verified by composing smaller gadgets and verifying their properties.

Half-Cycle Path. The Domain-Oriented Masking (DOM) scheme and Threshold Implementations (TI) both guarantee glitch-immunity, which means they proveably stay probing secure for every possible occurrence of a glitch. This is achieved by introducing register stages, which essentially result in a 'free' pipelining of the datapath. The SecADD datapath is dominated by chaining non-linear

SecAND and SecOR gates, which require at least one register stage to stop the propagation of glitches when crossing domain borders.

We propose interleaving registers clocked at the positive and negative edge in the SecADD$_{BK}$, resulting in half-cycle path implementation [24,34]. This circuit-level technique can halve the latency of a tightly pipelined secure gadget, (ideally) without significantly impacting the maximal operating frequency of the implementation. From Table 4, for our first-order implementation, using halfcycle datapaths reduces the operating frequency by 21% (176 MHz vs. 139 MHz), while the latency is halved (5 cycles vs 10/11 cycles). As a result, the total execution time is reduced by 36.6%/42.4% compared to the fullcycle implementation, for A2B$_p$/B2A$_p$ respectively. For second order, the maximum operating frequency is naturally lower due to increased circuit complexity. Half-cycle data paths reduces the operating frequency by 9%, and the execution time is reduced by 42% up to 47%. In conclusion, the total execution time is significantly reduced because the latency is reduced while not massively impacting the maximum operating frequency, illustrating why highly non-linear operations are a good target for such circuit-level optimizations.

Table 4. Timing performance of half-cycle and full-cycle X2X hardware implementation (Kintex-7).

Masking Order	Design	Max. Freq. [MHz]	Latency[a] [cycles]	Time [ns]
$d=1$	FULL	**176**	10/11	56.8/62.5
	HALF	139	**5/5**	**36.0/36.0**
$d=2$	FULL	**144**	20/21	139.9/145.8
	HALF	130	**10/10**	**76.9/76.9**

[a] A2B$_p$/B2A$_p$

Similarly, this technique can be directly applied to HPC1 gadgets, performing the refresh and DOM AND gate in a single clock cycle instead of two. Still, since we only include refresh stages when explicitly required (to ensure independent inputs and simulability), our manual masking approach results in a lower total latency.

4.2 A2B and B2A

In our X2X implementation, the A2B and X2B are computed using (mostly) the same physical instances in hardware. A tree-structure of SecEXP and SecADD components is instantiated, maximizing the parallelism available in hardware by operating on all shares simultaneously. As seen in Fig. 2, this combination of operations first doubles the level of Boolean sharing, after which the amount of arithmetic shares is halved. This process is repeated on all shares in parallel, $L = \lceil \log(d+1) \rceil$ times to obtain $d+1$ Boolean shares.

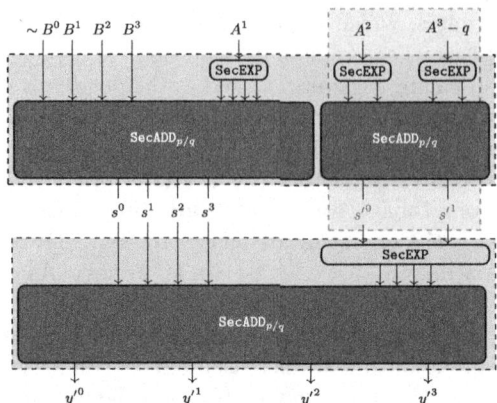

Fig. 2. 4-share X2B (& A2B) in hardware: SecEXP and SecADD. The right side (yellow) can be pre-computed. $y = B - A$ is directly computed during X2B, removing the need for a secure addition in post-processing. (Color figure online)

Technically, only the SecADD operations involving the actual, secret input data and final XOR (Line 13) need to be computed at run-time in order to obtain the final share $A^{\{d\}}$.

When computing the X2B for orders $d \geq 3$, minimal share count is no longer achieved, as a $d+1$ share secure adder is instantiated in all but the final layer. For prime moduli q, some pre-processing is required before the initial masking and the B2X2A requires additional post-processing, compared to the A2B. Interestingly, a portion of the X2B computation can be a target for pre-computation as it only involves random data (indicated in yellow). These operations can be computed when the random shares are generated and the result temporarily stored in memory. This optimization is left as future work.

5 Performance and Security Evaluation

5.1 Measurement Setup

In this section, we describe the practical evaluation of our masked designs on the Xilinx Kintex7 FPGA[2]. We utilize the *keep_hierarchy* pragma to prevent the compiler from optimizing masking countermeasures away. This may result in a less-than-optimal overhead but ensures the desired security.

For the security evaluation, we collect power traces from the measurement point on the SASIMI evaluation board [28] containing an Kintex7 XCKU040 FPGA. The traces are captured by a Tektronix DPO7254 oscilloscope at a sample rate of 1GS/s while the FPGA is externally clocked at 6MHz. We synchronized the oscilloscope and the external clock for all our measurements. Also, the mask conversion accelerator instance is duplicated several times on FPGA for lab

---

[2] XC7K160T & XCKU040, Xilinx Vivado v2021.1.

Table 5. Mask conversion hardware implementation: performance comparison.

Design	Mask. Tech.	Device	k	d	Util. [LUT/FF]	Freq. [MHz]	OP	mod	Rand.[a] [bits]	Lat. [cycles]	TP [coeff/cycle]
[58]	TI	Spartan-6	32	1	937/1,330	62	SecADD	2^k	32	6	0.167
				2	4,223/5,509	63			128	12	0.083
[27]	TI	Artix-7	32	1	2,464/1,323	454	SecADD	2^k	-	6	-
[1]	TI	Spartan-6	32	1	487/2352	280	SecADD	2^k	31	9	1
[1]	PINI (HPC)	Spartan-6	32	1	1588/4317	173	SecADD	2^k	74	18	1
				2	1666/7122	158			222	18	1
[13]	PINI (HPC)	-[c]	32	1	-	-	SecADD	2^k	122	10	1
				2	-	-			366	10	1
This Work (Full-cycle)	DOM	Kintex-7[d]	13	1	400/989	-	SecADD	2^k	114	9	1
				2	761/2,028	-			342	9	1
This Work (Half-cycle)	DOM	Kintex-7[d]	13	1	405/715	-	SecADD	2^k	114	5	1
				2	762/1515	-			342	5	1
[16][b]	PINI (HPC)	Artix-7	32	2	13,064/17,952	351	A2B	2^k	1,280	24	1
[9][b]	PINI (HPC)	Artix-7	32	2	2,234/20,423	512	A2B	2^k	124	124	0.008
[42]	PINI (HPC)	Artix-7	32	2	11,196/14,550	370	A2B	2^k	1,056	14	1
This Work (Full-cycle)	DOM	Kintex-7[d]	13	1	1,150/3,335	176	A2B	2^k	**140**	**10**	**2**
								3329	**255**	**20**	**1**
							B2A	2^k	**140**	**11**	**2**
								3329	**255**	**21**	**1**
				2	3,128/16,774	144	A2B	2^k	**534**	**20**	**2**
								3329	**993**	**40**	**1**
							B2A	2^k	**534**	**21**	**2**
								3329	**993**	**41**	**1**
This Work (Half-cycle)	DOM	Kintex-7[d]	13	1	1,133/2,170	139	A2B	2^k	**140**	**5**	**2**
								3329	**255**	**10**	**1**
							B2A	2^k	**140**	**5**	**2**
								3329	**255**	**10**	**1**
				2	3,105/9,376	130	A2B	2^k	**534**	**10**	**2**
								3329	**993**	**20**	**1**
							B2A	2^k	**534**	**10**	**2**
								3329	**993**	**20**	**1**

[a] Total random bits (full operation, per coefficient).
[b] Numbers taken from [42].
[c] No numbers for FPGA given, only ASIC.
[d] XC7K160T

evaluations, to guarantee satisfactory SNR for statistical analysis, illustrated in the mean measurement traces. All instances operate on a single, identical input data and fresh randomness in parallel. The randomness required by our design is supplied by a PRNG that runs on the crypto FPGA. The PRNG consists of an AES-CTR and Trivium cipher implementation, which is re-seeded with fresh randomness for each mask conversion. We interleave the execution of the PRNG with the execution of the full mask conversion to decrease the impact of noice induced by the PRNG.

5.2 Performance Comparison

We now give an overview of existing implementations and our optimized design for different mask conversions in hardware (Table 5). It is important to note that the compared hardware implementations target different operations, platforms, data word sizes, masking strategies, and more. As a result, a direct and/or fair comparison is not always possible. We compare our work with other (SecADD-based) A2B/B2A strategies, which are favored for hardware implementations as both operations rely on similar arithmetic and benefit physical from instance reuse. Through algorithmic, gadget- and circuit-level optimizations, we reduce latency, maximize throughput and minimize area cost.

Firstly, we observe that our design is the only one to directly support the computation all of the types of mask conversions required in the Kyber decapsulation (or any lattice-based PQC scheme). Our streaming hardware design can be dynamically reconfigured, maximally reusing physical instances between operations. The A2B and B2A operations require identical amounts of fresh randomness, thanks to the B2X2A gadget. For power-of-two modes, the throughput can be doubled by utilizing both instantiated SecADD gadgets.

As expected, the half-cycle design outperforms the full-cycle design (without circuit-level modifications): flipflop utilization is reduced due to the shorter pipeline, which also reduces latency at the cost of slightly decreased operating frequency.

We are aware of one other work which directly implements the (second order) A2B$_p$ operation [42], with $k = 32$ and using the PINI security notion (HPC gadgets). By relying on universal composability, this work significantly reduces the verification and design cost. However, the randomness cost and latency are $1.98\times$ and $1.4\times$ higher, respectively, compared to our design. For reference, this work also implements the designs proposed in [16] and [9] using HPC gadgets. Both are less efficient (throughput, latency and/or randomness) compared to the design proposed in [42]. We rely on manual masking and DOM gadgets, which allow to reduce the implementation overhead. We repeat that our design is optimized for Kyber parameters ($k = 13$) but supports four different modes of operation. While we note that it is difficult to compare implementations on different platforms, our design has a significantly lower area utilization and also maximum operating frequency. We would expect the operating frequency of this design to reduce if other types of mask conversions are supported, as the critical path is situated in the B2A and mod q circuit.

Next, we remark that our design achieves the highest throughput for power-of-two moduli by using both instantiated secure adders for two different inputs at once. As our design is fully pipelined, as is the case with HPC gadgets, one coefficient is processed per cycle. Oppositely, [9] achieves low area utilization by reusing physical instances over time (ripple-carry), resulting in a low throughput, high latency and lower randomness cost. More specifically, compared to our design, [9] requires $4.3\times$ less random bits but a $12.4\times$ lower throughput.

Several other works have presented performance results for secure adder implementations, the most crucial component for mask conversions. Where possible, we compare with the most optimized and/or Brent-Kung adder architecture with this work. In [58] a 32-bit secure adder is presented, which has a low randomness cost but has lower throughput and operating frequency compared to our implementation. Compared to the adders presented in [1], our full-cycle design has half the latency but requires around 50% more fresh randomness at first- and second-order. The authors also propose a first-order secure TI secure adder, which outperforms our design at first-order. The main disadvantage is that this design cannot be scaled to higher protection orders. In [13] techniques were presented to reduce latency of large chains of PINI gadgets, at the cost of increased fresh randomness requirements.

We conclude that using HPC gadgets and the PINI security notion results in a low verification cost, through universal composability. However the implementation overhead, especially randomness and latency, are higher compared to manually (algorithmically masked) designs for highly non-linear operations (A2B & B2A). In this case, switching away from HPC gadgets results in 62% improvement in randomness cost, 29% up to 92% lower latency and 45% up to 60%, at the cost of increased design and verification complexity, which is error-prone.

5.3 Test Vector Leakage Assessment Results

We verify that our implementations do not show first-order (or second-order) univariate and bivariate leakage. The *non-specific, fixed vs. random* t-test statistic [30] is calculated for the implementation of all different mask conversion operations. The TVLA results for the $A2B_p$ mode are shown below (Fig. 3), with all (extended) figures shown in Appendix F. The threshold value of the t-test commonly used by the side-channel research community is 4.5 which provides a confidence of roughly 0.99999. If the t-test value of the measured power trace grows over 4.5, the implementation under test is considered as insecure. The regions of interest are indicated on all figures between vertical red lines, which indicate the start and end of mask conversion.

Figure 9 illustrates the TVLA results of the first-order masked $A2B_p$, $A2B_q$, $B2A_p$ and $B2A_q$ operations (i.e., Fig. 9a – 9d), which rely on the novel X2B and SecADDChain$_q$ gadgets. The mean trace, first- and second-order statistical moments with the PRNG activated are displayed. Each of the subplots confirm our theoretical expectation, as no significant evidence of first-order leakage was detected for 100 million measurements. The second-order leakages show as anticipated. In contrast, we also include t-test results for the implementation with the randomness turned off (set to zero), guaranteeing that our test set-up is sound and can detect leakage (Fig. 10a) with only 500K traces.

Figure 11 illustrates the TVLA result of the second-order masked A2B and B2A operations (mod 2^{13} and 3329). The mean trace and first, second (and third) order statistical moments with the RNG activated are displayed (Fig. 11a – 11d). First- and second-order (univariate) leakages are not present. Again, we verified our measurement setup by turning off the randomness source (Fig. 10b), with all present leakages not appearing when the randomness is turned on again.

We also performed second-order bivariate leakage detection tests [12], illustrated in Fig. 13. To alleviate the computational complexity of this analysis, we set the point of interests at every 10 sample points. First, we verified that our second-order implementation shows leakages with the PRNG turned off, with

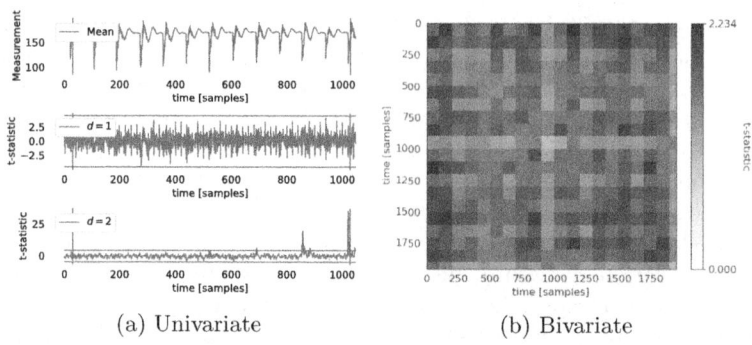

Fig. 3. Univariate and bivariate TVLA analysis (fixed-vs.-random) of 1st- and 2nd-order A2B$_{2^{13}}$, 100M traces, PRNG ON. The $\pm$ 4.5 threshold is marked by red lines and max-pooling guarantees that t-test peaks are visible.

only 500K traces (Fig. 12). We confirm the measurement setup is sound and can detect bivariate leakages (t-values exceeding 4.5). With the PRNG switched on, no excursions of the t-values beyond $\pm$ 4.5 occur and thus the test is passed with 100M traces. In our figures, we use max-pooling sub-sampling, displaying the largest (absolute) t-value for every 10×10 square in the bivariate plot.

Conclusion. From these first-and high-order univ- and bi-variate tests using TVLA methodology, we can conclude our proposed techniques and their first and second-order implementations are secure.

6 Conclusion

In this work, a first- and high-order hardware implementation of the mask conversion operation, secure against differential power analysis attacks were described. These leverage novel d−order secure gadgets and circuit-level optimizations to improve performance at all protection orders. Including a novel SecADDChain$_q$ gadget, which relies on repeated, implicit modular reduction for improved chaining and the B2X2A, which relies on the novel X2B. The univariate and multivariate security is formally proven and experimentally validated in various modes.

This work leverages careful, manual masking to achieve first- and high-order protection, which is demonstrated to lead to reasonable overheads. An interesting direction for future work is to investigate both the reuse of random masks and physical instances and machine-assisted verification of our implementation.

In summary, the presented techniques result in hardware implementations with the lowest area utilization, fresh randomness cost and latency published for Kyber parameters. The amount of clock cycles required for a mask conversion is reduced by 29% up to 92%, the required amount of fresh randomness by up to 62%. The presented second-order implementation requires 3,105/9,376 [LUT/FF] on FPGA, which is a reduction of 45% to 60% compared to the state-of-the-art and up to 62% fewer random bits.

Acknowledgements. We thank Lennert Wouters, Zhenda Zhang, John Gaspoz and Siemen Dhooghe for the interesting discussions. This work was partially supported by Horizon 2020 ERC Advanced Grant (101020005 Belfort), Horizon Europe (101070008 ORSHIN), CyberSecurity Research Flanders with reference number VOEWICS02, BE QCI: Belgian-QCI (3E230370) (see beqci.eu), and Intel Corporation.

Appendices

Appendix A Correctness and Security Proof SecADDChain$_q$ (Algorithm 2)

Note that Algorithm 2 is independent of the specific masked algorithms used for SecADD, SecNOT or SecREF. SecNOT refers to the sharewise $t-$NI computation of the Boolean negation, where only the first share of the Boolean-masked input is negated (Algorithm 7). SecADD denotes the (robust) $t-$NI arithmetic addition of Boolean shares, as from [5,16] or Appendix D. SecREF describes a $t-$SNI algorithm to refresh Boolean shares, as proposed in [5,14] and Algorithm 11. We note that explicit mask refresh operations can be avoided by switching to a more strict security notion, e.g., PINI [10]. We place the refresh in this position, in order to only have to refresh 1-bit shares (MSB), instead of $k-$bit shares. Furthermore, we use $\cdot$ to indicate the linear $t-$NI computation integer multiplication, on each of the shares separately. We use $\gg$ to denote the linear $t-$NI bitwise shift of Boolean shares, achieved by shifting each input share separately.

Correctness. For prime q, explicit modular reduction is performed on $z = x + y' = x + y - q \in [-q : q-2]$, because y' lies in $[-q : -1]$.

- $z \in [-q : -1]$: $c = q$, so $s = z + q$ lies in $[0 : q-1]$. $c' = 0$, because an uneven amount of carry bits cc will be '1' as both x and y are mod q. This ensures $s' = z + 0$ lies in $[-q : -1]$.
- $z \in [0 : q-2]$: $c = 0$, so $s = z + q$ lies in $[0 : q-2]$. $c' = -q$, because an even amount of carry bits cc will be '1' as both x and y are mod q. This ensures $s' = z - q$ lies in $[-q : -2]$.

The algorithm returns either a value modulo q, or (mod q) - q.

Security. To argue about the higher-order security of Algorithm 2, we prove it to be (word-level) $t-$NI with $t + 1$ shares. As a result, all gadgets are modeled to operate on word-level shares. This provides resistance against a probing adversary with t word-level probes and allows the use of the gadget in larger compositions. We show how probes on intermediate values in the algorithm can be perfectly simulated with only a limited number of input shares, by iterating over all possible intermediate variables. We provide formal arguments on how they can be simulated relying on the $t-$(S)NI properties of the sub-operations. We show that all word-level probes can be simulated with no more number of input shares.

Theorem 1. *The gadget* SecADDChain$_q$ *(Algorithm 2) is word-level t-NI secure.*

Proof. We model Algorithm 2 as a sequence of t-(S)NI gadgets, as shown in Fig. 4. For simplicity, we model (and combine) the linear operations in Lines 2 and 5/8 as t-NI gadgets (G_2 and G_4), which can be trivially shown as the operations are linear and process the inputs share-wise. We map all three $t-$NI SecADD gadgets as follows: G_1 (Line 1) and G_5 (Line 6 or 9). Due to the *if..else* statement, either Lines 5–6 or 8–9 are executed and can both be represented by gadgets G_4 and G_5. The t-SNI refresh gadget on Line 3 is mapped to gadget G_3. An adversary can probe the intermediate values and outputs of all gadgets G_i (except the output shares of the complete algorithm), t_{G_i} refers to the number of internal probes and o_{G_i} the number of output probes.

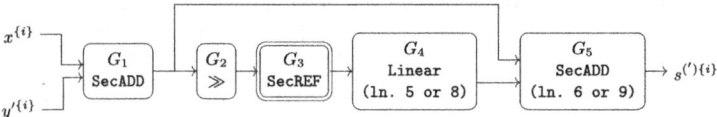

Fig. 4. An abstract diagram of $\texttt{SecADDChain}_q$ (Algorithm 2). The t-NI gadgets are depicted with a single border, the t-SNI gadgets with a double border.

To prove Theorem 1, we show that the internal (t_{G_i}) and output (o_{G_i}) probes of each gadget in Algorithm 2, except the output shares of the full composition, can be perfectly simulated with no more number of input shares $x^{\{i\}}$ and $y'^{\{i\}}$ ($\leq t_{A_2}$) with:

$$t_{A_2} = \sum_{i=1}^{5} t_{G_i} + \sum_{i=1}^{4} o_{G_i}$$

As defined earlier, for the t-NI notion, if any probes are placed on the final output of Algorithm 2 (entire composition), the simulator will get access to a same amount of input shares, for free. Or, as stated above, the simulation must succeed for any set of t intermediate probes. In contrast, for t-SNI security, an probing adversary can place t probes on intermediate values and at the final output and simulation must succeed without access to additional input shares. We rely on the $t-$(S)NI properties of each gadget to argue about their internal and output probes. For the simulation of a larger composition, the required shares are added up. To ensure the simulation is sound, we will show that it is necessary to insert a $t-$SNI SecREF gadget for the MSB of the result of the first SecADD and to ensure the inputs of the second SecADD are independent. This is because a $t-$SNI gadget stops the propagation of probes from the output shares to the input shares, allowing its simulation to be performed independent of the number of probed output shares.

To simulate the t_{G_5} intermediate probes of the $t-$NI gadget G_5, t_{G_5} shares of both inputs G_4 and G_1 are required. Given the share-wise operation of G_4, simulating $t_{G_4} + o_{G_4}$ intermediate and output probes requires $t_{G_4} + o_{G_4}$ shares of input G_3. Without a $t-$SNI refresh G_3, the simulation of gadgets G_1-G_5 would require t_{G_5} shares of both t_{G_1} and t_{G_4}. As a result, the required set of input shares (I) would include duplicate entries $2 \cdot t_{G_5}$, which cannot be simulated for $t_{G_5} = t$. From this it is clear that one of the inputs to G_5 needs to be refreshed. By further following the flow from gadgets G_3 through G_1 (the input), we conclude that the simulation of Algorithm 2 requires $|I| = t_{G_1} + o_{G_1} + t_{G_2} + o_{G_2} + t_{G_3} + t_{G_5} \leq t_{A_2}$ of the input shares, and thus is t−NI. □

Appendix B Security Proof X2B (Algorithm 4)

Note that the X2B gadget description is independent of the specific masked algorithm used for SecADD/SecADD$_q$. SecADD denotes the t−NI arithmetic addition of Boolean shares, as from [5] or Algorithm 2 & Appendix D. Furthermore, SecEXP refers to the t−NI expansion of Boolean shares, as proposed in [17] and formalised in Appendix E (Algorithm 10). As opposed to a t−SNI SecREF, it requires less fresh randomness (strictly $d + 1$ shares) and doubles the Boolean share count.

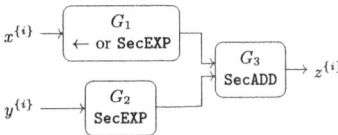

Fig. 5. An abstract diagram of X2B & A2B (Algorithm 4 & 3): the t-NI gadgets are depicted with a single border. This structure is recursively applied and combined for higher masking orders.

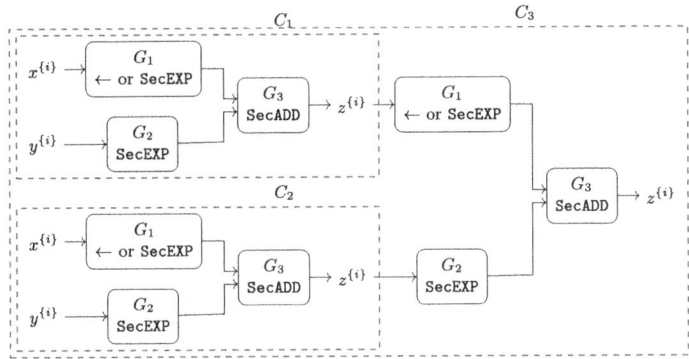

Fig. 6. Recursive structure of X2B (Algorithm 4) and A2B (Algorithm 3).

To argue about the higher-order security of Algorithm 3/4, we prove it to be word-level t-NI secure with $t+1$ shares. This provides resistance against a probing adversary (A2B) or allows the use of the gadget in larger compositions (X2B). We show how probes on intermediate word-level values in the algorithm can be perfectly simulated with only a limited number of input shares, by iterating over all possible intermediate variables. We show that all word-level probes can be simulated with no more number of input shares. To this end, we model all gadgets to operate on word-level data shares.

Theorem 2. *The gadgets A2B and X2B (Algorithm 3 & 4) are word-level t-NI secure.*

Proof. We model Algorithms 3 & 4 as a sequence of t-NI gadgets, as shown in Fig. 5. For the A2B gadget, the t-NI SecEXP gadgets (Line 5 and 7) are modeled as gadgets G_1 and G_2. For the X2B gadget, the signal assignment (Line 8) and/or t-NI SecEXP gadgets (Line 6 and 11) are modeled as gadgets G_1 and G_2. The t-NI gadget SecADD (Line 8 and 12, respectively) is modeled as gadget G_3. An adversary can probe the intermediate values and outputs of all gadgets G_i, except the output shares of the complete algorithm. The proof of Theorem 2 is a direct result from the direct chaining of t-NI gadgets G_1-G_3 resulting in a t-NI circuit (Fig. 5) and the recursive application also results in such a structure (Fig. 6). Each of the sub-circuits (C_1-C_3) is of the form shown in Fig. 5, as well as the larger circuit (A2B & X2B). All sub-circuits are t-NI and directly chained, from which it follows that the entire structure is t-NI. □

Appendix C Correctness and Security Proof B2X2A (Algorithm 5)

Note that Algorithm 5 is independent of the specific masked algorithms used for SecNOT, X2B or FullXOR. SecNOT refers to the $t-$NI computation of the Boolean negation, where only the first share of the Boolean-masked input is negated (Algorithm 7). FullXOR is a t-NI secure unmasking of a Boolean sharing, consisting of a strong (free-t-SNI) mask refreshing and XOR'ing of all shares ([9,19] or Appendix E). X2B refers to the $t-$NI secure conversion of composite shares to Boolean shares encoding the same value (Sect. 3.2), a variant of the A2B operation (ALgorithm 4).

Correctness. Algorithm 5 securely converts Boolean shares B to arithmetic shares A encoding the same value. y' is equivalent to $R_A + (\sim B) = R_A - B - 1$, with R_A randomly sampled data. As a result y is equal to $(-R_A + B + 1) - 1$ or $B - R_A$ (SecNOT). All resulting shares are XOR'd into a single share in Line 13, ensuring the full output A is equal to $R_A + B - R_A = B$, which is the same data as input but shared differently.

Security. To argue about the higher-order security of Algorithm 5, we prove it to be word-level t-NI with $t+1$ shares. This provides resistance against a probing adversary with t word-level probes and allows the use of the gadget in larger compositions. Again, we show how probes on intermediate word values in the algorithm can be perfectly simulated with only a limited number of input shares, by iterating over all possible intermediate variables. We provide formal arguments on how they can be simulated relying on the t−NI properties of the sub-operations. We show that all probes can be simulated with no more number of input shares.

Theorem 3. *The gadget B2X2A (Algorithm 5) is word-level t-NI secure.*

Proof. We model Algorithm 5 as a sequence of t-NI gadgets, as shown in Fig. 7. All gadgets are assumed to operate on full data words. The operations in Lines 1–9 are not considered, as they operate on fresh random shares (non-input data). We model the linear operations in Line 10 and 12 as t−NI gadgets G_1 and G_3, respectively, which is trivially shown as they process their inputs in a share-wise manner. Line 11 (X2B) is mapped to t−NI gadget G_2. The final operation on Line 13 is represented by t−NI gadget G_4. An adversary can probe the intermediate values and outputs of all gadgets G_i, t_{G_i} refers to the number of internal probes and o_{G_i} the number of output probes.

Fig. 7. An abstract diagram of B2X2A (Algorithm 5), t-NI gadgets are depicted with a single border.

To prove Theorem 3, we show that any set of probes on intermediate values t_{G_i} and output shares o_{G_i} of complete Algorithm 5 (Gadget 1–4), except for the output shares of the full composition, can be perfectly simulated with no more number of input shares $B^{\{i\}}$ ($\leq t_{A_4}$), with:

$$t_{A_4} = \sum_{i=1}^{4} t_{G_i} + \sum_{i=1}^{3} o_{G_i}$$

To simulate the t_{G_4} intermediate probes of t−NI gadget G_4, t_{G_4} shares of its input is required. To simulate the t_{G_3} intermediate and o_{G_3} output probes of gadget G_3, $t_{G_3} + o_{G_3}$ shares of the output of G_2 are required. This reasoning can be directly extended for all remaining gadgets in Algorithm 5. By following the flow from the output, through all gadgets, to the input, we conclude that the simulation of Algorithm 5 requires $|I| = t_{G_1} + o_{G_1} + t_{G_2} + o_{G_2} + t_{G_3} + o_{G_3} + t_{G_4} \leq t_{A_4}$ of the input shares and thus is t-NI. □

Appendix D   Our Masked Brent-Kung SecADD (SecADD$_{BK}$) Design and Security Proof (Sect. 4.1)

We construct a secure Brent-Kung adder from several masked components: SecAND, SecOR, SecXOR and SecREF. SecAND refers to the t-NI masked computation of the logical AND (Algorithm 8). SecXOR refers to the sharewise t-NI computation of the logical XOR of Boolean shares (Algorithm 6). SecREF describes a t-SNI algorithm to refresh Boolean shares, as proposed in [5,14] and included in Appendix E. SecOR denotes the t-NI masked computation of the logical OR, as described in Appendix E.

Correctness. We refer to [8] for the correctness proof. Our Brent-Kung adder architecture is optimized for the parameters of CRYSTALS-Kyber ($q = 3329$). Increasing or decreasing the amount of carry-generation and carry-propagation stages, allows to increase or decrease the operand bit width.

Security. To argue about the higher-order security of SecADD_{BK} (Fig. 8), we prove it to be bit-level t-NI with $t + 1$ shares. This provides resistance against a probing adversary with t bit-level probes and allows the use of the gadget in larger compositions. We show how probes on intermediate values in the algorithm can be perfectly simulated with only a limited number of input shares, by iterating over all possible intermediate variables. We provide formal arguments on how they can be simulated relying on the t-(S)NI properties of the sub-operations. We show that all probes can be simulated with no more number of input shares.

Theorem 4. *The gadget SecADD_{BK} (Fig. 8) is bit-level t-NI secure.*

Proof. As depicted in Fig. 8, our SecADD_{BK} design is modeled as a sequence of t-(S)NI gadgets and mapped as follows:

- SecREF [t-SNI]: $G_4, G_7-G_{12}, G_{14}, G_{17}-G_{21}, G_{23}, G_{26}-G_{28}, G_{29}, G_{32}-G_{33}$,
- SecAND [t-NI]: $G_2, G_3, G_5, G_{13}, G_{15}, G_{22}, G_{24}, G_{30}$,
- SecOR [t-NI]: $G_1, G_6, G_{16}, G_{25}, G_{31}$,
- SecXOR [t-NI]: G_{34}.

The modelling of share-wise (linear) operations to t-NI gadgets can be trivially shown, as inputs are processed in a sharewise manner. An adversary can probe the intermediate values and outputs of all gadgets G_i (except the output shares of the complete algorithm), t_{G_i} refers to the number of internal probes and o_{G_i} the number of output probes.

To prove Theorem 4, we show that the internal (bit-level) probes of complete gadget SecADD_{BK} ($t_{A_{BK}}$) can be perfectly simulated with no more number of input shares $x^{\{i\}}$ and $y^{\{i\}}$ ($\leq t_{A_{BK}}$) with

$$t_{A_{BK}} = \sum_{i=1}^{34} t_{G_i} + \sum_{i=1}^{33} o_{G_i}$$

For t-NI security, simulation must succeed for an attacker which can probe any intermediate bit-value of all gadgets t_{G_i} and the output shares of all gadgets o_{G_i}, except the output of the full composition. We rely on the t-(S)NI properties of each gadget to argue about their internal and output probes. For the simulation of a larger composition, the required shares of the inputs are added up. To ensure the simulation is sound, we will show that it is necessary to insert t-SNI SecREF gadgets. This is because a t-SNI gadget stops the propagation of probes from

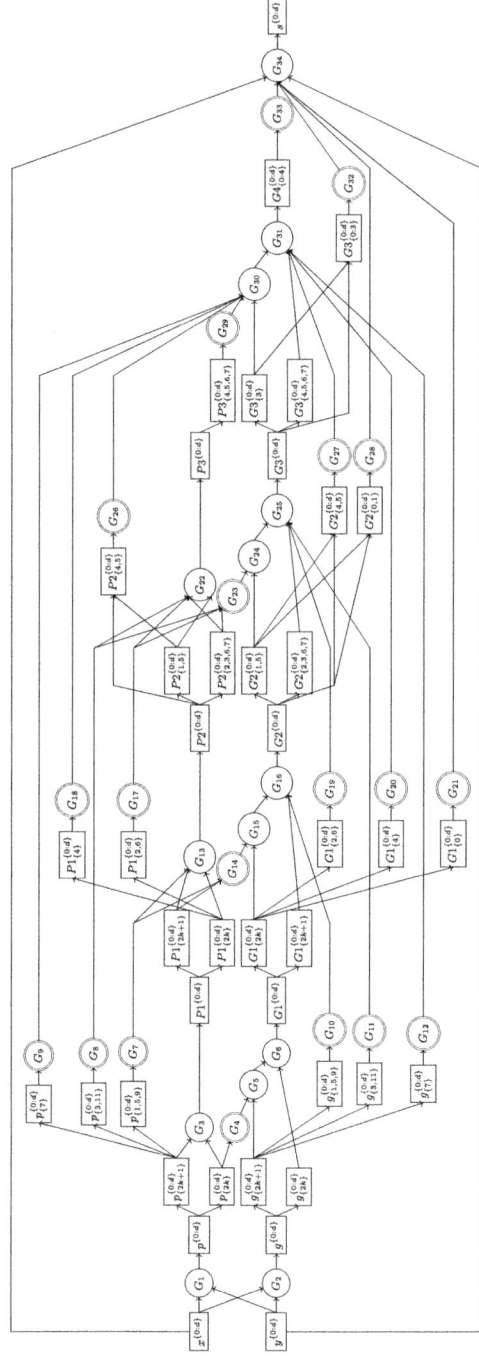

Fig. 8. The composition of $\texttt{SecADD}_{\text{BK}}$ (Theorem 4) from t–NI gadgets (single circle) and t–SNI gadgets (double circle). The even bits of variables are indicated in subscript by $2k$, uneven bits by $2k+1$.

the output shares to the input shares, allowing its simulation to be performed independent of the number of probed output shares.

Now, we go over the simulation of the entire design in detail. Starting with the output and gadget G_{34}, its $t_{G_{34}}$ internal probes can be simulated with $t_{G_{34}}$ shares of inputs $x^{\{i\}}$ and $y^{\{i\}}$, and $t_{G_{34}}$ of the output shares of G_{33}, G_{32}, G_{28} and G_{21}.

In order for the simulation of $G_3 - G_{33}$ to succeed, we model these gadgets to operate on the bit-level rather than on the complete variables. This means that we build multi-bit SecOR and SecAND gates, which operate on independent bits in parallel (1-bit gadgets), which are each t-NI. The simulation succeeds because the bits are independent. We now give an example of this construction, the simulation of G_{33}, which appears several times throughout the composition (four stages of the adder). To simulate $t_{G_{33}}$ of its internal probes and $o_{G_{33}}$ of its output shares, $t_{G_{33}} + t_{G_{31}} + o_{G_{31}} + t_{G_{30}} + o_{G_{30}}$ output shares of G_{25} are required. Because we model these gadgets to operate on individual bits (and these can' be probed), there is no problem in simulation: $t_{G_{33}} + t_{G_{31}} + o_{G_{31}} + t_{G_{30}} + o_{G_{30}}$ shares of bit $k = 3$ of the output of G_{25} ($G3$) are required, and $t_{G_{33}} + t_{G_{31}} + o_{G_{31}}$ shares of bits $k = 4, 5, 6, 7$ of $G3$ are required. If we the gadgets are defined on the word-level, $2 \cdot (t_{G_{33}} + t_{G_{31}} + o_{G_{31}})$ shares would be required which results in unsound simulation. However, as there are no duplicate entries (on the bit-level), the simulation succeeds.

Without the insertion of t-SNI refresh gadgets, the simulation of the entire design would not be sound. We now provide details for the simulation at particular points in the design, throughout the larger composition the shares required for simulation are added up. For G_{29} to G_{34}:

$$t_{G3\{i\}} = t_{G_{30}} + o_{G_{30}} + t_{G_{31}} + o_{G_{31}} + t_{G_{32}} + t_{G_{33}}$$

$$t_{P3\{i\}} = t_{G_{29}}$$

For G_{22} to G_{34}:

$$t_{G2\{i\}} = t_{G_{24}} + o_{G_{24}} + t_{G_{25}} + o_{G_{25}} + t_{G_{27}} + t_{G_{28}} + t_{G_{30}} + o_{G_{30}}$$
$$+ t_{G_{31}} + o_{G_{31}} + t_{G_{32}} + t_{G_{33}}$$

$$t_{P2\{i\}} = t_{G_{22}} + o_{G_{22}} + t_{G_{23}} + t_{G_{26}} + t_{G_{29}}$$

For G_{13} to G_{34}:

$$t_{G1\{i\}} = t_{G_{15}} + o_{G_{15}} + t_{G_{16}} + o_{G_{16}} + t_{G_{19}} + t_{G_{20}} + t_{G_{21}} + t_{G_{24}} + o_{G_{24}} + t_{G_{25}} + o_{G_{25}}$$
$$+ t_{G_{27}} + t_{G_{28}} + t_{G_{30}} + o_{G_{30}} + t_{G_{31}} + o_{G_{31}} + t_{G_{32}} + t_{G_{33}}$$

$$t_{P1\{i\}} = t_{G_{13}} + o_{G_{13}} + t_{G_{14}} + t_{G_{17}} + t_{G_{18}} + t_{G_{22}} + o_{G_{22}} + t_{G_{23}} + t_{G_{26}} + t_{G_{29}}$$

For G_3 to G_{34}:

$$t_{g\{i\}} = t_{G_5} + o_{G_5} + t_{G_6} + o_{G_6} + t_{G_{10}} + t_{G_{11}} + t_{G_{12}} + t_{G_{15}} + o_{G_{15}} + t_{G_{16}} + o_{G_{16}}$$
$$+ t_{G_{19}} + t_{G_{20}} + t_{G_{21}} + t_{G_{24}} + o_{G_{24}} + t_{G_{25}} + o_{G_{25}}$$
$$+ t_{G_{27}} + t_{G_{28}} + t_{G_{30}} + o_{G_{30}} + t_{G_{31}} + o_{G_{31}} + t_{G_{32}} + t_{G_{33}}$$

$$t_{p^{\{i\}}} = t_{G_3} + o_{G_3} + t_{G_4} + t_{G_7} + t_{G_8} + t_{G_9} + t_{G_{13}} + o_{G_{13}} + t_{G_{14}} + t_{G_{17}} + t_{G_{18}}$$
$$+ t_{G_{22}} + o_{G_{22}} + t_{G_{23}} + t_{G_{26}} + t_{G_{29}}$$

By following the flow from gadgets G_{34} through G_1, we conclude that the simulation of SecADD$_{\text{BK}}$ requires $|I| = |I_x| + |I_y| = t_{G_1} + o_{G_1} + t_{G_2} + o_{G_2} + t_{g^{\{i\}}} + t_{p^{\{i\}}} + t_{G_{34}} \leq t_{A_{BK}}$ of the input shares $x^{\{i\}}$ and $y^{\{i\}}$, and thus is t-NI. □

Appendix E Remaining Gadgets and their Security Proofs

E.1 SecXOR, SecNOT and SecAND

We include the SecXOR, SecNOT and SecAND gadgets for completeness. The SecXOR is a share-wise XOR of two Boolean shared (bit- or word-level) inputs, the SecNOT computes the logical inverse (e.g., Boolean negation) of two (bit- or word-level) Boolean shared inputs. Both are computed using strictly share-wise operations, and thus are t-NI.

Algorithm 6. SecXOR [t-NI]

Input Data : $x^{\{0:d\}}$ and $y^{\{0:d\}}$
Output Data : $z^{\{0:d\}}$ such that $\bigoplus_{i=0}^{d} z^{\{i\}} = \bigoplus_{i=0}^{d} x^{\{i\}} \oplus \bigoplus_{i=0}^{d} y^{\{i\}}$

1: **for** $i = 0$ upto d **do**
2: $\quad z^{\{i\}} \leftarrow x^{\{i\}} \oplus y^{\{i\}}$
3: **end for**

Algorithm 7. SecNOT [t-NI]

Input Data : $x^{\{0:d\}}$
Output Data : $y^{\{0:d\}}$ such that $y = \sim x$

1: $y^{\{0\}} \leftarrow \sim x^{\{0\}}$
2: **for** $i = 1$ upto d **do**
3: $\quad y^{\{i\}} \leftarrow x^{\{i\}}$
4: **end for**

The SecAND gadget, as proposed in [33], computes the bitwise logical AND of two Boolean shared values and is t-NI secure. We refer to [14] for its t-NI glitch-robust security proof. In Algorithm 8 we use $\otimes$ to denote a (field) multiplication.

E.2 SecOR

The SecOR gadget computes the OR of two Boolean shared inputs, following De Morgan's law.

Algorithm 8. SecAND [t-NI]

Input Data : $x^{\{0:d\}}$ and $y^{\{0:d\}}$
Output Data : $z^{\{0:d\}}$ such that $\bigoplus_{i=0}^{d} z^{\{i\}} = \bigoplus_{i=0}^{d} x^{\{i\}} \wedge \bigoplus_{i=0}^{d} y^{\{i\}}$

1: **for** $i = 0$ upto d **do**
2:     **for** $j = i + 1$ upto d **do**
3:         $r^{\{ij\}} \leftarrow \texttt{Rand}(k)$
4:         $u^{\{ij\}} \leftarrow x^{\{i\}} \otimes y^{\{j\}} \oplus r^{\{ij\}}$
5:         $u^{\{ji\}} \leftarrow x^{\{j\}} \otimes y^{\{i\}} \oplus r^{\{ij\}}$
6:     **end for**
7: **end for**
8: **for** $i = 0$ upto d **do**
9:     $z^{\{i\}} \leftarrow \texttt{Reg}[x^{\{i\}} \otimes y^{\{i\}}] \oplus \bigoplus_{j=0, j\neq i}^{d} u^{\{ij\}}$
10: **end for**

Algorithm 9. SecOR [t-NI]

Input Data : $x^{\{0:d\}}$ and $y^{\{0:d\}}$
Output Data : $z^{\{0:d\}}$ such that $\bigoplus_{i=0}^{d} z^{\{i\}} = \bigoplus_{i=0}^{d} x^{\{i\}} \vee \bigoplus_{i=0}^{d} y^{\{i\}}$

1: $a^{\{0:d\}} \leftarrow \texttt{SecNOT}(x^{\{0:d\}})$
2: $b^{\{0:d\}} \leftarrow \texttt{SecNOT}(y^{\{0:d\}})$
3: $z^{\{0:d\}} \leftarrow \texttt{SecAND}(a^{\{0:d\}}, b^{\{0:d\}})$
4: $z^{\{0:d\}} \leftarrow \texttt{SecNOT}(z^{\{0:d\}})$

Robust Probing Security: We now prove that the SecOR gadget is word-level t-NI with $t + 1$ shares, considering the leakage effects from Sect. 2.3.

We note that Algorithm 9 is independent of the specific masked algorithms used for SecNOT and SecAND. SecNOT refers to the t-NI computation of the Boolean negation, where the first share of the Boolean-masked input is negated. SecAND refers to the t-NI masked computation of the bitwise AND, e.g., DOM-indep AND [33].

Theorem 5. *The gadget SecOR (Algorithm 9) is word-level t-NI secure.*

Proof. This is a direct result from the linear SecNOT on both independently shared inputs and the SecAND gadget is t-NI secure. □

E.3 SecEXP, modified from [17]

The SecEXP gadget expands (and doubles) a Boolean sharing, using $d+1$ random shares $r^{\{i\}}$. The first half of the output $y^{\{0:2d+1\}}$ consists of the XOR-ing of r and input x, while the second half consists of r, resulting in an equivalent Boolean sharing. As such, the unshared output is equal to the unshared input.

Robust Probing Security: We now show that the SecEXP gadget is correct and prove it to be word-level t-SNI, considering the leakage effects from Sect. 2.3.

In Algorithm 10, SecXOR refers to the sharewise XOR operation, which is t-NI as it is linear. Reg[] corresponds to adding a register between the computation of $y^{\{0:2d+1\}}$ and the output of the gadget.

Algorithm 10. SecEXP [t-NI]

Input Data : $x^{\{0:d\}}$
Output Data : $y^{\{0:2d+1\}}$ such that $\bigoplus_{i=0}^{d} x^{\{i\}} = \bigoplus_{i=0}^{2d+1} y^{\{i\}}$

1: $r^{\{0:d\}} \leftarrow \text{Rand}(k)$
2: $y^{\{0:d\}} \leftarrow \text{SecXOR}(x^{\{0:d\}}, r^{\{0:d\}})$
3: $y^{\{d+1:2d+1\}} \leftarrow r^{\{0:d\}}$
4: $y^{\{0:2d+1\}} \leftarrow \text{Reg}[y^{\{0:2d+1\}}]$

Correctness. From the description in Algorithm 10, it is trivial that $\bigoplus_{i=0}^{d} x^{\{i\}} = \bigoplus_{i=0}^{2d+1} y^{\{i\}}$ and hence it is correct.

Security. To argue about the higher-order security of Algorithm 10, we prove it to be word-level t-NI with $t+1$ shares. This provides resistance against a probing adversary with t word-level probes and allows the use of the gadget in larger compositions, such as the X2B.

Theorem 6. *The gadget* SecEXP *(Algorithm 10) is word-level t-NI secure.*

Proof. This is a direct result from the share-by-share XOR with random shares, as all intermediate probes can be simulated with as many input shares. □

E.4 SecREF, from [14]

Below is the glitch-robust t-SNI refresh gadget, as proposed in [14], and which is used throughout this work. The main idea is to add a sharing of zero to the input x and register it. We refer to the original work for the correctness and security proofs.

Algorithm 11. SecREF [t-SNI]

Input Data : $x^{\{0:d\}}$
Input Data : $r^{\{0:d\}}$ such that $\bigoplus_{i=0}^{d} r^{\{i\}} = 0$ ▷ random 0-sharing
Output Data : $y^{\{0:d\}}$ such that $\bigoplus_{i=0}^{d} x^{\{i\}} = \bigoplus_{i=0}^{d} y^{\{i\}}$

1: $z^{\{0:d\}} \leftarrow \text{SecXOR}(x^{\{0:d\}}, r^{\{0:d\}})$
2: $y^{\{0:d\}} \leftarrow \text{Reg}[z^{\{0:d\}}]$

E.5 RefreshMasks, from [18]

The RefreshMasks gadget consists of $d+1$ mask refresh operations SecREF. As shown in [19], the gadget is (free-)t-SNI, which means all output variables except one can always be perfectly simulated. The gadget described in [18], which is recalled below, only requires $(d+1)d/2$ random values.

Algorithm 12. RefreshMasks [t-SNI]

Input Data : $x^{\{0:d\}}$
Output Data : $y^{\{0:d\}}$ such that $\bigoplus_{i=0}^{d} x^{\{i\}} = \bigoplus_{i=0}^{d} y^{\{i\}}$

1: $y^{\{0:d\}} \leftarrow x^{\{0:d\}}$
2: **for** $j = 0$ to d **do**
3: $\quad r^{\{j:d\}} \leftarrow \text{Rand}(k)$ $\qquad\qquad\qquad\qquad\qquad\qquad\qquad\qquad \triangleright \bigoplus_{i=j}^{d} r^{\{i\}} = 0$
4: $\quad y^{\{j:d\}} \leftarrow \text{SecREF}(x^{\{j:d\}}, r^{\{j:d\}})$
5: **end for**

E.6 FullXOR, from [5]

The FullXOR gadget first refreshes the input shares, before unmasking the shared value. As shown in [5,19], the gadget is t-NI.

Algorithm 13. FullXOR [t-NI]

Input Data : $x^{\{0:d\}}$
Output Data : $y^{\{0\}}$ such that $\bigoplus_{i=0}^{d} x^{\{i\}} = y^{\{0\}}$

1: $z^{\{0:d\}} \leftarrow \text{RefreshMasks}(x^{\{0:d\}})$
2: $y^{\{0\}} \leftarrow z^{\{0\}} \oplus \cdots \oplus z^{\{d\}}$

Appendix F   TVLA results

We want to bring the reader's attention to the complexities of observing higher-order leakages. For our second-order implementation, third-order leakages show for certain modes, as anticipated, and not for others. We can attribute this phenomenon to effects described in [47]. More specifically, to observe higher-order leakage one needs to collect much more traces. One could expect that if we continued acquiring traces up to 500M or even 1 billion traces, our second-order implementation would exhibit third-order leakages more clearly in other modes of operation too. We do not include such figures due to the practical and computational infeasibility.

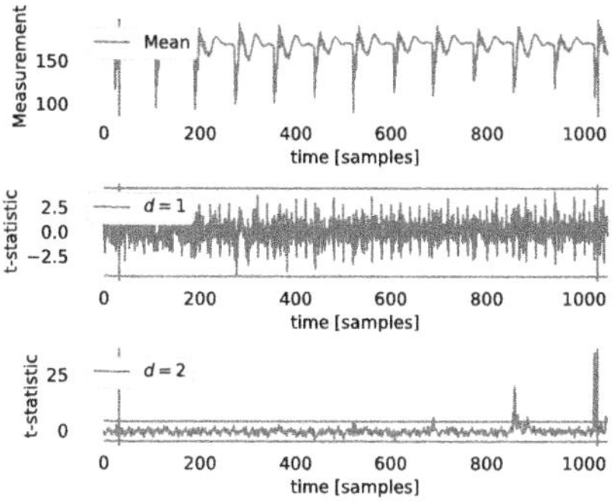

(a) A2B mod 2^{13}.

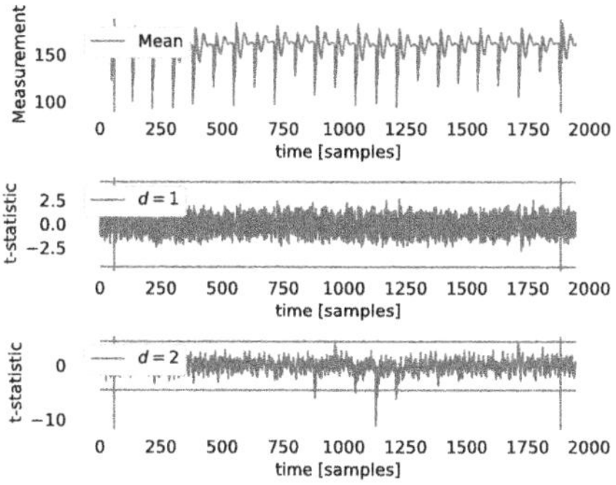

(b) A2B mod 3329.

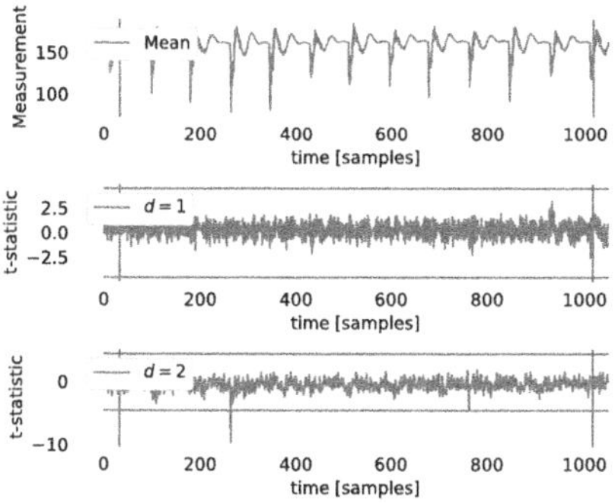

(c) B2A mod 2^{13}.

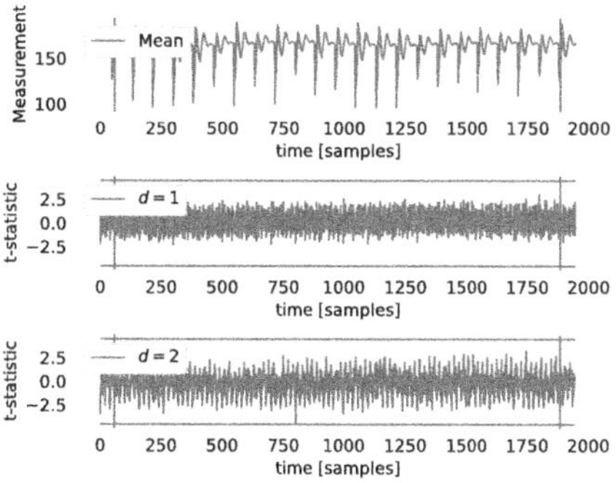

(d) B2A mod 3329.

Fig. 9. 1st & 2nd-order univariate fixed-vs.-random TVLA results for first-order mask conversions (2 shares) using 100M traces with PRNG ON. For each subfigure, the upper plot shows the mean trace. The ± 4.5 threshold is marked by red lines.

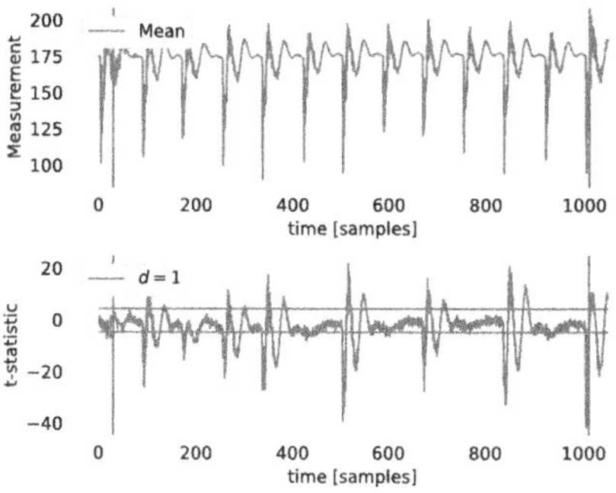

(a) 1st-order (2 share) implementation 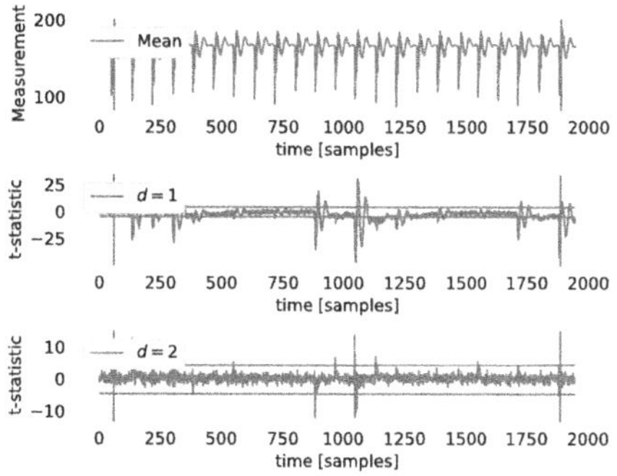 (b) 2nd-order (3 share) implementation

Fig. 10. 1st (& 2nd)-order univariate fixed-vs.-random TVLA results for A2B mod 2^{13} (2 and 3 shares) using 500K traces with PRNG OFF. For each subfigure, the upper plot shows the mean trace.

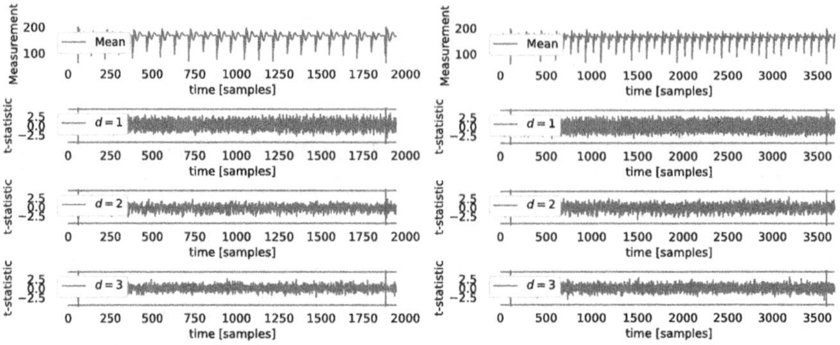

(a) A2B mod 2^{13}.

(b) A2B mod 3329.

(c) B2A mod 2^{13}.

(d) B2A mod 3329.

Fig. 11. 1st, 2nd (&3rd)-order univariate fixed-vs.-random TVLA results for second-order mask conversions (3 shares) using 100M traces with PRNG ON. For each subfigure, the upper plot shows the mean trace. The ± 4.5 threshold is marked by red lines.

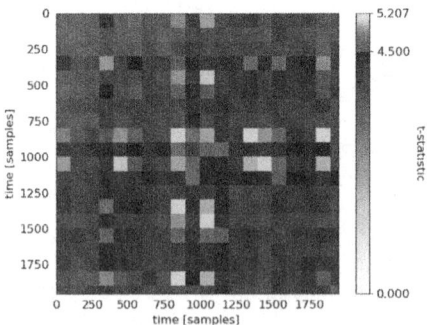

Fig. 12. Bivariate analysis of second-order mask conversion implementation (3 shares), 500K traces, PRNG OFF. Max-pooling guarantees that t-test peaks are visible.

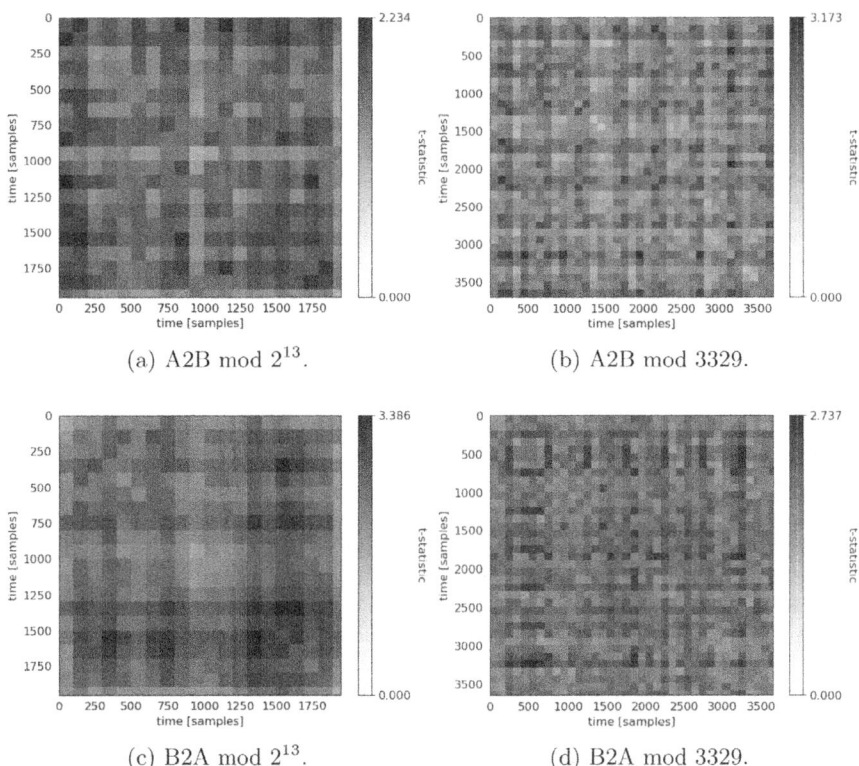

Fig. 13. (Best viewed on-screen.) Bivariate analysis of second-order mask conversion implementation (3 shares), 100M traces, PRNG ON. Max-pooling guarantees that t-test peaks are visible.

References

1. Bache, F., Güneysu, T.: Boolean masking for arithmetic additions at arbitrary order in hardware. Applied Sciences **12**(5) (2022). https://doi.org/10.3390/app12052274, https://www.mdpi.com/2076-3417/12/5/2274
2. Balasch, J., Gierlichs, B., Grosso, V., Reparaz, O., Standaert, F.-X.: On the cost of lazy engineering for masked software implementations. In: Joye, M., Moradi, A. (eds.) CARDIS 2014. LNCS, vol. 8968, pp. 64–81. Springer, Cham (2015). https://doi.org/10.1007/978-3-319-16763-3_5
3. Barthe, G., Belaïd, S., Dupressoir, F., Fouque, P.-A., Grégoire, B., Strub, P.-Y.: Verified proofs of higher-order masking. In: Oswald, E., Fischlin, M. (eds.) EUROCRYPT 2015. LNCS, vol. 9056, pp. 457–485. Springer, Heidelberg (2015). https://doi.org/10.1007/978-3-662-46800-5_18
4. Barthe, G., et al.: Strong non-interference and type-directed higher-order masking. In: Weippl, E.R., Katzenbeisser, S., Kruegel, C., Myers, A.C., Halevi, S. (eds.) ACM CCS 2016, pp. 116–129. ACM Press (2016). https://doi.org/10.1145/2976749.2978427

5. Barthe, G., Belaïd, S., Espitau, T., Fouque, P.-A., Grégoire, B., Rossi, M., Tibouchi, M.: Masking the GLP lattice-based signature scheme at any order. In: Nielsen, J.B., Rijmen, V. (eds.) EUROCRYPT 2018. LNCS, vol. 10821, pp. 354–384. Springer, Cham (2018). https://doi.org/10.1007/978-3-319-78375-8_12
6. Beirendonck, M.V., D'anvers, J.P., Karmakar, A., Balasch, J., Verbauwhede, I.: A side-channel-resistant implementation of saber. J. Emerg. Technol. Comput. Syst. **17**(2) (2021). https://doi.org/10.1145/3429983
7. Bos, J.W., Gourjon, M., Renes, J., Schneider, T., van Vredendaal, C.: Masking kyber: First- and higher-order implementations. IACR Trans. Cryptographic Hardware Embedded Syst. **2021**(4), 173–214 (2021). https://doi.org/10.46586/tches.v2021.i4.173-214, https://tches.iacr.org/index.php/TCHES/article/view/9064
8. Brent, Kung: A regular layout for parallel adders. IEEE Trans. Comput. **C-31**(3), 260–264 (1982). https://doi.org/10.1109/TC.1982.1675982
9. Bronchain, O., Cassiers, G.: Bitslicing arithmetic/Boolean masking conversions for fun and profit with application to lattice-based kems. IACR Trans. Cryptogr. Hardw. Embed. Syst. **2022**(4), 553–588 (2022). https://doi.org/10.46586/tches.v2022.i4.553-588
10. Cassiers, G., Standaert, F.X.: Trivially and efficiently composing masked gadgets with probe isolating non-interference. IEEE Trans. Inf. Forensics Secur. **PP**, 1–1 (2020). https://doi.org/10.1109/TIFS.2020.2971153
11. Cassiers, G.: Composable and efficient masking schemes for side-channel secure implementations. Ph.D. thesis, École polytechnique de Louvain and Université catholique de Louvain (2022)
12. Cassiers, G., Bronchain, O.: Scalib: A side-channel analysis library. Journal of Open Source Software **8**(86), 5196 (2023). https://doi.org/10.21105/joss.05196
13. Cassiers, G., Gigerl, B., Mangard, S., Momin, C., Nagpal, R.: Compress: generate small and fast masked pipelined circuits. Cryptology ePrint Archive, Paper 2023/1600 (2023). https://eprint.iacr.org/2023/1600
14. Cassiers, G., Grégoire, B., Levi, I., Standaert, F.X.: Hardware private circuits: from trivial composition to full verification. IEEE Trans. Comput. **70**(10), 1677–1690 (2021). https://doi.org/10.1109/TC.2020.3022979
15. Coron, J.-S., Giraud, C., Prouff, E., Renner, S., Rivain, M., Vadnala, P.K.: Conversion of security proofs from one leakage model to another: a new issue. In: Schindler, W., Huss, S.A. (eds.) COSADE 2012. LNCS, vol. 7275, pp. 69–81. Springer, Heidelberg (2012). https://doi.org/10.1007/978-3-642-29912-4_6
16. Coron, J.-S., Großschädl, J., Tibouchi, M., Vadnala, P.K.: Conversion from arithmetic to Boolean masking with logarithmic complexity. In: Leander, G. (ed.) FSE 2015. LNCS, vol. 9054, pp. 130–149. Springer, Heidelberg (2015). https://doi.org/10.1007/978-3-662-48116-5_7
17. Coron, J.-S., Großschädl, J., Vadnala, P.K.: Secure conversion between Boolean and arithmetic masking of any order. In: Batina, L., Robshaw, M. (eds.) CHES 2014. LNCS, vol. 8731, pp. 188–205. Springer, Heidelberg (2014). https://doi.org/10.1007/978-3-662-44709-3_11
18. Coron, J.-S., Spignoli, L.: Secure wire shuffling in the probing model. In: Malkin, T., Peikert, C. (eds.) CRYPTO 2021. LNCS, vol. 12827, pp. 215–244. Springer, Cham (2021). https://doi.org/10.1007/978-3-030-84252-9_8
19. Coron, J.S., Gérard, F., Montoya, S., Zeitoun, R.: High-order polynomial comparison and masking lattice-based encryption. IACR Transactions on Cryptographic Hardware and Embedded Systems, pp. 153–192 (2022). https://doi.org/10.46586/tches.v2023.i1.153-192

20. Coron, J.S., Gérard, F., Montoya, S., Zeitoun, R.: High-order table-based conversion algorithms and masking lattice-based encryption. IACR Trans. Cryptographic Hardware Embedded Syst. **2022**(2), 1–40 (2022). https://doi.org/10.46586/tches.v2022.i2.1-40, https://tches.iacr.org/index.php/TCHES/article/view/9479
21. Coron, J.S., Gérard, F., Trannoy, M., Zeitoun, R.: High-order masking of NTRU. IACR Transactions on Cryptographic Hardware and Embedded Systems **2023**(2), 180–211 (Mar 2023). https://doi.org/10.46586/tches.v2023.i2.180-211, https://tches.iacr.org/index.php/TCHES/article/view/10281
22. D'Anvers, J.P., Tiepelt, M., Vercauteren, F., Verbauwhede, I.: Timing attacks on error correcting codes in post-quantum schemes. In: Proceedings of ACM Workshop on Theory of Implementation Security Workshop. TIS'19, New York, NY, USA, pp. 2–9. Association for Computing Machinery (2019). https://doi.org/10.1145/3338467.3358948
23. De Cnudde, T., Bilgin, B., Gierlichs, B., Nikov, V., Nikova, S., Rijmen, V.: Does coupling affect the security of masked implementations? In: Guilley, S. (ed.) COSADE 2017. LNCS, vol. 10348, pp. 1–18. Springer, Cham (2017). https://doi.org/10.1007/978-3-319-64647-3_1
24. De Meyer, L., Reparaz, O., Bilgin, B.: Multiplicative masking for AES in hardware. IACR Trans. Cryptographic Hardware Embedded Syst. **2018**(3), 431–468 (2018). https://doi.org/10.13154/tches.v2018.i3.431-468, https://tches.iacr.org/index.php/TCHES/article/view/7282
25. D'Anvers, J.P.: One-hot conversion: towards faster table-based A2B conversion. In: In: Hazay, C., Stam, M. (eds.) EUROCRYPT 2023, Part IV. LNCS, pp. 628–657. Springer, Heidelberg (2023). https://doi.org/10.1007/978-3-031-30634-1_21
26. Faust, S., Grosso, V., Merino Del Pozo, S., Paglialonga, C., Standaert, F.X.: Composable masking schemes in the presence of physical defaults & the robust probing model. IACR Trans. Cryptographic Hardware Embedded Syst. **2018**(3), 89–120 (2018). https://doi.org/10.13154/tches.v2018.i3.89-120, https://tches.iacr.org/index.php/TCHES/article/view/7270
27. Fritzmann, T., et al.: Masked accelerators and instruction set extensions for post-quantum cryptography. IACR Transactions on Cryptographic Hardware and Embedded Systems **2022**(1), 414–460 (2021). https://doi.org/10.46586/tches.v2022.i1.414-460, https://tches.iacr.org/index.php/TCHES/article/view/9303
28. Fujimoto, D., Kim, Y., Hayashi, Y., Homma, N., Hashimoto, M., Sato, T., Danger, J.L.: Sasimi: Evaluation board for EM information leakage from large scale cryptographic circuits. In: 2022 IEEE International Symposium on Electromagnetic Compatibility & Signal/Power Integrity (EMCSI), pp. 299–302 (2022). https://doi.org/10.1109/EMCSI39492.2022.9889445
29. Gandolfi, K., Mourtel, C., Olivier, F.: Electromagnetic analysis: concrete results. In: Koç, Ç.K., Naccache, D., Paar, C. (eds.) CHES 2001. LNCS, vol. 2162, pp. 251–261. Springer, Heidelberg (2001). https://doi.org/10.1007/3-540-44709-1_21
30. Goodwill, G., Jun, B., Jaffe, J., Rohatgi, P.: A testing methodology for side channel resistance. https://csrc.nist.gov/csrc/media/events/non-invasive-attack-testing-workshop/documents/08_goodwill.pdf (2011). Accessed 6 Nov 2023
31. Goubin, L.: A sound method for switching between Boolean and arithmetic masking. In: Koç, Ç.K., Naccache, D., Paar, C. (eds.) CHES 2001. LNCS, vol. 2162, pp. 3–15. Springer, Heidelberg (2001). https://doi.org/10.1007/3-540-44709-1_2
32. Gross, H., Mangard, S.: Reconciling $d+1$ masking in hardware and software. In: Fischer, W., Homma, N. (eds.) CHES 2017. LNCS, vol. 10529, pp. 115–136. Springer, Cham (2017). https://doi.org/10.1007/978-3-319-66787-4_6

33. Gross, H., Mangard, S., Korak, T.: Domain-oriented masking: compact masked hardware implementations with arbitrary protection order. In: Proceedings of the 2016 ACM Workshop on Theory of Implementation Security. TIS '16, New York, NY, USA, p. 3. Association for Computing Machinery (2016). https://doi.org/10.1145/2996366.2996426
34. Gross, H., Schaffenrath, D., Mangard, S.: Higher-order side-channel protected implementations of KECCAK. In: 2017 Euromicro Conference on Digital System Design (DSD), pp. 205–212 (2017). https://doi.org/10.1109/DSD.2017.21
35. Guo, Q., Johansson, T., Nilsson, A.: A key-recovery timing attack on post-quantum primitives using the Fujisaki-Okamoto transformation and its application on FrodoKEM. In: Micciancio, D., Ristenpart, T. (eds.) CRYPTO 2020, Part II. LNCS, vol. 12171, pp. 359–386. Springer, Cham (2020). https://doi.org/10.1007/978-3-030-56880-1_13
36. Heinz, D., Kannwischer, M.J., Land, G., Pöppelmann, T., Schwabe, P., Sprenkels, D.: First-order masked kyber on ARM cortex-m4. Cryptology ePrint Archive, Paper 2022/058 (2022). https://eprint.iacr.org/2022/058
37. Ishai, Y., Sahai, A., Wagner, D.: Private circuits: securing hardware against probing attacks. In: Boneh, D. (ed.) CRYPTO 2003. LNCS, vol. 2729, pp. 463–481. Springer, Heidelberg (2003). https://doi.org/10.1007/978-3-540-45146-4_27
38. Kocher, P.C.: Timing attacks on implementations of Diffie-Hellman, RSA, DSS, and other systems. In: Koblitz, N. (ed.) CRYPTO 1996. LNCS, vol. 1109, pp. 104–113. Springer, Heidelberg (1996). https://doi.org/10.1007/3-540-68697-5_9
39. Kocher, P., Jaffe, J., Jun, B.: Differential power analysis. In: Wiener, M. (ed.) CRYPTO 1999. LNCS, vol. 1666, pp. 388–397. Springer, Heidelberg (1999). https://doi.org/10.1007/3-540-48405-1_25
40. Krausz, M., et al.: Generic accelerators for costly-to-mask PQC components. Cryptology ePrint Archive, Paper 2023/1287 (2023). https://eprint.iacr.org/2023/1287, https://eprint.iacr.org/2023/1287
41. Kundu, S., D'Anvers, J.P., Beirendonck, M., Karmakar, A., Verbauwhede, I.: Higher-order masked saber. In: Galdi, C., Jarecki, S. (eds.) Security and Cryptography for Networks, pp. 93–116. Springer, Cham (2022). https://doi.org/10.1007/978-3-031-14791-3_5
42. Liu, J., et al.: A low-latency high-order arithmetic to Boolean masking conversion. Cryptology ePrint Archive, Paper 2024/045 (2024). https://eprint.iacr.org/2024/045
43. Mangard, S., Popp, T., Gammel, B.M.: Side-Channel Leakage of Masked CMOS Gates. In: Menezes, A. (ed.) CT-RSA 2005. LNCS, vol. 3376, pp. 351–365. Springer, Heidelberg (2005). https://doi.org/10.1007/978-3-540-30574-3_24
44. Mangard, S., Schramm, K.: Pinpointing the side-channel leakage of masked AES hardware implementations. In: Goubin, L., Matsui, M. (eds.) CHES 2006. LNCS, vol. 4249, pp. 76–90. Springer, Heidelberg (2006). https://doi.org/10.1007/11894063_7
45. Migliore, V., Gérard, B., Tibouchi, M., Fouque, P.-A.: Masking Dilithium. In: Deng, R.H., Gauthier-Umaña, V., Ochoa, M., Yung, M. (eds.) ACNS 2019. LNCS, vol. 11464, pp. 344–362. Springer, Cham (2019). https://doi.org/10.1007/978-3-030-21568-2_17
46. Moos, T., Moradi, A., Schneider, T., Standaert, F.X.: Glitch-resistant masking revisited: or why proofs in the robust probing model are needed. IACR Trans. Cryptographic Hardware Embedded Syst. **2019**(2), 256–292 (2019). https://doi.org/10.13154/tches.v2019.i2.256-292, https://tches.iacr.org/index.php/TCHES/article/view/7392

47. Moradi, A., Wild, A.: Assessment of hiding the higher-order leakages in hardware. In: Güneysu, T., Handschuh, H. (eds.) CHES 2015. LNCS, vol. 9293, pp. 453–474. Springer, Heidelberg (2015). https://doi.org/10.1007/978-3-662-48324-4_23
48. Müller, N., Knichel, D., Sasdrich, P., Moradi, A.: Transitional leakage in theory and practice: Unveiling security flaws in masked circuits. IACR Trans. Cryptographic Hardware Embedded Syst. **2022**(2), 266–288 (2022). https://doi.org/10.46586/tches.v2022.i2.266-288, https://tches.iacr.org/index.php/TCHES/article/view/9488
49. National Institute of Standards and Technology: Module-lattice-based digital signature standard. Technical report, U.S. Department of Commerce, Washington, D.C. (2024). https://doi.org/10.6028/NIST.FIPS.204
50. National Institute of Standards and Technology: Module-lattice-based key-encapsulation mechanism standard. Technical report, U.S. Department of Commerce, Washington, D.C. (2024). https://doi.org/10.6028/NIST.FIPS.203
51. Nikova, S., Rechberger, C., Rijmen, V.: Threshold implementations against side-channel attacks and glitches. In: Ning, P., Qing, S., Li, N. (eds.) ICICS 2006. LNCS, vol. 4307, pp. 529–545. Springer, Heidelberg (2006). https://doi.org/10.1007/11935308_38
52. NIST Computer Security Division: Post-quantum cryptography standardization (2016). https://csrc.nist.gov/projects/post-quantum-cryptography. Accessed 17 Aug 2023
53. NIST Computer Security Division: Comments requested on three draft fips for post-quantum cryptography. https://csrc.nist.gov/news/2023/three-draft-fips-for-post-quantum-cryptography (2023). Accessed 30 Oct 2023
54. NIST Computer Security Division: Post-quantum cryptography: Digital signature schemes (2023). https://csrc.nist.gov/projects/pqc-dig-sig/round-1-additional-signatures. Accessed 7 Sept 2023
55. Primas, R., Pessl, P., Mangard, S.: Single-trace side-channel attacks on masked lattice-based encryption. In: Fischer, W., Homma, N. (eds.) CHES 2017. LNCS, vol. 10529, pp. 513–533. Springer, Cham (2017). https://doi.org/10.1007/978-3-319-66787-4_25
56. Ravi, P., Sinha Roy, S., Chattopadhyay, A., Bhasin, S.: Generic side-channel attacks on CCA-secure lattice-based PKE and KEMs. IACR Trans. Cryptographic Hardware Embedded Syst. **2020**(3), 307–335 (2020). https://doi.org/10.13154/tches.v2020.i3.307-335, https://tches.iacr.org/index.php/TCHES/article/view/8592
57. Reparaz, O., Bilgin, B., Nikova, S., Gierlichs, B., Verbauwhede, I.: Consolidating masking schemes. In: Gennaro, R., Robshaw, M. (eds.) CRYPTO 2015. LNCS, vol. 9215, pp. 764–783. Springer, Heidelberg (2015). https://doi.org/10.1007/978-3-662-47989-6_37
58. Schneider, T., Moradi, A., Güneysu, T.: Arithmetic addition over Boolean masking. In: Malkin, T., Kolesnikov, V., Lewko, A.B., Polychronakis, M. (eds.) ACNS 2015. LNCS, vol. 9092, pp. 559–578. Springer, Cham (2015). https://doi.org/10.1007/978-3-319-28166-7_27
59. Schneider, T., Paglialonga, C., Oder, T., Güneysu, T.: Efficiently masking binomial sampling at arbitrary orders for lattice-based crypto. In: Lin, D., Sako, K. (eds.) PKC 2019. LNCS, vol. 11443, pp. 534–564. Springer, Cham (2019). https://doi.org/10.1007/978-3-030-17259-6_18
60. Shamir, A.: How to share a secret. Commun. ACM **22**(11), 612–613 (1979). https://doi.org/10.1145/359168.359176

61. Shor, P.W.: Polynomial-time algorithms for prime factorization and discrete logarithms on a quantum computer. SIAM J. Comput. **26**(5), 1484–1509 (1997). https://doi.org/10.1137/S0097539795293172
62. Van Beirendonck, M., D'Anvers, J.P., Verbauwhede, I.: Analysis and comparison of table-based arithmetic to boolean masking. IACR Trans. Cryptographic Hardware Embedded Syst. **2021**(3), 275–297 (2021). https://doi.org/10.46586/tches.v2021.i3.275-297, https://tches.iacr.org/index.php/TCHES/article/view/8975
63. Xu, Z., Pemberton, O., Roy, S.S., Oswald, D.F., Yao, W., Zheng, Z.: Magnifying side-channel leakage of lattice-based cryptosystems with chosen ciphertexts: The case study of kyber. IEEE Trans. Comput. **71**, 2163–2176 (2022). https://api.semanticscholar.org/CorpusID:220794801

Area Efficient Polynomial Arithmetic Accelerator for Post-quantum Digital Signatures and KEMs

Dina Kamel(✉)[iD] and François-Xavier Standaert[iD]

ICTEAM, Crypto Group, UCLouvain, Louvain-la-Neuve, Belgium
{dina.kamel,fstandae}@uclouvain.be

Abstract. Cryptographic schemes relying on Lattice-based hard learning problems are popular options for post-quantum signature and key encapsulation. This is for example witnessed by the selection of CRYSTALS-Dilithium and CRYSTALS-Kyber as new standards by the National Institute for Standards and Technology (NIST). Many other algorithms are currently being considered by the scientific community. All lattice-based algorithms rely on polynomial operations, among which the polynomial multiplication is generally one of the most expensive from the implementation viewpoint. As a result, the Number Theoretic Transform (NTT) is very frequently considered to speed up the implementations of these algorithms. For this purpose, we propose a semi-generic lightweight hardware architecture that supports polynomial operations for multiple lattice-based schemes, namely Dilithium, Hawk, Raccoon, Kyber and Polka. Implementation results on an Artix-7 FPGA show that our design features a relatively small footprint compared to state-of-the-art implementations. For example, our polynomial arithmetic core requires 2604 LUTs, 770 FFs and 4 DSPs for Dilithium and 1583 LUTs, 458 FFs and 2 DSPs for Kyber and can operate at 100 MHz. It computes NTT/INTT, point-wise-multiplication, multiply-accumulate and addition/subtraction in 519, 134, 135 and 131 clock cycles for Dilithium and in 455, 134, 135 and 131 clock cycles for Kyber, respectively.

Keywords: Kyber · Dilithium · HAWK · Raccoon · Polka · Number theoretic transform (NTT) · Polynomial arithmetic · Lightweight design · FPGAs

1 Introduction

Post-Quantum Cryptography (PQC) has gained a significant momentum in recent years to match the advancements on the development of quantum computers [24]. Indeed, implementing Shor's algorithm [37] on quantum computers can break current public key cryptosystems (e.g. Rivest-Shamir-Adleman (RSA) and Elliptic Curve Cryptography (ECC)) that rely on the hardness of integer factorization and discrete logarithms [9]. In 2016, the National Institute for Standards and Technology (NIST) launched a call for standardization of new post-quantum public key algorithms, covering both public-key encryption and digital signatures. The lattice-based CRYSTALS-Dilithium [4] is one of three digital signature schemes selected for standardization in 2022. CRYSTALS-Kyber [2], which belongs to the same CRYSTALS family as Dilithium, was the only selected scheme for Key Encapsulation Mechanism (KEM). On top of that, the NIST posted a call for additional signature proposals to be considered in the PQC standardization process to diversify its post-quantum signatures portfolio. The lattice-based signature schemes Hawk [8] and Raccoon [35] were submitted to this call and Hawk has been accepted for the second round.

All these lattice-based schemes use operations in the polynomial ring $\mathcal{R}_q = \mathbb{Z}_q[X]/(X^n+1)$, where n is the degree of the polynomial. One of the most costly operations is the multiplication of high-degree polynomials. The Number Theoretic Transform (NTT) reduces the complexity of high-order polynomial multiplication from $\mathcal{O}(n^2)$ (in case of direct school-book multiplication) to $\mathcal{O}(n \log n)$. As a result, most lattice-based schemes choose their parameters' sets to enable using the NTT allowing fast and efficient polynomial arithmetic computation. This leads the core module that handles all polynomial arithmetic to be quite similar. Hence, it suggests that having a generic design of a polynomial arithmetic module that can be tailored to the above-mentioned lattice-based schemes would be quite useful. At the same time, developing efficient implementations that satisfy a wide spectrum of applications from high-performance through mid-range to light-weight for different platforms (software and hardware) is a growing research field. In this work, we focus on light-weight hardware applications.

Many efficient hardware implementations of the polynomial arithmetic unit in the literature explore the trade off between the hardware cost and performance. Here are some examples in the case of Dilithium. Beckwith et al. [5] proposed a polynomial arithmetic unit featuring a radix-4 NTT that calculates two layers of NTT/INTT at a time. This allowed to reduce the latency and the cost of memory access while reordering coefficients during these operations to optimize the BRAM utilization. Similarly, Wang et al. [38] employed a radix-4 NTT to implement the polynomial multiplication. However, they opted for a conflict-free memory mapping scheme applied to four-bank Block RAMs. In contrast, Land et al. [23] opted for a radix-2 NTT that takes advantage of readily available DSPs on low-end FPGA. Another approach by Zhao et al. [43] is to use a radix-2 multipath delay commutator (R2MDC) NTT architecture that has fewer memory accesses and a simpler control logic compared to in-place NTT architectures. Gupta et al. [17] on the other hand used two dual-port RAMs in their radix-2 NTT implementation to allow reading and writing their internal data in a ping-pong fashion. A different strategy was presented by Pham et al. [34] emphasizing effective hardware resource reuse and minimizing redundancies.

Similarly, there exists many works in the literature that target resource-constrained hardware applications for Kyber. For example, Ni et al. [33] presented a compact polynomial arithmetic module promoting a BRAM-free radix-

2 NTT architecture where BRAM units are replaced with three smaller FIFOs. Both Nguyen et at. [31] and Xing et al. [39] adopted a similar approach. Zhang et al. [41] on the other hand implemented a ping-pong memory access scheme for their polynomial arithmetic module that uses a radix-2 NTT architecture.

Since Hawk is quite recently introduced, to our knowledge there has not been any hardware implementations for it yet in the literature. Besides the actual proposal, there has been one software implementation [15]. Nevertheless, as a lattice-based signature, the implementation of its polynomial arithmetic core is expected to be similar to that of Dilithium and Kyber.

Finally, and in order to cover a wider spectrum of algorithms, we also chose to implement Raccoon which is a lattice-based digital signature submitted to NIST in response to its call for additional digital signature schemes [35]. The reason behind our choice is the appealing argument of Raccoon being a masking-friendly scheme that should enable better resistance against side-channel analysis attacks [19]. This appears as a natural motivation given the significant cost of protecting Dilithium against leakage [3]. For a similar reason, we added Polka to our portfolio [18], which is a lattice-based encryption scheme developed to take side-channel leakage into account. The design is based, among others, on avoiding "leaky" functions such as the Fujisaki-Okamoto transform and adopting masking-friendly key-homomorphic computations.

Based on this state of the art, in this work, we therefore propose an efficient low-cost hardware design that is suitable to perform polynomial operations among which the complex NTT/INTT for any of the target lattice-based schemes mentioned above. Concretely, our main contributions are threefold:

- First, our polynomial arithmetic module design is semi-generic in a way that provides compile-time configurability for the scheme parameters allowing easy implementation of any of the aforementioned lattice-base standards. Depending on whether $\log n$ is even or odd and whether the choice of the prime modulus q allows a fully-splitting ring or not, only minor changes in the core implementation of the polynomial arithmetic unit will be required. Namely, the address generation of the polynomial coefficients and the twiddle factors in the address control logic are the target of such slight modifications. Besides, the modular reduction is not generic – hence the full design is only semi-generic. The reason behind this is the fact that customized optimizations are required to design the Barrett reduction module for each standard (as they obviously have different prime moduli) in order to minimize its resource utilization for our target low-cost applications.
- Second, our compact FPGA-based polynomial arithmetic architecture has a small area footprint for most implemented standards. On an Artix-7, our core uses 2604 Look-Up Tables (LUT)s, 770 Flip-Flops (FF)s and 4 Digital Signal Processor (DSPs) to implement Dilithium. For Hawk1024 and prime modulus p_2, our core occupies 4451 LUTs, 1139 FFs and 8 DSPs. In the case of Raccoon (using the prime modulus $q_2 = 33292289$), the resource utilization is 3458 LUTs, 998 FFs and 4 DSPs. For Kyber, our core uses 1583 LUTs, 458 FFs and 2 DSPs. Regarding Polka, it utilizes 2512 LUTs, 593 FFs and 2

DSPs. Our core operate at a maximum of 83 to 100 MHz depending on the standard.
- Third, we provide the Verilog code for our design at https://git-crypto.elen.ucl.ac.be/dkamel/genericpolyarithunit to support open source research, something currently lacking in the literature.

The rest of the paper is organized as follows. Section 2 introduces preliminaries. The proposed poly-arithmetic architecture and design details of its sub-blocks are presented in Sect. 3. Section 4 discusses the implementation results and compares with related work. Section 5 concludes the paper.

2 Preliminaries

2.1 Notations

We denote by $\mathbb{Z}_q$ the ring of integers modulo the prime q and by $\mathcal{R}_q = \mathbb{Z}_q[X]/(X^n + 1)$ the polynomial ring in X modulo $X^n + 1$, with n the degree of the polynomial. We represent a polynomial with regular lowercase (e.g. a), a vector of polynomials with bold lowercase (e.g. $\boldsymbol{a}$) and a matrix of polynomials with bold uppercase (e.g. $\boldsymbol{A}$). The i-th coefficient of a polynomial is denoted by a_i. The · symbol denotes the multiplication operation whereas ∘ refers to the point-wise polynomial multiplication. Letters with a hat symbol correspond to their representation after NTT (e.g. $\hat{a}$).

2.2 Standards

Our design covers several lattice-based post-quantum standards for both digital signature and Key Encapsulation Mechanism (KEM).

CRYSTALS-Dilithium. Dilithium is a lattice-based digital signature recently standardized by NIST as ML-DSA in FIPS 204 [29] for secure Post-Quantum Cryptography (PQC) in 2024. Its hardness is based on the Module Learning With Errors (MLWE) and the Module Short Integer Solution problems. The signature scheme design is based on the "Fiat-Shamir with Aborts" paradigm proposed in [26,27]. The initial proposal is described by Ducas et al. in [12] and later refined in the NIST PQC submission [4]. Its main characteristics are: randomness generation from a uniform distribution instead of a discrete Gaussian distribution which is difficult to implement securely and efficiently, [13], adhere the public key and signature sizes to a minimum, and easiness to vary the security level by changing the size of the module (dimensions of the matrices and vectors). Relying on an algebraic structured lattice (MLWE) problem rather than an ideal lattice (Ring-LWE) or completely unstructured lattice (LWE) problems was an optimal intermediate solution that moves further away from the weaknesses of ideal lattice problems while still profiting from their efficiency without the extra cost of using unstructured LWE [12]. As for the rational behind building the digital signature scheme using the "Fiat-Shamir with aborts" paradigm was to reduce the size of the mask randomness and thus the signature significantly [27].

An extra rejection sampling step is needed to perform the aborts. Dilithium uses a 23-bit prime modulus $q = 8380417$ and degree $n = 256$ for all security levels.

Hawk. Hawk is a lattice-based signature scheme whose hardness is based on the module Lattice Isomorphism Problem (LIP) that responded to the NIST PQC call for additional digital signature scheme. The scheme was first introduced in [13] and later optimized in [8]. The goal of this call was to diversify its post-quantum signature portfolio which is mostly based on structured lattices so far (namely; CRYSTALS-Dilithium and Falcon). Hawk has been recently selected to move forward to the second round of the standardization process. Its main features are: randomness generation is either from a centred binomial distribution (during key generation) or from uniform distribution (during signing), compact public key and signature sizes (even smaller than those of Dilithium), floating-point free arithmetic which enables its implementation on various (constrained) hardware devices, small memory footprint and no rejection-sampling. The basic idea was to combine the use of module lattice based on LIP and ideas from NTRUSign and Falcon in order to design a highly efficient signature scheme. Hawk uses two 31-bit primes $p_1 = 2147473409$ and $p_2 = 2147389441$. The degree n is either 512 or 1024 for security level I or IV, respectively.

Raccoon. As a response to the NIST PQC call for additional digital signature schemes Raccoon [35] was submitted, but was not selected in the second round. It is a masking-friendly lattice-based digital signature scheme based on the "Fiat-Shamir" paradigm. As Dilithium, its hardness is based on the MLWE problem. The main objective of Raccoon is to build a scheme that is inherently resistant against side-channel attacks by making its subroutines either masking friendly (with quasilinear overheads) or ones that do not need to be masked at all. This was motivated by the fact that even though the standardized lattice-based signatures Dilithium and Falcon and the hash-based signature SPHINCS are efficient and their black-box security is well-understood, they remain vulnerable against side-channel attacks if left unprotected [10,16,20,21,28] (as some examples). The cost of protecting these schemes using the masking countermeasure is extremely expensive. Indeed, lattice-based signatures contain subroutines (mainly the rejection loop and the hash functions) which when masked incur quadratic or worse than quadratic overheads, see for example [3]. Raccoon uses a 49-bit modulus $q = 549824583172097$ which is a composite number consisting of two primes: 24-bit $q_1 = 16515073$ and 25-bit $q_2 = 33292289$. The degree $n = 512$ for all security levels.

CRYSTALS-Kyber. Belonging to the same CRYSTALS family as Dilithium, Kyber is a lattice-based KEM recently standardized by NIST as ML-KEM in FIPS 203 [30] for post-quantum secure KEMs in 2022. It is based on the hardness of MLWE where a CPA-secure Public Key Encryption (PKE) scheme is used to create a CCA-Secure KEM by applying a variant of the Fujisaki-Okamoto (FO) transform. Its main characteristics are: secret and noise generation from a centred binomial distribution which is easily, efficiently, and securely sampled from, adopting an implicit rejection approach, using a compress function to discard some low-order bits in the ciphertext; thus reducing its size, and easiness to vary the security level by changing the size of the module (dimensions of the matrices and vectors). Kyber uses a 12-bit modulus $q = 3329$ and a degree $n = 256$ for all security levels.

Polka. Polka [18] is a lattice-based encryption scheme that relies on the recently introduced Learning With Physical Rounding (LWPR) assumption [14]. As Raccoon, the main goal of Polka is to enable efficient side-channel protected implementations, but for encryption schemes. To do that, Polka leverages various features such as the rigidity property introduced by Bernstein and Persichetti [6] which allows avoiding the FO transform that proved to be a source of side-channel leakage. It also proposes to randomize the decryption process and adopts key-homomorphic computations that are easily masked with linear overheads. Polka uses a 16-bit modulus $q = 5939$ and a degree $n = 1024$ that satisfies security level I.

2.3 Number Theoretic Transform

All the before-mentioned standards (and others) share the fact that their main algebraic operation is high-order polynomial multiplication (whether on a matrix, vector or a single polynomial). The NTT is the most efficient method for multiplying two high-order polynomials where the complexity is reduced from $\mathcal{O}(n^2)$ in case of school-book multiplication for example to $\mathcal{O}(n \log n)$ in case of NTT. The NTT is the special case of Discrete Fourier Transform (DFT) over finite-field polynomials in $\mathcal{R}_q = \mathbb{Z}_q[X]/(X^n + 1)$. This ring structure enables the implementation of the Negative Wrapped Convolution-based (NWC) NTT effectively. Accordingly, n is a power of two and the prime modulus q satisfies $q \equiv 1 \bmod 2n$, such that the primitive $2n$-th root of unity ζ in $\mathbb{Z}_q$ exists; thus allowing a "fully-splitting" of the NTT algorithm. The NTT transform can therefore be written as:

$$\hat{a}_j = \sum_{i=0}^{n-1} a_i \zeta^{(2j+1)i} \bmod q, \; j \in [0, n-1]$$

Conveniently, the inverse NTT (INTT) is also straightforward and can be written as:

$$a_i = n^{-1} \sum_{j=0}^{n-1} \hat{a}_j \zeta^{-(2i+1)j} \bmod q, \; i \in [0, n-1]$$

Now, one can compute polynomial multiplication efficiently using NTT as $a \cdot b =$ INTT(NTT(a) ∘ NTT(b)). The radix-2 NTT is the simplest form of NTT where a polynomial of length n is split into two parts of length $n/2$ and this can go on recursively until the original polynomial is reduced to degree 0. One efficient algorithm is the Cooley-Tukey (CT) butterfly that takes advantage of the fact that $\zeta^n \equiv -1 \bmod q$. As a result it holds that $X^n + 1 = X^n - \zeta^n = (X^{\frac{n}{2}} - $

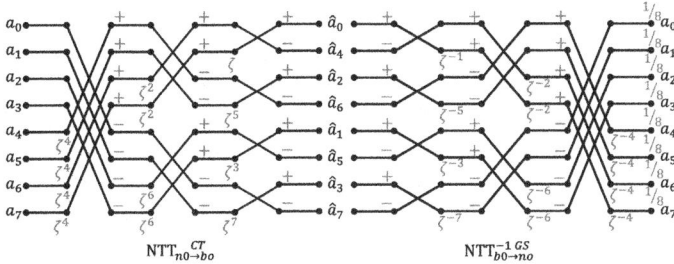

Fig. 1. Signal flow graph of radix-2 NTT/INTT for n = 8.

$\zeta^{\frac{n}{2}}) \times (X^{\frac{n}{2}} + \zeta^{\frac{n}{2}}) \bmod q$. If this step is repeated $\log n$ times then the polynomial $X^n + 1$ can therefore be written as

$$X^n + 1 = \prod_{i=0}^{n-1}(X - \zeta^{2i+1}) = \prod_{i=0}^{n-1}(X - \zeta^{2brv_{\log n}(i)+1}),$$

where the $brv_{\log n}(i)$ is the bit reversal of the unsigned $\log n$-bit integer i. This essentially implies that if the coefficients of the polynomial are kept in natural order (no), after the NTT operation they will be in bit-reversed order (bo). On the other hand, the INTT can be efficiently implemented using the Gentleman-Sande (GS) butterfly algorithm by inverting the mapping process. Keeping the inputs in bit-reversed order will result in naturally ordered coefficients after the INTT operation. This is quite convenient as it avoids the cost of reordering the polynomial coefficients [36]. Figure 1 shows the flow diagram for an 8-point radix-2 NTT and INTT using CT and GS algorithms, respectively.

2.4 NTT in Target Standards

The ring structure of Dilithium, Hawk, Raccoon and Polka were carefully chosen to enable the fully-splitting of the NWC NTT effectively without zero-padding. Accordingly, n is power of two and the prime modulus q satisfies $q \equiv 1 \bmod 2n$, such that the primitive $2n$-th root of unity ζ in $\mathbb{Z}_q$ exists. Therefore, the defining polynomial $X^n + 1$ of the ring $\mathcal{R}$ factors into n polynomials of degree 1 modulo q and the NTT of a polynomial $a \in \mathcal{R}_q$ is a vector of n polynomials of degree zero. Powers of ζ in the range $(0 : n - 1)$ are referred to as twiddle factors. Polynomial multiplication can be efficiently computed using NTT as described in the previous section.

As for Kyber the prime modulus q is chosen to satisfy $q \equiv 1 \bmod n$ (instead of $q \equiv 1 \bmod 2n$), such that the primitive n-th root of unity (instead of $2n$-th root of unity) ζ in $\mathbb{Z}_q$ exists. The idea of decreasing the prime modulus was presented in [44] citing the main advantage as enabling the reduction of both the public key and the ciphertext sizes. As a result of this choice, the NTT algorithm cannot fully split. However, the defining polynomial $X^n + 1$ of the ring $\mathcal{R}$ factors into $n/2$ polynomials of degree 2 modulo q and the NTT of a polynomial $a \in \mathcal{R}_q$ is a vector of $n/2$ polynomials of degree one. This leads to powers of ζ being in the range $(0 : n/2 - 1)$. Polynomial multiplication can be computed using NTT as $a \cdot b = \text{INTT}(\text{NTT}(a) \circ \text{NTT}(b))$. Nevertheless, $\text{NTT}(a) \circ \text{NTT}(b) = \hat{a} \circ \hat{b} = \hat{c}$ consists of the $n/2$ products in the form of $\hat{c}_{2i} + \hat{c}_{2i+1}X = (\hat{a}_{2i} + \hat{a}_{2i+1}X).(\hat{b}_{2i} + \hat{b}_{2i+1}X) \, mod(X^2 - \zeta^{2brv_{(\log n-1)}(i)+1})$, where i is the coefficient index and $brv_{(\log n-1)}$ is the bit reverse operation over $(\log n - 1)$−bits. As a result, an additional school-book multiplication is necessary to complete the polynomial multiplication.

For each of Dilithium, Kyber and Polka, the prime moduli used are all less than 31 bits which can easily fit on 32-bit platforms (mostly applicable to software). However in the case of Hawk and Raccoon, the moduli needed are larger than 32-bits. As a result, both schemes opted to apply the Chinese Remainder Theorem (CRT) and split the large modulus into two smaller primes to fit into 32-bit platforms, as explained in Sect. 2.2, then perform the necessary operations over these two primes.

3 Proposed Poly-Arithmetic Architecture

In this section, we describe the architecture of our proposed semi-generic poly-arithmetic core which is responsible for the computation of all polynomial operations in the target standards.

3.1 Architecture Overview

Figure 2a demonstrates the high-level architecture of the poly-arithmetic module. Our design consists of two butterfly units (BFUs) arranged in parallel (BFU 2X1), an address control unit with conflict-free memory access (thanks to an integrated address resolver block), a twiddle factor memory (TF ROM) as well as some data and control multiplexers. The proposed poly-arithmetic module is able to perform both radix-2 NTT and INTT as well as polynomial arithmetic operations such as pointwise multiplication (PWM), multiply and accumulate (MAC), addition (ADD) and subtraction (SUB) for all target standards. Additionally, the poly-arithmetic unit handles all interactions with the data RAMs where the polynomial coefficients are stored.

To meet the bandwidth requirement, the data RAMs are designed as a 4-bank memory block depicted in Fig. 2b similar to [23,42]. The goal is to ensure that the four different polynomial coefficients accessed in parallel during NTT/INTT are always located in four different banks to guarantee a conflict-free memory access without having to shuffle and reorder the coefficients. Although a more efficient BRAM configuration that has a higher utilization of each memory row was proposed by [5], their final BRAM cost of a full Dilithium implementation at security level 5 is slightly less than that of [23]. The banks are implemented with

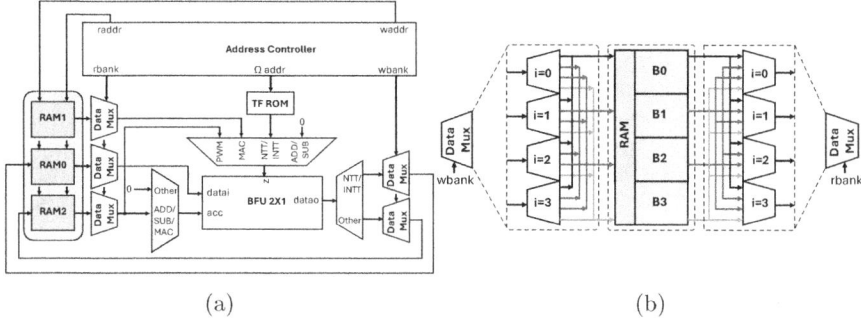

Fig. 2. (a) Proposed architecture and (b) internal RAM and data MUX structure.

dual-port 36-kbit block RAMs capable of reading and writing in the same clock cycle. Each BRAM is configured as 1024 × 36 memory. This configuration can store up to 16 polynomials of degree $n = 256$, 8 polynomials of degree $n = 512$ or 4 polynomials of degree $n = 1024$. Although the utilization of each memory row is not maximized for all target standards (66%, 86%, 69% in case of Dilithium, Hawk and Raccoon, respectively and 33% and 44% in case of Kyber and Polka, respectively), for the sake of generality we decided to keep such configuration. For NTT, INTT a single data RAM is needed. The addition, subtraction and pointwise multiplication operations require two data RAMs where coefficients of two distinct polynomials are stored. As for the MAC operation, three data RAMs are employed. Two RAMs store the coefficients of two polynomials to be multiplied and the third RAM stores their product which is later accumulated as required by operations over vectors of polynomials. The data multiplexers/demultiplexers are internally divided into 4 blocks, each connected to a bank RAM and controlled by the address controller via the *rbank* and *wbank* signals for read and write operations, respectively. The TFs are stored in a distributed memory (TF ROM). Details of each block are provided in the following sections.

3.2 Dual Butterfly Module

The butterflies arrangement in the BFU 2X1 block is illustrated in Fig. 3. The two BFUs, each capable of performing both CT and GS butterfly operations as well as basic arithmetic operations such as multiplication, addition and subtraction, are placed in parallel. They process either 4 coefficients per clock cycle during NTT/INTT or 2 coefficients per clock cycle during all other operations when the pipeline is fulfilled. The multiplexers at the inputs and outputs provide the design with the flexibility to change between the operating modes depending on the 3-bit mode signal as explained in Table 1.

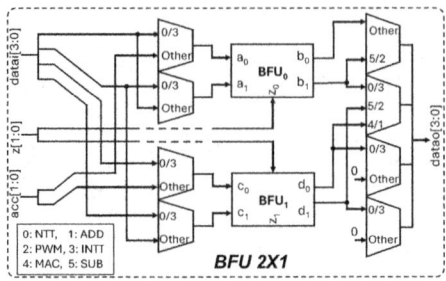

Fig. 3. Dual Butterfly unit.

Table 1. Dual butterfly unit in/out interconnections. 'X' represents a do not care state and '-' denotes an unconnected input.

	Operation	NTT	ADD	PWM	INTT	MAC	SUB
	mode[2:0]	0	1	2	3	4	5
In.	datai[0]	a_0	a_1	a_1	a_0	a_1	a_1
	datai[1]	a_1	c_1	c_1	a_1	c_1	c_1
	datai[2]	c_0	–	–	c_0	–	–
	datai[3]	c_1	–	–	c_1	–	–
	z[0]	z_0	X	z_0	z_0	z_0	X
	z[1]	z_1	X	z_1	z_1	z_1	X
	acc[0]	–	a_0	X	–	a_0	a_0
	acc[1]	–	c_0	X	–	c_0	c_0
Out.	datao[0]	b_0	b_0	b_1	b_0	b_0	b_1
	datao[1]	b_1	d_0	d_1	b_1	d_0	d_1
	datao[2]	d_0	0	0	d_0	0	0
	datao[3]	d_1	0	0	d_1	0	0

3.3 Modular Reduction

The modular reduction is the main operation that has to be tailored to the prime modulus adopted by each standard. Different modular reduction techniques exist in the literature. The most common are the Montgomery and the Barrett reduction algorithms. However, both of these algorithms require additional multiplications, which are expensive in time and hardware resources. Beckwith et al. [5] implemented Barrett reduction in hardware for Dilithium by only using shifts and additions. Nevertheless, their optimization method is highly customized to Dilithium's modulus using a complex Verilog code (available online [1]) and as a result difficult to reuse in case of other moduli. Another reduction technique recursively exploits the congruency relation within the prime modulus. For example in the case of Dilithium, $q = 2^{23} - 2^{13} + 1$, so by exploiting the relation $2^{23} \equiv 2^{13} - 1 \mod q$ recursively as in [23]. Other reduction techniques,

Algorithm 1. Optimized Barrett reduction [22,34]

Require: U, q, $l = \lceil \log q \rceil$, $T = \lfloor 2^{2l}/q \rfloor$
Ensure: $Z = U \bmod q$
1: $V = U >> (l-1)$
2: $W = (V \times T) >> (l+1)$
3: $X = (W \times q) \bmod 2^{l+1}$
4: $Y = U \bmod 2^{l+1}$
5: **if** $Y < X$ **then**
6:     $Z = 2^{l+1} + Y - X$
7: **else**
8:     $Z = Y - X$
9: **end if**
10: **if** $Z \geq q$ **then**
11:     $Z = Z - q$
12: **end if**

which are variants of Montgomery reduction, such as KRED, KRED-2X [25] and K²RED [7] are also proposed in the literature. They require the modulus to be a Proth prime of the form $q = q_h 2^\omega + 1$, where $\omega > \log q/2$ which is not the case for all supported standards.

An optimized Barrett reduction implementation customized for a specific modulus using only addition, subtraction and shift operation was proposed in [22] and used for the Dilithium modulus in [34]. The basic principle of the original Barrett reduction is to subtract the multiplication result between the quotient $\lfloor U/q \rfloor$ and the modulus q from the input number U. To avoid the expensive division of U and q, $1/q$ can be replaced by $T/2^k$ which is just a right-shift operation and $T = \lfloor 2^k/q \rfloor$ such that:

$$D = (U \times T) >> k,$$
$$U \bmod q = U - D \times q,$$

Algorithm 1 explains the optimized version of the Barrett reduction as in [22]. The input U is split into two overlapping parts, where the upper value V and the lower value Y intersect in minimum two bits. Instead of multiplying the $2 \log q$-bit value U by T, the smaller upper value V, which is the most-significant bits (MSB)s of U replaces it then the product is scaled by $\approx 1/q$ ($1/2^{\lceil \log q \rceil + 1}$). The scaled product is then multiplied by q as in the original Barrett reduction. Finally, the subtraction step is performed slightly different where the lower bits of this product is subtracted from the least-significant bits (LSBs) of the input Y. We follow the same path and optimize the modular reduction for each modulus of the target standards. Here we present the Barrett reduction of Dilithium and Kyber as examples due to space restrictions.

Dilithium. Figure 4 illustrates the optimized Barrett reduction for Dilithium, i.e. for the specific prime $q = 8370417$, where the parameter $l = 23$ and the constant $T = 8396807$. The figure first shows a full multiplication between two 23-bit integers A and B which requires two DSPs. The DSP48 slices available on the target Artix7 FPGA allow multiplication between signed 25-bit and 18-bit values. As a result, to multiply two 23-bit values, two DSPs are required as well as a shift and an addition operation which are available within the DSP slice. The modular reduction then follows the steps in Algorithm 1. A highly optimized method to perform the multiplication by constants (T, q) using only addition, subtraction, xor and shift operations was detailed in [34] and presented here. The reduction operation is divided into two parts. The upper half multiplier (UH-MULT) sub-block handles the multiplication of the most-significant bits of the full multiplier $V = U[45:22]$ by the constant value T:

$$\begin{aligned}
V \times T &= V[23:0] \times (2^{23} + 2^{13} + 2^2 + 2 + 1) \\
&= 2^{13}(2^{10}V[23:0] + V[23:0]) + 2(2V[23:0] + V[23:0]) + V[23:0] \\
&= 2^{13}(2^{10}V[23:0] + V[23:0]) + 2(2V[23:0] + V[23:0] + V[23:1]) \\
&\quad + V[0]
\end{aligned}$$

$$\begin{aligned}
V_1[34:0] &= 2^{10}V[23:0] + V[23:0] \\
&= concat\{V[23:0] + V[23:10], V[9:0]\}
\end{aligned}$$

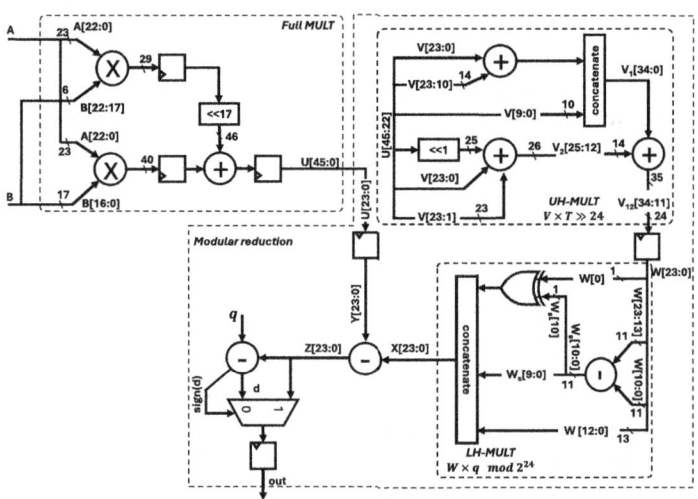

Fig. 4. Dilithium modular reduction module [34].

where, the concatenation from the MSB on the left to the LSB on the right is denoted by the *concat* function.

$$V_2[25:0] = 2V[23:0] + V[23:0] + V[23:1]$$
$$= (V[23:0] << 1) + V[23:0] + V[23:1]$$
$$V \times T = 2^{13}V_1[34:0] + 2V_2[25:0] + V[0]$$
$$= 2(2^{12}V_1[34:0] + V_2[25:0]) + V[0]$$
$$= concat\{V_1[34:0] + V_2[25:12], V_2[11:0], V[0]\}$$
$$V_{12} = V_1[34:0] + V_2[25:12]$$

Now, the output of the UH-MULT is computed as:

$$W[23:0] = (V \times T) >> 24$$
$$= V_{12}[34:11]$$

Next, the lower half multiplier (LH-MULT) manages the multiplication of $W[23:0]$ by Dilithium prime modulus q.

$$W \times q = W[23:0] \times (2^{23} - 2^{13} + 1)$$
$$= 2^{13}(2^{10}W[23:0] - W[23:0]) + W[23:0]$$
$$= concat\{2^{10}W[23:0] - W[23:0] + W[23:10], W[12:0]\}$$
$$X[23:0] = (W[23:0] \times q) \bmod 2^{24}$$
$$= concat\{2^{10}W[0] - W[10:0] + W[23:13], W[12:0]\}$$
$$W_s[10:0] = W[23:13] - W[10:0]$$

Then, the output of the LH-MULT is computed as:

$$X[23:0] = concat\{2^{10}W[0] + W_s[10:0], W[12:0]\}$$
$$= concat\{W[0] \oplus W_s[10], W_s[9:0], W[12:0]\}$$

The X value in fact represents the multiples of q that is closest to the LSB of the input to the reduction module Y. Finally, X is subtracted from Y at the output of the LH-MULT sub-block and stored in Z. A multiplexer is needed in case $Z \geq q$. The design consists of 4 pipeline stages, the first two are deployed within the full multiplier (inside the DSPs). The third pipeline stage is located at the output of the UH-MULT sub-block. To respect the timing, a pipeline stage is added on the LSB of the input to the reduction module $U[23:0]$. The fourth and final pipeline stage is placed at the output of the modular reduction block.

Kyber. Similar to the Barrett reduction for Dilithium, the one for Kyber is optimized for the specific prime $q = 3329$, where the parameter $l = 12$ and the constant $T = 5039$. Figure 5 first shows a full multiplication between two 12-bit integers A and B which takes place within a single DSP slice. The modular reduction then follows the steps in Algorithm 1. Using the same optimization techniques as in the Barrett reduction of Dilithium, multiplication by constants (T, q) needs only addition, subtraction, xor and shift operations.

The reduction operation is divided into two parts. The upper half multiplier (UH-MULT) sub-block handles the multiplication of the most-significant bits of the full multiplier $V = U[23:11]$ by the constant value T:

$$\begin{aligned}
V \times T &= V[12:0] \times (2^{12} + 2^9 + 2^8 + 2^7 + 2^5 + 2^3 + 2^2 + 2 + 1) \\
&= 2^5(2^7 V[12:0] + V[12:0]) + 2^2(2^7 V[12:0] + V[12:0]) \\
&\quad + 2(2^7 V[12:0] + V[12:0]) + (2^7 V[12:0] + V[12:0]) + 2^3 V[12:0] \\
V_1[20:0] &= 2^7 V[12:0] + V[12:0] \\
&= concat\{V[12:0] + V[12:7], V[6:0]\} \\
V \times T &= 2^5 V_1[20:0] + 2^2 V_1[20:0] + 2 V_1[20:0] + V_1[20:0] + 2^3 V[12:0] \\
&= 2^5 V_1[20:0] + 2(2 V_1[20:0] + V_1[20:0] + V_1[20:1]) + V_1[0] \\
&\quad + 2^3 V[12:0] \\
V_2[22:0] &= 2 V_1[20:0] + V_1[20:0] + V_1[20:1] \\
&= (V_1[20:0] << 1) + V_1[20:0] + V_1[20:1] \\
V \times T &= 2^5 V_1[20:0] + 2 V_2[22:0] + V_1[0] + 2^3 V[12:0] \\
&= concat\{V_1[20:0] + V_2[22:4], V[12:2], V[1:0] + V_2[3:2], V_2[1:0], \\
&\quad V_1[0]\} \\
V_{12} &= V_1[20:0] + V_2[22:4] + V[12:2]
\end{aligned}$$

Now, the output of the UH-MULT is computed as:

$$\begin{aligned}
W[12:0] &= (V \times T) >> 13 \\
&= V_{12}[21:8]
\end{aligned}$$

Next, the lower half multiplier (LH-MULT) manages the multiplication of $W[12:0]$ by Kyber prime modulus q.

$$\begin{aligned}
W \times q &= W[23:0] \times (2^{12} - 2^9 - 2^8 + 1) \\
&= 2^8(2^4 W[12:0] - 2W[12:0] - W[12:0]) + W[12:0] \\
&= concat\{2^4 W[12:0] - 2W[12:0] - W[12:0] + W[12:8], W[7:0]\} \\
X[12:0] &= (W[12:0] \times q) \bmod 2^{13} \\
&= concat\{2^4 W[0] - 2W[3:0] - W[4:0] + W[12:8], W[7:0]\} \\
W_s[4:0] &= W[12:8] - 2W[3:0] - W[4:0]
\end{aligned}$$

Then, the output of the LH-MULT is computed as:

$$X[12:0] = concat\{2^4W[0] + W_s[4:0], W[7:0]\}$$
$$= concat\{W[0] \oplus W_s[4], W_s[3:0], W[7:0]\}$$

The X value in fact represents the multiples of q that is closest to the LSB of the input to the reduction module Y. Finally, X is subtracted from Y at the output of the LH-MULT sub-block and stored in Z. A multiplexer is needed in case $Z \geq q$. The design consists of 4 pipeline stages as in the Barrett reduction of Dilithium. In order to preserve timing between the different standards' implementations, two pipeline stages are used inside the full multiplier even though, one would have been enough in the case of Kyber. The third and fourth pipeline stages are placed similar to the Dilithium Barrett reduction module.

3.4 Butterfly Unit

A compact fully pipelined butterfly architecture that supports all polynomial operations leveraging resource sharing is demonstrated in Fig. 6. It is inspired by the work of Pham et al. [34] where one of the four deployed computational elements efficiently implements the CT and the GS butterfly operations as well as the remaining arithmetic operations, such as addition, subtraction, pointwise multiplication and multiply-accumulate. The BFU unit is configured to operate in 4 modes (NTT/MAC, ADD/SUB, PWM and INTT) using only the 2 LSBs of the mode signal controlling the BFU 2X1 module. Since the MAC operation is basically the same as one NTT butterfly operation, but with outputs only from b_0 and not b_0 and b_1 so they both share mode[1:0] of 0. Similarly, the ADD and SUB operations are both done internally only outputed on different

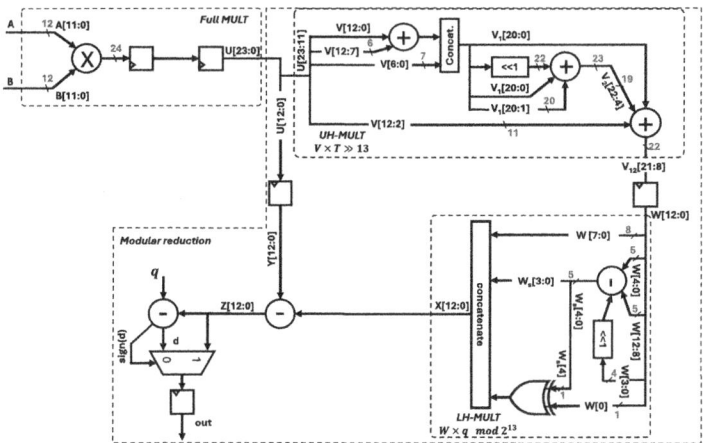

Fig. 5. Kyber modular reduction module.

outputs and they have the same mode[1:0] = 1 within the BFU block. They only differ at the BFU 2X1 level where we need the full 3-bit mode to route the correct outputs. These different modes of operations are facilitated by the integration of 9 q-bit 2-MUXs. The butterfly module also comprises a modular reduction block after the multiplication is performed. It uses the optimized form of Barrett reduction as detailed in Sect. 3.3. Instead of multiplying with 256^{-1} in the last step of the INTT, a divide-by-2 operation is incorporated inside the BFU module. This division operation only requires low-cost shift, addition and multiplexer blocks as explained in [42]. For all target standards, the BFU block is instantiated in the same way, only the sizes of the signals are adapted to each standard's data width and the corresponding Barrett reduction block is called explicitly for each standard. The BFU block performs its operations as follows. For NTT, the $b_0 = a_0 + a_1 \cdot z_0 \bmod q$ and $b_1 = a_0 - a_1 \cdot z_0 \bmod q$, where a_0 and a_1 are the input coefficients and the twiddle factor (stored in a distributed memory in the order of its fetch request) is applied to the z_0 input. The INTT operation is carried out as $b_0 = (a_0 + a_1)/2 \bmod q$ and $b_1 = (a_0 - a_1) \cdot z_0^{-1}/2 \bmod q$. In this case to compute z_0^{-1}, the twiddle factor is loaded from the memory in reverse order (at the layer level) and subtracted from q, allowing the reuse of the twiddle factors of NTT. This is inline with the symmetry property of the twiddle factor $\zeta^{k+n} = -\zeta^k$ where k is an integer. For modular multiplication, the factors are the inputs a_1 and z_0, whereas input a_0 is only used to accumulate the product of previous multiplications in case of the MAC mode (used for matrix-vector and vector-vector polynomial multiplications). As for modular addition and subtraction, the polynomial coefficients are entered through the inputs a_0 and a_1 that have direct access to the adder/subtracter blocks through a few independent multiplexers and FFs. Similar to the NTT, INTT and multiplication operations, a few extra registers are required to balance the pipeline latency. For NTT, INTT and MAC operations, the latency is 7 clock cycles. As for PWM, ADD and SUB operations, the latency is 6, 3 and 3 clock cycles, respectively. The cost of NTT/INTT operations is $n/4 \cdot \log n + c$ clock cycles whereas that of the other operations is $n/2 + c$, where c is the latency.

3.5 Address Controller

The address controller module is responsible for generating the read/write addresses of the polynomial coefficients for all six operations as well as the read addresses of the twiddle factors in the case of NTT/INTT. It also provides the select signals to the data and address multiplexers connected to the external RAM blocks. It supports all target standards by simple and inexpensive tweaks. In the case of NTT/INTT, two main factors affect how the address controller block generates the read addresses according to the required standard. The first is the number of NTT levels $\log n$ whether it is even or odd. The second factor is whether the NTT fully splits into degree 0 polynomials or not as in Kyber. Since the design consists of two parallel butterfly units, four polynomial coefficients are processed per clock cycle. For any standard, the read addresses of every four coefficients in each two successive levels are the same, only in different order.

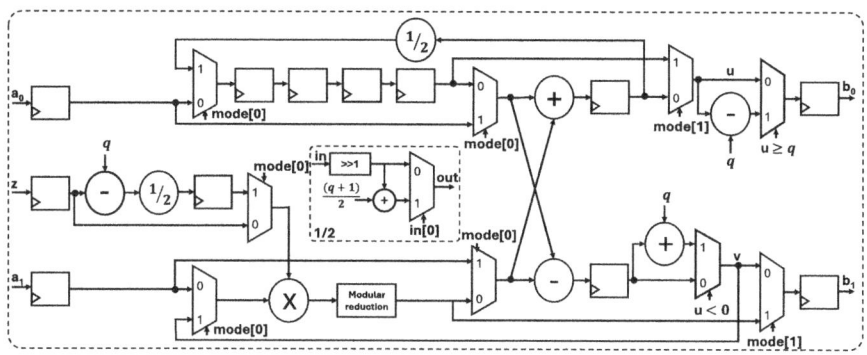

Fig. 6. Butterfly unit block diagram.

The first and fourth coefficients remain unchanged and only the second and third ones that switch places between even and odd stages. Figure 7 illustrates the read address call sequences of the twiddle factors for the NTT/INTT operation and the polynomial coefficients for all operations applicable to Dilithium as an example of a standard that has a fully splitting polynomial ring and the number of its NTT levels is even. Two brackets per line represent address(es) of polynomial coefficients (or twiddle factors) required by the two BFUs. Regarding NTT/INTT, four addresses of different coefficients from the same polynomial and two twiddle factor addresses are generated. As for the remaining operations, a single address is produced per BFU since they operate on the same coefficient in two different polynomials placed in different memories.

If the number of NTT levels is odd, read address generation for all successive pairs of the NTT stages remain the same as explained before. However, the coding of addresses of the last stage which is odd is different. In a fully-splitting NTT, the last stage must process consecutively ordered coefficients. Finally for Kyber where the NTT does not fully split, the modification is quite trivial where the level count stops at $\log n - 1$, but the read address generation remains unchanged.

Since the polynomial coefficients are placed in a data RAM designed as a four-bank memory, the read addresses generated so far need to be mapped to real RAM addresses as presented in [23,42] using an integrated address resolver block within the address controller module. The bank address for selecting the memory banks and the new addresses of the coefficients are computed as follows:

$$BankAddr = \sum_{i=0}^{\lceil \frac{1}{2}\log_2(n) \rceil - 1} RawAddr[2i+1:2i] \bmod 4$$

$$NewAddr = RawAdrr \gg 2,$$

where i is the bit position. This guarantees a conflict-free memory access.

To generate the write addresses, one straightforward method is to use shift registers to propagate the read addresses for the necessary number of clock cycles

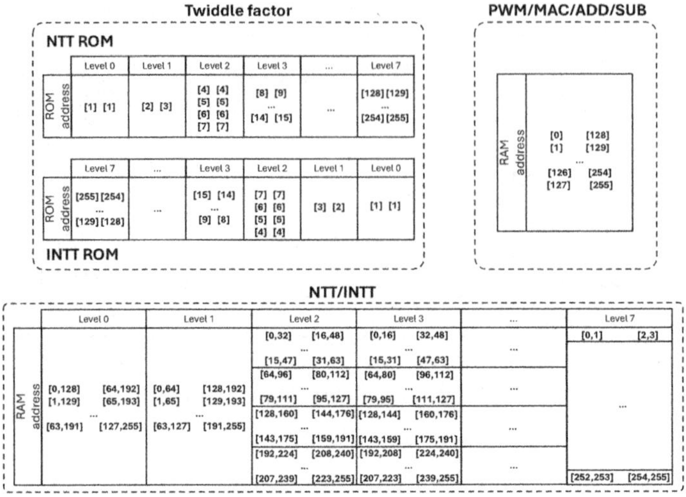

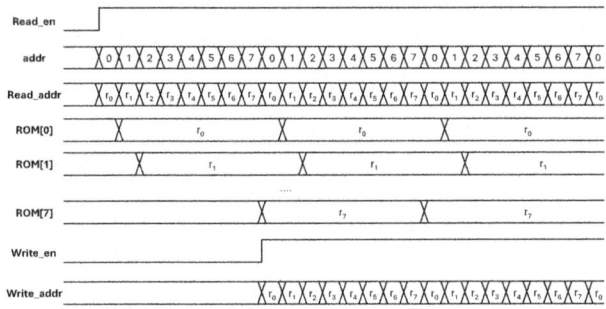

Fig. 7. Address generation of twiddle factors and polynomial coefficients for standards supporting fully-splitting NTT with even number of levels.

Fig. 8. Write address generation timing diagram for an NTT operation.

according to the pipeline depth of each operation. However instead of delaying the read addresses, we opted to store them in a small ROM (distributed memory) of length that equals the maximum pipeline depth (which is that of the NTT/INTT operation). The address of this ROM is a simple 3-bit counter. The polynomial coefficient read addresses are written inside the ROM upon a read enable signal. Similarly, the write addresses are read from the ROM upon a write enable signal that is activated after the pipeline is fulfilled for each operation. Figure 8 shows the timing diagram of the write operation taking the pipeline depth of the NTT/INTT as an example.

4 Implementation Results

Our proposed architecture was implemented on an Xilinx XC7A100T Artix-7 FPGA using Vivado 2022.1. For each standard, post-place and route (PnR) simulations using the Vivado simulator were performed. Table 2 details the resource utilization of our butterfly and modular reduction (MR) units and compares them to the state-of-the-art. Our Dilithium BFU is similar to the first control element (CE0) of [34]. The nubmer of required LUTs is slightly higher as for the number of FFs, we report 48% more because we deploy registers at the input and output of the BFU whereas in [34] they do not show these registers in their FF count, but from their NTT latency it is evident that they also implement these registers, but most probably at a higher level. Compared to [33]'s lookup-table-based modular reduction, our Kyber MR unit needs 64% more LUTs and only 4 more FFs. In [11] the number of LUTs and FFs of the BFU are almost the same for both Dilithium and Kyber. This is because the authors unified the butterfly unit to support multiple lattice-based PQC schemes at run time. Our Dilithium and Kyber BFUs (that are tailored at design time) require 43% and 65% less LUTs and similar percentages less FFs, respectively. Table 3 shows the implementation results of the polynomial arithmetic unit and comparison with state-of-the-art.

Table 2. Detailed Resource utilization comparison with state-of-the-art implementations of the butterfly and the modular reduction units.

Work	Module	LUT	FF	DSP	Work	Module	LUT	FF	DSP
	Dilithium					Kyber			
[34]	BFU	351	209	2	[33]	BFU			
	⌊ MR	69	71	0		⌊ MR	50	34	0
[11]	BFU	705	488	8	[11]	BFU	703	474	8
	⌊ MR					⌊ MR			
★	**BFU**	**400**	**310**	**2**	★	**BFU**	**241**	**167**	**1**
	⌊ **MR**	**114**	**72**	**0**		⌊ **MR**	**82**	**39**	**0**

For Dilithium, our proposed architecture fairly occupies overall less resources compared to other existing implementations. It requires 2604 LUTs, 770 FFs and 4 DSPs. Since our design targets low-cost area-constraint applications, we opted to optimize each sub-block individually while promoting resource sharing wherever possible. Using the same FPGA, Nguyen et al. [32] designed a configurable high-speed NTT accelerator suitable for both Dilithium and Kyber and supports both radix-2 and radix-4 MDC NTT operation. Compared to their radix-2 implementation, our design occupies 2.85× less LUTs and 6.85× less FFs, at the expense of an extra 4 DSPs. Land et al. [23] proposed a mid-range implementation that focused on optimizing the usage of LUTs and FFs by exploiting DSPs

Table 3. Resource utilization comparison with state-of-the-art implementations of the poly arithmetic unit.

Work	Plat.	n	$\lceil log_2(q) \rceil$	Resources				Freq. [MHz]	Latency (CCs)		
				LUT	FF	DSP	BRAM		NTT	INTT	PWM
Dilithium											
[32]	A7	256	23	7451	5275	0	0	180	319	319	
[23]	A7	256	23	5676	1218	41	1	311	533	536	
[5]	VUS+	256	23	4509	3146	8	0				
[43]	Z7000	256	23	2812	1748	10	2		296	296	
[17]	ZUS+	256	23	2759	2037	4	7		606	614	147
[34]	ZUS+	256	23	2637	1071	8	1	385	268	268	
[38]	Z7000	256	23	2386	932	8	1	217	264		
[11]	A7	256	23	2119	1058	8	3	117	1052	1318	3688
⋆	A7	256	23	2604	770	4	0	100	519	519	134
Hawk											
⋆	A7	512	31	3801	1135	8	0	83	1159	1159	262
		512	31	3968	1135	8	0	83	1159	1159	262
		1024	31	4287	1139	8	0	83	2567	2567	518
		1024	31	4451	1139	8	0	83	2567	2567	518
Raccoon											
⋆	A7	512	24	3194	912	4	0	83	1159	1159	262
		512	25	3458	998	4	0	83	1159	1159	262
Kyber											
[32]	A7	256	12	4834	4683	0	1	250	247	247	
[11]	V7	256	12	2128	1144	8	3	174	922	1184	3812
[39]	A7	256	12	1579	1058	2	3		512	448	256
[31]	A7	256	12	1416	1074	2	1.5	227	448	448	256
[33]	A7	256	12	1154	1031	2	0	300	456	456	265
[40]	A7	256	12	948	352	1	2.5	190	904	904	3359
[41]	A7	256	12	609	640	2	4	257	490	490	
⋆	A7	256	12	1583	458	2	0	100	455	455	134
Polka											
⋆	A7	1024	16	2512	593	2	0	100	2567	2567	518

available in low-end FPGAs. Their design consists of three modules (NTT based on two radix-2 BFUs, Multiply-Accumulate and Matrix-Vector Mult.) that collectively perform the poly arithmetic functions. Our design needs 2× less LUTs, 1.6× less FFs and far less DSPs. A single BRAM is needed to store the twiddle factors whereas we decided to use a distributed ROM instead. In [5] the authors targeted a high-performance implementation. They use a radix-4 2 × 2 NTT

BFU arrangement to speed up the NTT and INTT operations. As a result, their design requires 1.7×, 4× and 2× more LUTs, FFs and DSPs than our design, respectively. Zhao et al. [43] proposed a compact and high-speed hardware design that employs four BFUs in a radix-2 R2MDC NTT architecture. Our design utilizes slightly less LUTs, 2.3× less FFs and 2.5× less DSPs. The two BRAMs are reportedly used to store the twiddle factors and to replace large shift registers (required by the R2MDC NTT). The work by Gupta et al. [17] reports a lightweight hardware implementation that invested in resource and control logic sharing as well as pre-computed LUTs among other optimization strategies. Their design requires two radix-2 BFUs and two 64×256 dual-port RAMs to transfer internal computations of NTT in a ping-pong fashion until all the layers have been processed. Our design requires slightly less LUTs, 2.6× less FFs and the same number of DSPs. As for the BRAM cost, their design uses 7 BRAMs, however, it is not clear how they are exploited. The polynomial arithmetic module introduced in [34] targets a lightweight hardware implementation even though it implements a radix-4 NTT. Our design employs almost the same number of LUTs and 1.4× less FFs, but half the DSPs. Wang et al. [38] targets a high-performance efficient design that uses a radix-4 NTT block. Among the reported state-of-the-art, Wang's implementation is the smallest even though it requires 4 BFUs. Yet, our design still uses less FFs (18%), slightly higher LUTs (9%) and half the DSPs. An interesting implementation by [11] offers both run-time and compile-time configurability to cover a wide base of parameter sets (n and q) and performance requirements of various platforms. Compared to their one BFU implementation, our design uses 23% more LUTs, but it requires 27% less FFs and half the DSPs. Our design can run at a maximum frequency of 100 MHz on Artix-7 FPGA. Indeed, this is less than the state-of-the-art reported frequencies. Nevertheless, they mostly used high-speed FPGAs and targeted efficient high-performance applications. In addition, our target is area-constrained applications, therefore the maximum frequency requirement can be relaxed. We also provide latency figures for all polynomial operations which admittedly lie mid-range the state-of-the-art spectrum.

For Kyber, our proposed architecture requires 1583 LUTs, 458 FFs and 2 DSPs. Compared to the configurable design of Nguyen et al. [32], our implementation needs 1.9× less LUTs, 7.9× less FFs at the expense of an extra 2 DSPs. Compared to the one BFU implementation of [11], our design uses 1.3× less LUTs, 1.88× less FFs and 4× less DSPs. Xing et al. [39] implemented a compact hardware design. Our design needs slightly more LUTs, but 2.3× less FFs. Works such as [31,33] opted to rearrange the order of the polynomial coefficients at all NTT/INTT stages instead of changing the data addresses to access the coefficients stored in the RAMs in a conflict-free memory access fashion. This requires the use of a reordering unit that also acts a temporary memory to hold coefficients after each stage. Their design eliminates the need for additional memory usage in the iterative NTT design claiming to simplify the control logic. Our design again requires slightly more LUTs, but 2.3× less FFs. Yaman et al. [40] proposed three different hardware architectures (lightweight, balanced, high-performance), we compare our work to their lightweight implementation that employs one BFU. Indeed their design occupies 1.67× less LUTs, 23% less FFs and half the DSPs compared to ours. Zhang et al. [41] reported an efficient implementation that favors a ping-pong memory access to read/write the polynomial coefficients from/to the block RAMs. Their approach avoids read/write conflicts without the cost of reordering the coefficients. Indeed, our design occupies 2.3× more LUTs, but 1.4× less FFs which makes the overall resource utilization in favor of [41]. Also, the maximum frequency of most reported works is higher than ours which is 100 MHz even though all implementations are done on the same Artix-7 FPGA. As for the latency of the NTT and INTT operations, they are quite comparable to similar designs that use two butterflies. Regarding the point-wise multiplication we report nearly half the clock cycles compared to similar works. This is because the polynomial arithmetic unit does not compute the last step of polynomial multiplication needed after NTT. It is left to be implemented on the upper level. We also provide the resource utilization for Hawk, Raccoon and Polka, but comparison to the literature was not possible since there is no available hardware implementations that we know of.

A cautionary note, since the block RAMs used to store the coefficients are shared among other higher level modules, they are not considered part of the BRAM cost within the poly arithmetic unit in our design and in most state-of-the-art works.

5 Conclusion

This paper presents a lightweight polynomial arithmetic hardware architecture for post-quantum digital signatures and KEMs, suitable for low-cost and area-constrained applications. Our approach uses an in-place NTT without reordering of coefficients during the NTT and INTT operations, which reduces the complexity and the area cost of the control unit. In addition, storing the NTT twiddle factors in LUTs avoids occupying unnecessary BRAM footprint and reusing them during INTT avoids redundancy. The proposed architecture also establishes a straightforward address generation mechanism with simple conflict-free memory access which further facilitates the usage of lower resources. For most algorithms, our work utilizes fewer hardware resources than state-of-the-art lightweight implementations.

Acknowledgment. François-Xavier Standaert is a senior research associate of the Belgian Fund for Scientific Research (F.R.S.-FNRS). This work has been funded in part by the European Research Council (ERC) Advanced Grant BRIDGE (number 101096871). Views and opinions expressed are those of the authors and do not necessarily reflect those of the European Union or the ERC. Neither the European Union nor the granting authority can be held responsible for them.

References

1. CERG, dilithium. https://github.com/GMUCERG/Dilithium
2. Avanzi, R., et al.: CRYSTALS,-kyber algorithm specifications and supporting documentation (version 3.02). https://pq-crystals.org/kyber/data/kyber-specification-round3-20210804.pdf
3. Azouaoui, M., et al.: Protecting dilithium against leakage revisited sensitivity analysis and improved implementations. IACR Trans. Cryptogr. Hardw. Embed. Syst. **2023**(4), 58–79 (2023). https://doi.org/10.46586/TCHES.V2023.I4.58-79
4. Bai, S., et al.: CRYSTALS,-dilithium algorithm specifications and supporting documentation (version 3.1). https://pq-crystals.org/dilithium/data/dilithium-specification-round3-20210208.pdf
5. Beckwith, L., Nguyen, D.T., Gaj, K.: High-performance hardware implementation of crystals-dilithium. In: 2021 International Conference on Field-Programmable Technology (ICFPT), pp. 1–10 (2021). https://doi.org/10.1109/ICFPT52863.2021.9609917
6. Bernstein, D.J., Persichetti, E.: Towards KEM unification. Cryptology ePrint Archive, Paper 2018/526 (2018), https://eprint.iacr.org/2018/526
7. Bisheh-Niasar, M., Azarderakhsh, R., Kermani, M.M.: High-speed ntt-based polynomial multiplication accelerator for crystals-kyber post-quantum cryptography. IACR Cryptol. ePrint Arch, p. 563 (2021), https://eprint.iacr.org/2021/563
8. Bos, J.W., et al.: HAWK version 1.0.2, September 26 2024. https://hawk-sign.info/hawk-spec.pdf
9. Chen, L., et al.: Report on post quantum cryptography. https://nvlpubs.nist.gov/nistpubs/ir/2016/NIST.IR.8105.pdf, April 2016, nathional Institute of Standards and Technology, Technical Report, NIST IR 8105
10. Chen, Z., Karabulut, E., Aysu, A., Ma, Y., Jing, J.: An efficient non-profiled side-channel attack on the crystals-dilithium post-quantum signature. In: 39th IEEE International Conference on Computer Design, ICCD 2021, Storrs, CT, USA, 24–27 October 2021, pp. 583–590. IEEE (2021). https://doi.org/10.1109/ICCD53106.2021.00094
11. Derya, K., Mert, A.C.,Öztürk, E., Savaş, E.: CoHA-NTT: a configurable hardware accelerator for NTT-based polynomial multiplication. Cryptology ePrint Archive, Paper 2021/1527 (2021), https://eprint.iacr.org/2021/1527
12. Ducas, L., et al.: Crystals-dilithium: a lattice-based digital signature scheme. IACR Trans. Cryptogr. Hardw. Embed. Syst. **2018**(1), 238–268 (2018). https://doi.org/10.13154/TCHES.V2018.I1.238-268
13. Ducas, L., Postlethwaite, E.W., Pulles, L.N., van Woerden, W.P.J.: Hawk: module LIP makes lattice signatures fast, compact and simple. In: Agrawal, S., Lin, D. (eds.) Advances in Cryptology - ASIACRYPT 2022 - 28th International Conference on the Theory and Application of Cryptology and Information Security, Taipei, Taiwan, 5–9 December 2022, Proceedings, Part IV, LNCS, vol. 13794, pp. 65–94. Springer (2022). https://doi.org/10.1007/978-3-031-22972-5_3
14. Duval, S., Méaux, P., Momin, C., Standaert, F.: Exploring crypto-physical dark matter and learning with physical rounding towards secure and efficient fresh re-keying. IACR Trans. Cryptogr. Hardw. Embed. Syst. **2021**(1), 373–401 (2021). https://doi.org/10.46586/TCHES.V2021.I1.373-401
15. Eum, S., Lee, M., Seo, H.: Optimizing hawk signature scheme performance on armv8. Appl. Sci. **14**(19) (2024). https://doi.org/10.3390/app14198647

16. Guerreau, M., Martinelli, A., Ricosset, T., Rossi, M.: The hidden parallelepiped is back again: Power analysis attacks on falcon. IACR Trans. Cryptogr. Hardw. Embed. Syst. **2022**(3), 141–164 (2022). https://doi.org/10.46586/TCHES.V2022.I3.141-164
17. Gupta, N., Jati, A., Chattopadhyay, A., Jha, G.: Lightweight hardware accelerator for post-quantum digital signature crystals-dilithium. IEEE Trans. Circuits Syst. I Regul. Pap. **70**(8), 3234–3243 (2023). https://doi.org/10.1109/TCSI.2023.3274599
18. Hoffmann, C., Libert, B., Momin, C., Peters, T., Standaert, F.: POLKA: towards leakage-resistant post-quantum cca-secure public key encryption. In: Boldyreva, A., Kolesnikov, V. (eds.) Public-Key Cryptography - PKC 2023 - 26th IACR International Conference on Practice and Theory of Public-Key Cryptography, Atlanta, GA, USA, 7–10 May 2023, Proceedings, Part I, LNCS, vol. 13940, pp. 114–144. Springer (2023). https://doi.org/10.1007/978-3-031-31368-4_5
19. Kamel, D., Standaert, F., Bronchain, O.: Information theoretic evaluation of raccoon's side-channel leakage. IACR Commun. Cryptol. **1**(3), 44 (2024)
20. Kannwischer, M.J., Genêt, A., Butin, D., Krämer, J., Buchmann, J.: Differential power analysis of XMSS and SPHINCS. In: Fan, J., Gierlichs, B. (eds.) Constructive Side-Channel Analysis and Secure Design - 9th International Workshop, COSADE 2018, Singapore, 23–24 April 2018, Proceedings, LNCS, vol. 10815, pp. 168–188. Springer (2018). https://doi.org/10.1007/978-3-319-89641-0_10
21. Karabulut, E., Aysu, A.: FALCON down: breaking FALCON post-quantum signature scheme through side-channel attacks. In: 58th ACM/IEEE Design Automation Conference, DAC 2021, San Francisco, CA, USA, 5–9 December 2021, pp. 691–696. IEEE (2021). https://doi.org/10.1109/DAC18074.2021.9586131
22. Kim, S., Lee, K., Cho, W., Cheon, J.H., Rutenbar, R.A.: Fpga-based accelerators of fully pipelined modular multipliers for homomorphic encryption. In: Andrews, D., Cumplido, R., Feregrino, C., Platzner, M. (eds.) 2019 International Conference on ReConFigurable Computing and FPGAs, ReConFig 2019, Cancun, Mexico, 9–11 December 2019, pp. 1–8. IEEE (2019). https://doi.org/10.1109/RECONFIG48160.2019.8994793
23. Land, G., Sasdrich, P., Güneysu, T.: A hard crystal - implementing dilithium on reconfigurable hardware. In: Grosso, V., Pöppelmann, T. (eds.) Smart Card Research and Advanced Applications - 20th International Conference, CARDIS 2021, Lübeck, Germany, 11–12 November 2021, Revised Selected Papers, LNCS, vol. 13173, pp. 210–230. Springer (2021). https://doi.org/10.1007/978-3-030-97348-3_12
24. Liu, Y.K., Moody, D.: Post-quantum cryptography, and the quantum future of cybersecurity. https://doi.org/10.1103/PhysRevApplied.21.040501, April 2024, nathional Institute of Standards and Technology,Physical Review Applied
25. Longa, P., Naehrig, M.: Speeding up the number theoretic transform for faster ideal lattice-based cryptography. In: Foresti, S., Persiano, G. (eds.) Cryptology and Network Security - 15th International Conference, CANS 2016, Milan, Italy, 14–16 November 2016, Proceedings. LNCS, vol. 10052, pp. 124–139 (2016). https://doi.org/10.1007/978-3-319-48965-0_8
26. Lyubashevsky, V.: Fiat-shamir with aborts: applications to lattice and factoring-based signatures. In: Matsui, M. (ed.) Advances in Cryptology - ASIACRYPT 2009, 15th International Conference on the Theory and Application of Cryptology and Information Security, Tokyo, Japan, 6–10 December 2009, Proceedings. LNCS, vol. 5912, pp. 598–616. Springer (2009). https://doi.org/10.1007/978-3-642-10366-7_35

27. Lyubashevsky, V.: Lattice signatures without trapdoors. In: Pointcheval, D., Johansson, T. (eds.) Advances in Cryptology - EUROCRYPT 2012 - 31st Annual International Conference on the Theory and Applications of Cryptographic Techniques, Cambridge, UK, 15–19 April 2012. Proceedings. LNCS, vol. 7237, pp. 738–755. Springer (2012). https://doi.org/10.1007/978-3-642-29011-4_43
28. Marzougui, S., Ulitzsch, V., Tibouchi, M., Seifert, J.: Profiling side-channel attacks on dilithium: a small bit-fiddling leak breaks it all. IACR Cryptol. ePrint Arch, p. 106 (2022), https://eprint.iacr.org/2022/106
29. National Institute of Standards and Technology: Module-lattice-based digital signature standard. Technical Report, Federal Information Processing Standards Publications (FIPS PUBS) 204, U.S. Department of Commerce, Washington, D.C. (2024). https://doi.org/10.6028/NIST.FIPS.204
30. National Institute of Standards and Technology: Module-lattice-based key-encapsulation mechanism standard. Technical Report, Federal Information Processing Standards Publications (FIPS PUBS) 203, U.S. Department of Commerce, Washington, D.C. (2024). https://doi.org/10.6028/NIST.FIPS.203
31. Nguyen, T.H., Dam, D.T., Duong, P.P., Kieu-Do-Nguyen, B., Pham, C.K., Hoang, T.T.: Efficient hardware implementation of the lightweight crystals-kyber. IEEE Trans. Circ. Syst. I: Regular Papers 1–13 (2024). https://doi.org/10.1109/TCSI.2024.3443238
32. Nguyen, T., Kieu-Do-Nguyen, B., Pham, C., Hoang, T.: High-speed NTT accelerator for crystal-kyber and crystal-dilithium. IEEE Access **12**, 34918–34930 (2024). https://doi.org/10.1109/ACCESS.2024.3371581
33. Ni, Z., Khalid, A., Liu, W., O'Neill, M.: Towards a lightweight crystals-kyber in fpgas: an ultra-lightweight bram-free NTT core. In: IEEE International Symposium on Circuits and Systems, ISCAS 2023, Monterey, CA, USA, 21–25 May 2023, pp. 1–5. IEEE (2023). https://doi.org/10.1109/ISCAS46773.2023.10181340
34. Pham, T.X., Duong-Ngoc, P., Lee, H.: An efficient unified polynomial arithmetic unit for crystals-dilithium. IEEE Trans. Circuits Syst. I Regul. Pap. **70**(12), 4854–4864 (2023). https://doi.org/10.1109/TCSI.2023.3316393
35. del Pino, R., Prest, T., Rossi, M., Saarinen, M.O.: High-order masking of lattice signatures in quasilinear time. In: 44th IEEE Symposium on Security and Privacy, SP 2023, San Francisco, CA, USA, 21–25 May 2023, pp. 1168–1185. IEEE (2023). https://doi.org/10.1109/SP46215.2023.10179342
36. Pöppelmann, T., Oder, T., Güneysu, T.: High-performance ideal lattice-based cryptography on 8-bit atxmega microcontrollers. In: Lauter, K.E., Rodríguez-Henríquez, F. (eds.) Progress in Cryptology - LATINCRYPT 2015 - 4th International Conference on Cryptology and Information Security in Latin America, Guadalajara, Mexico, 23–26 August 2015, Proceedings. LNCS, vol. 9230, pp. 346–365. Springer (2015). https://doi.org/10.1007/978-3-319-22174-8_19
37. Shor, P.: Algorithms for quantum computation: discrete logarithms and factoring. In: Proceedings 35th Annual Symposium on Foundations of Computer Science, pp. 124–134 (1994). https://doi.org/10.1109/SFCS.1994.365700
38. Wang, T., Zhang, C., Cao, P., Gu, D.: Efficient implementation of dilithium signature scheme on fpga soc platform. IEEE Trans. Very Large Scale Integr. (VLSI) Syst. **30**(9), 1158–1171 (2022). https://doi.org/10.1109/TVLSI.2022.3179459
39. Xing, Y., Li, S.: A compact hardware implementation of cca-secure key exchange mechanism CRYSTALS-KYBER on FPGA. IACR Trans. Cryptogr. Hardw. Embed. Syst. **2021**(2), 328–356 (2021). https://doi.org/10.46586/TCHES.V2021.I2.328-356

40. Yaman, F., Mert, A.C., Öztürk, E., Savas, E.: A hardware accelerator for polynomial multiplication operation of CRYSTALS-KYBER PQC scheme. In: Design, Automation & Test in Europe Conference & Exhibition, DATE 2021, Grenoble, France, 1–5 February 2021, pp. 1020–1025. IEEE (2021). https://doi.org/10.23919/DATE51398.2021.9474139
41. Zhang, C., Liu, D., Liu, X., Zou, X., Niu, G., Liu, B., Jiang, Q.: Towards efficient hardware implementation of ntt for kyber on fpgas. In: 2021 IEEE International Symposium on Circuits and Systems (ISCAS), pp. 1–5 (2021). https://doi.org/10.1109/ISCAS51556.2021.9401170
42. Zhang, N., Yang, B., Chen, C., Yin, S., Wei, S., Liu, L.: Highly efficient architecture of newhope-nist on FPGA using low-complexity NTT/INTT. IACR Trans. Cryptogr. Hardw. Embed. Syst. **2020**(2), 49–72 (2020). https://doi.org/10.13154/TCHES.V2020.I2.49-72
43. Zhao, C., et al.: A compact and high-performance hardware architecture for crystals-dilithium. IACR Trans. Cryptogr. Hardw. Embed. Syst. **2022**(1), 270–295 (2022). https://doi.org/10.46586/TCHES.V2022.I1.270-295
44. Zhou, S., Xue, H., Zhang, D., Wang, K., Lu, X., Li, B., He, J.: Preprocess-then-ntt technique and its applications to kyber and newhope. In: Guo, F., Huang, X., Yung, M. (eds.) Information Security and Cryptology - 14th International Conference, Inscrypt 2018, Fuzhou, China, 14–17 December 2018, Revised Selected Papers. LNCS, vol. 11449, pp. 117–137. Springer (2018). https://doi.org/10.1007/978-3-030-14234-6_7

Efficient Error Detection Methods for the Number Theoretic Transforms in Lattice-Based Algorithms

Mohamed Abdelmonem[1,2](✉), Lukas Holzbaur[2], Håvard Raddum[1], and Alexander Zeh[2]

[1] Simula UiB, Bergen, Norway
{mohameda,haavardr}@simula.no
[2] Infineon Technologies AG, Munich, Germany
{lukas.holzbaur,alexander.zeh}@infineon.com

Abstract. The Number Theoretic Transform (NTT) is a crucial component in many post-quantum cryptographic (PQC) algorithms, enabling efficient polynomial multiplication. However, the reliability of NTT computations is an important concern, especially for safety-critical applications. This work presents novel techniques to improve the fault tolerance of NTTs used in prominent PQC schemes such as Kyber, Dilithium, and Falcon. The work first establishes a theoretical framework for error detection in NTTs, exploiting the inherent algebraic properties of these transforms. It derives necessary and sufficient conditions for constructing error-detecting vectors that can identify single faults without the need for costly recomputation. For the Dilithium scheme, the work further advances the state-of-the-art by developing the first algorithm capable of detecting up to two maliciously placed faults. The proposed error detection methods are shown to reduce the number of required multiplications by half, leading to significant improvements in computational efficiency compared to existing single error-detecting algorithms. Concrete implementations for Kyber, Dilithium, and Falcon demonstrate the practicality and effectiveness of the error-detection scheme.

Keywords: Error Detection · Fault Countermeasures · Lattice-Based Cryptography · Number Theoretic Transform · Post-Quantum Cryptography

1 Introduction

The advent of quantum computing poses a significant challenge to the security of current cryptographic systems. Traditional public-key cryptography, which underpins much of today's digital security infrastructure, relies on the computational difficulty of problems such as integer factorization and the discrete logarithm problem. Algorithms such as RSA are fundamental to secure communications but are vulnerable to quantum attacks by Shor's algorithm [18], which can solve these problems in polynomial time on a sufficiently large quantum computer. In particular, long-lived products such as automotive microcontrollers, as well as sensitive data with long shelf life, need to be secured now against the future threat of quantum computers.

This threat has catalyzed the development of Post-Quantum Cryptography (PQC), which aims to establish secure cryptographic protocols in the face of quantum computing capabilities. In 2016, the National Institute of Standards and Technology (NIST) announced a competition to standardize PQC alternatives, and in July 2022, they selected four algorithms. Three of these four algorithms are from the class of lattice-based schemes, i.e., they rely on complex problems over lattices for their security. The lattices in these schemes are represented by elements of a polynomial ring, and arithmetic over this ring, therefore, plays a crucial role in their execution. The Number Theoretic Transform (NTT) is used to speed up this arithmetic, particularly the multiplication of polynomials. This approach is a generalization of the Fast Fourier Transform (FFT), which has long been established in fields such as signal processing. Since a significant part of the computational complexity of these algorithms lies in the NTT, it is a prime candidate for hardware acceleration, and many papers in the literature have proposed such accelerators [4,7,13–15].

While considerable efforts have been made to provide fast and lean NTT accelerators, the issue of fault tolerance has received little attention. The importance of this is described in [16], where the authors identify a critical vulnerability in the NTT, which enables practical key recovery and message recovery attacks on Kyber KEM, as well as existential forgery and verification bypass attacks on the Dilithium signature scheme.

In safety-critical applications, such as those in the industrial sectors, error resilience is an essential feature that the hardware must provide. This can be achieved by recomputation techniques as presented in [17]. On the other hand, these techniques are traditionally price-sensitive, so the additional chip area required for these features should be minimal. However, current approaches that guarantee error detection, such as those introduced by Sarker et al. [17], impose a large area (or latency) overhead as they rely on recomputation.

This paper addresses this gap by investigating and developing new methods for error-resilient NTT computation. By exploiting insights from existing error detection techniques in FFT computation and adapting them to the NTT context, this work aims to improve the fault tolerance of lattice-based algorithms without incurring prohibitive overheads.

1.1 Related Work

In [17], the authors introduced the first error detection architecture for the NTT. Their technique is based on recomputation, which ensures the detection of any number of computational faults. However, it does not address errors during data loading and storage and significantly increases the computational complexity, requiring $N/2 \log N$ additional multiplications, where N is the ring degree.

Since the hardware architecture of the NTT and the FFT are quite similar as they both rely on a network of so-called butterfly operations, many well-studied techniques used to detect faults in the FFT can be applied to the NTT as well.

In 1988, Jou and Abraham [11] introduced the first algorithm-based fault tolerance (ABFT) scheme, which does not rely on recomputation. Instead, they encode the inputs and decode the outputs of the FFT. Afterwards, they compare these two results. If there is no error, the encoded inputs and decoded outputs should be equal; if there is an error, they should not. The authors use the sum of a normal Discrete Fourier Transform (DFT) and a rotated DFT as the encoder and derive the decoder accordingly. Based on that, the authors in [1] present their similar error detection algorithm on the NTT. It requires only N additional multiplications. Despite this efficiency, it lacks proven error detection, making it less reliable and not able to prevent faults in malicious attacker models.

In [19,20], the authors use weighted checksums for encoding and decoding, which means they multiply the outputs by an error-detection vector, multiply the inputs by the FFT of that vector, and compare the results. This method guarantees the detection of single errors with low overhead. The technique presented in [3] for the NTT is similar to that. Here the authors use polynomial evaluation and interpolation to protect the computation of the NTT against fault injection attacks. It requires the execution of $2N - 1$ additional multiplications, guarantees the detection of at least one fault, and offers the potential for probabilistic detection of additional faults if these faults are to occur randomly. The method described in [3] can be seen as a special case of the method presented in this work for single error detection. However, it requires twice the number of multiplications and is only introduced in the case of a single error, whereas our method can be extended to detect multiple errors efficiently.

In [10], the authors provide methods for the protection of arithmetic operations in lattice-based cryptography, including the NTT, against side-channel and fault attacks. They do this by using the redundant number representation (RNR) described in [21], which introduces redundancy by expanding the modulus q. Its effectiveness and cost depend heavily on the hardware architecture. Unlike the probabilistic detection of this method, our approach guarantees the detection of up to two faults.

1.2 Contribution

Our error detection technique extends concepts used in [19,20] for the FFT to the NTT. This paper shows that single error-detection vectors exist for NTT with complete splitting, as used in Dilithium and Falcon, and NTT without complete splitting, as used in Kyber. We have also provided a concrete choice for these error-detecting vectors, which are more general than the one presented in [3]. Our choice of error-detecting vectors also requires fewer multiplications, namely N instead of $2N$. Furthermore, our work introduces the necessary and

Table 1. Comparison of different NTT Error Detection Techniques.

Method	Error Detection	Mult
[17]	Calculation errors guaranteed, load/store errors not	$N/2 \log N$
[1]	Probabilistic	N
[3]	One guaranteed	$2N$
This work	One guaranteed	N
	Two guaranteed	$2.5N$

sufficient conditions that guarantee the detection of two errors in Theorem 4. Using this, we introduced the first non-recomputation-based technique that can detect every error that results from injecting faults on two different wires in the NTT network for Dilithium while requiring only $2.5N$ additional multiplications, even if these faults are maliciously placed. This balance of efficiency and reliability makes our method particularly suitable for applications in fault-sensitive environments. Similar to [3], our method is also compatible with masking and shuffling countermeasures. Table 1 provides a comparative analysis of various NTT error detection techniques.

1.3 Notation

In this paper, we use the ring $R_q = \mathbb{Z}_q[X]/(X^N + 1)$, where q is a prime number satisfying $q \equiv 1 \mod 2N$ and N being a power of two. The following notation is used throughout this document:

- **Scalars** are denoted by lowercase italic letters, e.g., a, b, c.
- **Vectors** are denoted by bold lowercase letters, e.g., $\mathbf{v}, \mathbf{w}, \mathbf{x}$.
- **Matrices** are denoted by bold uppercase letters, e.g., $\mathbf{A}, \mathbf{B}, \mathbf{C}$.
- **Polynomials** are denoted by lowercase roman letters, e.g., $\text{f}(X), \text{g}(X), \text{h}(X)$.

The coefficients in $\mathbb{Z}_q$ of the polynomial $\text{f}(X) = f_0 + f_1 X + \ldots + f_{N-1} X^{N-1} \in R_q$ are $f_0, f_1, \ldots, f_{N-1}$. Additionally, a polynomial $\text{f}(X)$ is assumed to define a vector $\mathbf{f}$ by its coefficients, i.e., $\mathbf{f} = \begin{pmatrix} f_0 & f_1 & \cdots & f_{N-1} \end{pmatrix}$.

2 Preliminaries

2.1 Number Theoretic Transform

The NTT is a powerful technique for polynomial multiplication that exploits the properties of modular arithmetic to achieve efficient computation. The essence of the NTT is to decompose the multiplication task into operations on lower-degree polynomials, ideally scalars, and then combine these results to obtain the final product.

Let $R_q = \mathbb{Z}_q[X]/(X^N + 1)$, as defined in Sect. 1.3. Then the negative cyclic NTT (which is commonly used in lattice-based algorithms since it can be implemented efficiently) of a polynomial $f \in R_q$ is defined by its evaluation at the odd powers of the $2N$th root of unity ω_{2N}

$$\mathsf{NTT}(f) := \begin{pmatrix} \hat{f}_0 & \hat{f}_1 & \hat{f}_2 & \cdots & \hat{f}_{N-1} \end{pmatrix} \tag{1}$$
$$:= \begin{pmatrix} f(\omega_{2N}^1) & f(\omega_{2N}^3) & f(\omega_{2N}^5) & \cdots & f(\omega_{2N}^{2N-1}) \end{pmatrix}. \tag{2}$$

This definition allows us to look at the NTT as a linear transform similar to the DFT, where

$$\hat{f}_j = \sum_{i=0}^{N-1} \omega_{2N}^{(2j+1)i} f_i. \tag{3}$$

Given the matrix

$$\mathbf{A} = \begin{pmatrix} 1 & \omega_{2N}^1 & \omega_{2N}^2 & \cdots & \omega_{2N}^{N-1} \\ 1 & \omega_{2N}^3 & \omega_{2N}^{3 \cdot 2} & \cdots & \omega_{2N}^{3 \cdot (N-1)} \\ 1 & \omega_{2N}^5 & \omega_{2N}^{5 \cdot 2} & \cdots & \omega_{2N}^{5 \cdot (N-1)} \\ \vdots & \vdots & \vdots & \ddots & \vdots \\ 1 & \omega_{2N}^{(2N-1)} & \omega_{2N}^{(2N-1) \cdot 2} & \cdots & \omega_{2N}^{(2N-1) \cdot (N-1)} \end{pmatrix} \tag{4}$$

the NTT of a vector $\mathbf{f} \in \mathbb{Z}_q^N$ can written as

$$\hat{\mathbf{f}} = \mathbf{f}\mathbf{A}.$$

The inverse Number Theoretic Transform (INTT) is the interpolation polynomial defined by the evaluation points $(\omega_{2N}^1, \hat{f}_1), (\omega_{2N}^3, \hat{f}_3), \ldots, (\omega_{2N}^{2N-1}, \hat{f}_{2N-1})$. It can also be written as a linear transform

$$f_i = \frac{1}{N} \sum_{j=0}^{N-1} \omega_{2N}^{-(2i+1)j} \hat{f}_j. \tag{5}$$

It is well known that the product of two polynomials $h = f \cdot g \in R_q$ can be calculated using the NTT and INTT

$$h = \mathsf{INTT}\left[\mathsf{NTT}(f) \circ \mathsf{NTT}(g)\right], \tag{6}$$

where $\circ$ is component-wise multiplication. In addition to that, the NTT can be calculated similarly to the FFT with a Cooley-Tukey algorithm [6], making it run in quasi-linear time. This means that the product can be calculated in time $\mathcal{O}(N \log N)$ instead of $\mathcal{O}(N^2)$.

This is achieved by using the ring isomorphism

$$\mathbb{Z}_q[X]/\left(X^{\frac{N}{2^l}} - \omega_{2N}^{\frac{N}{2^l}}\right) \longrightarrow \mathbb{Z}_q[X]/\left(X^{\frac{N}{2^{l+1}}} - \omega_{2N}^{\frac{N}{2^{l+1}}}\right) \times \mathbb{Z}_q[X]/\left(X^{\frac{N}{2^{l+1}}} + \omega_{2N}^{\frac{N}{2^{l+1}}}\right),$$
$$p(X) \mapsto \left[p(X) \mod \left(X^{\frac{N}{2^{l+1}}} - \omega_{2N}^{\frac{N}{2^{l+1}}}\right), p(X) \mod \left(X^{\frac{N}{2^{l+1}}} + \omega_{2N}^{\frac{N}{2^{l+1}}}\right)\right],$$

for $l = 0, \ldots, \log_2(N) - 1$, since

$$p(X) \mod X^{N/2^{l+1}} - \omega_{2N}^{N/2^{l+1}} = \sum_{i=0}^{N/2^{l+1}-1} (p_i + \omega_{2N}^{N/2^{l+1}} p_{i+N/2^{l+1}}) X^i \qquad (7)$$

and

$$p(X) \mod X^{N/2^{l+1}} + \omega_{2N}^{N/2^{l+1}} = \sum_{i=0}^{N/2^{l+1}-1} (p_i - \omega_{2N}^{N/2^{l+1}} p_{i+N/2^{l+1}}) X^i. \qquad (8)$$

hold. Calculations (7) and (8) can be done simultaneously in one single butterfly unit as displayed in Fig. 1. This leads to a butterfly network consisting of $\log N$ layers of butterfly operations where the output of one layer is the input to the next, starting with the input vector and ending with the output vector, as shown in Fig. 2. Each layer consists of $N/2$ butterfly units, so to calculate a complete NTT $N/2 \log_2 N$ butterfly operations are needed.

Note that this split is possible because ω_{2N} is a $2N$th root of unity. If we are given only an Nth root of unity ω_N, then the last split is impossible. In this case we end up with $N/2$ linear polynomials

$$f(X) \mod X^2 - \omega_N^{2j+1}, \qquad j = 0, 1, \ldots, N/2 - 1. \qquad (9)$$

Equation (6) can still be applied here, but instead of doing N scalar multiplications, we have to perform $N/2$ multiplications of linear polynomials followed by reductions modulo the quadratic polynomials in (9). This leads to the following well-known result that an incomplete NTT can be calculated with two half-sized complete NTTs.

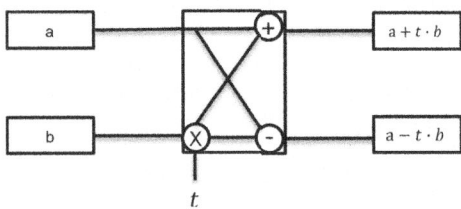

Fig. 1. Cooley-Tukey Butterfly.

Lemma 1. *Let* $f(X)$ *be an N-degree polynomial, and* $f^{(even)}(X)$ *and* $f^{(odd)}(X)$ *be $N/2$-degree polynomials with the even/odd coefficients of* $f(X)$

$$f^{(even)}(X) = f_0 + f_2 X^2 + \cdots + f_{N-2} X^{N-2},$$
$$f^{(odd)}(X) = f_1 X + f_3 X^3 + \cdots + f_{N-1} X^{N-1}.$$

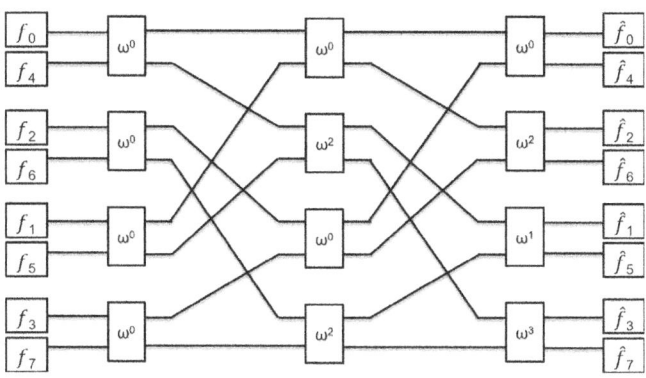

Fig. 2. Cooley-Tukey Butterfly Network for $N = 8$.

Let $\hat{\mathbf{f}}^{(lin)}$ and $\hat{\mathbf{f}}^{(const)}$ be the linear/constant part of the output of the incomplete NTT

$$\hat{\mathbf{f}} = \hat{\mathbf{f}}^{(lin)} X + \hat{\mathbf{f}}^{(const)}$$

Then using half-sized complete NTTs

$$\hat{\mathbf{f}}^{(const)} = \mathsf{NTT}(\mathrm{f}^{(even)}) \quad and \quad \hat{\mathbf{f}}^{(lin)} = \mathsf{NTT}(\mathrm{f}^{(odd)})$$

holds.

Proof. We have

$$\hat{\mathbf{f}} = \mathrm{f}(X) \mod X^2 - \omega_{2N}^j$$
$$= \sum_{i=0}^{N/2-1} f_i^{(even)} X^{2i} \mod X^2 - \omega_{2N}^j + \sum_{i=0}^{N/2-1} f_i^{(odd)} X^{2i+1} \mod X^2 - \omega_{2N}^j$$
$$= \sum_{i=0}^{N/2-1} f_i^{(even)} X^{2i} \mod X^2 - \omega_{2N}^j + X \sum_{i=0}^{N/2-1} f_i^{(odd)} X^{2i} \mod X^2 - \omega_{2N}^j$$
$$= \mathsf{NTT}(\mathrm{f}^{(even)}) + X\mathsf{NTT}(\mathrm{f}^{(odd)}).$$

□

2.2 NIST Standards

Dilithium [2] is a general-purpose lattice-based digital signature scheme based on the Module Learning with Errors (M-LWE) problem. It has been selected for standardization by NIST under the name ML-DSA [8]. The ring modulus is $q = 8380417$, and the ring degree is $N = 256$. Signatures are generated through several polynomial multiplications, typically arranged in matrix form.

The security levels of Dilithium are determined by the size of these matrices, with larger matrices providing stronger security.

Falcon [9] is another digital signature algorithm NIST will also standardize for scenarios where Dilithium signature sizes may be too large. Falcon uses a ring modulus $q = 12289$ and offers two levels of security: Falcon-I with a ring degree of $N = 512$ and Falcon-V with a ring degree of $N = 1024$. The NTT is used in the key generation, signature generation, and signature verification routines.

Kyber [5] is a lattice-based key encapsulation mechanism based on the M-LWE problem. It has been selected for standardization by NIST under the name ML-KEM [12]. The ring modulus is $q = 3329$, and the ring degree is $N = 256$. In contrast to Dilithium and Falcon, the ring used in Kyber has no $2N$th root of unity but an Nth root of unity. However, as we showed in the previous chapter, this allows us to do an incomplete NTT, which can be done with two NTTs of size $N = 128$.

3 Error Detection

In this section, we introduce our error detection method, beginning with a description of the fault and attacker model. Based on this model, we present our single fault detection technique for complete NTTs and explain its applicability to the Kyber cryptographic scheme. Additionally, we highlight how our method relates to the similar approach presented in [3]. Following this, we describe the first non-recomputation-based technique capable of detecting two errors for Dilithium and conjecture that they also exist for Kyber and Falcon, even under a strong attacker model. Since the only difference between the NTT and the inverse NTT is that ω is replaced by its inverse and an additional scaling factor of $1/N$, all the concepts we will present in the following sections can be adapted to the inverse NTT as well.

3.1 Fault Model

As discussed in Sect. 2.1, the NTT is computed in multiple layers, each consisting of a fixed number of butterfly operations. These layers are typically computed sequentially, with intermediate results stored and loaded from memory. We start with some assumptions on our fault model, which are the same as in [11,19,20]. We assume that additive errors in loading, storing, or calculating a value can occur within a single NTT network butterfly unit, as shown in Fig. 3. The errors can occur either due to random hardware faults or error injection by malicious attackers. Errors of type $\{2, 5\}$ can be considered equivalent to errors of type $\{8\}$, and errors of type $\{3, 6\}$ equivalent to errors of type $\{9\}$. Therefore, we only need to consider errors occurring at each butterfly's inputs and outputs. We also distinguish between two attacker models. A weak attacker can only inject faults at random locations, and a strong attacker can control the location and the error value.

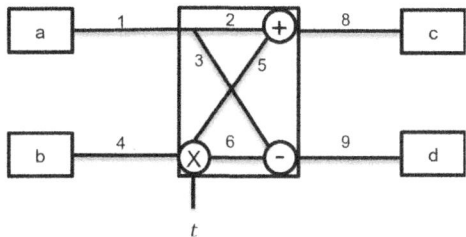

Fig. 3. Illustration of the Fault Model.

An NTT network of dimension N consists of $\log_2 N$ layers. The inputs to the 0th layer are $f_0, \ldots, f_{N-1}$, while $\hat{f}_0, \ldots, \hat{f}_{N-1}$ form the outputs of the $(\log_2 N)$th layer. Each layer contains N wires. For each layer $l = 0, \ldots, \log_2 N$, we can express the wth wire uniquely as

$$w = \frac{N}{2^l}\mu_1 + \mu_2, \tag{10}$$

where $\mu_1 \in \{0, \ldots, 2^l - 1\}$ and $\mu_2 \in \{0, \ldots, N/2^l - 1\}$. This representation is advantageous as it illustrates the propagation of an error through the network until it reaches the output layer, as seen in Fig. 4. If an error happens at the line (l, w), it will affect all outputs with index

$$m = 2^l m_1 + m_2 \tag{11}$$

where $m_2 = \mu_1$ and $m_1 \in \{0, \ldots, N/2^l - 1\}$.

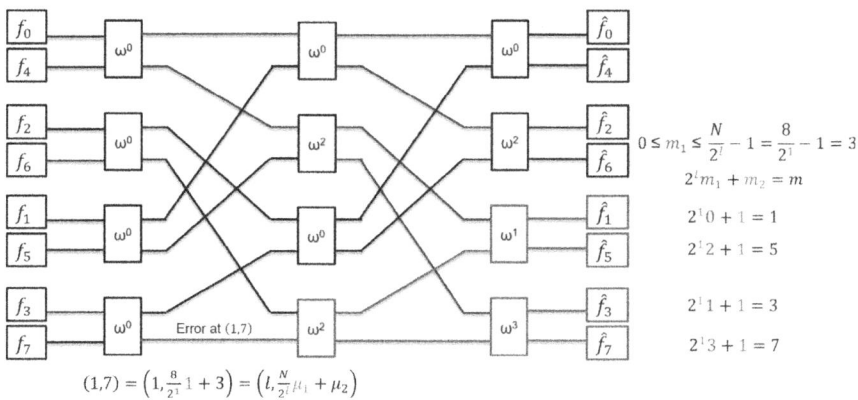

Fig. 4. Error Propagation in the NTT Network. Error occurring in $(l, \frac{N}{2^l}\mu_1 + \mu_2)$ affects all outputs where $m \bmod 2^l = \mu_1$.

We now derive the exact value that a propagated error has on the output layer.

Definition 1. *For a given* $(l, w) \in \{0, \ldots, \log N\} \times \{0, \ldots, N-1\}$ *the* **error function** $\mathbf{E}^{(l,w)}(e) = [E_0^{(l,w)}(e), \ldots, E_{N-1}^{(l,w)}(e)]$, *is defined for each* $e \in \mathbb{Z}_q$ *by the expression*

$$E_m^{(l,w)}(e) = E_{2^l m_1 + m_2}^{(l, \frac{N}{2^l}\mu_1 + \mu_2)}(e) = \begin{cases} e \sum_{r=0}^{\frac{N}{2^l}-1} \omega_{2N}^{(2(2^l r + \mu_1)+1)\mu_2} & \text{if } m_2 = \mu_1, \\ 0 & \text{if } m_2 \neq \mu_1, \end{cases} \quad (12)$$

where $(l, m_1, m_2, \mu_1, \mu_2)$ *are defined as in* (10) *and* (11).

We proceed to demonstrate that (12) is the error at the output layer after one fault has been injected. We show this by applying the same techniques used in [19] on the FFT.

Theorem 1. *A fault* $e \in \mathbb{Z}_q$ *injected on line* $(l, \frac{N}{2^l}\mu_1 + \mu_2)$ *will cause the error vector* $\mathbf{E}^{(l,w)}(e)$, *i.e.*,

$$NTT_{faulty}(\mathbf{f}) = NTT(\mathbf{f}) + \mathbf{E}^{(l,w)}(e). \quad (13)$$

Proof. Consider the mth output of the NTT given by

$$\hat{f}_m = \sum_{n=0}^{N-1} f_n \omega_{2N}^{n \cdot (2m+1)}, \quad \text{for } 0 \leq m < N.$$

Decomposing m and n as

$$m = 2^l m_1 + m_2,$$
$$n = \frac{N}{2^l} n_1 + n_2,$$

with $0 \leq m_2, n_1 < 2^l$ and $0 \leq m_1, n_2 < N/2^l$, we can express $\hat{f}_m$ as

$$\hat{f}_m = \hat{f}_{2^l m_1 + m_2}$$

$$= \sum_{n=0}^{N-1} f_n \omega_{2N}^{n(2(2^l m_1 + m_2)+1)}$$

$$= \sum_{n_2=0}^{\frac{N}{2^l}-1} \sum_{n_1=0}^{2^l-1} f_{\frac{N}{2^l}n_1 + n_2} \omega_{2N}^{(2(2^l m_1 + m_2)+1)(\frac{N}{2^l}n_1 + n_2)}$$

$$= \sum_{n_2=0}^{\frac{N}{2^l}-1} \left[\sum_{n_1=0}^{2^l-1} f_{\frac{N}{2^l}n_1 + n_2} \omega_{2N}^{(2(2^l m_1 + m_2)+1)(\frac{N}{2^l}n_1)} \right] \omega_{2N}^{(2(2^l m_1 + m_2)+1)n_2}$$

$$= \sum_{n_2=0}^{\frac{N}{2^l}-1} \underbrace{\left[\sum_{n_1=0}^{2^l-1} f_{\frac{N}{2^l}n_1 + n_2} \omega_{2N}^{(2m_2+1)\frac{N}{2^l}n_1} \right]}_{\frac{N}{2^l}m_2 + n_2 \text{ output of the } l\text{th stage}} \omega_{2N}^{(2(2^l m_1 + m_2)+1)n_2}.$$

Let $\hat{\mathbf{f}}'$ be the NTT output with an error $e \in \mathbb{Z}_q$ in line $(l, \frac{N}{2^l}\mu_1 + \mu_2)$. Then it will affect only the outputs whose indices have the form $2^l m_1 + \mu_1$. This gives

$$\hat{f}'_{2^l m_1 + m_2} = \hat{f}_{2^l m_1 + m_2},$$

when $\mu_1 \neq m_2$ and when $\mu_1 = m_2$ holds:

$$\hat{f}'_{2^l m_1 + m_2} = \sum_{n_2=0}^{\frac{N}{2^l}-1} \left[\sum_{n_1=0}^{2^l-1} f_{\frac{N}{2^l}n_1 + n_2} \omega_{2N}^{(2m_2+1)\frac{N}{2^l}n_1} + \omega_{2N}^{(2(2^l m_1 + m_2)+1)n_2} \right]$$

$$+ e \sum_{r=0}^{\frac{N}{2^l}-1} \omega_{2N}^{(2(2^l r + \mu_1)+1)\mu_2}$$

$$= \hat{f}_{2^l m_1 + m_2} + e \sum_{r=0}^{\frac{N}{2^l}-1} \omega_{2N}^{(2(2^l r + \mu_1)+1)\mu_2}$$

$$= \hat{f}_m + E_m^{(l,w)}(e).$$

□

It should be noted that in the context of our fault model, a single fault is defined as a single faulty butterfly unit. An alternative attack vector could be to falsify the value of a single twiddle factor, which would be loaded on multiple butterflies, or a zeroization of all twiddle factors, using a single targeted attack, as demonstrated in [16]. In our fault model, this would result in multiple faulty butterflies. We will show in Sect. 3.3 that, in this case, errors will be detected with $1 - 1/q$ probability.

3.2 Single Error Detection

Error detection is achieved by encoding the NTT's input, decoding the output, and then comparing the two results. We need to show that if no error has occurred, the encoded input and decoded output will match; conversely, if a single error has occurred, they will not.

Let the output of the NTT be denoted by the vector $\hat{\mathbf{f}} = \begin{pmatrix} \hat{f}_0 & \hat{f}_1 & \cdots & \hat{f}_{N-1} \end{pmatrix}^T$, and let the error detecting vector be $\mathbf{a} = \begin{pmatrix} a_0 & a_1 & \cdots & a_{N-1} \end{pmatrix}$. We compute the error detection value over the output as

$$C_{\text{out}} := \mathbf{a}\hat{\mathbf{f}}. \tag{14}$$

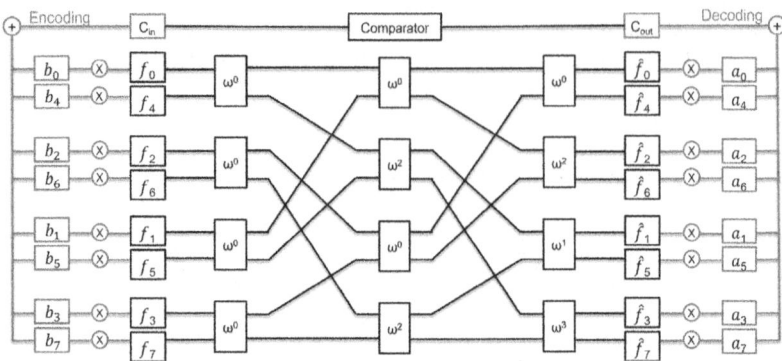

Fig. 5. Proposed error detection technique in which the inputs and outputs of the NTT are pointwise multiplied by vectors **b** and **a**, respectively. The resulting sums are then compared.

To determine the error detection value for the input, we substitute the definition of the NTT for $\hat{\mathbf{f}}$

$$C_{\text{out}} = \begin{pmatrix} a_0 & a_1 & \cdots & a_{N-1} \end{pmatrix} \underbrace{\begin{pmatrix} 1 & \omega_{2N}^{(2\cdot 0+1)\cdot 1} & \cdots & \omega_{2N}^{(2\cdot 0+1)\cdot (N-1)} \\ 1 & \omega_{2N}^{(2\cdot 1+1)\cdot 1} & \cdots & \omega_{2N}^{(2\cdot 1+1)\cdot (N-1)} \\ \vdots & \vdots & \ddots & \vdots \\ 1 & \omega_{2N}^{(2\cdot(N-1)+1)\cdot 1} & \cdots & \omega_{2N}^{(2\cdot(N-1)+1)\cdot (N-1)} \end{pmatrix}}_{=:\begin{pmatrix} b_0 & b_1 & \cdots & b_{N-1} \end{pmatrix}} \begin{pmatrix} f_0 \\ f_1 \\ \vdots \\ f_{N-1} \end{pmatrix}.$$

(15)

We define the input to the comparator as:

$$C_{\text{in}} := \mathbf{b}\mathbf{f}. \tag{16}$$

This way, we guarantee that if no error occurs, $C_{\text{in}} = C_{\text{out}}$ holds. The question is whether $C_{\text{in}} \neq C_{\text{out}}$ holds for any **a** when an error occurs. In the following theorem, we provide necessary and sufficient conditions on the choice of **a** so that no single error can go undetected.

Theorem 2. *An error* $e \in \mathbb{Z}_q \backslash \{0\}$ *occurring at line* $(l, \frac{N}{2^l}\mu_1 + \mu_2) \in \{0, \ldots, \log_2 N\} \times \{0, \ldots, N-1\}$ *is detectable with a vector* $\mathbf{a} = (a_0, \ldots, a_{N-1}) \in \mathbb{Z}_q^N$ *if and only if the sum* $S^l_{\frac{N}{2^l}\mu_1 + \mu_2}(\mathbf{a})$ *defined by*

$$S^l_{\frac{N}{2^l}\mu_1 + \mu_2}(\mathbf{a}) := \sum_{r=0}^{\frac{N}{2^l}-1} \omega_{2N}^{(2(2^l r + \mu_1)+1)\mu_2} a_{2^l r + \mu_1} \tag{17}$$

is nonzero.

Proof. From Theorem 1 we know that $\hat{f}'_{2^l m_1 + m_2}$, the mth output the faulty NTT with $m = 2^l m_1 + m_2$ defined as in (11), is given by

$$\hat{f}'_m = \hat{f}_m + E_m^{(l,w)}(e).$$

Applying the definitions of C_{out}, C_{in} and taking their difference, we obtain

$$\begin{aligned}
C_{out} &= \sum_{m=0}^{N-1} \hat{f}'_m a_m \\
&= \sum_{m=0}^{N-1} \hat{f}_m a_m + E_m^{(l,w)}(e) a_m \\
&= \sum_{m=0}^{N-1} \hat{f}_m a_m + e \sum_{r=0}^{\frac{N}{2^l}-1} \omega_{2N}^{(2(2^l r + \mu_1)+1)\mu_2} a_{2^l r + \mu_1} \\
&= \sum_{m=0}^{N-1} \hat{f}_m a_m + e \cdot S^l_{\frac{N}{2^l} \mu_1 + \mu_2}(\mathbf{a})
\end{aligned}$$

and

$$\begin{aligned}
C_{in} &= \sum_{m=0}^{N-1} f_m b_m \\
&= \sum_{m=0}^{N-1} \hat{f}_m a_m.
\end{aligned}$$

Then we obtain:

$$C_{out} - C_{in} = e \cdot S^l_{\frac{N}{2^l} \mu_1 + \mu_2}(\mathbf{a}).$$

Therefore, an error is detectable if and only if this difference is nonzero, which is equivalent to the condition

$$S^l_{\frac{N}{2^l} \mu_1 + \mu_2}(\mathbf{a}) \neq 0.$$

□

The subsequent theorem provides conditions under which an error-detecting vector exists and describes a recursive method for constructing such a vector.

Theorem 3. *If the inequality $q > 2N - 1$ holds, then there exists at least one single error-detecting vector.*

Proof. We describe a constructive method for building such a vector that always works as long as $q > 2N - 1$. The idea is to choose the first term in every

$S^l_{\frac{N}{2^l}\mu_1+\mu_2}(\mathbf{a})$ such that the sum is nonzero. This will give us a number of restrictions on each element a_i. These restrictions are kept track of with sets $\mathbb{B}_i$ that will contain values that a_i can not take. In the end, we can simply pick values for a_i that avoid $\mathbb{B}_i$ for $0 \leq i \leq N-1$. We explain the process in more detail.

Starting with $l = \log_2 N$ and hence $\mu_2 = 0$, we have N sums (one for each $\mu_1 \in \{0, \ldots, N-1\}$), consisting of only one term

$$S^{\log_2 N}_{\mu_1}(\mathbf{a}) = \omega_{2N}^0 a_{\mu_1}.$$

By choosing all the elements of $\mathbf{a}$ to be nonzero, $S^{\log_2 N}_{\mu_1}(\mathbf{a})$ will be nonzero, hence we initialize all the sets $\mathbb{B}_{\mu_1} = \{0\}$ for $0 \leq \mu_1 \leq N-1$.

In the next step, $l = \log_2 N - 1$, we also have $N-1$ sums, but each sum has two terms, where the first term is always a_{μ_1}, with $\mu_1 \in \{0, \ldots, N/2 - 1\}$

$$S^{\log_2 N - 1}_{2\mu_1+\mu_2}(\mathbf{a}) = \omega_{2N}^{(2\mu_1+1)\mu_2} a_{\mu_1} + \omega_{2N}^{(2(\frac{N}{2}+\mu_1)+1)\mu_2} a_{\frac{N}{2}+\mu_1}.$$

We now fix a_i for $\frac{N}{2} \leq i \leq N-1$, to any value not in $\mathbb{B}_i$, i.e., anything nonzero. For the remaining indices, we now get two additional constraints

$$a_{\mu_1} \neq -\frac{\omega_{2N}^{(2(2^l+\mu_1)+1)\mu_2} a_{\frac{N}{2}+\mu_2}}{\omega_{2N}^{(2\mu_1+1)\mu_2}},$$

for $\mu_2 = 0, 1$. These two values are added to $\mathbb{B}_{\mu_1}$ for $0 \leq \mu_1 \leq N/2 - 1$. This process can be continued with $l = \log_2 N - 2$, which will fix a_i for $N/4 \leq i \leq N/2 - 1$ and add four values to $\mathbb{B}_{\mu_1}$ for $0 \leq \mu_1 \leq N/4 - 1$.

Finally, for $l = 0$ (and hence $\mu_1 = 0$), we get N forbidden values added to $\mathbb{B}_0$, in addition to the $\sum_{l=1}^{\log_2 N} \frac{N}{2^l}$ values that were added in previous stages, and all other a_i's have been fixed. All the values a_0 must avoid might be different, so the maximum size of $\mathbb{B}_0$ is

$$\sum_{l=0}^{\log_2(N)} \frac{N}{2^l} = 2N - 1, \tag{18}$$

and all other $\mathbb{B}_i$ will have smaller maximum sizes. So when $q > 2N - 1$, we are guaranteed that it will always be possible to choose $a_i \in \mathbb{Z}_q \setminus EX_i$ for all $i = 0, 1, \ldots, N-1$. □

Theorem 2 proves that if the conditions are fulfilled, suitable error detection vectors exist, thereby showing that it is possible to guarantee error detection for a wide selection of parameters. In practice, other vectors might be more suitable for implementation. In particular, for Kyber, Dilithium, and Falcon, it suffices to set $\mathbf{b} = (1\ 1\ \ldots\ 1)$ and $\mathbf{a} = \mathbf{bA}^{-1}$, because in this case $S^l_{\frac{N}{2^l}\mu_1+\mu_2}(\mathbf{a}) \neq 0$ holds for all l, mu_1, μ_2, as we will demonstrate in Sect. 4.1.

Application to Kyber. Using Lemma 1, we can apply our error detection method on Kyber as well by simply checking the two half-sized NTTs. That means our error-detecting vector has length $N/2$ but has to be used twice.

Error Detection Through Evaluation and Interpolation. In [3], the authors have derived an error detection technique based on polynomial evaluation and interpolation. This work has been done independently and during the same time as ours. The advantage of our scheme, aside from the reduction in the number of multiplications required, is that the general description of the method allows for an efficient extension to more than single errors, as shown in the next section. This technique can be seen as a special case of ours because the evaluation of the polynomial $f \in R_q$ at $u \in \mathbb{Z}_q$ is simply a checksum over the input coefficients of the NTT

$$w := f(u) = \sum_{i=0}^{N-1} f_i u^i. \tag{19}$$

Using Lagrangian interpolation, they do another checksum over the outputs of the NTT

$$w' := f(u) = \sum_{i=0}^{N-1} \hat{f}_i L_i(u), \tag{20}$$

where $L_i(x)$ is the ith Lagrange polynomial.

By setting
$$\mathbf{b} = \begin{pmatrix} b_0 & b_1 & \cdots & b_{N-1} \end{pmatrix} = \begin{pmatrix} u^0 & u^1 & \cdots & u^{N-1} \end{pmatrix}, \tag{21}$$

and
$$\mathbf{a} = \begin{pmatrix} a_0 & a_1 & \cdots & a_{N-1} \end{pmatrix} = \begin{pmatrix} L_0(u) & L_1(u) & \cdots & L_{N-1}(u) \end{pmatrix}, \tag{22}$$

for $i = 0, 1, \ldots, N-1$, we can see that their method is a special case of ours.

3.3 Double Error Detection

Since the NTT is linear, it is easy to see that the output error of two faults in the butterfly network is the same as the sum of the output errors of two single faults. That means if we apply the same error-detecting technique as in Chap. 3, we get

$$C_{out} - C_{in} = S_w^l(\mathbf{a})e_1 + S_\gamma^\lambda(\mathbf{a})e_2,$$

for two errors $e_1, e_2 \in \mathbb{Z}_q \backslash \{0\}$ that occur on the lines (l, w) and (λ, γ). The error will not be detected if

$$e_2 = -\frac{S_w^l(\mathbf{a})e_1}{S_\gamma^\lambda(\mathbf{a})}.$$

If e_2 is random and independent from e_1, the probability for that is $1/q$. This probability also holds for the case of more than two errors. Depending on the application, this might be sufficient. However, for settings requiring higher assurance of error detection or considering strong attackers with the ability to select the positions and values of the errors, stronger guarantees are required.

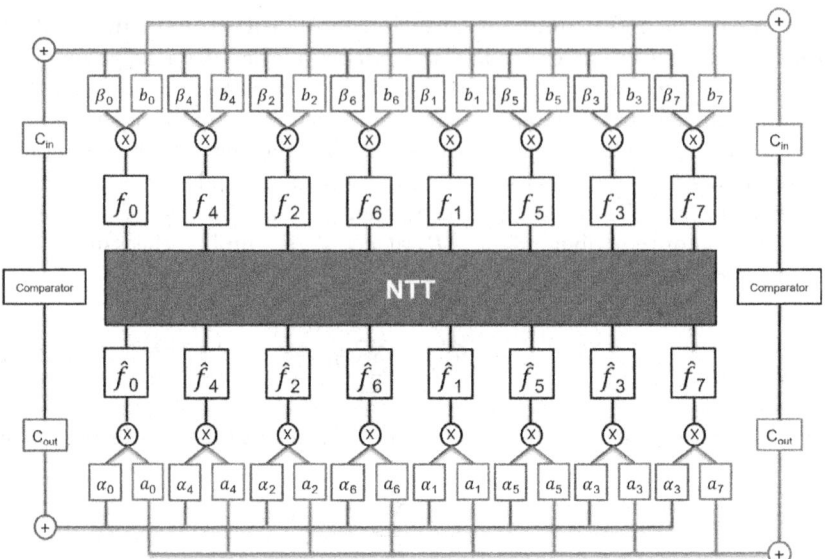

Fig. 6. Proposed error detection method for identifying two errors. The inputs are first pointwise multiplied by vectors **b** and β, and their sums are computed. These sums are then compared to the sum of the pointwise multiplication of the NTT output with vectors **a** and α.

If we want to detect any two errors with 100% probability, we must use two checksums, as shown in Fig. 6.

In the following theorem, we derive conditions on the two error-detecting vectors **a** and α so that two errors are always detected.

Theorem 4. *Two errors e_1 and e_2 occurring at lines (l, w) and (λ, γ) are detectable with two vectors $\mathbf{a} = (a_0, \ldots, a_{N-1}), \boldsymbol{\alpha} = (\alpha_0, \ldots, \alpha_{N-1}) \in \mathbb{Z}_q^N$ if and only if $S_w^l(\mathbf{a}) \neq 0$ and $S_\gamma^\lambda(\boldsymbol{\alpha}) \neq 0$ and*

$$S_w^l(\boldsymbol{\alpha}) S_\gamma^\lambda(\mathbf{a}) - S_w^l(\mathbf{a}) S_\gamma^\lambda(\boldsymbol{\alpha}) \neq 0. \tag{23}$$

Proof. If $(l, w) = (\lambda, \gamma)$, then the two errors can be regarded as one single error and will then be detected using only one vector. So, for the rest of the proof, we assume that the lines are distinct.

The errors will be detected if and only if

$$\begin{pmatrix} 0 \\ 0 \end{pmatrix} \neq \begin{pmatrix} C_{out}^1 - C_{in}^1 \\ C_{out}^2 - C_{in}^2 \end{pmatrix}.$$

We know

$$\begin{pmatrix} C^1_{out} - C^1_{in} \\ C^2_{out} - C^2_{in} \end{pmatrix} = \begin{pmatrix} S^l_w(\mathbf{a})e_1 + S^\lambda_\gamma(\mathbf{a})e_2 \\ S^l_w(\boldsymbol{\alpha})e_1 + S^\lambda_\gamma(\boldsymbol{\alpha})e_2 \end{pmatrix}$$
$$= \begin{pmatrix} S^l_w(\mathbf{a}) & S^\lambda_\gamma(\mathbf{a}) \\ S^l_w(\boldsymbol{\alpha}) & S^\lambda_\gamma(\boldsymbol{\alpha}) \end{pmatrix} \begin{pmatrix} e_1 \\ e_2 \end{pmatrix}.$$

Since $(e_1, e_2) \neq (0, 0)$ we know that

$$\begin{pmatrix} C^1_{out} - C^1_{in} \\ C^2_{out} - C^2_{in} \end{pmatrix} \neq \begin{pmatrix} 0 \\ 0 \end{pmatrix}$$

if and only if

$$\begin{vmatrix} S^l_w(\mathbf{a}) & S^\lambda_\gamma(\mathbf{a}) \\ S^l_w(\boldsymbol{\alpha}) & S^\lambda_\gamma(\boldsymbol{\alpha}) \end{vmatrix}$$
$$= S^l_w(\boldsymbol{\alpha})S^\lambda_\gamma(\mathbf{a}) - S^l_w(\mathbf{a})S^\lambda_\gamma(\boldsymbol{\alpha}) \neq 0.$$

□

Let

$$\mathbf{S} := \left(S^0_0(\mathbf{a})\ S^0_1(\mathbf{a})\ \cdots\ S^0_{N-1}(\mathbf{a})\ S^1_0(\mathbf{a})\ \cdots\ S^1_{N-1}(\mathbf{a})\ \cdots\ S^{\log_2 N}_0(\mathbf{a})\ \cdots\ S^{\log_2 N}_{N-1}(\mathbf{a}) \right),$$

$$\boldsymbol{\sigma} := \left(S^0_0(\boldsymbol{\alpha})\ S^0_1(\boldsymbol{\alpha})\ \cdots\ S^0_{N-1}(\boldsymbol{\alpha})\ S^1_0(\boldsymbol{\alpha})\ \cdots\ S^1_{N-1}(\boldsymbol{\alpha})\ \cdots\ S^{\log_2 N}_0(\boldsymbol{\alpha})\ \cdots\ S^{\log_2 N}_{N-1}(\boldsymbol{\alpha}) \right),$$

and

$$\mathbf{D} := (D(\mathbf{S}, \boldsymbol{\sigma})_{ij}) := (\mathbf{S}_i \boldsymbol{\sigma}_j - \mathbf{S}_j \boldsymbol{\sigma}_i) \in \mathbb{Z}_q^{N(\log_2 N+1) \times N(\log_2 N+1)}.$$

Now, (23) translates to $D(\mathbf{S}, \boldsymbol{\sigma})_{ij} \neq 0$ for $i \neq j$. Note that $\mathbf{D}$ is antisymmetric, meaning $D(\mathbf{S}, \boldsymbol{\sigma})_{ij} = -D(\mathbf{S}, \boldsymbol{\sigma})_{ji}$. That means

$$\binom{N(\log_2 N + 1)}{2} = \frac{(N(\log_2 N + 1) - 1)N(\log_2 N + 1)}{2}$$

inequalities have to be satisfied. Each of these conditions that are satisfied corresponds to a pair of wires in the NTT network and assures that any possible fault injection in these two wires will always be detected.

Similar to Theorem 3, we present here a sufficient condition that guarantees the existence of an error-detecting vector pair $\mathbf{a}$ and $\boldsymbol{\alpha}$ that satisfies the conditions in Theorem 4.

Theorem 5. *When $q > (2N - 1)N(\log_2 N + 1)$ there exists at least one pair $(\mathbf{a}, \boldsymbol{\alpha})$ such that $\mathbf{a}$ and $\boldsymbol{\alpha}$ will detect any two errors in the NTT computation.*

Proof. Let $s = |\mathbf{S}| = |\boldsymbol{\sigma}|$ be the number of values in $\mathbf{S}$ and $\boldsymbol{\sigma}$, that is

$$s = N(\log_2 N + 1).$$

The total number of distinct determinants given by pairs of these values is given by:
$$\binom{s}{2} = \frac{s(s-1)}{2}.$$

These represent the number of distinct wire pairs to be tested for the determinant condition.

Now, fix $\boldsymbol{\alpha}$ as done in the proof of Theorem 3. Fixing $\boldsymbol{\alpha}$ will also determine all values in $\boldsymbol{\sigma}$. We proceed to select the values in $\mathbf{a}$, making sure to avoid the banned values in $\mathbb{B}_i$ for each i. When fixing the a_i's as explained in the proof of Theorem 3, the values in $\mathbf{S}$ also become fixed. To satisfy the determinant condition we must fix the a_i such that all determinants $\mathbf{S}_i\boldsymbol{\sigma}_j - \mathbf{S}_j\boldsymbol{\sigma}_i$ are also non-zero. Therefore, values for a_i that would make any determinant zero must also be added to $\mathbb{B}_i$.

As in the proof of Theorem 3, the last value to fix is a_0, and this is the value that must meet the largest number of constraints. So, in the following, we focus on selecting a_0. Among the s sums in $\mathbf{S}$, there are $2N-1$ sums that start with a_0, as established in Theorem 3. The values for each of these $2N-1$ sums form determinants with the $s-1$ values in $\boldsymbol{\sigma}$, so the number of determinants that include a_0 is $(2N-1)(s-1)$. In the worst case, this leads to the same number of unique values to be added to $\mathbb{B}_0$. From the proof of Theorem 3, we know that there are up to $2N-1$ additional values in $\mathbb{B}_0$ to avoid that, make sure each $\mathbf{S}_i$ is non-zero. So in total we have

$$|\mathbb{B}_0| \leq (2N-1)(s-1) + (2N-1) = (2N-1)N(\log_2 N + 1).$$

As long as q is larger than this bound, we can always select a value for a_0 that avoids making any $\mathbf{S}_i$ or any determinant 0. □

In Sect. 4.2, we will demonstrate that the bound in this theorem is not sharp enough to construct error-detecting vectors for Kyber and Falcon, because the ring modulus q is too small for these schemes. For Dilithium, we will use this construction to give a pair of error-detecting vectors that can detect up to two errors.

4 Implementation

This section introduces effective implementations for our error detection techniques. An NTT without error detection requires $\frac{N \log_2 N}{2}$ multiplications. In order to apply our error detection method with one checksum, we have to multiply the inputs of the NTT with $\mathbf{b}$ and the outputs with $\mathbf{a}$, which both require N multiplication. So we would need $2N$ extra multiplications. If we want to use two checksums, we would need $4N$ extra multiplications. However, by choosing as many multipliers equal to one as possible, we can demonstrate that we only need N extra multiplication for detecting a single error and $2.5N$ extra multiplication for detecting two errors.

4.1 One Checksum

Let $\mathbf{b} = (1\ 1\ \cdots\ 1)$, we can show that the corresponding $\mathbf{a}$ can always detect one fault by calculating all $S_w^l(\mathbf{a})$ and confirming they are all nonzero for Kyber, Dilithium, and Falcon parameters. The exact vectors for guaranteed single error detection are given in the appendix.

4.2 Two Checksums

For our two error detection methods, we use the same $\mathbf{a}$ and choose

$$\alpha_{N-1} = \alpha_{N-2} = \cdots = \alpha_{\frac{N}{2}-1} = 1.$$

We choose the remaining α_i recursively as described in the proof of Theorem 5, so that $D(\mathbf{S}, \boldsymbol{\sigma})_{ij}$ is nonzero for all $i \neq j$. After that, we compute $\boldsymbol{\beta} := \boldsymbol{\alpha}\mathbf{A}$. Since half of the elements of $\boldsymbol{\alpha}$ are one, we only need $1.5N$ multiplications more compared to the one checksum case, meaning in total, we need $2.5N$ extra multiplications. The condition in Theorem 5 is satisfied for Dilithium. We provided $\boldsymbol{\alpha}$ and $\boldsymbol{\beta}$ for Dilithium in the appendix as well.

For Kyber and Falcon, it is not feasible to find values for low indices of $\boldsymbol{\alpha}$ using this method because this condition is not met. That means we can only guarantee two fault detection on a certain percentage of all wire pairs. As long as this percentage is not a 100%, meaning there is at least one wire pair where errors can go undetected, a strong attacker can compute $\mathbf{S}$ and $\boldsymbol{\sigma}$ and thereby also $\mathbf{D}$ and thus find the wire pair where errors can go undetected and exploit this by injecting the two faults there. The fact that the Kyber and Falcon parameters do not meet the condition in Theorem 5 does not exclude that a two error-detecting vector pair exists. In Sect. 3.3 we have shown that

$$\binom{N(\log_2 N + 1)}{2}$$

elements must be nonzero. Choosing $\mathbf{a}$ and $\boldsymbol{\alpha}$ randomly and assuming each $D(\mathbf{S}, \boldsymbol{\sigma})_{ij}$ is random in $\mathbb{Z}_q$, the probability, that they are all nonzero is

$$\left(1 - \frac{1}{q}\right)^{\binom{N(\log_2 N+1)}{2}}.$$

Since $\mathbf{a}, \boldsymbol{\alpha} \in \mathbb{Z}_q^N$, there are q^N possible values for each, so the expected number of vectors satisfying all the non-zero conditions is

$$q^N \left(1 - \frac{1}{q}\right)^{\binom{N(\log_2 N+1)}{2}} \gg 1.$$

Hence, we conjecture that two error-detecting pairs of vectors exist. We leave proving/disproving the existence of such a pair and finding it for the Falcon and Kyber parameters as an open problem. We have shown that N additional

Table 2. Relative cost of our error detection techniques in terms of multiplications.

Scheme	1 CS	2 CS
complete NTT	$\frac{2}{\log_2 N}$	$\frac{5}{\log_2 N}$
Incomplete NTT	$\frac{2}{\log_2 N - 1}$	$\frac{5}{\log_2 N - 1}$

Table 3. Relative cost of our error detection techniques in terms of multiplications for Kyber, Dilithium and Falcon.

Scheme	1 CS	2 CS
Dilithium	0.25	0.625
Falcon I	0.222	0.556
Falcon V	0.2	0.5
Kyber	0.286	0.714

multiplications are required for one checksum, while $2.5N$ are needed for two checksums. A complete NTT (used in Dilithium and Falcon) requires $\frac{N \log_2 N}{2}$ multiplications, and an incomplete NTT (used in Kyber) requires $\frac{N(\log_2 N - 1)}{2}$ since the last layer is omitted. The cost of applying our error detection methods, using one and two checksums (CS), relative to the cost of the NTT in terms of multiplications is given in Table 2. The numbers are computed as the additional number of multiplications required for the checksums and dividing it by the number of multiplications needed for a complete or incomplete NTT. Now, setting N to the numbers presented in Sect. 2.2 results in the numbers presented in Table 3.

Our proposed technique using one checksum reduces the number of required multiplications compared to both [3,17] methods while still guaranteeing the detection of one error. This highlights the efficiency of the approach, especially for larger values of N. Note that unlike in the recomputation method, additional storage is needed for the coefficients in our method and in [3]. We need to store N coefficients for Dilithium and Falcon, whereas we only need $\frac{N}{2}$ coefficients for Kyber because the same coefficients can be used for each half-sized NTT performed for Kyber.

5 Conclusion

We have introduced a generalized error detection technique that improves the security of implementations using the NTT. Our approach is capable of detecting a single fault injected into a wire in the NTT network, requiring only N additional multiplications, significantly reducing the overhead compared to previous methods. We have further extended our technique to detect up to two faults with 100% reliability for Dilithium. This extended capability is achieved with an overhead of only $2.5N$ multiplications.

We leave finding an efficient algorithm that gives us **a** and **α** that guarantee the finding of two faults as an open problem. Note that this technique can be extended to detect more than two errors by adding more checksums. However, this is not practical as the additional cost is close to the cost of recomputation.

A Input and Output Multipliers for Techniques

This appendix presents the input and output multipliers for the four schemes: Dilithium, Kyber, Falcon I, and Falcon V. The multipliers a and α represent the output multipliers, while b and β represent the input multipliers.

A.1 Dilithium

Table 4. Dilithium Multipliers

Multiplier	Values
b	$\{1\}^{256}$
a	7511306, 7268830, 5474525, 5631597, 117126, 2894273, 5415375, 6137690, 5412937, 879351, 7630876, 7950048, 2707004, 2223415, 7757689, 6794386, 4413478, 1434037, 6593365, 2371240, 3775900, 2069059, 3050174, 2348902, 885454, 950158, 391593, 800539, 7946762, 7724623, 5651610, 7657810, 2346552, 5905197, 5542002, 7885504, 2266250, 295216, 2670256, 3902893, 3120930, 2207058, 4168676, 7836275, 6401582, 3423687, 8256204, 7633393, 1059210, 2645505, 2868862, 5530426, 2218396, 6414667, 5248249, 5834839, 2638709, 8231049, 856716, 4909726, 317499, 2591320, 566630, 7259347, 6220539, 3522895, 5398834, 120765, 626895, 3309814, 6419699, 6297723, 1949702, 3647406, 993985, 5264941, 5720329, 317292, 6501330, 8088966, 2307577, 2816303, 5278157, 3404063, 5743422, 7610229, 6838252, 6520254, 7614068, 3264328, 94014, 3796289, 372831, 1903233, 7842375, 2906811, 5023664, 1466781, 3010429, 3141092, 8212262, 1157548, 2840242, 5561907, 907175, 1740496, 7577840, 3098394, 4536213, 3727033, 7910907, 910323, 6456321, 7599170, 1993767, 3785916, 5655461, 141639, 2230157, 3832335, 1244577, 8243668, 5047276, 8140557, 7668172, 6349172, 1865577, 458640, 7856305, 6449368, 1965773, 646773, 174388, 3267669, 71277, 7070368, 4482610, 6084788, 8173306, 2659484, 4529029, 6321178, 715775, 1858624, 7404622, 404038, 4587912, 3778732, 5216551, 737105, 6574449, 7407770, 2753038, 5474703, 7157397, 102683, 5173853, 5304516, 6848164, 3291281, 5408134, 472570, 6411712, 7942114, 4518656, 8220931, 5050617, 700877, 1794691, 1476693, 704716, 2571523, 4910882, 3036788, 5498642, 6007368, 225979, 1813615, 7997653, 2594616, 3050004, 7320960, 4667539, 6365243, 2017222, 1895246, 5005131, 7688050, 8194180, 2916111, 4792050, 2094406, 1055598, 7748315, 5723625, 7997446, 3405219, 7458229, 83896, 5676236, 2480106, 3066696, 1900278, 6096549, 2784519, 5446083, 5669440, 7255735, 681552, 58741, 4891258, 1913363, 478670, 4146269, 6107887, 5194015, 4412052, 5644689, 8019729, 6048695, 429441, 2772943, 2409748, 5968393, 657135, 2663335, 590322, 368183, 7514406, 7923352, 7364787, 7429491, 5966043, 5264771, 6245886, 4539045, 5943705, 1721580, 6880908, 3901467, 1520559, 557256, 6091530, 5607941, 364897, 684069, 7435594, 2902008, 2177255, 2899570, 5420672, 8197819, 2683348, 2840420, 1046115, 803639

(*continued*)

Table 4. (*continued*)

Multiplier	Values
β	5791121, 3876506, 1812116, 6910599, 858961, 6913584, 1646428, 6089601, 1687322, 1692175, 8209040, 6038377, 3135400, 2658623, 5231154, 2825832, 7459415, 1536327, 673249, 8185212, 4466516, 4563857, 1324194, 1484330, 3250522, 6133580, 7011383, 3192114, 4672318, 852807, 734578, 1733239, 1530988, 2107944, 3476597, 4659735, 6931191, 3307246, 931936, 4318748, 3365542, 6899902, 5065856, 4622758, 1397997, 2951382, 754023, 1798099, 3195823, 3497845, 2416746, 6363325, 2797313, 7003747, 950818, 4537049, 3176956, 3716664, 3285715, 266803, 6849160, 863625, 725468, 2606776, 730552, 3686374, 878625, 4948166, 6650739, 7231932, 6848492, 820998, 2281956, 7314383, 58338, 283191, 587775, 5464612, 7304239, 2482172, 6313754, 5290807, 8091398, 2174999, 2840257, 7268978, 8085971, 3356631, 7419232, 1759623, 806177, 7326295, 5529423, 6049846, 6216333, 2683516, 4445040, 7884559, 3614972, 4621250, 3674006, 8096164, 4710879, 8243928, 959352, 2153760, 4194460, 2974857, 3417856, 7195563, 2452187, 6961339, 1097918, 4887793, 1147063, 6037604, 2152775, 6064359, 5454959, 7637950, 1036440, 3903066, 1624500, 2136616, 2488859, 3153127, 3709896, 5919480, 6466532, 4260647, 7762914, 8168859, 236105, 3298174, 447552, 3583058, 738963, 4792049, 6900868, 758349, 3272429, 3782168, 6597079, 2273128, 4607808, 1627153, 5103035, 7052454, 1405956, 3874393, 6113179, 4036651, 8149804, 4536498, 5262283, 456865, 7206170, 6825363, 8262546, 6872768, 6539836, 2760140, 7695741, 5619060, 3179045, 977927, 26228, 1912650, 4046403, 5715759, 5274874, 1804365, 695873, 4825361, 3914766, 1509198, 153827, 4966095, 1260046, 5380686, 4291999, 5707936, 7547877, 6232755, 1886681, 8174088, 7939977, 7936308, 2490571, 1780044, 5225834, 1798941, 6229697, 5730199, 2872745, 6764240, 1587611, 3918125, 2630225, 2908370, 739846, 1155391, 460911, 5297629, 2123787, 7670502, 1321504, 6147571, 6271373, 1671981, 2956561, 6354100, 185111, 151819, 4115853, 4922346, 1514357, 5212543, 3076389, 2485910, 1094922, 1153739, 7128445, 5878944, 8305779, 1056013, 3403448, 2243480, 402191, 1486893, 139458, 3216086, 7897803, 6272279, 138104, 4482737, 4426582, 8353746, 6751744, 3709583, 4836134, 6647156, 2451104, 1386815, 8279168, 6690625, 3490424, 7603346, 5219632, 2792155, 7179649, 6558019, 3076511, 6226001, 6144737, 1144017
α	$\{1\}^{128}$, 5240616, 6625160, 3870293, 451475, 4098101, 3509475, 4720287, 3204487, 2633339, 8261277, 5371451, 4802163, 1052454, 7985202, 7011421, 1789078, 2482935, 2162795, 2130324, 6911940, 8224373, 7975065, 7362675, 5318767, 256384, 2940530, 1953642, 2284237, 7680329, 4798738, 182096, 6420995, 6262728, 6853579, 1467056, 6679038, 3384943, 1364494, 1815539, 7173684, 381074, 5963412, 378030, 4343637, 1345703, 7882546, 7249321, 3605300, 2415392, 591713, 2396687, 7518040, 2221840, 8100078, 4900106, 5263091, 4483921, 6097599, 5483953, 5444106, 117789, 1529228, 6899376, 3873271, 4699322, 4450988, 1726840, 679011, 2219822, 4140793, 466656, 2203965, 6509925, 7787412, 603082, 2094235, 7492608, 5969231, 1342993, 5182765, 6680762, 3437557, 2969525, 2295436, 4479817, 4814112, 2440657, 2484460, 7892496, 237306, 530634, 816529, 6541158, 7820662, 5399117, 6330948, 3594342, 5863786, 3924672, 251287, 5757005, 7867614, 309896, 217175, 5619146, 2193097, 2578525, 7908807, 4382588, 6137892, 97233, 5691157, 6645351, 4427738, 6988557, 8131464, 431981, 1572591, 4052322, 508107, 748762, 3306458, 289281, 6956158, 7513153, 4539509, 3758126, 4320940

A.2 Kyber

Table 5. Kyber Multipliers

Multiplier	Values
b	$\{1\}^{128}$
a	777, 1317, 3320, 2467, 2492, 857, 2702, 6, 2870, 1105, 2433, 2589, 2739, 424, 2713, 1618, 2499, 1982, 225, 3045, 17, 3301, 1812, 2207, 472, 2128, 3204, 260, 2400, 3200, 459, 2102, 30, 1819, 3051, 3042, 2998, 1225, 1479, 1831, 2198, 1035, 312, 2126, 725, 2730, 1983, 1482, 2930, 9, 298, 2832, 2875, 36, 2231, 1321, 369, 2224, 1289, 373, 1042, 1305, 1550, 367, 2910, 1727, 1972, 2235, 2904, 1988, 1053, 2908, 1956, 1046, 3241, 402, 445, 2979, 3268, 347, 1795, 1294, 547, 2552, 1151, 2965, 2242, 1079, 1446, 1798, 2052, 279, 235, 226, 1458, 3247, 1175, 2818, 77, 877, 3017, 73, 1149, 2805, 1070, 1465, 3305, 3260, 232, 3052, 1295, 778, 1659, 564, 2853, 538, 688, 844, 2172, 407, 3271, 575, 2420, 785, 810, 3286, 1960, 2500

A.3 Falcon I

Table 6. Kyber Multipliers

Multiplier	Values
b	$\{1\}^{512}$
a	9731, 10896, 3629, 5768, 3702, 10752, 248, 5700, 894, 9075, 10343, 4800, 3736, 871, 1204, 3480, 6457, 5172, 1052, 7314, 10097, 7279, 836, 4745, 9877, 6410, 398, 7342, 7766, 6782, 6180, 11927, 2683, 3917, 8355, 292, 4446, 9568, 2659, 9230, 9949, 9749, 7319, 2216, 10032, 2960, 4485, 8998, 3331, 1247, 3997, 10227, 3656, 1473, 1039, 2347, 11136, 6413, 4135, 11082, 12276, 4709, 11349, 5174, 1338, 6381, 9557, 1752, 9842, 9356, 5253, 8858, 4562, 4643, 3078, 6293, 10951, 1048, 3042, 2500, 5139, 6229, 11523, 89, 3604, 520, 7321, 7150, 11840, 2406, 6780, 4399, 8453, 12240, 8969, 3360, 9846, 3866, 11229, 334, 266, 6548, 436, 4370, 11150, 7583, 5479, 25, 3109, 2808, 362, 8252, 1297, 4898, 6620, 7979, 1259, 10963, 5598, 11425, 4118, 9719, 6575, 10156, 11834, 1814, 10318, 7408, 9487, 3574, 9042, 1460, 9783, 11047, 8008, 1578, 10159, 1353, 4960, 7734, 303, 11821, 12175, 4413, 4983, 1439, 5183, 4518, 2723, 9038, 8559, 12001, 11286, 11302, 10582, 11585, 2034, 4579, 1031, 6169, 6774, 11430, 7864, 6385, 7147, 236, 704, 440, 7054, 7612, 5758, 572, 4756, 838, 1613, 10544, 11291, 6950, 5478, 4185, 9697, 7392, 2272, 3915, 8770, 12209, 10436, 2502, 10604, 9615, 3677, 3711, 10766, 11568, 3398, 2158, 8879, 10687, 6024, 10045, 1002, 9224, 8275, 4464, 8985, 5095, 2064, 3690, 1872, 5593, 2315, 6927, 3838, 9050, 4040, 9973, 8868, 1043, 11281, 1279, 4952, 8041, 3197, 10803, 414, 3684, 7917, 7302, 5368, 9701, 6023, 8313, 7977, 8892, 11156, 203, 1242, 10163, 4006, 7187, 3006, 616, 3257, 8552, 5295, 2163, 1155, 8409, 2140, 11540, 10048, 2588, 10907, 1160, 138, 3080, 9161, 12103, 11081, 1334, 9653, 2193, 701, 10101, 3832, 11086, 10078, 6946, 3689, 8984, 11625, 9235, 5054, 8235, 2078, 10999, 12038, 1085, 3349, 4264, 3928, 6218, 2540, 6873, 4939, 4324, 8557, 11827, 1438, 9044, 4200, 7289, 10962, 960, 11198, 3373, 2268, 8201, 3191, 8403, 5314, 9926, 6648, 10369, 8551, 10177, 7146, 3256, 7777, 3966, 3017, 11239, 2196, 6217, 1554, 3362, 10083, 8843, 673, 1475, 8530, 8564, 2626, 1637, 9739, 1805, 32, 3471, 8326, 9969, 4849, 2544, 8056, 6763, 5291, 950, 1697, 10628, 11403, 7485, 11669, 6483, 4629, 5187, 11801, 11537, 12005, 5094, 5856, 4377, 811, 5467, 6072, 11210, 7662, 10207, 656, 1659, 939, 955, 240, 3682, 3203, 9518, 7723, 7058, 10802, 7258, 7828, 66, 420, 11938, 4507, 7281, 10888, 2082, 10663, 4233, 1194, 2458, 10781, 3199, 8667, 2754, 4833, 1923, 10427, 407, 2085, 5666, 2522, 8123, 816, 6643, 1278, 10982, 4262, 5621, 7343, 10944, 3989, 11879, 9433, 9132, 12216, 6762, 4658, 1091, 7871, 11805, 5693, 11975, 11907, 1012, 8375, 2395, 8881, 3272, 1, 3788, 7842, 5461, 9835, 401, 5091, 4920, 11721, 8637, 12152, 718, 6012, 7102, 9741, 9199, 11193, 1290, 5948, 9163, 7598, 7679, 3383, 6988, 2885, 2399, 10489, 2684, 5860, 10903, 7067, 892, 7532, 12254, 1159, 8106, 5828, 1105, 9894, 11202, 10768, 8585, 2014, 8244, 10994, 8910, 3243, 7756, 9281, 2209, 10025, 4922, 2492, 2292, 3011, 9582, 2673, 7795, 11949, 3886, 8324, 9558, 314, 6061, 5459, 4475, 4899, 11843, 5831, 2364, 7496, 11405, 4962, 2144, 4927, 11189, 7069, 5784, 8761, 11037, 11370, 8505, 7441, 1898, 3166, 11347, 6541, 11993, 1489, 8539, 6473, 8612, 1345, 2510

A.4 Falcon V

Table 7. Dilithium Multipliers

Multiplier	Values
b	$\{1\}^{1024}$
a	5134, 848, 11089, 10938, 1011, 817, 2526, 9283, 782, 4219, 4751, 4902, 2193, 10753, 7706, 7898, 1171, 3639, 10713, 5439, 784, 11574, 7926, 12186, 3206, 4153, 4812, 7629, 696, 9045, 2514, 1858, 3783, 7541, 7222, 9668, 11459, 7212, 3677, 3807, 8190, 3655, 638, 5306, 6388, 235, 2885, 3353, 11680, 6854, 6079, 2426, 3500, 7777, 410, 257, 3888, 7642, 10472, 5288, 11453, 4349, 11933, 1838, 1912, 4377, 11043, 2822, 18, 8304, 6192, 3765, 4226, 2437, 3861, 8720, 7305, 4458, 3292, 8020, 9047, 8749, 11742, 4556, 7955, 8762, 5931, 11216, 10554, 758, 5264, 4577, 868, 12268, 4361, 12151, 6181, 9100, 11291, 10817, 5551, 8305, 158, 11465, 9595, 5815, 8785, 556, 8120, 9183, 9073, 2054, 7786, 10275, 321, 4321, 12222, 8887, 6048, 6501, 2053, 5318, 8165, 7372, 2348, 2222, 11053, 3465, 2471, 11883, 6716, 1438, 4119, 808, 305, 9401, 200, 3504, 417, 3936, 9027, 5682, 6292, 6939, 2220, 6545, 3447, 192, 10231, 11654, 3309, 11467, 1612, 2624, 2351, 1663, 600, 9333, 6039, 11273, 7588, 4972, 10760, 1306, 1464, 8269, 7051, 7911, 10815, 11337, 10774, 10680, 8923, 11610, 4844, 2006, 11589, 10511, 4242, 12180, 9547, 3882, 9440, 6655, 11862, 9356, 1038, 1814, 686, 6747, 5654, 9212, 7531, 8289, 1821, 10063, 3362, 7017, 9825, 3445, 10249, 5996, 4930, 7246, 9218, 6691, 7543, 2736, 12067, 3893, 1816, 9025, 9894, 6551, 12250, 9031, 3409, 6197, 8768, 2945, 10242, 372, 11116, 11828, 9532, 5820, 10618, 10328, 11597, 3667, 6131, 4312, 7679, 2651, 4059, 5621, 5483, 8308, 9906, 5631, 7658, 7748, 1820, 6429, 4275, 9685, 5127, 6917, 7651, 12006, 2761, 7896, 3755, 2036, 11315, 9806, 6702, 11153, 852, 5113, 5284, 4978, 442, 5487, 10773, 3948, 7498, 11245, 10142, 10828, 7108, 4628, 10709, 5876, 10410, 4217, 5394, 5168, 6024, 11967, 8264, 84, 6231, 6205, 3002, 2677, 2112, 9094, 1001, 7895, 4596, 5266, 1642, 9752, 5130, 6806, 11323, 8186, 9766, 6032, 2074, 11766, 10565, 10171, 11311, 5455, 1572, 209, 2758, 8920, 9037, 9223, 5665, 3777, 8595, 6748, 7881, 10688, 8986, 9030, 5477, 1953, 9397, 2347, 11577, 2867, 9412, 3068, 2716, 7144, 8755, 12115, 7971, 11029, 3537, 274, 3727, 3207, 10748, 4143, 10084, 4992, 3701, 3737, 7447, 6323, 8009, 6582, 7186, 2872, 5807, 790, 5080, 4984, 4730, 10831, 2343, 4034, 3587, 2591, 11731, 7015, 2592, 7484, 7939, 10529, 5082, 9502, 2502, 6382, 6126, 8700, 8467, 7722, 2127, 2306, 7799, 4562, 2026, 6601, 12243, 9939, 8285, 5249, 8322, 711, 384, 2779, 9481, 1566, 7864, 10200, 7341, 426, 10189, 10939, 8607, 5966, 5353, 6465, 6067, 8687, 6351, 4987, 507, 3282, 10497, 10710, 7071, 11987, 1733, 5261, 10459, 38, 5210, 8600, 8767, 7657, 4, 4680, 154, 10749, 10617, 10979, 4042, 10875, 8218, 4327, 4443, 195, 2496, 3884, 5496, 226, 3386, 8619, 2403, 759, 10059, 11929, 7172, 915, 11213, 2441, 1046, 1462, 10261, 550, 8929, 560, 11905, 11442, 6471, 6313, 1205, 5017, 10175, 11636, 6280, 12109, 4464, 2058, 5583, 8325, 6620, 10665, 9540, 8621, 3066, 5584, 6171, 10506, 6842, 994, 9909, 6989, 9352, 11132, 3600, 1076, 2196, 8599, 2239, 5195, 263, 4390, 10008, 5594, 7417, 7066, 4271, 2952, 10390, 9637, 10732, 6979, 4394, 6478, 9858, 10722, 78, 6673, 7409, 12153, 3559, 2254, 2330, 9574, 5146, 7436, 2217, 7668, 4597, 10048, 4829, 7119, 2691, 9935, 10011, 8706, 112, 4856, 5592, 12187, 1543, 2407, 5787, 7871, 5286, 1533, 2628, 1875, 9313, 7994, 5199, 4848, 6671, 2257, 7875, 12002, 7070, 10026, 3666, 10069, 11189, 8665, 1133, 2913, 5276, 2356, 11271, 5423, 1759, 6094, 6681, 9199, 3644, 2725, 1600, 5645, 3940, 6682, 10207, 7801, 156, 5985, 629, 2090, 7248, 11060, 5952, 5794, 823, 360, 11705, 3336, 11715, 2004, 10803, 11219, 9824, 1052, 11350, 5093, 336, 2206, 11506, 9862, 3646, 8879, 12039, 6769, 8381, 9769, 12070, 7822, 7938, 4047, 1390, 8223, 1286, 1648, 1516, 12111, 7585, 12261, 4608, 3498, 3665, 7055, 12227, 1806, 7004, 10532, 278, 5194, 1555, 1768, 8983, 11758, 7278, 5914, 3578, 6198, 5800, 6912, 6299, 3658, 1326, 2076, 11839, 4924, 2065, 4401, 10699, 2784, 9486, 11881, 11554, 3943, 7016, 3980, 2326, 22, 5664, 10239, 7703, 4466, 9959, 10138, 4543, 3798, 3565, 6139, 5883, 9763, 2763, 7183, 1736, 4326, 4781, 9673, 5250, 534, 9674, 8678, 8231, 9922, 1434, 7535, 7281, 7185, 11475, 6458, 9393, 5079, 5683, 4256, 5942, 4818, 8528, 8564, 7273, 2181, 8122, 1517, 9058, 8538, 11991, 6728, 1236, 4294, 150, 3510, 5121, 9549, 9197, 2853, 9398, 688, 9918, 2868, 10312, 6788, 3235, 3279, 1577, 4384, 5517, 3670, 8488, 6600, 3042, 3228, 3345, 9507, 12056, 10693, 6810, 954, 2094, 1700, 499, 10191, 6233, 2499, 4079, 942, 5459, 7135, 2513, 10623, 6999, 7669, 4370, 11264, 3171, 10153, 9588, 9263, 6060, 6034, 12181, 4001, 298, 6241, 7097, 6871, 8048, 1855, 6389, 1556, 7637, 5157, 1437, 2123, 1020, 4767, 8317, 1492, 6778, 11823, 7287, 6981, 7152, 11413, 1112, 5563, 2459, 950, 10229, 8510, 4369, 9504, 259, 4614, 5348, 7138, 2580, 7990, 5836, 10445, 4517, 4607, 6634, 2359, 3957, 6782, 6644, 8206, 9614, 4586, 7953, 6134, 8598, 668, 1937, 1647, 6445, 2733, 437, 1149, 11893, 2023, 9320, 3497, 6068, 8856, 3234, 15, 5714, 2371, 3240, 10449, 8372, 198, 9529, 4722, 5574, 3047, 5019, 7335, 6269, 2016, 8820, 2440, 5248, 8903, 2202, 10444, 3976, 4734, 3053, 6611, 5518, 11579, 10451, 11227, 2909, 403, 5610, 2825, 8383, 2718, 85, 8023, 1754, 676, 10259, 7421, 655, 3342, 1585, 1491, 928, 1450, 4354, 5214, 3996, 10801, 10959, 1505, 7293, 4677, 992, 6226, 2932, 11665, 10602, 9914, 9641, 10653, 798, 8956, 611, 2034, 12073, 8818, 5720, 10045, 5326, 5973, 6583, 3238, 8329, 11848, 8761, 12065, 2864, 11960, 11457, 8146, 10827, 5549, 382, 9794, 8800, 1212, 10043, 9917, 4893, 4100, 6947, 10212, 5764, 6217, 3378, 43, 7944, 11944, 1990, 4479, 10211, 3192, 3082, 4145, 11709, 3480, 6450, 2670, 800, 12107, 3960, 6714, 1448, 974, 3165, 6084, 114, 7904, 12286, 11397, 7688, 7001, 11507, 1711, 1049, 6334, 3503, 4310, 7709, 523, 3516, 3218, 4245, 8973, 7807, 4960, 3545, 8404, 9828, 8039, 8500, 6073, 3961, 12247, 9443, 1222, 7888, 10353, 10427, 332, 7916, 812, 6977, 1793, 4623, 8377, 12008, 11855, 4488, 8765, 9839, 6186, 5411, 585, 8912, 9380, 12030, 5877, 6959, 11627, 8610, 4075, 8458, 8588, 5053, 806, 2597, 5043, 4724, 8482, 10407, 9751, 3220, 11569, 4636, 7453, 8112, 9059, 79, 4339, 691, 11481, 6826, 1552, 8626, 11094, 4367, 4559, 1512, 10072, 7363, 7514, 8046, 11483, 2982, 9739, 11448, 11254, 1327, 1176, 11417, 7131

References

1. Ahmadi, K., Aghapour, S., Kermani, M.M., Azarderakhsh, R.: Efficient Algorithm Level Error Detection for Number-Theoretic Transform used for Kyber Assessed on FPGAs and ARM (2024). https://arxiv.org/abs/2403.01215
2. Bai, S., et al.: Supporting documentation: Crystals-dilithium: algorithm specifications and supporting documentation. NIST PQC (2020)
3. Bauer, S., Santis, F.D., Koleci, K., Aghaie, A.: A fault-resistant NTT by polynomial evaluation and interpolation. Cryptology ePrint Archive, Paper 2024/788 (2024). https://eprint.iacr.org/2024/788
4. Bisheh-Niasar, M., Azarderakhsh, R., Mozaffari-Kermani, M.: High-speed NTT-based polynomial multiplication accelerator for post-quantum cryptography. In: 2021 IEEE 28th Symposium on Computer Arithmetic (ARITH), pp. 94–101 (2021)
5. Bos, J., et al.: CRYSTALS-Kyber: a CCA-secure module-lattice-based KEM. In: 2018 IEEE European Symposium on Security and Privacy (EuroS&P), pp. 353–367 (2018)
6. Cooley, J.W., Tukey, J.W.: An algorithm for the machine calculation of complex fourier series. Math. Comput. **19**(90), 297–301 (1965)
7. Derya, K., Mert, A.C., Öztürk, E., Savaş, E.: CoHA-NTT: a configurable hardware accelerator for NTT-based polynomial multiplication. Microprocess. Microsyst. **89**, 104451 (2022)
8. Digital-Signature, N.M.L.B.: Mechanism standard. Gaithersburg, MD, USA, NIST Post-Quantum Cryptography Standardization Process; NIST (2024)
9. Fouque, P.A., et al.: Falcon: Fast-fourier lattice-based compact signatures over ntru. Submission to the NIST's post-quantum cryptography standardization process **36**(5), 1–75 (2018)
10. Heinz, D., Pöppelmann, T.: Combined fault and DPA protection for lattice-based cryptography. IEEE Trans. Comput. **72**(4), 1055–1066 (2022)
11. Jou, J.Y., Abraham, J.A.: Fault-tolerant FFT networks. IEEE Trans. Comput. **37**(5), 548–561 (1988)
12. Key-Encapsulation, N.M.L.B.: Mechanism standard. Gaithersburg, MD, USA, NIST Post-Quantum Cryptography Standardization Process; NIST (2024)
13. Li, D., Pakala, A., Yang, K.: MeNTT: a compact and efficient processing-in-memory number theoretic transform (NTT) accelerator. IEEE Trans. Very Large Scale Integration (VLSI) Syst. **30**(5), 579–588 (2022)
14. Nejatollahi, H., Cammarota, R., Dutt, N.: Flexible NTT accelerators for RLWE lattice-based cryptography. In: 2019 IEEE 37th International Conference on Computer Design (ICCD), pp. 329–332 (2019)
15. Nguyen, T.H., Kieu-Do-Nguyen, B., Pham, C.K., Hoang, T.T.: High-speed NTT Accelerator for CRYSTAL-Kyber and CRYSTAL-Dilithium. IEEE Access (2024)
16. Ravi, P., Yang, B., Bhasin, S., Zhang, F., Chattopadhyay, A.: Fiddling the twiddle constants-fault injection analysis of the number theoretic transform. IACR Trans. Cryptographic Hardware Embedded Syst. (2023)
17. Sarker, A., Canto, A.C., Kermani, M.M., Azarderakhsh, R.: Error detection architectures for hardware/software co-design approaches of number-theoretic transform. IEEE Trans. Comput. Aided Des. Integr. Circuits Syst. **42**(7), 2418–2422 (2022)
18. Shor, P.W.: Polynomial-time algorithms for prime factorization and discrete logarithms on a quantum computer. SIAM Rev. **41**(2), 303–332 (1999)

19. Tao, D.L., Hartmann, C.R.: A novel concurrent error detection scheme for FFT networks. IEEE Trans. Parallel Distrib. Syst. **4**(2), 198–221 (1993)
20. Wang, S.J., Jha, N.K.: Algorithm-based fault tolerance for FFT networks. IEEE Trans. Comput. **43**(7), 849–854 (1994)
21. Zijlstra, T., Bigou, K., Tisserand, A.: FPGA implementation and comparison of protections against SCAs for RLWE. In: Hao, F., Ruj, S., Sen Gupta, S. (eds.) INDOCRYPT 2019. LNCS, vol. 11898, pp. 535–555. Springer, Cham (2019). https://doi.org/10.1007/978-3-030-35423-7_27

A Fault-Resistant NTT by Polynomial Evaluation and Interpolation
Application to ML-KEM and ML-DSA

Sven Bauer, Fabrizio De Santis, Kristjane Koleci, and Anita Aghaie(✉)

Foundational Technologies, Siemens AG, Munich, Germany
{svenbauer,fabrizio.desantis,kristjane.koleci,anita.aghaie}@siemens.com

Abstract. In computer arithmetic operations, the Number Theoretic Transform (NTT) plays a significant role in the efficient implementation of cyclic and nega-cyclic convolutions with the application of multiplying large integers and large degree polynomials. Multiplying polynomials is a common operation in lattice-based cryptography. Hence, the NTT is a core component of several lattice-based cryptographic algorithms. Two well-known examples are the key encapsulation mechanism ML-KEM and the digital signature algorithm ML-DSA. In this work, we introduce a novel and efficient method for safeguarding the NTT against fault injection attacks. This new countermeasure is based on polynomial evaluation and interpolation. We prove its error detection capability, calculate the required additional computational effort, and show how to concretely use it to secure the NTT in ML-KEM and ML-DSA against fault injection attacks. Finally, we provide concrete implementation results of the proposed novel technique on a resource-constrained ARM Cortex-M4 microcontroller, e.g., the technique exhibits a 72% relative overhead, when applied to ML-DSA, and 67%, when applied to ML-KEM.

Keywords: Lattice-Based Cryptography · Post-Quantum Cryptography · ML-KEM · ML-DSA · Kyber · Dilithium · NTT · Fault Countermeasures

1 Introduction

The Number Theoretic Transform (NTT) is a core building block of a number of cryptographic schemes defined over polynomial rings. It plays a central role in various lattice-based cryptographic schemes that rely on the difficulty of certain computational problems in structured lattices. Both the post-quantum key encapsulation mechanism ML-KEM [28] and the post-quantum digital signature scheme ML-DSA [29] make use of the NTT to efficiently compute polynomial multiplication. Both algorithms have recently been standardized by the US National Institute of Standards and Technology (NIST) [20]. In this paper, we refer to ML-KEM and ML-DSA but older literature that is still applicable usually refers to their predecessors Kyber and Dilithium, respectively. Therefore, when citing previous work, we often use both names and write ML-KEM/Kyber and ML-DSA/Dilithium. ML-KEM and ML-DSA were designed with NTT-friendly parameters, in order to allow for an efficient implementation of polynomial multiplication using the NTT. While the NTT provides significant benefits in terms of speed and memory, it is also an attractive target for side-channel and fault injection attacks [1,16,23]. While there have been several studies focusing on protecting the NTT against side-channel attacks [4,6,8,19,22], there has been comparatively little research conducted on the fault resistance of the NTT itself [4,11,23].

Note that, although our proposed countermeasure primarily targets software implementations, it can also be suitable for hardware implementations. However, differently from NTT re-computing strategies that can re-use the same NTT hardware units, our countermeasure may require additional hardware for evaluation and interpolation circuits.

Related Work

Fault attacks. Various fault injection attacks against BLISS, ring-TESLA, and the GLP-scheme have been reported in [5]. Differential fault injection attacks against deterministic variants of ML-DSA and Falcon have been presented in [2,7]. fault injection attacks against signature verification in ML-DSA/Dilithium and Falcon have been considered in [3,21,23]. In [15], a chosen-ciphertext fault attack against ML-KEM/Kyber is introduced where the fault can be injected during almost the entire decapsulation or at more specific locations during re-encryption. This proposed approach involves manipulating the ciphertext and correcting it by fault injection to obtain inequalities and recover the secret key using belief propagation. It has been demonstrated that this method can bypass several countermeasures such as straightforward shuffling and boolean masking methods [15]. In [30], single instruction skip fault injections during the decapsulation are considered for various KEM algorithms such as ML-KEM/Kyber. More precisely, the attack approach involves exploiting the Fujisaki-Okamoto (FO) transform used in ML-KEM/Kyber. The attacker implements a skipping-the-equality-test attack by carefully injecting faults during the decapsulation process. This fault injection causes the algorithm to skip a critical equality test between the original and re-encrypted ciphertexts, consequently bypassing this security check. It has been shown that this method can be effective in compromising the security of ML-KEM/Kyber implementations. In addition, the attack has been improved in [9] considering single bit flips. In [10] the attack presented in [15] has been improved to include binomial sampling and NTT butterflies and by relaxing the fault model to include random faults and instruction skips. This work also shows that the countermeasure proposed in [15] is not effective against the improved attacks. In [23] a fault attack involving the manipulations of the NTT twiddle factors is proposed. The attack is based on fault injection in the Cooley-Tukey butterfly operation to zeroize the twiddle factor. Therefore, the corresponding changes result in a significant reduction in the entropy of the NTT's output. By extending this fault to an entire stage of the NTT, and eventually to the whole NTT, the output entropy is greatly reduced.

Countermeasures. A number of countermeasures including detection and correction are investigated in previous research works [1,4,11,14,23,24]. The paper [23] presents an integrated redundancy technique within the NTT butterfly operations that detects faults in the twiddle constants. The work [1] introduces an efficient algorithm-level error detection method for FPGA and ARM platforms that minimizes the number of multiplications and latency. The article [25] proposes hardware/software co-design-based detection architectures that guarantee error detection under specific fault models. Different ways of re-computing the entire NTT in hardware to detect fault attacks are presented in [24]. The quasi-linear masking scheme proposed in [4] mitigates side channel leakage and benefits from error detection capabilities to strengthen an implementation against fault injection attacks. The works [11,14] use redundant number representation to detect faults.

Contributions. In this work, we present a novel technique to protect the NTT against fault injection attacks based on polynomial evaluation and interpolation. Our main idea is illustrated in Fig. 1.

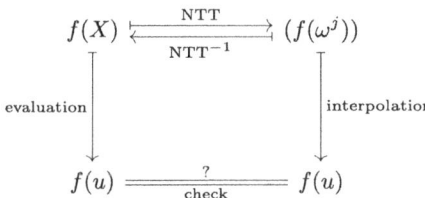

Fig. 1. The basic idea behind our countermeasure against fault injection.

To protect the computation of NTT(f) against fault injection for some polynomial f, we suggest an implementation of the NTT that evaluates the polynomial f on a selected point u. To verify the correctness of the output of the NTT, the implementation reconstructs the value $f(u)$ by polynomial interpolation. The inverse NTT^{-1} can be protected analogously. This implies that a complete ring multiplication, i.e., NTT transformations and the point-wise multiplication, can be protected with the proposed novel technique, hence providing full protection for this operation.

We describe the details of this countermeasure, the choice of the interpolation point u, the error detection properties of the proposed countermeasure and its adaption to different forms of the NTT with application to ML-DSA and ML-KEM. We also investigate the additional computational effort required by this countermeasure. Finally, we provide practical evaluations of the proposed method on an ARM Cortex-M4 microcontroller. In the exemplary cases of ML-DSA and ML-KEM, the results indicate that the proposed technique incurs a computational overhead of 72% and 67%, respectively.

Structure. This paper is structured as follows. Section 2 provides background information about the NTT, ML-KEM and ML-DSA. Section 3 presents the proposed method for safeguarding the NTT against fault injection attacks, the error detection properties of the proposed countermeasure and its application to ML-KEM and ML-DSA. Section 4 describes practical evaluation results of the proposed countermeasures on an ARM Cortex-M4 microcontroller with applications to ML-DSA and ML-KEM. Conclusions and an outlook are in Sect. 5.

2 Background

This section provides background information regarding the Number Theoretic Transform (NTT), ML-DSA and ML-KEM. Furthermore, it fixes the notation used throughout this paper.

2.1 The Number Theoretic Transform

Let K be a field and $\phi(X) = X^n + 1$ with $n = 2^k$ for some integer $k \geq 0$. Let us assume that K contains a $2n$-th root of unity ω. Then $\phi(X)$ can be factored as follows:

$$\begin{aligned}\phi(X) &= (X^{n/2} - \omega^{n/2})(X^{n/2} - \omega^{3n/2}) \\ &= (X^{n/4} - \omega^{n/4})(X^{n/4} - \omega^{5n/4})(X^{n/4} - \omega^{3n/4})(X^{n/4} - \omega^{7n/4}) \\ &= \cdots \\ &= \prod_{j=0}^{n-1}(X - \omega^{2\mathrm{br}_k(j)+1}),\end{aligned} \quad (1)$$

where $\mathrm{br}_k(j)$ denotes the bit-reversal of a k-bit number j, i.e., $\mathrm{br}_k\left(\sum_{i=0}^{k-1} a_i 2^i\right) = \sum_{i=0}^{k-1} a_{k-1-i} 2^i$. Of course the order of the factors is arbitrary. We use the bit-reversal in the index, because it is consistent with the algorithmic representation of the NTT we will introduce later.

The factorization of $\phi(X)$ in Eq. (1) leads to a series of ring isomorphisms over multiple layers ℓ:

$$\begin{array}{ll}\ell = 0: & K[X]/(X^n + 1) \\ & \quad\quad \downarrow \cong \\ \ell = 1: & K[X]/(X^{n/2} - \omega^{n/2}) \times K[X]/(X^{n/2} - \omega^{3n/2}) \\ & \quad\quad \downarrow \cong \\ \vdots & \vdots \\ & \quad\quad \downarrow \cong \\ \ell = k-1: & \prod_{j=0}^{n-1} K[X]/(X - \omega^{2\mathrm{br}_\ell(j)+1})\end{array} \quad (2)$$

The chain of isomorphisms defined in Eq. (2) is canonical and simply given by modular reduction as follows:

$\ell = 0:$ $\qquad\qquad\qquad\qquad f(X)$
$\qquad\qquad\qquad\qquad\qquad\quad \downarrow$
$\ell = 1:$ $\qquad (f(X) \bmod (X^{n/2} - \omega^{n/2}), f(X) \bmod (X^{n/2} - \omega^{3n/2}))$

$\qquad\qquad\qquad\vdots \qquad\qquad\qquad\qquad\quad \vdots$
$\qquad\qquad\qquad\qquad\qquad\qquad\qquad\quad \downarrow$
$\ell = k-1:$ $\qquad\qquad (f(\omega^{2\mathrm{br}_2(j)+1}))_{j=0,\ldots,n-1}$

where in the last layer $k-1$ we identify $f(X) \bmod X - \omega^{2\mathrm{br}_2(j)+1}$ with $f(\omega^{2\mathrm{br}_2(j)+1})$

We define the NTT : $K[X]/(\phi) \to K^n$ as the concatenation of the isomorphisms in Eq. (2), so we have:

$$\mathrm{NTT}(f) = (f(\omega^{2\mathrm{br}_k(0)+1}), f(\omega^{2\mathrm{br}_k(1)+1}), \ldots, f(\omega^{2\mathrm{br}_k(n-1)+1})). \qquad (3)$$

If we equip K^n with component-wise addition and multiplication, then the NTT is a ring isomorphism. In other words, $\mathrm{NTT}(f + g) = \mathrm{NTT}(f) + \mathrm{NTT}(g)$ and $\mathrm{NTT}(f \cdot g) = \mathrm{NTT}(f) \odot \mathrm{NTT}(g)$, where $\odot$ denotes component-wise multiplication.

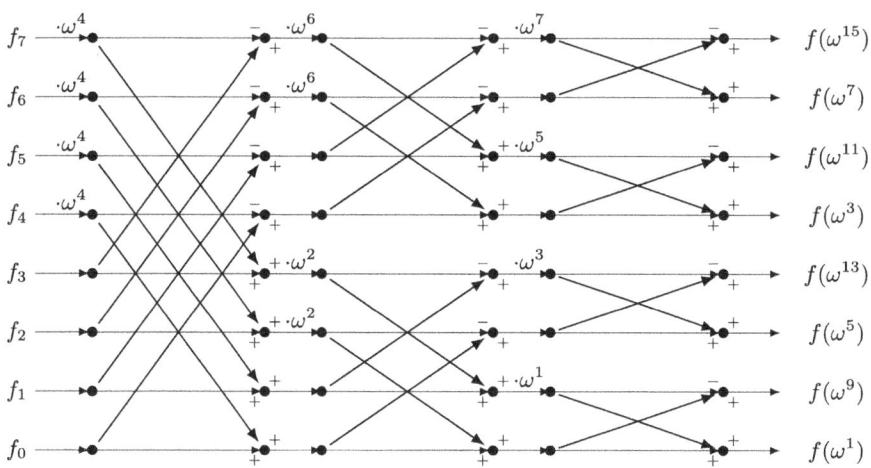

Fig. 2. The Cooley-Tukey algorithm for computing NTT.

The latter property is the reason why the NTT plays such an important role in many cryptographic schemes. It turns the computationally expensive multiplication of two polynomials of degree n into n field multiplications. This comes at the cost of first computing the NTT for the two polynomials and then computing NTT^{-1} of the component-wise product. In many applications, however, one of the polynomials is fixed, so an application can simply store and use $\text{NTT}(f)$ without recomputing it every time. For this reason, many cryptographic schemes specify explicitly that the NTT of a polynomial is to be stored or transmitted to another party, rather than the polynomial in its usual representation as a string of coefficients.

2.2 Implementing the NTT

The representation of the NTT as a series of isomorphisms in Eq. (2) leads directly to an efficient implementation, namely the well-known Cooley-Tukey butterfly construction. Let $f(X)$ be a polynomial of degree $n - 1$:

$$f(X) = \sum_{j=0}^{n-1} f_j X^j, \tag{4}$$

then the modular reductions mapping layer 0 to layer 1 in Eq. (2) are described by the following equations:

$$f(X) \bmod (X^{n/2} - \omega^{n/2}) = \sum_{j=0}^{n/2-1} (f_j + \omega^{n/2} f_{j+n/2}) X^j \tag{5}$$

and

$$f(X) \bmod (X^{n/2} - \omega^{3n/2}) = \sum_{j=0}^{n/2-1} (f_j - \omega^{n/2} f_{j+n/2}) X^j. \tag{6}$$

Repeating this for all layers gives the Cooley-Tukey butterfly structure of a typical NTT implementation, illustrated for $n = 8$ in Fig. 2. Reversing all operations gives the Gentleman-Sande implementation of the inverse NTT. A single butterfly does the following:

$$a' = b - a \cdot \omega^j \tag{7}$$
$$b' = b + a \cdot \omega^j \tag{8}$$

So to recover a, b from a', b' we compute:

$$a = \frac{1}{2}(b' - a')\omega^{-j} \tag{9}$$
$$b = \frac{1}{2}(b' + a') \tag{10}$$

The multiplication with $\frac{1}{2}$ can be deferred by multiplying every result by $2^{-\log_2 n}$ in a final step. Equation (9) and (10) lead to the inverse scheme of Fig. 2 shown in Fig. 3.

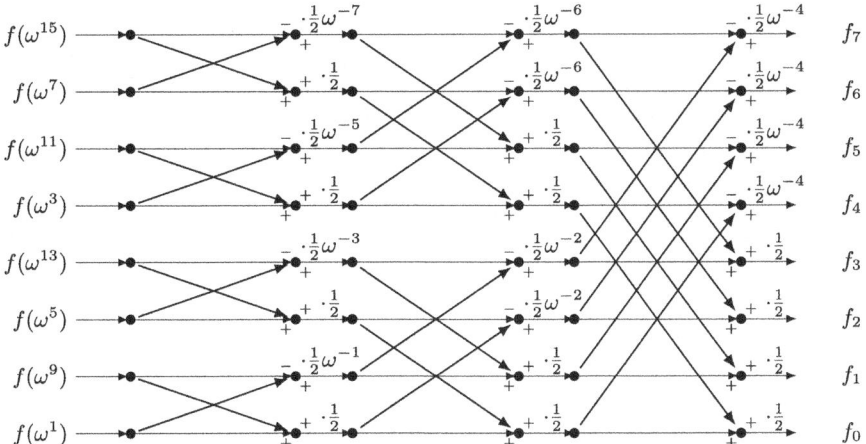

Fig. 3. The Gentleman-Sande algorithm for computing NTT^{-1}.

2.3 ML-DSA

ML-DSA [29] is a lattice-based general purpose digital signature scheme based on the Module Small Integer Solutions (M-SIS) and Module Learning with Errors (M-LWE) problems. The module is of dimension $k \times t$ over the polynomial ring $\mathcal{R}_q = \mathbb{Z}_q[X]/(X^n + 1)$, where $n = 256$ and $q = 2^{23} - 2^{13} + 1 = 8380417$. We see that $2n$ divides $q - 1$, so the NTT as constructed in Sect. 2 can be applied to multiply elements of $\mathcal{R}_q$. Because $n = 256 = 2^8$, it requires eight butterfly layers like the ones shown in Fig. 2. The reference implementation that is part of [18] implements the NTT in this way. For its inverse NTT^{-1} it uses the Gentleman-Sande algorithm. There are currently three versions ML-DSA-44, ML-DSA-65, ML-DSA-87 targeting the NIST security level 1, 3, 5, respectively. The parameters consist of the module dimension (k, t), the sampling bound of the secret η, and the rejection thresholds β and ω, cf. Table 1. The NTT is used in the key generation, signature generation, and signature verification routines of ML-DSA to perform the $(k \times t) \times (t \times 1)$ matrix-to-vector polynomial multiplications $\boldsymbol{A s_1}$, $\boldsymbol{A y}$, and $\boldsymbol{A z}$, respectively.

2.4 ML-KEM

ML-KEM [28] is a lattice-based key encapsulation mechanism based on the Module Learning With Errors (M-LWE) problem. The module is of dimension $t \times t$ over the polynomial ring $\mathcal{R}_q = \mathbb{Z}_q[X]/(X^n + 1)$, where $n = 256$ and $q = 13 \cdot 2^8 + 1 = 3329$. Note that n divides $q - 1$ but $2n$ does not. Therefore, the chain of isomorphisms in Eq. (2) breaks off at the penultimate seventh layer. Hence, in ML-KEM, the NTT reduces multiplication in $\mathcal{R}_q$ to multiplying a sequence of polynomials of degree one modulo a polynomial of degree two. The reference implementation that is part of [26] implements the NTT in this way.

For its inverse NTT^{-1} it uses the Gentleman-Sande algorithm, starting at the second layer. There are currently three versions ML-KEM-512, ML-KEM-768, ML-KEM-1024 targeting the NIST security levels 1, 3, 5, respectively. Each variant is specified by a parameter set, cf. Table 1, where t denotes the module dimension, (d_1, d_2) are the rounding parameters, and η is the width of the centered binomial distribution. The NTT is used in the key generation and encryption routines of ML-KEM to perform the $(t \times t) \times (t \times 1)$ matrix-to-vector polynomial multiplications $\boldsymbol{A}^t\boldsymbol{s}$ and $\boldsymbol{A}\boldsymbol{s}'$.

Table 1. ML-KEM and ML-DSA parameter sets.

	NIST	t	(d_1, d_2)	$\eta(s, s')$	$\eta(e, e', e'')$		NIST	(k, t)	η	β	ω
ML-KEM-512	1	2	(10, 4)	6	4	ML-DSA-44	1	(4, 4)	2	78	80
ML-KEM-768	3	3	(10, 4)	4	4	ML-DSA-65	3	(6, 5)	4	196	55
ML-KEM-1024	5	4	(11, 5)	4	4	ML-DSA-87	5	(8, 7)	2	120	75

3 Fault Resistant NTT Using Polynomial Evaluation and Interpolation Techniques

This section presents the proposed method for safeguarding the NTT against fault injection attacks and its error detection capability. Furthermore, it provides a calculation of the additional computational effort required and shows how to concretely use it to secure the NTT in ML-KEM and ML-DSA.

3.1 Proposed Countermeasure

The idea behind our countermeasure is shown in Fig. 1. More precisely, let $u \in K$, where the criteria for choosing u are given in Lemma 3, then our countermeasure consists of the following steps:

1. Compute $w = f(u)$ by evaluating f at u;
2. Compute $\mathrm{NTT}(f) = (f(\omega^{2\mathrm{br}_k(0)+1}), f(\omega^{2\mathrm{br}_k(1)+1}), \ldots, f(\omega^{2\mathrm{br}_k(n-1)+1}))$ with, e.g., the usual Cooley-Tukey algorithm;
3. Compute $w' = f(u)$ by interpolating the n output values $\mathrm{NTT}(f)$;
4. Check that $w = w'$. If this is not the case, then a fault in the computation of $\mathrm{NTT}(f)$ has been detected.

Let us first look at the computational cost of this countermeasure. Its error detection properties will be analyzed in Sect. 3.2.

Lemma 1. *Let $u \in K$ and $f \in K[X]$ of degree $n - 1$. Then computing $f(u)$ requires at most $n - 1$ multiplications and $n - 1$ additions in K.*

Proof. This refers to Horner's method. We write

$$f(X) = \sum_{j=0}^{n-1} f_j X^j = ((\cdots((f_{n-1}X + f_{n-2})X + f_{n-3})\cdots)X + f_1)X + f_0 \quad (11)$$

and count the operations on the right. □

```
49      void ntt(int32_t a[N]) {
50          unsigned int len, start, j, k;
51          int32_t zeta, t;
52
53          k = 0;
54          for(len = 128; len > 0; len >>= 1) {
55              for(start = 0; start < N; start = j + len) {
56                  zeta = zetas[++k];
57                  for(j = start; j < start + len; ++j) {
58                      t = montgomery_reduce((int64_t)zeta
59                          * a[j + len]);
60                      a[j + len] = a[j] - t;
61                      a[j] = a[j] + t;
62                  }
63              }
64          }
65      }
```

Listing 1.1. Excerpt from ref/ntt.c in [27]

As we have clearly shown in Eq. (3), the NTT maps a polynomial f to n values of f. By interpolation, the polynomial f can be reconstructed from these n values.

In detail, we write

$$L_j(X) = \prod_{\substack{0 \leq i < n \\ i \neq j}} \frac{X - \omega^{2i+1}}{\omega^{2j+1} - \omega^{2i+1}}, \qquad j = 0, 1, \ldots, n-1 \qquad (12)$$

for the n Lagrange polynomials for the points $\{\omega, \omega^3, \omega^5, \ldots, \omega^{2n-1}\}$. These polynomials form a basis of the K-vector subspace of polynomials of degree at most $n-1$ in $K[X]$ and have the property that

$$L_j(\omega^{2i+1}) = \begin{cases} 1 & \text{if } i = j \\ 0 & \text{if } i \neq j \end{cases} \qquad (13)$$

Then

$$f(X) = \sum_{j=0}^{n-1} f(\omega^{2j+1}) L_j(X) \qquad (14)$$

For our countermeasure, we do not want to reconstruct f from $f(\omega^{2j+1})_{j=0,\ldots,n-1}$ but just evaluate f at a single point u. We note that the values $L_j(u)$ can be precomputed as soon as u is fixed. The interpolated value can then be calculated with Eq. (14). In particular, if the point u is fixed at compile-time and only f varies at run-time, then we can precompute the values $L_j(u)$ and link them as a table to the code.

Lemma 2. *Let $u \in K$ and $f \in K[X]$ of degree $n-1$. Then computing $f(u)$ given $f(\omega^{2j+1})_{j=0,\ldots,n-1}$ and $(L_j(u))_{j=0,\ldots,n-1}$ requires at most n multiplications and $n-1$ additions.*

Proof. Count the operations on the right-hand side of Eq. (14). □

An algorithmic description of the proposed countermeasures is provided in Appendix A.

3.2 Error Detection Properties

Let us now have a look at the error detection capability of our countermeasure. We will first discuss how low-level faults like instruction skips or changed register values lead to higher level mathematical faults in the NTT. Listing 1.1 shows a typical example for an implementation of the NTT in software. Let us restrict our attention to the innermost loop body in lines 58–60. This corresponds to a single Cooley-Tukey butterfly as illustrated in Fig. 4:

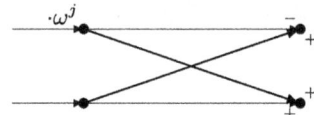

Fig. 4. A single Cooley-Tukey butterfly from Fig. 2.

We assume a single instruction skip or a register fault affects one of the lines 58–60 in Listing 1.1 and hence can cause any of the following types of errors:

1. An error in one of the input coefficients (caused by skipping of loading a[j] or a[j+1] or a register fault).
2. An error in the multiplication with ω^j. This is equivalent to an error in the input coefficient that is being multiplied by ω^j.
3. An error in the subtraction. This is equivalent to an error in an input coefficient in the following layer.
4. An error in the addition. This is also equivalent to an error in an input coefficient in the following layer.

We see that all four types of errors can be reduced to an error in an input coefficient in one of the layers of the Cooley-Tukey implementation of the NTT.

A fault in a single coefficient somewhere in the NTT means that the polynomial in one of the ring isomorphisms of Eq. (2) is changed. Let us assume this happens in layer ℓ and write $g(X) \in K[X]/(X^{n/2^\ell} - \omega^{(2\mathrm{br}_\ell(i)+1)n/2^\ell})$ for the affected polynomial. Then $g(X)$ is changed to

$$\tilde{g}(X) = g(X) + DX^m \tag{15}$$

for some $D \in K$ and some integer m, $0 \le m < n/2^\ell$.

We need to determine how the error propagates through the following layers in the NTT implementation. To do this, we translate the error in layer ℓ to an error in layer 0. Define a polynomial

$$e(X) := D\Big(\prod_{j=0, j \ne i}^{2^\ell-1} \frac{X^{n/2^\ell} - \omega^{(2\mathrm{br}_\ell(j)+1)n/2^\ell}}{\omega^{(2\mathrm{br}_\ell(i)+1)n/2^\ell} - \omega^{(2\mathrm{br}_\ell(j)+1)n/2^\ell}}\Big) X^m. \tag{16}$$

Now

$$e(X) \bmod (X^{n/2^\ell} - \omega^{(2\mathrm{br}_\ell(j)+1)n/2^\ell}) = \begin{cases} DX^m & \text{if } i = j \\ 0 & \text{if } i \ne j \end{cases}. \tag{17}$$

Hence, the error that replaces $g(X)$ with $\tilde{g}(X)$ is equivalent to an error that replaces the input $f(X)$ with

$$\tilde{f}(X) = f(X) + e(X) \tag{18}$$

Therefore, the injected error changes the output of the NTT to

$$\mathrm{NTT}(\tilde{f}) = \mathrm{NTT}(f) + \mathrm{NTT}(e) \tag{19}$$

and the interpolation in our countermeasure will compute $\tilde{f}(u) = f(u) + e(u)$.

Lemma 3. *Let $u \in K \setminus \{0\}$ such that $u^{n/2^\ell} \ne \omega^{(2\mathrm{br}_\ell(j)+1)n/2^\ell}$ for any $0 \le \ell \le k$ and any $0 \le j < 2^\ell$. Then the countermeasure described in Sect. 3.1 detects an error in a single coefficient in an NTT implementation as in Sect. 2.2.*

Proof. We have just seen that the interpolation step of the countermeasure computes $\tilde{f}(u) = f(u) + e(u)$, whereas the evaluation step computes $f(u)$. We notice from the definition of $e(X)$ in Eq. (16) that $e(u) \ne 0$. Hence, $\tilde{f}(u) \ne f(u)$ and therefore the error is detected. □

Such a u is easy to find by just picking a random u, testing the condition and, if necessary, repeat the procedure until a suitable u is found.

If an attacker injects several faults or a single fault causes several errors on the mathematical level (e.g., an early loop abort that skips entire parts of the NTT), we cannot provide an absolute guarantee of detecting them with our countermeasure. However, such faults are still detected with a high probability. It seems reasonable to assume that an attack with several faults will affect interpolated value in such a way that the probability of it being correct is the same as for a random guess. In this case, the probability that an attack of this type is detected, is $1 - 1/q$ if K has q elements.

If an attacker can inject several faults, there is of course the possibility that the comparison $w = w'$ in step 4 in Sect. 3.1 is attacked. This, however, is a generic problem for any kind of fault detection mechanism. Setting all twiddle constants to zero as in [23] corresponds to many faults of type 2 in Sect. 3.2.

3.3 Applying the Countermeasure to the Inverse NTT

All the concepts presented in the previous section can be adapted to the NTT^{-1} operation and the Gentleman-Sande algorithm as well.

Specifically, the order of the operations in Sect. 3.1 changes. If the input to NTT^{-1} is $\text{NTT}(f)$ for some polynomial f, then our countermeasure, applied to NTT^{-1} becomes:

1. Compute $w = f(u)$ by interpolating $\text{NTT}(f)$, the input to NTT^{-1};
2. Compute $f = \text{NTT}^{-1}(\text{NTT}(f))$;
3. Compute $w' = f(u)$ by evaluating f on u;
4. Check that $w = w'$. If this is not the case, then a fault in the computation of NTT^{-1} has been detected.

From Eq. (9) and Eq. (10) we see that a single Gentleman-Sande butterfly looks like in Fig. 5.

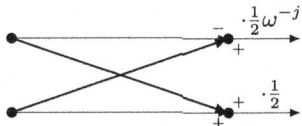

Fig. 5. A single Gentleman-Sande butterfly from Fig. 3

As in Sect. 3.2, we pointed out that the four types of errors listed there can again each be reduced to an error in a single coefficient. Such an error can again be described by the addition of a monomial DX^m as in Eq. (15). The resulting error in the output of NTT^{-1} is then provided by Eq. (16). The faulty output of NTT^{-1} is given by Eq. (18). So, in this case, the interpolation step of the countermeasure computes $f(u)$, whereas the evaluation computes $\tilde{f}(u)$. The proof of Lemma 3 shows that, if u is chosen as in Lemma 3, then $e(u) \neq 0$. Hence, $\tilde{f}(u) \neq f(u)$ and the error in the computation of NTT^{-1} is detected.

3.4 Compatibility of the Countermeasure with Ring Operations

When used as part of a cryptographic algorithm, the purpose of the NTT is typically to accelerate multiplication. Polynomial addition, although not accelerated by the NTT, is also a common operation in cryptographic algorithms that use the NTT. Therefore, it is worth exploring the compatibility of our countermeasure with these operations and determining if it can be utilized to provide protection for them as well.

The ring multiplication $h = f \cdot g$ can efficiently be computed using the NTT as $h = \text{NTT}^{-1}(\text{NTT}(f \cdot g)) = \text{NTT}^{-1}(\text{NTT}(f) \odot \text{NTT}(g))$. Therefore, our countermeasure can be extended to protect the multiplication and not just the NTT by following the steps outlined below:

1. Compute $w_1' = f(u)$, $w_2' = g(u)$, by interpolating the n output values of NTT(f) and NTT(g), respectively;
2. Compute $w = h(u)$ by evaluating the result of the multiplication at u;
3. Check that $w = w_1' w_2'$. If this is not the case, then a fault in the computation of the ring multiplication has been detected.

Note that in some algorithm specifications, e.g., ML-KEM, some inputs are already NTT-transformed, so that the transformations NTT(f) and NTT(g) in the first step are not always needed. For error detection to cover the NTT operations as well as the multiplication, the checksums w_1' and w_2' have to be verified as described in Sect. 3.1. Otherwise, if, for example, $w_1' = 0$, errors in the computation of NTT(g) may go undetected.

Analogously, our countermeasure is compatible with polynomial addition. This is particularly interesting when a polynomial is split into two shares as a countermeasure against side-channel attacks. If $f = f_1 + f_2$ and $w_1 = f_1(u)$, $w_2 = f_2(u)$, then we can check that $f(u) = w_1 + w_2$, hence providing combined side-channel and fault resistance.

3.5 Comparison with Other Countermeasures

An obvious way of securing an NTT implementation against single faults is to compute the NTT twice and compare the results. Computing the NTT with the Cooley-Tukey method costs $\frac{n}{2} \log_2(n)$ multiplications and $n \log_2(n)$ additions. From Lemmas 1 and 2 we see that the total cost of our countermeasure is $2n-1$ multiplications and $2n-2$ additions. Hence, the cost of our countermeasure relative to the cost of the NTT in terms of multiplications is

$$\frac{2n-1}{\frac{n}{2}\log_2(n)} = \frac{4-2/n}{\log_2(n)} \tag{20}$$

and in terms of additions it is

$$\frac{2n-2}{n\log_2(n)} = \frac{2-2/n}{\log_2(n)}. \tag{21}$$

In the case of ML-DSA we have $n = 256$ and hence the cost of our countermeasure is about an extra 50% multiplications and an extra 25% additions. This is significantly less than the overhead of 100% for computing the NTT a second time. In practice, the exact performance cost depends on the implementation details (cf. Sect. 4).

In [13], a different type of countermeasure against fault injection attacks is presented. The authors enlarge the modulus q and use this 'extra space' to introduce redundancy into the coefficients of the NTT. The cost of this countermeasure depends very much on the hardware architecture underlying the implementation. The idea is to use registers which are wide enough to hold numbers significantly larger than q. Similarly, the effectiveness of this countermeasure depends very much on exactly this register width. An important difference between the countermeasure in [13] and the one presented in this paper is that our countermeasure guarantees the detection of a single fault in a coefficient, while the error detection property in [13] is probabilistic.

As we have seen at the end of Sect. 3.2, our countermeasure can also detect errors beyond the guaranteed detection with a certain probability. How this compares to the probabilistic error detection of [13] again depends very much on the concrete implementation. However, if we assume implementation on a 32-bit platform and if we further assume that the size of q is roughly 16 bit, then the probabilistic error detection capability of our countermeasure and that of [13] are similar.

3.6 Adapting the Countermeasure to ML-KEM

As far as possible, we will keep our description generic to apply to any 'ML-KEM-like' NTT, i.e., we will continue working with the letters q, n etc. rather than concrete numbers. As we have described in Sect. 2.4, the NTT in ML-KEM leaves out the final layer. In other words, the NTT computes $n/2$ polynomials $a_j X + b_j$ of degree one such that

$$a_j X + b_j = f(X) \bmod (X^2 - \zeta^{2\mathrm{br}_{k-1}(j)+1}), \tag{22}$$

where ζ is an n-th root of unity. So, instead of computing $f(u)$ for our countermeasure as in the previous section, it seems natural to compute $f(X) \bmod (X^2 \bmod u)$ instead.

To adapt our countermeasure, we define polynomials for $j = 0, 1, \ldots, n/2-1$:

$$M_j(X) := \prod_{i=0, i \neq j}^{2^{k-1}-1} \frac{X^2 - \zeta^{2\mathrm{br}_{k-1}(i)+1}}{\zeta^{2\mathrm{br}_{k-1}(j)+1} - \zeta^{2\mathrm{br}_{k-1}(i)+1}} \tag{23}$$

In ML-KEM we have $n = 256$, and the specification of ML-KEM [28] uses the 256-th root of unity $\zeta = 17$ in $\mathbb{F}_{3329}$.

Lemma 4. *With the notation as above:*

$$f(X) = \sum_{j=0}^{n/2-1} (a_j X + b_j) M_j(X) \tag{24}$$

Proof. Observe that

$$M_j(X) \bmod (X^2 - \zeta^{2\mathrm{br}_{k-1}(i)+1}) = \begin{cases} 1 & \text{if } j = j \\ 0 & \text{if } j \neq i \end{cases}. \tag{25}$$

Hence, we have for all $i = 0, 1, \ldots, n/2 - 1$:

$$\sum_{j=0}^{n/2} (a_j X + b_j) M_j(X) \bmod (X^2 - \zeta^{2\mathrm{br}_{k-1}(i)+1}) = a_i X + b_i \tag{26}$$

$$= f(X) \bmod (X^2 - \zeta^{2\mathrm{br}_{k-1}(i)+1}).$$

$\square$

Let $u \in K$. Then, before the NTT, we can compute

$$f(X) \bmod (X^2 - u) = \Big(\sum_{j=0}^{n/2-1} f_{2j+1} u^j \Big) X + \Big(\sum_{j=0}^{n/2-1} f_{2j} u^j \Big) \qquad (27)$$

Both sums can be computed efficiently with Horner's method again. This requires $n/2 - 1$ multiplications and $n/2 - 1$ additions in K for each sum.

Looking at the definition of $M_j(X)$ in Eq. (23), we see that $M_j(X) \bmod (X^2 - u) =: m_j \in K$ for all $j = 0, 1, \ldots, n/2 - 1$.

Hence, using Lemma 4, we can compute $f(X) \bmod (X^2 - u)$ from the NTT output, i.e., from the polynomials $a_j X + b_j$ as:

$$\begin{aligned}
\sum_{j=0}^{n/2-1} (a_j X + b_j) M_j(X) \bmod (X^2 - u) &= \sum_{j=0}^{n/2-1} (a_j X + b_j) m_j \\
&= \Big(\sum_{j=0}^{n/2-1} a_j m_j \Big) X + \Big(\sum_{j=0}^{n/2-1} b_j m_j \Big)
\end{aligned} \qquad (28)$$

Computing both sums on the right requires $n/2$ multiplications and $n/2 - 1$ additions for each, and so n multiplications and $n - 2$ additions in total.

Hence, for polynomial evaluation and interpolation together $2n - 2$ multiplications and $2n - 4$ additions are required in total. The cost of our countermeasure relative to the cost of the NTT in terms of multiplications is therefore

$$\frac{2n - 2}{\frac{n}{2}(\log_2(n) - 1)} \qquad (29)$$

and in terms of additions it is

$$\frac{2n - 4}{n(\log_2(n) - 1)} \qquad (30)$$

For the concrete parameter $n = 256$ in ML-KEM this gives a cost of about 57% extra multiplications and about 28% additions.

Lemma 5. *Let $u \in K \setminus \{0\}$ such that $u^{n/2^{\ell+1}} \neq \zeta^{(2\mathrm{br}_\ell(j)+1)n/2^{\ell+1}}$ for any $0 \leq \ell < k$ and any $0 \leq j < 2^\ell$. Then the countermeasure as described in this section detects an error in a single coefficient in the ML-KEM NTT.*

Proof. Based on the same arguments as before, any error is equivalent to an error of the type $e(X)$ as in Eq. (16). The checksum in Eq. (28) will be wrong by $e(X) \bmod (X^2 - u)$. We have chosen u such that this is non-zero. Hence, the error will be detected. □

4 Practical Evaluation

To verify the feasibility of our approach and our estimates for its performance impact, we implemented our countermeasure on a 'black pill' board with an STM32F401CCU6 microcontroller [12]. This microcontroller is based on an ARM Cortex-M4 CPU architecture. Please note that our countermeasure requires storing $n \log_2(q)$ bits if precomputed values are used to speed up the interpolation. This overhead accounts for 5888 bits in case of ML-DSA and 2996 bits in case of ML-KEM. The precomputed values can be stored in ROM or computed on-the-fly at startup and stored in RAM. The results of evaluation w and interpolation w' require $2 \log_2(q)$ bits and can be stored in RAM or registers (in total, 46-bit for ML-DSA and 24-bit for ML-KEM, respectively).

4.1 Practical Evaluation for ML-DSA

We implemented our countermeasure for ML-DSA. So the field is $\mathbb{F}_q$ with $q = 8380417$, and we are working in the ring $\mathbb{F}_q[X]/(X^{256} + 1)$.

We took the NTT from the ML-DSA implementation by the pqm4 library [17], a well-known library that provides optimized implementations of post-quantum cryptographic schemes for microcontroller-based platforms.

The results of our performance measurements for ML-DSA are summarized in Table 2.

Table 2. Performance numbers for our countermeasure applied to ML-DSA.

operation	clock cycles (avg.)
evaluate f	2879
interpolate NTT(f) and evaluate	3160
compute NTT(f)	8406

The relative cost of our countermeasure applied to ML-DSA can easily be computed from the numbers in Table 2 as:

$$\frac{(\text{cost of evaluating } f) + (\text{cost of interpolating NTT}(f) \text{ and evaluating})}{(\text{cost of NTT})} \equiv 72\%$$

This is close to the expected overhead from the theoretical estimate given in Sect. 3.5. The implementation of our countermeasure has not been optimized for the ML-DSA NTT or a particular point in the evaluation. So there may be some potential for further optimizations. The NTT implementation in the pqm4 library, on the other hand, is highly optimized.

4.2 Practical Evaluation for ML-KEM

We also implemented our countermeasure for ML-KEM. In this case, the field is $\mathbb{F}_q$ with $q = 3329$, and we are working in the ring $\mathbb{F}_q[X]/(X^{256}+1)$. As we explained in Sect. 2.4, compared to ML-DSA the NTT in ML-KEM is truncated. Again, we took the NTT implementation for ML-KEM from the pqm4 library [17] to have an optimized implementation in the public domain as a benchmark.

The results of our performance measurements for ML-KEM are summarized in Table 3.

Table 3. Performance numbers for our countermeasure applied to ML-KEM.

operation	clock cycles (avg.)
evaluate f	1752
interpolate NTT(f) and evaluate	2150
compute NTT(f)	5822

We see that the relative overhead of our countermeasure is 67%, and hence our countermeasure is significantly cheaper than re-computation as expected. As with ML-DSA, the overhead is higher than expected from the theoretical estimate in Sect. 3.6. We put this down to the fact that the pqm4 code is highly optimized.

5 Conclusion

We have presented a countermeasure that protects an implementation of the NTT or its inverse against a single fault in one of the coefficients. We have seen that this fault model also covers faults in a twiddle factor, the multiplication with a twiddle factor and the addition in a butterfly operation. Our countermeasure requires $2n - 1$ multiplications and $2n - 2$ additions in the field K, hence is significantly faster than a redundant computation. We have also shown how to adapt our countermeasure to situations where the computation of the NTT is 'incomplete', as it is the case for ML-KEM. Our countermeasure can be safely combined with further masking and shuffling countermeasures to achieve combined fault and side-channel protections. Finally, it is worth noting that the countermeasure presented in this paper can also be applied to other schemes using the NTT operation, e.g., other cryptographic schemes based on structured lattices.

Acknowledgments. This work was partly funded by the German Federal Ministry for Economic Affairs and Climate Action in the project PoQsiKom through grant number 13I40V010 and by the German Federal Ministry of Education and Research in the project Quoryptan through grant number 16KIS2033.

A Algorithmic Countermeasure

This section provides an algorithmic description of the proposed fault countermeasure to protect the NTT operation. Algorithm 1 describes a fault resistant NTT for $\mathcal{R}_q = \mathbb{Z}_q[X]/(X^n + 1)$ and $K = \mathbb{Z}_q$, while Algorithm 2 and Algorithm 3 describe algorithms for polynomial evaluation and interpolation using the Horner and Lagrange techniques, respectively. In particular, Algorithm 3 takes advantage of a precomputation algorithm specified in Algorithm 4.

Algorithm 1. Algorithmic description of the fault resistant NTT for $\mathcal{R}_q = \mathbb{Z}_q[X]/(X^n + 1)$ and $K = \mathbb{Z}_q$.

Require: $f \in \mathcal{R}_q$ with $f = (f_0, ..., f_{n-1})$, $u \in K$ as defined in Lem. 3 (or Lem. 5 in the case of a 'truncated' NTT as in ML-KEM) and $L = \text{Precompute}(u)$
Ensure: $\hat{f} \in K^n$ s.t. $\hat{f} = (\hat{f}_0, ..., \hat{f}_{n-1})$ with $\hat{f}_j = f(\omega^{2\text{br}_k(j)+1})$ for $0 \leq j < n-1$
1: **procedure** FaultResistant-NTT(f, u, L)
2:    $w \leftarrow \text{Eval}(f, u)$
3:    $\hat{f} \leftarrow \text{NTT}(f)$
4:    $w' \leftarrow \text{Interpolate}(\hat{f}, L)$
5:    **if** $w \neq w'$ **then**
6:        Error()
7:    **end if**
8:    **return** $\hat{f} = (\hat{f}_0, ..., \hat{f}_{n-1})$
9: **end procedure**

Algorithm 2. Evaluation by Horner's rule for $\mathcal{R}_q = \mathbb{Z}_q[X]/(X^n + 1)$ and $K = \mathbb{Z}_q$.

Require: $f \in \mathcal{R}_q$ s.t. $f = (f_0, ..., f_{n-1})$ and $u \in K$
Ensure: $w \in K$
1: **procedure** Eval(f, u)
2:    $w \leftarrow f_{n-1}$
3:    **for** $i \leftarrow 0$ **to** $n-2$ **do**
4:        $w \leftarrow f_{n-2-i} + wu$
5:    **end for**
6:    **return** w
7: **end procedure**

Algorithm 3. Lagrange interpolation with immediate evaluation for $K = \mathbb{Z}_q$.

Require: $\hat{f} \in K^n$ with $\hat{f} = (\hat{f}_0, ..., \hat{f}_{n-1})$, $u \in K$ and $L = \text{PRECOMPUTE}(u)$
Ensure: $w' \in K$
1: **procedure** INTERPOLATE($\hat{f}, L$)
2:     $w' \leftarrow 0$
3:     **for** $i \leftarrow 0$ **to** $n-1$ **do**
4:         $w' \leftarrow w' + \hat{f}_i \cdot L[i]$
5:     **end for**
6:     **return** w'
7: **end procedure**

Algorithm 4. Precompute the $L_i(u)$ for interpolation, where L_i is defined in Eq. (12) and $K = \mathbb{Z}_q$.

Require: $u \in K$
Ensure: $L = (L_0(u), L_1(u), \ldots, L_{n-1}(u))$
1: **procedure** PRECOMPUTE(u)
2:     **for** $i \leftarrow 0$ **to** $n-1$ **do**
3:         $L[i] \leftarrow L_i(u)$
4:     **end for**
5:     **return** L
6: **end procedure**

References

1. Ahmadi, K., Aghapour, S., Kermani, M.M., Azarderakhsh, R.: Efficient algorithm level error detection for number-theoretic transform used for kyber assessed on FPGAs and arm. arXiv preprint arXiv:2403.01215 (2024)
2. Bauer, S., De Santis, F.: A differential fault attack against deterministic falcon signatures. IACR Cryptology ePrint Archive, p. 422 (2023). https://eprint.iacr.org/2023/422
3. Bauer, S., De Santis, F.: Forging dilithium and falcon signatures by single fault injection. In: 2023 Workshop on Fault Detection and Tolerance in Cryptography (FDTC). IEEE Computer Society (2023)
4. Berthet, P., Tavernier, C., Danger, J., Sauvage, L.: Quasi-linear masking to protect kyber against both SCA and FIA. IACR Cryptology ePrint Archive, p. 1220 (2023). https://eprint.iacr.org/2023/1220
5. Bindel, N., Buchmann, J., Krämer, J.: Lattice-based signature schemes and their sensitivity to fault attacks. Cryptology ePrint Archive, Report 2016/415 (2016). https://eprint.iacr.org/2016/415
6. Bos, J.W., Gourjon, M., Renes, J., Schneider, T., van Vredendaal, C.: Masking kyber: first- and higher-order implementations. IACR TCHES **2021**(4), 173–214 (2021). https://doi.org/10.46586/tches.v2021.i4.173-214

7. Bruinderink, L.G., Pessl, P.: Differential fault attacks on deterministic lattice signatures. IACR TCHES **2018**(3), 21–43 (2018). https://doi.org/10.13154/tches.v2018.i3.21-43
8. Coron, J., Gérard, F., Trannoy, M., Zeitoun, R.: Improved gadgets for the high-order masking of dilithium. IACR Trans. Cryptogr. Hardw. Embed. Syst. **2023**(4), 110–145 (2023). https://doi.org/10.46586/TCHES.V2023.I4.110-145
9. Delvaux, J.: Roulette: a diverse family of feasible fault attacks on masked kyber. IACR TCHES **2022**(4), 637–660 (2022). https://doi.org/10.46586/tches.v2022.i4.637-660
10. Delvaux, J., Merino Del Pozo, S.: Roulette: Breaking kyber with diverse fault injection setups. Cryptology ePrint Archive, Report 2021/1622 (2021). https://eprint.iacr.org/2021/1622
11. Duparc, M., Taha, M.: Improved NTT and CRT-based RNR blinding for side-channel and fault resistant kyber. Cryptology ePrint Archive (2025)
12. Gravekamp, T.: WeAct Black Pill V3.0. https://stm32-base.org/boards/STM32F401CEU6-WeAct-Black-Pill-V3.0.html. Accessed 21 Dec 2023
13. Heinz, D., Pöppelmann, T.: Combined fault and DPA protection for lattice-based cryptography. Cryptology ePrint Archive, Report 2021/101 (2021). https://eprint.iacr.org/2021/101
14. Heinz, D., Pöppelmann, T.: Combined fault and DPA protection for lattice-based cryptography. Cryptology ePrint Archive, Paper 2021/101 (2021). https://eprint.iacr.org/2021/101
15. Hermelink, J., Pessl, P., Pöppelmann, T.: Fault-enabled chosen-ciphertext attacks on kyber. In: Adhikari, A., Küsters, R., Preneel, B. (eds.) Progress in Cryptology - INDOCRYPT 2021 - 22nd International Conference on Cryptology in India, Jaipur, India, December 12–15, 2021, Proceedings. LNCS, vol. 13143, pp. 311–334. Springer (2021). https://doi.org/10.1007/978-3-030-92518-5_15
16. Hermelink, J., Streit, S., Strieder, E., Thieme, K.: Adapting belief propagation to counter shuffling of NTTS. IACR Trans. Cryptogr. Hardw. Embed. Syst. **2023**(1), 60–88 (2023). https://doi.org/10.46586/TCHES.V2023.I1.60-88 https://doi.org/10.46586/TCHES.V2023.I1.60-88
17. Kannwischer, M.J., Petri, R., Rijneveld, J., Schwabe, P., Stoffelen, K.: PQM4: post-quantum crypto library for the ARM Cortex-M4. https://github.com/mupq/pqm4
18. Lyubashevsky, V., et al.: CRYSTALS-DILITHIUM, Technical report, National Institute of Standards and Technology (2022). https://csrc.nist.gov/Projects/post-quantum-cryptography/selected-algorithms-2022
19. Migliore, V., Gérard, B., Tibouchi, M., Fouque, P.: Masking dilithium - efficient implementation and side-channel evaluation. In: Deng, R.H., Gauthier-Umaña, V., Ochoa, M., Yung, M. (eds.) Applied Cryptography and Network Security - 17th International Conference, ACNS 2019, Bogota, Colombia, June 5-7, 2019, Proceedings. LNCS, vol. 11464, pp. 344–362. Springer (2019). https://doi.org/10.1007/978-3-030-21568-2_17
20. NIST: NIST announces first four quantum-resistant cryptographic algorithms (2022). https://www.nist.gov/news-events/news/2022/07/nist-announces-first-four-quantum-resistant-cryptographic-algorithms
21. Ravi, P., Chattopadhyay, A., Baksi, A.: Side-channel and fault-injection attacks over lattice-based post-quantum schemes (kyber, dilithium): survey and new results. Cryptology ePrint Archive, Report 2022/737 (2022). https://eprint.iacr.org/2022/737

22. Ravi, P., Poussier, R., Bhasin, S., Chattopadhyay, A.: On configurable SCA countermeasures against single trace attacks for the NTT - a performance evaluation study over kyber and dilithium on the ARM cortex-m4. In: Batina, L., Picek, S., Mondal, M. (eds.) Security, Privacy, and Applied Cryptography Engineering - 10th International Conference, SPACE 2020, Kolkata, India, December 17-21, 2020, Proceedings. LNCS, vol. 12586, pp. 123–146. Springer (2020). https://doi.org/10.1007/978-3-030-66626-2_7
23. Ravi, P., Yang, B., Bhasin, S., Zhang, F., Chattopadhyay, A.: Fiddling the twiddle constants - fault injection analysis of the number theoretic transform. IACR Trans. Cryptogr. Hardw. Embed. Syst. **2023**(2), 447–481 (2023). https://doi.org/10.46586/TCHES.V2023.I2.447-481
24. Sarker, A.: Secure hardware constructions for fault detection of lattice-based post-quantum cryptosystems, Ph.D. thesis, University of South Florida (2022)
25. Sarker, A., Canto, A.C., Kermani, M.M., Azarderakhsh, R.: Error detection architectures for hardware/software co-design approaches of number-theoretic transform. IEEE Trans. Comput. Aided Des. Integr. Circuits Syst. **42**(7), 2418–2422 (2023). https://doi.org/10.1109/TCAD.2022.3218614
26. Schwabe, P., et al.: CRYSTALS-KYBER, Technical report, National Institute of Standards and Technology (2022). https://csrc.nist.gov/Projects/post-quantum-cryptography/selected-algorithms-2022
27. Seiler, G., et al.: Official reference implementation of the Dilithium signature scheme. https://github.com/pq-crystals/dilithium
28. Natiopnal Institute of Standards Technology: FIPS 203 module-lattice-based key-encapsulation mechanism standard, Technical report, U.S. Department of Commerce (2024). https://doi.org/10.6028/NIST.FIPS.203
29. Natiopnal Institute of Standards Technology: FIPS 204 module-lattice-based digital signature standard, Technical report, U.S. Department of Commerce (2024). https://doi.org/10.6028/NIST.FIPS.204
30. Xagawa, K., Ito, A., Ueno, R., Takahashi, J., Homma, N.: Fault-injection attacks against NIST's post-quantum cryptography round 3 KEM candidates. In: Tibouchi, M., Wang, H. (eds.) ASIACRYPT 2021, Part II. LNCS, vol. 13091, pp. 33–61. Springer, Heidelberg (2021). https://doi.org/10.1007/978-3-030-92075-3_2

Homomorphic Encryption and White-Box Cryptography

Hybrid Homomorphic Encryption Resistance to Side-Channel Attacks

Pierugo Pace[1,2](✉), Hervé Pelletier[2], and Serge Vaudenay[1]

[1] EPFL, Lausanne, Switzerland
pierugo.pace@gmail.com, serge.vaudenay@epfl.ch
[2] Nagra Kudelski Group, Cheseaux-sur-Lausanne, Switzerland
herve.pelletier@nagra.com

Abstract. This work performs a side-channel analysis on the Hybrid Homomorphic Encryption cipher `Elisabeth-b4`. In particular, a Correlation Power Analysis allows to recover the 2048-bit key with 35,000 traces. Mounting template attacks or using Machine Learning decreases this number to 1,000. We then implement 2-share masking and shuffling, which completely eliminates the leakage measure – a Test Vector Leakage Assessment (TVLA) – and mitigates the Correlation Power Analysis and template attacks. Using a Divide and Conquer Deep Learning approach, we manage to bypass them but the number of required traces increases to 250,000.

Keywords: Hybrid homomorphic encryption · Side-channel analysis · Correlation power analysis · Template attacks · Deep machine learning · Countermeasures

1 Introduction

1.1 Context

We currently live in a world where the smallest Internet of Things (IoT) devices are able to collect useful data on the field at low cost and are used in combination with the largest cloud computers, that have the computing capabilities to process this data. This motivating process immediately raises privacy concerns if the data sent by the IoT contains sensitive information. A discovery from 2009 showed that *Fully Homomorphic Encryption* (FHE) could be used to tackle this problem [15]. FHE provides confidentiality and arbitrary computation on encrypted data, which allow cloud servers to process sensitive data that stays encrypted. While having practical realisations, Homomorphic Encryption is a costly operation that still remains a challenge for IoT devices.

Recent work thus came up with the Hybrid Homomorphic Encryption (HHE) framework, providing the same guarantees as FHE but shifting the overhead from the IoT device to the server [30]. The framework consists in the IoT device sending symmetrically-encrypted data and the server needing to *transcipher* it to get the equivalent data homomorphically encrypted and process it. The overhead induced by this transciphering heavily depends on the underlying symmetric cipher used by the parties. In particular, not all operations have the same cost and multiple symmetric schemes have been designed for HHE with different applications in mind [2,5,19,28]. In particular, as Deep Machine Learning inference is getting widely popularized as a cloud service, researchers designed Elisabeth-4 [9] to optimize for this use case.

1.2 Motivation

When designing a cryptographic cipher, researchers always provide theoretical security guarantees that are mathematically sound but do not consider any implementation details, to be as generic as possible. In reality though, practical implementations on an electronic device often lead to a loss of security. Indeed, information about cryptographic secrets, like keys, can be obtained by observing the environment of the device. This process is called side-channel analysis and examples of the environment are timing [22], current consumption [23], or electromagnetic radiation [12]. It is very powerful but often requires some sort of physical access to the target device to observe the leakage.

Elisabeth-b4 is a good candidate for the emerging HHE but IoT devices intrinsically suffer from physical access and it is thus essential to provide a secure implementation of the algorithms running on those devices. Our work aims to analyze the complexity of side-channel attacks on an IoT device and study the efficiency of countermeasures.

1.3 Related Work

One year after its release, an algebraic attack compromised Elisabeth-4, demonstrating its vulnerability to such methods [17]. In response, the original authors proposed multiple different alternatives, including an adjusted cipher named Elisabeth-b4 [20], specifically designed to resist the attack in [17]. Our work, however, focuses on analyzing and attacking Elisabeth-b4 using a distinct approach – side-channel analysis – and demonstrates that, despite the modifications, the newer version remains vulnerable to this class of attacks.

To the best of our knowledge, we have not seen any research done on the side-channel analysis of hybrid homomorphic ciphers and our work is innovative in that sense. Another hybrid homomorphic cipher called FRAST [8], beating Elisabeth-b4 in terms of both latency and throughput, has been designed after the start of our work, but it still does not consider the threat of side-channel analysis in its design, and our work could probably be extended to this cipher as well. A differential fault attack was recently mounted on Elisabeth-4 [33] but they did not study side-channel analysis either.

1.4 Contributions

Our work provides results of side-channel attacks using electromagnetic radiation traces from Elisabeth-b4 executions. We show how to recover the 2048-bit key with 350,00 traces with Correlation Power Analysis and with 1,000 traces using a template attack.

By integrating known protections like masking [6] and shuffling [32], the previously mounted Correlation Power Analysis becomes impossible and the template attack is much more complex. By using multiple Deep Learning models instead of templates, we still manage to recover the key by predicting the mask shares and shuffling. Though, it increases the number of traces on the target device to 250,000.

1.5 Outline

After a background on `Elisabeth-b4` and side-channel tools in Sect. 2, we describe our attack setup in Sect. 3 and show how we recover the entire key from the algorithm using different attacks in Sect. 4. In Sect. 5, we describe the countermeasures we implemented to increase the attacks' complexity and analyze their effectiveness in Sect. 6. We then present the use of Deep Learning as a new attack method in Sect. 7. Finally, we conclude our work in Sect. 8.

2 Background

2.1 Homomorphic Encryption

A homomorphic encryption scheme includes a plaintext space, a ciphertext space, a pair of public-private key space and a circuit space. It provides the following algorithms:

- The key generation **KeyGen** (1^λ) for security parameter λ returns a public-private key pair (HK^{pub}, HK^{priv}) satisfying λ bits of security.
- The encryption **HEnc** (p, HK^{pub}) for plaintext p and public key HK^{pub} returns the ciphertext c corresponding to the encryption of p with HK^{pub}.
- The decryption **HDec** (c, HK^{priv}) for ciphertext c and private key HK^{priv} returns the plaintext p corresponding to the decryption of c with HK^{priv}. For correctness, $Pr\left(\textbf{HDec}\left(\textbf{HEnc}\left(p, HK^{pub}\right), HK^{priv}\right) = p\right) = 1$ must be satisfied.
- The evaluation **HEval** $(HK^{pub}, C, c_1, ..., c_n)$ returns the encryption of circuit C evaluated at the decrypted inputs, i.e., if $c_i = \textbf{HEnc}(p_i, HK^{pub})$, then **HEval** $(HK^{pub}, C, c_1, ..., c_n) = \textbf{HEnc}(C(p_i, ..., p_n), HK^{pub})$.

The second and third provide confidentiality on the plaintexts and the last provides certain computation on encrypted data. If the circuit C can be arbitrary, then we call such a scheme a *Fully* Homomorphic Encryption (FHE) one and it provides arbitrary computation on encrypted data.

Hybrid Homomorphic Encryption (HHE). A HHE scheme consists of a FHE scheme with operations (**HEnc, HDec, HEval**) and keys

(HK^{pub}, HK^{priv}) combined with a symmetric encryption scheme with operations (**SEnc**, **SDec**) and key SK. The client sends $SK^{\text{HE}} := \textbf{HEnc}\left(SK, HK^{pub}\right)$ once at the very start and then sends the symmetric encryption $p^{\text{SE}} := \textbf{SEnc}\left(p, SK\right)$ of input p (instead of $p^{\text{HE}} := \textbf{HEnc}\left(p, HK^{pub}\right)$ for FHE). The server can then retrieve p^{HE} by homomorphically evaluating the symmetric decryption circuit C^{SDec} on inputs $p^{\text{SE}^{\text{HE}}} := \textbf{HEnc}\left(p^{\text{SE}}, HK^{pub}\right)$ and SK^{HE}: $\textbf{HEnc}\left(C^{\text{SDec}}\left(p^{\text{SE}}, SK\right), HK^{pub}\right) = p^{\text{HE}}$, an operation called *transciphering*.

The HHE scheme provides the same guarantees as FHE but removes the overhead of performing any homomorphic encryptions on the client except one on SK, which is ideal for IoT devices. The challenge lies in finding a symmetric cipher whose decryption circuit is efficient homomorphically to reduce the overhead from transciphering as much as possible. `Elisabeth-4` and `Elisabeth-b4` are examples of such an optimized cipher.

2.2 Elisabeth-4 and Elisabeth-b4

`Elisabeth-4` [9] is a symmetric stream cipher operating in $\mathbb{Z}_{16}$. It encrypts one plaintext element of $\mathbb{Z}_{16}$ (i.e. 4 bits) at a time by summing it with the keystream generated by the algorithm depicted in Fig. 1a. The latter consists of the following two parts.

- We refer to the first part as **Random Whitened Subset (RWS)**. A public initialization vector (IV), is used as a seed to a forward secure PRNG that selects a random subset of 60 elements of $\mathbb{Z}_{16}$ from the 256 of the key, permutes them and adds a uniformly distributed whitening to each element. This results in a vector of 60 elements of $\mathbb{Z}_{16}$ that we will call *keyround* throughout the rest of the document.
- The keyround is then divided into 12 blocks of 5 elements called x_1, x_2, x_3, x_4, x_5 where each block is fed into the filtering function f depicted in Fig. 1b. The outputs of the 12 independent evaluations of f are summed to get the keystream. All S-boxes are instances of Negacyclic Look-Up Tables (NLUTs), i.e. $S[i+8] = -S[i] \mod 16 \; \forall i \in \{0, \ldots, 7\}$ for a NLUT S of length 16. Their first halves were generated taking the output of the SHA-256 hash of a string chosen by the authors.

The decryption algorithm consists in generating the same keystream using the initialization vector and subtracting it to the ciphertext to get the plaintext. `Elisabeth-4`'s key has a length of 256 elements of $\mathbb{Z}_{16}$, so 256 nibbles or 1,024 bits.

`Elisabeth-b4` [20] is designed to mitigate the attacks against `Elisabeth-4` discovered by [17]. The design is very similar to `Elisabeth-4`. The differences lie in the size of the key, which now has 512 elements, or 2,048 bits, and the size of the keyround which has a length of 98 elements. The latter is now divided into 14 blocks of length 7 that are fed to its adapted filtering function shown in Algorithm 1. The S-boxes are also NLUTs and their first halves were also generated taking the output of the SHA-256 hash of a string chosen by the authors. The

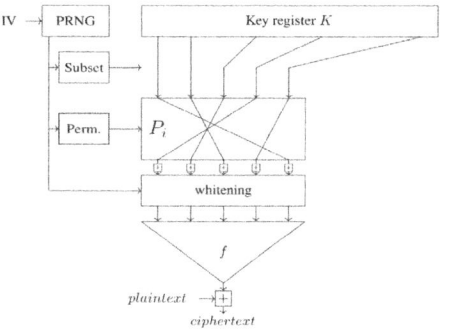 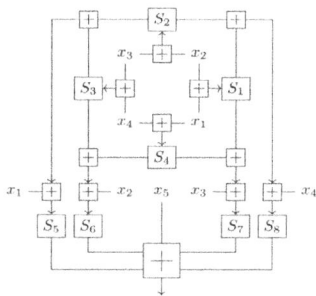

(a) Elisabeth-4's encryption algorithm   (b) Elisabeth-4's filtering function

Fig. 1. Elisabeth-4 description

initial copy of the inputs on line 3 of the algorithm corresponds to their manipulation when copying them in the function's stack frame. The copy is necessary because the function would modify the inputs in place otherwise.

2.3 Side-Channel Analysis Tools

Points of Interests. Faced with the very large number of samples present in the traces, it is essential to identify and select the points that carry the useful information for our attacks. Numerous methods have been studied [13] to detect leakage regions, also called Points of Interests (PoIs). Examples of these include *Difference Of Means based method* [7] (DOM), *Signal-to-Noise Ratios based method* [25] (SNR), *Correlation Power Analysis based method* [25] (CPA), *Principal Component Analysis based method* [3] (PCA), and *Sum Of Squared pairwise T-differences based method* [16] (SOST). In our experiments, the most effective one was the last. Its formula reads:

$$\mathbf{f}[t] = \sum_{s_1 \neq s_2} \left(\frac{\mathbf{M}_{\mathbf{s_1}}[t] - \mathbf{M}_{\mathbf{s_2}}[t]}{\sqrt{\mathbf{S}^2_{\mathbf{s_1}}[t]/|G_{s_1}| + \mathbf{S}^2_{\mathbf{s_2}}[t]/|G_{s_2}|}} \right)^2 \quad (1)$$

where s_1 and s_2 are all the possible critical values, G_s is the set of traces associated to s, $\mathbf{M_s} = \frac{1}{|G_s|} \sum_{\mathbf{t_i} \in G_s} \mathbf{t_i}$, $\mathbf{S^2_s} = \frac{1}{|G_s|} \sum_{\mathbf{t_i} \in G_s} (\mathbf{t_i} - \mathbf{M_s}) \odot (\mathbf{t_i} - \mathbf{M_s})$

2.4 Evaluation Metrics

Rank. The rank of a subkey hypothesis is the position of the correct value in the corresponding vector of prediction probabilities sorted in decreasing order. If the rank is 0, then the correct value is predicted with highest probability and the prediction is correct. If the number of possible values the subkey can take is K, a trivial attack consisting in uniformly selecting one of the K values yields an expected rank of $(K-1)/2$.

Algorithm 1: Elisabeth-b4's filtering function

input : $(x_0, x_1, x_2, x_3, x_4, x_5, x_6) \in \mathbb{Z}_{16}^7$
output: $z \in \mathbb{Z}_{16}$

1. **begin**
2.   **for** j in range(7) **do**
3. $x'_j \leftarrow x_j$
4.   **for** j in range(3) **do**
5. $x'_{2j+1} \leftarrow x'_{2j+1} + x'_{2j}$
6.   **for** j in range(6) **do**
7. $y_j \leftarrow S_j(x'_j)$
8.   **for** j in range(3) **do**
9. $z_{2j} \leftarrow y_{2j+5 \mod 6} + y_{2j}$
10. $z_{2j+1} \leftarrow y_{2j+4 \mod 6} + y_{2j+1}$
11.   **for** j in range(6) **do**
12. $z_j \leftarrow z_j + x'_{j+2 \mod 6}$
13. $z_j \leftarrow S_{j+6}(z_j)$
14.   **for** j in range(2) **do**
15. $t_{3j} \leftarrow z_{3j} + z_{3j+1} + z_{3j+2}$
16. $t_{3j+1} \leftarrow z_{3j+1} + z_{3j+3 \mod 6}$
17. $t_{3j+2} \leftarrow z_{3j+2} + z_{3j+3 \mod 6} + y_{3j}$
18. $x\_perm \leftarrow [5, 4, 3, 1, 0, 2]$
19.   **for** j in range(6) **do**
20. $t_j \leftarrow t_j + x'_{x\_perm[j]}$
21. $z \leftarrow x'_6$
22.   **for** j in range(6) **do**
23. $u_j \leftarrow S_{j+12}(t_j)$
24. $z \leftarrow z + u_j$
25.   **return** z

Success Rate. The success rate is the ratio of subkeys correctly retrieved by the attacker. The same trivial attack for each element of the key yields an expected success rate of $1/K$. In the case of Elisabeth-b4, this is $1/16 = 6.25\%$.

3 Threat Model and Attack Setup

The very long key length – 2048 bits compared to the usual 256 bits – for this stream cipher represents a new challenge in terms of side-channel analysis. After considering a first threat model consisting of collecting traces directly on the target device, we then assume a different one in which the attacker can access a cloned component, where they can run any code. In both cases, the attacker gathers thousands of traces, each encrypted with the same key, while seeds (IVs) vary for each encryption.

We took inspiration from the authors' implementation of Elisabeth-4 in Rust[1] to implement it in C. Adapting it for Elisabeth-b4 was straight-forward. The PRNG was implemented by generating the byte stream from the output of the ChaCha20 cipher, using the seed as the cipher's key. The stream was produced by encrypting null plaintexts with null initialization vectors and subsequently used to produce numbers for the subsetting, permutation, and whitening operations of Elisabeth-b4's key. We embedded the compiled code on an *Arduino DUE*, featuring an ARM Cortex-M3 32-bit processor operating at 84MHz. In addition to the previous work on stream ciphers in [24], we show that it is possible to attack 4-bit data words on a 32-bit processor.

By using the electromagnetic radiation with a dedicated probe instead of the power, it is possible to focus on the CPU part in charge of code execution only and eliminate other sources of noise (USB stack, analog part). Moreover, as shown in [26], glitches in CMOS circuitry have a high-frequency component which is more easily measurable in the EM field (a shunt resistor, for power, acts as a combination of resistance, inductance, and capacitance at high frequency). Finally, in modern processors, since nowadays dynamic power continues to dominate static power [29], it is in the interest of collecting the signal in the high-frequency domain with an electromagnetic probe.

To improve the quality of the leakage signal, we also thinned the chip by the back side, until it was about 100 μm long and moved the probe until we got the best signal. We finally select the sampling frequency of the oscilloscope at the value of 500 MS/s, by quantifying the collected values over 8 bits.

Indeed, measurements with a lower sampling rate showed that the amplitude and the number of leaks in the signal decreased. In contrast, a greater sampling rate produced new brief leaks, but this required the collection of a very large number of points per trace and led to a dataset which was too large to manage.

Each time we collected a trace, we executed the target 10 times and average them to reduce the noise. The collected trace corresponds to the algorithm executed to generate one keystream element of 4 bits as described in Sect. 2.2.

To evaluate the proposed methods, we collected four distinct sets of traces, referred to as Datasets A, B, C, and D, referenced throughout this document:

- **Dataset A:** Collected without countermeasures. It is divided into two populations of 125,000 traces each: one uses a fixed seed, while the other varies the seed. Both populations use the same fixed key.
- **Dataset B:** Collected without countermeasures. It contains 256,000 traces, each generated with a different seed but under the same fixed key.
- **Dataset C:** Collected with countermeasures and structured similarly to Dataset A, with two populations of 125,000 traces each: one with a fixed seed and the other with varying seeds. The seeds and keys are different from those in Dataset A.
- **Dataset D:** Collected with countermeasures. It comprises 1,000,000 traces, each generated with a different seed but under the same fixed key.

---

[1] Available on GitHub.

The unprotected algorithm (Datasets A and B) runs in 160 μs, resulting in traces of 80,000 time points, while the protected one (Datasets C and D) runs in 400 μs, producing traces of 200,000 time points.

The machine mounting the CPA, template and ML-based attacks consists of an *AMD Ryzen Threadripper 7970X* processor with 256 GB RAM, using Python and NumPy, SciPy, scikit-learn. Our neural networks were trained on two *NVIDIA RTX 4500 Ada Generation* graphics cards and six *NVIDIA GeForce RTX 2080 Ti* graphics cards, using TensorFlow.

4 Attacks on an Unprotected Implementation

4.1 Trace Analysis

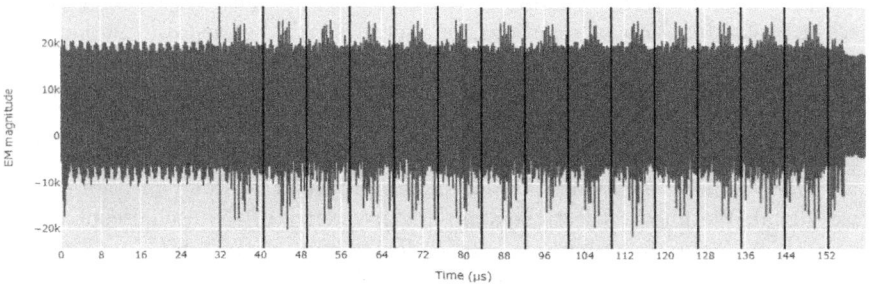

Fig. 2. Example of trace of `Elisabeth-b4`'s keystream generation

Figure 2 displays an example of a trace from Dataset B (unprotected). The scale of the electromagnetic field amplitude correspond to mV within a multiplicative factor: collected samples are encoded on 16 bits, ranging from $-32{,}768$ to $32{,}767$. We can already identify the **RWS** from the start to the red line, as well as each of the 14 sequential executions – or *rounds* – of the filtering function, separated by the black lines.

4.2 Attack Strategy

The adversary's goal could either be to recover the plaintext or the symmetric key. The key is more often targeted since it can be used to recover not only the current plaintext but also future plaintexts. Also, as opposed to the plaintext, the same key is used in multiple messages, giving the adversary lots of traces to recover it. Therefore, the targeted critical values are the 512 key elements in our case. `Elisabeth-b4`'s keystream generation leaks in two distinctive parts:

Random Whitened Subset (RWS). The key elements are directly manipulated by the device to shuffle and whiten them. Even though the key is 512 elements long, only 98 are selected – and thus, leaked – during this procedure.

Filtering Function. The key elements are manipulated but are shuffled and whitened. Since both operations are deterministically derived from the public seed, they are reversible. The method to revert them is described below. Each of the 14 different executions of the filtering function leaks information about 7 elements of the key, totalling in the same 98 key elements as during the **RWS** from the previous paragraph.

We use $\mathbf{S_i} \in \{A \subseteq \{0,\ldots,511\} \mid |A| = 98\}$ and $\mathbf{W_i} \in \mathbb{Z}_{16}^{98}$ to respectively refer to the sample/permutation and whitening during **RWS** of trace $\mathbf{t_i}$. To get prediction probabilities for the original key $\mathbf{K} \in \mathbb{Z}_{16}^{512}$ from prediction probabilities for the keyrounds $\mathbf{k_i} \in \mathbb{Z}_{16}^{98}$, we revert the random sample, shuffling and whitening as follows:

$$p\left(\mathbf{K}[j] = \hat{k} \mid \mathbf{t_i}\right) = \begin{cases} p\left(\mathbf{k_i}\left[\mathbf{S_i^{-1}}[j]\right] = \hat{k} + \mathbf{W_i}\left[\mathbf{S_i^{-1}}[j]\right] \mod 16 \mid \mathbf{t_i}\right), & \text{if } j \in \mathbf{S_i}. \\ \frac{1}{16}, & \text{otherwise.} \end{cases}$$

Indeed, the key element is uniformly distributed if it has not been sampled (i.e., $j \notin \mathbf{S_i}$), as no information can be gathered from the trace. Also, note that $p(\mathbf{k_i}[\cdot] = \cdot \mid \mathbf{t_i}) \propto p(\mathbf{t_i} \mid \mathbf{k_i}[\cdot] = \cdot)$ because $p(\mathbf{k_i}[\cdot] = \cdot) = 1/16$, a useful property to compute probabilities of keyround elements from the templates. In both cases, and even if we target both parts simultaneously, only 98 out of the 512 elements of the key are used. This implies that, to recover the entire key, its 512 elements must appear at least once. A strict minimum of $\lceil \frac{512}{98} \rceil = 6$ traces are thus needed by the pigeonhole principle, but 33 in expectation.[2]

4.3 Test Vector Leakage Assessment (TVLA)

We perform a TVLA on Dataset A. It is shown in Fig. 3, zoomed on the last round of the algorithm – the other rounds are similar.

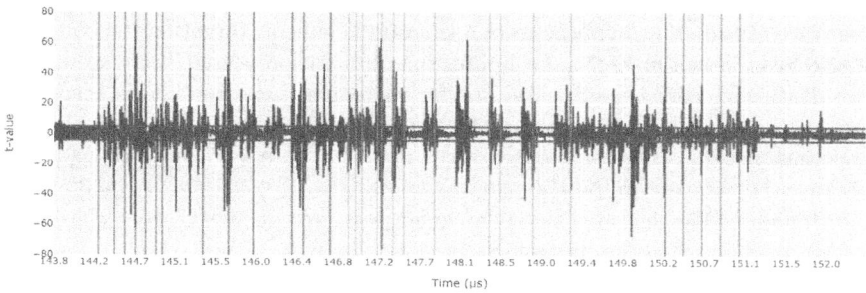

Fig. 3. TVLA on last round of `Elisabeth-b4`

The red horizontal lines highlight a t-value of 4.5, which is the threshold corresponding to a confidence level of 99.999% in our setting, with nearly 250,000

---
[2] See Appendix A for more details.

degrees of freedom at each time point. By disassembling the code and applying a Pearson correlation calculation between the manipulated data and the trace, we identify the leakage points associated with different colors in Fig. 3. These colors correspond to operations that we found leaked the most, such as the output of the first round of S-Boxes for the red regions (Algorithm 1, line 7).

4.4 Correlation Power Analysis

Previous results showed that the **Hamming Weight** was a good model to assess leakage. This model was thus retained for the attack. We targeted non-linear operations, i.e. the S-boxes. S-boxes S_0, S_2, and S_4 caught our attention because they depend only on a single keyround element which corresponds to a search space of 4 bits. Other S-boxes depend on up to six elements, corresponding to a larger search space of 24 bits. Examples of correlations with the correct key are shown in Fig. 4. This step was performed on Dataset B.

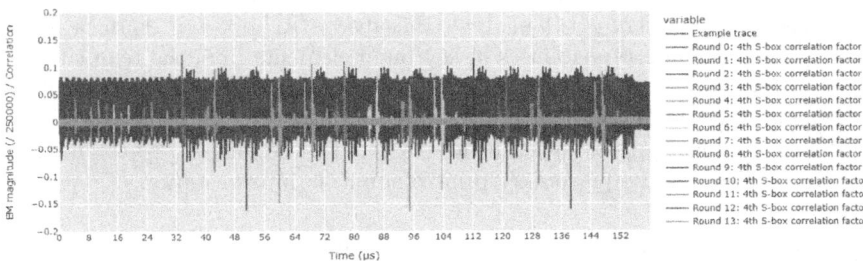

Fig. 4. Correlation factor of the Hamming Weight of the output of S-box S_4

An example of a graph showing the maximum correlation factor throughout the trace for different hypotheses of a keyround element, targeting the output of S-box S_4 is shown in Fig. 5. An interesting observation is that there are always two distinctive correlation peaks: one for the correct key hypothesis k and one for $k + 8 \mod 16$. This increases the number of traces to distinguish the two and thus increases the complexity of the attack. The phenomenon is explained because the S-boxes are NLUTs, i.e., $S_4[k + 8 \mod 16] = -S_4[k] \mod 16$ and the Hamming Weights of the respective outputs are thus heavily correlated.

We only used the output of S_4 because it gave the best results. We only considered the last two rounds for simplicity. Concretely, we correlate the second to last round's traces with values $\mathbf{HW}(S_4[x])$ and the last round's traces with values $\mathbf{HW}(S_4[x'])$ with $x, x' \in \mathbb{Z}_{16}$ hypotheses for $\mathbf{K}[\mathbf{S_i}[88]] + \mathbf{W_i}[88] \mod 16$ and $\mathbf{K}[\mathbf{S_i}[95]] + \mathbf{W_i}[95] \mod 16$ respectively. By removing the whitening, we thus have a hypothesis for a key element.

As two different elements of the key are leaked in each trace ($\mathbf{K}[\mathbf{S_i}[88]]$ and $\mathbf{K}[\mathbf{S_i}[95]]$), we collected 256,000 traces so that we have about 1,000 traces for each key element (Dataset B) and successfully recovered the entire key. We

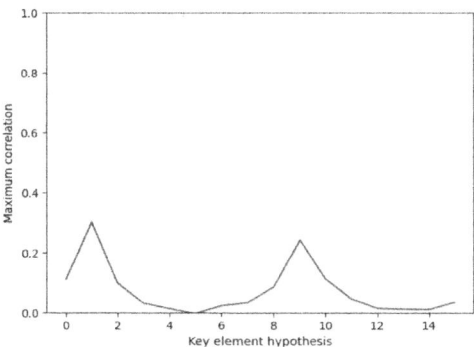

Fig. 5. Example of maximum correlation factors across the entire trace for different hypotheses. Correct key element is 1.

expect that the number of traces required is divided by 7 when targeting all 14 rounds instead of the last two, involving about 35,000 traces. This number could probably be even further reduced by also exploiting more information than simply the output of S_4, such as other S-boxes or the **HW** of the inputs at the beginning of the rounds. We observe that the attack is feasible with a model leakage based on 4 bits only (the **HW** of an S-box) even though the processor is 32-bit. In our case, it is difficult to find a model on more bits, since every operation is in $\mathbb{Z}_{16}$, but doing so could also reduce the complexity of the attack.

4.5 Template Attack

The objective of our template attack is to predict the values of the 98 keyround elements. Compared to other PoI detection methods, SOST gave us the clearest ones and were in accordance with the previously computed TVLA. We thus compute 98 SOSTs, one for each of the 98 targeted keyround elements. Examples of such SOSTs are shown in Fig. 6. We notice in particular that keyround values leak once during **RWS** and once during its respective round, validating the claim in Sect. 4.2.

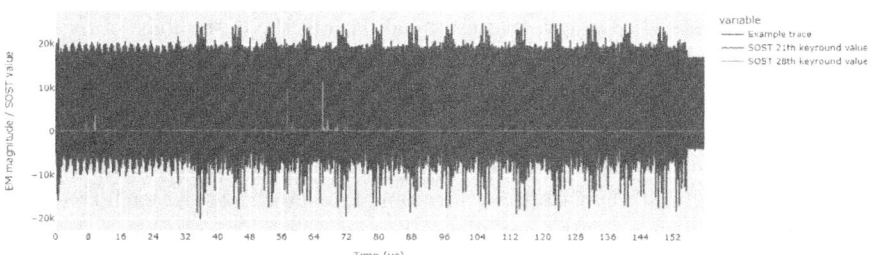

Fig. 6. Example of SOSTs on top of a trace

We build $98 \cdot 16 = 1,568$ templates during the profiling phase – one for every possible value of every keyround element. Each template is defined over $N = 40$ points from the trace, chosen as the largest N values of the SOST corresponding to the target element. The precise values of N was 5-fold cross-validated based on the success rate.

During the extraction phase, we compute the 16 probabilities of each keyround value for each of the 98 elements, follow Sect. 4.2 to revert the **RWS** and select the Maximum-Likelihood Estimator for every j:

$$\hat{\mathbf{K}}[j] = \arg\max_{\dot{k}\in\mathbb{Z}_{16}} \prod_{\mathbf{t_i}} p\left(\mathbf{t_i} \mid \mathbf{K}[j] = \dot{k}\right) = \arg\max_{\dot{k}\in\mathbb{Z}_{16}} \sum_{\mathbf{t_i}} \log p\left(\mathbf{K}[j] = \dot{k} \mid \mathbf{t_i}\right) \quad (2)$$

where we used that $p\left(\mathbf{K}[j] = \dot{k}\right) = 1/16 \; \forall \dot{k}$ and applied the logarithm to tackle numerical instabilities that arise when multiplying small probabilities together. This method preserves the order of probabilities when selecting the maximum due to the logarithm's monotonic increase while staying numerically stable.

We also used Dataset B for this attack. When using 100,000 profiling traces, this attack gives an average accuracy of 13.33 ± 0.20 % for keyround elements. After applying the Maximum-Likelihood Estimator, we recover the complete key with 1,000 extraction traces. The average rank of a key element is 0.005 at 1,000 extraction traces. To practically compute this number, we computed each key element's average rank across 100 sets of size 1,000 sampled from 10,000 traces not seen during the training. We then averaged the ranks from all elements.

4.6 Machine Learning-Based Attack

Using Machine Learning is almost identical as with templates: For each one of the 98 targeted elements, we first select a subset of the trace using SOST, and then train an ML model predicting its value between 0 and 15. Each model outputs probabilities for each possible keyround value, we revert the **RWS** following Sect. 4.2, add all the logarithms of probabilities and choose the highest one as the final prediction. We tried different configurations of ML models:

SVMs [10]: We rapidly abandoned the use of SVMs due to their long training times, independently of the kernel or of the regularization parameter.

Random Forests [4]: Using 5-fold cross-validation, the best choice of hyperparameters were to choose a subset of length $N = 40$ from the SOST, train 300 trees, let them grow indefinitely but have at least 6 samples left at each leaf.

Gradient Boosting [14]: Using 5-fold cross-validation, the best choice of hyperparameters were to choose a subset of length $N = 60$ from the SOST, iterate for at most 300 iterations with the multinomial deviance loss, let each tree grow indefinitely but have at least 6 samples left at each leaf. This method performed best consistently.

Also using Dataset B and choosing Gradient Boosting with 100,000 profiling traces results in 11.14 ± 0.18 % accuracy for keyround elements. We recover the entire key with 1,500 extraction traces, performing slightly worse than template attacks. We did not try any more complex models as our results were already satisfactory. All our attack results are summarized in Table 1. The *Baseline* row indicates the accuracy one would get with a trivial estimator that would select a uniform random value for every keyround element.

Table 1. Overall attack results without countermeasures

Method	# Traces		Test element accuracy (%)	Success rate (%)
	Profiling	Extraction		
CPA	0	~350,00	-	100
Template	100,000	1,000	13.33 ± 0.20	100
Random Forest	100,000	2,500	10.93 ± 0.17	100
Gradient Boosting	100,000	1,500	11.14 ± 0.18	100
Baseline	0	0	6.25 ± 0.00	6.25

5 Countermeasures Implementation

5.1 Masking

Masking is a countermeasure that has already been proven to exponentially increase the attack complexity with respect to the number of shares used [6]. To protect a sensitive value s with M-share masking, we uniformly sample M shares such that they all sum to s. This leads to the masking vector $\mathbf{m} \in \mathbb{Z}_{16}^M$, where $\sum_{i=0}^{M-1} \mathbf{m}[i] \mod 16 = s$. Then, the algorithm uses $\mathbf{m}$ instead of s and the value of s is never manipulated directly.

Implementing this countermeasure means redefining all operations that use sensitive values into ones that use masking vectors. In our case, the sensitive values are the 98 keyround elements and the operations that use them are additions and S-box evaluations.

The addition of two masked values $\mathbf{m_1}$ and $\mathbf{m_2}$ that respectively correspond to sensitive s_1 and s_2 is $\mathbf{m_3}$, where $\mathbf{m_3}[i] = \mathbf{m_1}[i] + \mathbf{m_2}[i] \mod 16$, such that the corresponding s_3 is $s_1 + s_2 \mod 16$. The time complexity of the addition is multiplied by M.

To evaluate S-box $\mathbf{S} \in \mathbb{Z}_{16}^{16}$ on sensitive s, we pre-compute a table $\mathbf{S}'$ corresponding to the evaluation of S-box $\mathbf{S}$ for every possible share combination, inspired by the implementation of [1]. What follows applies only for $M = 2$, protecting against first-order attacks. For higher order attacks where $M > 2$, we refer the reader to [31]. The new table is $\mathbf{S}' \in \mathbb{Z}_{16}^{16 \times 16}$, where $\mathbf{S}'[i_1][i_2] = \mathbf{S}[i_1 + i_2 \mod 16] - i_1 \mod 16$ and we store $\mathbf{S}'$ in memory instead of $\mathbf{S}$. When we want to evaluate it with masked $\mathbf{m}$, we compute $[\mathbf{m}[0] \ \mathbf{S}'[\mathbf{m}[0]][\mathbf{m}[1]]] = [\mathbf{m}[0] \ \mathbf{S}[\mathbf{m}[0] + \mathbf{m}[1] \mod 16] - \mathbf{m}[0] \mod 16]$, a vector whose sum is the expected $\mathbf{S}[s]$. The memory complexity is multiplied by 16 to store $\mathbf{S}'$.

We chose $M = 2$ for performance reasons. An important improvement we realized is that we could pack the 2 shares inside the same 32-bit word in memory since they are 4 bits long, as elements of $\mathbb{Z}_{16}$. This has the advantage of being able to add two masked values in a single addition instead of two and with less memory fetches. Concretely, our packed number is a single word in memory instead of a vector: $m' = (2^8 \cdot \mathbf{m}[0]) \vee \mathbf{m}[1]$. We use the notation $[\cdot : \cdot]$ for bit indexing. We thus have $m'[11:8] = \mathbf{m}[0]$ and $m'[3:0] = \mathbf{m}[1]$. Additions are defined as (the $\wedge$ is used here to prevent overflows):

$$\texttt{MaskedAdd}(m'_1, m'_2) := (m'_1 + m'_2) \wedge \texttt{0b0000111100001111}, \qquad (3)$$

and S-boxes evaluations as:

$$\texttt{MaskedSBox}(\mathbf{S}', m') := (2^8 \cdot m'[11:8]) \vee \mathbf{S}'[m'[11:8]][m'[3:0]]. \qquad (4)$$

We mask every keyround element. Since there is also some shuffling (see Sect. 5.2), the masks do not appear in the same order during **RWS** and during the rounds. We will thus refer to them respectively as $\mathbf{m}^{\textbf{rws}}_{\mathbf{j}} \in \mathbb{Z}^2_{16}, j \in \{0, ..., 97\}$ and $\mathbf{m}^{\textbf{rounds}}_{\mathbf{r},\mathbf{b}} \in \mathbb{Z}^2_{16}, (r,b) \in \{0, ..., 13\} \times \{0, ..., 6\}$ (the bth mask of the rth round), in order where they appear in the trace. There is thus a total of 392 variables for mask shares, all ranging between 0 and 15.

5.2 Shuffling

Shuffling is another countermeasure that was thoroughly studied previously [32] whose purpose is to randomize the execution order of independent operations. This does not alter the outcome of the operations and an attacker now cannot directly know which operation is executed at which point in time. We implemented it with Random Start Indices (RSI) [32], i.e., the operations are executed in order but starting from a random index, for performance reasons. We shuffled the following for `Elisabeth-b4`:

- The order in which the key elements are manipulated during **RWS** is indifferent. We will refer to this RSI as $p_{rws} \in \mathbb{Z}_{98}$.
- The order in which the 14 executions of the filtering function are executed is indifferent. We will refer to this RSI as $p_{round} \in \mathbb{Z}_{14}$.
- For each round $r \in \{0, \ldots, 13\}$, the order in which the block inputs are copied is indifferent (Line 3). We will refer to the corresponding r^{th} round's RSI as $p_{block_r} \in \mathbb{Z}_7$.
- For each of the 7 remaining loops of the 14 rounds, the order in which they are executed is indifferent. The RSIs take values respectively from $\mathbb{Z}_3, \mathbb{Z}_6, \mathbb{Z}_3, \mathbb{Z}_6, \mathbb{Z}_2, \mathbb{Z}_6, \mathbb{Z}_6$ (see Algorithm 1).

Our shuffling countermeasure thus contains 114 different RSIs, but we target only 16 of them ($p_{rws}, p_{round}, p_{block_r}$) to retrieve the key.

The pseudo-code containing this countermeasure as well as the 2-share masking can be found in Algorithms 2 and 3. Note: we use the vector notation for masks, but our implementation pack the shares in the same 32-bit word in memory, as described in Sect. 5.1.

The countermeasures bring a x2.5 time overhead, as traces now last 400 µs.

Algorithm 2: Masked and shuffled `Elisabeth-b4`'s keystream generation

input : Masked key $(\mathbf{K_0},\ldots,\mathbf{K_{511}}) \in \mathbb{Z}_{16}^{512\times 2}$, Sampling/Permutation $\mathbf{S_i} \in \{A \subseteq \{0,\ldots,511\} \mid |A| = 98\}$ and Whitening $\mathbf{W_i} \in \mathbb{Z}_{16}^{98}$
output: Masked keystream $\mathbf{z} \in \mathbb{Z}_{16}^2$

1 **Function** Perm(*max*):
2     $rsi \leftarrow rand()\mod max$
3   **return** $[rsi \mod max, rsi+1 \mod max, \ldots, rsi+(max-1) \mod max]$
4 **begin**
5   // Masked RWS:
6   **for** j in Perm(98) **do** // Targeted RSI p_{rws}
7        $\mathbf{m_j} \leftarrow$ MaskedAdd$(\mathbf{K_{S_i[j]}}, \mathbf{W_i}[j])$ // Targeted masks $\mathbf{m_j^{rws}}$
8   // Masked rounds:
9     $\mathbf{z}[0] \leftarrow rand() \mod 16$
10     $\mathbf{z}[1] \leftarrow 0 - \mathbf{z}[0] \mod 16$
11   **for** j in Perm(14) **do** // Targeted RSI p_{round}
12        $\mathbf{z} \leftarrow$ MaskedAdd$(\mathbf{z}, \text{Algorithm3}(\mathbf{m_{7*j}}, \ldots, \mathbf{m_{7*j+6}}))$
13   **return** $\mathbf{z}$

6 Attacks on a Protected Implementation

6.1 TVLA and CPA

To assess the impact of these countermeasures, we enabled them and mounted the same attacks from Sect. 4. As a first step, we redo a TVLA, this time on Dataset C. It is shown in Fig. 7, zoomed on the last round of the algorithm – the other rounds are similar. We observe that the first-order leakage of the key elements has in this case completely disappeared. This is explained because random mask shares are manipulated instead of the key elements. The leakage is further reduced due to the order of operations depending on those elements that are consistently shuffled.

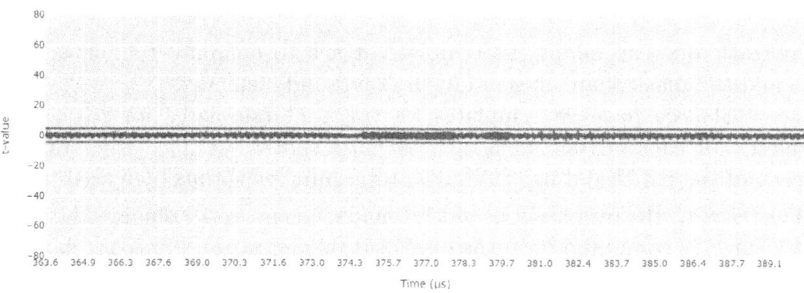

Fig. 7. TVLA on last round of `Elisabeth-b4` with 2-share masking and shuffling

Algorithm 3: Masked and shuffled `Elisabeth-b4`'s filtering function

input : Mask shares $(\mathbf{m}_0, \mathbf{m}_1, \mathbf{m}_2, \mathbf{m}_3, \mathbf{m}_4, \mathbf{m}_5, \mathbf{m}_6) \in \mathbb{Z}_{16}^{7 \times 2}$
output: Mask shares $\mathbf{z} \in \mathbb{Z}_{16}^2$

1 **begin**
2   **for** j in Perm(7) **do** // Targeted RSI p_{block_r}
3       $\mathbf{m}'_j \leftarrow \mathbf{m}_j$ // Targeted masks $\mathbf{m}_{r,b}^{rounds}$
4   **for** j in Perm(3) **do**
5       $\mathbf{m}'_{2j+1} \leftarrow \mathtt{MaskedAdd}\left(\mathbf{m}'_{2j+1}, \mathbf{m}'_{2j}\right)$
6   **for** j in Perm(6) **do**
7       $\mathbf{y}_j \leftarrow \mathtt{MaskedSBox}\left(\mathbf{S}'_j, \mathbf{m}'_j\right)$
8   **for** j in Perm(3) **do**
9       $\mathbf{z}_{2j} \leftarrow \mathtt{MaskedAdd}\left(\mathbf{y}_{2j+5 \mod 6}, \mathbf{y}_{2j}\right)$
10      $\mathbf{z}_{2j+1} \leftarrow \mathtt{MaskedAdd}\left(\mathbf{y}_{2j+4 \mod 6}, \mathbf{y}_{2j+1}\right)$
11   **for** j in Perm(6) **do**
12      $\mathbf{z}_j \leftarrow \mathtt{MaskedAdd}\left(\mathbf{z}_j, \mathbf{m}'_{j+2 \mod 6}\right)$
13      $\mathbf{z}_j \leftarrow \mathtt{MaskedSBox}\left(\mathbf{S}'_{j+6}, \mathbf{z}_j\right)$
14   **for** j in Perm(2) **do**
15      $\mathbf{t}_{3j} \leftarrow \mathtt{MaskedAdd}\left(\mathtt{MaskedAdd}\left(\mathbf{z}_{3j}, \mathbf{z}_{3j+1}\right), \mathbf{z}_{3j+2}\right)$
16      $\mathbf{t}_{3j+1} \leftarrow \mathtt{MaskedAdd}\left(\mathbf{z}_{3j+1}, \mathbf{z}_{3j+3 \mod 6}\right)$
17      $\mathbf{t}_{3j+2} \leftarrow \mathtt{MaskedAdd}\left(\mathtt{MaskedAdd}\left(\mathbf{z}_{3j+2}, \mathbf{z}_{3j+3 \mod 6}\right), \mathbf{y}_{3j}\right)$
18   $m\_perm \leftarrow [5, 4, 3, 1, 0, 2]$
19   **for** j in Perm(6) **do**
20      $\mathbf{t}_j \leftarrow \mathtt{MaskedAdd}\left(\mathbf{t}_j, \mathbf{m}'_{m\_perm[j]}\right)$
21   $\mathbf{z} \leftarrow \mathbf{m}'_6$
22   **for** j in Perm(6) **do**
23      $\mathbf{u}_j \leftarrow \mathtt{MaskedSBox}\left(\mathbf{S}'_{j+12}, \mathbf{t}_j\right)$
24      $\mathbf{z} \leftarrow \mathtt{MaskedAdd}\left(\mathbf{z}, \mathbf{u}_j\right)$
25   **return** $\mathbf{z}$

6.2 Template Attack on Countermeasures

In contrast, one can adapt the template attack to compute templates for the RSIs and the mask shares instead of the keyround elements.

For RSIs, we have 98 templates for p_{rws}, 14 templates for p_{round} and 7 templates for each of the 14 p_{block_r}. For mask shares, we have $16 \cdot 2$ templates for each of the $\mathbf{m}_j^{rws}$ and $\mathbf{m}_{r,b}^{rounds}$. The total number is thus increased to 6,482.

For trace $\mathbf{t_i}$, the probabilities of keyround element $\mathbf{k_i}[j]$, renamed here $\hat{k}_j$ for convenience, is computed from the ones of RSIs and mask shares as follows [27]:

$$p_{\hat{k}_j}\left(\hat{k} \mid \mathbf{t_i}\right) = p_{\hat{k}_j^{rws}}\left(\hat{k} \mid \mathbf{t_i}\right) \cdot p_{\hat{k}_{\lfloor j/7 \rfloor, j \mod 7}^{rounds}}\left(\hat{k} \mid \mathbf{t_i}\right) \quad (5)$$

where

$$p_{\dot{k}_j^{rws}}\left(\dot{k} \mid \mathbf{t_i}\right) = \sum_{p=0}^{97} p_{p_{rws}}\left(p \mid \mathbf{t_i}\right) \cdot \left(\sum_{m=0}^{15} p_{\mathbf{m}_{j'}^{rws}[0]}\left(m \mid \mathbf{t_i}\right) \cdot p_{\mathbf{m}_{j'}^{rws}[1]}\left(\dot{k}-m \mod 16 \mid \mathbf{t_i}\right)\right),$$

$$p_{\dot{k}_{r,b}^{rounds}}\left(\dot{k} \mid \mathbf{t_i}\right) = \sum_{p_r=0}^{13} p_{p_{round}}\left(p_r \mid \mathbf{t_i}\right) \cdot \left(\sum_{p_b=0}^{6} p_{p_{block_{r'}}}\left(p_b \mid \mathbf{t_i}\right)\right.$$

$$\left. \cdot \left(\sum_{m=0}^{15} p_{\mathbf{m}_{r',b'}^{rounds}[0]}\left(m \mid \mathbf{t_i}\right) \cdot p_{\mathbf{m}_{r',b'}^{rounds}[1]}\left(\dot{k}-m \mod 16 \mid \mathbf{t_i}\right)\right)\right),$$

with $j' = j - p \mod 98$, $r' = r - p_r \mod 14$, and $b' = b - p_b \mod 7$. Just like without the countermeasures, we then revert the **RWS**, add all the logarithms of probabilities and choose the highest one as the final prediction for each key element.

During the profiling phase, we compute the PoIs of every predicted variable (RSI and mask share) using SOST, select the N highest time points, and build the templates using those. The value of N is 5-fold cross-validated to be 1,000 for p_{rws}, 200 for p_{round} and p_{block_r}, and 20 for $\mathbf{m}_j^{rws}$ and $\mathbf{m}_{r,b}^{rounds}$. We used 675,000 profiling traces and 250,000 extraction traces from Dataset D and got the results displayed in Table 2.

Even though we see that mask shares have an accuracy slightly better than the baseline, it was not enough to reconstruct the complete key without a large number of extraction traces. Indeed, only 20.7% of the key was recovered with 250,000 extraction traces.

We also tried predicting both shares together instead of separately, i.e. compute 16^2 templates for every masked variable. Our validation accuracies in this case were worse and it required more computing power as more than 50,000 templates needed to be computed. Overall, predicting each share separately would give a more consistent performance.

We did not evaluate the ML-based attack with the countermeasures since it already performed worse than the template without them. The latter thus successfully mitigate the attacks that we were able to mount previously: CPA, template attack and ML-based attack from Sect. 4. We will now study the usage of Deep Learning as a more complex method to bypass them.

7 Deep Learning Application to Bypass Protections

7.1 Straightforward Monolithic Approach

Since our implemented countermeasures were very similar to the ones attacked by Masure and Strullu [27], we adapt their `MultiResNetSCA-1` to our use-case. Their architecture predicts 34 variables each between 0 and 255 by taking a trace of 15,000 time points and feeding it to a residual network, whose output is then fully connected to each output variable through 1024-node hidden layers, totalling in 137,396,064 trainable parameters.

In our case, we predict 408 variables, counting all RSIs and mask shares. This large number of output variables and the large trace size (200,000 time points) results in a neural network with 20,871,800,210 trainable parameters if we use the exact same architecture. Even if we wanted to, we do not have the computing capabilities to train such a gigantic model. To reduce the number of parameters, we modify the architecture in three ways:

- We compute the second order Haar wavelet that divides our trace size by 4 while keeping most information of the trace [11].
- We select the parts of the trace that leak the variables using SOST on the wavelets and concatenate them. Combined with the previous wavelet transform, this reduces the number of input points to 12,150, a number similar to the original architecture.
- We reduce the number of hidden nodes from 1,024 to 512 for RSIs and to 128 for mask shares.

These modifications result in an architecture with 188,046,738 parameters. A graphical representation is shown in Appendix B. We kept the same loss function – the categorical cross-entropy – and trained it during 30 epochs with a dataset of 675,000 training traces.

The mean test accuracies for all predicted variables using Dataset D are displayed in Table 2. It resulted in a success rate of 12.5%, slightly better than the baseline of 6.25% but not even reaching the performance of the template attack from Sect. 6.2. We explain this poor performance due to the wavelet transform discarding useful information found in higher frequencies. Indeed, the PoIs identified by the SOST were less clear after the wavelet transform, compared to the original traces. Another explanation could be that the model architecture is not complex enough to capture the data structure and that the optimizer gets stuck in a local minimum – our model is underfitting.

7.2 A Better Modular Approach

Instead of prematurely using wavelets to reduce our input space, we only detect the PoIs of our variables using SOST and train multiple smaller – but with more capabilities – models on subsets of the trace, following the *Divide & Conquer* paradigm. Concretely, we train 20 models that have similar architectures but with different input and output sizes.

- ResNetRWSPerm, taking the entire **RWS** of 19,850 time points and predicting p_{rws}. This model has 11,497,410 trainable parameters.
- ResNetRoundPerm, taking the PoIs of p_{round} of 700 time points and predicting p_{round}. This model has 4,389,998 trainable parameters.
- {ResNetRWS-0,...,ResNetRWS-3} each taking one quarter of the **RWS** of 4,860 (5,270 for ResNetRWS-3) time points and each predicting 48 (52 for ResNetRWS-3) of the m_j^{rws}. Splitting **RWS** in less than four led to models too complex to be trained. These models have 63,107,168 (74,680,480 for ResNetRWS-3) trainable parameters.

Table 2. Overall attack results with countermeasures

Method	# Traces		Mean test accuracies (%)					Success rate (%)
	Profiling	Extraction	p_{rws}	p_{round}	p_{block_r}	$\mathbf{m}_j^{rws}$	$\mathbf{m}_{r,b}^{rounds}$	
CPA	mitigated	mitigated	-	-	-	-	-	0
Template	675,000	250,000	69.96	65.92	58.01	7.71	7.37	20.7
Single NN	675,000	250,000	74.12	58.93	37.71	6.85	6.98	12.5
20 NNs	675,000	250,000	99.35	75.11	60.23	9.58	8.44	100
Baseline	0	0	1.02	7.14	14.29	6.25	6.25	6.25

– {ResNetRound-0, ..., ResNetRound-13} each taking round $r \in \{0, \ldots, 13\}$ of 1,400 time points (identified with the SOSTs of involved variables) and predicting their respective p_{block_r} and $\mathbf{m}_{r,b}^{rounds}$. These models have 26,213,447 trainable parameters.

This sums up to a total of 646,877,650 trainable parameters but that can be trained on multiple GPUs in parallel. A graphical representation is shown in Appendix C. We used 675,000 traces for training, 75,000 for validation and chose the Adam optimizer with default values except an exponential decay β_1 of 0.99 to escape local minima [21]. We early stopped the training by monitoring the validation loss with a patience of 10 epochs.

ResNetRWSPerm converged after 3 epochs, while the rest after 10 to 15 epochs. Mean test accuracies for all predicted variables are displayed in Table 2, requiring 250,000 extraction traces to recover the entire key.

Figure 8 depicts the expected rank of each of the 512 elements of the key for different numbers of extraction traces. We practically computed the expected rank of a key element for a given number of extraction traces using the same method as in Sect. 4.5, sampling this time from 250,000 traces not seen during the training. The average rank of a key element is 0.003 at 250,000 extraction

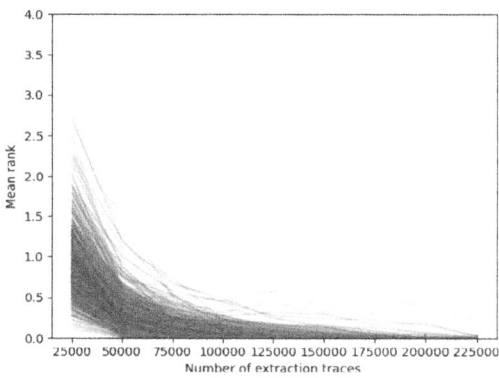

Fig. 8. 20 Neural Networks with 2-share masking and shuffling: Expected key ranks

traces. We notice that few key elements still have a mean rank not steadily converging to 0. We do not have a rational explanation for this behaviour, even though there are only 4 of them out of 512 and that they are still below rank 1, meaning they are still ranked between first and second in average.

8 Conclusion

Elisabeth-b4 offers a lightweight solution for preserving user privacy in cloud computing as an HHE scheme. Our side-channel analysis showed that a 2048-bit key could be extracted with a limited number of traces. In side-channel analysis, non-linear operations typically exhibit the highest leakage, which we observed as the CPA specifically targeted the S-boxes. These S-boxes, structured as NLUTs with a minimal output size of just 4 bits, introduced uncertainty regarding whether any exploitable leakage would be present. Nevertheless, our attack proved successful even on a 32-bit processor. Moreover, other classic techniques such as template attacks enabled key recovery with as few as 1,000 traces.

Using well-known mitigations like masking and shuffling, the previous attack is mitigated but a stronger attacker can still train 20 independent deep neural networks and acquire 250 times more traces on the target to retrieve the key.

As a direction for future work, we doubt that the same analysis could be transposed to power analysis as we suspect most of our leaking information to be found in higher frequencies of the leakage signal. With a lot of the leakage coming from the **RWS**, we wonder whether the latter could be modified to keep the security level while avoiding to unnecessarily manipulate all keyround elements for every plaintext nibble. Instead, it could be thought of precomputing the keyrounds in advance once per seed.

A Expected Number of Traces Before Every Key Element Is Observed

The key has $N = 512$ elements and $n = 98$ of them are uniformly sampled at each trace. We would like to compute the expected number of traces after which all N elements are chosen. This problem is a variant of the Coupon collector's problem but instead of choosing one element with replacement at a time, we choose n of them.

We model the problem as a discrete-time Markov chain where its states represent the number of key elements that were already selected. We are interested in the expected number of steps to go from state 0 to state N. The probability $p_{i,j}$ to go from state i to state j can be computed as:

$$p_{i,j} = \begin{cases} \frac{\binom{N-i}{j-i}\binom{i}{n-(j-i)}}{\binom{N}{n}}, & \text{if } i \leq j \leq i+n. \\ 0, & \text{otherwise.} \end{cases}$$

Indeed, we cannot decrease our number of selected elements so $p_{i,j} = 0$ if $i > j$. We can select a maximum of n elements at each step so $p_{i,j} = 0$ if $j > i+n$. In the remaining case, we count the number of ways of selecting $j-i$ new elements from the $N-i$ remaining to be selected, while also selecting the rest $(n-(j-i))$ from the i already selected. We then divide by the total number of ways of selecting n elements from N.

Our chain is an instance of an absorbing Markov chain, i.e., $\exists i, p_{i,i} = 1$, and its only absorbing state is N because we can always increase the number of already selected elements except if all of them have been so. There exists a useful theorem that allows us to compute the expected number of steps before the chain is absorbed starting from any state [18]. In our case, we start at state 0. Applying the theorem shows that the expected number of steps is the sum of the first row of $(\mathbf{I_N} - \mathbf{Q})^{-1}$ where $\mathbf{Q} = \begin{pmatrix} p_{0,0} & \cdots & p_{0,N-1} \\ \vdots & \ddots & \vdots \\ p_{N-1,0} & \cdots & p_{N-1,N-1} \end{pmatrix}$.

Replacing N with 512 and n with 98 leads to an expected number of steps of 32.61, rounding up to 33.

B Adapted `MultiResNetSCA-1` architecture

We adapted the `MultiResNetSCA-1`'s architecture, originally proposed by [27] into the one shown in Fig. 9, with $f.(\cdot)$ being probability density functions.

C Our 20 Neural Network Architectures

`ResNetRWSPerm`, `ResNetRoundPerm`, {`ResNetRWS-0`,..., `ResNetRWS-3`} and {`ResNetRound-0`,..., `ResNetRound-13`} are shown in Fig. 10, with $f.(\cdot)$ being probability density functions.

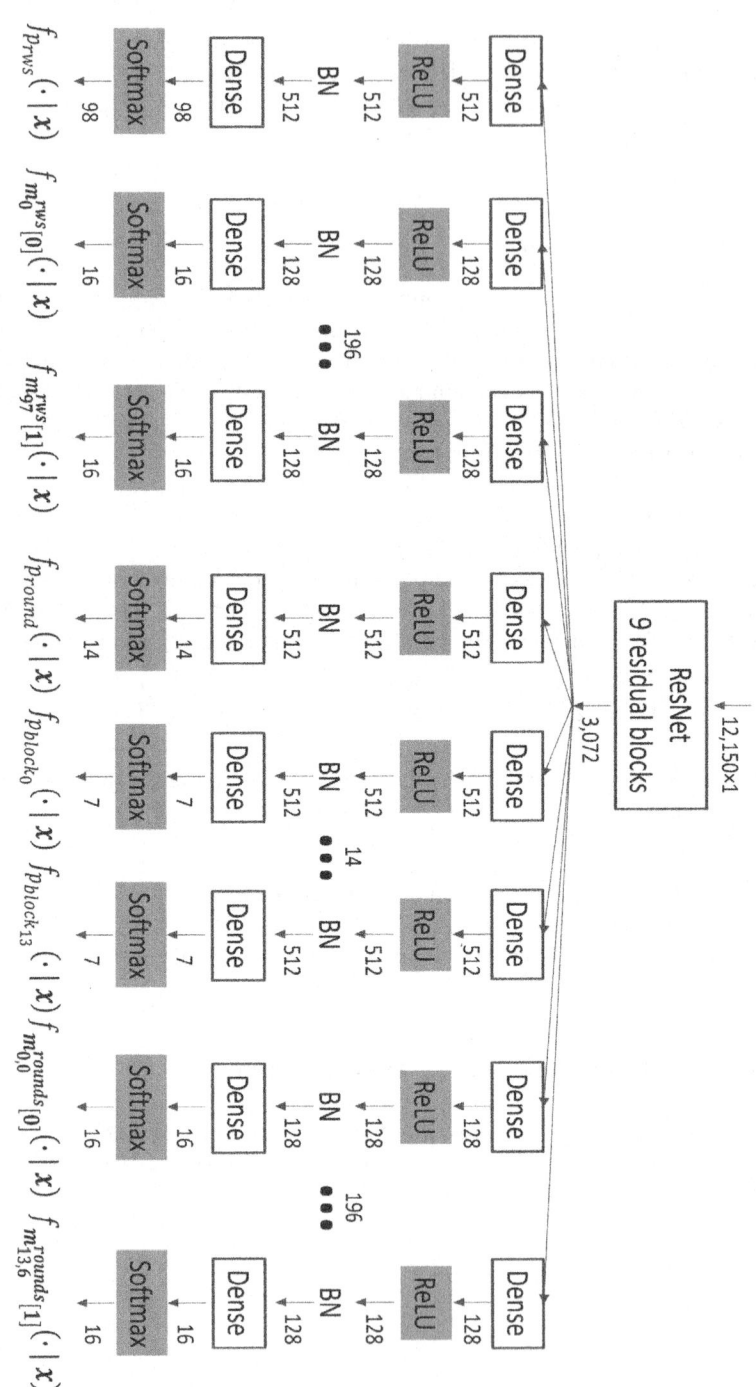

Fig. 9. Adapted `MultiResNetSCA-1` [27].

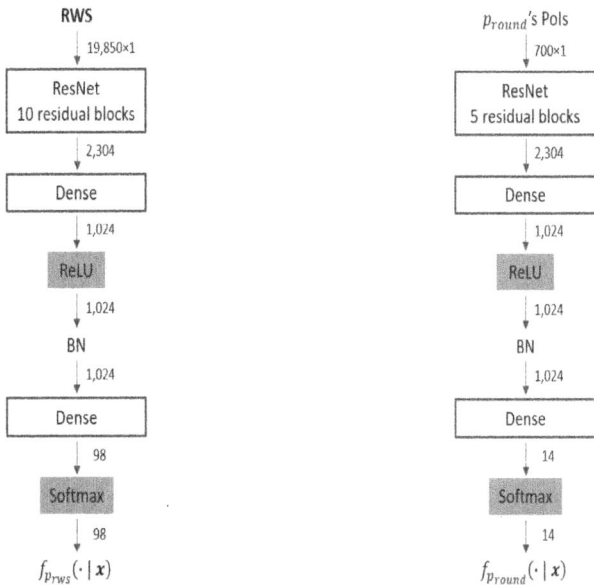
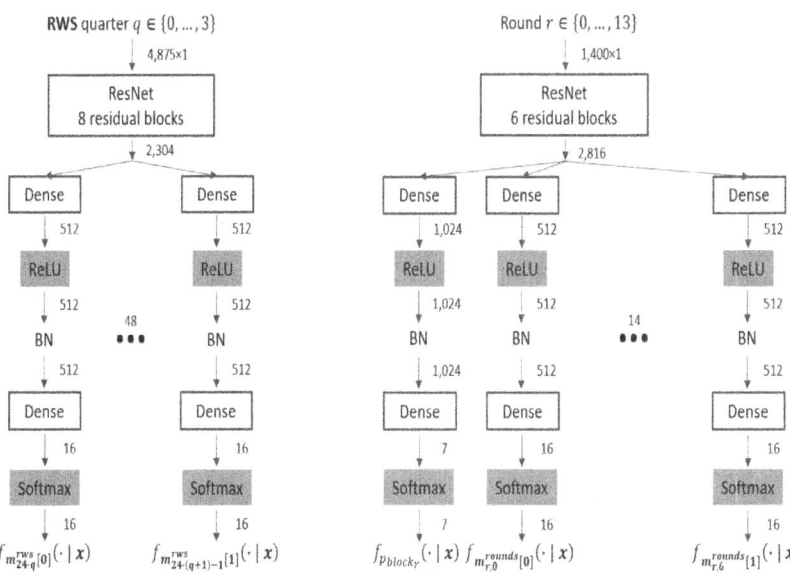

Fig. 10. Our 20 neural networks architectures.

References

1. Akkar, M.-L., Giraud, C.: An implementation of DES and AES, secure against some attacks. In: Koç, Ç.K., Naccache, D., Paar, C. (eds.) CHES 2001. LNCS, vol. 2162, pp. 309–318. Springer, Heidelberg (2001). https://doi.org/10.1007/3-540-44709-1_26
2. Albrecht, M.R., Rechberger, C., Schneider, T., Tiessen, T., Zohner, M.: Ciphers for MPC and FHE. In: Oswald, E., Fischlin, M. (eds.) EUROCRYPT 2015. LNCS, vol. 9056, pp. 430–454. Springer, Heidelberg (2015). https://doi.org/10.1007/978-3-662-46800-5_17
3. Archambeau, C., Peeters, E., Standaert, F.-X., Quisquater, J.-J.: Template attacks in principal subspaces. In: Goubin, L., Matsui, M. (eds.) CHES 2006. LNCS, vol. 4249, pp. 1–14. Springer, Heidelberg (2006). https://doi.org/10.1007/11894063_1
4. Breiman, L.: Random forests. Mach. Learn. **45**(1), 5–32 (2001). https://doi.org/10.1023/A:1010933404324
5. Canteaut, A., et al.: Stream ciphers: a practical solution for efficient homomorphic-ciphertext compression. J. Cryptol. **31**(3), 885–916 (2018). https://doi.org/10.1007/S00145-017-9273-9
6. Chari, S., Jutla, C.S., Rao, J.R., Rohatgi, P.: Towards sound approaches to counteract power-analysis attacks. In: Wiener, M. (ed.) CRYPTO 1999. LNCS, vol. 1666, pp. 398–412. Springer, Heidelberg (1999). https://doi.org/10.1007/3-540-48405-1_26
7. Chari, S., Rao, J.R., Rohatgi, P.: Template attacks. In: Kaliski, B.S., Koç, K., Paar, C. (eds.) CHES 2002. LNCS, vol. 2523, pp. 13–28. Springer, Heidelberg (2003). https://doi.org/10.1007/3-540-36400-5_3
8. Cho, M., Chung, W., Ha, J., Lee, J., Oh, E., Son, M.: FRAST: tfhe-friendly cipher based on random s-boxes. IACR Cryptol. ePrint Arch., p. 745 (2024). https://eprint.iacr.org/2024/745
9. Cosseron, O., Hoffmann, C., Méaux, P., Standaert, F.: Towards globally optimized hybrid homomorphic encryption - featuring the elisabeth stream cipher. IACR Cryptol. ePrint Arch. p. 180 (2022), https://eprint.iacr.org/2022/180
10. Cristianini, N., Shawe-Taylor, J.: An Introduction to Support Vector Machines and Other Kernel-based Learning Methods. Cambridge University Press (2000). https://doi.org/10.1017/CBO9780511801389
11. Debande, N., Souissi, Y., Elaabid, M.A., Guilley, S., Danger, J.: Wavelet transform based pre-processing for side channel analysis. In: 45th Annual IEEE/ACM International Symposium on Microarchitecture, MICRO 2012, Workshops Proceedings, Vancouver, BC, Canada, December 1-5, 2012, pp. 32–38. IEEE Computer Society (2012). https://doi.org/10.1109/MICROW.2012.15
12. van Eck, W.: Electromagnetic radiation from video display units: An eavesdropping risk? Comput. Secur. **4**(4), 269–286 (1985). https://doi.org/10.1016/0167-4048(85)90046-X
13. Fan, G., Zhou, Y., Zhang, H., Feng, D.: How to choose interesting points for template attacks? IACR Cryptol. ePrint Arch., p. 332 (2014). http://eprint.iacr.org/2014/332
14. Friedman, J.H.: Greedy function approximation: a gradient boosting machine. Annal. Stat. **29**(5), 1189 – 1232 (2001). https://doi.org/10.1214/aos/1013203451

15. Gentry, C.: Fully homomorphic encryption using ideal lattices. In: Mitzenmacher, M. (ed.) Proceedings of the 41st Annual ACM Symposium on Theory of Computing, STOC 2009, Bethesda, MD, USA, May 31 - June 2, 2009, pp. 169–178. ACM (2009). https://doi.org/10.1145/1536414.1536440
16. Gierlichs, B., Lemke-Rust, K., Paar, C.: Templates vs. stochastic methods. In: Goubin, L., Matsui, M. (eds.) CHES 2006. LNCS, vol. 4249, pp. 15–29. Springer, Heidelberg (2006). https://doi.org/10.1007/11894063_2
17. Gilbert, H., Boissier, R.H., Jean, J., Reinhard, J.: Cryptanalysis of elisabeth-4. In: Guo, J., Steinfeld, R. (eds.) Advances in Cryptology - ASIACRYPT 2023 - 29th International Conference on the Theory and Application of Cryptology and Information Security, Guangzhou, China, December 4-8, 2023, Proceedings, Part III. LNCS, vol. 14440, pp. 256–284. Springer (2023). https://doi.org/10.1007/978-981-99-8727-6_9
18. Grinstead, C.M., Snell, J.L.: Introduction to probability. American Mathematical Soc. (2012)
19. Hebborn, P., Leander, G.: Dasta - alternative linear layer for rasta. IACR Trans. Symmetric Cryptol. **2020**(3), 46–86 (2020). https://doi.org/10.13154/TOSC.V2020.I3.46-86
20. Hoffmann, C., Méaux, P., Standaert, F.: The patching landscape of elisabeth-4 and the mixed filter permutator paradigm. In: Chattopadhyay, A., Bhasin, S., Picek, S., Rebeiro, C. (eds.) Progress in Cryptology - INDOCRYPT 2023 - 24th International Conference on Cryptology in India, Goa, India, December 10-13, 2023, Proceedings, Part I. LNCS, vol. 14459, pp. 134–156. Springer (2023). https://doi.org/10.1007/978-3-031-56232-7_7
21. Kingma, D.P., Ba, J.: Adam: a method for stochastic optimization. In: Bengio, Y., LeCun, Y. (eds.) 3rd International Conference on Learning Representations, ICLR 2015, San Diego, CA, USA, May 7-9, 2015, Conference Track Proceedings (2015). http://arxiv.org/abs/1412.6980
22. Kocher, P.C.: Timing attacks on implementations of Diffie-Hellman, RSA, DSS, and other systems. In: Koblitz, N. (ed.) CRYPTO 1996. LNCS, vol. 1109, pp. 104–113. Springer, Heidelberg (1996). https://doi.org/10.1007/3-540-68697-5_9
23. Kocher, P.C., Jaffe, J., Jun, B., Rohatgi, P.: Introduction to differential power analysis. J. Cryptogr. Eng. **1**(1), 5–27 (2011). https://doi.org/10.1007/S13389-011-0006-Y
24. Kumar, S., Dasu, V.A., Baksi, A., Sarkar, S., Jap, D., Breier, J., Bhasinl, S.: Side channel attack on stream ciphers: a three-step approach to state/key recovery. IACR Trans. Cryptogr. Hardw. Embed. Syst. p. 166 (2022). https://doi.org/10.46586/tches.v2022.i2.166-191
25. Mangard, S., Oswald, E., Popp, T.: Power analysis attacks - revealing the secrets of smart cards. Springer (2007)
26. Mangard, S., Popp, T., Gammel, B.M.: Side-Channel Leakage of Masked CMOS Gates. In: Menezes, A. (ed.) CT-RSA 2005. LNCS, vol. 3376, pp. 351–365. Springer, Heidelberg (2005). https://doi.org/10.1007/978-3-540-30574-3_24
27. Masure, L., Strullu, R.: Side channel analysis against the anssi's protected AES implementation on ARM. IACR Cryptol. ePrint Arch., p. 592 (2021). https://eprint.iacr.org/2021/592
28. Méaux, P., Carlet, C., Journault, A., Standaert, F.-X.: Improved Filter Permutators for Efficient FHE: Better Instances and Implementations. In: Hao, F., Ruj, S., Sen Gupta, S. (eds.) INDOCRYPT 2019. LNCS, vol. 11898, pp. 68–91. Springer, Cham (2019). https://doi.org/10.1007/978-3-030-35423-7_4

29. Moradi, A.: Side-channel leakage through static power – should we care about in practice? IACR Cryptol. ePrint Arch., p. 562 (2014). https://eprint.iacr.org/2014/025.pdf
30. Naehrig, M., Lauter, K.E., Vaikuntanathan, V.: Can homomorphic encryption be practical? In: Cachin, C., Ristenpart, T. (eds.) Proceedings of the 3rd ACM Cloud Computing Security Workshop, CCSW 2011, Chicago, IL, USA, October 21, 2011, pp. 113–124. ACM (2011). https://dl.acm.org/citation.cfm?id=2046682
31. Vadnala, P.K.: Provably Secure Countermeasures against Side-channel Attacks. Ph.D. thesis, University of Luxembourg (2015). http://orbilu.uni.lu/handle/10993/21653
32. Veyrat-Charvillon, N., Medwed, M., Kerckhof, S., Standaert, F.-X.: Shuffling against side-channel attacks: a comprehensive study with cautionary note. In: Wang, X., Sako, K. (eds.) ASIACRYPT 2012. LNCS, vol. 7658, pp. 740–757. Springer, Heidelberg (2012). https://doi.org/10.1007/978-3-642-34961-4_44
33. Wang, W., Tang, D.: Differential fault attack on he-friendly stream ciphers: Masta, pasta and elisabeth. IACR Cryptol. ePrint Arch., p. 1005 (2024). https://eprint.iacr.org/2024/1005

White-Box Implementation Techniques for the HFE Family

Pierre Galissant and Louis Goubin[✉]

Laboratoire de Mathématiques de Versailles, UVSQ, CNRS, Université Paris-Saclay,
78035 Versailles, France
pierre.galissant@gmail.com, louis.goubin@uvsq.fr

Abstract. Cryptography is increasingly deployed in applications running on open devices in which the software is extremely vulnerable to attacks, since the attacker has complete control over the execution platform and the software implementation itself. This creates a challenge for cryptography: designing implementations of cryptographic algorithms that are secure, not only in the black-box model, but also in this attack context that is referred to as the white-box adversary model. Moreover, emerging applications such as mobile payment, mobile contract signing or blockchain-based technologies have created a need for white-box implementations of public-key cryptography, and especially of signature algorithms.

However, while many attempts were made to construct white-box implementations of block-ciphers, almost no white-box implementations have been published for what concerns asymmetric schemes. We present here the first white-box implementation technique of HFE signature primitives, for a specific set of internal polynomials. For instance our implementations of the signature primitive range from about 94 MB for security level $\lambda = 80$ to 752 MB for $\lambda = 128$ for variations of the C^{*+-} primitive, and similar ranges for pC^{*-}. To motivate the study of the security of the techniques we use, we also propose a challenge implementation and the white-box compiler used to produce this implementation.

Keywords: White-box cryptography · Public-key cryptography · Multivariate cryptography

1 Introduction

Since the seminal paper of Chow et al. in 2002, the research in the white-box model has mainly been focused on standard symmetric block-ciphers such as DES and AES. Many candidate implementations have been proposed [10,12,13,27,28,43] but all have later been broken due to very powerful generic attacks (such as [7,8,24,25]) or specific structural attacks (for instance [4,23]). The goal of these implementations is to provide security, with respect to stronger attack models, but weaker cryptographic notions than in the black box model:

unbreakability (being unable to extract the key from the code), incompressibility (being unable to compress the code) or one-wayness (being unable to invert the implementation).

Regarding asymmetric candidates, very few solutions have been proposed: the implementation of Barthelemy [3] does not stand against generic attacks and the implementations of Shamir's signature [40] in [19] and of an IEEE P1363 signature in [44] only focus on key-extraction, ignoring the incompressibility, while modifying the verifying algorithm in the white-box version of the scheme. Recently unbreakable implementations of ECDSA have been investigated in the WhibOx21 and WhibOx24 contests [41,42]. However, among the hundreds of implementations, all were broken in few days (see [1] and the websites of the contests [41,42]). After almost two decades of research, it is safe to say that getting a secure white-box implementation for an existing algorithm is a hard open problem.

In this paper, we propose the first investigation of white-box implementations of the HFE signature primitive (Hidden Field Equation) [35], that we quickly recall in Sect. 2.2. Our study shows that the richness of multivariate cryptography allows new possibilities for asymmetric white-box cryptography, and we design and analyze an explicit construction based on these new ideas.

The techniques we use are radically different from the usual techniques used in constructions for white-box symmetric cryptography. Moreover, they do not rely on security through obscurity, *i.e.* our compiler is described according to Kerckhoffs' principle and does not use any heuristic code obfuscation techniques.

Our Contribution. In the present paper, we exhibit the first white-box implementation of asymmetric multivariate signature algorithms, in the following sense:

- We propose a new white-box implementation technique for nude HFE instances and incorporate the p, $-$ and $\hat{+}$ perturbations into our implementations. This design technique follows Kerchkoffs' principle and does not rely on any hidden information or procedure.
- The *unbreakability* property of our implementation in the white-box model is proven under a reasonable assumption about the *Isomorphism of Polynomials* (IP) problem: a key-recovery attack on the white-box implementation is not easier than in the black-box model.
- We also revisit the notion of *incompressibility* in the white-box model, giving a more precise definition, and state a precise security conjecture in the case of our implementation : under this assumption, an attack aiming at obtaining a smaller implementation is not easier than all the standard attacks in the black-box model.
- We propose different parameters and choices of internal polynomials to derive concrete instantiations for different security parameters : from about 94 MB for security level $\lambda = 80$ to 752 MB for $\lambda = 128$ for variations of the $C^{*\hat{+}-}$ primitive, and similar ranges for pC^{*-}.

- We propose a challenge implementation as well as the white-box compiler used to produce it to motivate the study of the techniques used in the paper: https://github.com/p-galissant/WBHFE

Note that more material can be found in the extended version of the present paper, with additional details about multivariate cryptography, and other variants of HFE-based signature implementations in the white-box model.

Remark: From a practical point of view, the white-box implementations presented here are quite heavy, which is somewhat inherent to the white-box model (and is especially related to the concept of code incompressiblity). Nevertheless, the obtained sizes (from dozens to hundreds of MB) leave the possibility of using them in realistic contexts, typically smart-phone applications, or cloud-based applications for the strongest security levels. As an example, MasterCard Cloud-Based Payments (MCBP) [30] is a secure and scalable software-based solution developed to digitize card credentials and enable both contactless and remote payment transactions. In this context, MasterCard has specifically recommended the use of white-box implementation for the secure storage of payment tokens [31]. In addition, from a more theoretical point of view, it should be noted that our construction provides the first white-box implementation of a public key algorithm together with an extensive security analysis.

Technical Overview. Technically, our proposal is heavily based on the structure and flexibility of multivariate cryptography. The main idea is as follows. We consider the HFE (Hidden Field Equation) cryptosystem; its design involves an internal polynomial transformation F defined on the field extension $\mathbb{K} = \mathbb{F}_{2^n}$, such that all the monomials have an exponent of Hamming weight ≤ 2. It is then composed with affine secrets S and T to get the public key P.

The usual way to invert P is to use the structure of F in the field extension and the trapdoor consisting in the knowledge of S and T. However, we introduce a second trapdoor with the concept of affine multiple that allows to invert P while not revealing S and T. Namely, for our purpose, we intentionally choose F such that it has an *affine multiple* $A \in \mathbb{K}[X,Y]$ of low degree in Y, that is:

- All the exponents of X involved in $A(X,Y)$ have a Hamming weight ≤ 1;
- Any solution of the equation $F(a) = b$ is also a solution of $A(a,b) = 0$.

In a nutshell, the white-box implementation of the signature algorithm is derived from this affine multiple $A(X,Y)$ and the secret key, and its size can be kept moderate since the degree of A in Y is low. We then adapt this technique to also include perturbations of the public key P.

As a consequence, we obtain the following results: for an attacker who only knows the public key of this HFE signature scheme, recovering the white-box implementation is not easier than breaking the scheme in the black-box model; and from the white-box implementation, it is computationally difficult for the legitimate user to recover the secret key, or even to compress the white-box implementation.

Related Work. In the present paper, we consider and target the traditional (white-box) notions of *unbreakability* and *incompressibility*. We adapt the usual definition (see [14] for instance) to the public-key setting in Sect. 4. In this context, we describe a white-box implementation of an HFE signature primitive, which belongs to a family of algorithms that has been extensively studied in the black-box model and belongs to state-of-the-art cryptography.

The notion of unbreakability is a very intuitive security notion for white-box cryptography and has been studied since the seminal paper of Chow et al. in 2002 [13]. Ever since, cryptographers have tried to propose white-box implementations of usual cryptographic algorithms, with mitigated success. Block-ciphers have been the most studied as seen above. Recently, the WhibOx 2021 contest [41] showed the interest of the community to produce an unbreakable implementation of the ECDSA signature algorithm and the hundreds of implementations have all been broken. For the 2024 edition, the contest is still focused on ECDSA [42].

The notion of incompressibility is a stronger security notion, first formally defined in [14] where the study of this notion is motivated as a software countermeasure against code-lifting attacks. In the same paper, the authors also propose an incompressible implementation of a special private-key RSA in the Ideal Group Model. Since then, works like [5,6,20] or [26] have worked on defining incompressibility and studying designed symmetric algorithms to achieve their definitions. However, they focus only on symmetric algorithms.

We also refer to [21,22] for a recent survey on all these white-box security notions.

2 Background and Motivations

For any program or mathematical object P, we define $Size(P)$ to be the size in bits of its representation.

$(M, S, K_\mathcal{V} \times K_\mathcal{S}, \mathcal{V}, \mathcal{S})$ is an asymmetric signature scheme where M is the message space, S is the signature space, $K_\mathcal{V} \times K_\mathcal{S}$ is the key space, $\mathcal{S}$ is the signature algorithm, and $\mathcal{V}$ is the verification algorithm.

For any keyed cryptographic function f with key k we note C_f the compiler specified to f and $C_f(k)$ the white box implementation of f with the key k.

For two programs $\mathcal{A}$ and $\mathcal{B}$ we note $\mathcal{A} \approx \mathcal{B}$ when $\mathcal{A}$ and $\mathcal{B}$ are functionally equivalent; *i.e.* they agree on all inputs with probability 1.

Regarding polynomials, we note $\sigma(n,d)$ to be the number of monomials in at most n variables of at most degree d and $M(n,d)$ is the cost of multiplying polynomials of degree d with coefficients of size n. The rest of the notations are usual.

2.1 Public-Key White-Box Implementations

While many candidates have been publicly proposed to construct white-box implementations of block-ciphers, almost no white-box implementations for public-key algorithms have been published up to now, in spite of numerous research efforts.

The works of [19] and [44] achieve unbreakability but modify the verification algorithm and do not address incompressibility. It is well known that white-box security is easier to obtain if we allow ad-hoc designs. The present paper deals with a well-known and general-purpose family of signature algorithms, that was not specifically designed for the white-box scenario.

The WhibOx 2021 and WhibOx 2024 contests [41,42] showed that for the ECDSA algorithm, even with hidden design, getting an unbreakable implementation of small size is out of reach. The implementations, bound by the challenges benchmarks - 100MB source code, 50MB executable size and RAM usage and 10sec running time for Whibox24 for instance - were all broken few days after their publications. The report of Barbu et al. [1] goes through the generic attacks and problems the implementations of the Whibox21 contest suffered. Especially, they show that due to the fact that implementing a robust randomness generator is hard in the white-box model, all the implementations can be broken using classic techniques such as fault attacks or lattice attacks.

Despite the hardness of the problem, there is a growing need for such implementations, motivated by mobile payment [17], mobile contract signing (following the eIDAS regulation (EU Reg. N°910/2014) for instance) or blockchain technologies.

2.2 Multivariate Cryptography

We will assume that the reader is familiar with multivariate cryptography, especially with "Big Field" trapdoors.

Description of HFE. First described by Patarin in [35], the HFE scheme is a direct descendant of C^* [32,33]. For any positive integers n and $D \in \mathbb{N}$, the central map $F \in \mathbb{F}_{q^n}[X]$ is defined by:

$$F(X) = \sum_{\substack{0 \leq i < j < n \\ q^i + q^j \leq D}} a_{i,j} X^{q^i + q^j} + \sum_{\substack{0 \leq i < n \\ q^i \leq D}} b_i X^{q^i} + c$$

where the $a_{i,j}$, the b_i and c are elements of $\mathbb{F}_{2^n}$. As the integer D bounds the actual degree of any such F, we call D the degree of the HFE instance. As the quantity $\lceil log_q(D) \rceil$ will be important in the description of attacks, we set $d = \lceil log_q(D) \rceil$.

The secret key is the list of such polynomial F and a couple of affine bijective transformations $(S,T) \in AFF_n(\mathbb{F}_q)$. We note it (S, F, T). We remark that F is efficiently invertible on its image due to the Berlekamp algorithm if D is not too big and that S and T are trivially invertible as long as q^n is not too big.

To compute the public key, let us fix a basis $(e_1, ..., e_n) \in (\mathbb{F}_{q^n})^n$ of $\mathbb{F}_{q^n}$ over $\mathbb{F}_q$. It induces an isomorphism π from $(\mathbb{F}_q)^n$ to $\mathbb{F}_{q^n}$ such that $\pi(x_1, ..., x_n) = \sum_{i=1}^n x_i e_i$. The public key P is the map from $\mathbb{F}_q^n$ to $\mathbb{F}_2^n$ is then defined by:

$$P = T \circ \pi^{-1} \circ F \circ \pi \circ S$$

The public key is represented by the n coordinates of P: for each $0 \leq i < n$ we note its i-th coordinate $P_i \in \mathbb{F}_q[x_1, ..., x_n]$.

Usually, a "nude" instance (that is, an instance without perturbations) is not enough to resist the state-of-the-art attacks. That is why perturbations were introduced to reinforce these nude instances, while keeping the trapdoor property.

We assume that the reader is familiar with the perturbations $-$, p ([15,34]) and $\hat{+}$ ([18]).

Security of HFE Instances. As we will precisely tune our HFE instances to optimize the trade-off between security and implementation size, we recall briefly the best attacks found in the state-of-the-art against various HFE instances using different perturbations. These attacks can mostly be split in two categories : message-recovery attacks and key-recovery rank attacks. For the complexity of message-recovery attacks, we follow [2]. As this complexity depends on the degree of regularity of the public-key, we use the estimation of this degree following [11,18,37,39]. For the complexity of rank attacks, we follow the works of [18,34].

3 The Implementation Technique

For the rest of the paper, unless specified otherwise, we consider HFE instances over $\mathbb{F}_2$.

3.1 Affine Multiple Attacks

The starting point of our construction is the concept of affine multiple. It was introduced by Patarin in [35] to generalize an inversion attack on C^* to HFE. The central idea of this attack is that for any polynomial $F \in \mathbb{F}_{2^n}[x]$ there always exists a polynomial $A(x,y) \in \mathbb{F}_{2^n}[x,y]$ that is $\mathbb{F}_2$-linear in x and a multiple of the polynomial $F(x) + y$. This means that if $y = F(x)$, then $A(x,y) = 0$.

Definition 1. *Let $F \in \mathbb{F}_{2^n}[x]$. The polynomial $A(x,y) \in \mathbb{F}_{2^n}[x,y]$ is said to be an affine multiple of F if $A(x,y) = 0 \mod F(x) + y$ and A is $\mathbb{F}_2$-linear in x.*

The goal of the original affine multiple attack is to recover A via interpolation. When A is known to an attacker, they can plug any value of y to get a linear system in x of reasonable size they can solve to efficiently sign without using the structure of the equation in $\mathbb{F}_{2^n}$.

To further detail this attack, let us define the affine degree d_{aff} of an affine multiple:

Definition 2. *Let A be an affine multiple of $F(x) + y$, that is, $A(x, y) = a + \sum_{i=0}^{D-1} a_i x^{2^i}$ with $a, a_o, ..., a_{D-1} \in \mathbb{F}_{2^n}[y]$, if $Mon(a_k)$ is the set of the monomials of a_k we define d_{aff} the affine degree of A by:*

$$d_{\text{aff}} := \max_k \left(\max_{m \in Mon(a_k)} HW(deg_y(m)) \right).$$

i.e. the maximum Hamming weight of the monomials in y in the polynomial $A(x, y)$.

We then remark that the composition by these affine transformations S and T leads to a new affine multiple that has the same d_{aff} degree. Now, to start the attack, just notice that $A(x, y)$ is composed of about $n \times \sigma(n, d_{\text{aff}})$ unknown coefficients over $\mathbb{F}_2^n$, where $\sigma(n, d_{\text{aff}})$ is the number of monomials in at most n variables in degree d. We will go through this in more details in Sect. 3. This means that with enough queries $(x, P(x))$, the unknown coefficients of A are the solution of a linear system of n equations with $n \times \sigma(n, d_{\text{aff}})$ unknowns that we can obtain with a Gaussian reduction. This gives us an attack, if F is known to have such affine multiple, in space $n^2 \times \sigma(n, d_{\text{aff}})$ and in time $(n \times \sigma(n, d_{\text{aff}}))^\omega$.

This attack is quite inefficient in general as the degree d_{aff} is usually quite high. Also, it is well known that the perturbation minus ($-$) protects from affine multiple attacks [35]. It is important to remark that the cost of computing an affine multiple of $F(x) + y$ is easier when the private key (S, F, T) is known than when only the public key P is known, especially when modifiers like minus are used. This means that an affine multiple might be accessible with the knowledge of (S, F, T) but not with the knowledge of P only.

3.2 Rationale of the Construction

The main point of our construction is to use the affine multiple relation over $\mathbb{F}_2$ as an alternative way to inverse a public key P: the affine multiple will be our white-box implementation. Indeed, if we take $y = F(x)$ in the image of F, computing x knowing an affine multiple $A(x, y)$ boils down to plugging y onto the expression and then solving linear system in x. If the affine multiple is of a reasonable size, computing x is as easy as evaluating the affine multiple in y.

The feasability of the construction is due to the fact that computing an affine multiple from the secrets is easier than from the public key. As we will see later, the security is expected from the hardness to extract the secret key from the affine multiple and the hardness to compress it.

3.3 Construction for Nude Public-Keys

Computing the Affine Multiple. We now detail the existence of affine multiples and expose an algorithm to efficiently compute them if possible.

To prove the existence of affine multiple, let us assume that $D = deg(F)$ is such that $D < n$ and let us consider the vector space $\mathbb{F}_{2^n}(y)[x]/_{(P(x)+y)}$ of dimension $D = deg(F)$ over $\mathbb{F}_2(y)$. Now, the $(D+1)$ $\mathbb{F}_2$-linear polynomials $(1, x^{2^0}, x^{2^1}, ..., x^{2^{D-1}})$ are linearly dependent:

$$\exists a, a_o, ..., a_{D-1} \in \mathbb{F}_2(y), a + \sum_{i=0}^{D-1} a_i x^{2^i} = 0 \mod (F(x)+y)$$

To compute the coefficients a_k, we can use the reductions of the monomials x^{2^i} modulo $F(x) + y$:

$$\exists b_{i,0}, ..., b_{i,D-1} \in \mathbb{F}_2(y), x^{2^i} = \sum_{j=0}^{D-1} b_{i,j} x^j \mod (F(x)+y)$$

We then reinject into the previous equation:

$$a + \sum_{i=0}^{D-1} a_i \sum_{j=0}^{D-1} b_{i,j} x^j = 0$$

This clearly translates into the linear system:

$$\begin{pmatrix} 1 & b_{0,0} & \cdots & b_{D-1,0} \\ 0 & b_{0,1} & \cdots & b_{D-1,1} \\ \vdots & \vdots & \ddots & \vdots \\ 0 & b_{0,D-1} & \cdots & b_{D-1,D-1} \end{pmatrix} \times \begin{pmatrix} a \\ a_0 \\ \vdots \\ a_{D-1} \end{pmatrix} = \begin{pmatrix} 0 \\ 0 \\ \vdots \\ 0 \end{pmatrix}$$

We can then solve this system with Gaussian reduction in $\mathbb{F}_2(y)$. Multiplying this relation by the LCM of the $a'_k s$ denominators leads to an affine multiple polynomial $A(x,y)$. We now note $a_k \in \mathbb{F}_2[y]$ the polynomials in y obtained that way. This proves the existence of an affine multiple, and gives us at the same time an algorithm to compute it.

Remark: We do not claim the uniqueness of the affine multiple. It is indeed clear that considering D other $\mathbb{F}_2$-linear monomials leads to a similar relation, but it is not clear how it affects the coefficients a_k obtained.

The White-Box Construction. We now detail the construction of our white-box compiler and how to use it in practice. As we mentioned earlier, we focus on implementing the P^{-1} functionality as it is enough to guaranty unbreakability and incompressibility (see Sect. 4.4).

Now, to start the white-box transformation from an HFE secret key (S, F, T) over n bits - with bijective affine transformation $S : \mathbb{F}_2^n \to \mathbb{F}_2^n$ and bijective affine transformation T: $\mathbb{F}_2^n \to \mathbb{F}_2^n$ and the public transformation π - the compiler computes first the affine multiple $A(x,y)$ of F over $\mathbb{F}_{2^n}$ following the algorithm described in the previous section.

From the polynomial $A(x,y)$, the compiler can now compute the coordinates $A_i(x_1, ..., x_n, y_1, ..., y_n)$ (for $i \in [\![1,n]\!]$) of A through the isomorphism π, and its composition with the secret maps S and T:

$$\tilde{A}_i(x_1, ..., x_n, y_1, ..., y_n) = A_i(S(x_1, ..., x_n), T^{-1}(y_1, ..., y_n))$$

Now, to compute $P^{-1}(y)$, one can plug the coordinates $y_1, ..., y_n$ of y into the polynomials $\tilde{A}_i$ to get a linear system of n equations in $x_1, ..., x_n$ that can be solved through Gaussian inversion for instance. However, one should worry that $(F(x) = y)$ only implies $(A(x,y) = 0)$, and not the reciprocate. Indeed, when we plug y in, we might get a solution x such that $(A(x,y) = 0$ and $F(x) \neq y)$. To avoid such cases, we have to verify that for the chosen y, the signature is valid (i.e. $F(x) = y$). As the verification is made with the public key, the time needed to perform this check is negligible. We define the collection of the n polynomials $\tilde{A}_i$, the code for evaluation and the code for linear inversion to be the white-box implementation of the computation of P^{-1}. We note this compiler *WBHFE*. This leads to the compiling Algorithm 1 :

Algorithm 1: White-box compiler *WBHFE*

input : A HFE secret key (S, F, T) with affine S and T
output: $WBHFE(S, F, T)$ the white-box implementation of P^{-1} with key (S, F, T)

- Compute the affine multiple $A(x,y)$ of F with algorithm of section 3.3
- Compute the composition with secrets S and T and projection maps to get the coordinates of $\tilde{A}_i$:

$$\tilde{A}_i(x_1, ..., x_n, y_1, ..., y_n) = A_i(S(x_1, ..., x_n), T^{-1}(y_1, ..., y_n))$$

- Produce a code that partially evaluates the $\tilde{A}_i$ over the $y_1, ..., y_n$
- Produce a code that compute a pre-image of the vector 0 through linear application given by the partial evaluations of the $\tilde{A}_i$, and output "NONE" if no solution can be found.
- Produce a code that check if the message to be signed is in the image of P.
- Concatenate the produced codes to get the whole white-box implementation $WBHFE(S, F, T)$.

3.4 Dimensioning of the Construction

The study of size of our solution boils down to two points: the computation of the multiple A over $\mathbb{F}_{2^n}$ and the size of its coordinates $\tilde{A}_i$ over $(\mathbb{F}_2)^n$. Indeed, the code size needed to perform evaluations of polynomials and Gaussian inversion is negligible. For the representation of polynomials, we use the so-called "sparse" representation to get the smallest size possible. The size analysis is of course to be linked with the white-box incompressibility which is detailed later on.

Cost of Computing an Affine Multiple. To compute the coefficients $b_{i,j}$, we have to go through the reduction of the monomials x^{2^i} modulo $F(x) + y$, with $0 \leq i < D$. Due to the reduction modulo $F(x) + y$, the degree of $b_{i,j}$ can be as big as 2^D and the $b_{i,j}$ can have up to 2^D monomials. The last part of the algorithm only solves a $D \times D$ system, leading to a worst case complexity if the polynomials $b_{i,j}$ are dense:

$$\mathcal{O}(M(n, 2^D)D^\omega)$$

where $M(n, 2^D)$ is the cost of multiplying polynomials of degree 2^D with coefficients of size n. This means that with $D = \mathcal{O}(n)$, computing this relation is usually impossible. However, we will use it with smaller polynomials than in usual HFE, i.e. $D = O(1)$.

Size and Running Time of the WBHFE Implementation. The central part of this analysis is the affine degree d_{aff} (definition 2), the greatest Hamming weight that appears in the description of the affine multiple A over $\mathbb{F}_2$. Over $\mathbb{F}_2$, $d_{\text{aff}} + 1$ is the highest degree of the monomials encountered in the expression of $A(x, y)$. Indeed, $A(x, y)$ is linear in the x_i but of degree d_{aff} in the y_i.

If we note $\sigma(n, d_{\text{aff}})$ to be the number of monomials in at most n variables of degree at most d_{aff}, this means that we have about $n \times \sigma(n, d_{\text{aff}})$ coefficients in $\mathbb{F}_2^n$ needed to compute a coordinate A_i of $A(x, y)$. When we compose by S and T to get $\tilde{A}$, the overall degree does not change since S and T are affine transformations. This means that each coordinate $\tilde{A}_i$ is composed of at most $n \times \sigma(n, d_{\text{aff}})$ monomials since S is a map from n bits to n bits.

As we are computing n coordinates, a lot of monomials will be shared in the expressions of the $\tilde{A}_i$ and it is more efficient to compute all the monomials that appear in these expressions, and then sum them. Since we want to only evaluate these polynomials in y_i to get a linear system in x_i, to then inverse it, we will represent the n polynomials $\tilde{A}_i$ as a matrix of polynomials over the y_i. This transformed expression is of the same size but will be more suited to our goals. To do so, we define the polynomials $\tilde{A}_{i,j}(y_1, ..., y_n)$ by the expression:

$$\tilde{A}_i(x_1, ..., x_{n-p}, y_1, ..., y_n) = \sum_{j=0}^{n} \tilde{A}_{i,j}(y_1, ..., y_n) \times x_j$$

Key Elements of WBHFE: We can now precisely state the size of our construction. Since we will need to use great values of n, we will say in our size study that code sizes are "negligible" if they are small - that is a few kB. Our construction is composed of:

- A code that evaluates, on an input $m = (m_1, ..., m_n)$ of size n, all the monomials of at most degree 2 in the m_i. As we compute all the monomials, a generic code can be made. This means that this part is negligible in code size. However, this code will produce $\sigma(n, d_{\text{aff}})$ bits during its execution. We will also suppose - without loss of generality - that these monomials are computed in an ordered way, with a label from 1 to $\sigma(n, d_{\text{aff}})$.

- The $n \times n$ files $File_{i,j}$ $i,j < n$ for which the k-th bit of the file $File_{i,j}$ is 1 if the k-th monomial computed by the precedent code is in the expression of the polynomial $\tilde{A}_{i,j}$. These files are the heaviest part of our implementation: their size is $\sigma(n, d_{\text{aff}})$ bits. As we need each of the coordinates, the whole size is $n^2 \times \sigma(n, d_{\text{aff}})$. We divide the n^2 polynomials into n^2 files so we can load them one at a time during evaluation, with potential for parallelization.
- A code that computes the evaluation of $\tilde{A}_{i,j}(m_1, ..., m_n)$ given the evaluations of the monomials of degree 2 in m_i and the file $File_{i,j}$. To do so, one just has to go through the file $File_{i,j}$ and sum the corresponding monomials as they go. This code is negligible and can load one file $File_{i,j}$ at a time.
- A code that computes the n by n binary matrix $Mat_{\tilde{A}}$ such that $(Mat_{\tilde{A}})_{i,j} = \tilde{A}_{i,j}(m_1, ..., m_n)$. This code is also negligible.
- A code that computes a solution for the linear system $Mat_{\tilde{A}} X = 0$, $X = (x_1, ..., x_n)^T$. This can be done by Gaussian elimination. Hence, it is negligible.
- A code that checks whether m was in the image of P, i.e. if $P(x) = m$. This can be done with the public key, whose size is $n \times \sigma(n, 2)$. The rest of the code is negligible.

Size and Time. This means that the code is composed of the n^2 $File_{i,j}$ for $n^2 \times \sigma(n, d_{\text{aff}})$ bits, the matrix $Mat_{\tilde{A}}$ of n^2 bits, the public key of $n \times \sigma(n, 2)$ bits, and some negligible code. The full size is then:

$$n^2 \times \sigma(n, d_{\text{aff}}) + n^2 + n \times n^2 + negl \approx n^2 \times \sigma(n, d_{\text{aff}})$$

For the rest of the paper we will define:

$$\sigma_{WB} := n^2 \times \sigma(n, d_{\text{aff}})$$

Regarding time, it is interesting to note that the computation of P^{-1} can be parallelized. Indeed, the $n \times n$ polynomials in the files $File_{i,j}$ can be computed independently. When the polynomials are evaluated, there is only a small n by n system to solve. If the evaluation of polynomials in the files $File_{i,j}$ is parallelized $n_p < n^2$ times, the time for inverting P^{-1} is:

$$\tau_{WB} := n^\omega + \frac{n^2}{n_p} \times \sigma(n, d_{\text{aff}})$$

Discussion on the Affine Degree. As seen in the previous section, the size of our construction is exponential in the affine degree d_{aff}, so it is important for us to understand its variations depending on F. As a consequence of the algorithm we used to prove the existence of a multiple affine, we know that the degrees involved in the computation of the multiple are upper bounded by 2^D where D is the degree of F. The affine degree is then bounded by D but this bound is clearly an overestimate. Through our experimentation we found that polynomials with degree of at most degree 12 can reach any affine degree ranging from 2 to 6.

These experiments show that most of small d_{aff} can be reached and that there are many polynomials reaching these values. We give examples of some families of these polynomials with $d = 3$ in the following table but these are just mere examples and any polynomial with the desired affine degree can be used in our construction (Table 1).

Table 1. For the polynomials F proposed, the affine multiple is easily computable with the algorithm of Sect. 3.2. The values d_{aff} are exact, provided that – for our choice of A and B – the terms of degree d_{aff} do not vanish (this only happens on few singular points).

Internal Polynomial F, $\forall A, B \in \mathbb{F}_2^n$	d_{aff}
$x^{12} + Ax^{10} + Bx^6$	2
$x^{12} + Ax^4 + Bx^3$	3
$x^{10} + Ax^6 + Bx^3$	4
$x^{10} + Ax^5 + Bx^3$	4
$x^{12} + Ax^{10} + Bx^5$	5
$x^{12} + Ax^5 + Bx^3$	5
$x^{10} + Ax^6 + Bx^4$	6

Besides our experiments on low degree polynomials, there are some examples that are really far from any expected bound. For instance, the Dobbertin polynomial $x^{2^{m+1}+1} + x^3 + x$ (see [16]) has a multiple affine of affine degree 3 over $\mathbb{F}_{2^{2m+1}}$ for every value m [35], which is – in general – really different from the observed values.

3.5 Using Perturbations

Usually, nude HFE instances are not sufficient by themselves to get reasonable black-box security. The goal of this section is to explain how we can turn the implementation of a nude HFE instance into a perturbed one. We will focus on three of them: p, $-$, and $\hat{+}$. For each perturbation on the public-key, we associate a perturbation or a list of perturbations between parentheses (p corresponding to (p) for instance) that are applied on the affine multiple of the nude HFE instance to match the perturbations made to the public-key. Note that these methods to incorporate perturbations into affine multiples do not change state-of-the-art perturbations on the public-key.

The p Perturbation. To transform a nude public key to one perturbed with p, one only needs to replace the bijective affine application $S : \mathbb{F}_2^n \to \mathbb{F}_2^n$ with an affine transformation of full rank $S_p : \mathbb{F}_2^{n-p} \to \mathbb{F}_2^n$ for a small integer p.

This replacement can be made in the affine multiple representation by also replacing S by S_p, so the perturbation is compatible with the affine multiple structure.

For a HFE instance perturbed with "p", we associate its affine multiple where S is replaced by S_p. When we use this perturbation on the affine multiple, we note that $\tilde{A}$ is perturbed by (p).

The − Perturbation. To transform a nude public-key to a one perturbed with −, one needs to remove some coordinates from the public-key. Let a be the number of equations removed. To sign with the private key, one needs to select at random these last a coordinates, and then proceed to the normal signing procedure.

The fact that the a last coordinates are random or at least secret is important to avoid any reduction to a nude public-key. Indeed, if the values of these coordinates are known for each signature produced, an attacker can then interpolate them and completely remove the − modifier from the key: the last a coordinates cannot be freely chosen in the white-box model.

For instance, one could try to replace the last a coordinates of y with any linear combination of the first $n - a$ coordinates. Then, the attacker knows that the missing polynomials in x are equal to a linear application in y and can then interpolate them from some couples message-signature (even in the black-box model). Note that, in practice, the choices we can make here are limited. If we take polynomials of degree 2 in the first $n - a$ coordinates for instance, the degree of the affine multiple increases. If these coordinates depend on x the affine multiple is not linear in x anymore.

If the HFE instance is itself resistant enough in the white-box model, one possibility is to let the last a coordinate free to be chosen at random for signing:

For a HFE instance perturbed with "-", we can associate its affine multiple without any modification from the nude one, but the last a coordinate of the signature are taken at random. When we use this perturbation on the affine multiple, we note that $\tilde{A}$ is perturbed by $(-,1)$.

Remark: Even if the affine multiple is not modified we can remark that in the black-box model, the last a coordinate are random so the reduction to an HFE instance without minus is not possible in the black-box model. This means that the $(-,1)$ perturbation on the affine multiple does not carry the security from minus in the white-box model but keeps it in the black-box model. More on the security of $(-,1)$ in Sect. 4.

A direct consequence of the previous remark is that the − perturbation is not directly compatible with the affine multiple structure. To partially go around this problem, we propose a countermeasure. To efficiently interpolate the missing equations of the public key, the attacker needs to know that the a last coordinates depend from x and y in a simple way. We will then try to hide these coordinates in a single special affine multiple.

First, through the isomorphism π, we decompose $y = y' + y_-$ from a direct sum $\mathbb{F}_2^n = \mathbb{F}_2^{n-a} \oplus \mathbb{F}_2^a$. The idea is to have an affine multiple that represents at least 2 fixed choices for the last a coordinates y_-. To do so, let us take any integer $n_s > 0$ and split $\mathbb{F}_2^a = \cup_{i=1}^{n_s} U_i$ where $\#U_i = \epsilon_i \geq 2$. We set $U_i = \{u_{i,1}, ..., u_{i,\epsilon_i}\}$. Now consider the polynomials:

$$G_i(x, y') = \prod_{j=1}^{\epsilon_i}(y' + u_{i,j} - F(x))$$

We now want an object that is similar to an affine multiple for the polynomial F, but for the polynomials G_i. To do so, we introduce the composite affine multiple:

Definition 3. *Let $\delta \in \mathbb{N}$, $\forall i$, $F_i \in \mathbb{F}_{2^n}[x]$ and $G(x, y) = \prod_{i=1}^{\delta}(F_i(x) - y)$. The polynomial $A(x, y) \in \mathbb{F}_{2^n}[x, y]$ is said to be a composite affine multiple of G if $A(x, y) = 0 \mod G(x, y)$ and A is $\mathbb{F}_2$-linear in x.*

Remark: It is obvious that the algorithm of Sect. 3.3 can be adapted to compute a composite affine multiple. The modulus simply needs to be changed to the product G. Its functionality is then similar to a regular affine multiple, except the solution satisfies one of the equations $F_i(x) = y$.

A composite affine multiple $B_i(x, y')$ of G_i in unknowns x and y' can produce signatures for which the last a coordinates of the message can be any element of U_i (relatively to the nude public key). When signing in the white-box model, the value of the $u_{i,j}$ are then not revealed and the signature can be chosen randomly among the ones satisfying the $n - a$ first coordinates. An attacker can then, at best, guess that the missing coordinates lie in a set of ϵ_i values to interpolate.

To incorporate the "$-$" perturbation in the white-box model, we will use the polynomials G_i and apply the affine multiple construction:

> For a HFE instance perturbed with "-", we can associate the collection of the affine multiples of the G_i. When we use this perturbation, we note that the implementation is perturbed by $(-, 2)$ with parameters $(\epsilon_1, ..., \epsilon_{n_s})$.

Remark: In the $(-, 2)$ perturbation, we provide a collection of n_s affine multiple to cover the whole vector space $\mathbb{F}_2^a$. Note that it is possible to do it for only few values, only one of the U_i for instance, and then get an implementation that produces a signature only when the last a coordinates are in U_i. This will lead to a smaller signature space and a smaller implementation size. More details on this technique will be given in Sect. 5.

The $\hat{+}$ Perturbation. To transform a nude public key to a one perturbed with $\hat{+}$, one needs to change the central polynomial F into $F+Q$ where Q is quadratic over $\mathbb{F}_2$ and of high degree over $\mathbb{F}_2^n$ such that $\forall x \in \mathbb{F}_2^n$, $Q(x) \in V$, where V is a small vector space of dimension t.

Similarly to the "$-$" modifier, the value of $Q(x)$ for any message y cannot be known to an attacker, otherwise Q can be interpolated. That is why the $\hat{+}$ perturbation is not directly compatible with the affine multiple construction.

Also, it is not possible to propose a perturbation close to $(-,1)$ as the values of Q cannot be left to be freely chosen.

We propose the same kind of perturbation as $(-,2)$ to not reveal the values of $Q(x)$. To do so, let us take any integer $m_s > 0$ and split $Im(Q) = \cup_{i=1}^{m_s} V_i$ where $\#V_i = \delta_i \geq 2$. We set $V_i = \{v_{i,1}, ..., v_{i,\delta_i}\}$. Now consider the polynomials:

$$H_i(x,y) = \prod_{j=1}^{\delta_i} (y - F(x) - v_{i,j})$$

A composite affine multiple $C_i(x,y)$ of H_i in unknowns x and y and fixed v_k can produce signatures for which the value of Q can be any $v_{i,j}$. An attacker can then at most guess that the missing coordinates lie in a set of δ_k values to interpolate.

For a HFE instance perturbed with "$\hat{+}$", we can associate the collection of the affine multiples of the H_i. When we use this perturbation, we note that the implementation is perturbed by $(\hat{+})$ with parameters $(\delta_1, ..., \delta_{m_s})$.

Remark: In the same spirit as the remark on the $(-,2)$ perturbation, it is possible to not use the whole collection of the H_i, but only few, or one of them. More details on this technique will be given in Sect. 5.

Combining Perturbations. Usually, multiple perturbations are used on a nude-HFE to achieve satisfactory security parameters be it pHFE$^-$ or the more recent HFE$^{\hat{+}-}$.

For our white-box implementation, we proceed similarly, although the compatibility depends on the perturbation used. For instance, the (p) and $(-,1)$ perturbation are easily compatible with $(\hat{+})$ but $(-,2)$ and $(\hat{+})$ needs more a subtle adaptation to work together: instead of splits of $\mathbb{F}_2^a$ and $Im(Q)$, one needs to work with a split of $\mathbb{F}_2^a \times Im(Q)$ and work with affine multiples of products of polynomials of the form $(y + u - F(x) - v)$, with $u \in \mathbb{F}_2^a$ and $v \in Im(Q)$.

In Sect. 5, we detail more on the compatibility of perturbations for affine multiples in a case by case basis on the implementation.

4 Security Analysis

In this section, we define the white-box security notions of unbreakability and incompressibility for public-key signature algorithms. We then analyse the security of our construction for these notions. For the rest of this section we suppose that A is an affine multiple of F or a composite affine multiple with respect to perturbations of Sect. 3.5.

4.1 White-Box Security Notions

The usual software white-box security notions that are discussed in the literature are unbreakability, incompressibility, one-wayness and traceability. While we study the first two, we do not consider traceability, and one-wayness does not make sense for decryption or signature in asymmetric cryptography: the one-wayness of decryption/signature in a public-key setting would mean that public-key encryption/verification is impossible, which is a contradiction by definition.

We follow [14] to extend the security notions of (τ, ϵ)-unbreakability and (σ, τ, ϵ)-incompressibility and adapt it to in the public-key setting. Furthermore, we shortly show that the unbreakability and incompressibility of the HFE one-way function is the key element to study.

4.2 Unbreakability

Let us describe the game for unbreakability of a compiler $\mathcal{C}_S$:

- Draw at random a key k in private keyspace K_S
- The adversary $\mathcal{A}$ gets the program $\mathcal{C}_S(k)$ from the compiler
- The adversary $\mathcal{A}$ returns a key guess $\hat{k}$ in time τ knowing $\mathcal{C}_S(k)$
- The adversary $\mathcal{A}$ succeeds if $k = \hat{k}$

Definition 4. *Let S be an asymmetric signature algorithm, $\mathcal{C}_S$ a white-box compiler and let $\mathcal{A}$ be any adversary. We define the probability of the adversary $\mathcal{A}$ to succeed in the unbreakability game by:*

$$Succ_{\mathcal{A},\mathcal{C}_S} := \mathbb{P}[k \leftarrow K; \mathcal{P} = \mathcal{C}_S(k), \mathcal{A}(\mathcal{P}) = \hat{k}; k = \hat{k}]$$

We say that $\mathcal{C}_S$ is (τ,ϵ)-unbreakable if for any adversary $\mathcal{A}$ running in time τ, $Succ_{\mathcal{A},\mathcal{C}_S} \leq \epsilon$.

Remark 1: Here, we do not set $\mathcal{A}$ to be a polynomial adversary depending on a security parameter λ and hope that ϵ is exponentially small in λ, as we are interested in concrete security for our chosen parameters.

Remark 2: This definition can usually be found with a parameter δ that allows the program $\mathcal{P}$ to agree with the targeted function with probability δ. As no known attack exploits this fact, we did not include it for sake of clarity.

4.3 Incompressibility

We now describe, for any $\sigma > 0$ the game for incompressibility for a compiler $\mathcal{C}_S$:

- Draw at random a key k in private keyspace K_S
- The adversary $\mathcal{A}$ gets the program $\mathcal{C}_S(k)$ from the compiler

- The adversary $\mathcal{A}$ returns a program $\mathcal{P}$ knowing $\mathcal{C}_\mathcal{S}(k)$
- The adversary $\mathcal{A}$ succeeds if $\mathcal{P} \approx \mathcal{C}_\mathcal{S}(k)$ and $size(\mathcal{P}) \leq \sigma$

Definition 5. *Let $\mathcal{S}$ be an asymmetric signature algorithm, $\mathcal{C}_\mathcal{S}$ a white-box compiler and let $\mathcal{A}$ be any adversary. We define the probability of the adversary $\mathcal{A}$ to succeed in the σ-incompressibility game by:*

$$Succ_{\mathcal{A},\mathcal{C}_\mathcal{S}} := \mathbb{P}[k \leftarrow K; \mathcal{P} = \mathcal{A}(\mathcal{C}_\mathcal{S}(k)); \mathcal{P} \approx \mathcal{C}_\mathcal{S}(k); (size(\mathcal{P}) \leq \sigma)]$$

Moreover, we say that $\mathcal{C}_\mathcal{S}$ is (σ,τ,ϵ)-incompressible if for any adversary $\mathcal{A}$, Time($\mathcal{A}$)+Time($\mathcal{P}$) $< \tau$ implies $Succ_{\mathcal{A},\mathcal{C}_\mathcal{S}} \leq \epsilon$.

The definition of incompressibility we propose here is a slightly corrected version from the usual one used in [14]. Indeed, this one is flawed as it does not constrain the running time of the program $\mathcal{P}$. If the running time is not bounded we can propose a compression of any white-box algorithm by using brute force: an attacker can compute few pairs plaintext-ciphertext, and code the brute force attack on the primitives that is white-boxed, and then code the computation of the primitive with the key found. This program can be made with few lines of code, is identically functional to the white-box code, but has an unreasonable running time. That is why we add a new time constraint: we want that the sum of the running time of the attacker and the program produced is less than a constant τ representing the whole computation time allowed.

4.4 White-Boxing the Inversion of a Secure Trapdoor One-Way Function is Enough

The goal of this section is to show that for notions like unbreakability and incompressibility, it is sometime enough to look at the white-box implementation of a core component of the signature algorithm, and not the entire algorithm itself. Note that all the following remarks also work for encryption for instance.

It is common to have signature built from a secure trapdoor one-way function (OWF) and extended into complete signature algorithm following the so-called 'hash-and-sign' paradigm. This is the case for RSA, with FDH or PSS and for instance it is also the case for HFE with Feistel-Patarin (used in GeMSS [11]). It is natural to study the white-box properties of these functions and how they extend to their corresponding signature schemes. In this case, what is interesting is the implementation of the inversion of f, for which a secret is needed.

For the rest of the paragraph, $f : \mathcal{X} \times \mathcal{K} \to \mathcal{Y}$ is a secure trapdoor one-way function and $\mathcal{C}_{f^{-1}}$ is a white-box compiler for the inversion of this function. We define unbreakability and incompressibility similarly as we did for signatures. The game for unbreakability for the compiler $\mathcal{C}_{f^{-1}}$ is as follows:

- Draw at random a key k in private keyspace $\mathcal{K}$
- The adversary $\mathcal{A}$ gets the program $\mathcal{C}_{f^{-1}}(k)$ from the compiler
- The adversary $\mathcal{A}$ returns a key guess $\hat{k}$ in time τ knowing $\mathcal{C}_{f^{-1}}(k)$

– The adversary $\mathcal{A}$ succeeds if $k = \hat{k}$

Definition 6. *Let f be a secure trapdoor one-way function, $\mathcal{C}_{f^{-1}}$ a white-box compiler of its inversion and let $\mathcal{A}$ be any adversary. We define the probability of the adversary $\mathcal{A}$ to succeed in the unbreakability game by:*

$$Succ_{\mathcal{A},\mathcal{C}_{f^{-1}}} := \mathbb{P}[k \leftarrow K; \mathcal{P} = \mathcal{C}_{f^{-1}}(k), \mathcal{A}(\mathcal{P}) = \hat{k}; k = \hat{k}]$$

We say that $\mathcal{C}_{f^{-1}}$ is (τ,ϵ)-unbreakable if for any adversary $\mathcal{A}$ running in time τ, $Succ_{\mathcal{A},\mathcal{C}_{f^{-1}}} \leq \epsilon$.

Remark 1: This definition can also be extended to incompressibility as in Sect. 4.1.

We now study signature schemes that are built "on top" of the inversion of a trapdoor OWF, which a general term to qualify many existing techniques like FDH, PSS or Feistel-Patarin cited before.

Definition 7. *We say that a signature algorithm S is built "on top" of a trapdoor one-way function f if it can decomposed in two algorithms:*

– *Algorithm A: On the input of an element in $Im(f)$, outputs one of its pre-image*
– *Algorithm B: On the input of a message, outputs a signature $S(m)$ of m. The B can only perform computations using the message m, public data, data drawn at random and calls to A.*

With such algorithms we can reduce the unbreakability of the signature algorithm to the unbreakability of the trapdoor OWF.

Proposition 1. *Let f be a secure trapdoor one-way function. Let $\mathbf{WBf}^{-1}$ be any (τ,ϵ)-unbreakable implementation of f^{-1}. If S is a signature algorithm built "on top" of f (Definition 8) then there exist a (τ,ϵ)-unbreakable implementation of S.*

Proof: If $\mathbf{WBf}^{-1}$ is such implementation (τ,ϵ)-unbreakable, build the implementation of S by replacing any call to f^{-1} by a call to $\mathbf{WBf}^{-1}$ and note this implementation $\mathbf{WBS}$. Now, if any attacker $\mathcal{A}$ breaks the (τ,ϵ)-unbreakability, one can build an attacker $\mathcal{A}'$ breaking WBf^{-1} by simply building WBS and running $\mathcal{A}$. This is absurd by unbreakability of WBf^{-1}.

This result does not seems to be easily extendable to incompressibility. Indeed, it is not trivial to obtain a compression of f^{-1} from a compression of S. However, for the usual "reasonable" constructions (FDH, PSS, Feistel-Patarin, ...) we still conjecture that the security of the one way-function carries onto the complete signature algorithm.

Remark: There exist algorithms S that are easily compressible even if f has an incompressible implementation. For instance, if we use full domain hash with a hash function of the form $h \circ f$, trivial compression arises if h has a short description. This encourages to further the study of the incompressibility of $f \circ g$ when f or g are incompressible.

4.5 Attack by Reduction to a Weaker HFE Instance

This paragraph only deals with HFE implementations with perturbations. If perturbations are used on an implementation (Sect. 3.5), one idea to perform an attack is to try to remove the perturbation on the affine multiple construction, in the same way attackers try to remove perturbations on public-keys for attacks in the black-box model. As we will focus the study the unbreakability and incompressiblity of our challenge construction, we will focus on perturbations $\hat{+}$ and (-,1). A reduction for (-,2) can be made similarly to $\hat{+}$.

Reduction for (-,1). If we have an implementation perturbed with (-,1), we can remove the perturbation - on the public-key by recovering the missing coordinates. We can fix the last a coordinates to any constant and gather enough signatures to solve a linear system with the coefficients of the monomials of our missing coordinates as unknowns. Experimentally, this allows us to recover vector space of dimension a that contains these equations, which is sufficient to recover an equivalent HFE public key. Since there are $\binom{n}{2}$ unknowns, the cost of this attack is $\mathcal{O}(n^{2\omega} + n^2 \times \tau_{WB})$.

Remark 1: The time τ_{WB} can be increased by other used perturbations, and needs to be taken into account for concrete security analysis.

Reduction ($\hat{+}$). For the ($\hat{+}$) perturbation, with the notations of Sect. 3.5, notice that for the affine multiples C_i of the polynomials H_i the only possible values of $Q(x)$ are in V_i. The signatures from B_i will satisfy:

$$\prod_{j=1}^{\delta_i}(Q(x) + v_{i,j}) = 0$$

This product can then be interpolated by gathering signatures using the same method as for the reduction for $(-,1)$. Then, a recovery of $Q(x)$ can be attempted. In our setting, the exact values $v_{i,j}$ are unknown. To the best of our knowledge, recovering $Q(x)$ can only be made by factoring $\prod_{j=1}^{\epsilon_i}(Q(x)+v_{i,j}) = 0$, which is hard for any instance we will use later.

Remark 2: Note that these equations can be gathered for any $\text{HFE}^{\hat{+}}$ instance in black-box for $V_i = Im(Q)$. This means that any algorithm solving this problem if $\#V_i = 2^t$ can break the corresponding $\text{HFE}^{\hat{+}}$ instance. Even if this perturbation is young, no attack of this kind has been reported by the authors of [18] which confirms our security analysis.

4.6 The Implementation as a ($d_{\text{aff}} + 1$)-IP1S Problem

To analyse unbreakability and incompressibility directly on the affine multiple, we rely on two properties of the polynomials describing our white-box implementation. The first will be the key recovery of the underlying ($d_{\text{aff}} + 1$)-IP1S instance. The IP (Isomorphism of Polynomials) problem – studied in papers such as [9,29,36,38] – has been introduced to explore the security of multivariate cryptography in general. We quickly recall that for an integer d, an d-IP instance is defined by a system of polynomials $g = b \circ f \circ a$ where F is a known system of n polynomials in n variables, and hidden a and b affine bijective n-by-n transformations. To solve the IP instance, one needs to find a, b. When there is only one secret b, the instance is usually called a IP instance with one secret abbreviated d-IP1S.

The second one is a variant of the regular IP1S problem that we call "incompressibility of IP instances". We detail these two properties, how they are linked to our problem and how well studied they are. For this section, let A be an affine multiple of any HFE instance with perturbations (p), (-,1), (-,2) or ($\hat{+}$).

Secret Recovery on $(d_{\text{aff}}+1)$-IP1S. Let us first recall that our white-box implementation is composed of the n polynomials $\tilde{A}_i$ and a deterministic generic way to evaluate them (compute all the monomials then sum them up). The polynomials $\tilde{A}_i$ are defined by a composition with two affine transformations S and T such that:

$$\tilde{A}_i(x_1, ..., x_n, y_1, ..., y_n) = A_i(S(x_1, ..., x_n), T^{-1}(y_1, ..., y_n))$$

It is then obvious that $\tilde{A}_i$ is an instance of a $(d_{\text{aff}}+1)$-IP1S problem over $2n$ variables, with A_i as the known polynomials and a block-affine transformation composed of S and T. This problem has a structured secret, so it is not generic, but we do not know any other attack against it (as an IP problem) than the generic ones. To the best of our knowledge, the best generic attack on 3–IP1S with affine secrets has complexity $\mathcal{O}(n^6 q^n)$ [9]. This means that the best known attack against 3–IP1S instances is exponential in n. For our instances, $(d_{\text{aff}} + 1) \geq 3$, these pieces of evidence allow us to conjecture that our instances are secure for the desired security level.

Remark 1: For the perturbation (p), the secret $S : \mathbb{F}_2^{n-p} \to \mathbb{F}_2^n$ is not a bijection, this instance is different from the one studied in general. However, since the projection variant is efficient against key recovery for HFE instances, one can hope that it will help our IP instance to stand against secret recovery for the same reasons.

Remark 2: For perturbations $(-, 2)$ and $(\hat{+})$, the polynomial $\tilde{A}$ are composite affine multiples, but the same analysis can be made.

Incompressibility of IP1S Instances. The main goal of this part is to highlight a specificity of multivariate cryptography in general that will help us to prove the incompressibility of our white-box construction. To do so, we formalize a new problem around IP instances, and analyse it on our instance $(\tilde{A}_i)_{i \in [\![1,n]\!]}$.

We define the (σ, τ)-incompressibility of an IP instance with known polynomials $(P_i)_{i \in [\![1,m]\!]}$:

- Draw at random two secret affine transformations S, T in $AFF_n(\mathbb{F}_2)$

- The adversary $\mathcal{A}$ is given an IP instance $(\tilde{P}_i)_{i\in[\![1,m]\!]}$ composed of $(P_i)_{i\in[\![1,m]\!]}$, S and T
- The adversary $\mathcal{A}$ returns a program $\mathcal{P}$ that allows to evaluate $(\tilde{P}_i)_{i\in[\![1,m]\!]}$ for every element $(\mathbb{F}_2)^n$
- The adversary $\mathcal{A}$ wins if $size(\mathcal{P}) \leq \sigma$

Definition 8. *Let $(\tilde{P}_i)_{i\in[\![1,m]\!]}$ be an IP instance with polynomials in n variables over $\mathbb{F}_2$, with known polynomials $(P_i)_{i\in[\![1,m]\!]}$ and secrets S, T and let $\mathcal{A}$ be an adversary. We say that $(\tilde{P}_i)_{i\in[\![1,m]\!]}$ is (σ,τ,ϵ)-incompressible if there is no adversary $\mathcal{A}$ that wins the σ-incompressibility game with probability ϵ and $Time(\mathcal{A})+Time(\mathcal{P}) < \tau$.*

Remark 1: We could also consider, similarly to the incompressibility for white-box, that $\mathcal{A}$ does not have to agree with $(P_i)_{i\in[\![1,m]\!]}$ on all inputs or that it can be probabilistic. However, known attacks do not use this flexibility.

It is well known that, for truly random polynomials, compressibility is not possible by definition in the sense of Kolmogorov, even with an unbounded computation power. In contrast, in our context, a compressed version of the $\tilde{A}_i$ polynomials is obviously given if we can recover the secrets S and T. This problem of secret recovery on an IP instance corresponds to the extreme case $\sigma = size(S)+size(T)$ in Definition 4, and boils down to the unbreakability problem, for which the best known attacks require large computational efforts - see paragraph above, about Secret recovery on $(d_{\text{aff}} + 1)$-IP1S. In the intermediate cases $size(S) + size(T) < \sigma \leq size(P_i)$, to the best of our knowledge, no attack has been found in the literature.

4.7 Generic White-Box Attacks on Multivariate Cryptography

In the literature, generic automated attacks are proven to be very efficient against the state-of-the-art white-box implementations of block-ciphers due to the techniques used (*i.e.* masking or internal encodings for instance). These attacks include Differential Computation Analysis (DCA) and Differential Fault Analysis (DFA) as their most potent representatives. In this section we argue against their usefulness against our technique.

The main point of this section is to understand how IP instances are secure against these attacks, even if they are used in HFE schemes and hence have a trapdoor. A first example of this is how HFE public keys are not vulnerable to DPA attacks or their white-box DCA counterpart. Indeed, even if the inversion of the public key can be attacked because it decomposes the inversion of P into the inversion of S, T and F separately, the public key itself is not vulnerable against DCA, even if it contains the complete key (S, T). This is due to the structure of the IP problem. Indeed, all the bits of S and T are diffused by polynomial composition into the coefficients of the public key P. This means that unless a specific computation depending on few key bits is found on a specific instance, the probability is negligible that a "nice" target exists for generic white-box attacks, as the complexity of DCA is exponential in the number of key bits on which the target depends. The state of the art HFE security ignores these attacks for such reasons. For DFA, it is easy to make faults on the evaluation of P, but any evaluation of any function depending on the polynomials' coefficients of the public is already allowed to solve IP and hence does not provide new information. This is a huge difference compared to state-of-the-art targets of these attacks, which usually are S-Boxes in SPN schemes, and most often specifically those of the AES algorithm.

For our implementation, the affine multiple structure allows to diffuse S and T into A, in the same way they are diffused into the public key. Unless a specific relation is found for this particular instance, the DCA has no more chances to succeed than the ones targeting the public key. The same argument also stands for DFA. In summary, such a DCA-like (resp. DFA-like) attack is not expected to be able to circumvent the similar hard-to-solve algebraic problem on which the algorithm's black-box security relies.

Remark 1: We can think of the following factorization-flavoured analogy. Assume that an attacker is given an RSA public key. Since n depends on the secrets primes p and q, one could wonder if DCA (resp. DFA) could be applied to n (or to a computation making use of n) to recover the secret elements p and q. However, it is also easy to see that in this case the algebraic complexity of the bits of n (as functions of the bits of p and q) quickly gets so high that this kind of DCA (resp. DFA) strategy is not relevant here.

4.8 Conclusion of the Analysis of Security

In the sections above, we considered all the known attacks in the white-box context. The conclusion of the analysis is that, with the best of our knowledge, none of these attacks is able to retrieve the secret key (unbreakability) nor to compress the implementation (incompressibility). Nevertheless, we are able to formulate the security of our white-box implementation as a set of two conjectures, explicitly stating the links between the (white-box) security of our implementation and natural hypotheses about well-known objects of multivariate cryptography (HFE, modifiers, IP1S problem, affine multiple).

> **Unbreakability Conjecture:**
>
> Let P be a HFE public key with modifiers chosen among $-$, p and $\hat{+}$. Let **WBHFE** be the white-box implementation of P^{-1} and A an associated composite affine multiple with corresponding perturbations. Let $\epsilon < 1$ be a small probability and λ be our security level. If
>
> 1. The HFE instance associated to the public key P is secure against key recovery in the black-box model up to security level λ.
> 2. The knowledge of A does not help to remove modifiers from P (Section 4.2) in less than 2^λ operations.
> 3. The affine multiple A is $(2^\lambda, \epsilon)$-unbreakable as a $(d_{\text{aff}} + 1)$-IP1S instance. (Section 4.3)
>
> then the implementation **WBHFE** of the primitive P^{-1} is $(2^\lambda, \epsilon)$-unbreakable in the white-box model.

Remark 1: The first point of this conjecture is trivial if we want our HFE instance to be of any use. However, as we will see in Sect. 5, this is an important dimensioning parameter to optimize the implementation size. This is why we make it part of the conjecture.

> **Incompressibility Conjecture:**
>
> Let P be a HFE public-key with modifiers chosen among $-$, p and $\hat{+}$. Let **WBHFE** be the white-box implementation of P^{-1} and A an associated composite affine multiple with corresponding perturbations. Let $\epsilon < 1$ be a small probability and λ be our security level. If :
>
> 1. The HFE instance associated to the public-key P is secure against key recovery in the black-box model up to security level λ.
> 2. The knowledge of A does not help to remove modifiers from P (Section 4.2) in less than 2^λ operations.
> 3. The affine multiple A is $(\sigma_{WB}, 2^\lambda, \epsilon)$-incompressible as a $(d_{\text{aff}} + 1)$-IP1S instance. (Section 4.3)
>
> then the implementation **WBHFE** of the primitive P^{-1} is $(\sigma_{WB}, 2^\lambda, \epsilon)$-incompressible in the white-box model.

Remark 2: This conjecture is very similar to the unbreakability one. This is due to the fact that the only compression we know from the public key is key recovery.

Of course, proving this conjecture still requires new insights, in particular to clarify the deep algebraic links between the polynomial systems arising from

$A(x, y)$ on the one hand, and from P^{-1} on the other hand. However, we believe this paves the way for a better understanding of the incompressibility property, which up to now could be formally verified only for white-box implementations of symmetric cryptosystems in very restricted models (see the proof of incompressibility of an RSA-like symmetric encryption scheme in [14], using an Ideal Group Model).

5 Challenge Implementation

In this section, we propose an instance close to $C^{*\hat{+}-}$ for our challenge implementation. For more details about C^*, please refer to [32,33].

In this section, the instance includes the perturbations $\hat{+}$ and $-$. To do so, we include perturbations $(\hat{+})$ and $(-, 1)$ in the affine multiple. This means that the implementation is composed of the composite affine multiples of the polynomials H_i:

$$H_i(x, y) = \prod_{j=1}^{\delta_i} (y + v_{i,j} - F(x))$$

and the last a coordinates of y are chosen at random for signing. We will choose internal polynomials of the form $F = x^3 + Ax^2$, thus close to C^*.

Security Analysis. The black-box security of this unusual instance can be checked using attacks of Sect. 2.2: our instance needs to stand against direct inversion with Gröbner bases and key-recovery rank attacks, hence the high value of t. The affine multiple attack is not applicable to public keys with $\hat{+}$ and $-$.

For white-box security, according to the conjecture, our instance needs to stand against attacks on d_{aff}-IP1S instances of Sect. 4.4, *i.e.* we only need to ensure that the attack of Sect. 4.3 cannot be used. To do so, we take $\delta_i = 3$ so that the polynomial

$$\prod_{j=1}^{\delta_i} (Q(x) + v_{i,j}) = 0$$

is not linear in $Q(x)$.

Parameter Choices. To reduce the affine degree, we choose polynomials F of the form $x^3 + Ax^2$, $A \in \mathbb{F}_2^n$ and take $\epsilon_i = 3$. Indeed, with these parameters, we get affine multiples with $d_{\text{aff}} = 3$. We then optimize n, t and a for the desired level of security (Table 2).

Remark: A signature can be computed if its image through Q lies in V_i. This means that a message drawn at random will be signed with roughly probability $\frac{3}{2^t}$. This probability is quite low but this remark can be used to have a smaller signature algorithm in the white-box model while not changing the public-key and the verification algorithm.

Table 2. Set parameters d_{aff}, a, t and n which satisfies a particular security level λ. The value $log_2(size(C_i))$ is the corresponding log_2 of size of an affine multiple in bits. The values C_G and C_R are the log_2 of the complexity of respectively best Gröbner basis attacks and best rank attacks

Target	(n, d, t, a)	$log_2(size((C_i))$	C_G	C_R
Smallest for $\lambda = 80$	(85,2,9,5)	29.5	82.4	80.3
Smallest for $\lambda = 90$	(96,2,11,6)	30.3	106.5	91.3
Smallest for $\lambda = 128$	(132,2,18,4)	32.6	138.3	128.9

Challenge: To motivate the cryptanalysis of our technique, we propose a challenge implementation corresponding to the line $(85, 2, 9, 5)$ on the previous table. The code in Sage is available at https://github.com/p-galissant/WBHFE. It contains the public-key, one affine multiple and resources to manipulate them.

Acknowledgments. This research was partly supported by ANR grant SWITECH (ANR-19-CE39-0014-01) and PEPR PQ-TLS (the France 2030 program under grant agreement ANR-22-PETQ-0008 PQ-TLS).

References

1. Barbu, G., et al.: ECDSA white-box implementations: attacks and designs from whibox 2021 contest. Cryptology ePrint Archive, Paper 2022/385 (2022). https://eprint.iacr.org/2022/385
2. Bardet, M., Faugère, J., Salvy, B.: On the complexity of the F5 gröbner basis algorithm. J. Symb. Comput. **70**, 49–70 (2015). https://doi.org/10.1016/j.jsc.2014.09.025
3. Barthelemy, L.: A First Approach To Asymmetric White-Box Cryptography and a Study of Permutation Polynomials Modulo 2^n in Obfuscation. Ph.D. thesis, Sorbonne Université, Paris (2020)
4. Billet, O., Gilbert, H., Ech-Chatbi, C.: Cryptanalysis of a white box AES implementation. In: Handschuh, H., Hasan, M.A. (eds.) SAC 2004. LNCS, vol. 3357, pp. 227–240. Springer, Heidelberg (2004). https://doi.org/10.1007/978-3-540-30564-4_16
5. Biryukov, A., Bouillaguet, C., Khovratovich, D.: Cryptographic schemes based on the **ASASA** structure: black-box, white-box, and public-key (extended abstract). In: Sarkar, P., Iwata, T. (eds.) ASIACRYPT 2014, Part I. LNCS, vol. 8873, pp. 63–84. Springer, Heidelberg (2014). https://doi.org/10.1007/978-3-662-45611-8_4
6. Biryukov, A., Perrin, L.: On Reverse-engineering S-boxes with hidden design criteria or structure. In: Gennaro, R., Robshaw, M. (eds.) CRYPTO 2015. LNCS, vol. 9215, pp. 116–140. Springer, Heidelberg (2015). https://doi.org/10.1007/978-3-662-47989-6_6
7. Bock, E.A., et al.: White-box cryptography: don't forget about grey-box attacks. J. Cryptol. **32**(4), 1095–1143 (2019). https://doi.org/10.1007/s00145-019-09315-1

8. Bos, J.W., Hubain, C., Michiels, W., Teuwen, P.: Differential computation analysis: hiding your white-box designs is not enough. In: Gierlichs, B., Poschmann, A.Y. (eds.) CHES 2016. LNCS, vol. 9813, pp. 215–236. Springer, Heidelberg (2016). https://doi.org/10.1007/978-3-662-53140-2_11
9. Bouillaguet, C., Faugère, J.-C., Fouque, P.-A., Perret, L.: Practical cryptanalysis of the identification scheme based on the isomorphism of polynomial with one secret problem. In: Catalano, D., Fazio, N., Gennaro, R., Nicolosi, A. (eds.) PKC 2011. LNCS, vol. 6571, pp. 473–493. Springer, Heidelberg (2011). https://doi.org/10.1007/978-3-642-19379-8_29
10. Bringer, J., Chabanne, H., Dottax, E.: White box cryptography: another attempt. IACR Cryptol. ePrint Arch. p. 468 (2006). http://eprint.iacr.org/2006/468
11. Casanova, A., Faugère, J.C., Macario-Rat, G., Patarin, J., Perret, L., Ryckeghem, J.: GeMSS. Technical report, National Institute of Standards and Technology (2020). https://csrc.nist.gov/projects/post-quantum-cryptography/round-3-submissions
12. Chow, S., Eisen, P., Johnson, H., Oorschot, P.C.: White-box cryptography and an AES implementation. In: Nyberg, K., Heys, H. (eds.) SAC 2002. LNCS, vol. 2595, pp. 250–270. Springer, Heidelberg (2003). https://doi.org/10.1007/3-540-36492-7_17
13. Chow, S., Eisen, P., Johnson, H., Oorschot, P.C.: A white-box DES implementation for DRM applications. In: Feigenbaum, J. (ed.) DRM 2002. LNCS, vol. 2696, pp. 1–15. Springer, Heidelberg (2003). https://doi.org/10.1007/978-3-540-44993-5_1
14. Delerablée, C., Lepoint, T., Paillier, P., Rivain, M.: White-box security notions for symmetric encryption schemes. In: Lange, T., Lauter, K., Lisoněk, P. (eds.) SAC 2013. LNCS, vol. 8282, pp. 247–264. Springer, Heidelberg (2014). https://doi.org/10.1007/978-3-662-43414-7_13
15. Ding, J., Schmidt, D., Werner, F.: Algebraic attack on HFE revisited. In: Wu, T.-C., Lei, C.-L., Rijmen, V., Lee, D.-T. (eds.) ISC 2008. LNCS, vol. 5222, pp. 215–227. Springer, Heidelberg (2008). https://doi.org/10.1007/978-3-540-85886-7_15
16. Dobbertin, H.: Almost perfect nonlinear power functions on gf(2n): the welch case. IEEE Trans. Inf. Theory **45**, 1271–1275 (1999)
17. EMV: Integrated circuit card specifications for payment systems. Book 2. Security and Key Management. Version 4.2. June 2008 (2008). www.emvco.com
18. Faugère, J., Macario-Rat, G., Patarin, J., Perret, L.: A new perturbation for multivariate public key schemes such as HFE and UOV. IACR Cryptol. ePrint Arch. p. 203 (2022). https://eprint.iacr.org/2022/203
19. Feng, Q., He, D., Wang, H., Kumar, N., Choo, K.R.: White-box implementation of shamir's identity-based signature scheme. IEEE Syst. J. **14**(2), 1820–1829 (2020). https://doi.org/10.1109/JSYST.2019.2910934
20. Fouque, P.-A., Karpman, P., Kirchner, P., Minaud, B.: Efficient and provable whitebox primitives. In: Cheon, J.H., Takagi, T. (eds.) ASIACRYPT 2016. LNCS, vol. 10031, pp. 159–188. Springer, Heidelberg (2016). https://doi.org/10.1007/978-3-662-53887-6_6
21. Galissant, P.: Contributions to white-box cryptography : models and algebraic constructions. Theses, Université Paris-Saclay (2023). https://theses.hal.science/tel-04457255
22. Galissant, P., Goubin, L.: Introduction to White-Box Cryptography. In: Embedded Cryptography, vol. 3. Sciences Collection. Wiley (2025)

23. Goubin, L., Masereel, J.-M., Quisquater, M.: Cryptanalysis of white box DES implementations. In: Adams, C., Miri, A., Wiener, M. (eds.) SAC 2007. LNCS, vol. 4876, pp. 278–295. Springer, Heidelberg (2007). https://doi.org/10.1007/978-3-540-77360-3_18
24. Goubin, L., Paillier, P., Rivain, M., Wang, J.: How to reveal the secrets of an obscure white-box implementation. J. Cryptogr. Eng. **10**(1), 49–66 (2020). https://doi.org/10.1007/s13389-019-00207-5
25. Goubin, L., Rivain, M., Wang, J.: Defeating state-of-the-art white-box countermeasures with advanced gray-box attacks. IACR Trans. Cryptogr. Hardw. Embed. Syst. **2020**(3), 454–482 (2020). https://doi.org/10.13154/tches.v2020.i3.454-482
26. Hosoyamada, A., Isobe, T., Todo, Y., Yasuda, K.: A modular approach to the incompressibility of block-cipher-based AEADS. In: Agrawal, S., Lin, D. (eds.) ASIACRYPT 2022, Part II. LNCS, vol. 13792, pp. 585–619. Springer, Cham (2022). https://doi.org/10.1007/978-3-031-22966-4_20
27. Karroumi, M.: Protecting white-box AES with dual ciphers. In: Rhee, K.H., Nyang, D. (eds.) ICISC 2010. Lecture Notes in Computer Science, vol. 6829, pp. 278–291. Springer (2010). https://doi.org/10.1007/978-3-642-24209-0_19
28. Lee, S., Kim, T., Kang, Y.: A masked white-box cryptographic implementation for protecting against differential computation analysis. IEEE Trans. Inf. Forensics Secur. **13**(10), 2602–2615 (2018). https://doi.org/10.1109/TIFS.2018.2825939
29. Macario-Rat, G., Plut, J., Gilbert, H.: New Insight into the isomorphism of polynomial problem IP1S and its use in cryptography. In: Sako, K., Sarkar, P. (eds.) ASIACRYPT 2013. LNCS, vol. 8269, pp. 117–133. Springer, Heidelberg (2013). https://doi.org/10.1007/978-3-642-42033-7_7
30. Mastercard: Mastercard cloud-based payments – mobile payment application functional description. Version 1.0, August 2014
31. Mastercard: Mastercard mobile payment SDK security guide for MP SDK v1.0.6. Version 2.0, January 2017. https://developer.mastercard.com/media/32/b3/b6a8b4134e50bfe53590c128085e/mastercard-mobile-payment-sdk-security-guide-v2.0.pdf
32. Matsumoto, T., Imai, H.: Public quadratic polynomial-tuples for efficient signature-verification and message-encryption. In: Barstow, D., et al. (eds.) EUROCRYPT 1988. LNCS, vol. 330, pp. 419–453. Springer, Heidelberg (1988). https://doi.org/10.1007/3-540-45961-8_39
33. Matsumoto, T., Imai, H., Harashima, H., Miyakawa, H.: A class of asymmetric cryptosystems using obscure representations of enciphering functions. In: 1983 National Convention Record on Information Systems, IECE Japan (1983)
34. Øygarden, M., Smith-Tone, D., Verbel, J.: On the effect of projection on rank attacks in multivariate cryptography. In: Cheon, J.H., Tillich, J.-P. (eds.) PQCrypto 2021 2021. LNCS, vol. 12841, pp. 98–113. Springer, Cham (2021). https://doi.org/10.1007/978-3-030-81293-5_6
35. Patarin, J.: Hidden Fields Equations (HFE) and Isomorphisms of Polynomials (IP): two new families of asymmetric algorithms. In: Maurer, U. (ed.) EUROCRYPT 1996. LNCS, vol. 1070, pp. 33–48. Springer, Heidelberg (1996). https://doi.org/10.1007/3-540-68339-9_4
36. Patarin, J., Goubin, L., Courtois, N.: Improved algorithms for isomorphisms of polynomials. In: Nyberg, K. (ed.) EUROCRYPT 1998. LNCS, vol. 1403, pp. 184–200. Springer, Heidelberg (1998). https://doi.org/10.1007/BFb0054126
37. Patarin, J., Macario-Rat, G., Bros, M., Koussa, E.: Ultra-short multivariate public key signatures. Cryptology ePrint Archive, Report 2020/914 (2020). https://eprint.iacr.org/2020/914

38. Perret, L.: A fast cryptanalysis of the isomorphism of polynomials with one secret problem. In: Cramer, R. (ed.) EUROCRYPT 2005. LNCS, vol. 3494, pp. 354–370. Springer, Heidelberg (2005). https://doi.org/10.1007/11426639_21
39. Petzoldt, A.: On the complexity of the hybrid approach on hfev-. IACR Cryptol. ePrint Arch. p. 1135 (2017). http://eprint.iacr.org/2017/1135
40. Shamir, A.: Identity-based cryptosystems and signature schemes. In: Blakley, G.R., Chaum, D. (eds.) CRYPTO 1984. LNCS, vol. 196, pp. 47–53. Springer, Heidelberg (1985). https://doi.org/10.1007/3-540-39568-7_5
41. WhibOx Organizing Committee: Ches 2021 ctf challenge – whibox contest (2021). https://whibox.io/contests/2021/
42. WhibOx Organizing Committee: Ches 2024 ctf challenge – whibox contest (2024). https://whibox.io/contests/2024/
43. Xiao, Y., Lai, X.: A secure implementation of white-box aes. In: 2009 2nd International Conference on Computer Science and its Applications, pp. 1–6 (2009). https://doi.org/10.1109/CSA.2009.5404239
44. Zhang, Y., He, D., Huang, X., Wang, D., Choo, K.R., Wang, J.: White-box implementation of the identity-based signature scheme in the IEEE P1363 standard for public key cryptography. IEICE Trans. Inf. Syst. **103-D**(2), 188–195 (2020). http://search.ieice.org/bin/summary.php?id=e103-d_2_188

Attacks on Symmetric Cryptography

The Dangerous Message/Key Swap in HMAC

Antoine Wurcker[✉] and David Marçais

Serma Safety and Security, Pessac, France
{a.wurcker,d.marcais}@serma.com

Abstract. Classical usage of Hash-based Message Authentication Code (HMAC) is known to be subject to Side-Channel Attacks (SCA). In case physical leakage of information occurs, and without proper countermeasures, the variability of known message endangers the secret key through statistical attacks. These attacks are not always applicable due to strict constraints on attacker model. However, some protocols can choose not to use the HMAC the way it was designed by swapping the roles of message and key, and therefore modify the condition of applicability of such attacks.

In this paper, we describe a new attack method that takes advantage of the reduction of constraints induced by the choice to swap roles. Moreover, we describe two methods that can optimize previously existing attacks against HMAC. One allowing to reduce the trace cost of some attacks by $\sim 25\%$, the other allowing to adapt existing attacks even in presence of partial countermeasures.

Keywords: HMAC · SHA-2 · SCA · Side-Channel · DPA · Masking · HKDF

1 Introduction

Side-Channel Attacks (hereafter called SCA) are a type of attack that use an unplanned source of information (side-channel) leaking from hardware component. When such a component runs an algorithm, fluctuations can appear on physical measurements that are related to the values processed by the chip. If algorithms are processing data related to secret information, such as in cryptographic algorithms, the related leakages can lead to disclosure of secret information. The first paper to consider these information leakages was focusing on execution time of operations [11]. Once the potential of SCA discovered, other leakage mediums were exploited such as: power consumption [12], electromagnetic emissions [8], light emissions [6], acoustic emissions [9]. These sources of information can since be exploited by attackers, allowing to target secrets during their processing in an hardware component.

Differential Power Analysis (hereafter called DPA) is a statistical SCA described in [12]. Other enhancements of this attack exist such as the *Correlation Power Analysis* [5]. In an attack of this family (hereafter called *DPA-like*), the attacker performs numerous executions of code on a physical component that involve the targeted secret information. For each execution, a measurement through a side-channel is performed. Attack will then be possible depending on the presence of leakage resulting from the combination of i) a known variable (e.g. message) and ii) an unknown constant (e.g. key). The variations of the measured leakages are expected to correlate the best when the known variable is combined with the correct guess for the unknown constant.

In order to retrieve the used secret key, DPA-like attacks are known to be able to target hash based algorithms such as *Hash-based Message Authentication Code* (hereafter called HMAC) described in [4]. Several publications show how to target HMAC with different leakages assumptions [3,14,17,19].

As HMAC needs an underlying hash function, *Secure Hash Algorithm 2* (hereafter called SHA-2), detailed in [15], is the most targeted algorithm in these publications. However, these attacks are often also applicable on *Secure Hash Algorithm 1* (hereafter called SHA-1) as this algorithm partially shares the same structures as SHA-2. Our contribution also focus on SHA-2 as main example, however, we will show later that it can also be applied to SHA-1.

In these publications, state-of-the-art methods only consider classical usages of HMAC. However, there exists protocols where the role of the message and the key registers are swapped, such as *HMAC-based extract-and-expand Key Derivation Function* (hereafter called HKDF) or *HMAC based Deterministic Random Bit Generator* (hereafter called HMAC-DRBG). For example, in HKDF specification, the usage of a known value (called salt) as the HMAC key and a secret fixed value (called IKM for Input Key Material) as the HMAC message is depicted. We cannot consider usages where the salt value is fixed [1,18]. This is due to DPA-like attacks that require a variable known input and are therefore not applicable. We only consider protocols where the salt can be variable as a diversifier, as suggested in [7,10,13]. Our contributions intend to show that such a swap in the roles of message and key registers of HMAC can be dangerous as it may remove a lot of constraints on attacker model.

In this paper, notations are detailed in Sect. 2, then the attack methods of state-of-the-art and the evolution of the constraints on attacker model are described in Sect. 3. Finally, our contributions are detailed in Sect. 4.

2 Notations

SHA-2 is in fact a set of several hash functions based on the same algorithm but with several buffer sizes and different initial values, as described in [15]. All these functions are based on the process described in Fig. 1. The message is padded and cut in equal chunks depending on the chosen version of algorithm block size. Then, starting with a constant known Initial Value (IV_0), IV value is mixed together with a message block by function f to produce the next block IV.

Function f processes 64 rounds R_i where IV is progressively mixed with message block transformed into 64 words (W_i). Finally, IV is added to the state before being exited as the next IV. The output of last f is the hash value. $'+'$ means addition performed modulo 2 to the size of the word in bits corresponding to the chosen algorithm. $'\oplus'$ means bitwise exclusive-or operation. $'\wedge'$ means bitwise $'$and$'$ operation. $'\neg'$ means bitwise $'$not$'$ operation.

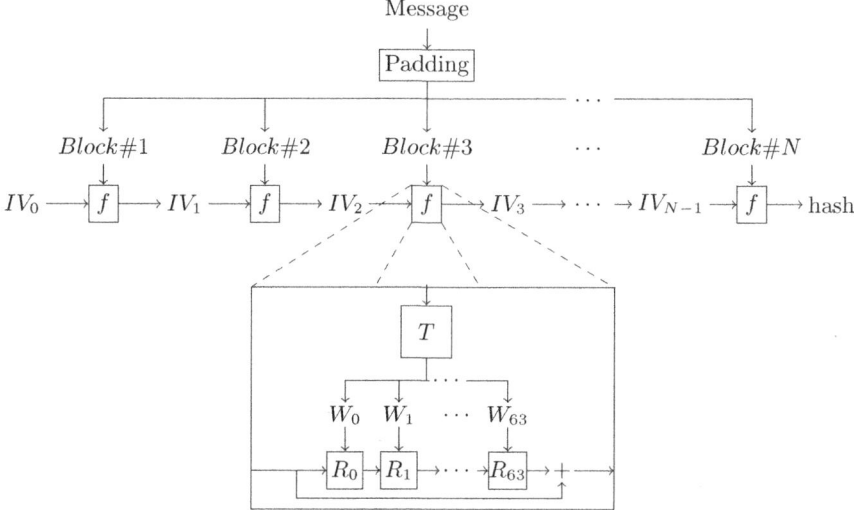

Fig. 1. Scheme of SHA-2 process.

Transformed message parts (W_i), have the property that the first 16 words are the message block split in 16 words when the last 48 words are computed as combinations of the previous ones. As this is not relevant in this paper, the exact computation of later value is omitted but can be found in specifications [15]. This means that an attacker controlling the message has control over the first 16 W_i values and has knowledge of the next 48.

Entering f function, IV value is split in 8 words ($A_0, \ldots, H_0$), updated through rounds to produce 8 words as output of the loop ($A_{64}, \ldots, H_{64}$). A final word by word addition between ($A_{64}, \ldots, H_{64}$) and initial ($A_0, \ldots, H_0$) is performed to produce the IV of next block. Focusing on round R_i, equations are:

$$T1_i = H_i + \Sigma_1(E_i) + \mathscr{C}(E_i, F_i, G_i) + K_i + W_i \tag{1}$$
$$T2_i = \Sigma_0(A_i) + \mathscr{M}(A_i, B_i, C_i) \tag{2}$$
$$A_{i+1} = T1_i + T2_i \tag{3}$$
$$B_{i+1} = A_i \tag{4}$$
$$C_{i+1} = B_i \tag{5}$$
$$D_{i+1} = C_i \tag{6}$$
$$E_{i+1} = T1_i + D_i \tag{7}$$
$$F_{i+1} = E_i \tag{8}$$
$$G_{i+1} = F_i \tag{9}$$
$$H_{i+1} = G_i \tag{10}$$

With some sub-operations ('Choice' $\mathscr{C}$ and 'Majority' $\mathscr{M}$):

$$\mathscr{C}(E_i, F_i, G_i) = (E_i \wedge F_i) \oplus (\neg E_i \wedge G_i)$$
$$\mathscr{M}(A_i, B_i, C_i) = (A_i \wedge B_i) \oplus (A_i \wedge C_i) \oplus (B_i \wedge C_i)$$

Σ_0 and Σ_1 are not detailed here. The data passed as input of these transformation functions do not undergo changes in properties required for our attack. E.g. a known value passed though these functions will remains known (the same stands for properties: unknown, fix and variable).

$T1_i$ and $T2_i$ are temporary variables used to combine current round inputs $(A_i, \ldots, H_i)$ with round constant K_i and round message part W_i. Then, these temporary variables are used to compute the current round outputs, denoted $(A_{i+1}, \ldots, H_{i+1})$.

To ease further explanations, we set up several intermediate data references that are not dependent on known constants K_i and on message part W_i:

$$\delta E_{i+1} = H_i + \Sigma_1(E_i) + \mathscr{C}(E_i, F_i, G_i) + D_i$$
$$\delta A_{i+1} = H_i + \Sigma_1(E_i) + \mathscr{C}(E_i, F_i, G_i) + \Sigma_0(A_i) + \mathscr{M}(A_i, B_i, C_i)$$

These references are involved in the following equations:

$$A_{i+1} = \delta A_{i+1} + K_i + W_i$$
$$E_{i+1} = \delta E_{i+1} + K_i + W_i$$

HMAC SHA-2 is composed of two successive calls to SHA-2. The first is called *inner* hash when the second is called *outer* hash. The key is processed through a padding process to be of the size of one block. Then, the result is combined with a constant called *ipad* by exclusive-or. Finally, the concatenation of the modified key and the message to process is hashed. The result is used as a message for a second pass of the same process except that *ipad* is now replaced by another constant called *opad*. This process is described in Fig. 2. In this figure, message padding method is replaced by Padding' as the message bit length has a role in padding and must then take into account the concatenation of first block from key part.

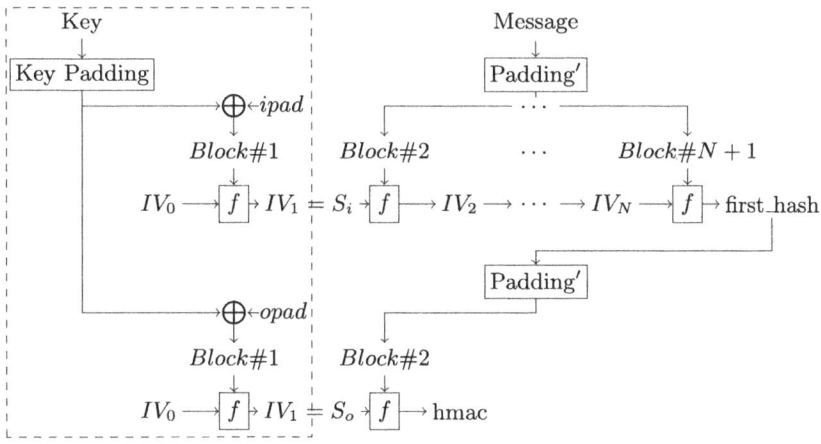

Fig. 2. Scheme of HMAC- SHA-2 process.

In a classical usage of HMAC, the key is constant and therefore the dashed area on Fig. 2 identifies a part of computation that is constant and does not depend on the message. Most attacks from state-of-the-art aim at retrieving (S_i, S_o). This pair of constant values allows an attacker to forge a valid HMAC output by performing the non framed part of algorithm on Fig. 2 with any message.

HKDF is a key derivation function based on HMAC. The used inputs are the secret source named IKM (e.g. shared secret during Diffie-Hellman key exchange) and a publicly known salt. The key derivation consists in two steps:

- **Extract** that produces a Pseudo-Random Key (PRK) by using a HMAC with the salt as the key and the secret IKM as the message:

$$PRK = \text{HMAC}(\text{salt}, \text{IKM})$$

- **Expand**[1] that uses obtained PRK as a key in a HMAC with a chosen message (called info) to produce a derived key:

$$\text{Key}_{\text{info}} = \text{HMAC}(\text{PRK}, \text{info})$$

3 State-of-the-Art Attacks

During attacks explanations below, the known constants K_i will often be associated with known variables (e.g. W_i) as it does not have an impact (e.g. $K_i + W_i$ is also a known variable if W_i is). It could also have been included in targeted constant and then been subtracted once the whole constant is recovered.

3.1 Early Attacks

Short Description: Early attacks are described in [2,14] where authors propose the first attacks allowing to recover secret information of HMAC-SHA-2 through a DPA-like attacks. Both does not apply constraints on attacker model, as only a known message is required. However, specific constraints on the leakage model must be met in order to be able to apply the attacks.

In [14], authors propose an attack in a context where Hamming distance leakages appear on intermediate values of $T1_i$, and on results of bitwise-and operations inside of $\mathscr{C}$ and $\mathscr{M}$ functions.

In [2], authors propose a variation that needs Hamming weight leakages of the same intermediate values.

The attack principle consists in using message variability (W_i) to attack S_i value when used as an IV ($A_0, \ldots, H_0$) during second block absorption of first hash in HMAC. Once recovered, S_i allows to compute the rest of inner hash. The output produced is the input message of outer hash, then the exact same attack can be conducted on S_o.

Step-By-Step Description: Is given hereafter, an example derived from early attacks principle. At each step a constant, called here χ_i, is recovered through a DPA-like attack.

1. Target E_1 leakage, use the variability of W_0 to recover the value of $\chi_1 = \delta E_1$ constant:

$$E_1 = \underbrace{D_0 + H_0 + \Sigma_1(E_0) + \mathscr{C}(E_0, F_0, G_0)}_{\delta E_1 : \text{Unknown Constant}} + \underbrace{K_0 + W_0}_{\text{Known Variable}}$$

From now on, E_1 becomes a known variable.

---

[1] Details about the *Expand* part of the computation are omitted here as we only focus on *Extract* part. For more details, please consult [13].

2. Target A_1 leakage, use the variability of W_0 to recover the value of $\chi_2 = \delta A_1$ constant:

$$A_1 = \underbrace{H_0 + \Sigma_1(E_0) + \mathscr{C}(E_0, F_0, G_0) + \Sigma_0(A_0) + \mathscr{M}(A_0, B_0, C_0)}_{\delta A_1: \text{Unknown Constant}} + \underbrace{K_0 + W_0}_{\text{Known}}$$

From now on, A_1 becomes a known variable.

3. Target $E_1 \wedge E_0$ leakage, use the variability of E_1 to recover the value of $\chi_3 = E_0$ constant:

$$\mathscr{C}(E_1, F_1, G_1) = \mathscr{C}(E_1, E_0, F_0)$$
$$= \underbrace{(E_1 \wedge E_0)}_{\text{Expected Leakage}} \oplus (\neg E_1 \wedge F_0)$$

4. Target $\neg E_1 \wedge F_0$ leakage, use the variability of E_1 to recover the value of $\chi_4 = F_0$ constant:

$$\mathscr{C}(E_1, F_1, G_1) = \mathscr{C}(E_1, E_0, F_0)$$
$$= (E_11 \wedge E_0) \oplus \underbrace{(\neg E_1 \wedge F_0)}_{\text{Expected Leakage}}$$

5. Target $A_1 \wedge A_0$ leakage, use the variability of A_1 to recover the value of $\chi_5 = A_0$ constant:

$$\mathscr{M}(A_1, B_1, C_1) = \mathscr{M}(A_1, A_0, B_0)$$
$$= \underbrace{(A_1 \wedge A_0)}_{\text{Expected Leakage}} \oplus (A_1 \wedge B_0) \oplus (A_0 \wedge B_0)$$

6. Target $A_1 \wedge B_0$ leakage, use the variability of A_1 to recover the value of $\chi_6 = B_0$ constant:

$$\mathscr{M}(A_1, B_1, C_1) = \mathscr{M}(A_1, A_0, B_0)$$
$$= (A_1 \wedge A_0) \oplus \underbrace{(A_1 \wedge B_0)}_{\text{Expected Leakage}} \oplus (A_0 \wedge B_0)$$

7. Target E_2 leakage, use the variability of W_1 and E_1 and the knowledge of E_0 and F_0 to recover the value of $\chi_7 = (C_0 + G_0)$ constant:

$$E_2 = D_1 + H_1 + \Sigma_1(E_1) + \mathscr{C}(E_1, F_1, G_1) + K_1 + W_1$$
$$= \underbrace{C_0 + G_0}_{\text{Unknown}} + \underbrace{\Sigma_1(E_1) + \mathscr{C}(E_1, E_0, F_0) + K_1 + W_1}_{\text{Known Variable}}$$

8. Target A_2 leakage, use the variability of W_1, E_1 and A_1 and the knowledge of E_0, F_0, A_0 and B_0 to recover the value of $\chi_8 = G_0$ constant:

$$A_2 = H_1 + \Sigma_1(E_1) + \mathscr{C}(E_1, F_1, G_1) + \Sigma_0(A_1) + \mathscr{M}(A_1, B_1, C_1) + K_1 + W_1$$
$$= G_0 + \underbrace{\Sigma_1(E_1) + \mathscr{C}(E_1, E_0, F_0) + \Sigma_0(A_1) + \mathscr{M}(A_1, A_0, B_0) + K_1 + W_1}_{\text{Known Variable}}$$

Therefore, the resulting system of equation can be solved:

$$\chi_1 = D_0 + H_0 + \Sigma_1(E_0) + \mathscr{C}(E_0, F_0, G_0) \tag{11}$$
$$\chi_2 = H_0 + \Sigma_1(E_0) + \mathscr{C}(E_0, F_0, G_0) + \Sigma_0(A_0) + \mathscr{M}(A_0, B_0, C_0) \tag{12}$$
$$\chi_3 = E_0 \tag{13}$$
$$\chi_4 = F_0 \tag{14}$$
$$\chi_5 = A_0 \tag{15}$$
$$\chi_6 = B_0 \tag{16}$$
$$\chi_7 = C_0 + G_0 \tag{17}$$
$$\chi_8 = G_0 \tag{18}$$

A_0, B_0, E_0, F_0 and G_0 are directly known (Eqs. 15, 16, 13, 14, 18). Knowledge of G_0 allows to get C_0 (Eq. 17). H_0 can now be recovered as the only unknown value in Eq. 12. Then, the same applies to D_0 being now the only unknown value in Eq. 11.

Summary of Early Attack: Early attacks have several constraints:

- Known message.
- Varying message with sufficient entropy.
- Leakage on two end-of-turn stored variables (E_i, A_i) over two first rounds.
- Leakage on four intermediate bitwise-and operations during second round ($E_1 \wedge F_1$, $\neg E_1 \wedge G_1$, $A_1 \wedge B_1$ and $A_1 \wedge C_1$)

Later works pointed a drawback of such an attack in that it requires leakages for two different processed values. One from round-end memory (A_i and E_i) that will be stored, read and manipulated several times and one from temporary sub-operations (bitwise-and) that can be harder to target for an attacker depending on the attack conditions.

3.2 Partial Attack with Fewer Constraints

Short Description: Methodology was furnished in slides from [17], briefly showing an update of early attacks. Authors implied that leakage of bitwise-and operations used in Sect. 3.1 are not necessary anymore in counterpart of a chosen message constraint. This short description was later detailed in [19].

Step-By-Step Description: Description is given here as some part were still omitted in [19]. The new attack process needs four different sets of acquisitions:

- Set $\mathscr{S}_0$ with W_0 varying.
- Set $\mathscr{S}_1$ with W_0 fixed to any known value and W_1 varying.
- Set $\mathscr{S}_2$ with W_0 and W_1 fixed to any known value and W_2 varying.
- Set $\mathscr{S}_3$ with W_0, W_1 and W_2 fixed to any known value and W_3 varying.

Then the attack becomes:

1. Focusing on set $\mathscr{S}_0$ they use the same steps (1) and (2) of early attack method described in Sect. 3.1 to recover δE_1 and δA_1 as conditions are identical (W_0 varying):

$$E_1 = \underbrace{\delta E_1}_{\text{Unknown Constant}} + \underbrace{K_0 + W_0}_{\text{Known Variable}}$$

$$A_1 = \underbrace{\delta A_1}_{\text{Unknown Constant}} + \underbrace{K_0 + W_0}_{\text{Known Variable}}$$

   From now on, δE_1 and δA_1 become known constants.

2. Focusing on set $\mathscr{S}_1$, as W_0 is fixed to any constant value W_0^*, then E_1 becomes fixed to a known constant value $E_1^* = \delta E_1 + K_0 + W_0^*$. The same stands for A_1 that is fixed to a constant known value $A_1^* = \delta A_1 + K_0 + W_0^*$. Then, δE_2 and δA_2 become also constant as the only variable inside them are E_1 and A_1. Then, the exact same attack than step (1) can be applied to recover δE_2^* and δA_2^*:

$$E_2 = \underbrace{\delta E_2^*}_{\text{Unknown Constant}} + \underbrace{K_1 + W_1}_{\text{Known Variable}}$$

$$A_2 = \underbrace{\delta A_2^*}_{\text{Unknown Constant}} + \underbrace{K_1 + W_1}_{\text{Known Variable}}$$

   From now on, $E_1^*, A_1^*, \delta E_2^*$ and δA_2^* become known constants.

3. The same principle propagates for set $\mathscr{S}_2$ when (W_0, W_1) are fixed to constant values (W_0^*, W_1^*), then (E_2, A_2) becomes known fixed too (E_2^*, A_2^*) and finally $(\delta E_3, \delta A_3)$ become fixed to constant values and the same attack becomes applicable to recover them:

$$E_3 = \underbrace{\delta E_3^*}_{\text{Unknown Constant}} + \underbrace{K_2 + W_2}_{\text{Known Variable}}$$

$$A_3 = \underbrace{\delta A_3^*}_{\text{Unknown Constant}} + \underbrace{K_2 + W_2}_{\text{Known Variable}}$$

   From now on, $E_2^*, A_2^*, \delta E_3^*$ and δA_3^* become known constants.

4. Again, the same principle propagates for set $\mathscr{S}_3$ when (W_0, W_1, W_2) are fixed to constant values (W_0^*, W_1^*, W_2^*), then (E_3, A_3) become known fixed too

(E_3^*, A_3^*) and finally $(\delta E_3, \delta A_3)$ become fixed to constant values and the same attack becomes applicable to recover them:

$$E_4 = \underbrace{\delta E_4^*}_{\text{Unknown Constant}} + \underbrace{K_3 + W_3}_{\text{Known Variable}}$$

$$A_4 = \underbrace{\delta A_4^*}_{\text{Unknown Constant}} + \underbrace{K_3 + W_3}_{\text{Known Variable}}$$

From now on, E_3^*, A_3^*, δE_4^* and δA_4^* become known constants.

Therefore, the resulting system of equation can be solved:

$$\delta E_1 = D_0 + H_0 + \Sigma_1(E_0) + \mathscr{C}(E_0, F_0, G_0) \tag{19}$$

$$\delta A_1 = H_0 + \Sigma_1(E_0) + \mathscr{C}(E_0, F_0, G_0) + \Sigma_0(A_0) + \mathscr{M}(A_0, B_0, C_0) \tag{20}$$

$$\delta E_2^* = D_1 + H_1 + \Sigma_1(E_1^*) + \mathscr{C}(E_1^*, F_1, G_1)$$
$$= C_0 + G_0 + \Sigma_1(E_1^*) + \mathscr{C}(E_1^*, E_0, F_0) \tag{21}$$

$$\delta A_2^* = H_1 + \Sigma_1(E_1^*) + \mathscr{C}(E_1^*, F_1, G_1) + \Sigma_0(A_1^*) + \mathscr{M}(A_1^*, B_1, C_1)$$
$$= G_0 + \Sigma_1(E_1^*) + \mathscr{C}(E_1^*, E_0, F_0) + \Sigma_0(A_1^*) + \mathscr{M}(A_1^*, A_0, B_0) \tag{22}$$

$$\delta E_3^* = D_2 + H_2 + \Sigma_1(E_2^*) + \mathscr{C}(E_2^*, F_2, G_2)$$
$$= B_0 + F_0 + \Sigma_1(E_2^*) + \mathscr{C}(E_2^*, E_1^*, E_0) \tag{23}$$

$$\delta A_3^* = H_2 + \Sigma_1(E_2^*) + \mathscr{C}(E_2^*, F_2, G_2) + \Sigma_0(A_2^*) + \mathscr{M}(A_2^*, B_2, C_2)$$
$$= F_0 + \Sigma_1(E_2^*) + \mathscr{C}(E_2^*, E_1^*, E_0) + \Sigma_0(A_2^*) + \mathscr{M}(A_2^*, A_1^*, A_0) \tag{24}$$

$$\delta E_4^* = D_3 + H_3 + \Sigma_1(E_3^*) + \mathscr{C}(E_3^*, F_3, G_3)$$
$$= A_0 + E_0 + \Sigma_1(E_3^*) + \mathscr{C}(E_3^*, E_2^*, E_1^*) \tag{25}$$

$$\delta A_4^* = H_3 + \Sigma_1(E_3^*) + \mathscr{C}(E_3^*, F_3, G_3) + \Sigma_0(A_3^*) + \mathscr{M}(A_3^*, B_3, C_3)$$
$$= E_0 + \Sigma_1(E_3^*) + \mathscr{C}(E_3^*, E_2^*, E_1^*) + \Sigma_0(A_3^*) + \mathscr{M}(A_3^*, A_2^*, A_1^*) \tag{26}$$

E_0 can be recovered in Eq. 26 as it is the only unknown value. Then, A_0 becomes the only unknown value in Eq. 25. This phenomenon is cascading for F_0 in Eq. 24, B_0 in Eq. 23, G_0 in Eq. 22, C_0 in Eq. 21, H_0 in Eq. 20 and finally D_0 in Eq. 19. Eventually, all targeted values $(A_0, \ldots, H_0)$ are recovered.

Application on HMAC: Attack on HMAC is incomplete as stated in [17]. The chosen message requirement allows to attack inner hash but this property is lost for outer hash where message is only known. It has to be noted that this partial attack still reduces the security of HMAC.

Summary of Partial Attack: the given methodology releases the constraint from early attacks where several types of leakages were needed. However, in counterpart, the message now requires to be chosen. The constraints of this attack version are:

- Chosen message.
- Leakage on two end-of-turn stored variables (A_i, E_i) over four first rounds.
- Four sets of traces.

This attack can endanger HMAC but remains only a partial threat to its security. Author of [19] have pursued this work to present a full attack path.

3.3 Complete Attack with Fewer Constraints

Short Description: In [19], author starts from the partial attack suggested in [17] and completes it in order to lead to a full secret recovery. The same conditions are used (A_i and E_i leakages and chosen message constraint). However, in exchange to complete the attack with recovery of S_o, the HMAC output must now be known.

Step-By-Step Description: The main idea is to attack by the end of the algorithm as an addition is performed between targeted initial values ($A_0, \ldots, H_0$) and the output of rounds that ingested the message block ($A_{64}, \ldots, H_{64}$). However, attacking the addition itself (as proposed in [2]) requires of another kind of leakage. In order to respect the constraint to use only A_i and E_i leakages during rounds, author of [19] makes use of the following equations:

$$hash_0 = A_0 + A_{64} \Rightarrow A_{64} = hash_0 - A_0$$
$$hash_1 = B_0 + B_{64} = B_0 + A_{63} \Rightarrow A_{63} = hash_1 - B_0$$
$$hash_2 = C_0 + C_{64} = C_0 + A_{62} \Rightarrow A_{62} = hash_2 - C_0$$
$$hash_3 = D_0 + D_{64} = D_0 + A_{61} \Rightarrow A_{61} = hash_3 - D_0$$
$$hash_4 = E_0 + E_{64} \Rightarrow E_{64} = hash_4 - E_0$$
$$hash_5 = F_0 + F_{64} = F_0 + E_{63} \Rightarrow E_{63} = hash_5 - F_0$$
$$hash_6 = G_0 + G_{64} = G_0 + E_{62} \Rightarrow E_{62} = hash_6 - G_0$$
$$hash_7 = H_0 + H_{64} = H_0 + E_{61} \Rightarrow E_{61} = hash_7 - H_0$$

hash values being the variable known HMAC output split in 8 words. B_{64}, C_{64} and D_{64} are related to A_i in the 4 last rounds when F_{64}, G_{64} and H_{64} are related to E_i in the 4 last rounds. This allows to target, through a DPA-like attacks, initial values ($A_0, \ldots, H_0$) when leakages from A_i and E_i computed in the four last rounds are leaking.

It has to be noted that author of [19] details methods to palliate if A_{64} and E_{64} are missing which will not be detailed here.

Summary of Complete Attack: This methodology fixes the partial HMAC attack from [17] in counterpart to the HMAC output that requires now to be known. The constraints of this attack version are:

- Chosen message.

- Known HMAC output.
- Leakage on two end-of-turn stored variables (A_i, E_i) over four first rounds of inner hash.
- Leakage on two end-of-turn stored variables (A_i, E_i) over four last rounds of outer hash.
- Four sets of traces.

4 Our Contribution

Our contribution lies in two parts. On first hand, we will describe how the choice to swap the roles of the message and the key in HMAC usage can open a very low constraint attack path compared to those of the state-of-the-art. On second hand, we will describe some variations of state-of-the-art attacks on HMAC that could reduce the number of traces needed by 25% or allow the attack even in presence of some countermeasures (partial masking).

4.1 The Dangerous Message/Key Swap

In this section, we will show how switching the roles of message and key in HMAC algorithm can seriously endanger the secret's confidentiality. This permutation is, for example, performed in protocols such as HKDF and HMAC-DRBG.

Swapping the roles means that the "Key" from Fig. 2 becomes known or controlled by the attacker, when the "Message" becomes a constant value, unknown from the attacker. We will denote Key* the known variable key and Message* the unknown varying message. For sake of clarity of explanations, Message* will be considered as entirely secret and constant, and only E_i leakages will be considered. These assumptions will be relaxed later.

As a consequence, S_i becomes known to the attacker as it can be computed from the known Key* through key padding, then combined by exclusive-or with ipad constant and then mixed in f function with known IV (IV_0). In fact, the whole dashed section of Fig. 2 becomes known by the attacker, even if only S_i is used here. On the other side, any W_i derived from Message* block values becomes unknown and constant.

Thus, considering the second block absorption of inner hash, IV value is composed of known variables ($A_0, \ldots, H_0$) and W_i values are unknown constants. As a reminder, the equation for E_1 used in previous attacks was:

$$E_1 = \underbrace{D_0 + H_0 + \Sigma_1(E_0) + \mathscr{C}(E_0, F_0, G_0)}_{\delta E_1:\text{ Unknown Constant}} + \underbrace{K_0 + W_0}_{\text{Known Variable}}$$

When roles are swapped, this equation becomes:

$$E_1 = \underbrace{D_0 + H_0 + \Sigma_1(E_0) + \mathscr{C}(E_0, F_0, G_0) + K_0}_{\text{Known Variable}} + \underbrace{W_0}_{\text{Unknown Constant}}$$

Our attack is much easier compared to previous ones, as the constant to recover per round is directly part of secret information (W_i) instead of the aggregation of constants (δE_1).

Step by Step Description of Our Attack Process: Based on same leakage assumptions done in [17,19] we can mount a DPA-like attack recovering any unknown constant (W_i values) in intermediate computations by using the variability of known IV:

1. Using the knowledge of varying Key* to compute, for each acquisition, the value of S_i, which is the IV of second compression function (f) call of inner hash.
2. Targeting E_1 leakage, use the variability of known $S_i = (A_0, \ldots, H_0)$ to recover the value of constant W_0:

$$E_1 = \underbrace{D_0 + H_0 + \Sigma_1(E_0) + \mathscr{C}(E_0, F_0, G_0) + K_0}_{\text{Known Variable}} + \underbrace{W_0}_{\text{Unknown Constant}}$$

3. The acquired knowledges of W_0 and the one of $(A_0, \ldots, H_0)$ allow to compute the values of $(A_1, \ldots, H_1)$ by applying the Eqs. (1) to (10).
4. Same as step 2. but targeting E_2 leakage and using the variability of known $(A_1, \ldots, H_1)$ to recover W_1.
5. Same as step 3. but computing $(A_2, \ldots, H_2)$ from knowledge of W_1 and $(A_1, \ldots, H_1)$.
6. By inference, step 2 and 3 can be repeated (with increment on indexes) to recover W_2 to W_{15} at respective rounds.

The secret W_0 to W_{15} can therefore be recovered. There is no need to go beyond W_{15} as the following values are only combinations of the previous ones.

Discussing Using A Instead of E: The equation detailed above in step-by-step description only made usage of E_i leakages but the same equations stand with only A_i kind of leakage by using:

$$A_1 = \underbrace{H_0 + \Sigma_1(E_0) + \mathscr{C}(E_0, F_0, G_0) + \Sigma_0(A_0) + \mathscr{M}(A_0, B_0, C_0) + K_0}_{\text{Known Variable}} + W_0$$

Discussing Using A Or/and E: As A_i equations and E_i equations both target the same W_{i-1}, both can be used if available to potentially reduce the number of traces needed to ensure that the correct value is recovered.

Also, if leakages are inconsistent from one round to another, roles can be mixed (e.g. if implementation or hardware specificity induces best leakage of A_i on some rounds and best leakage of E_i on other ones).

Discussing the Low Variability Messages: If a protocol uses a low variability known input (such as a counter), this could thwart state-of-the-art attacks. Indeed, variability of message is used during DPA-like attack to target the constant secret and a low variability could keep part of the secret out of reach.

However, in our attack scenario, the known input is Key* that is passed through hash process f before using it to attack the secret. Therefore, as soon as there are enough different values that can be used as known input to perform the DPA-like attack, our attack benefits from good entropy properties offered by hash sub-function f and is therefore not affected by low variability input.

Discussing the Secret Length: The example given in step-by-step description considers a secret of size up to the length of one block. However, the method can be pursued in case of longer secret Message*. Indeed, once the first Message* block recovered, the output of the second f call of inner hash can be computed and therefore the IV of next call to function f becomes known and is varying. Then the same process can be applied recovering, any number of Message* blocks until fully recovered.

Discussing the Discontinuity of Secret: If portions of Message* are known (varying or not), the attack can still recover the constant secret part. Indeed:

- if a full W_i word is known (varying or not), the equations still apply and the attacker may directly target the next word W_{i+1} or the next Message* block.
- if a portion of a W_i word is known (varying or not) and another is unknown and constant, then it can be split in two parts $W_i = W_{i,\text{Known}} + W_{i,\text{Unknown}}$. Then the equation becomes:

$$E_1 = \underbrace{D_0 + H_0 + \Sigma_1(E_0) + \mathscr{C}(E_0, F_0, G_0) + K_0 + W_{0,\text{Known}}}_{\text{Known Variable}} + \underbrace{W_{0,\text{Unknown}}}_{\text{Unknown Constant}}$$

and therefore the unknown part can still be recovered.

An example of this situation can be found in the HMAC-DRBG process. A simplification of the HMAC-DRBG process is presented here, for more details please refer to specifications in [16]. In HMAC-DRBG, HMAC are performed in a loop ($\|$ being the concatenation operator):

1. X, Y and Z are set to known values
2. $HMAC(X, Y\|Z\|\text{Seed})$
3. X is updated
4. Y is updated
5. Random bits are generated
6. Return to step 2.

Seed is the main target for an attacker as it is the real secret here. Its recovery allows to predict the generated deterministic bit sequence. X and Y initial values are known but their update can remain non-revealed to an attacker. Thus, if another attack allows to recover some (X,Y) pairs, our attack can then be applied even in presence of varying content inside the Message* (here Y).

Summary of Our Attack: Swapping the roles Message/Key relaxes constraints applied on previous attacks. The constraints applied onto our attack are:

- Swap of roles between message and key.
- Leakage of A_i or E_i intermediate values on rounds corresponding to targeted secret round of appearance.

Constraints per attacks are summarized in Table 1.

Table 1. Summary of constraints per attack.

	Early [2,14]	Partial [17]	Complete [19]	Our Method
Input with high entropy	X			
Leakage of A and E	X	X	X	
Other leakages types	X			
Chosen input		X	X	
Several set of traces		X	X	
Known HMAC output			X	
Leakage of A or E				X
Swap Message/key roles				X

Applicability to SHA-1: Our attack presented here takes advantage of the way the message part (W_i) is mixed with IV ($A_0, \ldots, H_0$) in SHA-2. As this algorithm has huge design similarities with its predecessor SHA-1, the applicability of our method on this algorithm can be questioned. Here, briefs extracts from specifications of SHA-1 [15] are used. The notations are kept but equations that transform values are different. The attack is found applicable on SHA-1 by using:

$$A_1 = \underbrace{\text{Rotation}(A_0) + \mathscr{C}(B_0, C_0, D_0) + E_0 + K_0}_{\text{Known Variable}} + \underbrace{W_0}_{\text{Unknown Constant}}$$

4.2 Simulations

Previous work in [19] has already described a use case where no leakage can be found, except for A_i and E_i intermediate values. Author has shown that such a leakage can be used to perform an attack.

We still performed simulations to ensure the viability of our attack process. The simulations were done on HMAC-SHA-2 algorithm, with hash size output of 256-bit. First, simulated traces are created:

- 5,000 HMAC executions are performed with varying Key* and fixed Message*. For each execution, 32-bit intermediate values E_i are gathered for each round of each call to f function inside of inner hash of HMAC.
- For each execution, the Hamming weight of gathered 32-bit words are computed and concatenated in order to produce one simulation trace.
- A random normal noise with scale σ is added to each trace in order to simulate measurement noise.

Then, we simulate an attacker that have N traces available:

- Value of known Key* are used to compute $S_i = (A_0, \ldots, H_0)$ values for N traces. δE_1 can then be computed.

- DPA-like attack (here CPA) is performed on N first traces of the set, using the least significant byte of δE_1 variability to target the least significant byte of first 32-bit word of Message* (W_0). Ranks of candidates were logged during the attack.
- The best ranking candidate (correct or not) is taken to perform carry computation and now another attack of same kind is performed on next least significant byte of W_0. The process is repeated for the 4 bytes of W_0.
- Eventually a best ranking candidate for W_0 (correct or not) is obtained, it can be combined with $(A_0, \ldots, H_0)$ to compute $(A_1, \ldots, H_1)$ as explained in our attack process. It must be noted that the candidate for W_0 can be incorrect if trace number is insufficient to correctly distinguish the good candidate. Therefore, an error will propagate to value of $(A_1, \ldots, H_1)$.
- The process can be repeated to target following W_i if necessary.

This attack simulation was performed for various N and σ values in order to control the attack feasibility and the number of traces needed for recovery. The simulations were positive to confirm the viability of the method: with $\sigma = 5$, nearly 400 traces were needed to recover the correct value for W_0, W_1 and W_2. The number raised to nearly $1,200$ traces for $\sigma = 10$ and nearly $3,500$ traces for $\sigma = 15$. Figures of attack result per byte are given in Appendix A.

4.3 Optimization of State-of-the-Art Techniques on HMAC

We also provide two tricks to enhance previous work of state-of-the-art. These tricks do not apply to our new attack methodology presented in Sect. 4.1.

25% Decrease of Number of Traces: An optimization can be realized in attacks on HMAC performed in [17,19]. As described in Sect. 3.2, the attack on inner hash requires that 4 sets are acquired. However, we point out that the fourth is not necessary, thus reducing the number of required traces.

The first set is required to start the attack and use variability of W_0 to attack δE_1 that is constant.

The second set is needed in order to fix W_0 to have a constant $E_1 = E_1^*$. Looking at Eq. 21, the need to have a constant E_1^* comes solely from choice function ($\mathscr{C}$). Indeed, E_1 known and variable is not a problem for $\Sigma_1(E_1)$ that is also a known variable and could have been transferred with W_1 out of the equation. As the attacker cannot process $\mathscr{C}(E_1, E_0, F_0)$, due to the ignorance of E_0 and F_0, this part becomes an unknown variable that thwarts DPA-like attacks.

The third set is needed for the exact same reasons. Looking at Eqs. 23, choice is again the problem here as if E_2 is kept variable, $\mathscr{C}(E_2, E_1^*, E_0)$ becomes a unknown variable due to the ignorance of E_0.

However for the next round, there is no need of a fourth set, the final attack can be done on the third one. Indeed, in Eq. 25, if E_3 is kept as a known variable, then $\mathscr{C}(E_3, E_2^*, E_1^*)$ is also a known variable and can then be transferred with $\Sigma_1(E_3)$ to the known variable part of the equation. In summary, the equation:

$$E_4 = \underbrace{A_0 + E_0 + \Sigma_1(E_3^*) + \mathscr{C}(E_3^*, E_2^*, E_1^*)}_{\text{Unknown Constant}} + \underbrace{K_3 + W_3}_{\text{Known Variable}}$$

becomes:

$$E_4 = \underbrace{A_0 + E_0}_{\text{Unknown Constant}} + \underbrace{\Sigma_1(E_3) + \mathscr{C}(E_3, E_2^*, E_1^*) + K_3 + W_3}_{\text{Known Variable}}$$

The exact same process can be applied on equation of A_4. Therefore, the attack can be done on 3 sets instead of 4 reducing the number of trace by $\sim 25\%$.

Shifting Start of Attack: As state-of-the-art attacks require leakages of intermediate values on rounds of hash function, a protection against SCA can be applied to mitigate/remove these leakages. As state-of-the-art attacks detailed in Sect. 3 need leakages only on first rounds, a choice can be made, for cost reduction purposes, to apply the protection only on first rounds.

In such a situation of partial protection and in chosen message context, we suggest to start the attacks on later rounds. As an example, if the n first rounds of hash function f are protected but the following are not, one can fix W_0 to W_{n-1} to thwart the protection. Doing so, the input of $(n+1)^{th}$ round $(A_n, \ldots, H_n)$ are fixed and unknown and can be targeted by the same methodology as $(A_0, \ldots, H_0)$ could be. Once $(A_n, \ldots, H_n)$ recovered, and with knowledge of W_{n-1}, Eqs. (1) to (10) can be inverted to recover $(A_{n-1}, \ldots, H_{n-1})$:

$$A_{n-1} = B_n$$
$$B_{n-1} = C_n$$
$$C_{n-1} = D_n$$
$$T2_{n-1} = \Sigma_0(A_{n-1}) + \mathscr{M}(A_{n-1}, B_{n-1}, C_{n-1})$$
$$T1_{n-1} = A_n - T2_{n-1}$$
$$D_{n-1} = E_n - T1_{n-1}$$
$$E_{n-1} = F_n$$
$$F_{n-1} = G_n$$
$$G_{n-1} = H_n$$
$$H_{n-1} = T1_{n-1} - \Sigma_1(E_{n-1}) - \mathscr{C}(E_{n-1}, F_{n-1}, G_{n-1}) - K_{n-1} - W_{n-1}$$

This process can be done again on previous rounds and thanks to knowledge of W_{n-1} to W_0, this allows to recover the targeted $(A_0, \ldots, H_0)$.

The limitation of this method is the control of W_i by attacker as only the first 16 words can be controlled[2]. Therefore, we recommend to mask at least the 16 first rounds to protect from this method.

---

[2] For SHA-2 algorithm.

5 Conclusion

After a detailed summary of state-of-the-art of DPA-like attacks against HMAC, we have shown that some protocols make a dangerous usage of HMAC by swapping the role of the message and the key. We conclude that this choice can drastically reduce the constraints on attacker, which can ease attack on such protocol, even in case of reduced leakages opportunities.

Moreover, we describe two methods that can optimize state-of-the-art attacks. One by reducing by $\sim 25\%$ the number of trace of some attacks. The second allowing to adapt existing attacks even in case a partial masking countermeasure is applied.

This work implies to further study the consequences of alternative usage of algorithms outside the way they are specified. As an open subject, adaptations of attacks to SHA-3 (and corresponding HMAC) should also be investigated as it does not share the same common design of SHA-1 and SHA-2.

A Simulations Results: Attack Score per Number of Traces

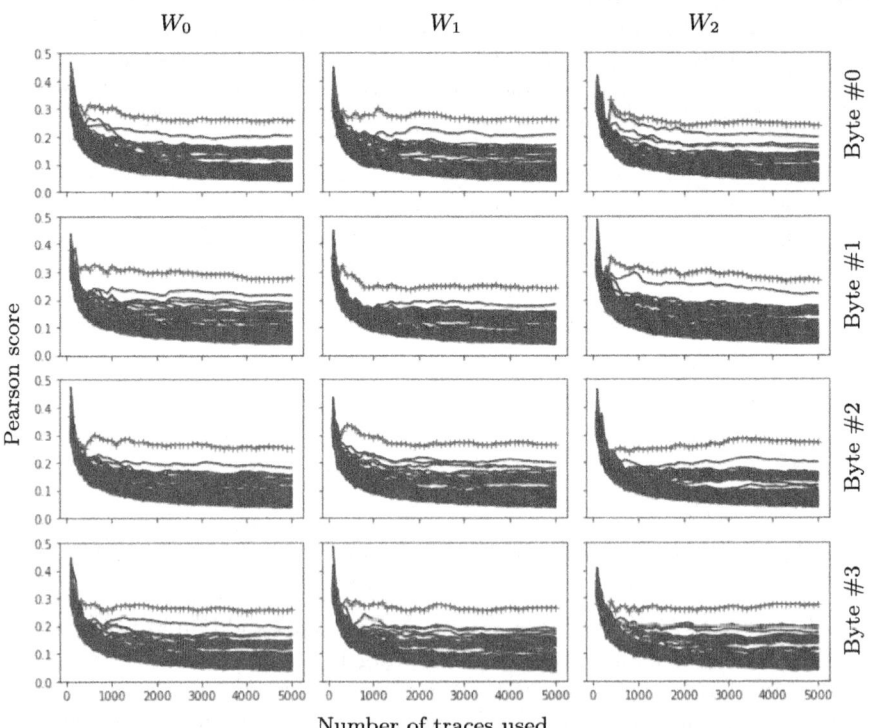

Fig. 3. Simulation score evolution per byte, noise $\sigma = 5$.

As described in Sect. 4.2, simulations have been run to verify the feasibility of the attack methodology described in this paper. Each sub-plot shows the evolution of the CPA score obtained per candidate for one targeted byte. Bytes are the ones from 32-bit words W_0, W_1 and W_2 values targeted during simulations. The good candidate is in red/plus sign marked line while wrong candidates are blue/straight lines. Figure 3 shows results when noise level is $\sigma = 5$ and Fig. 4 shows results when noise level is $\sigma = 15$.

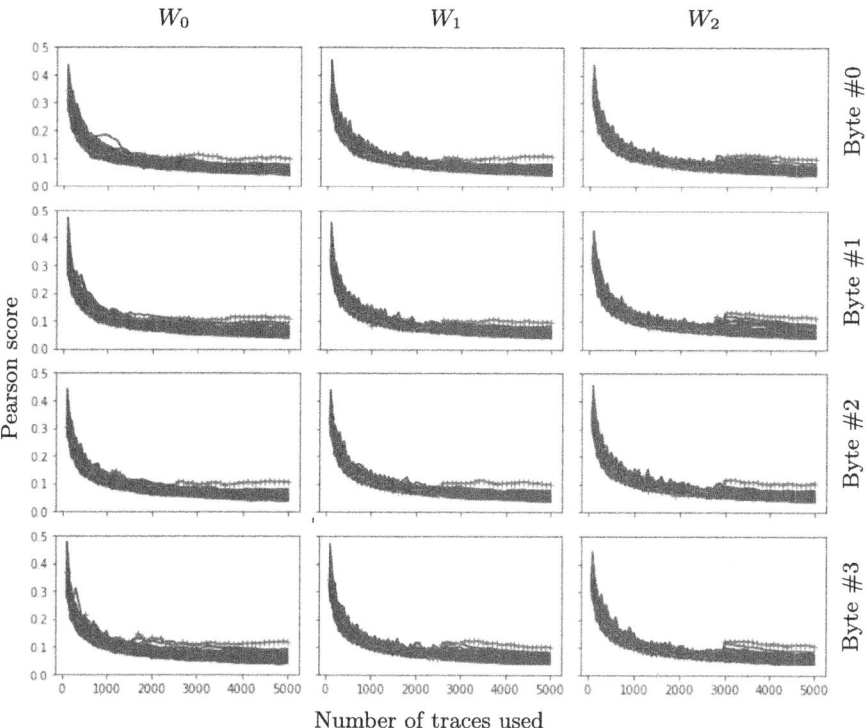

Fig. 4. Simulation score evolution per byte, noise $\sigma = 15$.

References

1. Barnes, R.L., Bhargavan, K., Lipp, B., Wood, C.A.: Hybrid public key encryption. RFC **9180**, 1–107 (2022). https://doi.org/10.17487/RFC9180
2. Belaïd, S., Bettale, L., Dottax, E., Genelle, L., Rondepierre, F.: Differential power analysis of HMAC SHA-2 in the hamming weight model. In: Samarati, P. (ed.) SECRYPT 2013 - Proceedings of the 10th International Conference on Security and Cryptography, Reykjavík, Iceland, 29–31 July 2013, pp. 230–241. SciTePress (2013). https://ieeexplore.ieee.org/document/7223170/

3. Belenky, Y., Dushar, I., Teper, V., Chernyshchyk, H., Azriel, L., Kreimer, Y.: First full-fledged side channel attack on HMAC-SHA-2. In: Bhasin, S., De Santis, F. (eds.) COSADE 2021. LNCS, vol. 12910, pp. 31–52. Springer, Cham (2021). https://doi.org/10.1007/978-3-030-89915-8_2
4. Bellare, M., Canetti, R., Krawczyk, H.: Keying hash functions for message authentication. In: Koblitz, N. (ed.) CRYPTO 1996. LNCS, vol. 1109, pp. 1–15. Springer, Heidelberg (1996). https://doi.org/10.1007/3-540-68697-5_1
5. Brier, E., Clavier, C., Olivier, F.: Correlation power analysis with a leakage model. In: Joye, M., Quisquater, J.-J. (eds.) CHES 2004. LNCS, vol. 3156, pp. 16–29. Springer, Heidelberg (2004). https://doi.org/10.1007/978-3-540-28632-5_2
6. Ferrigno, J., Hlaváč, M.: When AES blinks: introducing optical side channel. IET Inf. Secur. **2**(3), 94–98 (2008)
7. Fischlin, M., Janson, C., Mazaheri, S.: Backdoored hash functions: immunizing HMAC and HKDF. In: 31st IEEE Computer Security Foundations Symposium, CSF 2018, Oxford, United Kingdom, 9–12 July 2018, pp. 105–118. IEEE Computer Society (2018). https://doi.org/10.1109/CSF.2018.00015
8. Gandolfi, K., Mourtel, C., Olivier, F.: Electromagnetic analysis: concrete results. In: Koç, Ç.K., Naccache, D., Paar, C. (eds.) CHES 2001. LNCS, vol. 2162, pp. 251–261. Springer, Heidelberg (2001). https://doi.org/10.1007/3-540-44709-1_21
9. Genkin, D., Shamir, A., Tromer, E.: RSA key extraction via low-bandwidth acoustic cryptanalysis. In: Garay, J.A., Gennaro, R. (eds.) CRYPTO 2014. LNCS, vol. 8616, pp. 444–461. Springer, Heidelberg (2014). https://doi.org/10.1007/978-3-662-44371-2_25
10. Housley, R.: Use of the elliptic curve Diffie-Hellman key agreement algorithm with X25519 and X448 in the cryptographic message syntax (CMS). RFC **8418**, 1–18 (2018). https://doi.org/10.17487/RFC8418
11. Kocher, P.C.: Timing attacks on implementations of Diffie-Hellman, RSA, DSS, and other systems. In: Koblitz, N. (ed.) CRYPTO 1996. LNCS, vol. 1109, pp. 104–113. Springer, Heidelberg (1996). https://doi.org/10.1007/3-540-68697-5_9
12. Kocher, P., Jaffe, J., Jun, B.: Differential power analysis. In: Wiener, M. (ed.) CRYPTO 1999. LNCS, vol. 1666, pp. 388–397. Springer, Heidelberg (1999). https://doi.org/10.1007/3-540-48405-1_25
13. Krawczyk, H., Eronen, P.: HMAC-based extract-and-expand key derivation function (HKDF). RFC **5869**, 1–14 (2010). https://doi.org/10.17487/RFC5869
14. McEvoy, R., Tunstall, M., Murphy, C.C., Marnane, W.P.: Differential power analysis of HMAC based on SHA-2, and countermeasures. In: Kim, S., Yung, M., Lee, H.-W. (eds.) WISA 2007. LNCS, vol. 4867, pp. 317–332. Springer, Heidelberg (2007). https://doi.org/10.1007/978-3-540-77535-5_23
15. NIST: FIPS pub 180-4 secure hash standard (SHS) (2015). https://nvlpubs.nist.gov/nistpubs/FIPS/NIST.FIPS.180-4.pdf. Accessed 10 Dec 2024
16. NIST: Recommendation for random number generation using deterministic random bit generators (2015). https://nvlpubs.nist.gov/nistpubs/SpecialPublications/NIST.SP.800-90Ar1.pdf. Accessed 10 Dec 2024
17. Rohatgi, P., Marson, M.: NSA suite b crypto, keys, and side channel attacks (2013). https://www.rambus.com/wp-content/uploads/2015/08/2013-JunMarson-SuiteBAndSideChannel.pdf. Accessed 10 Dec 2024
18. Rescorla, E.: The transport layer security (TLS) protocol version 1.3. RFC **8446**, 1–160 (2018). https://doi.org/10.17487/RFC8446
19. Schuhmacher, F.: Canonical DPA attack on HMAC-SHA1/SHA2. In: Balasch, J., O'Flynn, C. (eds.) COSADE 2022. LNCS, vol. 13211, pp. 193–211. Springer, Cham (2022). https://doi.org/10.1007/978-3-030-99766-3_9

Practical Second-Order CPA Attack on ASCON with Proper Selection Function

Viet Sang Nguyen[✉], Vincent Grosso, and Pierre-Louis Cayrel

Université Jean Monnet Saint-Etienne, CNRS, Institut d Optique Graduate School, Laboratoire Hubert Curien UMR 5516, Saint-Etienne 42023, France
{viet.sang.nguyen,vincent.grosso,pierre.louis.cayrel}@univ-st-etienne.fr

Abstract. ASCON has recently been selected by the National Institute of Standards and Technology (NIST) as the lightweight cryptography standard. Consequently, it is utilized in a multitude of environments and devices. In this study, we examine the potential vulnerability of ASCON software implementations to Correlation Power Analysis (CPA) attacks. First, we conduct a comprehensive analysis of different approaches from the literature for choosing the selection function used to compute intermediate values in a CPA attack. Through both theoretical explanation and experimental validation, we demonstrate how these choices influence the success of the attack. Second, leveraging insights from our analysis, we present, to the best of our knowledge, the first successful and practical second-order CPA attack on a masked software implementation provided by the ASCON team running on a 32-bit microcontroller. Our results show that the full 128-bit key can be recovered in 4.7 h through the analysis of 360,000 traces on classical laptop.

Keywords: Correlation Power Analysis · ASCON · Masking

1 Introduction

Nowadays, the use of small computing devices, such as RFID tags, sensors, and smart cards, is increasingly common. Although being time-proven to be a robust cipher, the Advanced Encryption Standard (AES) [1] is often too resource-intensive for deployment in such low-end devices. This limit of the AES highlights the need for a more *lightweight* cipher. In this context, NIST initiated a lightweight cryptography competition to seek a new standard. After a rigorous selection process, ASCON [9] was announced as the new standard for lightweight cryptography in February 2023. Prior to this, ASCON had also been included in the final portfolio of the CAESAR competition. The careful analysis in these two selection processes enforces the confidence of the security of ASCON in a *black-box model*, in which the adversary only has access to the inputs and outputs.

However, the black-box model is not always sufficient to ensure security in practice. Especially when implemented and executed in embedded devices, cryptographic algorithms can be vulnerable to Side-Channel Attacks (SCA), which exploit *physical leakages* from the devices (*e.g.*, power consumption, execution time, electromagnetic radiations). Since the introduction of Differential Power Attack (DPA) by Kocher *et al.* [13], power analysis attacks have become a prominent research area. Over the years, many attack techniques have been developed, for example, Template Attacks (TA) by Chari *et al.* [8], Correlation Power Analysis (CPA) by Brier *et al.* [6], Mutual Information Analysis (MIA) by Batina *et al.* [2], Soft Analytical Side-Channel Analysis (SASCA) by Veyrat-Charvillon *et al.* [24], Deep Learning Side-Channel Attacks (DLSCA) by Maghrebi *et al.* [15].

With the expected widespread deployment of ASCON in embedded devices, where power leakages pose a significant threat, the need for studies on power analysis attacks against implementations of ASCON is growing. So far, there has not been much attention on this research area for ASCON. Samwel and Daemen [21] introduced the first successful CPA attack on a noisy hardware implementation. In their work, the authors constructed an effective *selection function* for computing the *intermediate variable* targeted by the attacks. Using the same selection function, Roussel *et al.* [20] and Weissbart and Picek [26] also successfully performed CPA attacks on a hybrid CMOS/MRAM hardware implementation and a ARMv7m software implementation, respectively. Ramezanpour *et al.* [18] conducted DPA and CPA attacks with a different selection function, but reported that they failed to recover the key. The authors later proposed a deep learning-based power analysis, which succeeded in key recovery. You *et al.* [27] introduced an efficient template attack on a 32-bit software implementation. Lou *et al.* [14] presented a SASCA attack with simulated traces for an 8-bit implementation.

To protect against power analysis attacks, *masking* [7,11] is one of the most widely studied countermeasures. The core concept behind masking is to split the sensitive variables into multiple shares and carry out the computations on these shares. ASCON's design, which features an efficient bitsliced implementation of the S-boxes, facilitates the use of masking. Several masked software implementations were published by the ASCON team.[1] Note that masking increases the attack complexity rather than offering complete protection. A method of attacking masked schemes is to combine the leakages from the individual shares and perform a CPA on the aggregated leakages. This technique is known as *higher-order* CPA [12,16,25]. When two shares are involved, the attack is referred to as a *second-order* CPA. Weissbart and Picek [26] attempted to perform a second-order CPA on a masked software implementation of ASCON, but reported a failure. The authors then proposed a successful deep learning-based power analysis, which was later improved by Rezaeezade *et al.* [19].

Most of the state-of-the-art power attacks on (protected) implementations of ASCON, including template attack [27], SASCA [14], deep learning attacks [19, 26], are *profiled attacks*, in which the powerful adversary is assumed to have full control on a copy of the targeted device and can obtain *a priori* knowledge about the implementation details. In contrast, the CPA attack, which our work focuses on, is a *non-profiled attack* corresponding to a weaker adversary. The adversary is only able to observe the device's leakages, *i.e.*, the power consumption when the

---

[1] See https://github.com/ascon/simpleserial-ascon.

cryptographic algorithm is executed. No detailed knowledge about the device is required. The CPA attack is univariate, assuming the real leakage function closely matches the chosen leakage model (*e.g.*, Hamming weight). Its goal is to recover the key through a statistical analysis of key-dependent physical leakages.

An important factor that significantly affects the success of a CPA attack is the choice of the selection function for computing intermediate values. In the literature, different approaches of choosing this function have been proposed, leading to either a success [21] or a failure [18] in key recovery. One approach relies on heuristics, such as using the S-box computation as the selection function [18], which has been well-studied in CPA attacks on AES. Another approach derives from observing of how processed data leaks into the power consumption [21]. In both cases [18,21], whether successful or not, there is a notable lack of analysis regarding the impact of these choices of the selection function on the success of the CPA attack.

Contributions. First, we provide a comprehensive analysis of the selection functions used in the literature. Through both theoretical explanation and experimental validation, we demonstrate that different choices of the selection function can determine the success or failure of a CPA attack on ASCON. Second, leveraging insights from our analysis, we present, to our knowledge, the first successful and practical second-order CPA attack against a masked software implementation of ASCON. We detail how the attack can be performed with modest resource requirements. To validate our attack path, we use the 32-bit ARMv6 masked implementation provided by the ASCON team. Power traces are recorded from executions of this implementation on a 32-bit STM32F303 microcontroller. Our results show that the full 128-bit key can be recovered successfully in 4.7 h using 360,000 traces.

For the sake of reproducibility, we publish the source code of the experiments at: https://github.com/nvietsang/socpa-ascon.

Outline. This paper is organized as follows. Section 2 provides the background knowledge. Section 3 presents a thorough analysis of the selection functions used in the literature. Section 4 presents the practical second-order CPA attack. Finally, Sect. 5 concludes our work and provides some perspectives.

2 Preliminaries

In this section, we first briefly recall the principle of the Correlation Power Analysis (CPA) attacks. Next, we present the self-contained background of the ASCON cipher. Finally, we provide the information on the devices and the setup in our experiments.

2.1 CPA Attacks

The goal of CPA is to recover the key based on a number of power traces recorded while the cryptographic algorithm is executed. The main advantage of CPA is that it does not require detailed knowledge about the cryptographic device. Knowing the algorithm that is executed by the device is usually sufficient. CPA attacks analyze the dependence between the power consumption at specific moments and the processed data. The attack procedure consists of the following five steps:

1. Choose an intermediate variable of the executed algorithm as the attack point. This intermediate variable needs to be a function $f(d,k)$, called *selection function*, of a part of the key k and the known non-constant data d (*e.g.*, plaintext).
2. Measure the power consumption of the device while it executes the cryptographic algorithm ℓ times. For each execution, the adversary records the data value d involved in the selection function and a power trace of s samples. Then, ℓ data values are written as a vector $\mathbf{d} = (d_1, \ldots, d_\ell)$, and ℓ power traces are written as a matrix $\mathbf{T}$ of size $\ell \times s$. It is important to note that the traces must be correctly aligned.
3. Calculate hypothetical intermediate values for every possible candidate of k. Let $\mathbf{k} = (k_1, \ldots, k_p)$ be the vector of p possible candidates for k, also usually referred to as key hypotheses. For each key hypothesis, the adversary uses the selection function $f(d,k)$ to calculate the hypothetical intermediate values corresponding to the vector $\mathbf{d}$. Performing this calculation for all key hypotheses results in a matrix of hypothetical intermediate values, denoted by $\mathbf{V}$, of size $\ell \times p$.
4. Map hypothetical intermediate values to hypothetical power consumption values. The adversary chooses a leakage model to estimate the power consumption (*i.e.*, hypothetical power consumption) exposed by the device when processing a value. In this work, we use the Hamming weight model. Each value in $\mathbf{V}$ is then mapped to a corresponding hypothetical power consumption value, resulting in a hypothetical power consumption matrix $\mathbf{H}$ of size $\ell \times p$.
5. Compare the hypothetical power consumption values with the power traces. The adversary uses the Pearson's correlation coefficient to examine the linear correlation between the hypothetical power consumption values of each key candidate with the measured traces at every position. Specifically, he calculates the correlation coefficient between each column $\mathbf{h}_i$ of the matrix $\mathbf{H}$ and each column $\mathbf{t}_j$ of the matrix $\mathbf{T}$, resulting the element $r_{i,j}$ of the matrix $\mathbf{R}$ of size $p \times s$, where

$$r_{i,j} = \frac{\sum_{u=1}^{\ell} \left(h_{u,i} - \overline{h}_i\right)\left(t_{u,j} - \overline{t}_j\right)}{\sqrt{\sum_{u=1}^{\ell}\left(h_{u,i}-\overline{h}_i\right)^2}\sqrt{\sum_{u=1}^{\ell}\left(t_{u,j}-\overline{t}_j\right)^2}}.$$

In the above equation, the values $h_{u,i}$ and $t_{u,j}$ (resp. $\overline{h}_i$ and $\overline{t}_j$) denote the u-th elements (resp. mean values) of the columns $\mathbf{h}_i$ and $\mathbf{t}_j$.

The key can be recovered based on the fact that the higher value $r_{i,j}$ indicates a stronger linear corelation between the columns $\mathbf{h}_i$ and $\mathbf{t}_j$, suggesting a better match under the assumed leakage model. Let ck be the index of the correct key k_{ck} (i.e., the key that is used in the device) in the vector **k**, and ct be the index of the power consumption values $\mathbf{t}_{\mathrm{ct}}$ that depend on the intermediate values $\mathbf{v}_{\mathrm{ck}}$. The columns $\mathbf{h}_{\mathrm{ck}}$ and $\mathbf{t}_{\mathrm{ct}}$ should be strongly correlated. Thus, the highest value $r_{\mathrm{ck,ct}}$ in the matrix **R** reveals the indexes of the correct key ck and the position ct.

2.2 ASCON

ASCON [9] is a suite of Authenticated Encryption with Associated Data (AEAD) and hashing algorithms, using the duplex sponge construction [4]. This paper considers the recommended version of authenticated cipher, ASCON-128 (referred to as ASCON throughout the paper). The encryption process of ASCON is depicted in Fig. 1. It takes as input a key K of 128 bits, a nonce N of 128 bits, associated data $A_1, \ldots, A_s$, each of 64 bits, and plaintexts $P_1, \ldots, P_t$, each of 64 bits. It produces as output a tag T of 128 bits and ciphertexts $C_1, \ldots, C_t$, each of 64 bits. This tag is used to authenticate the ciphertexts in the decryption process.

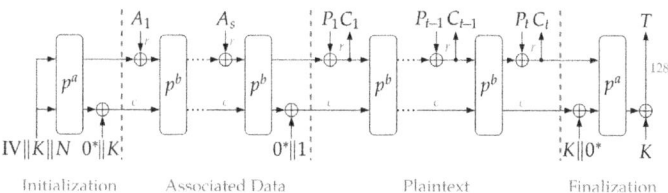

Fig. 1. Encryption in ASCON [9].

The permutations, denoted by p^a and p^b, are the core of the construction. These permutations consist of $a = 12$ rounds and $b = 6$ rounds, respectively. Each round is composed of three steps operating on a 320-bit state: (1) addition of constants, (2) substitution layer (S-box), and (3) linear diffusion layer, as depicted in Fig. 2. The 320-bit state is split into five words of 64 bits. These words can be stored in one or more registers, facilitating the translation from mathematical description to efficient implementation.[2]

Let $x_0, \ldots, x_4$ denote five 64-bit words of the round input. In the first step, a round constant is added to the rightmost eight bits of the word x_2. As the step of constant addition is not important in our attack, we simplify the notation by also denoting the output of the first step as $x_0, \ldots, x_4$. The second step is a non-linear transformation operating on five bits, one bit from each word of the first step output $x_0, \ldots, x_4$. Let $y_0, \ldots, y_4$ denote the output state of the S-box, and

---

[2] Implementations for 8-bit, 32-bit, 64-bit architectures can be found at https://github.com/ascon/ascon-c.

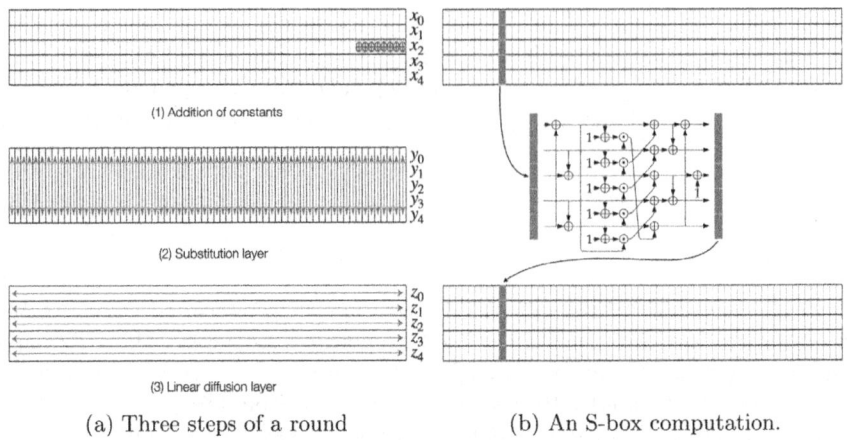

(a) Three steps of a round (b) An S-box computation.

Fig. 2. Each step in a round [9].

1 (in bold) denote a word of full 64 bit 1s. The algebraic normal form (ANF) of the S-box with operations performed on the entire 64-bit words (bitsliced form) can be written as:

$$\begin{aligned} y_0 &= x_4 x_1 \oplus x_3 \oplus x_2 x_1 \oplus x_2 \oplus x_1 x_0 \oplus x_1 \oplus x_0, \\ y_1 &= x_4 \oplus x_3 x_2 \oplus x_3 x_1 \oplus x_3 \oplus x_2 x_1 \oplus x_2 \oplus x_1 \oplus x_0, \\ y_2 &= x_4 x_3 \oplus x_4 \oplus x_2 \oplus x_1 \oplus \mathbf{1}, \\ y_3 &= x_4 x_0 \oplus x_4 \oplus x_3 x_0 \oplus x_3 \oplus x_2 \oplus x_1 \oplus x_0, \\ y_4 &= x_4 x_1 \oplus x_4 \oplus x_3 \oplus x_1 x_0 \oplus x_1. \end{aligned} \quad (1)$$

At the beginning of the initialization phase (Fig. 1), the 64-bit initialization vector IV is stored in the word x_0, the two 64-bit halves of the key $(k_0, k_1) = K$ are stored in the words x_1 and x_2, and the two 64-bit halves of the nonce $(n_0, n_1) = N$ are stored in the words x_3 and x_4. The S-box computation in the first round of the initialization phase, where our attack focuses on, thus can be written as (the constant addition step is omitted for the sake of simplicity):

$$\begin{aligned} y_0 &= n_1 k_0 \oplus n_0 \oplus k_1 k_0 \oplus k_1 \oplus k_0 \mathbf{IV} \oplus k_0 \oplus \mathbf{IV}, \\ y_1 &= n_1 \oplus n_0 k_1 \oplus n_0 k_0 \oplus n_0 \oplus k_1 k_0 \oplus k_1 \oplus k_0 \oplus \mathbf{IV}, \\ y_2 &= n_1 n_0 \oplus n_1 \oplus k_1 \oplus k_0 \oplus \mathbf{1}, \\ y_3 &= n_1 \mathbf{IV} \oplus n_1 \oplus n_0 \mathbf{IV} \oplus n_0 \oplus k_1 \oplus k_0 \oplus \mathbf{IV}, \\ y_4 &= n_1 k_0 \oplus n_1 \oplus n_0 \oplus k_0 \mathbf{IV} \oplus k_0. \end{aligned} \quad (2)$$

The third step, linear diffusion, rotates each word at the S-box output twice and XORs with itself. Let $z_0, \ldots, z_4$ denote the output of the linear diffusion layer. The linear functions applied to each word are:

$$z_0 = y_0 \oplus (y_0 \ggg 19) \oplus (y_0 \ggg 28),$$
$$z_1 = y_1 \oplus (y_1 \ggg 61) \oplus (y_1 \ggg 39),$$
$$z_2 = y_2 \oplus (y_2 \ggg 1) \oplus (y_2 \ggg 6), \qquad (3)$$
$$z_3 = y_3 \oplus (y_3 \ggg 10) \oplus (y_3 \ggg 17),$$
$$z_4 = y_4 \oplus (y_4 \ggg 7) \oplus (y_4 \ggg 41).$$

2.3 Experiment Setup

We use a ChipWhisperer Lite board, integrated with an STM32F303 32-bit ARM target microcontroller, to record the power consumption traces. The device is run with the default clock frequency 7.37 MHz. The ChipWhisperer board is connected to a MacBook Air M1 with 16 GB of RAM via a USB cable. All the analyses in this paper are also conducted on this computer. The details of the specific implementations used for our attack will be provided later.

3 Choices of Selection Function

The first and important step of a CPA is the selection of an intermediate variable as the attack point. This intermediate variable must be the output of a function (referred to as the selection function) that takes as input a small portion of the key and known non-constant data. As evidenced in certain prior works [18,20,21,26], an intermediate variable in the first round of the initialization phase seems well-suited for this purpose. This is due to the fact that the first round's inputs are the key and the nonce (see Fig. 1), where the nonce can be regarded as the known non-constant data.

In the literature, to our knowledge, there exists two approaches of choosing the intermediate variable and the selection function in the first round for CPA attacks on ASCON. The first approach, used by Ramezanpour et al. [18], is to straightforwardly choose the S-box output as the intermediate variable and the S-box computation as the selection function. This is similar to the choice of S-box output as the attack point in many well-studied CPA attacks on AES. Applying this approach, Ramezanpour et al. reported a failure for their attack (before introducing a successful deep learning attack), but did not provide any explanation. The second approach, proposed by Daemen and Samwel [21] and later used in [20,26], is to choose the linear diffusion layer output as the intermediate variable and *fine-tune* the S-box computation for the selection function. Applying this approach, the attacks in [20,21,26] succeeded in recovering the key. Daemen and Samwel provided the rationale behind their adjustment in the S-box computation to derive the selection function, but did not analyze how it impacts the success of the CPA attack. In other words, the authors did not explain why it is necessary to fine-tune the S-box computation instead of using it directly as the selection function.

In this section, we take a closer look into the two approaches. For each of them, we begin with a brief description of the selection function, and then analyze its impact on the success of the CPA attack. To simplify distinction, we refer the first approach as using the *pure* S-box computation (Subsect. 3.1), and the second approach as using the *fine-tuned* S-box computation (Subsect. 3.2), as the selection function.

3.1 Pure S-Box Computation as Selection Function

In Eq. 2, the S-box computation is written in a bitsliced form in which 64 parallel applications of the 5-bit S-box (corresponding to the entire 64-bit words) are performed at once. For analysis, we consider a single application of the S-box. Let the superscript j denote the index of the j-th bit of a 64-bit word, where $0 \leq j \leq 63$. The computation of the five S-box output bits $y_0^j, \ldots, y_4^j$ is written as:

$$
\begin{aligned}
y_0^j &= n_1^j k_0^j \oplus n_0^j \oplus k_1^j k_0^j \oplus k_1^j \oplus k_0^j \mathtt{IV}^j \oplus k_0^j \oplus \mathtt{IV}^j, \\
y_1^j &= n_1^j \oplus n_0^j k_1^j \oplus n_0^j k_0^j \oplus n_0^j \oplus k_1^j k_0^j \oplus k_1^j \oplus k_0^j \oplus \mathtt{IV}^j, \\
y_2^j &= n_1^j n_0^j \oplus n_1^j \oplus k_1^j \oplus k_0^j \oplus 1, \\
y_3^j &= n_1^j \mathtt{IV}^j \oplus n_1^j \oplus n_0^j \mathtt{IV}^j \oplus n_0^j \oplus k_1^j \oplus k_0^j \oplus \mathtt{IV}^j, \\
y_4^j &= n_1^j k_0^j \oplus n_1^j \oplus n_0^j \oplus k_0^j \mathtt{IV}^j \oplus k_0^j.
\end{aligned}
\tag{4}
$$

It can be observed that the values $y_0^j, y_1^j, y_2^j, y_3^j$ take as input two bits of the nonce (n_0^j, n_1^j) that are known non-constant data, and two bits of the key (k_0^j, k_1^j) that need to be guessed in our attack. The fifth bit corresponds to known constant data belonging to the $\mathtt{IV}$. Recall that $\mathtt{IV}$ is the 64-bit initialization vector, $\mathtt{IV}$ = 80400c0600000000 in hexadecimal. A small difference in y_4^j is that only one bit of the key (k_0^j) is involved.

A Single S-Box Output Bit as the Intermediate Variable. We now analyze the impact on the success of attacks if one chooses an output bit in $y_0^j, \ldots, y_4^j$ as the intermediate variable and the S-box computation as the selection function. Let us first consider the computation of y_0^j. There are 4 possible key candidates for (k_0^j, k_1^j), and 4 possible values of the known non-constant data (n_0^j, n_1^j). Table 1 presents the distribution of y_0^j corresponding to every possible key candidate. In the CPA attack on ASCON, we input (random) nonces into the algorithm and measure the corresponding power traces. The intermediate variable y_0^j, computed from (k_0^j, k_1^j) and (n_0^j, n_1^j), follows this distribution.

We examine the linear corelation between these distributions by computing Pearson's correlation coefficient between the distribution vectors for each key pair. For example, the vectors $(0, 0, 1, 1)$ and $(1, 1, 0, 0)$ represent the distributions of $(k_0^j, k_1^j) = (0,0)$ and $(k_0^j, k_1^j) = (0,1)$, respectively. These two vectors are correlated with a correlation coefficient of -1. Table 1 presents two correlation coefficients corresponding to the distribution vectors in red and blue. As observed, two key pairs result in distributions that are *fully correlated* (*i.e.*, with a correlation coefficient of ± 1).

Table 1 presents the correlation coefficients for only two key pairs. We then extend this analysis by performing similar calculations for all possible key pairs. Table 2 (top left) summarizes the correlation coefficients between their corresponding distributions for y_0^j. Suppose 1 among 4 possible key candidates is the correct key. This analysis of y_0^j implies that if y_0^j is selected as the intermediate variable, there will always exist an incorrect key candidate which hypothetical power consumption values correspond to are as highly correlated with the power traces as those of the correct key. Consequently, the correct key and this incorrect key cannot be distinguished in CPA, where the hypothetical power consumption values of the correct key are expected to exhibit the highest correlation with the power traces. As in Table 1, such pairs of correct key and incorrect key, for example, are $(0,0)$ and $(0,1)$, $(1,0)$ and $(1,1)$. Figure 3 illustrates the experiment for this analysis. It can be observed that the correlation traces for the candidate pairs $(0,0)$ and $(0,1)$ (in blue), as well as $(1,0)$ and $(1,1)$ (in red), are identical. Table 1 also shows that the value of the IV bit has no impact on the correlation score. This is expected, as when $\text{IV}^j = 1$, it either negates (for vectors in red) or has no effect (for vectors in blue) on all outputs of the selection function for $\text{IV}^j = 0$.

Table 1. Distribution of y_0^j corresponding to every possible key candidate when $\text{IV}^j = 0$ (left) and when $\text{IV}^j = 1$ (right). In each table, the correlation value in red (resp. blue) is computed using Pearson's correlation coefficient formula applied to the two vectors in red (resp. blue).

	(k_0^j, k_1^j)			
(n_0^j, n_1^j)	(0,0)	(0,1)	(1,0)	(1,1)
(0,0)	0	1	1	1
(0,1)	0	1	0	0
(1,0)	1	0	0	0
(1,1)	1	0	1	1
Correlation	-1		1	

	(k_0^j, k_1^j)			
(n_0^j, n_1^j)	(0,0)	(0,1)	(1,0)	(1,1)
(0,0)	1	0	1	1
(0,1)	1	0	0	0
(1,0)	0	1	0	0
(1,1)	0	1	1	1
Correlation	-1		1	

Note that the keys in those pairs are also not distinguishable in a DPA attack, where the values of y_0^j are used to divide the traces into two sets (one for $y_0^j = 0$ and the other for $y_0^j = 1$). For instance, the division into two sets will be identical for the two key candidates $(0,0)$ and $(0,1)$, or $(1,0)$ and $(1,1)$, as the resulting distributions of y_0^j for these candidates are identical, as shown in Table 1. As a consequence, the difference of means of the two sets will also be identical for the two candidates. In the DPA attack of Ramezanpour et al. [18], the authors chose y_0^j as the selection function. The authors reported that their DPA attack failed to find the correct key with more than 40K traces, but did not provide

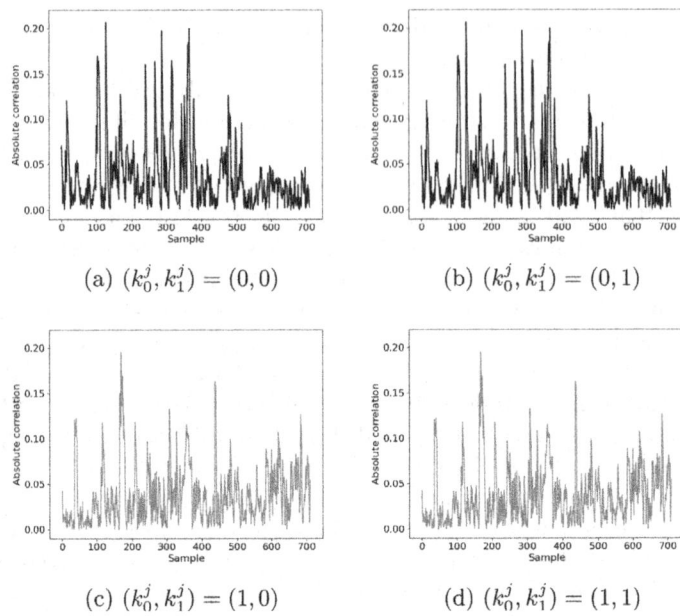

Fig. 3. Correlation traces when using y_0^j as the intermediate variable. The calculations use 1000 traces recorded from the execution of the reference implementation.

the reason. According to our analysis, their choice of the intermediate variable and the selection function could be the explanation for this failure.

We conduct a similar analysis for each of y_1^j, y_2^j, y_3^j and y_4^j, and present the correlations between the distributions of all possible key pairs for each case in Table 2. The results are similar to those of y_0^j, except for y_4^j. Specifically, for any given correct key in cases of y_1^j, y_2^j and y_3^j, there will always be an incorrect key that produces the same distribution, rendering the correct key indistinguishable from the incorrect one in DPA and CPA attacks. This is even worse in the cases of y_2^j and y_3^j (represented by the table of full correlations with values of 1 in Table 2), as all other incorrect key candidates yield identical distributions (or opposite distributions corresponding to the correlation coefficient of -1). Thus, we conclude that CPA attacks (resp. DPA attacks) using y_0^j, y_1^j, y_2^j or y_3^j as the intermediate variable, which aims to identify the key candidate corresponding to the highest value of correlation (resp. of the mean difference) as the correct one, will not succeed in obtaining a unique correct key, regardless the number of traces.

We observe an exception in the case of y_4^j (Table 2, bottom right). The distributions of the two possible key candidates (since only k_0^j is involved in y_4^j) are uncorrelated. This implies that y_4^j, when used as a selection function, could yield a unique key candidate given enough traces. This also suggests that if we fix, for example, $k_1^j = 0$ in y_0^j's table (i.e., removing the first and third columns

Table 2. Absolute correlations of distributions associated to all possible key pairs for $y_0^j, y_1^j, y_2^j, y_3^j, y_4^j$ when $\text{IV}^j = 0$. The entries with value 0 are indicated by "-" to facilitate reading. An interpretation example: the value 1 at row (0,0) and column (0,1) in the top-left table indicates a correlation coefficient of 1, meaning the the distribution vectors corresponding to the key candidates $(k_0^j, k_1^j) = (0,0)$ and $(k_0^j, k_1^j) = (0,1)$ are fully correlated.

(k_0^j, k_1^j)	(0,0)	(0,1)	(1,0)	(1,1)
(0,0)	1	1	-	-
(0,1)	1	1	-	-
(1,0)	-	-	1	1
(1,1)	-	-	1	1

y_0^j

(k_0^j, k_1^j)	(0,0)	(0,1)	(1,0)	(1,1)
(0,0)	1	-	-	1
(0,1)	-	1	1	-
(1,0)	-	1	1	-
(1,1)	1	-	-	1

y_1^j

(k_0^j, k_1^j)	(0,0)	(0,1)	(1,0)	(1,1)
(0,0)	1	1	1	1
(0,1)	1	1	1	1
(1,0)	1	1	1	1
(1,1)	1	1	1	1

y_2^j and y_3^j

k_0^j	0	1
0	1	0
1	0	1

y_4^j

as well as the first and third rows in the top-left table), the table reduces to one similar to y_4^j. A similar fix applies to the y_1^j's table. Using y_0^j and y_1^j with these fixes might also lead to a unique key candidate.

Later, in Subsect. 3.2, we will show that y_4^j or y_0^j and y_1^j with the fixes are similar to the fine-tuning in the second approach and will play an important role. However, using them directly as selection functions makes the DPA and CPA attacks prone to failure.

Hamming Weight of S-Box Output as the Intermediate Variable. We now consider the case where the Hamming weight of the 5-bit S-box output is used as the intermediate variable and the computations in Eq. 4 as the selection function.[3] Employing the Hamming weight of the S-box output, as done by Ramezanpour et al. [18] in their CPA attack on ASCON, is a very common approach in CPA attacks on AES. Recall that there are still 4 possible key candidates for (k_0^j, k_1^j) and 4 possible values for (n_0^j, n_1^j). As in the above analysis, we calculate the the Hamming weight distributions of the S-box output for every key candidate:

$$\text{HW}(y_0^j||y_1^j||y_2^j||y_3^j||y_4^j),$$

---

[3] This is specific to the hardware implementation design where a register stores a 5-bit S-box output, with 1 bit from each of the 5 words. In other words, the register is designed to operate along the vertical dimension in Fig. 2a. This design, adopted by Ramezanpour et al. [18], differs from the intent of the reference implementation, where a register is meant to store an entire word or part of a word, corresponding to the horizontal dimension in Fig. 2b.

where HW(·) denotes the Hamming weight and || denotes the concatenation. We then calculate the correlation between distributions generated by all possible key pairs, as shown in Table 3. We see that no key pairs with fully correlated distributions are observed. There are, however, still some very high correlations, for example, 0.90 between (1,0) and (1,1) in the left table, 0.93 between (0,1) and (0,0) in the right table. This suggests that the hypothetical power consumption values corresponding to some incorrect key candidates (besides the correct one) are also highly correlated to the power traces, making it difficult to distinguish the correct key. Especially in practical scenarios where the traces are heavily affected by noise, the CPA may fail or require a very large number of traces to find the correct key (similar to the remark of Brier et al. [6]).

Table 3. Absolute correlations between the Hamming weight distributions of the S-box output for each key pair when $\text{IV}^j = 0$ (left) and when $\text{IV}^j = 1$ (right).

(k_0^j, k_1^j)	(0,0)	(0,1)	(1,0)	(1,1)
(0,0)	1.00	0.15	0.89	0.87
(0,1)	0.15	1.00	0.48	0.09
(1,0)	0.89	0.48	1.00	0.90
(1,1)	0.87	0.09	0.90	1.00

(k_0^j, k_1^j)	(0,0)	(0,1)	(1,0)	(1,1)
(0,0)	1.00	0.93	0.52	0.17
(0,1)	0.93	1.00	0.48	0.27
(1,0)	0.52	0.48	1.00	0.09
(1,1)	0.17	0.21	0.09	1.00

Our analysis shows that using the Hamming weight of the S-box output as the intermediate variable is not effective for CPA attacks. In [18], Ramezanpour et al. adopted this approach for their CPA attack. The authors reported that their attack failed to recover the correct key even after using more than 40K traces, but they did not provide any justification. Since we do not have access to their implementation, we cannot determine the precise cause of the failure. However, we believe that the insights from our analysis here may contribute to explaining this outcome.

3.2 Fine-Tuned S-Box Computation as Selection Function

In the attack by Daemen and Samwel [21], the authors chose the output of the linear diffusion layer in their hardware implementation as the attack point, corresponding to the location of the registers. The activity of these registers at the end of each round (load/store) is assumed to leak information through power consumption. A notable contribution of their work is the adjustment applied to S-box computation before using it as the selection function. We now recall this adjustment and then analyze its impact on the success of CPA attacks.

As in [21], we only consider y_0^j, y_1^j and y_4^j in Eq. 4 as their computations contain non-linear terms between the key and the nonce. Let us focus on y_0^j as an example. Its computation in Eq. 4 is rewritten as follows:

$$y_0^j = k_0^j(n_1^j \oplus 1) \oplus n_0^j \oplus k_0^j k_1^j \oplus k_0^j \text{IV}^j \oplus k_1^j \oplus \text{IV}^j.$$

Following Bertoni et al. [3], the term $k_0^j k_1^j \oplus k_0^j \text{IV}^j \oplus k_1^j \oplus \text{IV}^j$ can be removed because, for the fixed correct key in the device, it is independent of the nonce and contributes a constant amount to the activity that drives the targeted power consumption of the register containing y_0. Note that this removal is similar to fixing $k_1^j = 0$ (and $\text{IV}^j = 0$) as discussed about the reduction for y_0^j in Table 2. The fine-tuned version of y_0^j, denoted by $\tilde{y}_0^j$, is:

$$\tilde{y}_0^j = k_0^j (n_1^j \oplus 1) \oplus n_0^j. \tag{5}$$

As the attack point is the activity of the register at the linear diffusion layer output (not at the S-box output), we take the operation of this layer into account. Recall from Eq. 1 that the first 64-bit output word z_0 of this layer is computed as:

$$z_0 = y_0 \oplus (y_0 \ggg 19) \oplus (y_0 \ggg 28).$$

The computation of the j-th bit of z_0 ($0 \leq j \leq 63$) thus is:

$$z_0^j = y_0^j \oplus y_0^{j+36} \oplus y_0^{j+45}. \tag{6}$$

The additions $j+36$ and $j+45$ are implicitly taken modulo 64. Applying Eqs. 5 to 6 results in the fine-tuned version of z_0^j, denoted by $\tilde{z}_0^j$, which is used as the selection function to recover k_0 (three bits at a time):

$$\begin{aligned}
\tilde{z}_0^j = & \left(k_0^j (n_1^j \oplus 1) \oplus n_0^j \right) \\
& \oplus \left(k_0^{j+36} (n_1^{j+36} \oplus 1) \oplus n_0^{j+36} \right) \\
& \oplus \left(k_0^{j+45} (n_1^{j+45} \oplus 1) \oplus n_0^{j+45} \right).
\end{aligned} \tag{7}$$

Similarly, we can derive the selection functions for recovering k_0 by fine-tuning y_4^j, and for recovering k_1 by fine-tunning y_1^j. The detailed derivation steps are provided in Sect. A. Here, we present the fine-tuned version of z_1^j, denoted by $\tilde{z}_1^j$, which is used as the selection function to recover k_1 (three bits at a time):

$$\begin{aligned}
\tilde{z}_1^j = & \left(n_0^j (k_{01}^j \oplus 1) \oplus n_1^j \right) \\
& \oplus \left(n_0^{j+3} (k_{01}^{j+3} \oplus 1) \oplus n_1^{j+3} \right) \\
& \oplus \left(n_0^{j+25} (k_{01}^{j+25} \oplus 1) \oplus n_1^{j+25} \right),
\end{aligned} \tag{8}$$

where $k_{01}^j = k_0^j \oplus k_1^j$. Note that k_1^j is not directly recovered, instead, k_{01}^j is recovered when $\tilde{z}_1^j$ is used as the selection. Then, k_1^j is derived as $k_1^j = k_{01}^j \oplus k_0^j$, with k_0^j recovered from the CPA using $\tilde{z}_0^j$ as the selection function.

Impact of Fine-Tuning. Let us analyze the selection function $\tilde{z}_0^j$. A similar analysis applies to $\tilde{z}_1^j$ and we present here the results for both $\tilde{z}_0^j$ and $\tilde{z}_1^j$. We begin by

Table 4. Distribution of $\tilde{y}_0^j$ (left) and $\tilde{y}_1^j$ (right) corresponding to every possible key candidate.

	k_0^j	
(n_0^j, n_1^j)	0	1
(0,0)	0	1
(0,1)	0	0
(1,0)	1	0
(1,1)	1	1
Correlation	0	

	k_{01}^j	
(n_0^j, n_1^j)	0	1
(0,0)	0	0
(0,1)	1	1
(1,0)	1	0
(1,1)	0	1
Correlation	0	

examining the core of $\tilde{z}_0^j$, which is $\tilde{y}_0^j$ (Eq. 5). As before, we calculate the distribution of $\tilde{y}_0^j$ for all possible candidates for k_0^j (2 candidates in total) in Table 4. It can be seen that the distributions produced by the two key candidates are uncorrelated to each other.

We then extend this calculation to the selection function $\tilde{z}_0^j$. Table 5 presents the correlations between distributions of all possible key pairs. Note that 3 key bits and 6 nonce bits involve in $\tilde{z}_0^j$. We thus have 8 key candidates. As we can see, the distribution associated with an arbitrary key is uncorrelated with that of any other key. This makes the correlation between the hypothetical power consumption associated with the correct key and the power traces stand out those of the incorrect keys. Figure 4 illustrates the experimental result for this analysis. It can be seen that the prominent peaks appear exclusively in the correlation trace of a single (correct) key candidate $(0,0,1)$. This explains the success of the attacks in [21], as opposed to the failure of the attack in [18], which relied on using the pure S-box computation as the selection function.

Table 5. Absolute correlations of distributions associated to all possible key pairs using the selection functions $\tilde{z}_0^j$ and $\tilde{z}_1^j$. The entries with value 0 are indicated by "-" to facilitate reading.

$(k_0^j, k_0^{j+36}, k_0^{j+45})$ or $(k_{01}^j, k_{01}^{j+3}, k_{01}^{j+25})$	(0,0,0)	(0,0,1)	(0,1,0)	(0,1,1)	(1,0,0)	(1,0,1)	(1,1,0)	(1,1,1)
(0,0,0)	1	-	-	-	-	-	-	-
(0,0,1)	-	1	-	-	-	-	-	-
(0,1,0)	-	-	1	-	-	-	-	-
(0,1,1)	-	-	-	1	-	-	-	-
(1,0,0)	-	-	-	-	1	-	-	-
(1,0,1)	-	-	-	-	-	1	-	-
(1,1,0)	-	-	-	-	-	-	1	-
(1,1,1)	-	-	-	-	-	-	-	1

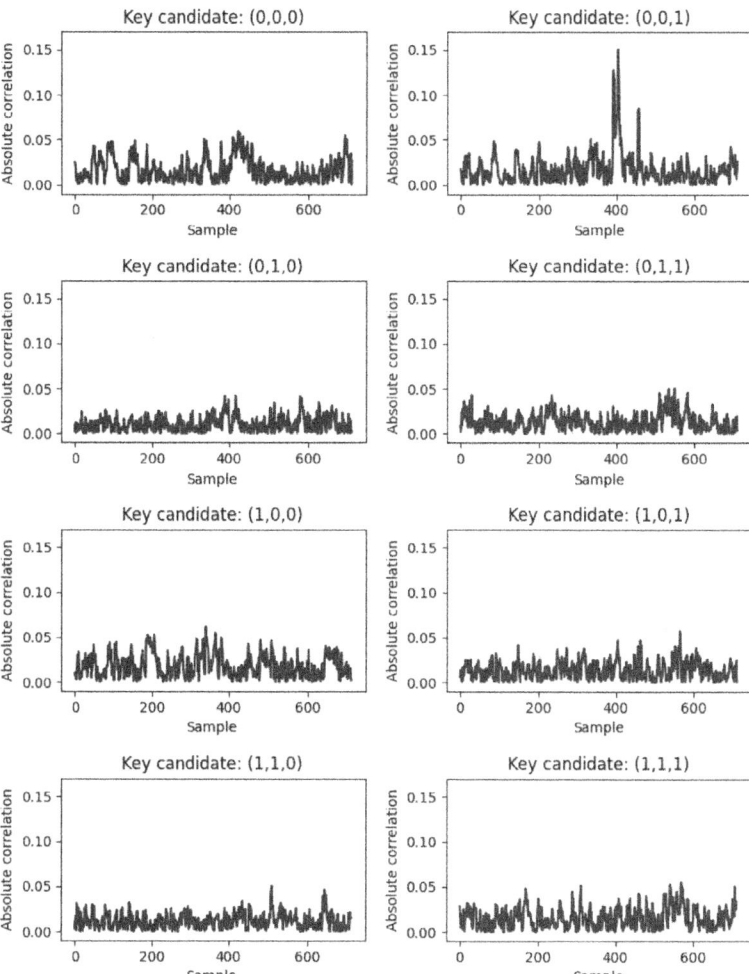

Fig. 4. Correlation traces for all key candidates when using $\tilde{z}_0^j$ as the intermediate variable. Peaks appear in the correlation trace corresponding to the correct key candidate $(k_0^j, k_0^{j+36}, k_0^{j+45}) = (0, 0, 1)$. The calculations use 1000 traces recorded from the execution of the reference implementation.

Impact of Linear Diffusion Layer. Recall that Daemen and Samwel [21] choose the linear diffusion layer output as the attack point since it is where the registers locate in their hardware implementation. In software implementations, the term "register" refers to variables or memory locations used to emulate the behavior of hardware registers. Thus, a variable update after an operation can be seen as a register activity consuming power. Previously, we demonstrated that the pure S-box output $(y_0^j, y_1^j, y_2^j, y_3^j)$ produce distributions that are correlated to each other for some pairs of key candidates (Table 2). This leads to the fact that employing one of $y_0^j, y_1^j, y_2^j, y_3^j$ as the intermediate variable results in multiple key candidates ranking equally with the correct key. We then showed that the fine-tuned S-box functions $(\tilde{y}_0^j, \tilde{y}_1^j, \tilde{y}_4^j)$ yield distributions that are uncorrelated for all possible pairs of key candidates (Table 4). Now, we are interested in investigating whether $\tilde{y}_0^j, \tilde{y}_1^j, \tilde{y}_4^j$ are also good choices for the intermediate variable (in addition to $\tilde{z}_0^j, \tilde{z}_1^j, \tilde{z}_4^j$) in software implementations. In other words, we aim to determine whether accounting for the linear operations really impacts the success of CPA attacks, or is just primarily relevant for attacks targeting hardware implementations with registers at the output of the linear diffusion layer (as in [21]).

Let us consider $\tilde{y}_0^j$ from Eq. 5 with two possible key candidates, $k_0^j = 0$ and $k_0^j = 1$. Below are the results of $\tilde{y}_0^j$ for each key candidate:

$$\tilde{y}_0^j = k_0^j(n_1^j \oplus 1) \oplus n_0^j = \begin{cases} n_0^j & \text{if } k_0^j = 0, \\ n_0^j \oplus n_1^j \oplus 1 & \text{if } k_0^j = 1. \end{cases}$$

We will use the visualization of peaks in correlation traces for explanation. First, when $k_0^j = 0$, $\tilde{y}_0^j = n_0^j$, meaning that the values of the intermediate variable $\tilde{y}_0^j$ are identical to the values of the nonce bit n_0^j. As a result, the values of $\tilde{y}_0^j$ become correlated with the power consumption caused by the activity of the registers containing n_0^j (in addition to that of the registers containing y_0^j). Consequently, many peaks appear in the correlation trace for $k_0^j = 0$, as the blue peaks shown in Fig. 5a. To support this explanation, we determine the locations where the activity of the registers containing n_0^j cause the power consumption, as illustrated by the light gray peaks in Fig. 5a.[4]

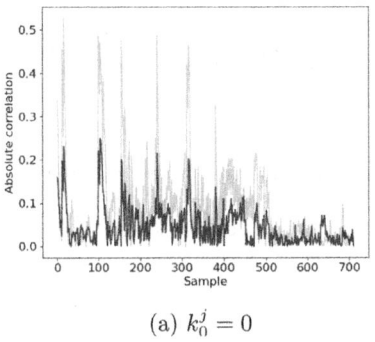
(a) $k_0^j = 0$

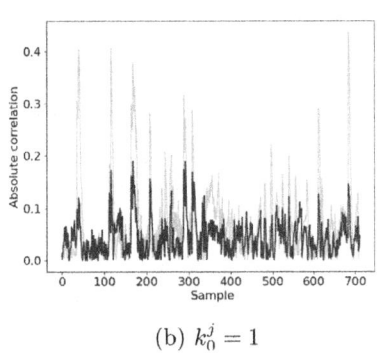
(b) $k_0^j = 1$

Fig. 5. Correlation traces when using $\tilde{y}_0^j$ as the intermediate variable. The calculations use 1000 traces recorded from the execution of the reference implementation. (Color figure online)

---

[4] For each of the recorded nonces, we extract a byte value from the 64-bit word n_0 that contains the bit n_0^j. We then compute the correlation between the Hamming weights of those values and the power traces.

Second, when $k_0^j = 1$, $\tilde{y}_0^j = n_0^j \oplus n_1^j \oplus 1$, meaning that the values of the intermediate variable $\tilde{y}_0^j$ are the inverse of $n_0^j \oplus n_1^j$ (correlation coefficient of -1). In the S-box computation shown in Listing 1.2 (Sect. C), there does exist the operation $n_0^j \oplus n_1^j$. As a result, the values of $\tilde{y}_0^j$ become correlated with the power consumption caused by this operation, leading to the appearance of many peaks in the correlation trace for $k_0^j = 1$, as the blue peaks shown in Fig. 5b. Similarly to before, we identify the locations where the activity of the operation $n_0^j \oplus n_1^j$ causes the power consumption, as illustrated by the light gray peaks in Fig. 5b, to support our argument.

To sum up, high peaks appear in correlation traces for all key candidates, making the CPA prone to failure in recovering the correct key. The analyses on $\tilde{y}_4^j$ and $\tilde{y}_1^j$ yield analogous results. In contrast, peaks appear only for the correct key candidate when the linear diffusion layer is accounted for, as in Fig. 4. This demonstrates that the linear diffusion layer in the selection functions of $\tilde{z}_0^j$ (Eq. 7) and $\tilde{z}_1^j$ (Eq. 8) plays an important role in the success of the CPA attacks, even in software implementations.

4 Second-Order Correlation Power Analysis

In the previous section, we thoroughly analyzed various approaches for choosing the intermediate variable and the selection function, along with their impact on the success of CPA attacks. Our analysis shows that $\tilde{z}_0^j$ (Eq. 7) and $\tilde{z}_1^j$ (Eq. 8) are effective choices for the intermediate variables to recover the first and the second halves of the key. In this section, we apply these two selection functions in order to perform a second-order CPA attack on a masked software implementation with two shares. For our experiment, we use the 32-bit ARMv6 implementation[5] submitted to the call for protected software implementations of finalists in the NIST lightweight cryptography standardization process by the ASCON team.[6]

We begin by configuring an encryption execution with the minimum number of rounds, using empty associated data and an empty plaintext (i.e., associated data and plaintext with length of 0) to skip the internal permutation blocks (see Fig. 1). The execution thus consists of 24 rounds: 12 rounds for the initialization phase and 12 rounds for the finalization phase. During an execution of these 24 rounds, we record a power consumption trace. Variance calculations are then applied to determine the length and starting index of each round, based on the assumption that the correctly aligned frames will minimize variance (i.e., 24 frames should align well when overlapped). Figure 6a shows the power consumption trace for the first 12 rounds of the initialization phase, while Fig. 6b illustrates the frame corresponding to the first round, consisting of 1400 samples. We focus on the power consumption of this first round, as our attack utilizes the linear diffusion layer outputs $\tilde{z}_0^j$ and $\tilde{z}_1^j$ as intermediate variables.

---

[5] https://github.com/ascon/simpleserial-ascon, in `protected_bi32_armv6`.
[6] https://cryptography.gmu.edu/athena/LWC/Call_for_Protected_Software_Imple mentations.pdf.

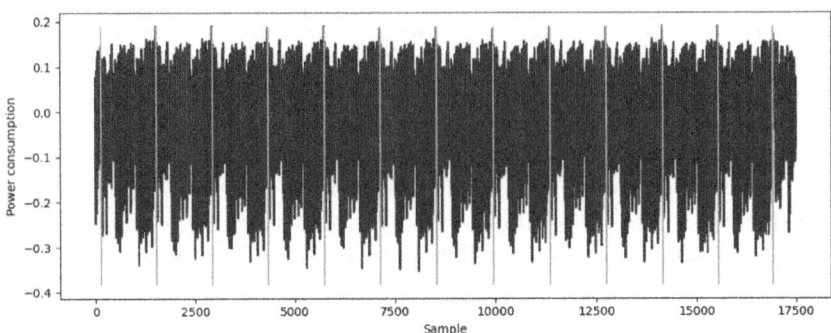

(a) Power consumption of the first 12 rounds.

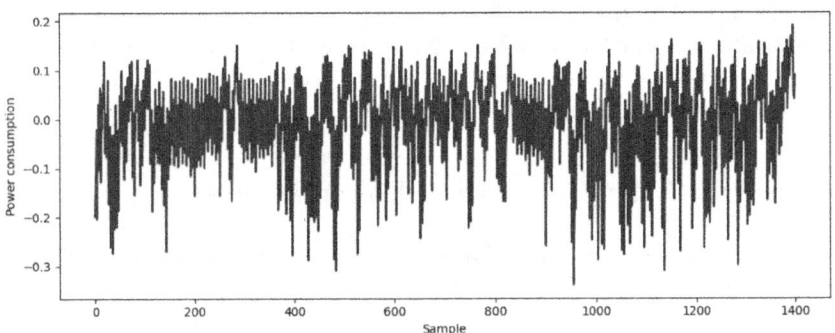

(b) Power consumption of the first round.

Fig. 6. Power consumption of initialization rounds.

4.1 First-Order Leakage Assessment

In the repository of the targeted masked software implementation,[6] the authors reported that the 2-share implementation might leak information due to potential collisions between the two shares in hardware. However, they introduced device-specific fixes to prevent first-order leakages, specifically by inserting an MOV instruction with a value of 0 at appropriate locations to avoid these collisions.

Using a similar hardware platform (STM32F303), we expect these fixes to remain effective in our experiment. To verify the absence of first-order leakages in the 2-share implementation under attack, we employ the widely used Test Vector Leakage Assessment (TVLA) [10]. This methodology applies a non-specific, fixed vs. random t-test statistic on two sets of traces, one with a fixed input and the other with random inputs. The t-score at the i-th sample, denoted as $\Delta[i]$, is computed as:

$$\Delta[i] = \frac{\mu_{\mathrm{f}}[i] - \mu_{\mathrm{r}}[i]}{\sqrt{\dfrac{\sigma_{\mathrm{f}}^2[i]}{n_{\mathrm{f}}} + \dfrac{\sigma_{\mathrm{r}}^2[i]}{n_{\mathrm{r}}}}}$$

where μ_f, σ_f, and n_f (resp. μ_r, σ_r, and n_r) represent the estimated mean, standard deviation, and the number of traces for the fix-input set (resp. random-input set). Leakage is detected if the absolute t-score exceeds the commonly used threshold of 4.5, in which case the null hypothesis that the means of the two sets are similar is rejected.

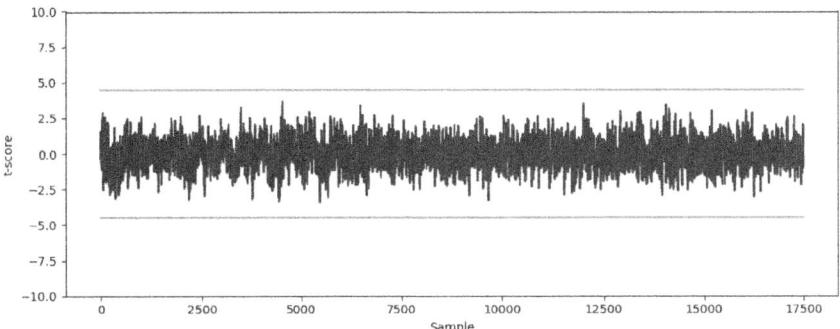

Fig. 7. Non-specific t-test on the first 12 rounds with 300,000 traces ($n_f = n_r = 150,000$).

Figure 7 shows the t-test results for all the time samples of the traces recorded during the execution of the first 12 rounds. As expected, no first-order leakages are observed, ensuring that we will not accidentally exploit them in our second-order CPA attack.

4.2 Pre-processing Power Traces

A second-order CPA attack consists of two phases: power traces pre-processing and the standard CPA. In the first phase, samples within a trace are combined to produce a *pre-processed trace*. This combination can cause the length of each trace to increase quadratically, significantly raising the attack complexity. Therefore, we detail the pre-processing steps below to ensure that the attack remains time and memory efficient in practice.

Let $\mathbf{t} = [t_1, \ldots, t_s]$ represent a power trace containing s samples, where in our case, $s = 1400$. We can combine the samples within $\mathbf{t}$ using various methods, such as normalized product, absolute difference, or sum [17,23]. Among these, the normalized product has been shown to be the most effective when applying Pearson's correlation coefficient with the Hamming weight leakage model [23]. In this work, we adopt the normalized product for trace pre-processing. According to this method, the sample $t'_{i,j}$ in the pre-processed trace $\mathbf{t}'$ derived from two power samples t_i and t_j ($1 \leq i, j \leq s$) in $\mathbf{t}$, is calculated as:

$$t'_{i,j} = (t_i - \bar{t}_i)(t_j - \bar{t}_j),$$

where $\bar{t}_i$ (resp. $\bar{t}_j$) is the estimated mean computed over all the traces at the i-th (resp. j-th) sample. There are a total of $s(s+1)/2 = 980700$ possible pairs (i,j) from $s = 1400$ samples. This large number will significantly increase the time and memory cost of the CPA. However, we note that the computation of the shares of the first round output occurs within a limited time span, making it unnecessary to consider all possible pairs. To address this, we introduce a parameter called the *window size*, denoted w, which estimates the maximum distance between the leakages of the two shares in the trace **t**. Thus, for the first $s-w$ samples ($i \in [1, s-w]$), there are w possible indexes j for each i. For the last w samples, there are a total of $w(w+1)/2$ possible pairs of (i,j). Consequently, the number of samples in the pre-processed trace **t'** (*i.e.*, the number of pairs (i,j)) becomes:

$$W = (s-w)w + \frac{w(w+1)}{2} = w\left(s - \frac{w-1}{2}\right).$$

To further reduce the number of samples s in **t**, we make an educated assumption that the S-box computation typically dominates the computation time in a round. Moreover, the less costly linear diffusion computation (*i.e.*, the attack point) occurs near the end of the round. Based on this insight, we focus on the last quarter of the samples in each trace. Specifically, we consider the last 350 samples (from 1050 to 1400 in Fig. 6b). This reduces the value of s to 350. Additionally, we set the window size to $w = 50$. With these parameters, the number of samples in each pre-processed trace becomes $W = 16275$.

4.3 Optimal Number of CPA Runs

In the second phase of the attack, the standard CPA, as described in Sect. 2, is applied to the pre-processed traces. Since this is a conventional approach, we omit the details and instead focus on optimizing the number of CPA runs required for the full key recovery.

Recall that each application of the CPA recovers three bits of k_0, indexed by $(j, j+36, j+45)$, or three bits of k_1, indexed by $(j, j+3, j+25)$, where $0 \le j \le 63$ (with additions implicitly modulo 64). To recover the full 128-bit key, the CPA must be applied multiple times to different tuples of key bit indexes. These tuples must collectively cover all indexes from 0 to 63 for both k_0 and k_1. Minimizing the number of such tuples is crucial to reduce the effort required for the attack. For example, performing the CPA three times to recover the key bits of k_0 at the tuples of indexes $(0, 36, 45)$, $(19, 55, 0)$ and $(28, 0, 9)$ (corresponding to $j = 0$, $j = 19$ and $j = 28$, respectively) results in the bit at index 0 being recovered three times, which is redundant.

To address this, we investigate the minimum number of index tuples. Weissbart and Picek [26] reported that 30 CPA runs are needed to recover k_0 and 33 runs to recover k_1, totaling 63 runs. In this work, we formalize the problem as a set cover problem and solve it using a SAT solver.

Let o_0 and o_1 be two offsets, $(o_0, o_1) = (36, 45)$ for k_0 and $(o_0, o_1) = (3, 25)$ for k_1. The problem is stated as follows: given a *universe* of elements $\mathcal{U} =$

$\{0, 1, \ldots, 63\}$ and a collection of 64 tuples $\mathcal{S} = \{(j, j + o_0, j + o_1) | j \in [0, 63]\}$ (with additions implicitly modulo 64), find the *smallest* sub-collection $\mathcal{S}' \subseteq \mathcal{S}$ whose union covers the universe, *i.e.* $\cup_{\text{tup} \in \mathcal{S}'} \text{tup} = \mathcal{U}$.

Although the set cover problem is known as NP-hard, it is conceivable that a solution may be found for problems of smaller scale. To this end, we represent the problem as a SAT problem. Each tuple $\text{tup}_j = (j, j + o_0, j + o_1) \in \mathcal{S}$ is represented by a Boolean variable b_j, where $b_j = 1$ (true) if $\text{tup}_j \in \mathcal{S}'$ and $b_j = 0$ (false) otherwise. To ensure full coverage of the universe, we impose that, for each $n \in [0, 63]$, at least one variable corresponding to the tuples that contains n should be true, *i.e.*, $\bigvee_{n \in \text{tup}_j} b_j = 1$. Additionally, we enforce a cardinality constraint to limit the number of selected tuples, $\sum_{j=0}^{63} b_j < \text{MAX}$, where MAX is a parameter, and the sum is over integers. We transform this constraint into SAT clauses following [22] and employ the SAT solver CryptoMiniSat[7] to find solutions for various values of MAX. The smallest MAX satisfying the SAT problem determines the minimum number of CPA runs. The Python script for this optimization is provided in Sect. B.

Our results show that only 23 CPA runs are needed for k_0 and 24 for k_1, reducing the total to 47 runs. These results are obtained within a few seconds after executing the Python script. It is worth noting that imposing a smaller cardinality constraint leads to unsatisfiable problems within seconds. Therefore, the reported number of CPA runs is optimal.

4.4 Results of Key Recovery

To efficiently perform the CPA with a large number of traces, we implement an *incremental* second-order CPA as introduced by Bottinelli and Bos [5]. This approach enables to gradually compute Pearson's correlation coefficients with a smaller, tunable number of traces instead of processing the entire dataset at once. Additionally, the trace pre-processing is performed on-the-fly. Recall that $\tilde{z}_0^j$ (Eq. 7) and $\tilde{z}_1^j$ (Eq. 8) are used to recover the two halves (k_0, k_1) of the key, three bits at a time.

Figure 8 shows the results of the second-order CPA for recovering three bits of k_0 using $\tilde{z}_0^j$ as the selection function. Several peaks corresponding to the correct key are clearly visible at around sample 2848. Figure 9 illustrates how the correlation coefficients depend on the number of traces. It can be observed that around 100K traces are required for the second-order CPA to reliably distinguish the correct key from the others.

We present the dependence between the success rate and the number of power traces for the full key recovery in Fig. 10. Since directly measuring the success rate for the full key recovery is time-consuming, we employ an estimation approach. Specifically, we measure the success rates of recovering three key bits of k_0 and k_1 by performing the CPA 100 times with different index tuples. These success rates obtained are then raised to the power of 23 and 24, respectively,

---

[7] https://github.com/msoos/cryptominisat.

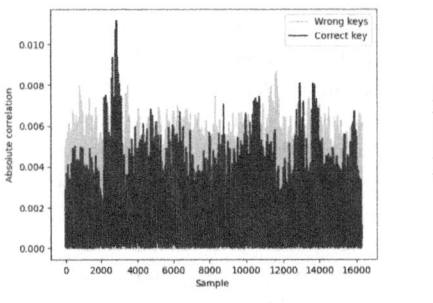 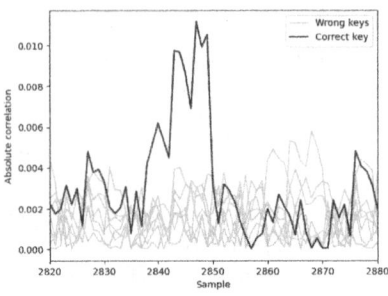

(a) Full-length correlation traces (b) Zoomed-in view of the peak

Fig. 8. Correlation traces for all key candidates. The calculations use 300K traces.

reflecting the number of CPA runs needed to recover the full 128-bit key. Multiplying these two results provide an estimate of the success rate for full key recovery. As in Fig. 10, about 360,000 traces are sufficient to achieve 100% success for the full key recovery. To validate this estimation, we perform an actual full key recovery experiment using 360,000 traces. As expected, we succeeded in recovering the full 128-bit key in about 4.7 h.

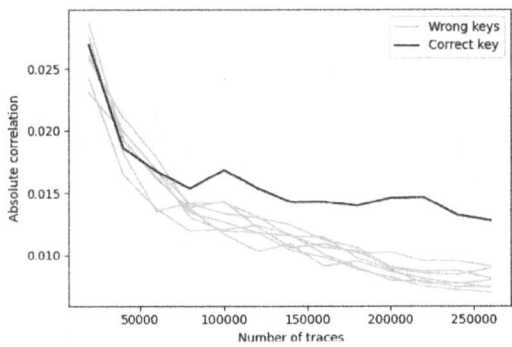

Fig. 9. Correlation for all key candidates depending on the number of traces.

In our second-order CPA, the analysis phase is very efficient as we implement the incremental computation [5] to process a small number of traces at a time. For example, if we set this number to 20,000, the computation consumes 0.06 GB of RAM and takes about 30 s. To recover three bits of the key with 100% success rate, we need to process 360,000 traces, which thus takes 9 min, while the memory cost (0.06 GB) does not change thanks to the incremental computation. We can run several CPAs on different tuples of key bit recoveries in parallel to accelerate the process. The most time-consuming phase of the attack is the collection of the power traces. With a collection speed of 448 traces per minute, acquiring 360,000 traces requires approximately 13.4 h to ensure a 100% success rate.

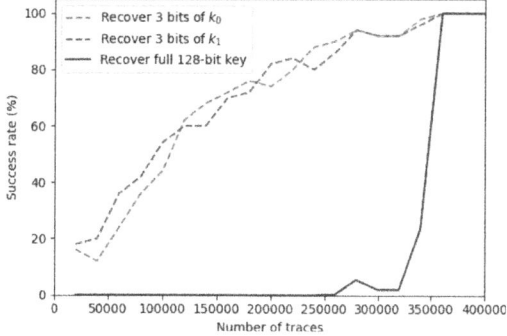

Fig. 10. Success rate of the full key recovery.

5 Conclusion and Perspectives

In this paper, we investigated various aspects of the CPA attack on (protected) software implementations of ASCON. We first provided a thorough analysis of the impact of different approaches for choosing the selection function on the success of the attack. Building on these insights, we presented the first practical and successful second-order CPA attack against a masked software implementation. We demonstrated how the attack can be performed efficiently with modest time and memory resources. By validating our attack path on the 32-bit ARMv6 masked implementation provided by the ASCON team, we successfully recovered the full 128-bit key in 4.7 h using 360,000 power traces. In conclusion, this work provides a deeper understanding of selection functions in CPA attacks and a concrete demonstration of their effectiveness against masked implementations.

This work focuses exclusively on 1-bit selection functions. A promising direction for future research is to explore how multi-bit selection functions could further reduce the number of traces required for successful attacks, potentially enhancing the efficiency of CPA attacks against protected implementations.

Acknowledgements. We sincerely thank the anonymous reviewers for their valuable suggestions, which helped improve this paper. This work was supported by the French *Agence Nationale de la Recherche* through the grant ANR-22-CE39-0008 (project PROPHY).

A Derivation of Selection Functions

The j-th bit of y_1 and y_4 are computed as:

$$y_1^j = n_0^j(k_1^j \oplus k_0^j \oplus 1) \oplus n_1^j \oplus k_1^j k_0^j \oplus k_1^j \oplus k_0^j \oplus \text{IV}^j,$$
$$y_4^j = n_1^j(k_0^j \oplus 1) \oplus n_0^j \oplus k_0^j \text{IV}^j \oplus k_0^j.$$

In y_1^j, we remove $k_1^j k_0^j \oplus k_1^j \oplus k_0^j \oplus \mathrm{IV}^j$ as they contribute a constant amount to the power consumption. For the same reason, $k_0^j \mathrm{IV}^j \oplus k_0^j$ is removed in y_4^j. The fine-tuned versions of y_1^j and y_4^j, denoted by $\tilde{y}_1^j$ and $\tilde{y}_4^j$, are:

$$\tilde{y}_1^j = n_0^j(k_{01}^j \oplus 1) \oplus n_1^j,$$
$$\tilde{y}_4^j = n_1^j(k_0^j \oplus 1) \oplus n_0^j,$$

where $k_{01}^j = k_0^j \oplus k_1^j$.

Recall the linear operations applied on the y_1 and y_4:

$$z_1 = y_1 \oplus (y_1 \ggg 61) \oplus (y_1 \ggg 39),$$
$$z_4 = y_4 \oplus (y_4 \ggg 7) \oplus (y_4 \ggg 41).$$

The j-th bit of z_1 and z_4 are thus computed as:

$$z_1^j = y_1^j \oplus y_1^{j+3} \oplus y_1^{j+25},$$
$$z_4^j = y_4^j \oplus y_4^{j+57} \oplus y_4^{j+23}.$$

We then apply the linear operations for $\tilde{y}_1^j$ and $\tilde{y}_4^j$. The fine-tuned versions of z_1^j and z_4^j, denoted by $\tilde{z}_1^j$ and $\tilde{z}_4^j$, are::

$$\tilde{z}_1^j = \left(n_0^j(k_{01}^j \oplus 1) \oplus n_1^j\right)$$
$$\oplus \left(n_0^{j+3}(k_{01}^{j+3} \oplus 1) \oplus n_1^{j+3}\right) \qquad (9)$$
$$\oplus \left(n_0^{j+25}(k_{01}^{j+25} \oplus 1) \oplus n_1^{j+25}\right).$$

$$\tilde{z}_4^j = \left(n_1^j(k_0^j \oplus 1) \oplus n_0^j\right)$$
$$\oplus \left(n_1^{j+57}(k_0^{j+57} \oplus 1) \oplus n_0^{j+57}\right) \qquad (10)$$
$$\oplus \left(n_1^{j+23}(k_0^{j+23} \oplus 1) \oplus n_0^{j+23}\right).$$

B Tuples of Indexes for Key Recovery

```
import pycryptosat as cs
import sys

# Cardinality constraint system proposed by Sinz
# sSat: the CNF system used
# setId: list of the variable id of the set
# nb_sets: number of sets
```

```python
# cc: cardinality constraint
# startextra: index of additional variable unused so far,
    can be a value large enough
# For more details C. Sinz, Towards an Optimal CNF Encoding
    of Boolean Cardinality Constraints.
def Cardinality_Constraints(sSat,setId,nb_sets,cc,
    startextra):
    sSat.add_clause([-(setId[0]), startextra])
    for j in range (2,cc+1):
        sSat.add_clause([-(startextra+j-1)])
    for i in range(2,nb_sets):
        sSat.add_clause([-(setId[i-1]),
                        startextra+(cc)*(i-1)])
        sSat.add_clause([-(startextra+(cc)*(i-2)),
                        startextra+(cc)*(i-1)])
        for j in range(2,cc+1):
            sSat.add_clause([-(setId[i-1]),
                            -(startextra+cc*(i-2)+j-2),
                            startextra+(i-1)*cc+j-1])
            sSat.add_clause([-(startextra+cc*(i-2)+j-1),
                            startextra+(i-1)*cc+j-1])
        sSat.add_clause([-(setId[i-1]),
                        -(startextra+cc*(i-2)+cc-1)])
    sSat.add_clause([-(setId[nb_sets-1]),
                    -(startextra+cc*(nb_sets-2)+cc-1)])
    startextra+=(nb_sets-1)*cc

if __name__ == "__main__":
    # Arguments
    # Run 'python3 64 36 45 23' for k0
    # Run 'python3 64 3 25 24' for k1
    n  = int(sys.argv[1]) # n = 64 indexes
    s1 = int(sys.argv[2]) # 1st shift
    s2 = int(sys.argv[3]) # 2nd shift
    ub = int(sys.argv[4]) # upper bound for number of
    subsets

    # Compute all subset
    list_set=[]
    for i in range(n):
        list_set.append([i,(i+s1)%n,(i+s2)%n])

    # Save the universe
    universe=list(range(n))

    # Create the solver object
    sSat=cs.Solver()

    # Add constraint
```

```python
    # For each element of the universe, we should select at least one subset containing the element
    for i in universe:
        # create an empty disjuction
        clause_presence=[]
        for j in list_set:
            # if subset j contains the element i, we add the variable corresponding to the set j to the disjunctions
            if i in j:
                clause_presence += [list_set.index(j)+1]
        # One variable in clause_presence must be set to true
        # Add disjunction to the conjunction
        sSat.add_clause(clause_presence)

    # Cardinality constraints
    Cardinality_Constraints(sSat,
                list(range(1,len(list_set)+1)),
                len(list_set),
                ub,
                len(list_set)+1)

    # solve it
    satq,solution=sSat.solve()
    # SAT or UNSAT
    print(satq)
    # if SAT print the solution
    if(satq):
        # for all variable corresponding to a subset
        for i in range(1,len(list_set)+1):
            # if True then the subset has been selected
            if solution[i]:
                print(list_set[i-1])
            # else the subset has not been selected each element of this subset should appear in at least one other selected subset
```

Listing 1.1. Python script to find the minimum number of tuples.

(Table 6)

Table 6. Tuples of indexes for each 3-bit key recovery. The number of tuples should be minimized while the range from 0 to 63 must be covered.

23 tuples for k_0		24 tuples for k_1	
$(j, j+36, j+45)$		$(j, j+3, j+25)$	
(1,37,46)	(29, 1,10)	(3, 6,28)	(34,37,59)
(2,38,47)	(32, 4,13)	(5, 8,30)	(39,42, 0)
(5,41,50)	(35, 7,16)	(6, 9,31)	(41,44, 2)
(8,44,53)	(39,11,20)	(7,10,32)	(43,46, 4)
(11,47,56)	(42,14,23)	(13,16,38)	(45,48, 6)
(12,48,57)	(45,17,26)	(15,18,40)	(50,53,11)
(15,51,60)	(49,21,30)	(17,20,42)	(51,54,12)
(18,54,63)	(52,24,33)	(22,25,47)	(52,55,13)
(19,55, 0)	(55,27,36)	(24,27,49)	(53,56,14)
(22,58, 3)	(59,31,40)	(26,29,51)	(58,61,19)
(25,61, 6)	(62,34,43)	(32,35,57)	(60,63,21)
(28, 0, 9)		(33,36,58)	(62, 1,23)

C Impact of Linear Layer in Selection Function

```
1  x0 = x0 ^ x4
2  x4 = x4 ^ x3           // n0 ^ n1 (in the first round)
3  x2 = x2 ^ x1
4  // Start of keccak S-box
5  t0 = x0 ^ (~x1 & x2)
6  t1 = x1 ^ (~x2 & x3)
7  t2 = x2 ^ (~x3 & x4)
8  t3 = x3 ^ (~x4 & x0)
9  t4 = x4 ^ (~x0 & x1)
10 // End of keccak S-box
11 y0 = t0 ^ t4
12 y1 = t1 ^ t0
13 y2 = ~t2
14 y3 = t3 ^ t2
15 y4 = t4
```

Listing 1.2. C implementation of Ascon S-box.

References

1. Advanced Encryption Standard (AES): National Institute of Standards and Technology, NIST FIPS PUB 197, U.S. Department of Commerce (2001)
2. Batina, L., Gierlichs, B., Prouff, E., Rivain, M., Standaert, F.X., Veyrat-Charvillon, N.: Mutual information analysis: a comprehensive study. J. Cryptol. **24**(2), 269–291 (2011). https://doi.org/10.1007/s00145-010-9084-8

3. Bertoni, G., Daemen, J., Debande, N., Le, T.H., Peeters, M., Van Assche, G.: Power analysis of hardware implementations protected with secret sharing. In: 2012 45th Annual IEEE/ACM International Symposium on Microarchitecture Workshops, pp. 9–16 (2012). https://doi.org/10.1109/MICROW.2012.12
4. Bertoni, G., Daemen, J., Peeters, M., Van Assche, G.: Duplexing the sponge: single-pass authenticated encryption and other applications. In: Miri, A., Vaudenay, S. (eds.) SAC 2011. LNCS, vol. 7118, pp. 320–337. Springer, Berlin, Heidelberg (2012). https://doi.org/10.1007/978-3-642-28496-0_19
5. Bottinelli, P., Bos, J.W.: Computational aspects of correlation power analysis. J. Cryptogr. Eng. **7**(3), 167–181 (2017). https://doi.org/10.1007/s13389-016-0122-9
6. Brier, E., Clavier, C., Olivier, F.: Correlation power analysis with a leakage model. In: Joye, M., Quisquater, J.J. (eds.) CHES 2004. LNCS, vol. 3156, pp. 16–29. Springer, Berlin, Heidelberg (2004). https://doi.org/10.1007/978-3-540-28632-5_2
7. Chari, S., Jutla, C.S., Rao, J.R., Rohatgi, P.: Towards sound approaches to counteract power-analysis attacks. In: Wiener, M.J. (ed.) CRYPTO 1999. LNCS, vol. 1666, pp. 398–412. Springer, Berlin, Heidelberg (1999). https://doi.org/10.1007/3-540-48405-1_26
8. Chari, S., Rao, J.R., Rohatgi, P.: Template attacks. In: Kaliski Jr., B.S., Koç, Çetin Kaya., Paar, C. (eds.) CHES 2002. LNCS, vol. 2523, pp. 13–28. Springer, Berlin, Heidelberg (2003). https://doi.org/10.1007/3-540-36400-5_3
9. Dobraunig, C., Eichlseder, M., Mendel, F., Schläffer, M.: Ascon v1.2: lightweight authenticated encryption and hashing. J. Cryptology **34**(3), 33 (2021). https://doi.org/10.1007/s00145-021-09398-9
10. Goodwill, G., Jun, B., Jaffe, J., Rohatgi, P.: A testing methodology for side channel resistance validation. NIST non-invasive attack testing workshop (2011). https://csrc.nist.rip/news_events/non-invasive-attack-testing-workshop/papers/08_Goodwill.pdf
11. Goubin, L., Patarin, J.: DES and differential power analysis (the "duplication" method). In: Koç, Çetin Kaya., Paar, C. (eds.) CHES'99. LNCS, vol. 1717, pp. 158–172. Springer, Berlin, Heidelberg (1999). https://doi.org/10.1007/3-540-48059-5_15
12. Joye, M., Paillier, P., Schoenmakers, B.: On second-order differential power analysis. In: Rao, J.R., Sunar, B. (eds.) CHES 2005. LNCS, vol. 3659, pp. 293–308. Springer, Berlin, Heidelberg (2005). https://doi.org/10.1007/11545262_22
13. Kocher, P.C., Jaffe, J., Jun, B.: Differential power analysis. In: Wiener, M.J. (ed.) CRYPTO 1999. LNCS, vol. 1666, pp. 388–397. Springer, Berlin, Heidelberg (1999). https://doi.org/10.1007/3-540-48405-1_25
14. Luo, S., Wu, W., Li, Y., Zhang, R., Liu, Z.: An efficient soft analytical side-channel attack on ascon. Springer-Verlag, Berlin, Heidelberg (2022). https://doi.org/10.1007/978-3-031-19208-1_32
15. Maghrebi, H., Portigliatti, T., Prouff, E.: Breaking cryptographic implementations using deep learning techniques. Cryptology ePrint Archive, Report 2016/921 (2016). https://eprint.iacr.org/2016/921
16. Messerges, T.S.: Using second-order power analysis to attack DPA resistant software. In: Koç, Çetin Kaya., Paar, C. (eds.) CHES 2000. LNCS, vol. 1965, pp. 238–251. Springer, Berlin, Heidelberg (2000). https://doi.org/10.1007/3-540-44499-8_19
17. Prouff, E., Rivain, M., Bévan, R.: Statistical analysis of second order differential power analysis. Cryptology ePrint Archive, Report 2010/646 (2010). https://eprint.iacr.org/2010/646

18. Ramezanpour, K., Abdulgadir, A., Diehl, W., Kaps, J.P., , Ampadu, P.: Active and passive side-channel key recovery attacks on Ascon. NIST Lightweight Cryptography Workshop (2020). https://csrc.nist.gov/CSRC/media/Events/lightweight-cryptography-workshop-2020/documents/papers/active-passive-recovery-attacks-ascon-lwc2020.pdf, https://csrc.nist.gov/CSRC/media/Events/lightweight-cryptography-workshop-2020/documents/papers/active-passive-recovery-attacks-ascon-lwc2020.pdf
19. Rezaeezade, A., Basurto-Becerra, A., Weissbart, L., Perin, G.: One for all, all for ascon: ensemble-based deep learning side-channel analysis. Cryptology ePrint Archive, Report 2023/1922 (2023). https://eprint.iacr.org/2023/1922
20. Roussel, N., Potin, O., Dutertre, J., Rigaud, J.: Security evaluation of a hybrid CMOS/MRAM ascon hardware implementation. In: Design, Automation & Test in Europe Conference & Exhibition, DATE 2023, Antwerp, Belgium, April 17–19, 2023, pp. 1–6. IEEE (2023). https://doi.org/10.23919/DATE56975.2023.10137126
21. Samwel, N., Daemen, J.: DPA on hardware implementations of Ascon and Keyak. In: CF 2017, Proceedings of the Computing Frontiers Conference, pp. 415–424. Association for Computing Machinery, New York, NY, USA (2017). https://doi.org/10.1145/3075564.3079067
22. Sinz, C.: Towards an optimal CNF encoding of boolean cardinality constraints. In: van Beek, P. (ed.) Principles and Practice of Constraint Programming - CP 2005, 11th International Conference, CP 2005, Sitges, Spain, October 1–5, 2005, Proceedings. Lecture Notes in Computer Science, vol. 3709, pp. 827–831. Springer (2005). https://doi.org/10.1007/11564751_73
23. Standaert, F.X., et al.: The world is not enough: another look on second-order DPA. In: Abe, M. (ed.) ASIACRYPT 2010. LNCS, vol. 6477, pp. 112–129. Springer, Berlin, Heidelberg (2010). https://doi.org/10.1007/978-3-642-17373-8_7
24. Veyrat-Charvillon, N., Gérard, B., Standaert, F.X.: Soft analytical side-channel attacks. In: Sarkar, P., Iwata, T. (eds.) ASIACRYPT 2014, Part I. LNCS, vol. 8873, pp. 282–296. Springer, Berlin, Heidelberg (2014). https://doi.org/10.1007/978-3-662-45611-8_15
25. Waddle, J., Wagner, D.: Towards efficient second-order power analysis. In: Joye, M., Quisquater, J.J. (eds.) CHES 2004. LNCS, vol. 3156, pp. 1–15. Springer, Berlin, Heidelberg (2004). https://doi.org/10.1007/978-3-540-28632-5_1
26. Weissbart, L., Picek, S.: Lightweight but not easy: side-channel analysis of the ascon authenticated cipher on a 32-bit microcontroller. Cryptology ePrint Archive, Paper 2023/1598 (2023). https://eprint.iacr.org/2023/1598
27. You, S.C., Kuhn, M.G., Sarkar, S., Hao, F.: Low trace-count template attacks on 32-bit implementations of ASCON AEAD. IACR TCHES **2023**(4), 344–366 (2023). https://doi.org/10.46586/tches.v2023.i4.344-366

Side-Channel Attacks

On the Success Rate of Simple Side-Channel Attacks Against Masking with Unlimited Attack Traces

Aymeric Hiltenbrand[1], Julien Eynard[2], and Romain Poussier[3(✉)]

[1] Univ Rennes, CNRS, Inria, IRISA Rennes, Rennes, France
[2] Rambus Inc., San Jose, USA
jeynard@rambus.com
[3] ANSSI, Pune, India
romain.poussier@inria.fr, romain.poussier@ssi.gouv.fr

Abstract. Side-channel attacks following a classical differential power analysis (DPA) style are well understood, along with the effect the masking countermeasure has on them. However, simple attacks (SPA) where the target variable does not vary thanks to a known value, such as the plaintext, are less studied. In this paper, we investigate how the masking countermeasure affects the success rate of simple attacks. To this end, we provide theoretical, simulated, and practical experiments. Interestingly, we will see that masking can allow us to asymptotically recover more information on the secret than in the case of an unprotected implementation, depending on the masking type. We will see that this is true for masking encodings that add non-linearity with respect to the leakages, such as arithmetic masking, while it is not for Boolean masking. We believe this context provides interesting results, as the average information of arithmetic encoding is proven less informative than the Boolean one.

Keywords: SPA · masking · success rate

1 Introduction

As opposed to classical cryptography, where an adversary has only access to the inputs and outputs of a primitive viewed as a black box, Side-Channel Attacks (SCAs) use additional information. This information comes from the physical implementation of a mathematical algorithm, and is referred to as leakage. This includes as an example the timing information [13], the power consumption [14], or the electromagnetic radiations [10]. This study concerns the last two types of leakages, where the adversary collects the corresponding information for each execution of a primitive, denoted as a power/electromagnetic trace.

Independently of the type of leakage used, SCAs can be divided into two categories: differential or simple. The former one, denoted as DPA, corresponds to the most usual case, where an adversary targets a sensitive variable that both depends on the secret and a known value. This can be the case when targeting the output of the AES Sbox for instance. Each trace comes from an AES execution, where the known plaintext is varying. Note that the "differential" term of DPA here refer to the dependency to a known *varying* variable, and not to Kocher's DPA [14]. The second type of attack, denoted as SPA, corresponds to the case where the target variable does not depend on any known varying value. This can happen for example when targeting the key scheduling of the AES [27], the key processing in Ascon [8], some Kyber [1] variables such as the output of the binomial sampler or a bus data transfer. The adversary can measure several executions of the algorithm, but the leakages will not include any variation regarding a known value. The existence or the lack of such dependency with a known value has a significant impact on these two types of attacks. For DPA, the use of an approximate leakage model can still allow to recover the secret, thanks to this dependency along with (e.g.) the non-linearity of the Sbox [20]. However, in the SPA context, the inaccuracy of the leakage model might have a significantly more negative impact. We further provide more description of the two attack scenarios in Sect. 2.6.

To protect against SCAs, independently of their nature, masking is a commonly used countermeasure [12]. It consists of splitting any sensitive value into independent shares using randomness, such that the combination of all shares is equal to the original sensitive value. For instance, the combination can be an addition over $\mathbb{F}_{2^k}$, such as Boolean masking [23], or an addition over $\mathbb{Z}_p$, as for arithmetic masking [18]. From a security perspective, the required number of traces to break an implementation increases exponentially with the number of shares, with respect to the noise level.

In this paper, we study the context of profiled SPAs against unprotected and 2-share masked (Boolean and arithmetic) implementations. For these different types of protection, we focus on the asymptotic success rates, denoting the probability of recovering a secret given an infinite number of attack traces. For a DPA, the asymptotic success rate is usually one even with a mediocre leakage model. This is true independently of the protection technique, as long as the attack order matches the masking level [15] and that the target variable has non-linearity such as an Sbox output. However, for SPA, we show that the asymptotic success rate can be lower, even assuming an infinite number of attack traces. Moreover, We further study the context of an imperfect profiling and its effect on the success rate, as real profiled attacks can never perfectly estimate the model. We believe that the specific context of SPA in combination with masking and asymptotic success rate is not well studied and can lead to counter-intuitive observations. More specifically, the contributions of this paper can be summarized as follows:

- First, we study the (unrealistic) context where the actual leakage function is known to the adversary, for both Hamming weight and bijective leakages. We show that arithmetic masking can help reaching a higher success rate than an unprotected implementation.

– Second, we study the more realistic context where an adversary approximates the leakage function through a profiling phase. This introduces incorrect profiling, where some classes can never be recovered. We show that this has more impact on non-linear encoding of arithmetic masking, even if it can reach higher success rates. Surprisingly, we also put in evidence cases where the asymptotic success rate is higher for an implementation with Boolean masking than for an unprotected one, for a similar profiling strength.
 – Finally, we validate the theoretical and simulated results using actual measurements.

The rest of the paper is organized as follows. First, Sect. 2 introduces the notions and background that are necessary for the rest of the paper, along with our simulated experimental setup. Second, Sect. 3 studies the unrealistic context where the adversary has perfect knowledge of the leakage function. Then, Sect. 4 shows what happens in a more realistic context, where an attacker can only estimate the actual leakage function through an actual profiling phase. Finally, Sect. 5 confirms the previous results using real leakages.

2 Background

2.1 Notations

We use capital letters for random variables and small caps for their realizations. We denote by $Pr\,[x]$ the probability a random variable X is equal to x. We denote the conditional probability of a random variable A given B with $Pr\,[A|B]$. We use a sans serif font for functions (e.g., F) and calligraphic fonts for sets (e.g., $\mathcal{A}$). Var denotes the variance, and HW denotes the Hamming weight function. We use bold notation for vectors (e.g. $\mathbf{v}$).

2.2 Leakage Model

Let X denote some n-bit variable processed at a given time. In the rest of this paper, we will assume an additive Gaussian noise [22,25] such that $L(X) = \mathsf{F}(X) + \mathcal{N}(0, \sigma^2_{noise})$. F denotes the deterministic part of the leakage, and $\mathcal{N}(0, \sigma^2_{noise})$ denotes the Gaussian noise with variance σ^2_{noise}. F can be generalized by the following linear polynomial [24] :

$$\mathsf{F}(x) = a + \sum_{i=0}^{n-1} a_i x_i \quad (1)$$

where x_i denotes the i-th bit of x. In the following, we will ignore the constant a without loss of generality. We will also study the common Hamming Weight leakage (HW) case where $\forall\, i,j \in [0, n-1]$, $a_i = a_j$.

2.3 Signal to Noise Ratio

The Signal-to-Noise Ratio [16] (SNR) is a commonly used information theory metric to measure the informativeness of the leakages. It is defined as the variance of F, representing the signal, divided by the noise level. Reusing the assumptions of the previous subsection, it can be computed as follows for a variable X:

$$\text{SNR} = \frac{\text{Var}_X(\mathsf{F}(X))}{\sigma_{noise}^2} \qquad (2)$$

2.4 Success Rate

The success rate is a security evaluation metric that is directly related to the number of traces necessary to mount an attack [25]. That is, the success rate is defined as the probability that the actual secret is completely recovered after the attack. If we define by $\mathbb{K}_V$ the random variable that outputs 1 if we guess the sensitive n-bit variable V properly for a given attack and 0 elsewise, we can define the success rate SR as:

$$\text{SR} = Pr\left[\mathbb{K}_V = 1\right] = \frac{1}{2^n} \sum_{v=0}^{2^n - 1} Pr\left[\mathbb{K}_V = 1 | V = v\right] \qquad (3)$$

Assuming that V has a uniform distribution. In our experiments, we will compute $Pr\left[\mathbb{K}_V = 1 | V = v\right]$ empirically by repeating an attack several times.

2.5 Masking

In this study, we will investigate the effect of the masking countermeasure in the context of SPA. Masking is a commonly used countermeasure to protect against side-channel attacks. The idea is to split any sensitive variable x into d shares s_i, $i \in [0, d-1]$, such that the knowledge of any $d-1$ shares does not give information on x. The corresponding circuit has to be modified into a masked circuit that computes over the shares instead of the original values, while still producing the correct result. There exist many masking types in the literature. In this study, we focus on Boolean and arithmetic ones.

Boolean Masking: This is the first masking proposal [12], and probably the most popular one in symmetric cryptography, such as the AES or hash functions. The d shares s_i are computed such that $x = \bigoplus_{0}^{d-1} s_i$, the addition being over $\mathbb{F}_{2^k}$.

Arithmetic Masking: Instead of having x as an element of a field of characteristic two, arithmetic masking [18] is typically used when x belongs to a ring of modular integers, not necessarily modulo a prime number. In this case, the d shares s_i are computed such that $x = \sum_{i=0}^{d-1} s_i \mod p$.

Security: The probing model [12] formalizes the security brought by the masking countermeasure. It ensures that the knowledge of any $d-1$ shares is independent of the original sensitive variable x. Upon a carefully masked implementation, the number of traces to recover a sensitive variable can grow exponentially with the number of shares, given enough noise [9].

2.6 Attack Type

Independently from the fact that an attack is profiled or not, one can split the context of the attack into two cases based on whether the target sensitive variable changes over the different runs of the algorithm, thanks to a varying known value.

DPA-like Scenario: In this paper, we denote by DPA-like (or simply DPA) any side-channel attack that targets some intermediate variable V using several traces such that $V = \mathsf{G}(K, M)$, where G denotes some function, K represents a fixed secret variable to recover and M a *known varying* variable over different observations. For instance, attacking the Sbox output of the AES falls into this category if the plaintext is known and varies over several trace acquisitions. Note that the scenario is independent of the attack method. Indeed, (e.g.) Kocher's DPA [14], CPA [4], MIA [11], template [7], Machine Learning [5] (and so on) all fall within the DPA scenario in this case.

SPA Scenario: As opposed to the DPA scenario defined above, in the SPA scenario, there is no dependency with a known varying value. An attack falls into this category if it targets some intermediate variable that only depends on the secret and potentially *unknown* varying values (e.g. randomness). Note that no assumption is made on the number of traces used for the attack. Attacking for example the key schedule of the AES, potentially using several observation traces, falls into this category as there is no variation at all. On the other hand, attacking the output of the AES Sbox with a single trace only or a fixed plaintext would also fall into this category. As for the DPA scenario, the category does not depend on the attack method.

Main Differences and Asymptotic Success Rate: This study will focus on the success rate of DPAs and SPAs when an infinite number of attack traces are used, which we refer to as *asymptotic success rate* and denote SR_∞.

In this context, the DPA scenario is well understood in the literature [25, 26]. The number of traces required to break an implementation depends on $\frac{1}{SNR^o}$ where o is the masking order ($o = 1$ for unprotected), when the SNR is low enough. An attack would eventually succeed given enough attack traces, assuming that the leakage model is close enough to the real one.

This is however quite different for SPAs. The secret might not be recovered even using an infinite number of attack traces, which can happen for several reasons. Assuming a non-bijective leakage function (e.g. HW), some hypotheses cannot be distinguished. Moreover, if the model is not perfect, a candidate might always be misclassified.

The asymptotic SR difference between DPA and SPA is due to the existence of the known varying input in the DPA context. In case of a wrong model or a non-bijective leakage function, the help of the other classes and the (hopefully) non-linearity of the function $\mathsf{G}(K, M)$ (e.g. an Sbox) will still help the attack to eventually succeed (assuming the model is not drastically far off the actual one).

In this study, we are interested in the impact of masking on the asymptotic success rate of an SPA. Up to our knowledge, this setting exhibits interesting observations which have not been shown before. The main intuition is that masking a fixed variable will introduce (unknown) variability, where there would be none in the unprotected SPA context. An example could be a masked implementation of the AES key schedule. We aim to study whether this added variability due to masking can improve the asymptotic complexity of a SPA, as opposed to an unmasked version of the algorithm. To answer this question, in the rest of this paper, we will compare the SPA results of an unmasked variable as opposed to its masked version. We will do so by considering two types of masking: Boolean and arithmetic. First, using a simulated setting, we will assume a perfect knowledge of the leakage function for the attacker, using both Hamming weight and a (more realistic) bijective linear leakage. Then, still using simulations, we will move to the more practical case where the actual leakages are not perfectly characterized. Finally, we will provide actual experiments to support our theoretical and simulated claims. From these settings, we will show that the question can be answered positively, showing that masking can increase SR_∞ of a SPA, especially for arithmetic masking.

Note that even if the asymptotic success rate of an attack can be improved thanks to masking, the main security property of the countermeasure still holds. That is, the required number of traces increases exponentially with the security order o [2]. However, this has no impact on this study as we are only interested in the asymptotic success rate given an infinite number of attack traces.

2.7 Simulation Setup

To exhibit the properties of SPAs, Sects. 3 and 4 will use the following simulated setting. We simulated leakages for four types of attacks: SPAs against unprotected, Boolean masking, arithmetic masking and finally a DPA against an unprotected implementation, used as a benchmark. All success rate calculations are done using 1000 repetitions. To speed up the computations, we targeted 4-bit values. To simulate the linear leakages introduced in Sect. 2.2, we randomly sampled each four coefficients a_i from a Normal distribution $\mathcal{N}(1, \sigma^2_{leakage})$ for each repetition of the experiment. The higher $\sigma^2_{leakage}$ is, the further from Hamming weight is the leakage function, as defined in 2.2, where a $\sigma^2_{leakage} = 0$ indicates an exact Hamming weight model. This allow us to control how far the leakage are from HW, and will use a value $\sigma^2_{leakage} = 10^{-4}$ in simulation as it will match its values obtained with real traces. The noise level σ^2_{noise} of the leakages is then set accordingly to match the desired SNR level.

Intermediate Values: For the DPA, we used the S-Box S of the Present cipher [3] and computed the intermediate value $v = \mathsf{S}(s \oplus p)$ for random plaintext p. The adversary is provided with the noisy leakage of v. For the unprotected SPA, we directly leak the noisy leakage of the sensitive variable. For the SPA against masked implementation, we leak two samples, one for each share.

Profiling: Except for Sect. 3 where we assume an adversary with perfect knowledge of the leakage function, we perform Gaussian template profiling. For each leakage sample (two in the case of masking), the adversary is provided with N_p leakages per value of the 4-bit variable, accounting for a total of $N_p \times 2^4$ traces for a 4-bit value. Note that this assumes a scenario where the adversary has access to the masking randomness for the profiling.

Attack: Using the profiled or known model, we use a maximum likelihood approach for the attacker, which computes $Pr[\mathbf{l}|k] = \prod_{i=1}^{N_a} Pr[l_i|k]$ using N_a attack traces. In case of masking, we compute $Pr[l_i|k] = \sum_{s_j} Pr[l_i|k, s_j] Pr[s_j]$ where s_j denotes the randomness guess used for the sharing. The masking randomness is not known during the attack phase. We emphasize that the conclusions of this study are independent of the distinguisher, and that similar results would be obtained with any profiled attack.

3 Perfect Profiling

In this section, we first study the (unrealistic) case where the adversary has perfect knowledge of the leakage function. More formally, during the attack, we assume the adversary knows exactly the deterministic part F of the leakages as introduced in Sect. 2.2. First, we will see the implication for a Hamming weight leakage function, before assuming more general linear leakages. For both cases, we study what SR_∞ can be achieved with and without the presence of masking in the context of SPA.

3.1 Hamming Weight Leakages

Assuming an adversary with the knowledge of $\mathsf{F} = \mathsf{HW}$, we are interested in evaluating SR_∞ for an unprotected, Boolean, and arithmetically masked value. We assume the attacker targets a uniformly distributed n-bit value v. We first show how the SR_∞ can be theoretically derived, before validating it using our simulated setting.

Unprotected: Without masking countermeasure, the adversary directly observes $\mathsf{HW}(v) + \mathcal{N}(0, \sigma_{noise}^2)$. In the perfect profiling setting, as we are interested with the asymptotic success rate, we can theoretically compute SR_∞ from Eq. 3 assuming noiseless leakages, where V denotes the n-bit sensitive variable:

$$SR_\infty = \frac{1}{2^n} \sum_{v=0}^{2^n-1} Pr\left[\not\models_V = 1 | V = v\right]$$

$$= \frac{1}{2^n} \sum_{v=0}^{2^n-1} \sum_{l=0}^{n} Pr\left[\not\models_V = 1 | V = v, \mathsf{HW}(v) = l\right] Pr\left[\mathsf{HW}(v) = l\right] \quad (4)$$

$$= \frac{1}{2^n} \sum_{v=0}^{2^n-1} \sum_{l=0}^{n} \frac{1}{\binom{n}{l}} \frac{\binom{n}{l}}{2^n} = \frac{1}{2^n} \sum_{v=0}^{2^n-1} \frac{n+1}{2^n} = \frac{n+1}{2^n}$$

Using $n = 4$ as an example, we would get $SR_\infty = 0.3125$. This success rate is computed assuming a uniformly distributed value v. Indeed, some values of v (e.g. $v = 0$ and $v = 15$) would be asymptotically recovered, while values such that $\mathsf{HW}(v) = 1$ would not.

Boolean masking: We now assume v is protected with 2-share Boolean masking. The adversary observes leakages on the shares s_0^v and s_1^v such that $v = s_0^v \oplus s_1^v$, which vary for each execution. That is, she is provided with $l_0 = \mathsf{HW}(s_0^v) + \mathcal{N}(0, \sigma_{noise}^2)$ and $l_1 = \mathsf{HW}(s_1^v) + \mathcal{N}(0, \sigma_{noise}^2)$. In this case, we can show that the asymptotic success rate is the same as for the unprotected case, which is derived from Proposition 1. The proof is provided in Appendix A.

Proposition 1. *Two unprotected values v_0 and v_1 have the same Hamming weight if, and only if, the two joint distributions of the Hamming weight of their shares are the same.*

Proposition 1 shows that, for noiseless Hamming weight leakages, the success rate for unprotected and Boolean masking are equivalent. The proof is finalized with Proposition 2.

Proposition 2. *The asymptotic success rate ($N_a = \inf$) of an attack with noiseless leakage given by a deterministic function F is the same as an attack with noisy leakages $\mathsf{F} + B$, where B denote the additive noise.*

In our context, if proposition 2 was false, then there would exist at least one secret value v such that its Hamming weight would not be recovered when adding noise to the leakages, while it would recovered with noiseless leakages. This cannot be in our asymptotic N_a setting, as masking can only increase the number of traces required to recover the secret, but not provide unconditional security. That is, adding noise will have no impact on the asymptotic success rate. As a result, in the context of Boolean masking, the SR_∞ is the same as for the unprotected version. Thus, the variability introduced by Boolean masking does not help nor hinder the attacker. A concrete example of this phenomenon is given in Table 1 for a 2-bit value v. The first column represents the value v written in binary, along with the corresponding Hamming weights. The remaining i columns correspond to all the possible sharings of v, also with their corresponding Hamming weights. We can see that for both $v = 01$ and $v = 10$ ($\mathsf{HW} = 1$), the corresponding possible Hamming weights of their shares are also equals up to a permutation. An attacker would thus not be able to distinguish these two values by observing their shared versions. However, this is not the case for $v = 00$ and $v = 11$, which have unique Hamming weights for their shared versions. These two values would thus be eventually recovered. We further note that this generalizes to any number of shares, and that the proof is independent of the bit size of the variable.

Table 1. Boolean sharings of a 2-bit value v, with their Hamming weight leakages. The first column corresponds to v, and the others show the possible sharings.

v	sharing 1	sharing 2	sharing 3	sharing 4
(00): HW=0	(00,00): HW=(0,0)	(01,01): HW=(1,1)	(10,10): HW=(1,1)	(11,11): HW=(2,2)
(01): HW=1	(00,01): HW=(0,1)	(01,00): HW=(1,0)	(10,11): HW=(1,2)	(11,10): HW=(2,1)
(10): HW=1	(00,10): HW=(0,1)	(01,11): HW=(1,2)	(10,00): HW=(1,0)	(11,01): HW=(2,1)
(11): HW=2	(00,11): HW=(0,2)	(01,10): HW=(1,1)	(10,01): HW=(1,1)	(11,00): HW=(2,0)

Arithmetic Masking: We now move to the context of a 2-share arithmetic masking, where the n bits sensitive value v is masked using $v = s_0^v + s_1^v \mod 2^n$, v_i being the shares. Again, the adversary is provided with two leakages l_i equal to the noisy Hamming weights of both shares and uses the actual model $\mathsf{F} = \mathsf{HW}$ for the attack.

As opposed to Boolean masking, where the XOR is solely performed bitwise, the addition adds some non-linearity due to the propagation of the carry. Thanks to this property, if two unprotected values v_0 and v_1 have the same Hamming weight, the sets of the Hamming weight of their shares might differ. For this reason, the SR_∞ will be higher than the unprotected/Boolean masked versions. We illustrate this in Table 2, which shows again the possible arithmetic sharing of a 2-bit value v and their Hamming weights. As for Table 1, the first column represents the value v, and the remaining 4 columns correspond to a possible sharing of v. As opposed to Boolean masking, we can see that there is no sharing equal to another (in terms of Hamming weights) up to any permutation. In that case, all values of v could be recovered, meaning $SR_\infty = 1$. Note that using more than 2-bit variables would provide different results for arithmetic masking, as some sharing could still share equalities, which we will show below.

SR_∞ for arithmetic is less trivial to derive using formulas as opposed to the unprotected or Boolean masking cases. Yet, it can be calculated in practice by computing the number of sets of shares having the same Hamming weight values up to a permutation for different sensitive values, as in Table 2. The corresponding results are shown in Fig. 1, where the SR_∞ in the Y-axis is given as a function of the bit size n in the X-axis. The blue (resp. green) curve corresponds to the unprotected/Boolean (resp. arithmetic) case.

Table 2. Arithmetic sharings of a 2-bit value v, with their Hamming weight leakages. The first column corresponds to v, and the others show the possible sharings.

v	sharing 1	sharing 2	sharing 3	sharing 4
(00): HW=0	(00,00): HW=(0,0)	(01,11): HW=(1,2)	(10,10): HW=(1,1)	(11,01): HW=(2,1)
(01): HW=1	(00,01): HW=(0,1)	(01,00): HW=(1,0)	(10,11): HW=(1,2)	(11,10): HW=(2,1)
(10): HW=1	(00,10): HW=(0,1)	(01,01): HW=(1,1)	(10,00): HW=(1,0)	(11,11): HW=(2,2)
(11): HW=2	(00,11): HW=(0,2)	(01,10): HW=(1,1)	(10,01): HW=(1,1)	(11,00): HW=(2,0)

We can see that the SR_∞ is much higher for arithmetic masking than for the unprotected case. In the latter, the asymptotic success rate decreases exponentially with the bit size of the variable. However, for arithmetic masking, SR_∞ is closer to a linear slope. From these observations, we can see that in the context of Hamming weight leakages (perfectly known to the adversary), arithmetic masking allows a SPA adversary to recover values that would otherwise not be recovered. However, the main property of masking still holds regarding the convergence rate. That is, reaching SR_∞ would be linear in the number of traces for the unprotected case, while it would be quadratic in the 2-share arithmetic one.

Note that while this study only focuses on 2-share versions of masking, we also computed SR_∞ for arithmetic masking for up to 8-bit values for a 3-share arithmetic masking. In this case, we still had SR_∞ equal to one for arithmetic masking. That is, adding more shares allows us to reach a higher asymptotic success rate for arithmetic masking.

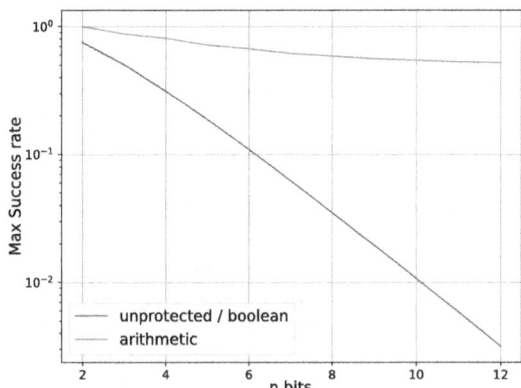

Fig. 1. Maximum success rate (Y-axis) as a function of the bit size n (X-axis) for Hamming weight leakage model, perfectly known to the adversary. The blue curve corresponds to the unprotected/Boolean masked cases. The green curve corresponds to arithmetic masking. (Color figure online)

Simulations: To validate the theoretical SR_∞ values derived above, we validate them using our simulated setting described in Sect. 3.2. As we assume perfect profiling, the actual probability density function (PDF), equal to a noisy Hamming weight function, is given to the adversary. For all cases, we ran experiments for 3 different SNRs levels equal to 0.1, 1, and 10, for 4-bit variables.

The results are shown in Fig. 2, which shows the success rate (Y-axis) as a function of the number of attack traces (X-axis). All curves are computed using 2000 repetitions. The red curves correspond to the success rate of DPA against an unprotected variable as a benchmark. The other colors represent the implementation type (unprotected, Boolean, arithmetic), and the curve type represents the SNR. A plain line is a for a SNR of 10, dashes for SNR of 1, and dots for SNR of 0.1. As a first observation, we can see that the unprotected and the Boolean masked versions indeed do reach the same SR_∞ value, slightly above 0.3 which validates what was theoretically shown before. On the other side, we reach SR_∞ slightly above 0.8 for arithmetic masking, which again validates what was previously computed. We can also observe that reducing the SNR does not impact SR_∞, but only the required number of attack traces to reach convergence, which is expected. Yet, we can see that for the unprotected version, there is a linear relationship between the required number of traces and the SNR, while there is one order of magnitude in the case of masking. This is due to the exponential benefit of masking [2], which is independent of the SR_∞ bound. Finally, we can observe that while arithmetic has a higher SR_∞ than Boolean, it takes more attack traces to reach this convergence. This is because the mutual information is lower for a 2-share arithmetic masking than for a Boolean one. This was previously observed in [17], which means that a single trace observation is on average less informative for arithmetic masking, which explains why more are needed to reach convergence. This also shows that mutual information is not the right tool to study the asymptotic success rate.

3.2 General Linear Leakages

The previous subsection assumed Hamming weight leakages. As this model is not bijective, it prevents SPA from reaching an asymptotic success rate of one. However, actual leakages are rarely linearly equivalent to the Hamming weight function, but rather close to it. That is, they would rather follow the general linear model given by Eq. 1 in Sect. 2.2 with fairly close coefficients a_i. As a result, the actual leakage function is bijective and more or less close to the Hamming weight one. In this subsection, we study how this affects the success rate of a SPA, where the leakage function is still known to the adversary (perfect profiling).

Convergence of the Success Rate: As we now assume a bijective leakage function G known to the adversary, we will have $SR_\infty = 1$. However, the convergence speed to reach SR_∞ will highly depend on G. More precisely, following the leakage model of 2.2, the convergence speed will be impacted by $\sigma^2_{leakage}$ as defined in . On one hand, if $\sigma^2_{leakage} \ll \sigma^2_{noise}$, then G will be hard to distinguish

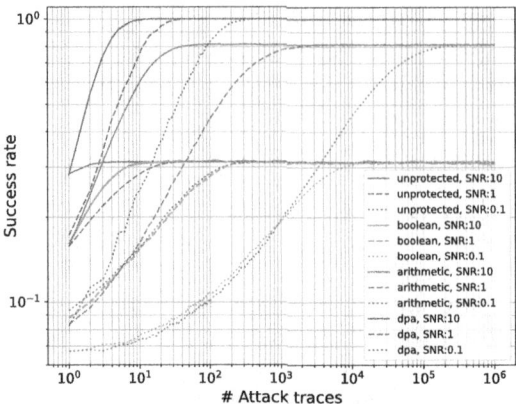

Fig. 2. Success rate (Y-axis) as a function of the number of attack traces (X-axis) for all 3 implementation types, computed with 2000 repetitions for perfectly known Hamming weight leakage. The curve color represents the implementation type (unprotected, Boolean, arithmetic, DPA), and the curve type represents the SNR. A plain line is a for a SNR of 10, dashes for SNR of 1, and dots for SNR of 0.1.

from a Hamming weight function. However, if $\sigma^2_{leakage}$ is larger, the bijectivity will be easier to capture. This is illustrated in Fig. 3, which represents the PDFs of a 3-bit variable leaking with the linear model. The dashed curve shows the Gaussian mixture, which represents what an adversary sees using attack traces. We arbitrarily chose the linear coefficients to illustrate this property, without loss of generality. The right part of the figure, denoted as high noise, shows the case where $\sigma^2_{leakage} = 0.014 \ll \sigma^2_{noise} = 0.0016$. On the opposite, the left shows the case with $\sigma^2_{leakage} = 0.014$ and $\sigma^2_{noise} = 0.0324$, denoted as low noise. For the low noise case on the left, we can see that observing the mixture still allows visually differentiating between the 8 possible classes, leading to a quick convergence to SR_∞. However, this is not the case for the high noise scenario, where observing the mixture would allow quickly differentiating the Hamming weight, but would struggle to distinguish the exact value of the Hamming weight equals 1 or 2. This would translates in a slower convergence to SR_∞.

Simulations: We used our simulated setting to validate the previous observation on the convergence for the different versions (unprotected, Boolean, and arithmetic masking, as well as unprotected DPA). We simulated the deterministic linear leakage function G using $\sigma^2_{leakage} = 0.0001$, as described in Sect. 3.2. The results are shown in Fig. 4. It shows the success rate (Y-axis) for different numbers of attack traces (X-axis). The red curve represents the unprotected DPA as a benchmark, and the other colors represent an implementation type, while the type of the curve represents a different SNR level.

As a first observation, we can now see that SR_∞ is not bounded anymore as it is for the Hamming weight case. While we do not reach a high enough number of attack traces for lower SNR values, all attacks would eventually reach a suc-

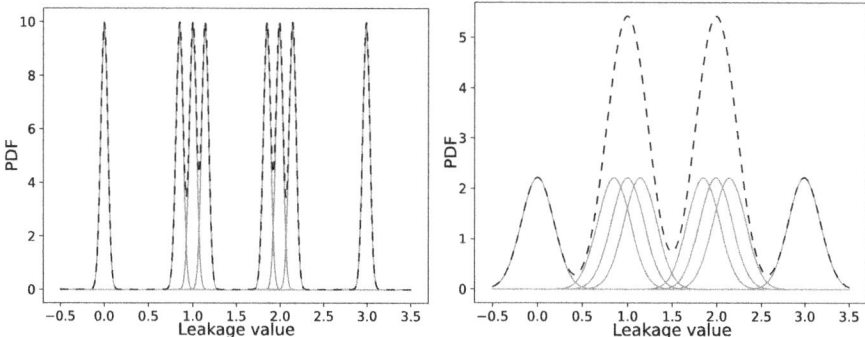

Fig. 3. Example of conditional PDFs (grey) and PDF mixture (black, dashed) for the bijective model in a low noise scenario (left) and in a high noise scenario (right). The values have been chosen to emphasize these differences. (Color figure online)

cess rate of one. Second, and most importantly, we can see that each SPA curve is composed of two parts with different slopes. Each implementation quickly reaches its Hamming weight SR_∞ (≈ 0.3 for unprotected/Boolean, and ≈ 0.8 for arithmetic). Then, the convergence rate decreases as the attack needs to distinguish the classes within the Hamming weights, which illustrates the convergence issue mentioned above. This is due to the information within a given Hamming weight class being inferior to the one between the different Hamming weights. Indeed, the second slope of the curve is equivalent to attacking with a new SNR, where the signal now depends on $\sigma^2_{leakage}$, which is much smaller for a same noise. The DPA does not suffer from this issue thanks to the dependency with a known varying value and the Sbox non-linearity.

Finally, we can see that this close-to-Hamming weight setting largely benefits arithmetic masking, which reaches high success rates more easily than for the unprotected case. An attacker would more easily attack an implementation with arithmetic masking than an unprotected one in this setting. However, for a sufficiently low SNR, this would reverse due to the masking security property.

4 Imperfect Profiling

The previous section studied the ideal case of perfect profiling, where the PDF of the leakages is given to the adversary. We now look at the more realistic case where the attacker aims at approximating the PDF through a profiling phase. She will use a set of N_p profiling traces per class, and estimate a model $\hat{\mathsf{F}}$, with $\hat{\mathsf{F}} \xrightarrow{N_p \to \infty} \mathsf{F}$. In this section, we study the impact of imperfect profiling in the context of SPA, comparing an unprotected secret to a masked one. As for the previous section, we first look at the particular case of non bijective Hamming weight leakages, before moving to the linear ones.

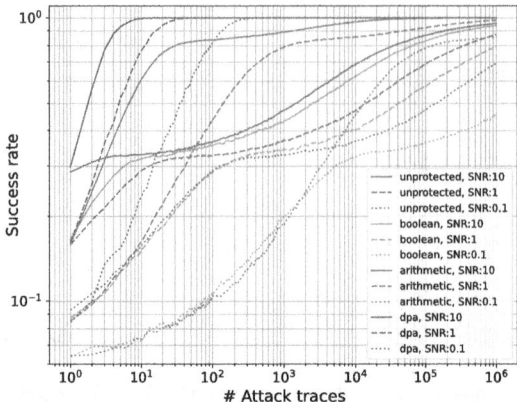

Fig. 4. Success rate (Y-axis) as a function of the number of attack traces (X-axis) for all 3 implementation types, computed with 2000 repetitions for perfectly known linear leakage. The curve color represents the implementation type (unprotected, Boolean, arithmetic, DPA), and the curve type represents the SNR. A plain line is for a SNR of 10, dots for SNR of 1, and dashes for SNR of 0.1.

4.1 Incorrect Profiling

We denote by $Pr_{\hat{\mathsf{F}}}[l|v]$ the probability of observing a leakage l for a value v using the estimated model. If the profiling has not converged enough, we might have consistent misclassifications. That is, when the actual value computed is v, we will have $\prod_i Pr_{\hat{\mathsf{F}}}[l_i|v] < \prod_i Pr_{\hat{\mathsf{F}}}[l_i|v']$ as soon as enough attack traces l_i are used, for some other value v'. In this case, v will never be recovered even with an infinite number of attack traces in a SPA context. As a result, SR_∞ would not reach one, even if the leakage function is bijective. We further refer to this as *incorrect profiling*, being stronger case of imperfect profiling. This is illustrated in Fig. 5, where the left (resp. right) part of the figure shows an imperfect (resp. incorrect) profiling. The two figures show the actual PDF of some theoretical leakages in black, which can take three values with means μ_i, $i \in [0, 2]$. The colored $\hat{\mu}_i$ correspond to the means calculated through profiling, i.e. the estimated model $\hat{\mathsf{F}}$. In the imperfect profiling on the left, we always have $|\hat{\mu}_i - \mu_i| < |\hat{\mu}_i - \mu_j|$ for $i \neq j$. In this case, all values would eventually be correctly classified given an infinite number of observations. However, for the incorrect profiling on the right, there are two means (shown in red) such that $\exists j \neq i, |\hat{\mu}_i - \mu_j| < |\hat{\mu}_i - \mu_i|$. This is the case for $\hat{\mu}_0$ being close to μ_1 than μ_0. In this case, the corresponding value would eventually be classified, and the SR_∞ bound would not be reached. The rest of this section will show how incorrect profiling impacts SPA for both Hamming weight and linear leakages.

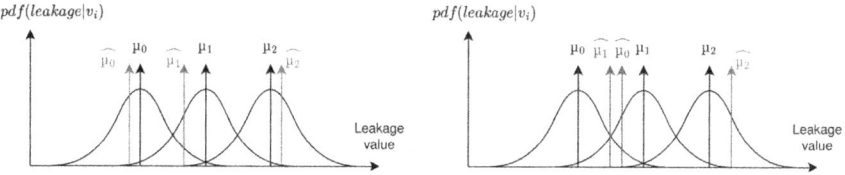

Fig. 5. Illustration of imperfect profiling (left) and incorrect profiling (right).

4.2 Hamming Weight Leakages

We first study the particular case where F = HW. From Sect. 3, we know that when F is known to the attacker, SR_∞ will reach a given SPA bound depending on the masking used. We now look at the impact of incorrect profiling in this context.

Simulations: We use our simulated setting of Sect. 3.2 on all implementation types, for different SNR values. To visualize the effect of imperfect profiling on SR_∞, we ran experiments where we varied the number of traces (per identity class, see Sect. 3.2) used during the profiling phase. The results are shown in Fig. 6, which shows the success rate (Y-axis) as a function of the number of attack traces (X-axis). The red curves represent the unprotected DPA as a benchmark, and the other colors represent an implementation type. The type of the curve (plain, dash, and dots) represents the strength of the profiling, measured as the number of profiling traces used. We used arbitrarily chosen values of N_p for both SNRs to illustrate the effect of an imperfect modeling. The plain curves represent the perfect profiling. The left (resp. right) part of the figure is for a SNR of 1 (resp. 0.1).

As a first observation, we can see that for the SPAs and all implementation types, SR_∞ does depend on the quality of the profiling. However, this is not the case for the DPA, which still reaches complete recovery even with a poor modeling. This exhibits the issue of incorrect profiling for SPA. However, we also notice that for SPA, the convergence speed does not depend on N_p. This is not the case for the DPA, which compensates for the incorrect profiling when using sufficient attack traces.

Second, we can see that in the case of a SNR of one, SR_∞ is higher for arithmetic masking with a poor profiling ($N_p = 5$) than the upper bound for the unprotected and Boolean cases. This means that given an unbounded number of attack traces, recovering the secrets with a SPA in case of arithmetic masking would be much easier than for an unprotected implementation, even if the profiling does not match well the attack traces (e.g. due to model transferability issues [6]). However, we can see that this advantage lessens when moving to a lower SNR of 0.1. Indeed, For $N_p = 20$, the success rate is about the same for arithmetic masking as for the unprotected case. Thus, for a low enough SNR and bad enough profiling, the non-linearity brought by arithmetic masking does not compensate for the information loss, as arithmetic masking is less informative [17].

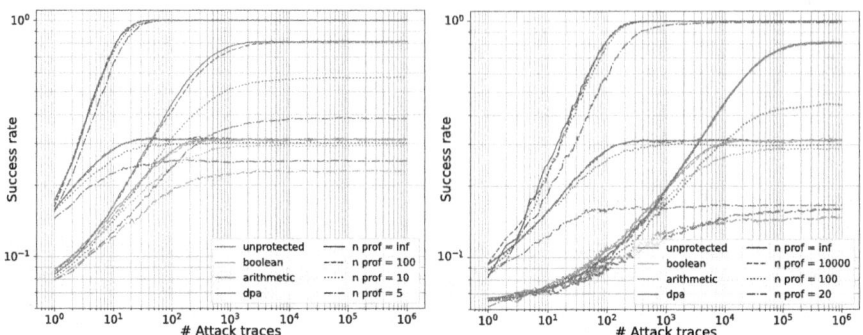

Fig. 6. Success rate (Y-axis) as a function of the number of attack traces (X-axis) for Hamming weight leakages and imperfect profiling. The color of a curve represent an implementation type, and the type of the curve (plain, dash) represents the strength of the profiling. The left (resp. right) part of the figure is for a SNR of 1 (resp. 0.1).

To provide a different view on the effect of the imperfect profiling, we additionally show the convergence SR_∞ as a function of the number of profiling traces, for which the results are shown in Fig. 7. It shows the SR_∞ bound (Y-axis) as a function of the number of profiling traces (X-axis). The curve color represents an implementation type (except the red curve for unprotected DPA), and the

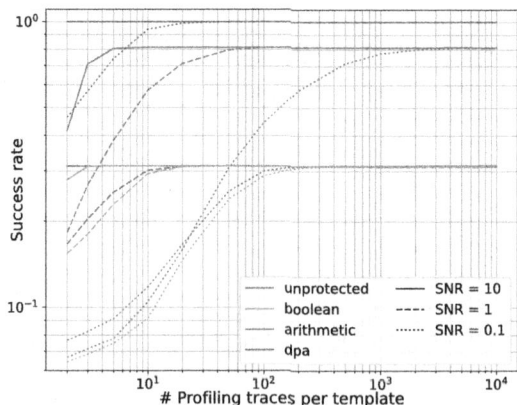

Fig. 7. SR_∞ (Y-axis) as a function of the number of profiling traces (X-axis) for Hamming weight leakages. Curve color represents an implementation type, and the type of curve represents a SNR level.

type of curve represents a SNR level. It uses 2000 repetitions, where SR_∞ is approximated using 1 million attack traces per class.

First, we can clearly see the resilience of DPA over SPA, where we only have $SR_\infty < 1$ for a SNR of 0.1 and less than 20 profiling traces per class. Next, for both unprotected and Boolean masking, we can see that we are bounded by the theoretical SR_∞ of about 0.3, while it goes up to about 0.8 for the arithmetic case. For a SNR of 1, the use of a really bad model (low N_p) still allows a higher SR_∞ in the presence of arithmetic masking than for an unprotected implementation. However, for a lower SNR of 0.1, SR_∞ starts with a higher value for the unprotected case until a better model is used ($N_p \approx 25$). This confirms the previous observation that the non-linearity provided by arithmetic masking benefits over the unprotected case only after a good enough profiling has been performed. We also see that the number of profiling traces to reach the SR_∞ bound is higher for arithmetic masking than for the Boolean case. This means that, in addition to arithmetic masking providing less informative leakages, it is also a more complex model to estimate. Yet, its non-linearity makes it to quickly reach a higher SR_∞ value.

Finally, we observe that for a fixed number of profiling traces, SR_∞ is higher for the unprotected implementation than for the Boolean masking case before reaching the bound. That is, given the same profiling strength, an attack against an unprotected implementation will perform better than against Boolean masking, given an unbounded number of attack traces. This is not a trivial observation, as we will see when moving to the linear leakages.

4.3 General Linear Leakages

After studying the effect of imperfect profiling in the case of Hamming weight leakages, we study the more realistic case where we assume a general linear leakage form. We investigate the effect on SR_∞ depending on the implementation.

Simulations: We apply our simulated setting with $\sigma^2_{leakage} = 0.0001$ to study the effect of imperfect profiling for linear leakages. Figure 8 shows the SR_∞ (Y-axis) as a function of the number of profiling traces (X-axis). The curve color represents an implementation type (except the red curve for unprotected DPA), and the type of curve (plain, dash, and dots) represents a SNR level. It uses 2000 repetitions, where SR_∞ is estimated using 1 million attack traces per class.

As for the Hamming weight case, we can first see that bad modeling affects the asymptotic success rate. However, for SPAs, we can see that each curve is decomposed into two parts. The first part is due to the profiling being quickly good enough for SR_∞ to reach the Hamming weight bounds. After this threshold, many more profiling traces are needed to get rid of the incorrect profiling within the Hamming weight classes. The DPA is however not affected by this, thanks to the varying known input and the Sbox non-linearity. Note that it is somewhat similar to what was observed with the SR convergence towards one in the perfect setting of Sect. 3.2. Yet, the difference here lies within the model accuracy with the Hamming weight classes, and not the attack part (which is here unbounded).

Second, this figure confirms that linear leakages benefit more arithmetic masking, as its SR_∞ gets above the one of an unprotected implementation with about $N_p = 15$, where we needed $N_p = 25$ for Hamming weight leakages in Fig. 7. Finally, and more surprisingly, we observe interesting results concerning the asymptotic success rate of the unprotected and Boolean cases. First, and for all SNR levels, SR_∞ starts with a higher value for the unprotected case up to the Hamming weight bound of 0.31. This confirms what was shown in the Hamming weight case of Fig. 7, where SR_∞ was higher for a given number of profiling traces. However, as soon as the model correctly classifies the Hamming weights ($SR_\infty > 0.31$), the asymptotic success rate becomes higher for Boolean masking than for the unprotected case. This remains until the profiling becomes better, where the SR_∞ against the unprotected value gets ahead again.

As a side note, we notice that SR_∞ seems to decrease for the Boolean case (SNR=0.1) when N_p is very high. We emphasize that this is not an actual trend, and is only due to the number of attack traces not being enough to get a proper approximation of SR_∞ in this case. Indeed, while the profiling gets more accurate, it takes many more attack traces to reach the SR_∞ bound due to the masking security property.

5 Practical Experiment

To validate the theoretical and simulated results of Sects. 3 and 4, we conducted actual experiments. We used a Chipwhisperer CW1200 with the CW308 STM32F target board [19]. The targeted microcontroller is a STM32F415RGT6 and is based on a 32-bits ARM cortex M4 architecture. The clock is generated by the chipwhisperer at 7.3MHz and fed to the target. We sampled the power traces at 29.7MHz (4 times per clock cycle).

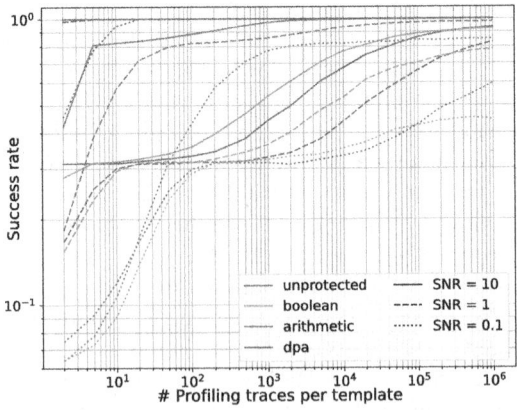

Fig. 8. SR_∞ (Y-axis) as a function of the number of profiling traces (X-axis) for linear leakages with $\sigma^2_{leakage} = 0.0001$. Curve color represents an implementation type, and the type of curve represents a SNR level.

As in our simulated settings, we used 4-bit values and obtained the same type of leakages as described in Sect. 3.2. For the DPA, we compute the Present Sbox. For the unprotected SPA, we simply directly load the sensitive variable in memory. For masked implementations, to validate the simulations, we study the security of the encoding by successively loading the two shares, with multiple NOP instructions in between. We used a gpio signal to trigger acquisitions. The SNR level is around 6, which is typical using the chipwhisperer.

5.1 Leakage Characterization

Before performing the different attacks, we performed a leakage characterization to determine how close to the Hamming weight model the leakages are. We performed a linear regression [24] with the 4 bits as a basis to compute the coefficients a_i as defined in Sect. 2.2. This gave us leakages with $\sigma^2_{leakage} = 0.00029$, which is close to our simulations. For completeness, the value of the coefficients are given in Appendix B.

To verify the bijectivity of the actual measurements, we computed the perceived information [21] (PI) for both linear regression with a Hamming weight and linear bases. The results are shown in Fig. 9, where the Y-axis shows the PI for a number of profiling traces given by the X-axis. The orange (resp. blue) curve corresponds to the Hamming weight (resp. linear) basis. The right part of the figure is a zoom where the two curves meet. As we can see, the orange PI converges much more quickly as it is a more simple basis. The two curves reach a very similar value, indicating that the leakages are almost as informative as the Hamming weight function. Yet, we reach a slightly higher PI for the linear basis, showing the bit coefficients are slightly different, which puts us in a similar setting as for the linear leakage ones used in simulations.

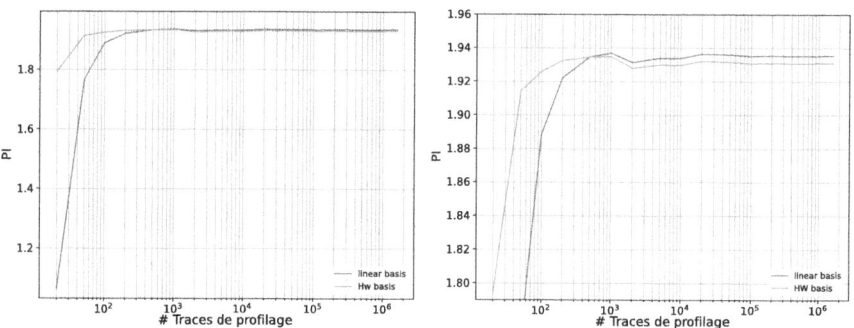

Fig. 9. Perceived information (Y-axis) for a number of traces given by the X-axis. The orange (resp. blue) curve is for the Hamming weight (resp. linear) basis. The right part of the figure is a zoom of the left one. (Color figure online)

5.2 Attack Results

After confirming the bijectivity of the leakages, and their proximity to the Hamming weight function, we applied a template attack on the different implementation types. The results are shown in Fig. 10. The Y-axis corresponds to the SR_∞ obtained for a number of profiling traces given by the X-axis. The curve color represents an implementation type. We used a dataset of 200,000 traces per class, with 10-fold cross validation.

As we can see, we get very similar results as for the simulated setting of Sect. 4.3. First, we can see that arithmetic masking allows to easily reach a higher success rate than the unprotected case. We also note that due to the SNR level being too high, we almost instantly reach a success rate higher than the Hamming weight bounds (0.3 for unprotected/Boolean, and 0.8 for arithmetic). The SR_∞ obtained is thus mainly defined by the information carried to distinguish within a given Hamming weight, from $\sigma^2_{leakage}$. Note that the DPA directly reaches $SR_\infty = 1$, which is not surprising given the high SNR.

Finally, we do observe the interesting relation between the unprotected and Boolean cases. Indeed, while the profiling strength is bad enough so that the Hamming weights are not distinguished ($SR_\infty \lesssim 0.31$), the unprotected case provides a higher SR_∞. After this threshold, this reverses, which holds until the profiling gets accurate enough. Overall, the practical experiments confirm the interesting properties of the SPA context, where the use of masking may give a higher success rate given enough attack traces.

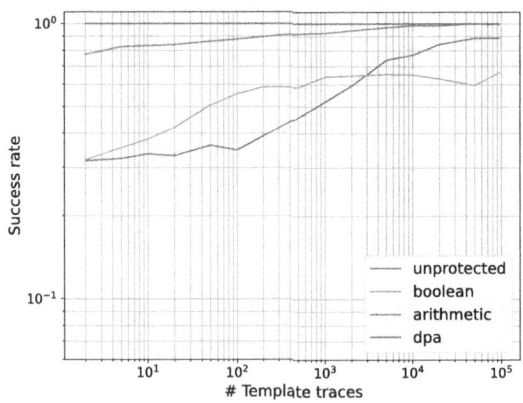

Fig. 10. SR_∞ (Y-axis) obtained for a number of profiling traces given by the X-axis for the real measurements. The curve color represents an implementation type.

6 Conclusion, Discussion

We studied the context of SPA against unprotected and masked implementations, with different assumptions on the leakage functions and the profiling strength of the adversary. To the best of our knowledge, this has not yet been investigated in the literature and shows interesting properties. In the perfect profiling setting, for Hamming weight leakages, we showed that arithmetic masking allows to reach a higher asymptotic success rate than an unprotected implementation, thanks to the non-linearity brought by the carry propagation. We showed that this still holds in the context of more realistic linear leakages, depending on the number of attack traces used. In this context, we showed the success rate has a two-phase convergence, where the second one is slower as it is equivalent to attacking with a new smaller SNR, where the signal now depends on $\sigma^2_{leakage}$.

When moving to the more practical context of imperfect profiling, we showed that the asymptotic success rate of SPA largely depends on the profiling strength, while DPA is much more resilient to incorrect profiling. Yet, we still showed that more information can be recovered when targeting arithmetic masking rather than an unprotected implementation, depending on the profiling strength and the SNR level. Additionally, we surprisingly exhibited a case where the asymptotic success rate is higher in the context of Boolean masking than for an unprotected implementation. Explaining this property formally would be an interesting future research direction.

Interesting future directions could study how other masking encodings behave, along with more shares. Additionally, as we assumed profiling with knowledge of the shares, one could investigate how the asymptotic success rate of a DPA behaves with it is not the case.

A Proof of Proposition 1

Proposition. *Two unprotected values v_0 and v_1 have the same Hamming weight if, and only if, the two joint distributions of the Hamming weight of their shares are the same.*

Proof. **Necessity:** $\mathsf{HW}(v_0) = \mathsf{HW}(v_1)$ implies that there exists a permutation of the bits, denoted P, such that $\mathsf{P}(v_0) = v_1$. The existence of P implies a bijective relationship between the sharings of v_0 and v_1. Indeed, letâĂŹs consider a sharing (a, b) such that $v_0 = a \oplus b$. Then $v_1 = \mathsf{P}(a) \oplus \mathsf{P}(b)$ by linearity of P, $(\mathsf{P}(a), \mathsf{P}(b))$ is a sharing for v_1 such that $(\mathsf{HW}(a), \mathsf{HW}(b)) = (\mathsf{HW}(\mathsf{P}(a)), \mathsf{HW}(\mathsf{P}(b)))$. Since the roles of v_0 and v_1 can be inverted, it proves the bijective relationship.

Sufficiency by Contraposition: If $\mathsf{HW}(v_0) \neq \mathsf{HW}(v_1)$, then there exists a sharing $(v_0, 0)$ of v_0. For this sharing, there cannot be a sharing (a, b) of v_1 such that $\mathsf{HW}(a) = \mathsf{HW}(v_0)$ and $b = 0$. As a result, the joint distribution of the Hamming weights of the shares differs between v_0 and v_1.

B Leakage Characterization and Linear Regression

We used the experimental setup described in Sect. 5 to perform a linear regression [24] with the 4 bits as a basis, and computed the coefficients a_i as defined in Sect. 2.2. The leakages are normalized so that the values are comparable to the simulated results. The results are shown in Fig. 11. The Y-axis corresponds to the leakage value for a coefficient a_i given in the X-axis. We show the median values as dots, along with the intervals containing 95% of the results (computed with 200 experiments using 50k traces each). As we can see, while the coefficients are very close, they seem to have small differences, indicating a bijective leakage function close to HW. We computed the corresponding $\sigma_{leakage}^2$, which results in a value of 0.00029, which is close to our simulations.

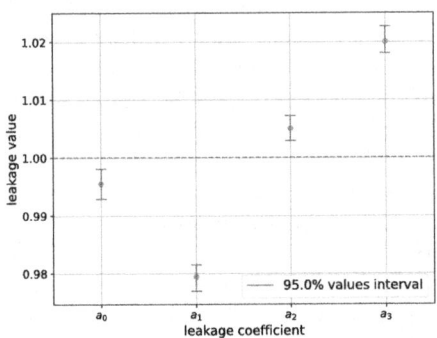

Fig. 11. Linear regression on the real measurements. The Y-axis corresponds to the values of the a_i coefficients given by the X-axis. Dots are the median values, with their confidence intervals in blue. (Color figure online)

References

1. Avanzi, R., et al.: Crystals-kyber algorithm specifications and supporting documentation. NIST PQC Round **2**(4), 1–43 (2019)
2. Barthe, G., Dupressoir, F., Faust, S., Grégoire, B., Standaert, F.-X., Strub, P.-Y.: Parallel Implementations of Masking Schemes and the Bounded Moment Leakage Model. In: Coron, J.-S., Nielsen, J.B. (eds.) EUROCRYPT 2017. LNCS, vol. 10210, pp. 535–566. Springer, Cham (2017). https://doi.org/10.1007/978-3-319-56620-7_19
3. Bogdanov, A., Knudsen, L.R., Leander, G., Paar, C., Poschmann, A., Robshaw, M.J.B., Seurin, Y., Vikkelsoe, C.: PRESENT: An Ultra-Lightweight Block Cipher. In: Paillier, P., Verbauwhede, I. (eds.) CHES 2007. LNCS, vol. 4727, pp. 450–466. Springer, Heidelberg (2007). https://doi.org/10.1007/978-3-540-74735-2_31
4. Brier, E., Clavier, C., Olivier, F.: Correlation Power Analysis with a Leakage Model. In: Joye, M., Quisquater, J.-J. (eds.) CHES 2004. LNCS, vol. 3156, pp. 16–29. Springer, Heidelberg (2004). https://doi.org/10.1007/978-3-540-28632-5_2
5. Cagli, E., Dumas, C., Prouff, E.: Convolutional Neural Networks with Data Augmentation Against Jitter-Based Countermeasures. In: Fischer, W., Homma, N. (eds.) CHES 2017. LNCS, vol. 10529, pp. 45–68. Springer, Cham (2017). https://doi.org/10.1007/978-3-319-66787-4_3

6. Cao, P., Zhang, C., Lu, X., Gu, D.: Cross-device profiled side-channel attack with unsupervised domain adaptation. IACR Transactions on Cryptographic Hardware and Embedded Systems, 27–56 (2021)
7. Chari, S., Rao, J.R., Rohatgi, P.: Template attacks. In: Cryptographic Hardware and Embedded Systems-CHES 2002: 4th International Workshop Redwood Shores, CA, USA, August 13–15, 2002 Revised Papers 4, pp. 13–28. Springer (2003)
8. Dobraunig, C., Eichlseder, M., Mendel, F., Schläffer, M.: Ascon v1. CAESAR Competition (2014)
9. Duc, A., Dziembowski, S., Faust, S.: Unifying Leakage Models: From Probing Attacks to Noisy Leakage. In: Nguyen, P.Q., Oswald, E. (eds.) EUROCRYPT 2014. LNCS, vol. 8441, pp. 423–440. Springer, Heidelberg (2014). https://doi.org/10.1007/978-3-642-55220-5_24
10. Gandolfi, K., Mourtel, C., Olivier, F.: Electromagnetic analysis: concrete results. In: Koç, Ç.K., Naccache, D., Paar, C. (eds.) CHES 2001. LNCS, vol. 2162, pp. 251–261. Springer, Heidelberg (2001). https://doi.org/10.1007/3-540-44709-1_21
11. Gierlichs, B., Batina, L., Tuyls, P., Preneel, B.: Mutual information analysis: a generic side-channel distinguisher. In: International Workshop on Cryptographic Hardware and Embedded Systems, pp. 426–442. Springer (2008)
12. Ishai, Y., Sahai, A., Wagner, D.: Private circuits: securing hardware against probing attacks. In: Boneh, D. (ed.) CRYPTO 2003. LNCS, vol. 2729, pp. 463–481. Springer, Heidelberg (2003). https://doi.org/10.1007/978-3-540-45146-4_27
13. Kocher, P.C.: Timing Attacks on Implementations of Diffie-Hellman, RSA, DSS, and Other Systems. In: Koblitz, N. (ed.) CRYPTO 1996. LNCS, vol. 1109, pp. 104–113. Springer, Heidelberg (1996). https://doi.org/10.1007/3-540-68697-5_9
14. Kocher, P., Jaffe, J., Jun, B.: Differential power analysis. In: Wiener, M. (ed.) CRYPTO 1999. LNCS, vol. 1666, pp. 388–397. Springer, Heidelberg (1999). https://doi.org/10.1007/3-540-48405-1_25
15. Lomné, V., Prouff, E., Rivain, M., Roche, T., Thillard, A.: How to estimate the success rate of higher-order side-channel attacks. In: Cryptographic Hardware and Embedded Systems–CHES 2014: 16th International Workshop, Busan, South Korea, September 23-26, 2014. Proceedings 16, pp. 35–54. Springer (2014)
16. Mangard, S.: Hardware countermeasures against DPA – a statistical analysis of their effectiveness. In: Okamoto, T. (ed.) CT-RSA 2004. LNCS, vol. 2964, pp. 222–235. Springer, Heidelberg (2004). https://doi.org/10.1007/978-3-540-24660-2_18
17. Masure, L., Méaux, P., Moos, T., Standaert, F.X.: Effective and efficient masking with low noise using small-mersenne-prime ciphers. In: Annual International Conference on the Theory and Applications of Cryptographic Techniques, pp. 596–627. Springer (2023)
18. Migliore, V., Gérard, B., Tibouchi, M., Fouque, P.-A.: Masking Dilithium. In: Deng, R.H., Gauthier-Umaña, V., Ochoa, M., Yung, M. (eds.) ACNS 2019. LNCS, vol. 11464, pp. 344–362. Springer, Cham (2019). https://doi.org/10.1007/978-3-030-21568-2_17
19. O'Flynn, C., Chen, Z.D.: ChipWhisperer: An Open-Source Platform for Hardware Embedded Security Research. In: Prouff, E. (ed.) COSADE 2014. LNCS, vol. 8622, pp. 243–260. Springer, Cham (2014). https://doi.org/10.1007/978-3-319-10175-0_17
20. Prouff, E.: Dpa attacks and s-boxes. In: International Workshop on Fast Software Encryption, pp. 424–441. Springer (2005)

21. Renauld, M., Standaert, F.-X., Veyrat-Charvillon, N., Kamel, D., Flandre, D.: A Formal Study of Power Variability Issues and Side-Channel Attacks for Nanoscale Devices. In: Paterson, K.G. (ed.) EUROCRYPT 2011. LNCS, vol. 6632, pp. 109–128. Springer, Heidelberg (2011). https://doi.org/10.1007/978-3-642-20465-4_8
22. Rivain, M.: On the exact success rate of side channel analysis in the gaussian model. In: International Workshop on Selected Areas in Cryptography, pp. 165–183. Springer (2008)
23. Rivain, M., Prouff, E.: Provably secure higher-order masking of AES. In: International Workshop on Cryptographic Hardware and Embedded Systems, pp. 413–427. Springer (2010)
24. Schindler, W., Lemke, K., Paar, C.: A Stochastic Model for Differential Side Channel Cryptanalysis. In: Rao, J.R., Sunar, B. (eds.) CHES 2005. LNCS, vol. 3659, pp. 30–46. Springer, Heidelberg (2005). https://doi.org/10.1007/11545262_3
25. Standaert, F.-X., Malkin, T.G., Yung, M.: A Unified Framework for the Analysis of Side-Channel Key Recovery Attacks. In: Joux, A. (ed.) EUROCRYPT 2009. LNCS, vol. 5479, pp. 443–461. Springer, Heidelberg (2009). https://doi.org/10.1007/978-3-642-01001-9_26
26. Standaert, F.-X., Veyrat-Charvillon, N., Oswald, E., Gierlichs, B., Medwed, M., Kasper, M., Mangard, S.: The World Is Not Enough: Another Look on Second-Order DPA. In: Abe, M. (ed.) ASIACRYPT 2010. LNCS, vol. 6477, pp. 112–129. Springer, Heidelberg (2010). https://doi.org/10.1007/978-3-642-17373-8_7
27. Strieder, E., Ilg, M., Heyszl, J., Unterstein, F., Streit, S.: Asca vs. sasca: a closer look at the aes key schedule. In: International Workshop on Constructive Side-Channel Analysis and Secure Design, pp. 65–85. Springer (2023)

A Comparison of Graph-Inference Side-Channel Attacks Against SKINNY

Stian Husum[✉][iD], Håvard Raddum[iD], and Martijn Stam[iD]

Simula UiB, Bergen, Norway
{stianh,haavardr,martijn}@simula.no

Abstract. Belief propagation can improve standard divide-and-conquer side-channel attacks by exploiting additional leakage both effectively and efficiently. The original approach for belief propagation against block ciphers uses factor graph inference (FGI). Recently, Costes and Stam (CHES'23) proposed the use of cluster graph inference (CGI) as a more effective and potentially more efficient alternative. In the context of SKINNY, they focus on exploiting leakage on the 44 S-boxes that each depend on at most two subkeys, surprisingly enabling exact inference. Expanding their cluster graph approach beyond the 44 S-boxes is intrinsically expensive, as it requires enumerating larger subkeys.

In contrast to CGI, FGI remains efficient regardless of the number of S-boxes exploited, yet in practice exploiting more rounds appears to quickly yield diminishing returns: against AES so far only two rounds have been exploited effectively. Costes and Stam provided a rough, qualitative comparison between cluster and factor graph inference, but without any quantitative experiments. Thus, it remains unclear how well FGI would fare against a low-diffusion cipher like SKINNY.

We provide a quantitative comparison of the two graph inference methods applied to SKINNY. We conclude that, when profiling is possible, both behave comparably when exploiting the aforementioned 44 S-boxes. Yet, FGI can easily exploit more S-boxes, comprehensively outperforming CGI. For the profiled scenarios originally considered by Costes and Stam, FGI on three leaking rounds from both sides of the cipher is best, both in terms of effectiveness and efficiency.

Keywords: Belief Propagation · Graph Inference · SKINNY

1 Introduction

Several approaches have been proposed to squeeze more information out of side-channel analysis (SCA) leakage than the typical divide-and-conquer strategies (D&C). In D&C the target key is attacked by dividing it into several subkeys. Each of those subkeys are attacked separately by applying a distinguisher to a set of attack traces, yielding a score for each possible subkey. The most likely subkey is then determined from the highest score. However, a full trace usually contains

© The Author(s), under exclusive license to Springer Nature Switzerland AG 2026
M. Rivain and P. Sasdrich (Eds.): CASCADE 2025, LNCS 15952, pp. 367–383, 2026.
https://doi.org/10.1007/978-3-032-01405-4_15

leakage in later rounds that relies on the master key in more complicated ways, which cannot be exploited by standard D&C.

The use of probabilistic graphical modeling and belief propagation algorithms has been proposed to exploit more of the observed leakage [5,24]. Two approaches, based on factor graphs and cluster graphs, respectively, look particularly promising, yet it is unclear how they relate to each other.

Veyrat-Charvillon et al. [24] advocated for factor graphs to model interactions between dependent variables in the cipher, followed by factor graph inference (FGI) to recover the full key. At its core, FGI builds a bipartite graph with nodes representing variables, respectively factors. For all nodes, local beliefs encode how likely the variables relevant to that node are deemed to be. Typically, for a select number of variable nodes, informative initial beliefs are available and subsequent belief propagation allows consolidating these partial, initial beliefs into a consistent, global belief on all the variables encoded by the graph.

In the context of SCA, the variables relate to the intermediate variables in the cipher, such as subkeys or S-box inputs and outputs, whereas the factors capture the operations on those variables, such as xors and S-boxes. Moreover, a typical SCA factor graph consists of a component encoding the key schedule and a component for the evaluation of the cipher proper. To combine information from multiple traces, we can use large FGI (LFGI), in which the cipher component is replicated for each trace and connected by a shared key schedule component. For the intermediate variables that leak directly during a computation, the initial beliefs correspond to the distinguisher scores for that particular intermediate (for intermediates that do not leak directly, say subkeys, a uniform prior can be used as initial belief). As beliefs are needed for intermediates appearing in a single trace, the distinguisher will have to be parameterized to obtain meaningful initial beliefs, which in turn requires a profiling stage to estimate the parameters involved (e.g. for Gaussian templates). Following the belief propagation, the final beliefs for the subkeys reveal the best guess for the full key.

A downside of FGI in SCA are the large and loopy graphs. Consequently, the belief propagation is only approximate and might not even converge. In principle, FGI-SCA could encode the full cipher and thus initial beliefs on all S-box inputs and outputs could be entered. Yet, when targeting a byte-wise implementation of AES, it turns out that leakage beyond the first round only provides marginal benefits [6,9] and the benefit of FGI over D&C lies in the former's ability to exploit leakage from the first round's MIXCOLUMNS.

Recently, Costes and Stam [5], henceforth CS23, introduced cluster graph inference (CGI) to SCA. Like factor graphs, cluster graphs are known from probabilistic graphical modeling, but they differ as they only have one type of nodes (for variables) and edges can be drawn between nodes to indicate shared variables. In the context of SCA, each node in the cluster graph contains a set of subkeys, and each possible value for the subkeys in that set must be enumerated for the attack. Thus, a node corresponding to two subkey bytes corresponds to an enumeration effort of 2^{16} values. This enumeration scales poorly with deeper rounds in a cipher where the leakage depends on more than two subkey bytes.

CS23 applied CGI to the lightweight cipher SKINNY. Due to SKINNY's slower diffusion, CS23 observed that 44 of its S-boxes each depend on at most two subkey bytes. The resulting cluster graph happens to be a clique tree, enabling exact inference. For this case, CS23 demonstrated that both in a profiled and unprofiled setting, the number of traces needed is roughly inversely proportional to the number of S-boxes exploited. So, using CGI against SKINNY's 44 bi-dependent S-boxes is $\approx 2.75 = 44/16$ times as efficient as exploiting only a single S-box per subkey in standard D&C.

When comparing CGI and FGI, attacking AES with FGI can exploit all rounds efficiently in principle, but in reality not effectively, as almost all useful leakage occurs in the first round [6]. After two full rounds of AES, every byte of the cipher state depends on the entire key. Conversely, with SKINNY's slower diffusion, in the third round some bytes in the cipher state still only depend on two keybytes. When attacking SKINNY with CGI, CS23 leverage this slow diffusion and effectively exploit deeper rounds in the cipher, but they cannot go deeper than three rounds efficiently. An open question is how well FGI might exploit slow diffusion by targeting variables deeper in a cipher and how well it compares to CGI, especially in scenarios where the latter still provides exact inference.

Our Contribution. We will compare CGI and FGI, specifically LFGI, using the lightweight blockcipher SKINNY as example, thus enabling a fair comparison with CS23's results (on CGI). We construct factor graphs for SKINNY, and use them to mount FGI attacks on synthetic traces with Gaussian noise, $\sigma^2 = 1$ and $\sigma^2 = 4$, as well as traces from two real implementations of SKINNY: one with a LUT implementation for the S-box and another with a circuit-based one representative of a scenario with low noise, respectively high noise. We compare those FGI attacks to the CGI attacks performed by CS23. For our comparison, we look at the success rates of the attacks over the number of traces and restrict ourselves to the profiled setting as, unlike CGI, FGI only works with profiled distinguishers.

We show that when FGI and CGI are exploiting the same leakage from the same 44 S-boxes, both attacks reach a similar success rate with the same amount of traces. However, unlike CGI, FGI can handle a larger amount of target S-boxes, and we demonstrate that additional S-box leakage leads to attacks with higher success rates. We targeted up to 128 S-boxes for the same scenarios as CS23, with a significant reduction in the traces needed for an attack. In addition, we investigated FGI in a synthetic scenario with even higher noise, $\sigma^2 = 16$, and saw that going beyond 128 S-boxes did not yield better results. Unlike FGI attacks on AES, where mainly the first round leads to leakage, FGI on SKINNY can exploit leakages from four rounds on each side of the cipher, leading to eight rounds, or 128 S-boxes, of leakage. Although FGI does exploit more S-boxes, the reduction in traces does not follow the linear relation suggested by CS23, with 96 S-boxes having a better reduction than the expected sixfold, and further rounds having a worse reduction than expected.

Related Works. Veyrat-Charvillon et al. [24] introduced FGI to target AES, and several papers since have studied and revised the method [6,7,9,23]. In addition, it has been employed to attack other targets than AES, such as Keccak [12,25], ASCON [14,26], and Clyde [2], as well as the number-theoretic transform, or NTT, used in lattice-based cryptography [19,20]

Several strategies have been suggested for scaling FGI for multiple traces, mainly large FGI (LFGI) and independent FGI (IFGI). The strategy of LFGI was employed in the initial attack by Veyrat-Charvillon et al. [24] and duplicates the graph for each trace and connects them through the key schedule. IFGI, on the other hand, introduced by Green et al. [6], uses a separate graph for each trace, and then consolidates the shared beliefs of the graphs after belief propagation. The main benefit of IFGI is improved efficiency with larger amounts of traces without significantly sacrificing the quality of the inference. As the trace count for our attacks are rather low, our focus will be on LFGI.

Prior to FGI, ASCA [21,22] and similar attacks [16,17] were suggested to exploit leakage in the traces beyond standard D&C. These attacks rely on an algebraic set of equations generated from the cipher, and augment that system with side-channel leakage before solving. The solvers used by ASCA use hard values and so cannot handle the noisy measurements from SCA directly. Strategies have been suggested to bridge the gap between solver and leakage in ASCA [18], but probabilistic belief propagation methods need no such bridge. Grosso and Standaert [7] compared FGI with ASCA arguing in favour of FGI, yet Strieder et al. [23] demonstrated an attack on the AES key schedule where ASCA outperforms FGI. We focus on FGI and leave algebraic side-channel attacks on SKINNY as open problem.

2 Preliminaries

2.1 SKINNY

SKINNY [1] is a family of lightweight tweakable blockciphers. A variant of it was a final-round candidate in the NIST lightweight cipher standardization [8]. It is constructed as a substitution-permutation network, similar to AES, but with slower diffusion, a lighter key schedule, and no key whitening. As SKINNY follows the tweakey framework [11], it uses in a tweakey instead of a key. A part of that tweakey is the secret key, and the rest is a public tweak.

Within the family, there are two different block sizes, 64 and 128 bits, as well as three different tweakey sizes, n, $2n$, and $3n$ bits, where n is the block size in bits. We describe each variant using these two values, so SKINNY-128-384 has a block size of 128 bits and a tweakey size of 384 bits ($3n$). The cipher state is divided into a 4×4 grid of cells, each cell holding either a nibble or a byte, depending on the size of the block. We index each cell in a block from 0 to 15 as a subscript. So, the top left cell of a state x is x_0 and the bottom right is x_{15}. The number of rounds depends on both the block and key size. The variants we will consider, SKINNY-128-128 and SKINNY-128-384, have 40 and 56 rounds, respectively. Below we provide a high level overview of SKINNY; for full details

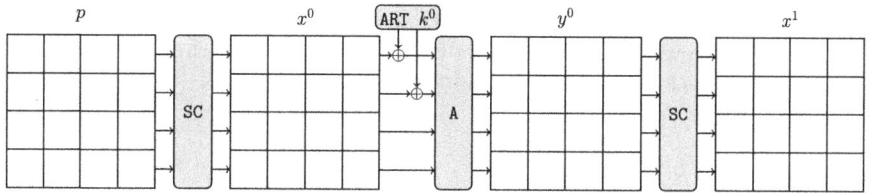

Fig. 1. The inital rounds of SKINNY. Adapted from [10].

please refer to the SKINNY specification [1]. We refer to the beginning rounds of the cipher, i.e., from the plaintext side, as the *initial* rounds, and to the ending rounds, i.e., from the ciphertext side, as the *final* rounds. The first round (and a bit) is illustrated in Fig. 1, starting with the plaintext p.

Round Structure and Round Functions. A round starts with applying an S-box function to each cell. We refer to this layer as the S-box layer (SC), and the S-box as S. After the S-box layer, the round tweakey is added to the upper half of the state (ART). After the tweakey addition, there is an affine layer consisting of adding round constants, shifting rows, and mixing columns. For simplicity, We depict the full affine layer as A.

As the first S-box layer comes before the first key addition, it contains no key material, and we can compute it without access to the key. Therefore, we choose to index rounds starting at the first S-box output as x^0. We denote the output of the affine layer, i.e., the end of a round, and input to the next S-box layer, as y^r. Consequently, the first S-box input with key material is y^0. Following this notion, the ciphertext is y^{39} or y^{55}, depending on the variant.

Key Schedule. The SKINNY key schedule is lightweight. First, the tweakey is divided into several blocks, each being a 4×4 grid of cells. Each block has the same size as the state, and the size of the tweakey denotes the number of blocks. So, SKINNY-128-128 has one block, and SKINNY-128-384 has three blocks. The secret key is stored in the last block of the tweakey; earlier blocks contain the public tweak. Between rounds, the blocks are updated independently of each other, by applying both a permutation to shuffle a block's cells and a bitwise-linear substitution on each of the block's cells. The permutation

$$P = [9, 15, 8, 13, 10, 14, 12, 11, 0, 1, 2, 3, 4, 5, 6, 7]$$

is the same for all blocks. This permutation is structured such that the two halves of the key are separate, so the first half of the key feeds into even rounds and the second half into odd rounds.

On the other hand, the linear substitution depends on the block. For the first block, and only block in SKINNY-128-128, it is the identity map (and can hence be omitted). For the two other blocks, present in SKINNY-128-384, a linear feedback shift register (LFSR) is applied to each cell in the upper half of the key state after the permutation. This LFSR is different for the two blocks, but since the last block is the one containing the secret key in SKINNY-128-384, we choose to denote that LFSR as L.

2.2 Side-Channel Analysis

In power analysis, the attacker measures a *trace* of the power drawn by a device during encryption to try to recover the secret key on the device. The trace contains multiple measurements per clock cycle, and therefore contains the power drawn by the operations in the cipher. We consider the plaintext and ciphertext to be known to the attacker, as is the cipher specification and the implementation running on the device.

The basis for most attacks is targeting some intermediate variables used during the computation of the cipher. A *distinguisher* is used on the traces to determine which value is the most likely for a given variable. The distinguisher is a function that takes a trace and outputs scores, a non-negative real number, for each possible value the intermediate variable can have. For variables that do not change between executions of the cipher, like subkeys and variables in the key schedule, a distinguisher might take several traces.

In traditional divide-and-conquer SCA attacks, the target key is divided into subkeys that are attacked independently. Such attacks are simple and efficient, however, they do not exploit points in the trace where the leakage is joint between several subkeys. As such, they do not exploit all available leakage in the traces. To remedy this, several approaches to combine the information from multiple intermediate variables have been proposed [5,21,22,24]. The details of two of those, FGI and CGI, will be described in Sects. 2.3 and 3.

2.3 Probabilistic Graphical Models

We can look at our side-channel leakage as a probabilistic system, with the leakage of each intermediate variable as a random variable. As the number of random variables in our system grows, the complexity of the distribution increases, and we need an efficient way to represent the system. Probabilistic graphical modeling provides one way of accomplishing this by using a graph-based representation of joint distributions. The graph representation allows us to run *inference* effectively on the system. We use uppercase letters to denote random variables in our systems. Our description of probabilistic graphical modeling is based on Koller and Friedman [13]. Further details can be found in their book.

A central concept in probabilistic graphical modeling is that of a *factor*. A factor is a mapping from the value space of some random variables to a non-negative real number. We use the Greek letter ϕ to denote factors. The set of random variables included in a factor are called the *scope*, so a factor $\phi(K_i, K_j)$ has scope K_i, K_j. When we evaluate a factor, we use lower case instantiations of the random variables, so an instantiation of the random variable K_i would be k_i.

We can look at distinguishing scores from SCA as factors. We use multiplicative notation for factors, so if we want to combine factors we multiply them like we would with probabilities. However, in our implementation we work additively, by taking the logarithm, for better numerical stability.

Factors as Nodes. Factors form the main basis for our graph representation. In cluster graphs, each node is a *cluster* of factors, i.e., each node represents a subset of all factors in our system. We then draw edges between nodes that share factors.

In factor graphs, we have a bipartite graph with two types of nodes: factors and variables. We represent every factor and every variable by a node. We draw edges from each factor node to the variable nodes in its scope. Our figures show factor nodes with boxes and variable nodes without.

Belief Propagation. We employ *belief propagation* to run inference on our graphical models. A *belief* is a real non-negative number associated with the possible values a variable can have, where a higher number indicates a stronger belief that a variable takes a particular value. As such, a factor can be described as a set of beliefs for its scope. In each node, we store a belief on the variables relating to that node, with the Greek letter β denoting that belief:

- A cluster node stores beliefs on the variables in the scope of its factors.
- A variable node stores beliefs on its variable.
- A factor node stores beliefs on its neighbouring variables, where beliefs on different variables are independent from each other.

After initializing some nodes in a graph with beliefs given by the traces, with unitialized nodes having uniform beliefs, we propagate those beliefs through the graph by *message passing*. Each node sends beliefs along its edges and then uses the beliefs it receives to update its own beliefs. We repeat sending messages, receiving messages, and updating beliefs until the overall beliefs in the graph are consolidated.

Non-loopy graphs consolidate their beliefs after a fixed number of iterations and yield an exact inference. However, if the graphs have loops, we must define a termination condition, such as a fixed number of iterations. With loopy graphs, the beliefs might not consolidate, and we only get an *approximate* inference.

Cluster Graph Inference. CS23 takes the cluster graph approach, and take the key byte variables as factors. They select each S-box dependent on exactly two key bytes and declare those pairs of key bytes as clusters. For SKINNY, this yields 12 clusters containing 13 of the 16 key bytes. Those clusters serve as the nodes for their cluster graph. Edges are drawn between the clusters to form a clique tree. The clique tree used they used for SKINNY-128-128 can be found in Fig. 6 in CS23. The key bytes not included in the graph are attacked separately with a standard divide-and-conquer approach.

To populate the inital beliefs for the nodes, CS23 uses either a profiled or unprofiled distinguisher to collect scores on keybytes and pairs of keybytes. Those scores are the factors. Each node is associated with three factors $\phi_1(K_i, K_j)$, $\phi_2(K_i)$ and $\phi_3(K_j)$. Then, for all $k_i, k_j \in \{0,1\}^8$, the belief $\beta(k_i, k_j)$ is initialized to $\phi_1(k_i, k_j) \cdot \phi_2(k_i) \cdot \phi_3(k_j)$.

After the beliefs on the nodes have been initialized, they run two passes of belief propagation: first from leaf nodes up to an arbitrary root node, then from the root node and back to the leaves. Once beliefs have been consolidated, they can be extracted from the nodes by *max-marginalization*, i.e., for a node K_i, K_j, the belief on $\beta(k_i) = \max_{k_j} \beta(k_i, k_j)$.

The nodes in the cluster graph contain factors relating to two key bytes, so computing the scores for those factors require a computational cost on the order of 2^{16}. Expanding the attack to more S-boxes, and therefore S-boxes dependent on three or more key bytes, would increase the cost to 2^{24} or beyond. For this reason CGI gets prohibitively expensive at deeper rounds.

On the other hand, only targeting the key bytes allows for a larger diversity of distinguishers, and therefore CGI can be used in both profiled and unprofiled scenarios. In addition, as the CGI graph for SKINNY-128-128 and SKINNY-128-384 using 44 S-boxes neatly forms an acyclic graph, we know that the inference we have is exact, and the attacker does not have to tweak parameters such as the number of message passing iterations.

3 Large Factor Graph Inference

Factor Graph Inference for SCA. Recall that factor graphs are bipartite graphs consisting of factor nodes and variable nodes. When applied to SCA, the variable nodes represent intermediate variables in the computation of the cipher, and the factor nodes correspond to operations in the cipher. This approach was first introduced by Veyrat-Charvillon et al. [24] to attack AES.

The graphs consist of two main components: the key schedule, whose values do not change between traces, and the cipher proper. For each target trace, we replicate the cipher component and connect them to the shared key schedule component. Green et al. [6] refer to this method of connected components as large FGI (LFGI, as opposed to independent or sequential FGI). They deem that method preferable when graphs remain small and will therefore be our approach.

We compute initial beliefs from the traces using a distiguisher and use those beliefs to initialize the variable nodes. Each variable node correspond to one intermediate variable, so if our variables are bytes, they store 2^8 beliefs. Hence, the size of the nodes does not increase the deeper we go into the cipher. However, to get beliefs on deeper intermediate variables, we need to use a distinguisher whose complexity also does not grow with depth. Therefore, FGI is better suited for use with profiled distinguishers.

After initializing the beliefs in the variable nodes, we propagate those beliefs using message passing. If the graph has no cycles propagation takes a fixed number of steps, yielding an exact inference. When the graph contains loops, we continue until either some convergence criteria is met, or after some heuristically set number of iterations. For loopy graphs, FGI only yields an approximate inference. After belief propagation, we can extract beliefs on subkeys from the variable nodes relating to the subkey variables.

3.1 Factor Graphs for SKINNY

To attack SKINNY using FGI, we first need a factor graph to describe the operations of the cipher. This graph can either be specific to one implementation, and hence generated from it, as in Veyrat-Charvillon et al. [24], or, as we choose to do, described manually from the cipher specification. Although our approach omits some potential leakage from real implementations, it provides a fairer comparison with CS23 and serves as the worst case for FGI (from an adversarial perspective). As we will be performing attacks on both SKINNY-128-128 and SKINNY-128-384, we need two constructions for our graphs. Both graph variants share the same cipher component, but differ in the key schedule.

For the cipher component we only need two types of factor nodes, S-boxes and XORs. The S-box nodes define a relationship between nodes x_i^{r+1} and y_i^r as

$$x_i^{r+1} = S[y_i^r]$$

where i is the index of the byte, r is the round number and S is the SKINNY S-box. For the XOR nodes, each node defines an XOR between several inputs and one output. An XOR node f_n has a set of neighbours V and defines the relation

$$\bigoplus_{v \in V} v = 0.$$

Figure 2 shows one round of the cipher component of the graph. We repeat this partial graph for each initial and final round we attack, and then the combined graph is replicated for each of our traces. Finally, we connect each of the graphs through the key schedule. Although we can construct a small loopless graph for slightly more than one round, such a graph becomes loopy once several subgraphs are connected through the key schedule. Thus, all the graphs we construct are loopy and the subsequent inference is heuristic.

For SKINNY-128-128, the key schedule is only a permutation. Therefore, we only need one set of key variable nodes k_n for $n \in \{0, ..., 15\}$ and k_n^r is only a renaming of that variable, i.e., $k_n^0 = k_n$ and

$$k_n^r = k_{P[n]}^{r-1}$$

where P is the key schedule permutation. As the first round of SKINNY contains no key material, we chose to exclude that round from the graph and start at the first S-box output.

For SKINNY-128-384, the key schedule contains an LFSR, so an additional factor node is needed. A node L defines, similar to the S-box nodes, a relation

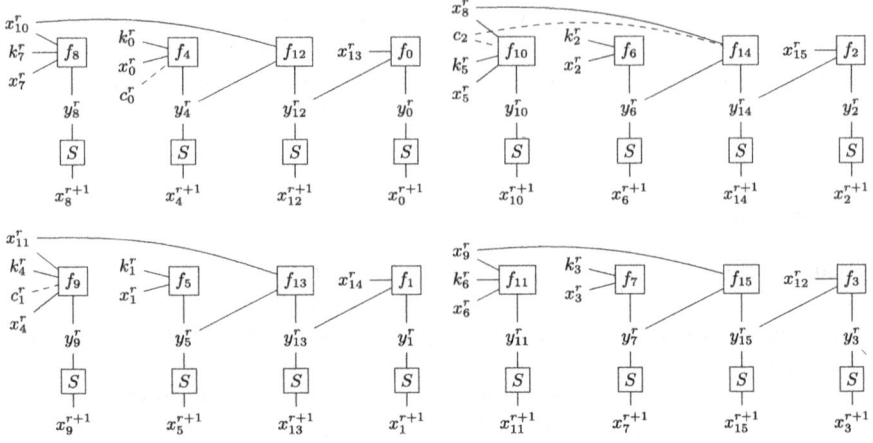

Fig. 2. One round of the FGI graph used for SKINNY. Square nodes are factors, and the rest are variables. Dashed lines indicate known values. Those are included in the factor calculation, but are not variable nodes in the graph for belief propagation.

between two variable nodes k_n and $k^r_{P^r[n]}$ as

$$k^r_n = L^{\lfloor \frac{r+1}{2} \rfloor}[k_{P^r[n]}]$$

where $L^{\lfloor \frac{r+1}{2} \rfloor}$ indicates $\lfloor \frac{r+1}{2} \rfloor$ applications of the SKINNY LFSR and P^r is r applications of the key schedule permutation. As the first round key is half of the initial key, we have $k^0_n = k_n$ for $n \in \{0, ..., 7\}$.

As SKINNY only uses half the key in each round, we only need to use eight key variable nodes for each of our rounds. We also add the known tweak to each XOR node that is already neighbour with a key variable.

We also constructed an alternative factor graph, where we connect k^i to k^{i-2} through a single invocation of L, instead of directly connecting k^i to k^0 through $L^{\lfloor \frac{r+1}{2} \rfloor}$. This approach increases the diameter of the graph and makes the path from each round key to the master key less direct. Especially the final rounds end up further from the master key. When we tried message passing on this alternative indirect graph it performed worse when attacking more than 96 S-boxes and performed the same for fewer S-boxes.

4 Experiments and Results

For our comparison between CGI and FGI, we consider the profiled scenarios from CS23: a simulated scenario targeting SKINNY-128-128 with noisy Hamming weight leakage from S-boxes, and a profiled attack on two implementations of SKINNY-128-384 collected on a ChipWhisperer. As there is no clear way to use FGI for an unprofiled attack, we do not compare against CS23's CPA attacks.

The results for CGI are taken directly from data provided to us by the authors of CS23, as are the traces used for our attacks on real traces. As CS23 we use the first order success rate of full key recovery as our metric for comparison.

Following CS23, we look at the leakage of S-box outputs of the initial rounds of encryption, and S-box inputs for the final rounds of the encryption.

4.1 FGI Setup

For the FGI attack, we use the SCALib library [3]. This library provides a full implementation of the FGI algorithm with access to APIs to: Create factor graphs from a text description, duplicate parts of those graphs to accommodate multiple traces, set known values, add initial beliefs to variables, run exact belief propagation on acyclic graphs, run approximate belief propagation on cyclic graphs with a fixed number of iterations, and reading out beliefs of variables. Therefore, the choices we have available are the structure of the graph, which nodes to add initial beliefs to, what those beliefs are, which belief propagation strategy to use, and the number of iterations.

For our attacks we generate a text representation of the graphs in Sect. 3.1 to describe the factor graphs. This representation skips the first S-box layer, as that layer does not contain any key material, so the known plaintexts must go through one S-box layer before being passed to SCALib. We chose to only look at S-box leakages, and therefore we only set initial beliefs for S-box input and/or outputs. Since the graphs are cyclic, we run approximate belief propagation. As we will be doing LFGI attacks, we use SCALib's built-in support for expanding the graphs. The code used for our experiments is available at https://github.com/Simula-UiB/SKINNY-LFGI and the trace dataset has been uploaded [4].

As noted earlier, the number of iterations of message-passing for approximate inference to consolidate, assuming it does, depend on the diameter of the graph. Going from one trace to two traces doubles the diameter, however, increasing from two to three or more makes no change. Therefore, the iteration count is independent of the number of traces. On the other hand, changing the number of rounds *does* change the diameter, and therefore impacts the iteration count. By taking the largest graph we look at, SKINNY-128-384 with 7 rounds on both sides, and increasing the iteration count of the attack until the increase in success rate started to diminish, we determined 60 iterations to be sufficient for our comparison. The success rates for FGI attacks on that graph with 25 target synthetic traces having a noise of $\sigma^2 = 16$ can be seen in Fig. 3. The noise was chosen such that the attack would not have a too high success rate at too few traces, and 25 target traces was chosen to not hit 100% success rate.

4.2 Synthetic Traces with Gaussian Noise

We start in the synthetic scenario, with leakage modeled as Hamming weights with Gaussian noise. As we know the parameter of the noise, we assume perfect templates and use those for the attack. That is, for each intermediate variable v, the leakage is sampled from $\mathcal{N}(\mathrm{HW}(v), \sigma^2)$. Let $f(x|\mu, \sigma^2)$ be the p.d.f. for

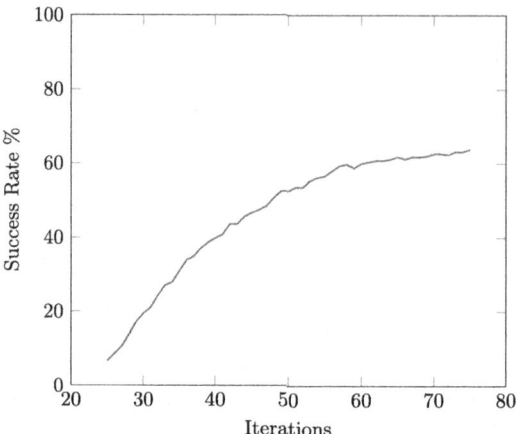

Fig. 3. Success rate as a function of number of iterations in the belief propagation step. Graph constructed as FGI targeting 224 S-boxes (7+7 rounds) of SKINNY-128-384 with 25 synthetic traces of noise $\sigma^2 = 16$. Success rate computed from 500 experiments.

$\mathcal{N}(\mu, \sigma^2)$, the normal distribution of mean μ and variance σ^2. Then the initial beliefs β for a node in the factor graph is computed as

$$\beta(i) = f(l|\text{HW}(i), \sigma^2) \tag{1}$$

for $0 \leq i \leq 255$.

CS23 only consider the leakage of S-boxes. With FGI, we could target all intermediate values, but for a more direct comparison, we chose to do the same as CS23, attacking only S-boxes. In each of the attacks, we look at the S-box outputs of initial rounds, and S-box inputs of final rounds. In addition, they only look at the 44 bi-dependent S-boxes, so for our initial comparison we will first look at an attack with only the same S-boxes to form our baseline. On the same scenarios as them, we then extend our attack to target up to four rounds from both sides, leading to a total of 128 S-boxes.

For each experiment, when another trace is added, the previous traces stay the same. So the experiments for n traces is the same as the experiment for $n-1$ traces, but with one additional trace added. For each plot, the experiments are repeated 500 times with new random traces.

Figure 4 shows the results for these scenarios for $\sigma^2 = 1$ and $\sigma^2 = 4$. We can see that for 44 S-boxes, the two approaches are comparable. However, FGI is able to exploit the information in the added S-boxes, and we can see that those additional S-boxes yield enough information for FGI to have a higher success rate with fewer traces.

Compared to a D&C approach, a fourfold increase in target S-boxes, from 16 to 64, yield a fourfold reduction in traces needed to reach similar success rates. The same linear relation between success rate and the number of S-boxes used approximately holds also when the number of target S-boxes is 44. However,

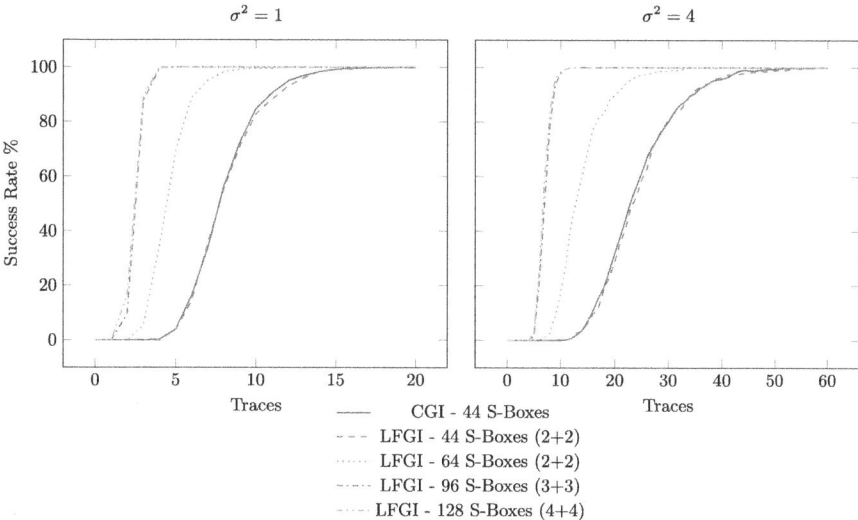

Fig. 4. Full key success rates over number of traces for FGI and CGI attacking generated Hamming weight traces of SKINNY. For the plaintext rounds, the S-box outputs are used, and for the ciphertext rounds, the S-box inputs are used.

for 96 S-boxes the reduction in traces needed is greater than sixfold reduction expected, and for 128 S-boxes there is no significant improvement over 96 S-boxes. Therefore, this relation does not seem to hold for deeper rounds.

Both $\sigma^2 = 1$ and $\sigma^2 = 4$ yield attacks with high success rates at only a handful of traces. Therefore, it is hard to see if more rounds would benefit the attack. To compare more rounds, we also attacked synthetic traces with higher noise, as seen in Fig. 5. Here, the noise level is $\sigma^2 = 16$ for synthetic SKINNY-128-128 traces, with 500 experiments for each number of traces. In addition to the success rates, we have computed estimated key ranks using SCALib and provide the average of the base two logarithm of those key ranks, following the suggestion of Martin et al. [15]. We can see from both success rates and average key ranks that there is an improvement going from 96 to 128 S-boxes, but going deeper is not beneficial for our approach. As the success rate shows a clearer separation between the different methods, we will stick to success rate henceforth.

4.3 Real Traces Produced by ChipWhisperer

For the real traces, we consider two implementations. One implements S-boxes as lookup tables (LUT) and the other with a circuit. Both of these implementations are of SKINNY-128-384, with the target key stored in the last block of the tweakkey. As the LUT leaks more, it will represent a scenario with low noise. As the circuit leaks less, it will be representative of a high-noise scenario. Since SKINNY-128-384 uses LFSRs in the key schedule, the graphs for FGI need to change to include them, as described in Sect. 3.1.

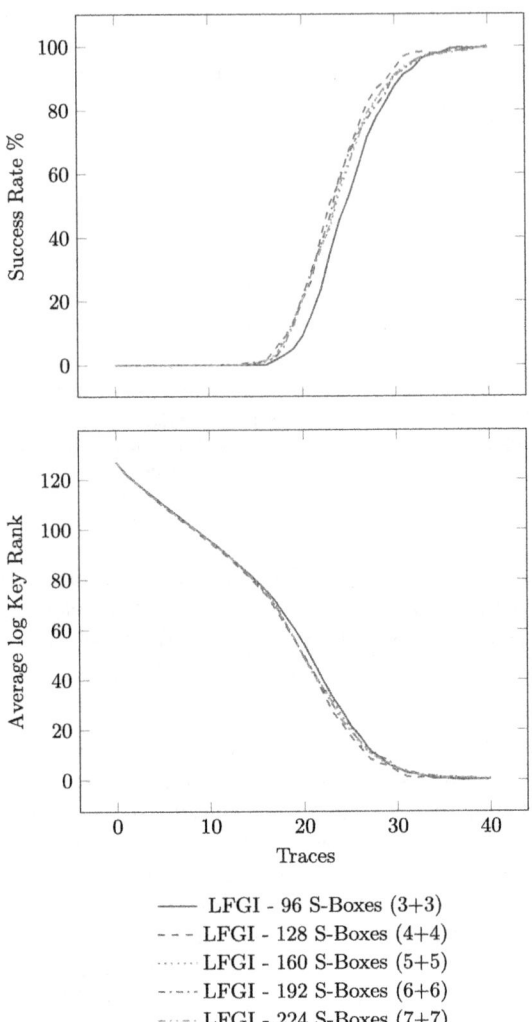

Fig. 5. Full key success rates and average $\log_2$ key ranks over number of traces for FGI attacking generated Hamming weight traces of SKINNY-128-128. For the plaintext rounds, the S-box outputs are used, and for the ciphertext rounds, the S-box inputs are used. Noise is $\sigma^2 = 16$.

For our profiled FGI attack we create profiles in the same way as CS23. For each of our target S-boxes, we select points of interest (PoI) using sum of differences, then we compute multivariate Gaussian templates for all 256 possible values of the S-boxes at those PoI.

For the attacks, we compute initial beliefs using our profiled templates on the attack traces. For the number of experiments we follow CS23 and do 500 exper-

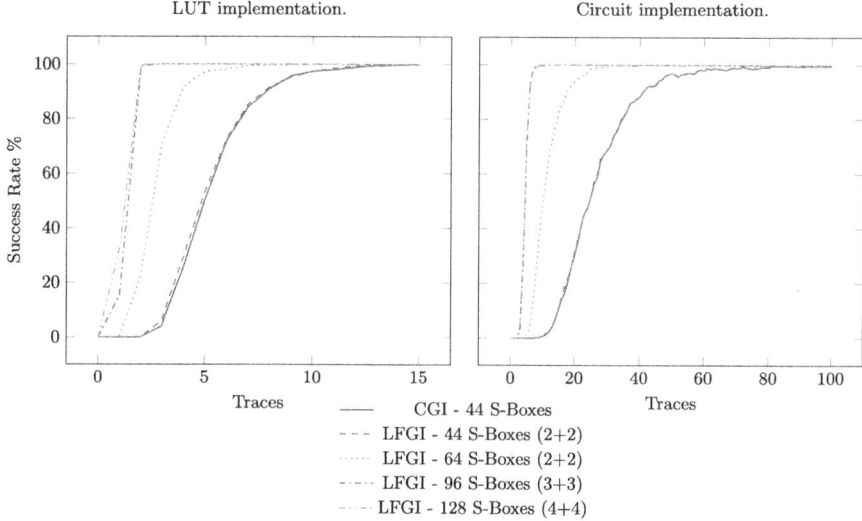

Fig. 6. Full key success rates over number of traces for FGI and CGI attacking SKINNY traces gathered on a ChipWhisperer. For both attacks, points of interest are found using sum of differences and scores are computed using Gaussian templates.

iments for the attacks on the circuit implementation and 1000 experiments for the attacks on the LUT implementation.

We can see from Fig. 6 that FGI is, again, on par with CGI with an equal amount of S-boxes, but FGI is able to exploit deeper rounds. Attacking 64 S-boxes yields an improved attack, which is further improved with 96 S-boxes, but there is no significant difference when going from 96 to 128 S-boxes.

5 Conclusion

We demonstrated an LFGI attack on SKINNY by constructing factor graphs for SKINNY-128-128 and SKINNY-128-384. We compared the performance of the attacks in a profiled setting with synthetic and real traces. Our attacks outperformed the previous state-of-the-art CGI attack by CS23, with the LFGI attacks exploiting leakage deeper into the cipher. However, unlike CGI, LFGI is not applicable in an unprofiled setting.

Our comparison focused on the graphical inference step in the attacks, as such, other aspects are left to optimize for a full attack. Our attack could be combined with deep learning based attacks, or improved dimensionality reduction techniques such as LDA. We also did not study the efficacy of our attack against masked implementations, so that remains a topic for future research.

For our experiments, we used success rate as our metric to compare the different attacks. An alternative approach would be comparing keyranks. However, we also believe key enumeration strategies is a potential point of improvement for graph based attacks, and leave that for future research.

Several open questions also remain for optimizing FGI for SCA. What is a good heuristic for the iteration count for loopy graphs? How do we quantify the impact of loops in our graphs, and what is a sensible heuristic for removing loops? How do we use FGI in an unprofiled setting?

References

1. Beierle, C., et al.: The SKINNY Family of Block Ciphers and Its Low-Latency Variant MANTIS. In: Robshaw, M., Katz, J. (eds.) CRYPTO 2016. LNCS, vol. 9815, pp. 123–153. Springer, Heidelberg (2016). https://doi.org/10.1007/978-3-662-53008-5_5
2. Bronchain, O., Standaert, F.X.: Breaking masked implementations with many shares on 32-bit software platforms. IACR TCHES **2021**(3), 202–234 (2021). https://doi.org/10.46586/tches.v2021.i3.202-234, https://tches.iacr.org/index.php/TCHES/article/view/8973
3. Cassiers, G., Bronchain, O.: Scalib: A side-channel analysis library. J. Open Source Softw. **8**(86), 5196 (2023). https://doi.org/10.21105/joss.05196
4. Costes, N., Husum, S., Stam, M., Raddum, H.: Side-channel analysis traces for SKINNY (2025). https://doi.org/10.5281/zenodo.14640175
5. Costes, N., Stam, M.: Pincering SKINNY by exploiting slow diffusion enhancing differential power analysis with cluster graph inference. IACR TCHES **2023**(4), 460–492 (2023). https://doi.org/10.46586/tches.v2023.i4.460-492
6. Green, J., Roy, A., Oswald, E.: A systematic study of the impact of graphical models on inference-based attacks on AES. In: Bilgin, B., Fischer, J.-B. (eds.) CARDIS 2018. LNCS, vol. 11389, pp. 18–34. Springer, Cham (2019). https://doi.org/10.1007/978-3-030-15462-2_2
7. Grosso, V., Standaert, F.-X.: ASCA, SASCA and DPA with enumeration: which one beats the other and when? In: Iwata, T., Cheon, J.H. (eds.) ASIACRYPT 2015. LNCS, vol. 9453, pp. 291–312. Springer, Heidelberg (2015). https://doi.org/10.1007/978-3-662-48800-3_12
8. Guo, C., Iwata, T., Khairallah, M., Minematsu, K., Peyrin, T.: Romulus v1.3 specification (2021)
9. Guo, Q., Grosso, V., Standaert, F.X., Bronchain, O.: Modeling soft analytical side-channel attacks from a coding theory viewpoint. IACR TCHES **2020**(4), 209–238 (2020).https://doi.org/10.13154/tches.v2020.i4.209-238, https://tches.iacr.org/index.php/TCHES/article/view/8682
10. Jean, J.: TikZ for Cryptographers. https://www.iacr.org/authors/tikz/ (2016)
11. Jean, J., Nikolic, I., Peyrin, T.: Tweaks and keys for block ciphers: the TWEAKEY framework. In: Sarkar, P., Iwata, T. (eds.) ASIACRYPT 2014, Part II. LNCS, vol. 8874, pp. 274–288. Springer, Heidelberg (Dec 2014). https://doi.org/10.1007/978-3-662-45608-8_15
12. Kannwischer, M.J., Pessl, P., Primas, R.: Single-trace attacks on KECCAK. Cryptology ePrint Archive, Report 2020/371 (2020). https://eprint.iacr.org/2020/371
13. Koller, D., Friedman, N.: Probabilistic Graphical Models - Principles and Techniques. MIT Press (2009)
14. Luo, S., Wu, W., Li, Y., Zhang, R., Liu, Z.: An efficient soft analytical side-channel attack on ASCON. In: Wang, L., Segal, M., Chen, J., Qiu, T. (eds.) WASA 2022. LNCS, vol. 13471, pp. 389–400. Springer, Heidelberg (2022). https://doi.org/10.1007/978-3-031-19208-1_32

15. Martin, D.P., Mather, L., Oswald, E., Stam, M.: Characterisation and estimation of the key rank distribution in the context of side channel evaluations. In: Cheon, J.H., Takagi, T. (eds.) ASIACRYPT 2016. LNCS, vol. 10031, pp. 548–572. Springer, Heidelberg (2016). https://doi.org/10.1007/978-3-662-53887-6_20
16. Oren, Y., Kirschbaum, M., Popp, T., Wool, A.: Algebraic side-channel analysis in the presence of errors. In: Mangard, S., Standaert, F.-X. (eds.) CHES 2010. LNCS, vol. 6225, pp. 428–442. Springer, Heidelberg (2010). https://doi.org/10.1007/978-3-642-15031-9_29
17. Oren, Y., Renauld, M., Standaert, F.-X., Wool, A.: Algebraic side-channel attacks beyond the hamming weight leakage model. In: Prouff, E., Schaumont, P. (eds.) CHES 2012. LNCS, vol. 7428, pp. 140–154. Springer, Heidelberg (2012). https://doi.org/10.1007/978-3-642-33027-8_9
18. Oren, Y., Wool, A.: Tolerant algebraic side-channel analysis of AES. Cryptology ePrint Archive, Report 2012/092 (2012). https://eprint.iacr.org/2012/092
19. Pessl, P., Primas, R.: More practical single-trace attacks on the number theoretic transform. In: Schwabe, P., Thériault, N. (eds.) LATINCRYPT 2019. LNCS, vol. 11774, pp. 130–149. Springer, Cham (2019). https://doi.org/10.1007/978-3-030-30530-7_7
20. Primas, R., Pessl, P., Mangard, S.: Single-trace side-channel attacks on masked lattice-based encryption. In: Fischer, W., Homma, N. (eds.) CHES 2017. LNCS, vol. 10529, pp. 513–533. Springer, Cham (2017). https://doi.org/10.1007/978-3-319-66787-4_25
21. Renauld, M., Standaert, F.X.: Algebraic side-channel attacks. Cryptology ePrint Archive, Report 2009/279 (2009). https://eprint.iacr.org/2009/279
22. Renauld, M., Standaert, F.-X., Veyrat-Charvillon, N.: Algebraic side-channel attacks on the AES: why time also matters in DPA. In: Clavier, C., Gaj, K. (eds.) CHES 2009. LNCS, vol. 5747, pp. 97–111. Springer, Heidelberg (2009). https://doi.org/10.1007/978-3-642-04138-9_8
23. Strieder, E., Ilg, M., Heyszl, J., Unterstein, F., Streit, S.: ASCA vs. SASCA - A closer look at the AES key schedule. In: Kavun, E.B., Pehl, M. (eds.) COSADE 2023. LNCS, vol. 13979, pp. 65–85. Springer, Heidelberg (2023). https://doi.org/10.1007/978-3-031-29497-6_4
24. Veyrat-Charvillon, N., Gérard, B., Standaert, F.-X.: Soft analytical side-channel attacks. In: Sarkar, P., Iwata, T. (eds.) ASIACRYPT 2014. LNCS, vol. 8873, pp. 282–296. Springer, Heidelberg (2014). https://doi.org/10.1007/978-3-662-45611-8_15
25. You, S., Kuhn, M.G.: Single-trace fragment template attack on a 32-bit implementation of KECCAK. In: Grosso, V., Pöppelmann, T. (eds.) CARDIS 2021. LNCS, vol. 13173, pp. 3–23. Springer, Heidelberg (2021). https://doi.org/10.1007/978-3-030-97348-3_1
26. You, S.C., Kuhn, M.G., Sarkar, S., Hao, F.: Low trace-count template attacks on 32-bit implementations of ASCON AEAD. IACR TCHES **2023**(4), 344–366 (2023). https://doi.org/10.46586/tches.v2023.i4.344-366

Physical Security

Robust and Reliable PUF Protocol Exploiting Non-monotonic Quantization and Neyman-Pearson Lemma

Neelam Nasir[1], Julien Béguinot[1], Wei Cheng[1,2], Ulrich Kühne[1(✉)], and Jean-Luc Danger[1]

[1] Télécom Paris, Institut polytechnique de Paris, Palaiseau, France
ulrich.kuhne@telecom-paris.fr
[2] Secure-IC S.A.S, Paris, France

Abstract. Strong physical unclonable functions (PUFs) provide a cost-effective authentication solution for resource-limited devices. However, they are susceptible to machine learning (ML) attacks. The lightweight defenses against ML rely on adding non-linearity in the PUF behavior (as the XOR-PUF), or limiting the number of challenges at protocol level (as the lockdown protocol) to constrain learning. Another low-cost approach is to use a non-linear quantization of the response when the PUF provides an integer response, like the RO-PUF. This paper studies the non-monotonic quantization (NMQ) which greatly enhances the security when a large number of quantization level is used. Unfortunately, this makes the PUF highly unreliable, rendering it impractical for authentication purposes. In this study, we propose a solution which circumvents the intrinsic PUF unreliability of NMQ to build an effective authentication protocol. It relies on the Neyman-Pearson test which transforms the native dependability of responses into an asset to get a reliable authentication protocol. To validate this approach, we evaluate our solution in FPGA using a loop PUF (ring oscillator-based PUF) which is a multi-bin PUF. The results show that an authentication success of nearly 100% can be obtained with a high resistance as up to 60% accuracy against three types of ML attacks.

Keywords: Hardware security · Physical unclonable functions · ML attacks · Reliability · Non-monotonic quantization · Neyman-Pearson test

1 Introduction

Physical unclonable functions (PUFs) have been proposed as a low-cost security anchor [1,2], notably for lightweight authentication protocol. This protocol relies on the physical input/output relationship (respectively challenge/response) of the PUF. The PUF called *strong* are well suited for this application as they provide many challenge-responses pairs(CRPs).

In the context of a challenge-response protocol, for a PUF to be *secure*, its output must be hard to predict. Strong PUFs relying on delay chains as entropy source (such as the arbiter PUFs [3] and RO PUFs [1]) have inherently a linear behavior or a limited entropy. Therefore they are attackable by machine learning (ML) techniques such as linear and/or logistic regressions by collecting challenge-response pairs (CRPs) [4]. In order to prevent such attacks, the PUF must be hard to model. One type of protection is to introduce non-linearity into the current PUF architectures. The composition of PUFs is one way to increase the non-linear behavior. The XOR-PUF [1] which is composed of arbiter PUFs whose outputs are XORed, and the interpose-PUF [5] are the most popular. The use of permutation of multiple delay lines [6] like the Beli PUF [7] is another type of protection. However, even if a deep security analysis of these structures has shown a great increase of robustness against ML attacks, they still remain vulnerable [6,8].

Another non-linear approach applicable to PUFs where the physical variable can be quantized with more than 1-bit, like the oscillation frequency of the RO-PUF, is to do the *non-monotonic quantization* (NMQ) [9]. The output distribution of these types of PUF is multi-bin PUF as their entropy is more than one bit, hence the values are $\{0,1,2,3\}$ for a 2-bit linear quantization. A generic multi-bin PUF is the *Alphabet PUF* [10] which takes advantage of a multi-threshold quantization stage and data encoding. The alphabet PUF has been originally studied for secret key generation with Helper data and ECC, but it can also be used as a strong PUF with a CRP protocol. The NMQ quantization principle is to transpose a n-bit PUF to a 1-bit PUF such that the values 1 and 0 values are interleaved, i.e. the values $\{0,1,2,3\}$ of the 2-bit PUF become $\{0,1,0,1\}$, thus generating a 1-bit output in a non-monotonic way. It has been shown in [9] that the resistance against ML grows with the quantization levels, denoted by Q in the sequel, but the reliability becomes so low with high Q that an authentication process becomes impossible. Indeed, Q values involves $Q-1$ thresholds to compare at the quantization stage, and consequently more unsteadiness due the environmental noise around these thresholds.

In this paper, we first study the PUF with NMQ quantization (NMQ-PUF) to better know the impact of the quantization level Q and the environmental noise on both the security against ML and the reliability. Then, we propose an authentication protocol based on the Neyman-Pearson Lemma [11] to compensate for the bad reliability of NMQ with high values of Q. It has to be noted that the security comes from the NMQ quantization, while the protocol helps to mitigate the low reliability of NMQ by exploiting the knowledge of the reliability itself for each challenge. Our simulations and experimental results with a multi-bin PUF – a Loop PUF [12] implemented in FPGA – show the effectiveness of the proposed approach, allowing for high values of Q, while compensating the resulting high bit error rate.

As a summary, the contributions of this paper are the following:

1. Present analyses on the reliability and security against modeling attacks with NMQ at various quantization levels.

2. Propose a new PUF authentication protocol using the Neyman-Pearson test in the presence of high bit error rates.
3. Validate the security and authentication success on a Loop PUF implemented in FPGA.

The remainder of this paper is structured as follows: Related work is discussed in Sect. 2. The main contributions on reliability, machine learning attacks and our proposed protocol are presented in Sects. 3 and 4, respectively. We show experimental results in Sect. 5. Section 6 discusses about the impact of the environment on the authentication method, and Sect. 7 concludes.

2 Related Work

In this section we present the context related to the ML attack against PUF when used for authentication. The protections against such attacks are either to build a natively robust PUF or to devise specific PUF protocols, or both. The robustness challenge is all the greater if the PUF has to keep the lightweight property.

2.1 Modeling Attacks on PUF

In the classical PUF Challenge-Response Pair (CRP) protocol, the input challenges and associated output responses can be eavesdropped and replayed by the attacker. A stronger model which is currently used in the literature and in this paper is that the attacker has full access to the device's interface. Thus, she can freely input any challenge and read the associated response to build a CRP dataset and feed Machine Learning (ML) algorithms to get a PUF model. The attack efficiency highly depends on the ML algorithms and the number of collected CRPs to get a high accuracy. The arbiter PUF [13] is one of the first silicon PUF which has been devised and attacked by the Support Vector Machine (SVM) algorithm [14]. More derivatives of Arbiter PUF have been attacked by the Logistic Regression algorithm (LR) in [4]. It takes advantage of the quasi-linear behavior of the arbiter PUF which relies on a delay chain. The progress in ML attack has followed the evolution of PUF. For instance the Covariance Matrix Adaptation Evolution Strategy (CMA-ES) [15] uses the information of reliability to increase the attack efficiency of XOR-PUF. The hyperparameters of Neural Networks (NN) have often to be tailored to target a great variety of strong PUFs [16].

2.2 ML Resistant PUFs

Many PUFs have been devised to have a more complex and non-linear behavior, mainly by using a composition of PUFs. One of the most common is the XOR Arbiter PUF [1]. It has been shown that the Neural Network (NN) is an efficient

ML algorithm to attack such PUF [17]. The Interpose PUF [5] provides a better security for the same complexity as the XOR PUF. Another variant is the Multiplexer Arbiter PUF where the XOR is replaced by a multiplexer [18]. A novel architecture relying on permutations of multiple delay lines like the Beli PUF [7] has been recently proposed. All these architectures significantly increase the security, especially with bigger size and composition of delay lines. But all the proposed PUFs can be attacked by learning bigger dataset and optimizing ML algorithms [6,8]. For instance the attack on the interpose PUF splits the composed PUF in subsets to perpetrate a divide and conquer approach.

2.3 PUF Protocols

In the survey by Delvaux et al. [19], it is shown than most PUF-based authentication protocols use cryptographic block, True Random Number Generator (TRNG) or Error Correcting Code (ECC). These tools allow to get a higher level of robustness, even if in [20] it is shown that many PUF protocols are attackable by tailored ML. The significant drawback of these protocols result in an heavyweight implementation which is not suitable for low-cost products like RFID or IoT devices. There are very few lightweight protocols which do not require complex blocks at device level. The Lockdown technique [21] is one of the more robust and lightweight protocol as it allows the authentication process to bound the number of CRPs, hence thwarting the ML attacks by limiting the dataset.

2.4 Contribution of the Proposed Method

We consider that the security against ML attack is ensured by the multi-bin PUF architecture which uses NMQ as quantizer. The authentication protocol uses the Neyman-Pearson test to enhance the bad reliability provided by NMQ when the number of quantization levels is high. Hence, from the security point of view, it mainly relies on the PUF rather than the protocol. This latter is to allow the NMQ-PUF to work properly when it has a high level of security. Another strong requirement of the method is its lightweight property. The only addition of complexity is the quantization block which consists of comparators between the PUF internal response and constant threshold values.

The next section is dedicated to the security and reliability of NMQ, notably the impact of the quantization level and noise on these two properties.

3 Non-monotonic Quantization

In this section, we first introduce the basic definitions and notations in order to reason about PUFs and present NMQ and its specific properties of reliability and security.

3.1 Basic Notions

We will denote the set of challenges as $\mathcal{C} = \{C_1, C_2, \ldots, C_N\}$. The response of a PUF is calculated in two steps: First we measure the raw response (in our case a delay difference) to a given challenge. The raw response is then quantized in a second step to a single bit response. The first step is modeled as a function $\mathcal{P}$ that maps a challenge to a delay difference value:

$$\mathcal{P}: C \mapsto \delta_C. \tag{1}$$

The raw response $\mathcal{P}$ can be modeled as a random[1] variable Δ following a normal distribution: $\Delta \sim \mathcal{N}(\mu, \Sigma^2)$. The standard deviation Σ depends on the underlying circuit technology. Note that the function $\mathcal{P}$ is an idealized model, since it does not take into account measurement noise. This raw response is then mapped to a single bit using some quantization function

$$b: \delta_C \mapsto \{0, 1\}. \tag{2}$$

We summarize both as the PUF's response

$$\mathcal{R}(C) = b(\mathcal{P}(C)). \tag{3}$$

A typical example for b is the sign of the raw response.

For a more realistic model, we need to take into account the noise, which will make the measurements of δ_C vary around their nominal values. Again, we model the noise as a random variable $Z \sim \mathcal{N}(0, \sigma^2)$. By adding the noise to the nominal output, we obtain a probabilistic version of our PUF model:

$$\hat{\mathcal{P}}: C \mapsto \delta_C + Z. \tag{4}$$

An important property of a PUF implementation is the ratio between the variance of the nominal response and the measurement noise. The higher the noise level with respect to the amplitude of the nominal response, the higher will be the probability to get a wrong response. We thus define the signal-to-noise ratio of the PUF as the ratio of the two variances:

$$\text{SNR} = \frac{\Sigma^2}{\sigma^2}. \tag{5}$$

Finally, we define the *bit error rate* (BER) as the probability to obtain a wrong response, i.e. that the response differs from the nominal response:

$$\text{BER}(C) = \mathbb{P}\left(b(\mathcal{P}(C)) \neq b(\hat{\mathcal{P}}(C))\right). \tag{6}$$

---

[1] Note that while the raw outputs δ_C follow a Gaussian distribution, $\mathcal{P}$ is not deterministic but it is considered as such at first, i.e. the environment is steady and the delays are fixed at fabrication time of the PUF. Section 6 will consider the impact of temperature and voltage.

3.2 NMQ Principle

As described above, in classic delay PUFs like the arbiter PUF, RO PUF, or Loop PUF, the response is based on whether a differential delay Δ is positive or negative, thus equivalent to 1-bit quantization. It has been shown in Sect. 2 that this simple decision-making process is vulnerable to ML attacks, even for composite PUF which are attackable by ML with a large dataset or a tailored ML. For multi-bin PUFs like RO PUF and Loop PUF, the raw output δ_C can be quantized on more than 1 bit, let us use Q as the quantization level. This allows the user to either increase the entropy of $\log_2(Q)$ bits or to keep a 1-bit entropy by using the non-monotonic quantization (NMQ) method. Figure 1 shows a typical quantization (equivalent to $Q=2$) and NMQ with $Q=4$ and 8.

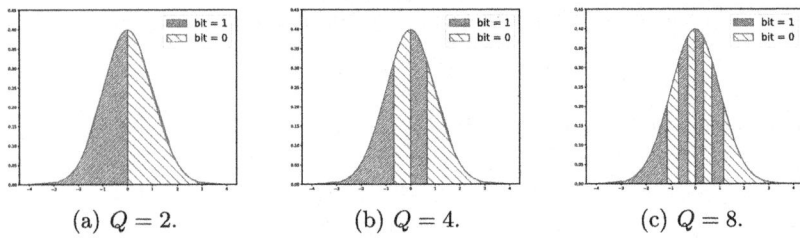

(a) $Q = 2$. (b) $Q = 4$. (c) $Q = 8$.

Fig. 1. Different NMQ quantization levels.

Given the raw response δ_C and an even quantization level Q, the non-monotonic quantization can be defined as

$$\text{NMQ}_Q(\delta_C) = \begin{cases} 1, & \text{if } T_{2i-1} < \delta_C \leq T_{2i} \text{ for } i \in \{1, \ldots, \frac{Q}{2}\} \\ 0, & \text{otherwise} \end{cases} \quad (7)$$

where the T_i are threshold values delimiting the quantiles of the distribution. In order to avoid bias, we want to use equiprobable quantiles. For example, for $Q = 4$, the thresholds can be determined as follows:

$$T_1 = \mu - 0.675\sigma, \quad T_2 = \mu, \quad T_3 = \mu + 0.675\sigma, \quad T_4 = \infty. \quad (8)$$

This new decision metric complicates the mapping between the challenge and the response, enhancing the resilience of PUFs against ML-based attacks.

3.3 Reliability of NMQ Implementation

In a PUF equipped with NMQ, its reliability tends to decrease as the quantization level Q increases. Figure 2 illustrates the BER of δ_C for different values of Q. The BER shown in the Figure has been calculated based on a simulated PUF using a SNR of 300, which corresponds to the SNR that we have measured for an FPGA implementation of a Loop PUF, and which is consistent with values

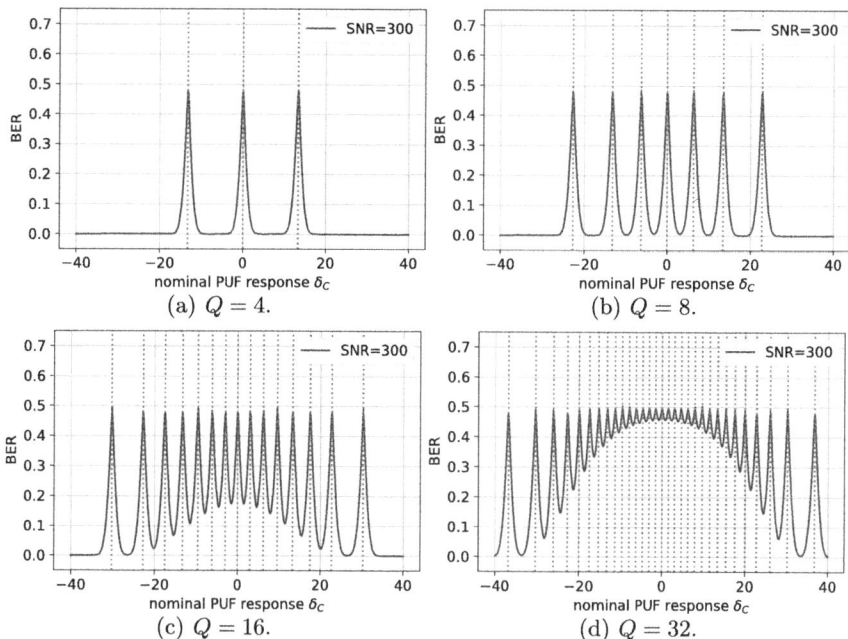

Fig. 2. BER estimation for different quantization levels and SNR = 300.

from the literature [22]. We can see that the BER greatly increases for δ_C being close to the quantization thresholds. At higher numbers of Q, as the number of thresholds increases in $Q-1$, the boundaries between quantization intervals become finer. Figure 3 shows the significant impact of SNR on the BER. The increased granularity associated with low SNR makes the PUF more sensitive to noise when Q is high. This leads to an higher average BER, and thus lower reliability.

The reduced reliability at higher Q poses a challenge for the authentication process. With a higher BER, it becomes more difficult to distinguish between a legitimate device and an adversary, thus creating a significant rate of false negatives. Although increasing the number of quantization level can enhance security by introducing more complex response patterns, this comes at the cost of reliability. Therefore, there is a trade-off between achieving higher security and reliability.

3.4 Security of NMQ Against Modeling Attacks

The question is to know if PUFs equipped with NMQ can really resist against the modeling attacks. The first study of NMQ [9] has shown that it is attackable by Convolutional Neural Network (CNN) with a low level of quantization. Increasing the quantization level increases the resistance but the PUF becomes

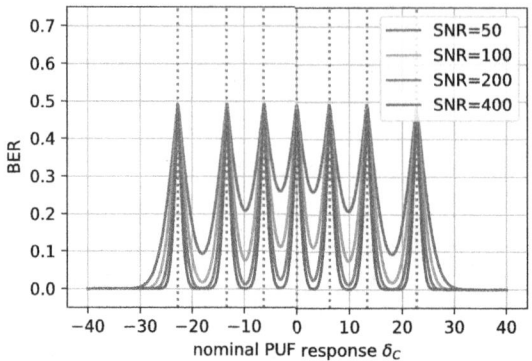

Fig. 3. BER estimation for $Q = 8$ and different noise levels.

unpracticable because of its very poor reliability. In order to assess the modeling attack resistance, we utilize Logistic regression (LR) [4], CNN, and multi-layer perceptron (MLP) as three attacking means[2].

In the sequel, we consider NMQ running on a Loop PUF as an exemplary target with various NMQ parameter. We launch experiments on both simulated CRP dataset and real-world CRP dataset acquired on an FPGA implementation.

Modeling Attacks on Simulated NMQ-LPUFs

We first simulate RO-PUFs equipped with NMQ as introduced in Sect. 3.2. In addition, we also consider the PUF process is perturbed by the environmental and electronic factors by adding extra noise as in Eq. 4. The main impact of this extra noise is the reliability of the PUF instance, which shall affect the learnable feature in CRPs and thus the attack accuracy of modeling attacks.

In this work, we have selected several noise levels to show their impact. In particular, we choose $\frac{1}{\text{SNR}} \in \{0, \frac{1}{1000}, \frac{1}{800}, \frac{1}{500}, \frac{1}{400}, \frac{1}{200}, \frac{1}{100}, \frac{1}{50}\}$ (namely, SNR ranges from noiseless to 50). This range of SNR includes typical SNR of FPGA-based and ASIC PUF implementations that have an SNR between 50 and 300. For instance, SNR = 220 has been measured on a PUF implementation using 65nm CMOS technology [22], or SNR ≈ 50 when using a 28nm CMOS FD-SOI technology [23]. In our FPGA experiments, we measured a value of around 300. We set the total number of CRPs for the training phase to 400,000[3], which is enough to get stable results, and use another 100,000 CRPs for the attack phase. Each experiment is repeated 10 times to reduce the numerical biases.

---

[2] In this work, we do not differentiate the conventional modeling attacks (like LR, support vector machine, etc.) with the deep learning-based attacks, since they typically act similarly in evaluating the security of PUFs.

[3] We have tested for other dataset size for verification, while obtained similar results starting from around 200,000 CRPs.

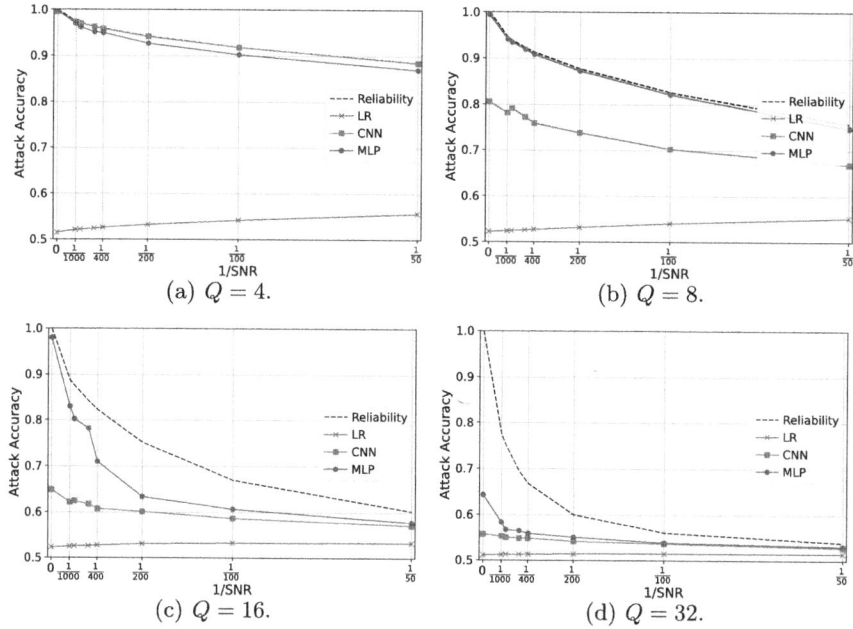

Fig. 4. Modeling attack results against NMQ-LPUF with $Q \in \{4, 8, 16, 32\}$ in simulated scenario.

The results are shown in Fig. 4. We show the attack accuracy of the three modeling attacks compared to the corresponding reliability results at each noise level. The main takeaway is that with increasing of the NMQ parameter, the modeling attack resistance is largely increased, especially when $Q = 32$. Secondly, the noise can have a distinct impact on the learning ability of modeling attack methods, which are consistent for both CNN and MLP results. Notably, the best attack accuracy is, as expected, upper-bounded by the reliability of the corresponding noise level.

Modeling Attacks on FPGA-Based NMQ-LPUFs

We next present the results on real-world FPGA-based PUF implementation. We implement NMQ-LPUFs on the Basys3 FPGA boards, which are based on the Xilinx Artix-7 28nm technology. It is worth noting that SNR ≈ 300 on the measured dataset containing 1,000,000 CRPs. The attack results are shown in Fig. 5 for $Q \in \{2, 4, 8, 16, 32\}$ where $Q = 2$ is selected as the baseline to demonstrate the security gains against the modeling attacks. Specifically, for each of LR, CNN and MLP, we vary the size of the training set from 10,000 to 800,000 CRPs and train the model with 50 epochs to show the impact of dataset size; while the attacking (test) set contains 100,000 CRPs (without overlapping

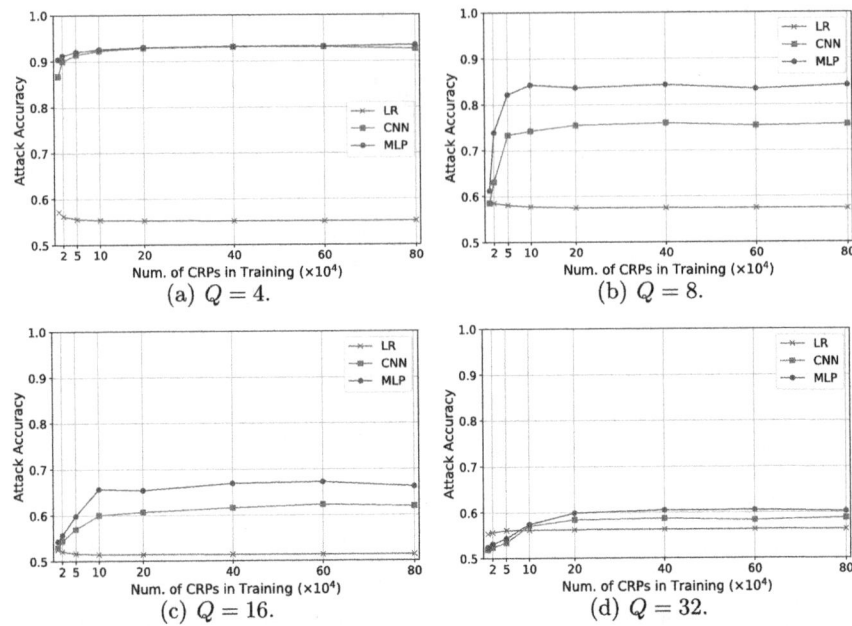

Fig. 5. Modeling attack results against NMQ-LPUF with $Q \in \{4, 8, 16, 32\}$ implemented on an FPGA board.

with training set). We repeat each experiments by 10 times and then take the average to have more stable results.

Notably, the results from the real-world devices are overall consistent with the simulated data as shown in Fig. 4. From Fig. 5, there are two main takeaways: Firstly, NMQ can resist against LR-based modeling attacks even with quite small Q (e.g., $Q = 4$). Secondly, NMQ seems to show significantly enhanced resistance against CNN-based and MLP-based modeling attacks when taking large values of Q (e.g., $Q \geq 16$). The underlying reason is that NMQ discloses less significant information on the delay difference in deciding the output rather than the sign function in many ideal PUFs [4]. However, NMQ with smaller Q is still ineffective, which the designers should be careful to avoid for potential vulnerability against CNN-based and MLP-based modeling attacks.

4 Neyman-Pearson Test for PUF Authentication

To address the issue of higher BER at higher Q, we propose the application of the Neyman-Pearson test in the PUF protocol.

4.1 Principle

The Neyman-Pearson framework provides a statistically rigorous method to differentiate between a legitimate device and an adversarial device. It takes advantage of the BER knowledge for each challenge. By the Neyman-Pearson Lemma [24, Theorem 11.7.1], this test is uniformly most powerful at level α. In other words, for fixed level of security (probability to accept an adversary) this test will minimize the probability to reject a legitimate device.

The proposed protocol works by using a fixed number of challenges, say n, to authenticate a device and by using their associated BER. Leveraging the BER knowledge helps in a sense to discard the least reliable response and consider reliable responses in the test outcome while not disclosing to the adversary which challenge response pair is unreliable.

The Neyman-Pearson test aims to distinguish between two hypotheses: the null hypothesis H_0 and the alternative hypothesis H_1, while focusing on controlling the probabilities of two types of errors. This test maximizes the probability of correctly rejecting H_1 (i.e., the *power* of the test) for a given threshold, ensuring that false positives do not exceed. In the context of device authentication, the Neyman-Pearson test can be used to distinguish between a legitimate device H_0 and an adversary device H_1. The attack efficiency is characterized by:

- The probability of rejecting the hypothesis that the device is legitimate (H_0) when it is actually legitimate: **false negative** or **missed authentication**).
- The probability of accepting the hypothesis that the device is illegitimate (H_1) when it is actually an adversary: **false positive** or **false authentication**.

4.2 Steps of the Neyman-Pearson Test

Four steps are required to carry out the test:

1. **Formulate the hypotheses**:

$$H_0 : \text{The device is legitimate,}$$
$$H_1 : \text{The device is an adversary.}$$

2. **Choose a threshold**: The threshold k defines the boundary for authentication process, it is chosen to yield a separation between the two hypotheses.
3. **Define the rejection region**: The test is based on the likelihood ratio:

$$\alpha = \frac{L(R|H_1)}{L(R|H_0)} = \frac{\prod_{i=0}^{n} \text{BER}(C_i)^{e_i} \left(1 - \text{BER}(C_i)\right)^{(1-e_i)}}{\left(\frac{1}{2}\right)^n} \qquad (9)$$

where $L(R|H_0)$ and $L(R|H_1)$ are the likelihood functions under the hypotheses H_0 (legitimate device) and H_1 (adversary device), respectively. Here, R represents the n responses from the device, and the likelihood ratio α is computed to compare the hypotheses.

In the formula, $\text{BER}(C_i)$ represents the BER for the i-th challenge, and e_i denotes the observed error for the i-th challenge. The test rejects H_0 if the likelihood ratio α is less than threshold k. In particular, errors on reliable challenge will be heavily penalized while errors on unreliable challenges are less significant (in the extreme case where a bit error rate is maximal equals to $\frac{1}{2}$ an error is completely ignored by the test).

4. **Make a decision**: Based on the observed data R, if $\alpha < k$, reject H_0 (consider the device as adversarial); otherwise, do not reject H_0 (consider the device as legitimate).

Overall, this procedure mitigates the high bit error rates of the challenges as long as some challenges are reliable.

4.3 Design of the PUF Authentication Protocol

The protocol is represented in Fig. 6. The enrollment phase is to prepare the Neyman-Pearson test by modeling the PUF and BER. The authentication phase is to check the two hypotheses of the Neyman-Pearson test.

The two phases are described below in a detailed manner:

1. Enrollment Phase. During the enrollment phase, the server collects the responses of Hadamard challenges. The Hadamard challenges are used because their response are theoretically uncorrelated [25,26] and the delay model D of the PUF can be easily reconstructed by a matrix inversion. This approach allows the server to calculate responses for any future challenges without storing a big set of CRPs. Furthermore, the Hadamard challenges can be used multiple times to reduce the effect of noise and create a more accurate model by averaging the raw responses δ_{c_H}.

To account for the impact of noise during the enrollment phase, the responses are sampled multiple (j) times during the enrollment phase[4]. Additionally, the BER model is created which is essential for the following Neyman-Pearson test. This BER model estimates the error rates for all challenges, quantifying the likelihood of errors due to noise, environmental variations, or quantization effects. The noise's standard deviation σ is calculated using a reference challenge and stored for use during the authentication phase. It is used to estimate the BER for each challenge at a given quantization level.

2. Authentication Phase. The server sends a set of n random challenges at a given quantification Q to the device. The device generates responses R_d using the PUF. The server, utilizing its stored PUF model, computes the expected raw responses δ_C and quantized responses R_s for the same set of random challenges. By comparing R_d and R_s, it identifies the error e_i for each challenge, creating an error vector e. The BER model is then used to estimate the probability of error $\mathbf{P}_{err}(C_i)$. The server subsequently applies the Neyman-Pearson test using the calculated BER for each challenge and the observed errors e from the comparison between the device's PUF responses and the expected responses from the server's PUF model. The likelihood ration α is computed and compared with

---

[4] We assume that the enrollment of the PUF takes place in a controlled environment, minimizing temperature and voltage variations as well as external electro-magnetic radiation.

Server		Device
Enrollment Phase		
Generate C_H	$\xrightarrow{C_H, i}$	
$D_i = C_{Hi}^{-1} . \delta_{di}$ Store D_i	$\xleftarrow{\delta_{di}}$	$\delta_d = PUF(C_H)$
Generate C_{ref}	$\xrightarrow{C_{ref}, j}$	
$std(noise) = \sigma(\delta_{ref})$ Store $std(noise)$	$\xleftarrow{\delta_{ref}}$	$\delta_{ref} = PUF(C_{ref})$
Authentication Phase		
Generates C_{random} and select Q	$\xrightarrow{C_{random}, Q}$	
$\delta_C = PUF_{model}(C_{random})$ $R_s = NMQ_Q(\delta_C)$		
$e_i = \begin{cases} 0, & \text{if } R_d = R_s \\ 1, & \text{if } R_d \neq R_s \end{cases}$	$\xleftarrow{R_d}$	$\delta_c = PUF(C_{random})$ $R_d = NMQ_Q(\delta_C)$
where $i = 1, 2, 3, \ldots, N$ $BER_i(\delta_C) = \mathbf{P}_{err}(C_i)$ $\alpha = NP_{test}(BER, e, N)$		
if $\alpha < k$, then $\begin{cases} \text{True, Authenticated,} \\ \text{False, Unauthenticated.} \end{cases}$		
where $k = Threshold$	$\xrightarrow{Auth/Unauth}$	

Fig. 6. Neyman-Pearson PUF authentication protocol: the enrollment and the authentication.

the predefined threshold k. If $\alpha < k$, the device is authenticated as legitimate; otherwise, the device is flagged as an adversary.

This PUF authentication protocol offers the following properties:

- The application of the Neyman-Pearson Lemma reduces the likelihood of false positives and false negatives by carefully choosing the threshold k and the number of challenges n. k guarantees the best trade-off between the false positives and false negatives, whereas n decreases both.
- The protocol increases the security for a high number of quantization level, thanks to NMQ.

4.4 PUF Delay and BER Models

The protocol requires at server side an accurate delay model and BER model. The build of the models is described below.

Delay Modeling

The responses obtained from the PUF for the Hadamard challenges are then used to calculate the delays of the physical elements in the PUF. For the delay PUF like the Loop PUF, the delay chain consists of M delay elements and the challenge is M bits long. Hence M Hadamard challenges and their corresponding responses are used. The delay model of the M elements can be computed using matrix multiplication, where the inverse of the matrix of M Hadamard challenges is multiplied by the vector of recorded responses. The delay for the i-th element is given by:

$$D_i = C_i^{-1} \cdot R_i. \qquad (10)$$

where C_i^{-1} is the inverse of the Hadamard challenge matrix, and R_i is the vector of responses for the i-th challenge. This method allows the server to model the delay characteristics of the PUF accurately and use this model for future challenge-response calculations without needing to store all CRPs.

BER Modeling

As shown in Fig. 7, the BER requires first the delay model and the noise model of the device. Then the quantization is executed according to the quantization level Q.

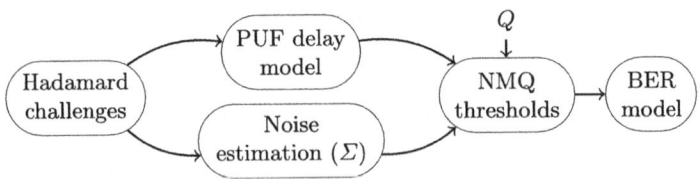

Fig. 7. BER estimation for Neyman-Pearson PUF Authentication Protocol.

Noise Model: At the enrollment phase, the server gathers several raw responses δ_{ref} for reference challenge C_{ref} to estimate the noise affecting the PUF. The standard deviation of the noise, namely $\sigma(\text{noise})$, is calculated based on these repeated observations.

More formally, we have

$$\sigma(\text{noise}) = \sqrt{\frac{1}{N}\sum_{i=1}^{N}(\delta_{ref_i} - \mu_{ref})^2} \quad . \tag{11}$$

where:

- δ_{ref_i} is the raw response to a reference challenge in ith iterations,
- μ_{ref} is the mean response over N iterations,
- N is the number of iterations or repeated raw responses collected.

By storing $\sigma(\text{noise})$ at the enrollment phase, the system can later predict how much variation is expected in the responses during the authentication phase.

BER Model: During the authentication phase, the BER is estimated by analyzing the probability of error in a response derived from the server-side PUF model, denoted as δ_s, when subjected to noise characterized by a standard deviation $\sigma(\text{noise})$.

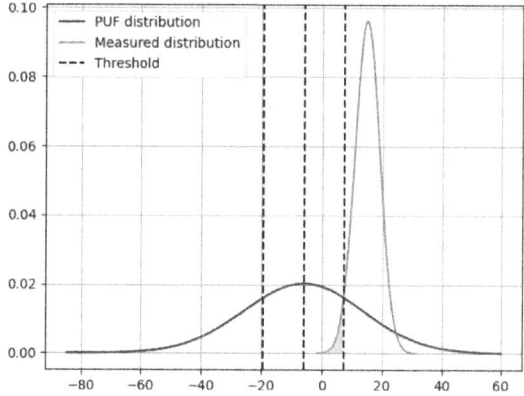

Fig. 8. BER estimation for a single challenge with $Q = 4$.

Figure 8 visualizes the relationship between the distributions of the PUF response values (in blue) and the measured distribution at δ_s (in red). The blue curve represents the distribution of the responses from the server-side PUF model. These values can vary slightly around a central value due to natural variations in the PUF's physical characteristics. The distribution is modeled as a normal distribution as follows.

$$pdf(\delta) = \mathcal{N}(0, \Sigma^2). \tag{12}$$

where Σ^2 represents the variance of the PUF response values. The red curve represents the measured response, which is the actual PUF response corrupted by noise. The noise is modeled as by a normal distribution as $\mathcal{N}(0, \sigma^2)$.

The error probability (shaded region) refers to the likelihood that the measured response is different from the actual PUF response. If the response is close to a threshold (the vertical dotted line), this likelihood increases. If the measured response lies in the overlapping region between the two curves, there is a higher chance of an error. The larger the overlap between the PUF response distribution and the measurement distribution, the higher the BER.

5 Results and Observations

5.1 Experimental Setup

The experiments were conducted on sixteen Basys3 FPGA boards, which are based on the Xilinx Artix-7 28nm technology. As a multi-bin delay PUF, we used a Loop PUF [12] with a delay chain of 64 elements and a δ_C response of 16 bits.

5.2 Neyman-Pearson PUF Authentication Protocol: Safety Window for Threshold

The safety window in the Neyman-Pearson PUF authentication protocol refers to the gap between the α-PUF and α-adversary values. This window plays a crucial role in distinguishing between legitimate devices and adversaries during authentication. A larger safety window indicates a significant difference between the responses of the PUF and the adversary, reducing the likelihood of wrong authentication. When the safety window is wide, the system can more reliably differentiate between legitimate responses and random guesses made by adversaries, even in the presence of noise or environmental variations. Conversely, a narrow safety window increases the risk of false positives or false negatives, as the adversary's response values may be too close to the legitimate PUF values.

Figure 9 shows the fluctuation in α-PUF and α-adversary due to system noise and physical factors, and predicts a region of safety to define a threshold. The green region in each graph represents the safety window, within which a threshold can be defined based on security requirements. The threshold is set closer to α-PUF to minimize the risk of false positives, which occur when an adversary is mistakenly accepted as a legitimate PUF. It can be observed that with a small number of challenges, it is difficult to distinguish between the PUF and the adversary as shown in Fig. 9(a). Therefore, it is crucial to choose a sufficient number of challenges for secure and reliable authentication. Figure 9(b) shows that a safety window (in green) is obtained with more challenges.

However, the safety window decreases with an increase in the quantization level, requiring more challenges to maintain the protocol's reliability.

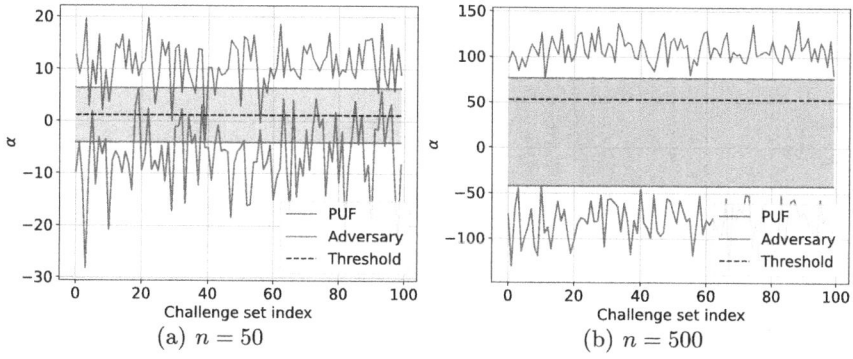

Fig. 9. Neyman-Pearson PUF authentication protocol with $Q = 16$: the legitimate PUF vs the adversary.

5.3 False Authentication Probabilities

Figure 10 represents two probability distributions in the context of an authentication protocol. The safety window depends on the proximity of these two distributions. Below is a breakdown of the components and what they represent:

- **Blue Curve (PUF)**: This curve represents the probability distribution of responses from a legitimate PUF. In an authentication scenario, these responses are from a trusted device or system.
- **Red Curve (Adversary)**: This curve represents the probability distribution of random responses from an adversary.
- **Threshold (Black Dashed Line)**: The vertical line represents the decision boundary or threshold. Responses to the right of this line are classified as legitimate, while those to the left are classified as adversarial.
- **Shaded Region (Red)**: The shaded region represents the *False Positive Rate (FPR)*. It corresponds to the portion of the adversary's responses (red curve) that are incorrectly classified as legitimate responses.

In Fig. 10(a), the false positive region is the area under the red curve to the right of the threshold, indicated by the black dashed line. The threshold is chosen such that there is no false negative for all the challenge sets. Thus the false negative rate is less than the inverse of the number of sets. This shaded region highlights the probability that the adversary's response, despite originating from a non-legitimate source, is incorrectly identified as a valid response by the server. The larger the shaded region, the higher the likelihood that the adversary will be able to deceive the authentication server. In particular, Fig. 10(b) shows a very small false positive region, which implies a very low probability of incorrectly accepting the adversary as legitimate.

Table 1 provides the range false authentication probability for different numbers of challenges and various quantization levels Q in an authentication protocol using 16 PUF devices. The rows represent different *numbers of challenges* (e.g.,

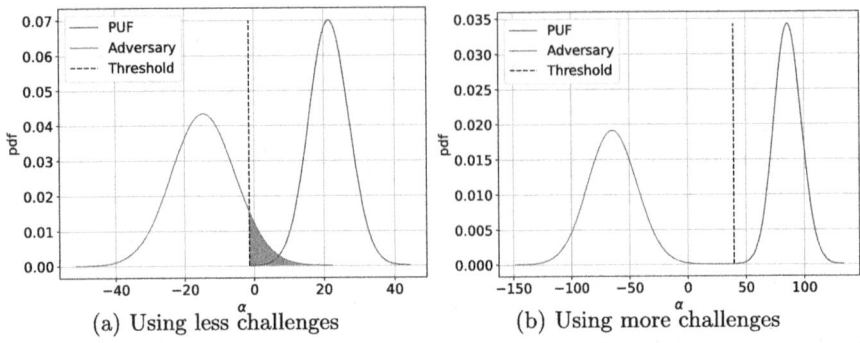

Fig. 10. Neyman-Pearson PUF Authentication Protocol: False Authentication Probability.

n equals 50, 100, 150, etc.), while the columns represent different *quantization levels* $Q \in \{4, 8, 16, 32\}$. Table 1 shows that the false authentication probability generally decreases as the number of challenges increases, while as the quantization level increases, the false authentication probability increases, highlighting the trade-off between security and complexity.

For each number of challenges, the false authentication probability generally *increases* as the quantization level Q increases. This suggests that higher values of Q require higher number of challenges for authentication but it provides better security against ML attacks. For small numbers of challenges (e.g., 50 challenges), the false authentication probabilities are higher for higher values of Q, meaning the authentication server is more vulnerable to attacks. As the number of challenges increases, the false authentication probability tends to decrease across all quantization levels. For example, with 400 challenges, the false authentication probability is as low as 2.4–4.3% for $Q = 32$, and with 600 challenges, it decreases further to 0.1–1.6%.

Table 1. Range of false authentication probability for 16 different PUFs.

Number of challenges	$Q = 4$ (Avg Rel: 93.7%)	$Q = 8$ (Avg Rel: 86.6%)	$Q = 16$ (Avg Rel: 72.5%)	$Q = 32$ (Avg Rel: 60.5%)
50	0.008 - 0.055	0.052 - 0.119	0.115 - 0.268	0.220 - 0.361
100	0.000 - 0.011	0.006 - 0.035	0.046 - 0.140	0.159 - 0.315
150	$3.605 \cdot 10^{-5}$ - 0.001	0.002 - 0.012	0.016 - 0.104	0.073 - 0.255
200	$1.345 \cdot 10^{-6}$ - $3.134 \cdot 10^{-4}$	0.001 - 0.004	0.010 - 0.068	0.050 - 0.211
250	$1.220 \cdot 10^{-5}$ - $2.509 \cdot 10^{-4}$	$2.527 \cdot 10^{-4}$ - 0.002	0.006 - 0.044	0.034 - 0.168
300	$1.090 \cdot 10^{-9}$ - $2.285 \cdot 10^{-7}$	$1.006 \cdot 10^{-5}$ - 0.001	0.002 - 0.034	0.036 - 0.134
350	$2.125 \cdot 10^{-10}$ - $2.484 \cdot 10^{-7}$	$1.250 \cdot 10^{-5}$ - $1.291 \cdot 10^{-4}$	0.001 - 0.029	0.024 - 0.129
400	$1.221 \cdot 10^{-6}$ - $1.781 \cdot 10^{-5}$	$3.727 \cdot 10^{-6}$ - $8.169 \cdot 10^{-4}$	0.001 - 0.015	0.005 - 0.105
450	$1.607 \cdot 10^{-9}$ - $3.337 \cdot 10^{-7}$	$1.478 \cdot 10^{-6}$ - $1.986 \cdot 10^{-4}$	$2.252 \cdot 10^{-4}$ - 0.007	0.006 - 0.079
500	$1.004 \cdot 10^{-10}$ - $1.195 \cdot 10^{-7}$	$4.542 \cdot 10^{-6}$ - $8.002 \cdot 10^{-6}$	$2.105 \cdot 10^{-4}$ - 0.004	0.004 - 0.076
550	$1.021 \cdot 10^{-13}$ - $4.862 \cdot 10^{-10}$	$1.579 \cdot 10^{-8}$ - $2.908 \cdot 10^{-7}$	$1.812 \cdot 10^{-5}$ - 0.001	0.004 - 0.065
600	0.0 - $1.519 \cdot 10^{-12}$	$1.014 \cdot 10^{-8}$ - $1.576 \cdot 10^{-5}$	$2.435 \cdot 10^{-5}$ - 0.001	0.004 - 0.052

6 Discussions

6.1 Comparison with Other Protocols

Contrary to protocols of the literature which are to increase the security against ML attacks, the proposed protocol relying on the Neyman-Pearson test is to increase the reliability, as the security is ensured by NMQ. As far as we know, the only lightweight security protocol against ML used in the literature is the *Lockdown protocol* [21]. This countermeasure has a relatively low complexity (PUF + PRNG). The countermeasure in our study is the PUF which takes advantage of the NMQ quantization. The complexity added by NMQ is very low (comparators for quantization stage). This NMQ-PUF is particularly unreliable when the security is high. The goal of the proposed protocol is to enhance its reliability. Hence, the Lockdown protocol can be used jointly with the Neyman-Pearson test. Table 2 summarized the main properties of 3 scenarios according to the criteria of security, reliability and hardware complexity. Concerning the reliability, it is indicated if it is exploited in order to strenghten the authentication process.

Table 2. Comparison of 3 different scenarios.

	Lockdown	This work: NMQ + Neyman-Pearson	Lockdown + Neyman-Pearson
Security	proven	high with high Q	proven
Reliability	not exploited	exploited	exploited
Complexity	PUF + PRNG	multi-bin PUF + quantizer	PUF + PRNG

6.2 Impact of Environmental Changes

The delays δ_C of a delay PUF are greatly impacted by the temperature, the voltage and the device aging [27]. Consequently, the quantization thresholds of NMQ have to be adapted as their values is the standard deviation Σ of the δ_C multiplied by constant numbers. A first scenario is to use a specific process between the PUF and the server to assess the new environment and consequently update the thresholds. A simpler solution when using a multi-bin PUF based on ring oscillators (ROs), is to use a reference clock which follows the same environmental changes. The PUF response corresponds to a difference of oscillations between two configurations of the RO (Loop PUF) or two different ROs (RO PUF). Let's call T_{osc1} and T_{osc2} the oscillation period of each RO, respectively. The measurement window lasts K oscillations of each RO configuration, K is a constant. During this time window, a counter is incremented with a clock having a period T. At the end of the measurement the counter reaches respectively n_1 and n_2. Hence the PUF response before quantization is $n_1 - n_2$ and can be written:

$$K \cdot T_{osc1} = n_1 \cdot T, \qquad K \cdot T_{osc2} = n_2 \cdot T \qquad (13)$$

$$\Rightarrow \quad n_1 - n_2 = \frac{K}{T} \cdot (T_{osc1} - T_{osc2}) \qquad (14)$$

If there is an environmental change with a factor α on T_{osc1} and T_{osc2}, the response is changed to $n_1 - n_2 = \alpha \cdot \frac{K}{T}(T_{osc1} - T_{osc2})$. Consequently the thresholds have to be updated. Now, if the clock period T comes from another ring oscillator which is also impacted by a factor α, the clock period becomes αT and the response stays the same whatever the environment. This solution assumes that all the elements of the PUF are impacted in the same way and that the noise remains stable over the measurement time. More experiments will be carried out to verify this hypothesis in a future study.

6.3 Scalability

The Neyman-Pearson test requires the knowledge of the BER for every challenge in order to be fully scalable. Thanks to the Hadamard challenges used during the enrollment phase, the BER model build on the server is fully generic. During the authentication phase, the BER for a given challenge is computed from this model. Therefore, the server does not need to store the BER for every challenge, thus ensuring scalability. On the client side (the PUF), no additional computation is needed.

6.4 ML Techniques with Reliability as Feature

If the considered adversary model is such that the PUF interface is open and the attacker can replay the CRPs or try new challenges, the reliability of the CRPs can be measured and the ML could use it as a feature. It has been shown that the Covariance Matrix Adaptation Evolution Strategy (CMA-ES) [15] is particularly efficient to attack the XOR-PUF by using the reliability information. More recently the gradient-based ML attack [28] has shown to be even more powerful against the interpose-PUF. In case of the NMQ-PUF, the reliability-based attacks should definitely be considered but they are not straightforward to implement in a multi-threshold PUF. They are parts of future works.

6.5 Feasibility for IoT Applications

The main properties to meet for the IoT domain are the cost, real-time and low-power. The cost, or hardware complexity, remain low for the NMQ-PUF as the only add-on is the quantizer with multiple thresholds. The real-time constraint may be more difficult to respect as a multi-bin PUF generally relies on a ring oscillator (RO-PUF) and could require at most $1ms$ to output a response. Hence the authentification process can last a few $100ms$. The multi-bin PUF relying on Ring oscillators is not optimal in terms of power consumption compared to arbiter PUF. However, in addition to the low-power RO-PUF proposed in the literature as [29,30], the authentication process remains a relatively short operation with a limited energy consumption when the PUF is in standby mode after authentication.

7 Conclusion

Non-Monotonic Quantization strengthens the resistance of multi-bin delay PUFs such as RO-PUFs against ML attacks by introducing non-linearity at the quantization stage. However, the price to pay for this security increase is a high drop of reliability. By using the Neyman-Pearson Lemma in the PUF protocol, we show that the native unreliability caused by the NMQ quantization can be tackled. More precisely, the unreliability is exploited to help distinguishing between legitimate and adversarial devices. We validated the efficiency of an authentication protocol relying on both an NMQ-PUF and the Neyman-Pearson test. The results obtained with a very high number of quantization levels display a perfect resistance against ML, thanks to NMQ and noise, and an authentication success without failure, thanks to the Neyman-Pearson test. Future works will be to validate the efficiency of the protocol to face environmental changes and to consider new approaches of reliability based attacks.

A Neural Network Structure and Parameters

In Table 3, we detail the network structure of our CNN and MLP models against NMQ-LPUF in Sect. 3.4. In addition, we implemented an adaptive loss function

Table 3. Network architecture of CNN/MLP models, and training parameters.

Network	Architecture	Epochs	Batch Size
CNN	Conv1D(16, 64) BatchNormalization Dropout(0.2) Conv1D(10, 64) BatchNormalization Dropout(0.2) Flatten() Dense(32) Dropout(0.2) Dense(2): Output layer	50	1000
MLP	Flatten() Dense(64) Dropout(0.2) Dense(32) Dropout(0.2) Dense(2): Output layer	50	1000

that is halved by every 10 epochs starting from 0.01 (which shows better attack performances among several settings).

References

1. Edward Suh, G., Devadas, S.: Physical unclonable functions for device authentication and secret key generation. In: Proceedings of the 44th Annual Design Automation Conference, DAC '07, pp. 9–14, New York, NY, USA (2007). Association for Computing Machinery
2. Maes, R., Verbauwhede, I.: Physically unclonable functions: a study on the state of the art and future research directions. Towards Hardware-Intrinsic Security: Foundations and Practice, pp. 3–37 (2010)
3. Gassend, B., Lim, D., Clarke, D., Dijk, M., Devadas, S.: Identification and authentication of integrated circuits. Concurrency Comput. Pract. Experience **16**(11), 1077–1098 (2004)
4. Rührmair, U., Sehnke, F., Sölter, J., Dror, G., Devadas, S., Schmidhuber, J.: Modeling attacks on physical unclonable functions. In: Proceedings of the 17th ACM Conference on Computer and Communications Security, pp. 237–249, Chicago Illinois USA (2010). ACM
5. Nguyen, P.H., Sahoo, D.P., Jin, C., Mahmood, K., Rührmair, U., Van Dijk, M.: Secure PUF design against state-of-the-art machine learning attacks. Cryptology ePrint Archive, The interpose PUF (2018)
6. Aghaie, A., Moradi, A., Tobisch, J., Wisiol, N.: Security analysis of delay-based strong PUFs with multiple delay lines. In: 2022 IEEE International Symposium on Hardware Oriented Security and Trust (HOST), pp. 125–128. IEEE (2022)
7. Wisiol, N.: Beli PUF. In: Modeling Attack Security of Physical Unclonable Functions based on Arbiter PUFs, pp. 79–87. Springer (2023)
8. Wisiol, N., et al.: Splitting the interpose PUF: a novel modeling attack strategy. In: IACR Transactions on Cryptographic Hardware and Embedded Systems, pp. 97–120 (2020)
9. Stangherlin, K., Wu, Z., Patel, H., Sachdev, M.: Enhancing strong PUF security with nonmonotonic response quantization. IEEE Trans. Very Large Scale Integr. (VLSI) Syst. **31**(1), 55–64 (2023). Conference Name: IEEE Transactions on Very Large Scale Integration (VLSI) Systems
10. Immler, V., Hiller, M., Liu, Q., Lenz, A., Wachter-Zeh, A.: Variable-length bit mapping and error-correcting codes for higher-order alphabet PUFs–extended version. J. Hardware Syst. Secur. **3**, 78–93 (2019)
11. Lehmann, E.: Introduction to Neyman and Pearson (1933) on the problem of the most efficient tests of statistical hypotheses. Breakthroughs in Statistics: Foundations and Basic Theory, pp. 67–72 (1992)
12. Cherif, Z., Danger, J.-L., Guilley, S., Bossuet, L.: An easy-to-design PUF based on a single oscillator: the loop PUF. In: 2012 15th Euromicro Conference on Digital System Design, pp. 156–162, Cesme, Izmir, Turkey (2012). IEEE
13. Lee, J.W., Lim, D., Gassend, B., Suh, G.E., Van Dijk, M., Devadas, S.: A technique to build a secret key in integrated circuits for identification and authentication applications. In: 2004 Symposium on VLSI Circuits. Digest of Technical Papers (IEEE Cat. No. 04CH37525), pp. 176–179. IEEE (2004)
14. Lim, D., Lee, J.W., Gassend, B., Suh, G.E., Van Dijk, M., Devadas, S.: Extracting secret keys from integrated circuits. IEEE Trans. Very Large Scale Integr. (VLSI) Syst. **13**(10), 1200–1205 (2005)

15. Becker, G.T.: The gap between promise and reality: on the insecurity of XOR Arbiter PUFs. In: Güneysu, T., Handschuh, H. (eds.) CHES 2015. LNCS, vol. 9293, pp. 535–555. Springer, Heidelberg (2015). https://doi.org/10.1007/978-3-662-48324-4_27
16. Santikellur, P., Bhattacharyay, A., Chakraborty, R.S.: Deep learning based model building attacks on arbiter PUF compositions. Cryptology ePrint Archive (2019)
17. Hospodar, G., Maes, R., Verbauwhede, I.: Machine learning attacks on 65nm arbiter PUFs: accurate modeling poses strict bounds on usability. In: 2012 IEEE International Workshop on Information Forensics and Security (WIFS), pp. 37–42. IEEE (2012)
18. Sahoo, D.P., Mukhopadhyay, D., Chakraborty, R.S., Nguyen, P.H.: A multiplexer-based arbiter PUF composition with enhanced reliability and security. IEEE Trans. Comput. **67**(3), 403–417 (2017)
19. Delvaux, J., Peeters, R., Dawu, G., Verbauwhede, I.: A survey on lightweight entity authentication with strong PUFs. ACM Comput. Surv. (CSUR) **48**(2), 1–42 (2015)
20. Delvaux, J.: Machine-learning attacks on PolyPUFs, OB-PUFs, RPUFs, LHS-PUFs, and PUF-FSMs. IEEE Trans. Inf. Forensics Secur. **14**(8), 2043–2058 (2019)
21. Meng-Day, Yu., Hiller, M., Delvaux, J., Sowell, R., Devadas, S., Verbauwhede, I.: A lockdown technique to prevent machine learning on PUFs for lightweight authentication. IEEE Trans. Multi-Scale Comput. Syst. **2**(3), 146–159 (2016)
22. Schaub, A., Danger, J.-L., Guilley, S., Rioul, O.: An improved analysis of reliability and entropy for delay PUFs. In: 2018 21st Euromicro Conference on Digital System Design (DSD), pp. 553–560 (2018)
23. Danger, J.-L., et al.: Analysis of mixed PUF-TRNG circuit based on SR-latches in FD-SOI technology. In: 2018 21st Euromicro Conference on Digital System Design (DSD), pp. 508–515 (2018)
24. Cover, T.M., Thomas, J.A.: Elements of information theory (2. ed.). Wiley (2006)
25. Rioul, O., Solé, P., Guilley, S., Danger, J.-L.: On the entropy of physically unclonable functions. In: 2016 IEEE International Symposium on Information Theory (ISIT), pp. 2928–2932. IEEE (2016)
26. Solé, P., Cheng, W., Guilley, S., Rioul, O.: Bent sequences over Hadamard codes for physically unclonable functions. In: IEEE International Symposium on Information Theory, ISIT 2021, Melbourne, Australia, July 12-20, 2021, pp. 801–806. IEEE (2021)
27. Kroeger, T., Cheng, W., Guilley, S., Danger, J.-L., Karimi, N.: Effect of aging on PUF modeling attacks based on power side-channel observations. In: 2020 Design, Automation & Test in Europe Conference & Exhibition, DATE 2020, Grenoble, France, March 9-13, 2020, pp. 454–459. IEEE (2020)
28. Tobisch, J., Aghaie, A., Becker, G.T.: Combining optimization objectives: new modeling attacks on strong PUFs. In: IACR Transactions on Cryptographic Hardware and Embedded Systems, pp. 357–389 (2021)
29. Cao, Y., Zhang, L., Chang, C.-H., Chen, S.: A low-power hybrid RO PUF with improved thermal stability for lightweight applications. IEEE Trans. Comput. Aided Des. Integr. Circuits Syst. **34**(7), 1143–1147 (2015)
30. Sahoo, S.R., Kumar, S., Mahapatra, K., Swain, A.: A novel aging tolerant RO-PUF for low power application. In: 2016 IEEE International Symposium on Nanoelectronic and Information Systems (iNIS), pp. 187–192. IEEE (2016)

Towards Package Opening Detection at Power-up by Monitoring Thermal Dissipation

Julien Toulemont, Geoffrey Chancel[(✉)], Frédérick Mailly, Philippe Maurine, and Pascal Nouet

University of Montpellier, CNRS, LIRMM 161 rue Ada 34095 Montpellier CEDEX 5, Montpellier, France
gchancel@lirmm.fr

Abstract. Among the various threats to secure ICs, many are semi-invasive in the sense that their application requires the removal of the package to gain access to either the front or back of the target IC. Despite this stringent application requirements, little attention is paid to embedded techniques aiming at checking the package's integrity. This paper explores the feasibility of verifying the package integrity of microcontrollers by examining their thermal dissipation capability.

Keywords: Security · hardware · fault attacks · reverse-engineering · countermeasure · thermal dissipation monitoring

1 Introduction

During the design of secure integrated circuits, it is important to address numerous threats and potential attacks as early as possible in the standard design flow. These include side-channel attacks, fault attacks, reverse-engineering, and counterfeits, to name a few.

1.1 Context and Related Works

These threats and attacks are considered non-invasive if they do not require any contact with or modification of the target device. If their application involves modifying the device, they are considered invasive. Eventually, they are classified as semi-invasive if it is necessary to remove either the front or back part of the package using mechanical and chemical means before application.

Among semi-invasive attacks, one can identify some probing attacks [1,3], laser fault injection (LFI) [5], Body Bias Injection (BBI) [14], electromagnetic (EM) side-channel or fault attacks [12] often performed , after package removal, with tiny probes really close to the IC surface for a better efficiency, etc.

Numerous embedded countermeasures have been proposed in the literature to increase resilience against semi-invasive attacks or reverse-engineering. While not exhaustive, some of these countermeasures aims:

- At detecting probing attacks, which consist in the direct measurement of some compromising signals by means of e-beams or a probing station directly in the target IC whose front panel has been removed. These countermeasures often consist of adding an active metal grid (called a shield) [7] in the top metal layers of ICs, grid whose electrical properties (e.g. its impedance or response to a specific stimulus) are monitored periodically or during IC boot-up.
- At detecting the presence of an EM probe in the close vicinity of the IC frontside. A possible solution to that aim has been proposed in [8] and consists in monitoring the resonance frequencies of some embedded loops which are modified by the proximity of a solenoid used by an adversary to perform an EM side-channel or fault attack. Again, the resonance frequencies are checked periodically or during the IC boot.
- At detecting the thinning of the substrate, a common practice to better concentrate the laser beam during LFI. According to [10], this can be achieved by adding etched holes into the substrate that weaken the substrate structure so that it breaks when mechanically polished. This can also be achieved by designing a shield penetrating the substrate thanks to the use of Through Silicon Vias (TSV) and metal wires [4]. Again, the electrical characteristics of the shield are checked during the boot.
- At reflecting as suggested in [13] the laser beam using micro-mirrors, with a random pyramidal shape, embedded in the substrate. These mirrors are called nano-pyramids.
- At integrating specialized embedded sensors detecting the occurrence of an EM pulse [6] in the vicinity of the chip, or a laser pulse [11], or an unexpected current in the substrate [2], or a voltage pulse on the power pads, etc.

All these embedded solutions require additional structures in ICs, resulting in significant area and cost overheads. It should be noted that solutions enabling the detection of intrusions by the backside of the IC are particularly expensive since they require the use of optional processing steps (such as TSV or nano-pyramids), which are only available in advanced CMOS technologies.

Eventually, up to the best of our knowledge, no solution has been proposed to check the integrity of the packaging instead of detecting a specific phenomenon (such as a parasitic current, a laser pulse, ...) induced by an intrusion attempt. This lack is perhaps a legacy of smart cards whose packaging is reduced to its strict minimum (a piece of plastic), or to the will of some manufacturers to protect their countermeasures by keeping them secret. As a reminder, the disclosure of a countermeasure has a direct impact on the Attack Potential score during an AVA_VAN (assurance vulnerability analysis) evaluation.

However, with the proliferation of secure applications in various domains, many ICs and especially microcontrollers are now exposed to hardware threats and attacks. It is therefore conceivable that specific embedded solutions could be developed to verify the integrity of the package during the boot sequence of ICs, such as microcontrollers, or to verify the integrity of a system as a whole in the case of a package-on-package integration, which is very common in mobile applications. This is all the more justified as common or complex packages are designed for different purposes, one of those being to facilitate the dissipation of the heat generated by the circuit operation. For this purpose, common packages (QFP, QFN, ...) embed a heat sink that must be removed in order to gain access to the IC backside.

Objective and Contributions.
While temperature has been pointed out as a potential side-channel vulnerability [9], to the best of our knowledge, there has been no work aimed at exploiting the thermal behavior of ICs to thwart physical attacks, although modern microcontrollers often include a temperature sensor (STM32, Kinetics, etc.). Within this context, this paper aims to determine if one can envisage exploiting such a sensor to check the integrity of the package by monitoring heat dissipation during the IC boot. This study, which aims to establish a low-cost countermeasure against semi-invasive attacks, has been done on an STM32F439 microcontroller, considered as our case study for the rest of the paper.

Experimental results reported in this paper suggest that with such a temperature sensor (which has moderate performance and seems to be calibrated after fabrication), one can envisage verifying the integrity of the backside of the package by performing a procedure at the end of each boot that takes less than 0.3 s to complete.

In addition to this, the paper also reports data related to the efficiency of obvious solutions adversaries could use to bypass the proposed countermeasure.

Paper Organization.
Section 2 reports information related to the Device Under Test (DUT) that is necessary for the reading of the paper. Section 3 describes and justifies the embedded software procedure developed to monitor heat dissipation of the DUT. The latter procedure only uses the embedded temperature sensor and the RAM of the DUT. The effect of removing the frontside or the backside of the package are then reported and analyzed in Sect. 4. Finally, natural solutions potentially allowing to bypass the package integrity check are tested in Sect. 5 before concluding in Section 6.

2 The Device Under Test

The chosen test case for our study is the STM32F439. The latter is designed in 90nm CMOS technology around an ARM Cortex M4. It occupies a silicon area of about $4.4\,mm \times 5.5\,mm$ and contains several cryptographic modules but also a temperature sensor with a resolution of $\pm 1.5°C$, $+ -40°C$ and $+125°C$. Its maximum sampling rate is about 100 kS/s, it can thus provide a measure each 10 µs, the time to convert its analog response into a 12 bits digital value.

Because of fabrication process variations, it is recommended to use it to monitor temperature changes rather than getting absolute temperature values. However, the effect of these variations can be partially mitigated thanks to calibration values, TS_CAL1 and TS_CAL2, which values are measured during post fabrication calibration and stored inside each device. They allow getting a better estimate of the current temperature with Eq. 1, in which $valTS$ is the temperature measurement provided by the integrated sensor and T^o the actual temperature after correction.

$$T^o = \frac{80}{TS\_CAL2 - TS\_CAL1} \cdot (valTS - TS\_CAL1) + 30 \qquad (1)$$

In our case study, the STM32F439 is encapsulated in a $20\,mm \times 20\,mm$ LQFP-144 package. The heat dissipation capabilities of this package are represented Fig. 1 in which θ_F, θ_B are the frontside and backside thermal resistances respectively.

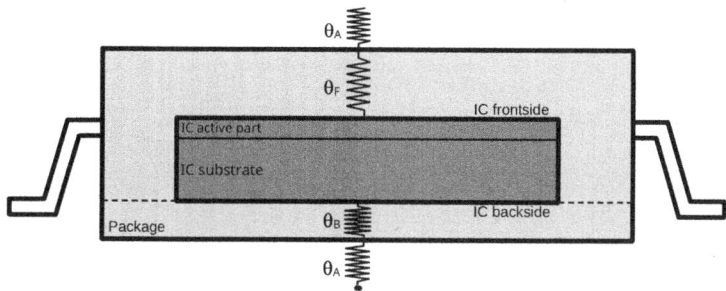

Fig. 1. Thermal dissipation of LQFP packages

The thermal resistance values (in $^\circ C \cdot W^{-1}$) of such packages typically follows the relation: $\theta_F \gg \theta_B$, because of the presence of an embedded metal heat sink inside the package on the IC backside. Thus, an attacker aiming at removing the package to get access, either to the IC frontside or the backside, necessarily removes θ_F or θ_B, that is to say set θ_F or θ_B equals to zero.

3 Monitoring the Thermal Dissipation Capability

The method to monitor the thermal dissipation capability of the DUT has been established after several experiments performed to better understand its thermal behavior assumed to be standard and shared with many ICs, at least those encapsulated in the same package. This section describes the performed experiments and the results we obtained. Eventually, the monitoring method, that must be fast, is introduced. Indeed, it is not acceptable to notably extend the IC boot sequence to check for the package integrity.

3.1 Analysis of the Thermal Behavior

This section describes the successive experiments that have led us to the proposed embedded solution for checking the package integrity during the IC boot. The latter is described at the end of this section.

3.2 Preliminary Tests

The first experiments aimed at observing differences between thermal behavior of ICs in non-tampered packages and in their counterpart with either frontside or backside removed. For this purpose, changes of temperature were monitored during a sequence which alternately wrote words into the flash memory for 180 s and remained idle for 180 s. It should be noted that the first phase of writing was set to start 180 s after power on.

Measured temperature changes with respect to the initial temperature are reported in Fig. 2 for three DUTs:

- one in an non-tampered package (black),
- one in a package with a frontside opening (blue),
- and one in package with a backside opening (red).

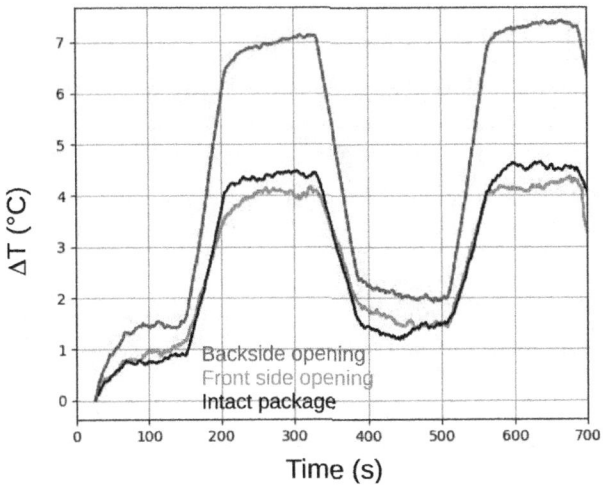

Fig. 2. Temperature changes, ΔT ($°C$), for an IC in an intact package (black), in a package with a frontside opening (green) and with a backside opening (red).(Color figure online)

For clarity, a moving average (with a window of 50 points) has been applied to the raw temperatures to reduce the effect of the sensor intrinsic noise and low accuracy. As one can observe, the IC temperature increases slowly after power-up and more sharply when flash memory writing starts. All chips demonstrate a similar periodic variation of their temperature which are representative of alternate writing and idle sequences. However, one can easily observe that the amplitude of temperature changes is significantly affected by the backside package removal. For an non-tampered package or a frontside opening of the package, amplitude of the temperature variations is about 3 °C, while it is almost doubled for a backside opening of the package. In addition, it can also be observed that the waveforms of the temperature changes is close to a square wave, a clear indication that the temperature change is fast enough to allow a quick detection of package removal.

From this preliminary experiment, we may conclude that creating an opening on the backside of the package, and thus destroying the heat sink, has a significant impact on the thermal behavior of such ICs. On the contrary, the effect of opening the frontside is much more limited. In addition, it can also be observed that the waveform of temperature changes is close to a square wave, a clear indication that the temperature changes are fast. In fact, it takes less than 30 s for the temperature to reach 90% of the semi-permanent state, depending on the state of the package. This encouraging observation led us to analyze the temperature transient that occurs just after IC power-up. Indeed, as shown in Fig. 2, the temperature of the IC with a backside opening rises much faster than the one of an IC in an non-tampered package or a frontside opened package.

3.3 Temperature Transients at Power-up

To monitor the temperature transients at power-up, we sampled the latter at 83333 samples per second, i.e. with one measurement every 12 µs. Figure 3 shows the observed linear temperature trends obtained for the same three ICs previously characterized in Fig. 2. However, the slope of the temperature variation with time is significantly greater (by about $3°C/s$) for a DUT with a backside opening. As a result, whether the package is intact or not, the temperature at power up can be modeled as follows:

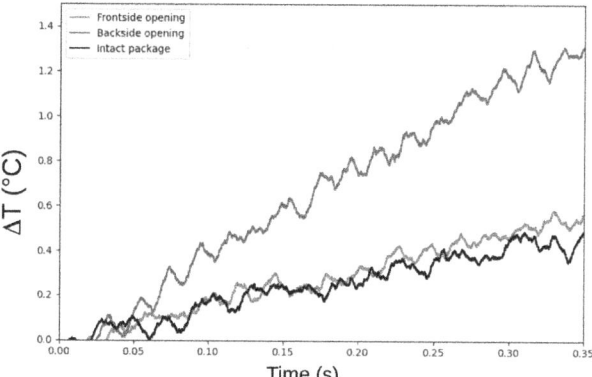

Fig. 3. Temperature changes during the first 0.35 s after power-up for ICs in an intact package (black), a package with a frontside opening (green) and a package with a backside opening (blue).(Color figure online)

$$T^o = \beta_1 \cdot t + \beta_0 + \epsilon \qquad (2)$$

with ϵ being a modeling error, β_1 the line slope, and β_0 the line constant coefficient.

3.4 Thermal Dissipation Metric at Boot

From the results above, it appears that the slope β_1 of the temperature transient is a good metric for checking the integrity of the package. A simple way to obtain this is to perform a linear regression of the temperature values provided by the embedded temperature sensor against time during IC boot. This results in the calculation of:

$$\beta_1 = \frac{cov(T^o, t)}{V(t)} \quad (3)$$

with V(t) being the variance of the temperature, and $cov(T^o, t)$ representing the covariance between temperature and time, which can be easily obtained on-chip using accumulators (registers) that store only the sums involved in the computation of means:

$$\beta_1 = \frac{\overline{T^o \cdot t} - \overline{T^o} \cdot \overline{t}}{\overline{t^2} - \overline{t}^2} \quad (4)$$

The soundness of the linear model can also be checked by computing the coefficient of determination, R^2. Its value ranges from 0 to 1 and is calculated using the following expression:

$$R^2 = \frac{cov(T^o, t)^2}{V(t)V(T^o)} = \frac{(\overline{T^o \cdot t} - \overline{T^o} \cdot \overline{t})^2}{(\overline{t^2} - \overline{t}^2) \cdot (\overline{T^o{}^2} - \overline{T^o}^2)} \quad (5)$$

The closer the value is to 1, the better the linear model reflects temperature changes over time. However, in our case, since the variance of temperature measurements is part of the denominator, R^2 is thus necessarily limited by the accuracy of the temperature sensor. In fact, R^2 is the ratio of the variance (of the temperature) explained by the model to the total variance. It is also the square of the Pearson correlation $\rho(T^o, t)$. Therefore, if there is no linear increase or decrease in temperature (an unlikely scenario in our context), the value of R^2 should be close to 0.

An embedded code has been written and stored in each DUT. It provides both β_1 and R^2 measurements. For this purpose, after power-on and during 300 ms, the temperature values are measured every 25 μs by the embedded sensor and are then stored in RAM. The value of 300 ms was empirically found to be sufficient to make the heat dissipation caused by the processing and RAM storage measurable with a sensor of such accuracy. Of course, it is possible to write embedded code that calculates β_1 values more quickly, but the aim of this work is not to calculate quickly, but rather to measure the slope of the temperature rise at start-up. Therefore, the number of RAM write operations (and thus the duration of the measurement phase) should be adapted to the device and to the sensor accuracy.

4 Impact of Package Removal : Experimental Results

This section presents initial experimental evidence of the ability to verify the integrity of the backside of the package during IC boot thanks to thermal dissipation. This initial evidence is supported by additional experiments conducted at various ambient temperatures using a climatic chamber. Experiments were also conducted on overpowered and underpowered ICs operating at room temperature.

4.1 Experimental Results at Room Temperature

We applied the embedded package integrity verification process to 13 devices, 7 of which have a backside opening. Table 1 shows the means and standard deviations of the β_1 and R^2 distributions obtained for each IC after 25 power-ups. Note that ICs were left in idle mode for 30 s between each power-up to avoid any cumulative effect due to the small time constant of thermal transients that might have distorted the verification process.

Table 1. Average values and standard deviation of 25 measurements of β_1 for the same IC batch before and after package opening. Units are expressed in $°C.s^{-1}$.

IC n°	$\overline{\beta_1}$	σ_{β_1}	$\overline{R^2}$	σ_{R^2}	Backside Opening
25	0.93	0.23	0.01	0.0	no
3	1.40	0.15	0.06	0.01	no
12	1.82	0.2	0.18	0.08	no
6	2.18	0.19	0.08	0.01	no
2	2.50	0.32	0.17	0.15	no
26	2.97	0.16	0.06	0.01	no
9	3.96	0.16	0.34	0.02	yes
7	4.56	0.14	0.28	0.02	yes
1	3.43	0.16	0.09	0.01	yes
10	4.34	0.19	0.14	0.1	yes
8	4.84	0.22	0.23	0.08	yes
11	6.53	0.24	0.39	0.09	yes
4	6.34	0.15	0.44	0.08	yes

The $\overline{\beta_1}$ values for ICs with a backside opening are significantly higher (by about $3\,°C/s$ for the average value) than those for ICs without backside opening. This is clear evidence that ICs with a backside opening heat up more than the others during power-up. Standard deviations, σ_{β_1}, range from 0.15 to $0.3\,°C/s$, a rather small value compared to the gap between the $\overline{\beta_1}$ values obtained for ICs with and without a backside opening. Consequently, $\overline{\beta_1}$ seems to be a reliable metric for checking the package integrity.

The same conclusion could be drawn for $\overline{R^2}$. However, due to the limited accuracy of the embedded temperature sensor, the difference between the values obtained for ICs with and without a backside opening is very limited, especially regarding the values of σ_R. However, one can expect to get higher (smaller) values of $\overline{R^2}$ (σ_R) with a more accurate temperature sensor. As a result, $\overline{\beta_1}$ appears to be a good indicator to identify a missing backside of the package. If the sensor had a better accuracy, $\overline{R^2}$ could have been an alternative indicator.

Regarding values listed in Table 1, we might be tempted to compare the values obtained for the two sets of ICs (with and without a backside opening) and see if the $\overline{\beta_1} + 3\sigma_{\beta_1}$ of all ICs with an intact package are lower than all $\overline{\beta_1} - 3\sigma_{\beta_1}$ of all ICs with a backside opening. However, this would create an overlapping gray area that could be a source of false alarms due to process variations from one IC to another. This limitation can easily be overcome if a post-fabrication characterization of $\overline{\beta_1}$ is undertaken in a trusted environment for each IC with its non-tampered package. An opening in the backside of the package at a later moment will then affect thermal dissipation, thus increasing $\overline{\beta_1}$ in a deterministic way due to an increase of the thermal resistance between the silicon chip and the air surrounding the package. Finally, reported $\overline{\beta_1}$ variation in Table 1 are more evidence of the effect of process variations at the IC, package, and board levels. This point is supported by additional data in the next section.

This analysis has consequences on how IC package integrity check should be performed. In fact, it is necessary to measure for each IC the $\overline{\beta_1} \pm 3\sigma_{\beta_1}$ after manufacturing and to store these values in an embedded non-volatile memory, as it is done for the embedded temperature sensor (through TS_CAL1 and TS_CAL2 mentioned previously). These values will then be considered as the upper and lower acceptable bounds for any measurement of β_1 during further boots during IC life.

4.2 Experimental Results at Different Ambient Temperatures

To further support the idea that thermal monitoring could be a way to detect a backside opening of an IC package, the effect of ambient temperature on the embedded measures of β_1 was analyzed. The idea was to verify that β_1 is indeed a reliable metric for checking package integrity. Twenty β_1 values were therefore collected for two ICs placed in a climatic chamber with temperature set successively at 15 °C and 45 °C. Again, ICs were left in idle mode for 30 s between each power-up. One of them had its package intact, the other a backside opening. This range, that could be perceived as limited, has been chosen to prevent our ICs and PCBs from being damaged by heat and humidity, as we cannot control the latter with our piece of equipment.

Figure 4 reports the values of β_1 obtained for these two ICs over 20 power-ups. The influence of the ambient temperature (at least a change of 30 °C) seems to be very limited. The means and the standard deviations are in the same order of magnitude than the ones reported in Table 1. This is not too surprising. In

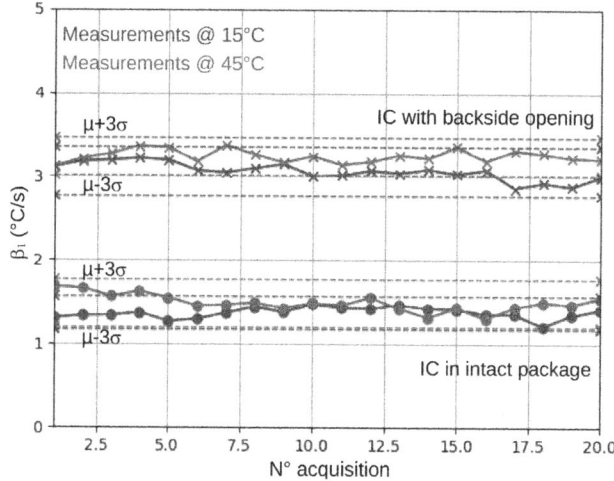

Fig. 4. Effect of ambient temperature on β_1 for two ICs : one had its package intact, the other had a backside opening.

fact, β_1 is an indirect measure of the thermal resistance of air and the material of which the package is made of, which are not expected to change much over this temperature range.

In support of this claim, we periodically measured β_1 for an IC in an non-tampered package over a period of 120 h (five days). One measurement was taken every 120 s. At the same time, the ambient temperature in the test room is recorded as well as the internal temperature of the device at the beginning and at the end of the β_1 measurement process. Figure 5 illustrates the results.

As can be seen, room temperature varied between 21 °C and 25 °C during these five days, while the internal temperature varied jointly with the latter between 23 °C and 28 °C. Correlations between the room temperature and the internal temperature at the beginning and at the end of the β_1 measurements are indeed equal to 0.96 and 0.97. During the same experiment, β_1 varied almost completely incoherently with the room temperature around its mean (1.71), as supported by the value of the correlation between them: -0.22. A linear regression between the room temperature and β_1 showed that β_1 decreases by 0.01 for an increase of one degree Celsius in the room temperature, as illustrated in Fig. 6.

Thus, for an increase of 30 °C, as it is the case in the preceding experiment, one can expect an increase of β_1 by 0.3 °C/s. This is what could be observed in Fig. 4. As a result, the reduced effect of room temperature on β_1 can be neglected unless:

- The device can experience large changes ($> 30°C$) of ambient temperature in its application context,
- The accuracy of the embedded temperature sensor used to verify package integrity is about 0.01°C.

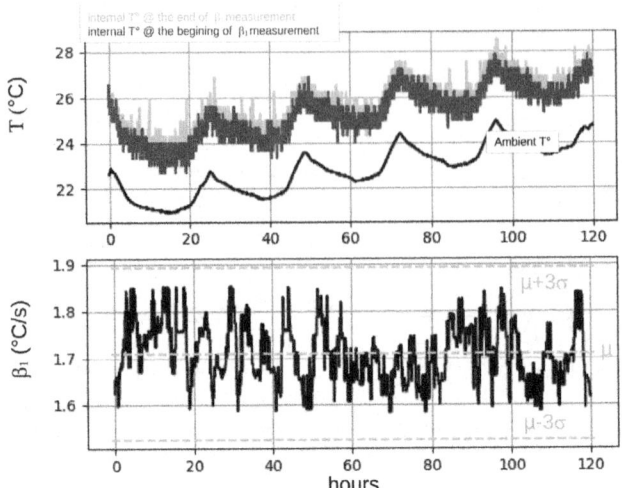

Fig. 5. Measurements of β_1 and of the ambient and internal temperatures over 120h for an IC in an intact package.

In these extreme cases, the upper and lower acceptable values of β_1 that allow the package integrity check should be defined according to the internal temperature of the IC at the beginning of the verification process. This has an additional cost in terms of IC customization after its fabrication. In other cases, most of the variance of β_1 is due to (explained by) the measurement errors done by the embedded sensor.

4.3 Experimental Results at Different Supply Voltages

Similarly, we studied the impact of the supply voltage, V_{dd}, variations of which are expected to change the heat dissipated by ICs in a quadratic way, since the power dissipation of ICs is proportional to $f_{ck} \cdot V_{dd}^2$ where f_{ck} is the clock frequency. Two ICs were used in the experiment: one with an intact package and one with a backside opening. Ten measurements of β_1 were performed for each IC while the ICs were supplied by either 3V, 3.3V or 3.6V. Again, the idea was to verify that β_1 remains a reliable metric for checking package integrity over a range of supply voltage conditions.

Figure 7 shows variations of β_1 during this experiment. For both circuits, variations of β_1 remain less than three times the standard deviations reported in the previous section. This was not a surprising result due to an on-chip regulator which is incorporated inside the DUT as in most modern microcontrollers. As a matter of fact, whatever is the supply voltage, power dissipation remains almost constant except the thermal dissipation of the regulator. We could not confirm this hypothesis because the on-chip regulator on the STM32F439 in LQFP144 package cannot be disabled (there is no $BYPASS\_REG$ pin).

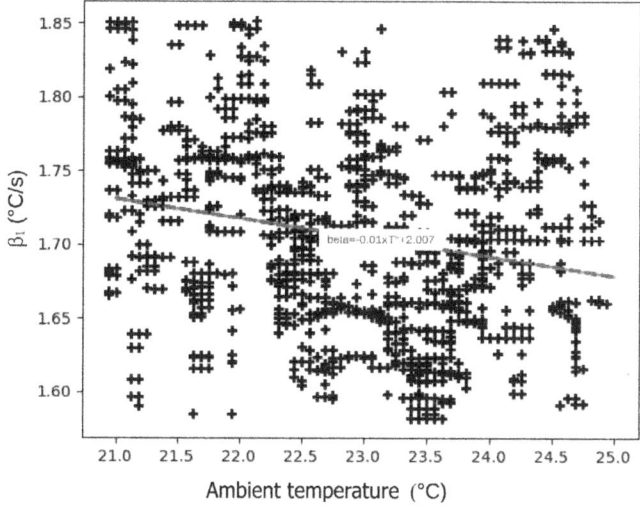

Fig. 6. The effect of the ambient temperature on β_1 measured during 120 h.

4.4 Final Validation

To further support the proposed package verification technique, we decided to perform experiments on different ICs before and after the opening of their backside. To that end, six ICs were selected: №2, 3, 6, 28, 26 and 25. For each of them, the experiment shown in Table 1 have been performed, first with the package intact and then with the backside removed. The results obtained are given in Table 2.

Table 2. Average values and standard deviation of 25 measurements of β_1 for the same IC batch before and after package opening. Units are expressed in $°C.s^{-1}$.

IC n°	Intact package		Backside opening		
	$\overline{\beta_1}$	$\overline{\sigma_{\beta_1}}$	β_1'	$\overline{\sigma_{\beta_1'}}$	$\beta_1' - \overline{\beta_1}$
2	1.400	0.125	7.470	0.063	6.070
3	1.608	0.147	5.899	0.089	4.291
6	1.636	0.112	5.642	0.068	4.006
28	2.095	0.195	4.097	0.077	2.002
26	2.970	0.175	5.817	0.084	2.847
25	3.101	0.453	5.660	0.059	2.559

Similar to the previous experiments, the β_1 values increase when the IC backside is removed. On average, they increase by 3.3 $°C.s^{-1}$, which is very similar

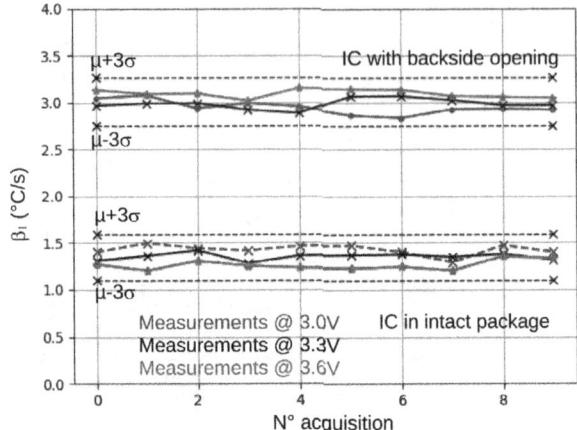

Fig. 7. Effect of supply voltage changes on β_1 : 10 measurements of β_1 for two ICs : one with an intact package, one with a backside opening of the package

to the previous observations and supports the proposed technique. Furthermore, it can now be seen that the β_1 distribution of an IC after backside opening does not overlap with the distribution obtained with its intact package. Therefore, the probability of not detecting the opening is limited.

4.5 Partial Conclusion

At this stage, it seems possible to detect a backside opening of the package by monitoring the heat dissipation capability of ICs with β_1 as metric. This metric appears to be stable with room temperature variations (at least between 15°C and 45°C) and supply voltage variations (at least if the IC integrates an on-chip regulator). To overcome die to die variations due to process variations, we have proposed to store two additional values, $\overline{\beta_1} - 3 \cdot \sigma_{\beta_1}$ and $\overline{\beta_1} + 3 \cdot \sigma_{\beta_1}$, into a secure non-volatile memory after manufacturing, and measuring β_1 at the end of each boot to verify that β_1 falls within the expected range. It is worth noting that the proposed add-on for backside package integrity testing is fully electrical and can be implemented by a few lines of code incorporated in the boot sequence that will store detection margins during first boot and secure backside of the package for the entire life of the microcontroller. Of course, such a countermeasure, as many others, could be still bypass using fault injection attack targeting the verification process or the thermal sensor. However, the presence of this countermeasure forces the adversary to successfully perform a preliminary fault attack before attacking cryptographic applications or other sensitive applications.

Of course, such countermeasure could still be bypassed using fault injection attacks targeting the thermal or the sensor verification process. However, the mere presence of this countermeasure forces the adversary to successfully perform a preliminary fault injection before attacking other sensitive ICs regions.

The response to the detection of an intrusion is not discussed in this work, as it could vary depending on the application. In fact, without being exhaustive, it could range from a total FLASH memory erasure, to a limitation of the user's privileges, or again to a halt in the boot process. In the latter case, a digital counter (in secure non-volatile memory), could be incremented so that if too many intrusion attempts are made, a FLASH erasure is performed.

Let us now switch our role from secure IC designers to that of malicious adversaries, fully aware of the presence of this embedded countermeasure in the target IC, that want to bypass it using tools commonly available in security characterization laboratories. Several methods come to mind. We have tested some of them and found three that can be sometimes successful. Those that sometimes gave positive results, i.e. bypassed the countermeasure, are presented in this section.

5 Bypassing the Package Integrity Verification

5.1 Fast Successive Power-Ups and Power-Downs

As previously explained, the verification is based on the measurement of the heat dissipation capability during the first 0.30 s after power-up. This verification procedure has been defined considering that the IC is at room temperature before being turned on. This explains why each measurement in previous sections was immediately followed by 30 s in the idle mode to allow chip cool-down.

One may thus wonder what might happen if the target IC is not at room temperature when it is turned-on. In other words, is there a way to bypass the countermeasure by using successive power-ups, each one interrupted before the end of the package verification process?

For the purpose of verification, an IC in a package with a backside opening (with its $\overline{\beta_1}$ close to 3) was forced to undergo a rapid sequence of power-ups and power-downs. Figure 8 shows the first 10 β_1 values when the measurements are separated by $\Delta m = 1\,s$, $3\,s$, $10\,s$ instead of $\Delta m = 30s$ as previously. Experiments were repeated three times.

One can notice that the coefficient starts to drop as soon as the duration between each measurement is not long enough (i.e. is lower than 3 s) and reaches a coefficient similar to the one of a circuit with an non-tampered package when measurements are separated by only 1 s. However, the first two measures are not in the range of validity for a circuit with an non-tampered package. Thus, to bypass the countermeasure, the adversary has to stop at least the two first boot sequence before the end of the package integrity verification. This is not so easy to do even if the adversary is aware of the countermeasure. Thus the countermeasure still makes semi-invasive attacks more difficult to perform.

5.2 Pre-heating the IC Before Power-Up

Like the previous bypass method, the one discussed in this section exploits the same major weakness of the proposed package integrity verification method,

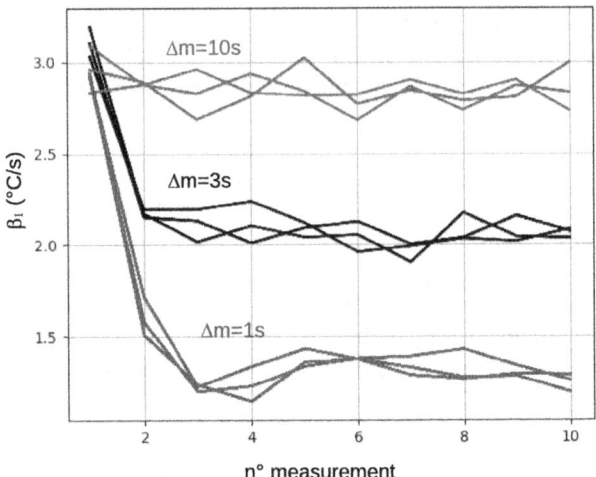

Fig. 8. Ten first measurements of β_1 provided by the IC when the measurements are separated by $\Delta m = 1\,s$, $3\,s$, $10\,s$ instead of $\Delta m = 30\,s$.

namely the need to stabilize at room temperature before powering up. The idea is to use a hot air station, a very common piece of equipment in electronics laboratories, to heat the circuit above room temperature before powering it up, so as to lower β_1 down to an acceptable range for an IC in an non-tampered package. The main difficulty for the adversary is, of course, to choose the duration and temperature of the hot air flow without any prior knowledge. Therefore, it is necessary to make several attempts. We were able to bypass the countermeasure after 10 to 15 attempts, depending on the target IC. Therefore, if an unlimited number of boots is possible, this method seems very easy to use. However, with a limited number of attempts, the game becomes more risky and difficult. One can easily imagine that an alarm during package integrity verification will at least temporarily block IC operation.

In fact, if the circuit is too hot at power-up, it will cool down instead of heating up during the boot sequence. This results in forcing the first three measurements of β_1 to be negative, as shown in Fig. 9 (green curve), which shows the first 10 measurements of β_1 for an IC in package with a backside opening. Conversely, if the circuit is not enough heat up, most of β_1 measurements are likely to remain in the range of a circuit with a backside opening of the package (blue curve). Finally, if the heating conditions are perfect (both in duration and temperature), the countermeasure will be bypassed (red curve). Note also the increase of β_1 during the successive measurements. After 10 measurements, the junction temperature is not in its steady state, except for the red curve.

These results show that there is room for improvement in the package verification procedure to make it more robust against a hot air station bypass attempt.

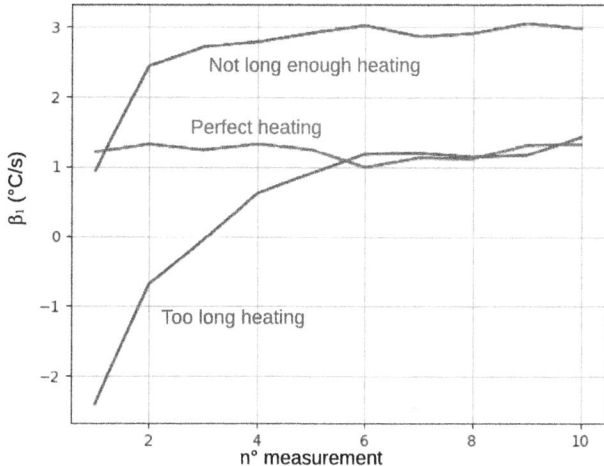

Fig. 9. Evolution of β_1 after an initial heating of the DUT with an hot air station.

In fact, an initial on-chip temperature measurement can be easily used to detect the bypassing attempt using pre-heating.

5.3 Removable Heatsink

A final way to bypass the package integrity verification countermeasure consists in placing a removable heatsink in contact with the IC backside (i.e. substrate), during power-up and β_1 verification. Then, one could remove it to perform fault injection attacks.

As a demonstration, we placed a 32 mm long and 3 mm wide copper cylinder with some thermal interface material as shown in Fig. 10 to try to replicate approximately the heat sink suppressed by the opening operation. The copper rod was estimated to have a 3 °C.W^{-1} thermal resistance. Then, we performed β_1 measurements with the heatsink on the IC batch considered in Sect. 4.4, i.e. ICs that were characterized before and after the backside opening procedure. Table 3 shows the results, where β_1'' stands for the value of β_1 measured in presence of the copper rod.

Firstly, it should be observed that the discrepancies between $\overline{\beta_1}$, $\overline{\beta_1'}$ and $\overline{\beta_1''}$ for a small set of ICs are significant. This confirms that defining an acceptable range of β_1 to check package integrity must be done considering die to die variations. It is therefore imperative to define an unique acceptable range for each IC after manufacturing and packaging since, as mentioned previously, removing the backside is expected to have a significant and deterministic effect on the IC thermal dissipation. The related additional cost induced might seem prohibitive, but in fact, is not, as such customization process is already used to calibrate the embedded temperature sensor (TS_CAL1 and TS_CAL2 values).

Fig. 10. The copper rod used as a removable heatsink.

Table 3. Average values and standard deviation of 25 measurements of β_1 for the same IC batch with the copper rod heatsink. Units are expressed in °C.s^{-1}.

IC №	Intact Package		Backside Opening		32 mm long rod	
	β_1	σ_{β_1}	β'_1	$\sigma_{\beta'_1}$	β''_1	$\sigma_{\beta''_1}$
26	2.970	0.453	5.660	0.059	0.709	0.047
3	1.608	0.147	5.899	0.089	0.735	0.047
6	1.636	0.112	5.642	0.068	0.708	0.109
28	2.095	0.195	4.097	0.077	0.516	0.073
2	1.400	0.125	7.470	0.063	0.816	0.142
25	3.101	0.453	5.660	0.059	0.714	0.095

Secondly, it should be noted that adding the copper rod and the thermal interface material reduces the average value of β_1 by about 5 °C.s^{-1}. This reduction is too important to bypass the proposed package detection technique. In fact, the distribution of β''_1 of all ICs has a mean value too low to overlap with that of β_1, i.e. the one of ICs in their intact package. Therefore, the probability of obtaining a legitimate β_1 value during a boot is quite low.

One can of course choose a different heatsink provoking a smaller β''_1 values reduction. However, this requires skill and knowledge about the DUT, so it is not straightforward. In addition to this, it is made all the more difficult by the fact that it seems impossible to select a heatsink that can be used for all ICs due to significant die-to-die variations.

Despite these difficulties, it is still possible for an adversary to bypass the countermeasure, either thanks to luck or skill. In this case, it should be noted that the thermal interface material is mandatory to effectively make a significant physical contact between the IC backside and the copper rod. Therefore, it appears possible to bypass the countermeasure, but the thermal interface material must be removed, without powering down the IC, before attacks can be carried out.

6 Conclusion

The spread of secure applications from smart cards to microcontrollers (IoT), which are encapsulated in plastic packages, raises the issue of verifying package integrity to thwart semi-invasive attacks; a topic which has not, up to the best of our knowledge be addressed up to now. We investigated the possibility of checking the integrity of the packaging using an embedded temperature sensor, a very common block in modern microcontrollers, to monitor at power-up the thermal dissipation of ICs. Experimental results reported in this paper suggest that it is possible to detect the creation of a backside opening during the boot sequence of microcontrollers. This is all the more encouraging as the sensor in question has a limited accuracy ($\pm$ 1.5 °C). Further work will consolidate these preliminary results and investigate the possibility of detecting the frontside opening of the package using a more accurate sensor, as well as the possibility of detecting fault injection attacks at runtime.

Acknowledgments. This work is supported by the "France 2030" government investment plan managed by the French National Research Agency (ANR), under the project ARSENE (ANR-22-PECY0004).

References

1. Anderson, R., Kuhn, M.: Tamper resistance – a cautionary note new. In 2nd USENIX Workshop on Electronic Commerce (EC 96), Oakland, CA, 1996. USENIX Association
2. Bastos, R.P., Torres, F.S., Dutertre, J.M., Flottes, M.L., Natale, G.D., Rouzeyre, B.: A bulk built-in sensor for detection of fault attacks. In: 2013 IEEE International Symposium on Hardware-Oriented Security and Trust (HOST), pages 51–54 (2013)
3. Boit, C., Schlangen, R., Kerst, U., Lundquist, T.: Physical techniques for chip-backside IC debug in nanotechnologies. IEEE Design Test Comput. **25** (2008)
4. Borel, S., et al.: A novel structure for backside protection against physical attacks on secure chips or SIP. In: 2018 IEEE 68th Electronic Components and Technology Conference (ECTC), pages 515–520, San Diego, United States, May 2018. IEEE
5. Dutertre, J.M., et al.: Laser fault injection at the CMOS 28 nm technology node: an analysis of the fault model. In: 2018 Workshop on Fault Diagnosis and Tolerance in Cryptography (FDTC), pages 1–6 (2018)
6. El-Baze, D., Rigaud, J.B., Maurine, P.: A fully-digital EM pulse detector. In: Fanucci, L., Teich, J., editors, 2016 Design, Automation & Test in Europe Conference & Exhibition, DATE 2016, Dresden, Germany, March 14-18, 2016, pages 439–444. IEEE, 2016

7. Gao, Y., Zhang, Q., Ma, H., He, J., Zhao, Y.: Eo-shield: a multi-function protection scheme against side channel and focused ion beam attacks. In: 2023 28th Asia and South Pacific Design Automation Conference (ASP-DAC), pages 670–675 (2023)
8. Homma, N., et al.: EM attack is non-invasive? - Design methodology and validity verification of EM attack sensor. In: CHES, pages 1–16. Springer (2014)
9. Hutter, M., Schmidt, J.M.: The temperature side channel and heating fault attacks. In: Smart Card Research and Advanced Applications: 12th International Conference, CARDIS 2013, Berlin, Germany, November 27-29, 2013. Revised Selected Papers, page 219–235, Berlin, Heidelberg (2014). Springer-Verlag
10. Manich, S., Arumi, D., Rodriguez-Montanes, R., Mujal, J., Hernandez, D.: Backside polishing detector: a new protection against backside attacks. In: Conference on Design of Circuits and Integrated Systems, vol. 1, 11 (2015)
11. Matsuda, K.,et al.: An IC-level countermeasure against laser fault injection attack by information leakage sensing based on laser-induced opto-electric bulk current density. Japanese J. Appl. Phys. 59(SG):SGGL02 (2020)
12. Ordas, S., Guillaume-Sage, L., Maurine, P.: Electromagnetic fault injection: the curse of flip-flops. J. Cryptogr. Eng. **7**(3), 183–197 (2017)
13. Shen, H., Asadizanjani, N., Tehranipoor, M., Forte, D.: Nanopyramid: an optical scrambler against backside probing attacks. volume ISTFA 2018: Conference Proceedings from the 44th International Symposium for Testing and Failure Analysis of International Symposium for Testing and Failure Analysis, pages 280–289, 11 2018
14. Tobich, K., Maurine, P., Liardet, P.Y., Lisart, M.,Ordas, T.: Voltage spikes on the substrate to obtain timing faults. In: 2013 Euromicro Conference on Digital System Design, DSD 2013, Los Alamitos, CA, USA, September 4-6, 2013, pages 483–486. IEEE Computer Society (2013)

Partial Key Overwrite Attacks in Microcontrollers: A Survey

Pcy Sluys[✉], Lennert Wouters, Benedikt Gierlichs, and Ingrid Verbauwhede

COSIC, KU Leuven, Kasteelpark Arenberg 10, Heverlee, Belgium
{pcy.sluys,lennert.wouters,benedikt.gierlichs, ingrid.verbauwhede}@esat.kuleuven.be

Abstract. Embedded devices can be exposed to a wide range of attacks. Some classes of attacks can be mitigated using security features or dedicated countermeasures. Examples include Trusted Execution Environments, and masking countermeasures against physical side-channel attacks. However, a system that incorporates such secure components is not automatically a secure system. Partial Key Overwrite attacks are one class of attacks that specifically target the interface between different components of the security system. These attacks may allow an adversary to extract otherwise protected cryptographic keys through careful manipulation of memory-mapped registers. So far this powerful class of attacks has received little attention in the academic literature. In this work, we provide an overview of known Partial Key Overwrite vulnerabilities and how they were used in real-world attacks. Additionally, we evaluated 31 common microcontrollers and embedded microprocessors from eleven distinct vendors and detail our findings. Based on a first high-level evaluation we selected 15 SoCs and performed an in-depth evaluation. This evaluation revealed that at least eight of these SoCs are vulnerable to partial key overwrite attacks.

Keywords: key overwrite attack · safe error analysis · microcontrollers · embedded security

1 Introduction

Microcontrollers and microprocessors are used in many embedded devices and deployed in a wide range of applications, from consumer IoT to industrial and automotive. As a result, a single microcontroller must be designed to withstand diverse threats depending on the context. This varies from attackers targeting software vulnerabilities in the firmware, to active and passive semi-invasive hardware attacks. Countermeasures against such attacks range from hardware features in the CPU to enhance software security such as Intellectual Property Encapsulation (IPE) and Trusted Execution Environments (TEEs) to defences in cryptographic accelerators against side-channel analysis and differential fault analysis attacks.

However, securing every individual component separately does not necessarily mean the entire system is secure. One overlooked attack that arises from a naive composition of individually secured components is the Partial Key Overwrite (PKO) attack: it allows an attacker to obtain a cryptographic key otherwise stored in a secure location, typically by careful manipulation of the memory-mapped input/output (MMIO) register interface.

While the concept of PKO attacks has been around for a few decades, they have received little academic attention. The aim of this paper is twofold: raise awareness of the existence of these attacks by listing a few real-world cases, and survey whether common microcontrollers are vulnerable to such attacks or if vendors incorporate any countermeasures against these attacks. We also provide the source code used for checking whether the microcontrollers and SoCs we tested are vulnerable.

1.1 Responsible Disclosure

For every microcontroller in which we discovered a vulnerability, the vendor has released a newer chip in which the vulnerability was mitigated. Hence, a full Coordinated Vulnerability Disclosure procedure was not deemed necessary, although we still notified all chip vendors with confirmed in-scope and vulnerable products of our upcoming publication.

Additionally, we found a peculiar strangeness in the behaviour of the cryptographic accelerator in the Renesas RA2E1 series of microcontrollers. Although its security implications are unclear, it was nonetheless disclosed to Renesas.

1.2 Structure of This Paper

This paper starts with background information in Sect. 2 and a theoretical description of partial key overwrite attacks in Sect. 3. Section 4 details a survey investigating which microcontrollers are vulnerable to PKO attacks. Finally, Sect. 5 provides possible countermeasures and Sect. 6 makes a few final notes.

2 Background and Related Work

A few publications exist that describe PKO attacks in OpenPGP [7,14] and the online file storage service MEGA [2,3]. OpenPGP private keys are stored at rest in an encrypted form, the user has to enter a password to decrypt and use the private key. Similarly, the MEGA service provider (which, in their threat model, should not be trusted by the user) stores the encrypted key material which is only decrypted client-side. However, in either case, parts of the key file can be corrupted, such as elliptic curve parameters stored in plaintext, or a single block of an ECB-encrypted private key. Intercepting a signature made with such a corrupted key allows an attacker to then derive the private key. With such a private key, they can decrypt the files of the user it belongs to.

The above attacks exist in a context rather different from embedded security. Examples of PKO attacks in the latter context are difficult to find in existing literature, though a few can be found. For instance, while [4] is best known as the seminal paper introducing Differential Fault Analysis, in its Sect. 3 the authors present a different attack, making use of partial key erasure. Their example presents a discrete encryption device with a built-in key stored in an EEPROM. An attacker sets a few key bits to 1 by exposing the target to ionising radiation. Similarly, the authors of [13] used the zeroisation of S-boxes as a method for key recovery, albeit in a white-box context (that is, they overwrite the part of a software program that implements the S-box). Almost a decade later, a similar attack was performed on an FPGA bitstream [28].

Meanwhile, hacking communities have been using partial key overwrite attacks against many targets. Informal sources describe its use on AES coprocessors in respectively the Nintendo DSi [15], Nvidia Tegra X1 [29] (used in the Nintendo Switch), and STM32H730 [12]; while [1] uses it on an RSA coprocessor in the Nintendo 3DS. In each of these cases, the system initialized the key registers of their coprocessors early during boot, with keys stored in e.g. one-time-programmable (OTP) memory. This memory is then made unreadable, after which the system executes lower-privilege code the attackers are able to exploit. Such an exploit is unable to read the keys from OTP memory or dump the system bootcode, but using a PKO attack, the keys can still be extracted from their accelerators. An attacker does not need a software exploit in the typical sense as a requirement for the PKO attack, in [12] direct debug access is used instead. The debugger cannot access flash memory (STM32 readout protection level 1 is used) but can still access peripheral registers. Finally, it is important to note that attackers have an explicit interest in recovering the key, rather than merely using the accelerator as a potential decryption oracle [9,16]. Game consoles typically encrypt and sign both the entire filesystem as well as individual games and software binaries. Installing unauthorized software on such a device thus requires circumventing every protection layer. Performing the encryption and decryption of full game install images—or even an entire filesystem—offline instead of having to query the console itself for this is much less of a hassle.

Table 1 gives a summary of all previously-published attacks, along with which cipher they targetted and which method was used to mount the attack.

2.1 Attack Categorisation

There is no real agreement to which class of attacks PKO attacks belong. The authors of [34, Section VI.B.3] mention PKO as a subtype of Safe Error Analysis (SEA) attacks[1]. However, SEA is more widely understood as a subclass of (physical) fault injection (FI) attacks similar to Ineffective Fault Analysis (IFA) [8,33,34]. Hence, referring to PKO attacks as SEA might lead to confusion.

---

[1] "Write-only cryptographic key registers should never allow partial update, otherwise the attacker can test a partial key guess by detecting these collisions.".

Table 1. Summary of published attacks making use of Partial Key Overwriting and similar techniques. The rows list the target attacked, the ciphers involved, the type of key storage used ('WO' means 'write-only'), the method used to mount the attack, whether the attack makes use of partial key overwrites, which community the attack was discovered in, and the relevant citation(s).

Target	Cipher	Key storage	Method	PKO?	Circle	Citation
OpenPGP	RSA, ECC	file	client-side malware	✔	academia	[7, 14]
MEGA	RSA, ECC	file	misbehaved server	✔	academia	[2, 3]
(vague)	generic	EEPROM	UV light	✔	academia	[4]
software	AES, DES	(vague)	software tampering	✘ (S-box)	academia	[13]
FPGA	AES, DES	bitstream	bitstream tampering	✘ (S-box)	academia	[28]
(vague)	RSA	(vague)	FI (SEA)	✔	academia	[33]
(vague)	DES	(vague)	FI (IFA)	✔	academia	[8]
Nintendo DSi	AES	WO MMIO reg	VRISKA (exploit)	✔	hobbyist	[15]
Nintendo 3DS	RSA	WO MMIO reg	VRISKA (exploit)	✔	hobbyist	[1]
Tegra X1	AES	WO MMIO reg	VRISKA (exploit)	✔	hobbyist	[29]
STM32H730	AES	WO MMIO reg	VRISKA (debug pins)	✔	hobbyist	[12]
Many	AES, RSA	WO MMIO reg	VRISKA	✔	academia	you are here

While referring to PKO as SEA makes sense from a purely cryptographic point of view, this paper focuses on PKO attacks in embedded devices, where they arise from imperfections in the interface between components. This is a property they have in common with Interrupt Oriented Programming [30], DMA-based attacks such as [6], the use of 'hardware gadgets' in [22], the `ntrcardhax` exploit in the Nintendo 3DS[2] [25] and the vulnerability in the Falcon TSEC coprocessor in the Tegra X1 [24].

As far as we are aware, no properly defined category for the attacks in the previous paragraph seems to exist. Yet, these attacks make use of vulnerabilities that have several elements in common: The vulnerabilities lie not in a single component of the system-on-chip (such as the CPU, memory, an accelerator, etc.), but rather arise from the combination of these components in a system, often due to complexities in the interface between them (such as their register interface, DMA, interrupts, 'event system/routing', etc.). We hence propose to name the category of attacks that exploit these vulnerabilities VULNERABLE

---

[2] Not to be confused with `ntrboot`, a *different* exploit in the 3DS system.

RESULT OF INDIVIDUALLY SECURE KOMPONENTS ATTACKs, or $VRISKAs$[3] for short.

We can view the PKO attacks treated in this paper as SEA mounted using a VRISKA. This differs from the attacks on OpenPGP and MEGA which are mounted using software vulnerabilities, and from 'traditional' SEA which is mounted using FI. Note that while more 'traditional' SEA attacks use transient faults, the modifications made to the key register in this work are more permanent in nature: they last until the next reset of the chip.

Similarly, with the above definition, `ntrcardhax` from [25] used a VRISKA on a time-of-check-vs-time-of-use vulnerability to perform a buffer overflow, [24] builds a ROP chain using a VRISKA, and [22] uses one as a source of side-channel information.

3 Theory of Partial Key Overwrite Attacks

In this section, we first define the attacker model. Afterwards, we describe how PKO attacks may be used against cryptographic coprocessors.

3.1 Attacker Model

In a PKO attack on a cryptographic coprocessor, the attacker can query the coprocessor as an encryption oracle and is able to overwrite parts of the key used. This key is never directly exposed to the attacker, it is often made inaccessible through some sort of privilege separation mechanism. It is the goal of the attacker to obtain the key.

Typically, the attacker takes control of the CPU to query the cryptographic coprocessor, but other possibilities exist as well, such as debug access. Similarly, the 'privilege separation mechanism' can come in many forms. Sometimes, the key is loaded into the coprocessor by firmware code running inside a TEE or otherwise locked away by an early system boot stage. In other cases, it might be loaded from some protected memory region such as one-time-programmable memory. In the case of debug access instead of software exploits, special code readout protection mechanisms serve as this privilege separation.

3.2 Attack Method for Symmetric-Key Coprocessors

The attack consists of two phases: obtaining ciphertexts with partly-overwritten keys, and a 'brute-force' calculation to obtain the key. These are depicted in Fig. 1.

In the first phase, the attacker will start by querying the encryption oracle with its original key K_0 using a known plaintext P, receiving a ciphertext C_0. The exact value of P does not matter, but it must be kept constant across all

---

[3] Yes, after the *Homestuck* character *Vriska Serket*.

queries. Then, the attacker proceeds by setting a single subkey[4] to an attacker-chosen value, resulting in the oracle using a key K_1. The attacker then queries the oracle again, obtaining the ciphertext C_1. We define n as the number of subkeys. This procedure continues until the key is fully overwritten by the attacker save for one word, resulting in a key K_{n-1} with corresponding ciphertext C_{n-1}.

In the second phase, a brute-force calculation with reduced complexity to obtain the original key K_0 is performed. The individual subkeys are sufficiently small to be within reach of brute-forcing (typically 32 bits at most in practice). The attacker can thus work backwards from K_{n-1} to K_{n-2} by knowledge of C_{n-1} and C_{n-2}, after which K_{n-3} is in computational reach, and so on. This continues until K_0 is recovered.

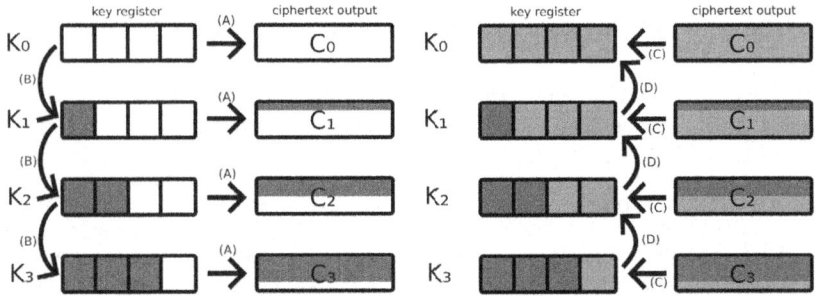

(a) Phase 1: the coprocessor, acting as an encryption oracle, is queried for ciphertexts (A). For each step, the attacker overwrites one more subword of the key (B), while keeping to receive ciphertexts. This ends when all but one subwords of the key are left

(b) Phase 2: in the last query, only one subword K_3 is left. The ciphertext C_3 obtained from the coprocessor makes it possible to brute-force the unknown key bits K_3 (C). This then makes it possible to obtain K_2, and so forth (D), until the full key is derived

Fig. 1. Diagram of a basic PKO attack on a symmetric-key coprocessor.

While the above matches the description in [4], variations of this attack are possible as well. For example, the register interface of the coprocessor may expose the key using a shift register instead. This has an influence on the bookkeeping, but the method is otherwise almost unchanged. This contrasts to [15], wherein Korth first queries the oracle with state K_0 to obtain C_0, but then starts writing to the same key register, iterating over every possible value of a subkey, until the same ciphertext C_0 is reached again. This procedure is repeated for every subkey.

---

[4] For example, an AES-128 coprocessor with a memory-mapped IO (MMIO) interface will have its 128-bit key accessible over this MMIO interface. However, it is likely that this key is larger than the width of the memory bus. Hence, the key is split into multiple subkeys (between 8 and 32 bits in size, typically) which may be written to individually.

This attack method thus performs both phases at the same time. Hence, the precise method of attack can be adapted depending on implementation details of the MMIO register interface. Countermeasures have to account for all of these variants.

3.3 Attack Method for RSA Coprocessors

In [1], Myria provided a novel technique for applying PKO attacks to RSA accelerators as well. It assumes the coprocessor has separate registers for message M, private exponent d, and public modulus N.

The attacker sets the message to a small prime M', and the modulus to a prime p greater than N and whose multiplicative order is a smooth number. The exponent register is left untouched. The attacker then queries the oracle, obtaining $C = M'^d \mod p$. With this specific choice of root M' and prime modulus p, it is computationally feasible to calculate $d = \mathrm{dlog}_{M'} C \mod p$ using the Pohlig-Hellman algorithm [21].

No iterative or recursive approach is required, unlike the symmetric-key variant explained in Sect. 3.2. The attacker must perform some offline computations, however: generating a suitable prime p of which its multiplicative order is a smooth number beforehand, and performing the Pohlig-Hellman algorithm afterwards. This contrasts to the symmetric-key approach, which cay be performed in an entirely online manner.

3.4 Attack Methods for ECC and PQC Coprocessors

It is possible to perform PKO attacks on Elliptic Curve Cryptography (ECC) and Post-Quantum Cryptography (PQC) coprocessors as well. Do note that, while the details of an attack depend on the register interface of the coprocessor, no vulnerable coprocessors implementing either ECC or PQC were found in the survey in Sect. 4. Hence, the below attacks are merely hypothetical.

Attacks on ECC coprocessors depend on the exact cryptosystem used. For ECDSA, a logical approach for an attacker would be to have a signing oracle generate two different signatures with the same nonce, or at least influence enough of the nonce to perform the lattice attack described in [17]. For Curve25519 and other systems, input parameters could be tweaked to perform an attack similar to the one described in Sect. 3.3.

For LWE-based PQC schemes such as ML-KEM (also known as Kyber), an attacker could iterate over possible values of every subkey of the secret key reminiscent of the symmetric-key case of [15] in Sect. 3.2. A decapsulation error would then inform the attacker on whether the subkey guess is correct, reminiscent of [33].

3.5 Practical Considerations

While the calculations required for a PKO attack are in the realm of the practical, these might still take a considerable amount of time on a small microcontroller.

This depends on several details, such as the subkey register word size used in the accelerator interface. Performing these attacks efficiently requires a bit of thought.

One may also carry out the second phase described in Sect. 3.2 in an offline manner. The need for offline attacks depends on the granularity with which the key subwords can be overwritten. If 8-bit writes are possible, a byte-by-byte bruteforce of an AES-128 key requires $16 \cdot 2^8 = 2^{12}$ steps, which is perfectly feasible even on an 8-bit 1 MHz microcontroller, and thus would need no extra offline processing. With a 32-bit write granularity, $4 \cdot 2^{32} = 2^{34} \approx 17$ billion iterations are instead required. Such a computation takes about 16 min single-threaded on an Intel Raptor Lake i7-13700 workstation using AES-NI, while it takes about 6 h on an STM32L562 at 110 MHz and making use of its AES accelerator.

Additionally, when performing a PKO attack on an RSA coprocessor, the prime modulus p can be chosen by constructing possible candidates of the form $2^x 3^y 5^z + 1$ for any natural numbers x, y and z, and selecting one that is prime and greater than the original RSA modulus. (In our experience, first constructing a number of smooth multiplicative order and then checking for primality yields a usable result much faster than generating a prime and checking for smoothness.) The root (and plaintext) is typically set to 11 or 13. A Python script implementing both this search and the Pohlig-Hellman algorithm needs less than 5 s to run either calculation on an Intel Skylake i7-6500U laptop, while performing these computations at all on a microcontroller can be challenging.

4 Prevalence Survey of Vulnerable Cryptographic Coprocessors

In this section, we perform a survey to check how many off-the-shelf microcontrollers and microprocessors contain cryptographic coprocessors vulnerable to PKO attacks as described in the previous section.

4.1 Method

This survey is performed in two parts: in the first part, datasheets and reference manuals of available microcontrollers and microprocessors are scanned, to find possibly-vulnerable candidates. In the second part, these chips are then ordered and some code is loaded onto them that tests for the presence of the vulnerability.

Compiling the list of candidates is done by first compiling a list of common microcontrollers and SoCs with cryptographic accelerators, then selecting chips with some form of software privilege separation, and finally reading their reference manuals to disqualify chips with software-readable key registers. The full list of chips considered (and some not considered) can be found in Table 2. Code used for vulnerability testing can be found at https://rdr.kuleuven.be/dataset.xhtml?persistentId=doi:10.48804/E5JSO7.

4.2 Limitations

The methodology described above skews towards not investigating chips without documentation on their cryptographic coprocessors. For example, for many microcontrollers made by Renesas and large microprocessors/SoCs made by Texas Instruments, Broadcom or NXP, the documentation on their cryptographic hardware is only available under NDA. Several other microprocessors made by e.g. Qualcomm, Mediatek, Samsung, Amlogic or Rockchip meanwhile have no publicly available documentation at all. Hence, smaller microcontrollers are overrepresented in this work.

Secondly, it would be interesting to know how many *devices* existing *in the wild* contain secrets that may be leaked using PKO attacks. However, performing such a study is much more impractical: it would require 1. buying a large number of off-the-shelf devices, 2. opening them up to discover which microcontroller or microprocessor is used inside (which is often not known before physical disassembly), 3. checking if the chip used has an accelerator vulnerable to a PKO attack, 4. extracting the firmware to check if the vulnerable accelerator is used in a manner in which the vulnerability is actually in scope (the 'privilege separation' explained in Sect. 3.1 has to be configured properly as well), 5. and finally try to exploit this vulnerability. Such a survey would require buying a large number of devices that might turn out to not use any vulnerable chips at all, while this cost cannot be recovered as the warranty will have to be void (due to disassembly of the device). Hence, this survey only concerns itself with researching which microcontrollers could *possibly* be configured in a way that will lead to key leakage through a PKO attack. We therefore cannot make any statements on the prevalence of PKO vulnerabilities in real-world devices.

4.3 Chip Selection

Most of the chips included in this study store the key in simple write-only MMIO registers (STM32 series, ESP32 RSA) or a shift register (TI MSP). A few chips with undocumented cryptographic accelerators were included as well (SAML11, RA2E1) of which we will reverse engineer the functioning, but doing this for every chip with undocumented accelerator is impractical.

The NXP i.MX series of microprocessors feature a 'CAAM' cryptographic accelerator, though its documentation is only available under NDA. However, besides CAAM, these chips also contain an HDMI encoder with hardware to perform HDCP (HDMI video DRM) cryptography. The HDCP key registers are readable, hence a PKO attack may not be necessary here.

The NXP LPC55S6x series also contains multiple accelerators: CASPER for RSA and ECC, PRINCE for flash memory contents, and an AES accelerator. CASPER, the public-key accelerator, only operates on units of 64 bits. It thus has to be called many times to perform a single full public-key operation. Hence, it cannot store a full private key. This limited design also makes it likely that its initial inputs are overwritten by temporary values. PRINCE only uses keys sourced from the system PUF. The AES accelerator uses the same MMIO registers for key and data input, rekeying is only possible by completely resetting the AES peripheral. With neither of these accelerators, PKO attacks seem possible.

Most other chips not further treated in this study (such as the NXP i.MX HDMI encoder, the TI MSP432E as well as several STM32G4 and STM32Fx chips from STMicroelectronics) have readable key registers. While they do not support TrustZone-M, they still have 'privilege separation' mechanisms, ranging from proprietary IPE features ('IP protection' and 'PCROP', respectively) to, in the case of the STM32, a debugger flash readout protection feature (RDP level 1). In these cases an attacker operating under the model defined in Sect. 3.1 may be able to directly read the key (otherwise stored in protected non-volatile storage) from the cryptographic accelerator, hence a PKO attack would not be relevant in these chips.

Table 2. List of all chips considered in this survey. The column 'ciphers' denotes the ciphers supported by the accelerators which were deemed relevant to this work. The column 'priv. sep.' lists the name of the privilege separation mechanism present in the microcontroller. 'TZ-A' and 'TZ-M' mean TrustZone-A and -M, respectively. 'PCROP', 'HDP' and 'IPE' are proprietary mechanisms that disallow read access to certain regions of code flash, c.f. [5,23]. The column 'used' shows whether this chip was then further investigated in this survey for the presence of vulnerabilities against PKO attacks.

Manufacturer	Name	Ciphers	Priv. sep.	Used	Notes
Espressif	ESP32S2, S3, C3	RSA	Encrypted keys	✔	AES key registers readable, thus focus on RSA
Microchip	SAML11	AES	TZ-M	✔	only access through ROM API
Renesas	RA2E1	AES	'Security MPU'	✔	No docs, reverse engineer
	RA4M2	AES	TZ-M	✔	No docs, reverse engineer
ST	STM32G0, STM32Fx	AES	PCROP	✔	Write-only key regs
	STM32L5	AES, RSA, ECC	TZ-M	✔	Write-only key regs
	STM32U0	AES	HDP	✔	Write-only key regs
	STM32H5, U5	AES, RSA, ECC	TZ-M	✔	Has mitigations for RSA & ECC, cf. [27]
	STM32MP1	AES	TZ-A	✔	Write-only key regs
TI	MSP430FR59	AES	IPE	✔	Key store is shift register
	MSP432P	AES	IPE	✔	same as MSP430
Microchip	ATXmega AU	AES, DES	N/A	✘	Key registers readable

(*continued*)

Table 2. (*continued*)

Manufacturer	Name	Ciphers	Priv. sep.	Used	Notes
NXP	i.MX 8M	AES, RSA, ECC	TZ-A	✗	Key registers readable (HDMI encoder, cf. [18])
	LPC55S6x	AES, RSA, ECC	TZ-M	✗	Countermeasures (cf. [19])
ST	STM32G4, STM32Fx	AES	PCROP	✗	Key registers readable (cf. e.g. [26])
	STM32H7	AES	PCROP	✗	Known vulnerability [12]
TI	MSP432E	AES	IPE	✗	Key registers readable (cf. [31])
GigaDevice	GD32L23	AES	N/A	✗	No priv. sep. to attack
	GD32VW55x	AES	key from OTP	✗	Priv. sep. trivially not vulnerable
Infineon	PSoC 64	AES	N/A	✗	No priv. sep. to attack (only accessible from high-privilege M0+)
Microchip	SAML2x	AES	N/A	✗	No priv. sep. to attack (but vulnerable key registers)
TI	SimpleLink, MSPM0	AES	N/A	✗	No priv. sep. to attack
	MSPM0Lx22x	AES	N/A	✗	Countermeasures (cf. [32]), chip not available
Allwinner	sun4i, 8i	AES	N/A	✗	No docs
Microchip	PIC32CMLx	AES	TZ-M	✗	No docs, only accessible through SDK
NXP	i.MX 6/7/8	AES, RSA, ECC	TZ-A	✗	No docs ('CAAM' module), NDA required
	i.MXRT10xx	AES	secure boot	✗	No docs ('DCP' module), NDA required
Renesas	RA, RX	AES	TZ-M (some)	✗	No docs, NDA required
Rockchip	RK3399, RK3588	AES	TZ-A	✗	No docs
TI	AM Sitara	AES	TZ-A	✗	No docs, NDA required
Xilinx	ZynqMP	AES	TZ-A	✗	No docs, NDA required

4.4 Results and Analysis

Table 3 presents a summary of the results of the survey.

Table 3. List of all evaluated chips, and an indication of whether their accelerators are vulnerable to PKO attacks or not (and if so, notes the complexity of the offline computations required for the attack, 'P-H' denotes use of the Pohlig-Hellman algorithm).

Manufacturer	Name	Year	Vuln.	Cplx.	Notes
TI	MSP430FR5994	2016	✔	$16 \cdot 2^8$	Cf. Sect. 4.4.5
	MSP432P401R	2015	✔	$16 \cdot 2^8$	same accel. as MSP430
ST	STM32L562 (AES)	2018	✔	$4 \cdot 2^{32}$	Cf. Sect. 4.4.1
	STM32G061	2018	✔	$4 \cdot 2^{32}$	Same accel. as L5
	STM32U083	2024	✔	$4 \cdot 2^{32}$	Same accel. as L5
	STM32MP157	2019	✔	$4 \cdot 2^{32}$	Same accel. as L5
	STM32H730	2019	✔	$4 \cdot 2^{32}$	Known vuln. [12]
	STM32L562 (RSA/ECC)	2018	?	N/A	Cf. Sect. 4.4.1
	STM32U5A5, H5 (RSA/ECC)	2021–2023	?	N/A	Cf. Sect. 4.4.1
Espressif	ESP32S2, S3, C3	2020–2021	✔/✘	P-H	Cf. Sect. 4.4.2
Microchip	SAML21	2015	N/A	N/A	Technically out of scope, cf. Sect. 4.4.3
	SAML11	2018	✘	N/A	Cf. Sect. 4.4.3
Renesas	RA2E1	2020	✘	N/A	Cf. Sect. 4.4.4
	RA4M2	2019	✘	N/A	Cf. Sect. 4.4.4
ST	STM32U5A5, H5 (AES)	2021–2023	✘	N/A	Cf. Sect. 4.4.1

Some of the results for particular chips are unclear or require further elaboration. These notes are listed below:

4.4.1 ST STM32 Series

The STM32L5, G0, MP1 and U0 all share the same AES accelerator, hence these are all equally vulnerable. Separate key words can be updated independently as long as the EN bit in the control register is set to zero.

The accelerator shared between the STM32U5 and H5 is based on the former one, but went through an Arm Platform Security Architecture (PSA) level 3 certification process [27]. Countermeasures against PKO attacks have now been implemented as well. This is reflected in the register interface, with an extra KEYVALID bit in the status register.

However, the public-key accelerator ('PKA') of the STM32 series is more troublesome. People have reported[5] having issues with getting the accelerator to

---

[5] https://community.st.com/t5/stm32-mcus-security/pka-modular-exponentiation-not-working-as-expected/m-p/699510.

work at all in the first place. We also faced this problem in our experimentation, and are thus unable to determine whether it is vulnerable to PKO attacks.

The STM32U5 extends the L5 PKA by adding different commands for computations using either the public or private key (automatically erasing remanent private key data in the latter case), while the L5 does not distinguish between the two. Hence, if the correct operation is used, the STM32U5 PKA should not be vulnerable to PKO attacks.

4.4.2 ESP32

The ESP32 RSA accelerator can be used in two modes: the 'normal' mode in which the accelerator is accessed directly and keys are supplied by the CPU, and the 'Digital Signature' (DS) mode in which the CPU uploads an encrypted key blob to the accelerator. The accelerator autonomously decrypts this key blob using a key from the one-time-programmable (OTP) memory, this key is not visible to the CPU.

In the 'normal' mode, the MMIO registers that store the RSA parameters are write-only. However, every parameter on its own (e.g. the modulus) can be changed without necessarily invalidating the others. Hence, a Pohlig-Hellman-based attack (c.f. Sect. 3.3) is possible. Though, the practicality of such an attack is questionable, as there is no memory protection measure (like PCROP or IPE) able to protect a key from an attacker-controlled CPU. Furthermore, the default Espressif driver code for the RSA peripheral immediately powers down said peripheral, erasing the keys stored in MMIO registers.

In the DS mode, there again seems to be an issue with the main functioning of the accelerator, and we struggled with inconsistent results here as well[6]. However, the output of the accelerator was still *deterministic*, unlike in the STM32L5. Although, in this case, overwriting only the base and modulus of the accelerator after a DS operation always results in an output of zero. Hence, it seems that after a DS operation, the MMIO registers for the RSA parameters are always cleared. Thus, in DS mode, the ESP32 RSA accelerator is not vulnerable to PKO attacks.

4.4.3 Microchip SAML11

The SAML11 has an AES accelerator, though the only documented way to make use of it is to use a runtime utility function which resides in the boot ROM. The contents of the boot ROM cannot be read by regular user code.

Using timer interrupts to trace execution flow (using the same method as described in [5, Sec. 3.3]), it is possible to obtain some information on the structure of the boot ROM code. We considered using DMA to create extra bus contention as a timing side channel leaking information on which memory is accessed at which point (cf. [6]). However, this is not useful, as the cryptographic accelerator hardware is attached to the Cortex-M23's single-cycle I/O bus, which is exclusively controlled by the CPU.

---

[6] As reported at e.g. https://esp32.com/viewtopic.php?f=12&t=42057.

The entire AES key schedule appears to be calculated entirely in software, with the cryptographic acceleration MMIO peripheral seemingly only responsible for the `SubBytes`, `ShiftRows` and `MixColumns` steps of AES, one round at a time. Hence, the key never leaves the CPU registers and does not get stored in any MMIO register. The SAML11 ROM AES routines are thus not vulnerable to a PKO attack.

Note that the older SAML2x series has an AES accelerator of which the key register allows partial overwrites. However, this older series does not contain any privilege separation mechanism (such as TrustZone, 'IP encapsulation', or a debug lockout level that disallows flash access but allows MMIO access) for an attack to be meaningful.

4.4.4 Renesas RA2E1 and RA4M1

Cryptographic accelerator designs in Renesas microcontrollers are often shared between multiple chips. These accelerators exist in several 'versions' or 'generations'. RA2xx MCUs have simple AES and TRNG peripherals, while RA4xx and up have a more comprehensive 'Secure Crypto Engine' (SCE). Different 'generations' of SCE exist, numbered 5, 5B, 7 and 9. The SCE peripherals support more ciphers (sometimes asymmetric ones as well) and block cipher modes of operation, as well as key 'wrapping'. Renesas does not publish documentation on the cryptographic accelerators in its microcontrollers. However, they do publish *obfuscated* driver code as part of their 'Flexible Software Package' (FSP).

For the RA2xx series, reverse-engineering this code revealed a rather standard AES accelerator, though it does incorporate PKO countermeasures (as evidenced by bits 24 and 25 in the 32-bit register at offset +4). However, there seems to be a 'secret' bit (#15) in this register that is unused by the FSP driver code. Setting this bit seems to cause a time-sensitive perturbation, where sometimes the result of a cryptographic operation is not propagated to the output registers. The exact functioning of this bit and its security implications are unclear.

The SCE peripheral (in RA4xx and up) has a 'command interface' where a 16-*byte* magic number must be supplied to perform a command, such as loading a key, setting the mode of operation, etc. The peripheral also mandates the use of 'wrapped' keys. 'Wrapped' keys are encrypted using an on-chip key residing inside the SCE hardware [10]. Next to this encryption layer, they are protected by a MAC as well, to protect against possible tampering [11]. A 'wrapped' key is thus twice the size of a plain key: an 128-bit AES key becomes 256 bits in size when wrapped, an AES-256 plain key turns into a 512-bit wrapped key.

Any key passed to the SCE meant for cryptographic operations must be supplied in its 'wrapped' form. These cannot be tampered with, hence PKO attacks are not possible on RA4xx/6xx/8xx MCUs either.

4.4.5 TI MSP430, MSP432 and MSPM0

This subsection concerns itself with the separate MSP430, MSP432 and MSPM0 lines of microcontrollers, all from Texas Instruments. While they have different

CPU cores and designs, they do share some peripherals, including the AES accelerator. TI MSP chips use a key MMIO register that acts as a shift register, as opposed to making any key word separately addressable as done on e.g. the STM32 series.

The AES accelerator keeps track of whether the key is fully written through the `AESKEYWR` bit in the `AESASTAT` register. However, this bit is writeable, and hence partial keys will be accepted as well.

Many MSP430 chips as well as the MSP432P incorporate some form of an 'IP protection' feature, as detailed in [5]. Most MSPM0 chips do *not* support this, except for the newer MSPM0Lx22x and MSPM0G351x models—currently the only PSA-certified microcontrollers in the MSPM0 series. However, these models instead incorporate an 'ADVAES' accelerator, which, according to their reference manual, does protect against PKO attacks [32]. At the time of writing, these MCUs are not yet available, and thus statements from the reference manual could not be verified.

5 Countermeasures

It should hopefully be clear by now that without countermeasures against PKO attacks, having write-only instead of read-write key registers makes little difference. However, care must be taken when implementing hardware countermeasures. The internal state machine that detects partially-overwritten keys must function regardless of the MMIO register access pattern, and there should be no 'force OK' bit (such as in the MSP430), yet it is possible to do this correctly (as seen in the STM32U5 and Renesas RA2E1). When designing the register interface of a cryptographic accelerator, a command-based interface (such as seen in the Renesas SCE) with which only a full key can be submitted at once may be a more prudent design option.

When using a vulnerable accelerator in a microcontroller, firmware engineers can mitigate PKO attacks in several ways. This mainly relies on redrawing the border between secure and nonsecure system components such that the accelerator falls entirely within the area marked as secure, instead of straddling the border. For example, if a TEE such as TrustZone-M is available, the cryptographic accelerator should be configured to only allow accesses from within TZ secure code (and expose a cryptographic software API to nonsecure code if needed). If no TEE exists in the chip, disabling interrupts during the operation of the accelerator and clearing the key registers afterwards should suffice against attackers taking over the CPU, though this could incur extra CPU time overhead. Chips with different debug readout protection levels should be configured to use the highest protection level (though downgrade attacks exist for this, e.g. [20] in the STM32 series).

6 Conclusion

As shown in Sect. 4.4, several off-the-shelf microcontrollers available on the market from different vendors are vulnerable to PKO attacks. Despite a lack of attention from academia, real-world attackers have demonstrated a sustained interest in these vulnerabilities. Note, however, that some chips included in the survey are in a worse situation where an adversary does not even need to use a PKO attack to extract keys from cryptographic accelerators, while those keys would still otherwise reside in protected nonvolatile memory.

Luckily, microcontroller manufacturers seem to move towards incorporating countermeasures: after having brought vulnerable chips to market, Microchip, TI and ST have all released newer models with countermeasures against PKO attacks. This seems to be correlated with the creation of the Arm PSA certification standard, of which the specifications were released in 2017. This could be an indication that such certification efforts increase the security of consumer products, though it is unclear to what extent PSA certification has actually influenced these matters: the only publicly available documentation with a certain degree of details belongs to level 1 certification only, and it is unclear which exact requirements are maintained by certification laboratories.

Code used for testing microcontrollers and microprocessors for vulnerability against PKO attacks can be found at https://rdr.kuleuven.be/dataset.xhtml?persistentId=doi:10.48804/E5JSO7.

Acknowledgments. We would like to thank dr. Anne Baanen for helping devise the wretched backronym VULNERABLE RESULT OF INDIVIDUALLY SECURE KOMPONENTS ATTACK (VRISKA).

This work was supported in part by the Flemish Government through the Cybersecurity Research Program with grant number VOEWICS02, by the European Commission through the Horizon 2020 research and innovation program under grant agreement Belfort ERC Advanced Grant 101020005 695305, and through the Horizon Europe research and innovation program under grant agreement HORIZON-CL3-2021-CS-01-02 101070008 ORSHIN.

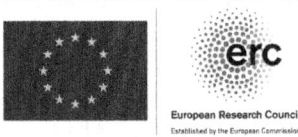

Disclosure of Interests. The authors have no competing interests to declare that are relevant to the content of this article.

References

1. 3dbrew, 3DS System Flaws, Archived at https://web.archive.org/web/20240829223013/https://www.3dbrew.org/wiki/3DS_System_Flaws#Hardware. https://www.3dbrew.org/wiki/3DS_System_Flaws%5C#Hardware. Accessed 08 Sept 2024
2. Albrecht, M.R., Haller, M., Mareková, L., Paterson, K.G.: Caveat Implementor! Key Recovery Attacks on MEGA, Cryptology ePrint Archive, Paper 2023/329 (2023). https://eprint.iacr.org/2023/329
3. Backendal, M., Haller, M., Paterson, K.G.: MEGA: Malleable Encryption Goes Awry, Cryptology ePrint Archive, Paper 2022/959 (2022). https://eprint.iacr.org/2022/959
4. Biham, E., Shamir, A.: Differential fault analysis of secret key cryptosystems. In: Kaliski, B.S. (ed.) Proceedings of the 17th Annual International Cryptology Conference on Advances in Cryptology. CRYPTO 1997, pp. 513–525. Springer, Heidelberg (1997). https://doc.lagout.org/security/Papers/DFA%20of%20Secret%20Key%20Cryptosystems.pdf
5. Bognár, M., Magnus, C., Piessens, F., Van Bulck, J.: Intellectual property exposure: subverting and securing intellectual property encapsulation in Texas instruments microcontrollers. In: 33rd USENIX Security Symposium (USENIX Security 2024), Philadelphia, PA, pp. 2155–2172. USENIX Association (2024). https://www.usenix.org/conference/usenixsecurity24/presentation/bognar
6. Bognár, M., Van Bulck, J., Piessens, F.: Mind the gap: studying the insecurity of provably secure embedded trusted execution architectures. In: 2022 IEEE Symposium on Security and Privacy (SP), pp. 1638–1655 (2022). https://doi.org/10.1109/SP46214.2022.9833735. https://mici.hu/papers/bognar2022gap.pdf
7. Bruseghini, L., Huigens, D., Paterson, K.G.: Victory by KO: attacking OpenPGP using key overwriting. In: Proceedings of the 2022 ACM SIGSAC Conference on Computer and Communications Security. CCS 2022, Los Angeles, CA, USA, pp. 411–423. Association for Computing Machinery (2022). https://doi.org/10.1145/3548606.3559363
8. Clavier, C.: Secret external encodings do not prevent transient fault analysis. In: Paillier, P., Verbauwhede, I. (eds.) CHES 2007. LNCS, vol. 4727, pp. 181–194. Springer, Heidelberg (2007). https://doi.org/10.1007/978-3-540-74735-2_13
9. Domke, F.T.: Almost Secure (2011). https://web.archive.org/web/20241119012300/https://debugmo.de/2011/11/almost-secure/. https://debugmo.de/2011/11/almost-secure/. Accessed 21 Nov 2024
10. RA6M5 Group: User's Manual: Hardware (2023). https://www.renesas.com/en/document/man/ra6m5-group-users-manual-hardware?r=1493931. Accessed 17 Dec 2024
11. Renesas RA Family Application note: Renesas Security Engine Operational Modes (2024). https://www.renesas.com/en/document/apn/renesassecurity-engine-operational-modes?r=1493931. Accessed 17 Dec 2024
12. GaryoderNichts, Looking into the Nintendo Alarmo (2024). https://archive.ph/4nhB8. https://garyodernichts.blogspot.com/2024/10/lookinginto-nintendo-alarmo.html. Accessed 31 Oct 2024
13. Kerins, T., Kursawe, K.: A Cautionary Note onWeak Implementations of Block Ciphers, (2006). https://web.archive.org/web/20221206234645/https://www.cosic.esat.kuleuven.be/wissec2006/papers/10.pdf

14. Klima, V., Rosa, T.: Attack on Private Signature Keys of the OpenPGP Format, PGP(TM) Programs and Other Applications Compatible with OpenPGP, Cryptology ePrint Archive, Paper 2002/076 (2002). https://eprint.iacr.org/2002/076
15. Korth, M.: GBATEK DSi AES I/O Ports (2021). https://web.archive.org/eb/20220829222918/http://problemkaputt.de/gbatek-dsi-aes-i-oports.htm. https://problemkaputt.de/gbatek-dsi-aes-i-o-ports.htm. Accessed 04 Oct 2022
16. Lu, Y.: The 3DS Cryptosystem (2016). https://web.archive.org/web/20240625001543/https://yifan.lu/2016/04/06/the-3ds-cryptosystem/. https://yifan.lu/2016/04/06/the-3ds-cryptosystem/. Accessed 08 Sept 2024
17. Minerva: The curse of ECDSA nonces: Systematic analysis of lattice attacks on noisy leakage of bit-length of ECDSA. IACR Trans. Cryptogr. Hardw. Embed. Syst. **2020**(4), 281–308 (2020). https://doi.org/10.13154/tches.v2020.i4.281-308. https://tches.iacr.org/index.php/TCHES/article/view/8684
18. NXP, i.MX 8M Dual/8M QuadLite/8M Quad Applications Processors Reference Manual, Sign-in required for download (2021). https://www.nxp.com/webapp/Download?colCode=IMX8MDQLQRM
19. NXP, LPC55S6x/LPC55S2x/LPC552x User manual, Sign-in required for download (2021). https://www.nxp.com/webapp/Download?colCode=UM11126
20. Obermaier, J., Tatschner, S.: Shedding too much Light on a Microcontroller's Firmware Protection. In: 11th USENIX Workshop on Offensive Technologies (WOOT 2017). USENIX Association, Vancouver, BC (2017). https://www.usenix.org/conference/woot17/workshop-program/presentation/obermaier
21. Pohlig, S., Hellman, M.: An improved algorithm for computing logarithms over GF(p) and its cryptographic significance (Corresp.) IEEE Trans. Inf. Theory **24**(1), 106–110 (1978). https://doi.org/10.1109/TIT.1978.1055817. https://www-ee.stanford.edu/~hellman/publications/28.pdf
22. Rodrigues, C., Oliveira, D., Pinto, S.: BUSted!!! Microarchitectural Side-Channel Attacks on the MCU Bus Interconnect. In: 2024 IEEE Symposium on Security and Privacy (SP) (2024). https://bustedattack.com/resources/BUSted.pdf
23. Schink, M., Obermaier, J.: Taking a look into execute-only memory. In: Proceedings of the 13th USENIX Conference on Offensive Technologies. WOOT 2019, p. 1. USENIX Association, Santa Clara, CA, USA (2019). https://www.usenix.org/system/files/woot19-paper_schink.pdf
24. SciresM, hexkyz, Je Ne Sais Quoi - Falcons over the Horizon (2021). https://archive.is/wNT42. https://hexkyz.blogspot.com/2021/11/je-nesais-quoi-falcons-over-horizon.html. Accessed 06 Dec 2024
25. plutoo derrek smea, s.: Console Hacking: Breaking the 3DS (2015). https://media.ccc.de/v/32c3-7240-console_hacking. Accessed 16 Dec 2024
26. STMicroelectronics, RM0440 Reference manual: STM32G4 series advanced Arm-based 32-bit MCUs (2024). https://www.st.com/resource/en/reference_manual/rm0440-stm32g4-series-advanced-armbased-32bit-mcus-stmicroelectronics.pdf. Accessed 08 Dec 2024
27. STMicroelectronics, RM0456 Reference manual: STM32U5 Series Arm-based 32- bit MCUs (2023). https://www.st.com/resource/en/reference_manual/rm0456-stm32u5-series-armbased-32bit-mcus-stmicroelectronics.pdf. Accessed 18 Nov 2024
28. Swierczynski, P., Fyrbiak, M., Koppe, P., Paar, C.: FPGA trojans through detecting and weakening of cryptographic primitives. IEEE Trans. Comput. Aided Des. Integr. Circ. Syst. **34**(8), 1236–1249 (2015). https://doi.org/10.1109/TCAD.2015.2399455

29. SwitchBrew, Switch System Flaws. https://web.archive.org/web/20240826033554/https://switchbrew.org/wiki/Switch_System_Flaws#Hardware. https://switchbrew.org/wiki/Switch_System_Flaws%5C#Hardware. Accessed 08 Sept 2024
30. Tan, S.J., Bratus, S., Goodspeed, T.: Interrupt-oriented bugdoor programming: a minimalist approach to bugdooring embedded systems firmware. In: Proceedings of the 30th Annual Computer Security Applications Conference. ACSAC 2014, pp. 116–125. Association for Computing Machinery, New Orleans, Louisiana, USA (2014). https://doi.org/10.1145/2664243.2664268
31. Texas Instruments, MSP432E4 SimpleLink Microcontrollers Technical Reference Manual (2018). https://www.ti.com/lit/ug/slau723a/slau723a.pdf. Accessed 08 Dec 2024
32. Texas Instruments, MSPM0 L-Series 32MHz Microcontrollers Technical Reference Manual (2024). https://www.ti.com/lit/pdf/slau847. Accessed 18 Nov 2024
33. Yen, S.-M., Joye, M.: Checking before output may not be enough against faultbased cryptanalysis. IEEE Trans. Comput. **49**(9), 967–970 (2000). https://doi.org/10.1109/12.869328. https://marcjoye.github.io/papers/YJ00chkb.pdf YJ00chkb.pdf
34. Yuce, B., Schaumont, P., Witteman, M.: Fault attacks on secure embedded software: threats, design, and evaluation. J. Hardw. Syst. Secur. **2**(2), 111–130 (2018). https://doi.org/10.1007/s41635-018-0038-13

RISC-V

Combined Masking and Shuffling for Side-Channel Secure Ascon on RISC-V

Linus Mainka[✉] and Kostas Papagiannopoulos

Informatics Institute, University of Amsterdam, Amsterdam, The Netherlands
{linus.mainka,kostas.papagiannopoulos}@uva.nl
https://ivi.uva.nl/

Abstract. Both masking and shuffling are very common software countermeasures against side-channel attacks. However, exploring possible combinations of the two countermeasures to increase and fine-tune side-channel resilience is less investigated. With this work, we aim to bridge that gap by both concretising the security guarantees of several masking and shuffling combinations presented in earlier work and additionally investigating their randomness cost. We subsequently implement these approaches to also analyse their performance. In this context, we present five different protected implementations of the new standard for lightweight cryptography, Ascon, on a 32-bit RISC-V architecture: A 3rd-order masked, unshuffled implementation and three combined 3rd-order masked and shuffled implementations. Additionally, we present a levelled implementation where only the particularly vulnerable keyed initialisation and finalisation of the permutation are masked and shuffled, while the rest is only shuffled. To further improve the security and performance of our implementations we make use of the Probe Isolating Non-Interference (PINI) masked AND gadget, coupled with techniques like bit-slicing and bit-interleaving. Utilising benchmarking and an MI-shortcut security analysis, we pinpoint the best masking-shuffling combinations that maximize security at reasonable overheads.

Keywords: Side-Channel Countermeasures · Cryptographic Implementations · RISC-V

1 Introduction

Side-Channel attacks such as Differential Power Analysis [22] pose one of the most significant threats to cryptographic implementations nowadays. How to prevent these kinds of attacks has thus become a major focus of research. Designers of cryptographic primitives have begun to consider side-channel resistance as one of the design concerns when devising new cryptographic algorithms. For example, the new standard for lightweight cryptography, Ascon [14], already incorporates features such as bitslicing [6] to prevent cache-timing attacks [4] and specifically tailored aspects of the encryption process to allow for easy integration of side-channel countermeasures such as masking [10] or shuffling [20].

Both of these techniques are able to provide standalone protection and can, in theory, be extended for an arbitrary amount of protection, given sufficient noise to amplify and sufficient independent operations to shuffle.

Related Work. The Ascon algorithm suite and the Ascon-128 variant in particular have undergone significant scrutiny and found to be cryptographically sound [15]. At the same time, it has been demonstrated that side-channel attacks on Ascon are feasible and can lead to partial or even full key recovery. Correlation power analysis (CPA) has been used to recover the complete encryption key from an unprotected Ascon implementation using 8,000 traces [24]. When augmenting the CPA with deep learning techniques, the number of traces can be reduced further to 1,000 and partial keys can be recovered even from 1st-order secure implementations [33], highlighting the need for strong higher-order secure implementations.

Several implementations of Ascon that make use of these side-channel countermeasures have been presented. A levelled 1st-order masked software implementation was presented in [1], yet it might not suffice for a thorough defense against SCAs. Two 2nd-order masked implementations of Ascon have been proposed in [19,27] for software and hardware, respectively. To the best of our knowledge, no implementations of Ascon with higher masking orders have been explored.

To achieve strong hardening against side-channel attacks, it is rarely the best choice to spend all effort on a single countermeasure. As suggested by Mangard et al. [23], it is more prudent to combine several cheap countermeasures and such combinations have been analysed in the past. In [29], Prouff et al. presented a probability-theoretic argument for the effectiveness of combining masking and shuffling. This was subsequently expanded by Azouaoui et al. in [2], where several different combinations of these countermeasures were discussed and evaluated.

Contribution. In this work, we expand and concretise the work of Azouaoui et al. [2]. We apply two of the combinations (Shuffle Tuples and Shuffle Shares) from that paper to a specific platform and algorithm and present an additional new combination that leverages bit-interleaving for a further increased security benefit. Additionally, we give a new way to shuffle a particular masked AND gadget, PINI-AND [9] and finally quantify the security increases the presented techniques provide according to the Mutual Information metric [30] by adapting the shortcut formulas put forward in [2].

Furthermore, we apply the discussed techniques to Ascon on a RISC-V 32-bit architecture, resulting in five side-channel protected implementations: One 3rd-order masked implementation, three versions combining 3rd-order masking with shuffling approaches and one levelled version, which exploits the fact that only the initialisation and finalisation of the Ascon scheme need to be heavily secured against side-channel attacks, whereas the associated data and message processing parts only need much lighter protection [3].

2 Background

2.1 Ascon

In 2023, the U.S. National Institute of Standards and Technology (NIST) concluded the lightweight cryptography (LWC) standardisation process by selecting the Ascon [14] family of algorithms as the winner [31]. For this work, we are concerned with the main recommendation of the Ascon suite, Ascon-128.

The encryption algorithm itself is permutation-based using a 320-bit state made up of 5 64-bit registers. An execution of the permutation consists of a certain number of rounds. During every round r, three steps are performed:

1. A one byte round constant c_r is added to the third state register.
2. A five-bit substitution layer (S-Box) is applied to the state. This S-Box iteratively processes a vertical slice of the five state registers, changing the values according to a look-up table.
3. A linear diffusion layer is applied, rotating every state register twice by different amounts and then XORing the two, as well as the unrotated state register, back together.

A visualisation of these operations can be found in Appendix B. The lookup table of the S-Box poses a significant hurdle in multiple regards. For one, lookup tables are often prone to side-channel attacks such as cache-timing attacks [4]. More significantly, since we want to mask the permutation, we need to have a way of performing the lookup without unmasking the current value. While it is technically possible to implement a masked lookup table, this quickly becomes infeasible with higher masking orders as the memory requirements to store these tables quickly grow larger than most embedded devices have at their disposal [12].

To circumvent these issues, bitslicing [6] can be used, which is often less computationally demanding and requires less memory. In fact, the design of the Ascon S-Box was created with bitslicing explicitly in mind. In the Ascon specification, the authors already provide a sequence of XOR, NOT, and AND operations to perform on the state that yields the same output as performing the "normal" lookup-table-based S-Box.

$$
\begin{array}{lllll}
x_0 = x_0 \oplus x_4; & x_4 = x_4 \oplus x_3; & x_2 = x_2 \oplus x_1; & & \\
t_0 = x_0; & t_1 = x_1; & t_2 = x_2; & t_3 = x_3; & t_4 = x_4; \\
t_0 = \neg t_0; & t_1 = \neg t_1; & t_2 = \neg t_2; & t_3 = \neg t_3; & t_4 = \neg t_4; \\
t_0 = t_0 \wedge x_1; & t_1 = t_1 \wedge x_2; & t_2 = t_2 \wedge x_3; & t_3 = t_3 \wedge x_4; & t_4 = t_4 \wedge x_0; \\
x_0 = x_0 \oplus t_1; & x_1 = x_1 \oplus t_2; & x_2 = x_2 \oplus t_3; & x_3 = x_3 \oplus t_4; & x_4 = x_4 \oplus t_0; \\
x_1 = x_1 \oplus x_0; & x_0 = x_0 \oplus x_4; & x_3 = x_3 \oplus x_2; & x_2 = \neg x_2; & \\
\end{array}
$$

2.2 Bit Interleaving

Considering that we are trying to implement an encryption based on a 64-bit state on a 32-bit system, we need to split each state register into two 32-bit registers without hampering performance too heavily. The naïve separation into two registers by simply splitting the register in the middle causes difficulties in the linear layer: With this separation, rotations of full state registers become cumbersome: A single rotation of a state register would require 7 instructions and three temporary registers in this scenario. Instead, we use a solution proposed by Bertoni et al. [5] called "Bit Interleaving": Rather than splitting the register in half, we separate the bits into even and uneven bits so that the first 32-bit register contains all the bits at even positions $b_0, b_2, \ldots, b_{62}$ of the original register and the second 32-bit register contains all the bits at odd positions $b_1, b_3, \ldots, b_{63}$. This configuration does not affect any operations except rotations. For a register x interleaved into x_e and x_o containing the even and odd bits of x, respectively, rotations by an even amount $2r$ can now be implemented by simply rotating both registers by r. Rotations by an uneven amount $2r + 1$ are implemented by rotating x_e by r, rotating x_o by $r + 1$ and then swapping the two registers. A visualisation of bit interleaving and these rotations is given in Appendix B. Although the RV32IM ISA we have chosen does not provide any rotation instructions[1], utilising this technique allows us to implement rotation with four shifts, two XORs, and one temporary register, meaning one less operation and two fewer temporary registers than the naïve version.

2.3 Masking

One of the most common countermeasures against SCAs is masking, which tries to prevent the leakage of intermediate values through the power consumption or electromagnetic emissions by "masking" relevant intermediate values with random values. More precisely, to mask a value x, it is split into $d + 1$ "shares" $x_0, \ldots, x_d$ using an involutory operation $\circ$ so that $x_0, \ldots, x_{d-1}$ contain random values $r_0, \ldots, r_{d-1}$ and $x_d = x \circ r_0 \circ \cdots \circ r_{d-1}$. One can then only obtain the original value by combining all d shares: $x_0 \circ \cdots \circ x_d = x$. This implies that an adversary trying to obtain x must now obtain all shares of the value to be able to unmask it. Consequently, there is no set of d shares an adversary can obtain that reveals any information about the original value. This is commonly referred to as d-th order security.

Commonly, $\circ$ denotes the XOR operation. Performing linear operations on masked values is straightforward. Difficulties arise when one tries to also perform non-linear operations such as AND on masked values. Several approaches have been presented to solve this, usually by incorporating additional randomness. A frequently used approach is that of Ishai, Sahai, and Wagner [21]. While this approach originally only promised $d/2$-th order security, adaptations of it have

---

[1] At the time of writing, no ratified extension to RISC-V implementing rotations exists yet.

been presented that promise d-th order security, albeit with special requirements for the individual shares that sometimes require mask refreshing when composing operations [28]. However, these mask refreshing procedures have also been shown to not be unconditionally d-th order secure [13].

Instead, we use a relatively novel scheme proposed by Cassiers and Standaert [9] for performing masked AND operations. In contrast to the ISW scheme, this approach has been proven to be d-th order secure as is. Moreover, it is arbitrarily composable, both with itself and any other masked operation, as long as the other operation also fulfils the notion of Probe Isolating Non-Interference (PINI) introduced in the paper. This includes any linear operation masked with the same number of shares as the PINI-AND gadget. The computation and randomness cost of a PINI-AND operation is the same as with the ISW scheme (both $\mathcal{O}(d^2)$). The original algorithm also requires $\mathcal{O}(d^2)$ amounts of memory. However, in the paper the authors hint at an adaptation of the gadget that gives the same security guarantees while only requiring linear memory. Our implementation makes use of this more efficient gadget. We give an explicit description of this adaptation in Sect. 3.4.

2.4 Shuffling

The idea of the shuffling countermeasure is to randomise the order of execution of a set of operations. Varying the point in execution at which a certain value is calculated between different executions of the encryption increases the difficulty for an adversary to correlate values from a given power trace or similar side-channel measurement [20].

Formally, shuffling takes an input vector y containing all inputs to process with a given operation $\mathsf{op}(\cdot)$. Additionally, a permutation $\theta \in \Theta_{|y|}$ is supplied where $\Theta_{|y|}$ is the set of all permutations of the sequence $[0, |y| - 1]$. During the execution of the cipher, the program iterates over θ so that at iteration i, y_{θ_i} is accessed, and $z_{\theta_i} = \mathsf{op}(y_{\theta_i})$ computed.

Two things need to be observed in particular when shuffling: First, the set of objects to shuffle must be sufficiently similar that an adversary cannot easily tell them apart in a power analysis. In practice, this usually means that all operations have to be the same and inputs to the operations need to be either all fixed or all random. For example, AND and XOR operations can already have distinct enough "leakage signatures" that an adversary can be able to tell them apart in a power trace. Secondly, one must be aware that if there is enough leakage of the permutation used to shuffle, an adversary can simply obtain this permutation and the benefit of shuffling vanishes.

2.5 Mutual Information

The Mutual Information (MI) framework [30] is a system of information-theoretic metrics created to measure the amount of information an implementation leaks while performing encryptions. Based on information theory, it employs metrics such as Shannon's Conditional Entropy to correlate leakages measured by an adversary to specific keys used in an encryption. It can thus give an estimation of the information leakage of a certain value (given sufficiently noisy conditions) and further be used to estimate the probability of success of an adversary recovering that value given a certain number of leakage measurements [11,16].

Concretely, let us assume we have a vector of secret keys K and a corresponding matrix of leakages L where every element of the matrix is a vector of leakages measured while using key k_i. We further assume that keys are uniformly randomly distributed, in which case we can calculate the conditional probability of a key given a leakage. Using this, we can estimate the mutual information $\mathrm{MI}(K; L)$ via the key entropy by sampling from this key distribution [7]. Generally, $\mathrm{MI}(K; L)$ is bound from above by the key entropy and is zero if leakages convey no information at all about the key used. Realistically, neither of these cases is likely. Usually, it is a value between 0 and 1 and should ideally be as small as possible. In that case, one can estimate the number of traces N needed to perform a statistical attack like correlation power analysis (CPA) very roughly using the mutual information: $N \geq \frac{c}{\mathrm{MI}(K;L)}$. Here, c is a constant depending on the key entropy and the desired success rate of the attack. We will use this formula to estimate the security improvements of our devised schemes in Sect. 5.

3 Combining Masking and Shuffling for Bit-Interleaved Schemes

As mentioned, the schemes presented in [2] serve as the baseline for this work. In this section, we discuss the adaptations of these schemes we devised to fit the specific structure of Ascon and the design choices made for this implementation. Although our focus here was Ascon, we want to highlight that the approaches presented can also be applied to other algorithms or platforms where the state register size of the algorithm is a multiple of two of the platform register size. For simplicity, the approaches here are shown with an interleaving factor of two. They could, however, be trivially adapted to other interleaving factors, e.g. using an interleaving factor of four if one were to implement Ascon on a 16-bit system.

Before we can discuss combinations of masking and shuffling, we need to establish how we mask values. A general algorithm for this masking and interleaving approach, independent of Ascon, is given in Algorithm 1.

To present our shuffling countermeasures in the following Sects. 3.1, 3.2, 3.3 and 3.4, we use the following notation: Let $A = [a_0, \ldots, a_{n-1}]$ and $B = [b_0, \ldots, b_{n-1}]$ be two lists each consisting of n d-th order masked, interleaved values as previously described, so e.g. $a_i = [[a_{i_e}^0, \ldots, a_{i_e}^d], [a_{i_o}^0, \ldots, a_{i_o}^d]]$. Furthermore, we define $C = [c_0, \ldots, c_{n-1}]$, where $c_i = \mathsf{op}(a_i, b_i)$ is the result of combining a_i and b_i with a binary linear operation $\mathsf{op}(\cdot)$ adapted to work on these masked, interleaved shares. A visualisation of all three approaches is given in Appendix B.

Algorithm 1. Masking and interleaving values

Inputs: $[a_0, \ldots, a_{n-1}]$, Masking order d
for $i = 0$ to n **do**
    $a_{i_e}, a_{i_o} \leftarrow \texttt{interleave}(a_i)$
    for $j = 0$ to $d - 1$ **do**
        $a_{i_e}^j \xleftarrow{\$} \mathbb{F}_{2^{32}}$
        $a_{i_o}^j \xleftarrow{\$} \mathbb{F}_{2^{32}}$
    end for
    $a_{i_e}^d \leftarrow a_{i_e} \oplus a_{i_e}^0 \oplus \cdots \oplus a_{i_e}^{d-1}$
    $a_{i_o}^d \leftarrow a_{i_o} \oplus a_{i_o}^0 \oplus \cdots \oplus a_{i_o}^{d-1}$
end for
Outputs:
$[[[a_{0_e}^0, \ldots, a_{0_e}^d], [a_{0_o}^0, \ldots, a_{0_o}^d]], \ldots, [[a_{n_e}^0, \ldots, a_{n_e}^d], [a_{n_o}^0, \ldots, a_{n_o}^d]]]$

3.1 Shuffling Tuples

The first and simplest approach to combining masking and shuffling countermeasures, as presented in [2], is to mask first and then shuffle in the same way as in an unmasked implementation. More precisely: given a permutation θ of $[0, n-1]$, we can shuffle the masked operations as we would if they were unmasked by performing them in the order $\texttt{op}(a_{\theta_0}, b_{\theta_0}), \ldots, \texttt{op}(a_{\theta_{n-1}}, b_{\theta_{n-1}})$. A precise algorithm for this procedure is given in Algorithm 2 and our interleaved implementation utilises it as is.

Algorithm 2. "Shuffling Tuples" masking and shuffling combination

Inputs: $a = [a_0, \ldots, a_{n-1}]$, $b = [b_0, \ldots, b_{n-1}]$, $\texttt{op}(\cdot)$, θ
for $i = 0$ to $n - 1$ **do**
    $k \leftarrow \theta_i$ ▷ Index to calculate next
    $c_k \leftarrow \texttt{op}(a_k, b_k)$ ▷ Perform the masked operation
end for
Outputs: $c = [c_0, \ldots, c_{n-1}]$ so that $\forall i : \texttt{op}(a_i, b_i) = c_i$

3.2 Shuffling Shares

For the following two shuffling approaches (Sects. 3.2, 3.3), the methods for shuffling linear and non-linear operations differ. Here, we will only discuss approaches for shuffling masked linear operations and extend our approach to non-linear operations in Sect. 3.4.

In this second approach, we do not shuffle the entire masked operations with each other but instead shuffle at the share-level. Note that there is no benefit to shuffling the order of processing of shares of the same value. This is because to successfully recover an unmasked value, an adversary needs to obtain all shares of that value, irrespective of the order in which they obtain them. Instead, we shuffle over the shares of different values in the following way: For two linear operations $a_0 \oplus b_0$ and $a_1 \oplus b_1$ we shuffle first the processing of all $a_{i_e}^k \oplus b_{i_e}^k$, where k is the current share index as dictated by the permutation used. In a second step, we process all $a_{i_o}^k \oplus b_{i_o}^k$. The sequences we shuffle over now are the sets of i-th shares of first the even, then the odd half of every interleaved register. Overall, this means we shuffle $d+1$ sets of n operations. See Algorithm 3 for a precise description of this procedure.

Algorithm 3. "Shuffling Shares" masking and shuffling combination

Inputs: $a = [a_0, \ldots, a_{n-1}]$, $b = [b_0, \ldots, b_{n-1}]$, $\mathsf{op}(\cdot)$, θ
  for $i \in \{e, o\}$ **do**   ▷ First process the shares of the even register, then the odd
    for $j = 0$ to d **do**   ▷ Iterate over the shares
      for $l = 0$ to $n-1$ **do**
        $k \leftarrow \theta_l$ ▷ Index to calculate next
        $c_{k_i}^j \leftarrow \mathsf{op}(a_{k_i}^j, b_{k_i}^j)$ ▷ Perform the masked operation
      end for
    end for
  end for
Outputs: $c = [c_0, \ldots, c_{n-1}]$ so that $\forall i : \mathsf{op}(a_i, b_i) = c_i$

3.3 Shuffling Everything "Light"

The third described countermeasure combination in [2] is called "Shuffling Everything", where the authors suggest combining all shares of all registers used into one permutation. Albeit technically possible, this approach grows significantly more complex when incorporating non-linear operations. Both due to suspected diminishing returns with respect to security and due to the scope of this work we elected not to investigate this, but instead to find more straightforward ways of shuffling more things with each other.

For shuffling shares, we only shuffle between registers at exactly the same position. This means that we differentiate between the "even" and "odd" registers of which one state register is comprised. However, this is not strictly necessary: in a linear operation (that is not a shift or rotation), the even and odd registers making up one state register never interact with each other. Thus, we can shuffle the i-th shares of an even and odd register with each other as well. We refer to this as "Shuffling Everything Light" (Shuffle EL). The permutation θ thus consists not only of the indices $[0, n-1]$ of the complete operations to shuffle, but also includes for every index an even and an odd variant. Consequently, the permutation is of the following form.

$$\theta = \{0_e, 0_o, 1_e, 1_o, \ldots, n-1_e, n-1_o\}, \quad |\theta| = 2n$$

This doubles the number of operations we can shuffle with one permutation. A more precise description is given in Algorithm 4.

Algorithm 4. "Shuffling Everything Light" masking and shuffling combination

Inputs: $a = [a_0, \ldots, a_{n-1}]$, $b = [b_0, \ldots, b_{n-1}]$, $\mathsf{op}(\cdot)$, $\theta = \{0_e, 0_o, \ldots, n-1_e, n-1_o\}$
for $j = 0$ to d **do** ▷ Iterate over the shares
    for $l = 0$ to $2n - 1$ **do** ▷ We now combine the even and odd part
        $k \leftarrow \theta_l$ ▷ Index to calculate next
        $c_k^j \leftarrow \mathsf{op}(a_k^j, b_k^j)$ ▷ Perform the masked operation
    end for
end for
Outputs: $c = [c_0, \ldots, c_{n-1}]$ so that $\forall i : \mathsf{op}(a_i, b_i) = c_i$

3.4 Shuffling PINI-AND Operations

When shuffling linear operations, there is a clear separation of when each share is processed. In a non-linear operation, this separation becomes much less clear, requiring us to devise specially crafted shuffling schemes, different from those for linear operations.

An algorithmic description of the gadget we use is given in Algorithm 5. It differs slightly from the original algorithm description given in [9], as we have implemented the hinted-at adapted version which requires only linear memory by directly calculating every z_{ij} and z_{ji} from each r_{ij}, removing the necessity to store each r_{ij}.

Algorithm 5. PINI AND gadget with linear memory requirements

Inputs: $a = [a_0, \ldots, a_d]$, $b = [b_0, \ldots, b_d]$
for $i = 0$ to d **do**
    $c_i \leftarrow a_i b_i$
end for
for $i = 0$ to d **do**
    for $j = i + 1$ to d **do**
        $r_{ij} \xleftarrow{\$} \mathbb{F}_{2^{32}}$; $r_{ji} \leftarrow r_{ij}$
        $z_{ij} = (a_i + 1) \cdot r_{ij} + a_i \cdot (b_j + r_{ij})$
        $z_{ji} = (a_j + 1) \cdot r_{ji} + a_j \cdot (b_i + r_{ji})$
        $c_i \leftarrow c_i + z_{ij}$
        $c_j \leftarrow c_j + z_{ji}$
    end for
end for
Outputs: $c = [c_0, \ldots, c_d]$ so that $c = a \wedge b$

To determine a shuffling approach for this gadget, we need to consider when each share is processed and which computed values have a dependence relation. When calculating the initial $c_i = a_i b_i$ in Algorithm 5 we can still clearly separate the share accesses but during the calculation of the values z_{ij}, different shares are accessed, muddying the distinction. This makes shuffling across shares infeasible for this gadget. On the other hand, note that the computation of every z_{ij} is independent from all other intermediate values computed in the gadget, meaning the order in which they are computed does not matter. This yields a first approach for shuffling. However, shuffling the computation of intermediate values inside one PINI gadget does not enhance security, similarly to how shuffling the processing of shares inside one linear gadget does not enhance security.

Consequently, we settled on shuffling the computation of $a_i b_i$ and z_{ij} for different a and b, thus shuffling across gadgets, instead of inside a gadget. This means we, for example, shuffle the computation of all $a_0 b_0$ for a given set of PINI AND operations. The same applies for the computation of all z_{01}, z_{10}, and so forth. The logic of *how* we shuffle across gadgets (i.e. whether we shuffle over each interleaved register separately or whether we combine these) is exactly the same as with linear gadgets, allowing for a seamless combination of linear and non-linear gadgets in our countermeasure combinations. For completeness, the algorithms for shuffling shares and shuffling everything light have also been written out in Algorithms 6 and 7, respectively. In these algorithms, $x \xleftarrow{+} y$ is a shorthand for $x \leftarrow x + y$.

Algorithm 6. "Shuffling Shares" masking and shuffling combination for PINI-AND

Inputs: $a = [a_0, \ldots, a_{n-1}]$, $b = [b_0, \ldots, b_{n-1}]$,
    Set Θ_n of permutations of length n to sample from
for $l \in \{e, o\}$ **do**   ▷ First process the shares of the even register, then the odd
  for $k = 0$ to d **do**   ▷ Iterate over the shares
    $\theta \xleftarrow{\$} \Theta_n$ ▷ Use a random permutation
    Shuffle$([a_{0_l}^k \wedge b_{0_l}^k, \ldots, a_{n-1_l}^k \wedge b_{n-1_l}^k], \theta)$ ▷ Shuffle the calculation of $a_i b_i$
  end for
  for $i = 0$ to d **do**
    for $j = i + 1$ to d **do**
      $\theta \xleftarrow{\$} \Theta_n$
      Shuffle$([c_{i0_l} \xleftarrow{+} z_{ij0_l}, \ldots, c_{i0_l} \xleftarrow{+} z_{ij0_l}], \theta)$ ▷ Shuffle the calculation of z_{ij}
      $\theta \xleftarrow{\$} \Theta_n$
      Shuffle$([c_{j0_l} \xleftarrow{+} z_{ji0_l}, \ldots, c_{j0_l} \xleftarrow{+} z_{ji0_l}], \theta)$ ▷ Shuffle the calculation of z_{ji}
    end for
  end for
end for
Outputs: $c = [c_0, \ldots, c_{n-1}]$ so that $\forall i : \text{op}(a_i, b_i) = c_i$

3.5 Randomness Cost

Generally, to mask a set of n r-bit values in our configuration with an interleaving factor of l, we need to generate $n \cdot r \cdot d$ bits of randomness. Note that the required randomness does not depend on the interleaving factor, as the overall size of the values to mask does not change. In the case of Ascon, for example, this results

Algorithm 7. "Shuffling Everything Light" masking and shuffling combination for PINI-AND

Inputs: $a = [a_0, \ldots, a_{n-1}]$, $b = [b_0, \ldots, b_{n-1}]$,
Set Θ_{2n} of permutations of length $2n$ to sample from
for $k = 0$ to d **do** ▷ Iterate over the shares
  $\theta \xleftarrow{\$} \Theta_{2n}$ ▷ Use a random permutation
  Shuffle$([a_{0_e}^k \wedge b_{0_e}^k, a_{0_o}^k \wedge b_{0_o}^k, \ldots, a_{n-1_e}^k \wedge b_{n-1_e}^k, a_{n-1_o}^k \wedge b_{n-1_o}^k], \theta)$
end for
for $i = 0$ to d **do**
  for $j = i+1$ to d **do**
    $\theta \xleftarrow{\$} \Theta_{2n}$
    Shuffle$([c_{i_{0_e}} \xleftarrow{+} z_{ij_{0_e}}, c_{i_{0_o}} \xleftarrow{+} z_{ij_{0_o}}, \ldots, c_{i_{0_e}} \xleftarrow{+} z_{ij_{0_e}}, c_{i_{0_o}} \xleftarrow{+} z_{ij_{0_o}}], \theta)$
    $\theta \xleftarrow{\$} \Theta_{2n}$
    Shuffle$([c_{j_{0_e}} \xleftarrow{+} z_{ji_{0_e}}, c_{j_{0_o}} \xleftarrow{+} z_{ji_{0_o}}, \ldots, c_{j_{0_e}} \xleftarrow{+} z_{ji_{0_e}}, c_{j_{0_o}} \xleftarrow{+} z_{ji_{0_o}}], \theta)$
  end for
end for
Outputs: $c = [c_0, \ldots, c_{n-1}]$ so that $\forall i: \text{op}(a_i, b_i) = c_i$

in a randomness requirement of $5 \cdot 64 \cdot d = 320d$ bits. The randomness cost of shuffling stems from generating the shuffling permutation alone. Generally, a permutation of length n can be generated with $\Theta(n \log_2 n)$ bits of randomness [17]. For shuffling tuples, a single permutation of length n is needed to shuffle the n operations. For shuffling shares, one permutation is needed per share index. Thus, for d-th order security, $\Theta((d+1)n \log_2(n))$ bits of randomness are required. For shuffling everything light, the situation is the same as for shuffling shares, with the only difference being the larger size of $2n$ for the permutation. Following, the randomness required is $\Theta((d+1)2n(\log_2(n)+1))$ bits.

On top of this, we need to account for the extra randomness required by all schemes for the computation of each PINI-AND gadget. Since every PINI-AND computation on an r-bit device requires $r \frac{(d+1)d}{2}$ bits of randomness, computing a set of n such operations requires an additional $n \cdot r \frac{(d+1)d}{2}$ bits of randomness. The randomness cost for shuffling PINI-AND operations with these schemes is not directly bound by the security order, but by the number of independent operations performed inside the non-linear gadget. Thus, in our case, shuffling shares requires $\Theta(d^2 n \log_2(n))$ bits of randomness and shuffling everything light requires $\Theta(d^2 2n(\log_2(n)+1))$ bits. Shuffling tuples does not require any extra randomness to shuffle the PINI-AND operations.

For clarity, the randomness values of all schemes, both in the linear and non-linear case, are also listed in Table 1. Refer to Appendix B for a graph showing the randomness requirement versus the masking order d. In Sect. 5, we will provide specific numbers for the randomness needed when applying these schemes to a third-order masked and a levelled version of Ascon.

Table 1. The randomness requirements of the different shuffling approaches, measured in bits. Values in the non-linear column do not include the randomness required in the computation of the non-linear gadgets.

	Linear	Non-linear
Shuffle tuples	$n \log_2(n)$	$n \log_2(n)$
Shuffle shares	$(d+1)n \log_2(n)$	$d^2 n \log_2(n)$
Shuffle EL	$(d+1)2n(\log_2(n)+1)$	$d^2 2n(\log_2(n)+1)$

4 Implementation

To benchmark the schemes proposed in a practical setting, we implemented five protected variants of the Ascon-128 encryption scheme. One implementation uses only 3rd-order masking for protection. Three implementations combine 3rd-order masking with Shuffle Tuples, Shuffle Shares and Shuffle EL respectively. Finally, we also implemented a levelled version, where only the initialisation and finalisation are masked and shuffled (with 3rd-order masking and Shuffle EL), while the rest of the cipher is shuffled (with Shuffle EL) but is not masked. All five variants were implemented in RV32IM assembly code and the source code can be found here: https://uva-hva.gitlab.host/l.mainka/side-channel-secure-ascon.

4.1 Optimising the S-Box

The bitsliced S-Box presented in the Ascon specification (shown again in Sect. 2.1) provides a good foundation for an initial implementation. There are, however, means to optimise it in our case. Concretely, the second and third row of the given bitsliced S-Box consist only of copy and NOT operations, respectively and can be combined into a single operation. Going further, we can also combine these two rows with the subsequent row of AND operations. While not a meaningful optimisation in an unprotected implementation, in a masked and shuffled implementation it saves a substantial amount of instructions because it reduces the number of instruction sets to shuffle by one. This means one less round of computing jump offsets and at least one less load and store for every share. In addition, as a masked negation is performed simply by negating an arbitrary share, integrating the negation into the AND should in theory only cost a single instruction. In reality, a few more instructions are required, but still many less than if we were performing the operations separately. The S-Box we now compute then looks as follows.

$x_0 = x_0 \oplus x_4; \quad x_4 = x_4 \oplus x_3; \quad x_2 = x_2 \oplus x_1;$
$t_0 = \neg x_0 \wedge x_1; \quad t_1 = \neg x_1 \wedge x_2; \quad t_2 = \neg x_2 \wedge x_3; \quad t_3 = \neg x_3 \wedge x_4; \quad t_4 = \neg x_4 \wedge x_0;$
$x_0 = x_0 \oplus t_1; \quad x_1 = x_1 \oplus t_2; \quad x_2 = x_2 \oplus t_3; \quad x_3 = x_3 \oplus t_4; \quad x_4 = x_4 \oplus t_0;$
$x_1 = x_1 \oplus x_0; \quad x_0 = x_0 \oplus x_4; \quad x_3 = x_3 \oplus x_2; \quad x_2 = \neg x_2;$

The number of instructions we save with this implementation varies between the different shuffling schemes. We report them in Table 2. The savings from this optimisation are so substantial in the latter two schemes because it reduces the number of operation sets we shuffle by one. When using Shuffling Shares and Shuffling EL, this saves us one whole iteration of computing jump offsets. Moreover, as alluded to previously we need to load/store all values before/after each computation, meaning this also reduces the number of times the entire state is loaded into registers and written back into memory by one.

For a brief discussion of other optimisations avenues that we decided against, refer to Appendix A.

Table 2. The instruction count of the masked S-Box without (Standard) and with (Optimised) combining the copy, NOT and AND per shuffling scheme.

	Shuffling Tuples	Shuffling Shares	Shuffling EL
Standard	2384	6175	6130
Optimised	2304	5797	5756

4.2 Shuffling

Generating the Permutation. For generating a (theoretically) unbiased random permutation of a sequence $s = [0, n-1]$, the algorithm presented in [17] is a common choice that we also utilised for this work. It generates the permutation in $\mathcal{O}(n)$ time and requires $\Theta(n \log_2 n)$ bits of randomness. While there are caveats to using this algorithm, such as possible bias, they do not pose hazards to the security of our implementation, since the bias induced by side-channel leakage is typically higher.

Implementing Shuffling. In [32], Veyrat-Charvillon et al. give a taxonomy of three possible paths for implementing shuffling. In the first, called "Double Indexing", an operand and a permutation vector are stored in memory. At every shuffling step, the permutation vector is accessed and the retrieved value is used as the index to access the operand vector. The retrieved operands are then fed into the operation. For the second approach, the authors propose writing out the code for each operation and giving it a label to store in an array in memory at compile time. At runtime, the order of this array is randomised and every entry is used successively to jump to the stored address and to perform the operation at that address. Finally, while the previous two approaches determined the next operation to execute at runtime, the third approach is to use the self-programming capabilities some chips have to reorder the program memory after compiling so that at runtime, the program can be executed without additional control logic.

In our work, approach three was not considered, as the number of times the flash memory of a chip can be rewritten is prohibitively low for use in practice. Similarly, we decided against approach one due to the significant performance overhead of creating operand vectors and then accessing memory twice for every operation.

The approach we chose is a modification of the second approach. Instead of giving every operation a label and assembling the addresses of these labels in an array at compile time, we place the operations sequentially in the program, set one label before the beginning of the first operation, one label after the last operation and determine the code size of the operations. At runtime, we then access a permutation vector in memory and calculate an address offset by multiplying the operation code size by the permutation index and adding the resulting value to the initial label. After all operations of one shuffling set have been performed, a final jump to the label after the last operation is done and the next instruction can be executed. Our approach allows us to determine the next operation to execute in only five instructions without requiring significant logic at compile-time and saves us from randomising the address vectors at runtime. Additionally, it ensures by design that all shuffled operations have exactly the same length, preventing potential side-channel leakage due to different operation sizes.

What to Shuffle. Our general motivation was to maximize the amount of shuffled components, meaning in particular that we try to shuffle the entire permutation. The bitsliced version of the S-Box as described in the Ascon specification has a natural structure of applying five operations at a time to the five state registers. Consequently, we chose to shuffle blocks of five masked operations. For the first and last XORs and the last NOT which do not comprise five operations, we introduced additional dummy operations. Accounting for the combining of the copy, NOT, and AND operations, this gives us five sets of operations across which we can shuffle.[2]

It is very important to note that shuffling significantly increases register pressure. Since there is no guarantee anymore that operations are performed in a particular order, a general rule is that results can not be written back to the same register immediately, but have to be stored in a temporary location until all operations of the current shuffling block have been performed. Take for example the first shuffling block of the S-Box. If we calculate $x_0 = x_0 \oplus x_4$ and then $x_4 = x_4 \oplus x_3$, everything is fine. Should we now shuffle with a permutation that performs these operations in inverted order, x_4 is updated before x_0 is, leading to incorrect results. Thus, we need to store the results of these operations in a

---

[2] The authors of [2] note that adding dummy operations in a masking-shuffling combination is rarely worth it from a security standpoint. We decided to add them regardless for two reasons: 1) Since in a levelled implementation a significant portion of the permutation will only be shuffled but not masked, the effect is more pronounced, and 2) With the dummy operations all shuffling sets will be of the same size, significantly simplifying the implementation.

temporary location before storing them back once all five have been completed. Naturally, these storing back operations can be (and are) shuffled, too.

In the linear layer, our use of bit interleaving posed a hurdle: Since the two bit interleaved registers need to be swapped for an odd rotation but not for an even rotation (cf. Section 2.2 or the visualisation in Appendix B), the operations needed to rotate by an even or an odd amount differ. Considering that we would like for all shuffled blocks to be of the same size to avoid distinguishing characteristics in time and power that can undo the benefit of shuffling, we introduced a dummy swap in the even rotation.

Due to the shape of the Ascon state, the linear layer also naturally lends itself to shuffling blocks of five operations. The granularity of the blocks to shuffle leaves more room for possibilities: For shuffling tuples, we considered each transformation of one state register as one block, thus giving us only a single set of operations to shuffle which each consists of two rotations and three XORs. For shuffling shares, we did separate the aforementioned blocks, giving us four sets of operations to shuffle: Two XORs and two rotations. As in the S-Box, we first shuffled the computation of the first 32-bit registers of the state registers and then performed the shuffled computation of the second. Shuffling Everything Light introduced a further difficulty, as the technique relies on the ability to process the two interleaved registers at the same time. Due to the two interleaved registers switching places in case of an uneven rotation, we can only have the rotation of both registers in the same shuffling set if the results are written to an intermediate location first and only moved to the correct place after all operations of the current shuffling set have been completed.

4.3 Randomness Requirements

Sect. 3 already discussed the theoretical randomness requirements for the three shuffling approaches. We will now use these formulas to provide explicit values for the number of bits of randomness required for all five implemented variants of Ascon-128. Since the randomness requirement of the PINI-AND operations does not differ between shuffling schemes and only depends on the masking order, we calculate this value once and add it to the requirements of every (masked) scheme: Every round of the permutation contains five non-linear PINI-AND operations on the state. Since we split the registers in two, this results in ten 32-bit PINI AND operations. These operations require an additional $10 \cdot 16(d+1)d = 160 \cdot 4 \cdot 3 = 1920$ bits of randomness.

Shuffling Tuples. The S-Box consists of three blocks of XORs, one block of PINI-AND and one block of NOTs we need to shuffle. On top of these, we need two blocks for shuffling the "storeback" operations mentioned in the previous section. Additionally, we have one further block for the linear layer. All eight of these blocks consist of five operations, meaning we have a rounded up randomness requirement of
$$8 \cdot (5 \log_2(5)) \approx 93 \text{ bits}$$
for generating the shuffling permutations for this approach.

Shuffling Shares. For shuffling shares, we still only shuffle blocks of five operations. However, since we are now shuffling the processing of shares across operations (in the case of linear operations) and separate the two halves of each state register into separate shuffling blocks, we now need eight shuffling blocks to complete one set of five operations in the S-Box. As we have the same amount of operations to perform as when shuffling tuples, this leaves us with $8 \cdot 6 = 48$ shuffling blocks in total for the linear operations of the S-Box. To shuffle the non-linear PINI-AND operations we require a total of 14 shuffling blocks to compute all intermediate values. Additionally, we need four more blocks to aggregate all intermediate values and to move them into the correct location, Finally, we need to double these numbers again to account for the separate processing of the interleaved halves of each state register. In total, we thus have 84 shuffling blocks in the S-Box. In the linear layer, each rotation and each subsequent XOR require one shuffling block, adding a further 16 blocks. This yields a total of

$$(84 + 16)(5\log_2(5)) \approx 1161 \text{ bits}$$

to generate all permutations for shuffling in this approach.

Shuffling Everything Light. For shuffling everything light, we now shuffle blocks of ten operations because we join the operations on each half of the state register into one shuffling block. This means that we only have six operations to shuffle for the S-Box. As we are masking with four shares, the total number of shuffling blocks for the S-Box is thus 24. In the linear layer we merged the rotations and following XOR into one operation, meaning we only have three operations to shuffle, resulting in a total of 12 shuffling blocks, Overall, we thus need

$$(24 + 12)(10\log_2(10)) \approx 1196 \text{ bits}$$

of randomness in this scheme.

5 Analysis

5.1 Performance

Section 4.1 already provides information regarding the performance of the proposed schemes in terms of instruction counts. This section will also present the number of cycles our schemes need on a device since the correspondence between cycles and instructions is not always one-to-one. To obtain these numbers we used a QEMU simulation of a SiFive HiFive 1 Rev B[3], a board built around a SiFive FE310-G002 chip which provides the RV32IMAC ISA. Cycle measurements were performed through the RISC-V provided RDCYCLE control-and-status register (CSR).

---

[3] https://www.sifive.com/boards/hifive1-rev-b.

Table 3. Number of clock cycles to process a single byte of plaintext and related throughput. All schemes are 3rd-order PINI masked.

	Unshuffled	ShuffleTuples	ShuffleShares	ShuffleEL	Levelled
No. Clock Cycles	16,395	20,842	50,326	51,481	7,301
Throughput (bits/cycle)	0.004	0.003	0.0013	0.0012	0.009

In Fig. 1 the number of cycles needed for one round of the permutation are shown per scheme. For comparison, we include an unmasked, but shuffled variant. In Table 3 we present the number of cycles needed to process a single block of plaintext, as well as the resulting throughput in bits per cycle.

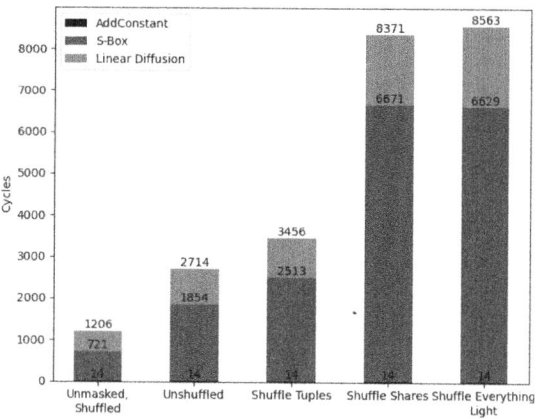

Fig. 1. The number of cycles needed to compute one round of the permutation per scheme, separated by the different steps. With the exception of the "Unmasked, Shuffled" variant, all others variants are 3rd-order PINI masked.

5.2 Security

To quantify what increases in security the implemented masking-shuffling combinations have brought, we performed an analysis using the Mutual Information framework and adapt the shortcut formulas from [2] to our customized shuffling variants.

When analysing a d-th order masked gadget, a potential attacker needs to obtain information about all $d+1$ shares of a key (Eq. 1). Instead, if attacking a shuffled gadget where a set of n operations are shuffled, the complexity of the attack increases linearly with the size of the permutation (Eq. 2).

$$N \geq \frac{c}{\prod_{j=0}^{d} \mathrm{MI}(K^j; L)} \quad (1) \qquad N \geq \frac{c \cdot n}{\mathrm{MI}_u(K; L)} \quad (2)$$

Here, $\mathrm{MI}_u(K; L)$ denotes the mutual information of an unshuffled implementation and we will assume that an adversary is attacking a single 32-bit chip register.

Shuffling Tuples. In the case of shuffling tuples, we are first masking an implementation and then shuffling the masked operations as a whole. An adversary thus needs to attack all n operations of a shuffling permutation to ensure that they obtain the specific value they are interested in. Furthermore, they need to obtain information about all shares of the value of interest, obtaining Eq. 3.

$$N \geq \frac{c \cdot n}{\prod_{j=0}^{d} \mathrm{MI}_u(K^j; L)} \quad (3)$$

Shuffling Shares. In the shuffling shares scenario, we no longer shuffle entire masked operations but instead shuffle across the shares of n operations. This implies that an attacker wishing to attack a particular masked value needs to perform multiple attacks on different shuffling permutations. The adversary has a probability of $\frac{1}{n}$ to obtain the share of the desired value in a shuffling permutation. Since they must additionally obtain all $d+1$ shares of the value, they must achieve this $d+1$ times, giving them a probability of $\left(\frac{1}{n}\right)^{d+1}$ to succeed.

$$N \geq \frac{c \cdot n^{d+1}}{\prod_{j=0}^{d} \mathrm{MI}_u(K^j; L)} \quad (4)$$

Shuffling Everything Light. Assuming an attacker recovering a single 32-bit register, this scheme effectively doubles the difficulty for an attacker to obtain the sought after register from the shuffling permutation. Therefore, all that changes from shuffling shares is the numerator increasing by a factor of two.

$$N \geq \frac{c \cdot (2n)^{d+1}}{\prod_{j=0}^{d} \mathrm{MI}_u(K^j; L)} \quad (5)$$

Scheme Comparison. We plotted the resulting number of traces needed according to these formulas for different values of $\mathrm{MI}_u(K; L)$. For this, we made two simplifying assumptions: First, c is a constant depending on the key entropy and the desired success rate of the attack and we simplify by equating it to the key entropy alone. Second, we assume that the mutual information between leakage and different shares of a value are equal simplifying all denominators from $\prod_{j=0}^{d} \mathrm{MI}_u(K^j; L)$ to $\mathrm{MI}_u(K^0; L)^{d+1}$. Table 4 also showcases the highest MI value such that the adversary needs 10^6 attack traces. We also show values for a lower security order of $d = 1$ there to also account for the case that the masking order of an actual implementation is reduced due to (micro-)architectural leakages of share combinations.

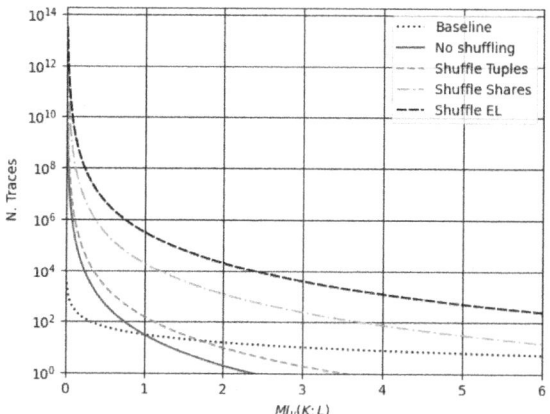

Fig. 2. Number of traces needed to mount a successful attack vs. the mutual information between masking shares and leakage. "Baseline" denotes an unmasked, unshuffled implementation while all others are 3rd-order PINI masked.

The plot is shown in Fig. 2. The maximum value $\mathrm{MI}_u(K; L)$ can take is 32 bits, if the mutual information between the leakage and the key contains all information about the key. The baseline shown is an assumed implementation that is neither masked nor shuffled. A simple 3rd-order masked, unshuffled implementation already shows a significant improvement over the baseline, given sufficiently low values for mutual information. Shuffling Tuples yields a further, albeit not substantial, improvement over the unshuffled variant. Both Shuffling Shares and Shuffling Everything Light exhibit a significant jump in the number of traces needed, with these variants offering security levels between 10^4 and 10^6 traces for MI ≈ 1.

Table 4. Highest $\text{MI}_u(K;L)$ value s.t. the adversary needs at least 1,000,000 attack traces. All implementations are 1st- or 3rd-order PINI masked.

	Unshuffled	Shuffle Tuples	Shuffle Shares	Shuffle EL
$d=3$	0.0752	0.1125	0.376	0.7521
$d=1$	0.0057	0.0126	0.0283	0.0566

6 Conclusion

Guided by the theoretical security evaluation we can conclude that all three shuffling schemes present notable increases in security compared to an implementation utilising only masking as a countermeasure. Overall, Shuffle Everything Light provides the best security gain in relation to performance cost, with a (theoretical) ten-fold increase in permissible mutual information at a roughly three-fold increase in clock cycles when compared to an only masked implementation. Shuffling Tuples proves to be a sound choice when there is not much spare performance available, with an almost 50% increase in security, again compared to an only masked implementation. While only increasing clock cycles by roughly 27%.

We also note that, while the schemes implemented are specific to the state structure of Ascon and the 32-bit RISC-V devices targetted, the general method of adapting countermeasures when the cipher state size is a multiple of 32 bits (and possibly interleaved) remains applicable.

Finally, we feel it is important to give a brief disclaimer: While the security estimates here are sound and the implementation should be secure from a theoretical standpoint, it is likely that through (micro-)architectural particularities such as overwrite- or memory remnant effects [26], the real security and masking order might be lower than the theoretical guarantees.

Future Work. While the theoretical analysis of the schemes devised in this work seems promising, an actual side-channel evaluation is an important next step to verify that the theoretical claims also hold up in practice, e.g. using countermeasure dissection [8]. Additionally, the exploration of possible schemes for combining masking and shuffling was far from exhaustive. It should certainly be possible to find schemes coming even closer to the "Shuffle Everything" scheme proposed in [2], thus further increasing the benefit to security. In the same vein, the existing approaches could be streamlined further, e.g. by unifying the computation of z_{ij} and z_{ji} for the PINI-AND gadgets into one shuffling block in the case of shuffling shares and shuffling everything light rather than using separate shuffling blocks for them. Finally, investigating avenues for reducing the randomness requirements for these schemes should prove useful to increase the feasibility of these implementations, as shown in [25].

Acknowledgements. This work was supported by an UvA starter grant.

A Implementation Paths Not Taken

In light of the optimisation presented in Sect. 4.1, we maintain that it is worthwhile to briefly discuss other means of implementing and optimising the encryption that we decided against using.

As discussed in Sect. 2.1, we decided against implementing the substitution layer as a masked lookup table [12]. While technically offering a performance improvement at runtime, the initial computation of these masked LUTs and the large memory requirement they impose for a four-share masked implementation make them infeasible for several resource-constrained devices.

An option for implementing the linear layer, and in particular circumventing the restriction of having no rotation instructions in RV32IM would have been to bitslice multiple encryption blocks by having one register for every bit of each state register and to then implement the rotations through "register renaming". Concretely, we could take 32 independent encryption blocks and bitslice them so that all first bits of each block go into one register, all second bits into the next, and so forth. In this case, the rotations of the linear layer would reduce to "renaming" e.g. the "register containing all first bits" would be renamed to the "register containing all second bits", in the case of a rotation by one. Apart from requiring a significant number of independent encryptions for efficient bitslicing (i.e. a bulk-encryption usecase), this approach is also infeasible due to the sheer number of registers needed. Since the Ascon state registers are 64 bits wide, we would need $5*64 = 320$ registers for storing all bits. The amount of loading and storing needed to realise this would very likely negate any performance gained from the free rotations.

Lastly, we could have approached the masking of the state differently in that we put multiple shares into one register, an approach also known as share-slicing. The benefit of this kind of slicing is that one can easily implement various operations on shares by rotating some of the share-sliced registers. This approach is especially appealing in architectures such as ARM, where certain instructions allow one of the operands to be rotated before the operation, effectively for free. Since such a construction does not exist for RV32IM, we cannot utilise this to our advantage. Furthermore, recent works have also discovered that share slicing also poses additional risks in a side-channel mitigation context [18] (Figs. 3, 4, 5, 6, 7 and 8).

B Additional Figures

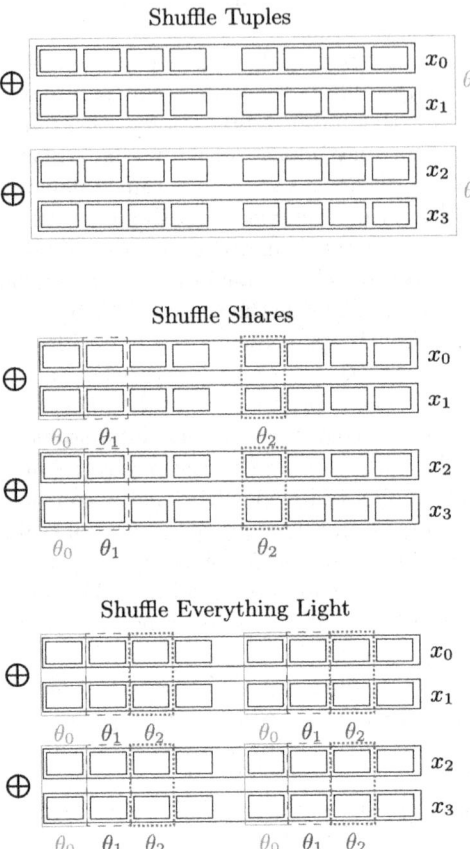

Fig. 3. A visualisation of the three different shuffling approaches selected for this implementation. Shown are two XOR operations on two 64-bit state registers, respectively split into two third-order masked 32-bit registers. Each θ denotes one set of operations to shuffle.

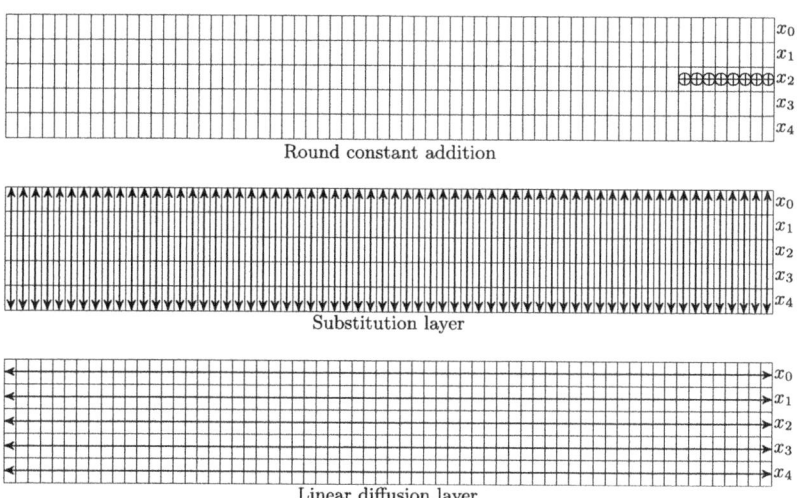

Fig. 4. The three steps performed on the state during each round of the Ascon permutation. Each rectangle represents one bit of the state.

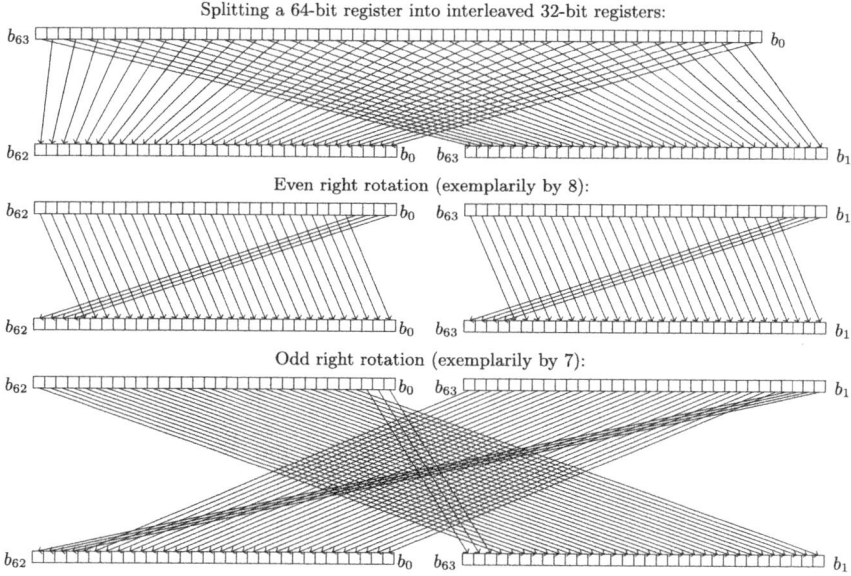

Fig. 5. A visualisation of interleaving and interleaved rotations.

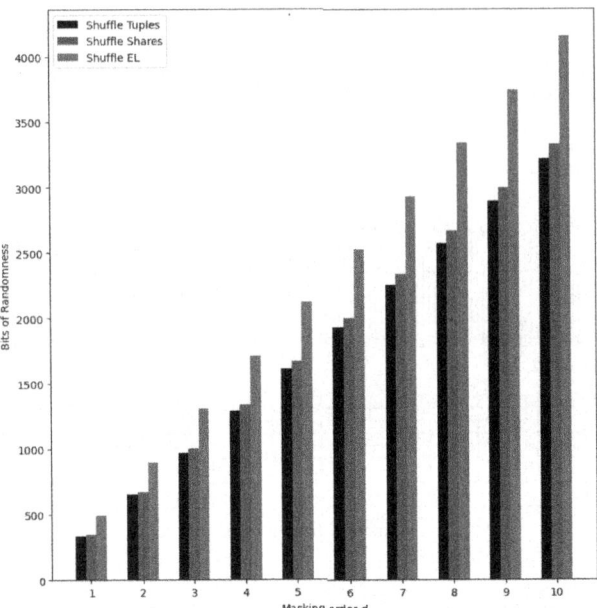

Fig. 6. Bits of randomness needed for linear operations per scheme depending on the chosen masking order d. Based on the formulas listed in Table 1 for $n = 5$ in the case of shuffle tuples and shuffle shares, and $n = 10$ for shuffle EL.

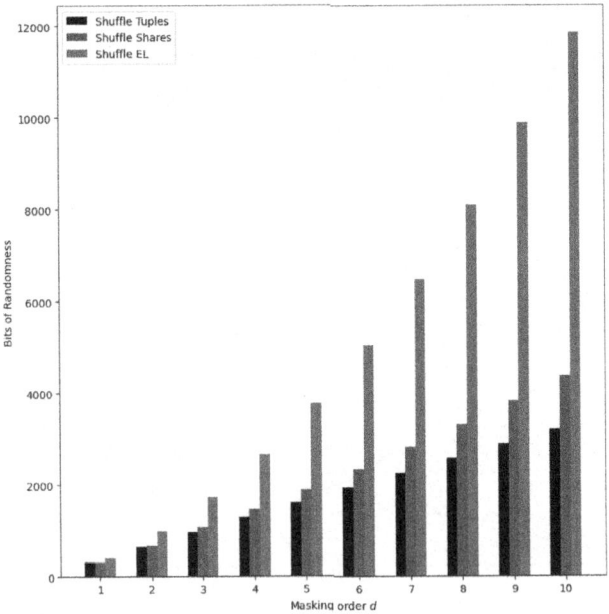

Fig. 7. Bits of randomness needed for non-linear operations per scheme depending on the chosen masking order d. Based on the formulas listed in Table 1 for $n = 5$ in the case of shuffle tuples and shuffle shares, and $n = 10$ for shuffle EL.

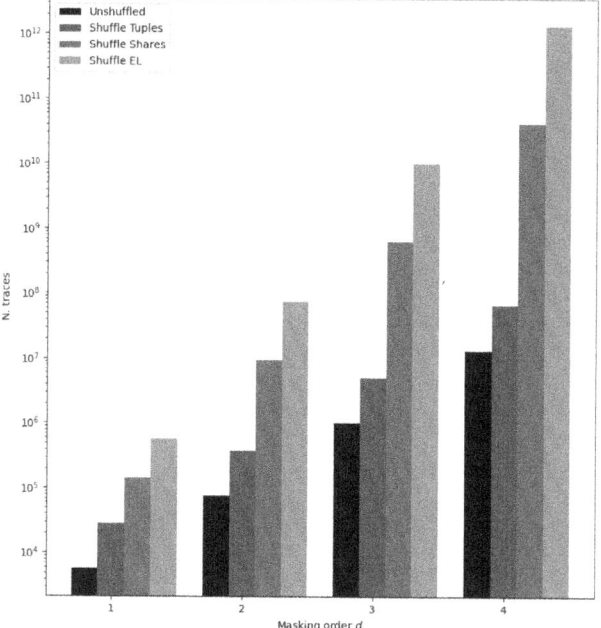

Fig. 8. The amount of traces needed to mount a successful attack per scheme and masking order. The $MI(K; L)$ is fixed to 0.0752, the amount where a third-order masked but unshuffled implementation would require 10^6 traces to be broken.

References

1. Adomnicai, A., Fournier, J.J.A., Masson, L.: Masking the lightweight authenticated ciphers ACORN and Ascon in software. Cryptology ePrint Archive, Paper 2018/708 (2018). https://eprint.iacr.org/2018/708
2. Azouaoui, M., Bronchain, O., Grosso, V., Papagiannopoulos, K., Standaert, F.X.: Bitslice masking and improved shuffling: how and when to mix them in software? IACR Trans. Cryptograph. Hardw. Embed. Syst. **2022**(2), 140–165 (2022). https://doi.org/10.46586/tches.v2022.i2.140-165
3. Bellizia, D., et al.: Mode-level vs. implementation-level physical security in symmetric cryptography. In: Micciancio, D., Ristenpart, T. (eds.) CRYPTO 2020. LNCS, vol. 12170, pp. 369–400. Springer, Cham (2020). https://doi.org/10.1007/978-3-030-56784-2_13
4. Bernstein, D.J.: Cache-timing attacks on AES (2005). https://api.semanticscholar.org/CorpusID:2217245
5. Bertoni, G., Daemen, J., Peeters, M., Van Assche, G., Van Keer, R.: KECCAK implementation overview (2012). https://keccak.team/files/Keccak-implementation-3.2.pdf
6. Biham, E.: A fast new DES implementation in software. In: Biham, E. (ed.) FSE 1997. LNCS, vol. 1267, pp. 260–272. Springer, Heidelberg (1997). https://doi.org/10.1007/BFb0052352

7. Bronchain, O., Hendrickx, J.M., Massart, C., Olshevsky, A., Standaert, F.X.: Leakage certification revisited: bounding model errors in side-channel security evaluations. Cryptology ePrint Archive, Paper 2019/132 (2019). https://eprint.iacr.org/2019/132
8. Bronchain, O., Standaert, F.: Side-channel countermeasures' dissection and the limits of closed source security evaluations. IACR Trans. Cryptogr. Hardw. Embed. Syst. **2020**(2), 1–25 (2020). https://doi.org/10.13154/TCHES.V2020.I2.1-25
9. Cassiers, G., Standaert, F.X.: Trivially and efficiently composing masked gadgets with probe isolating non-interference. IEEE Trans. Inf. Forensics Secur. **15**, 2542–2555 (2020). https://doi.org/10.1109/TIFS.2020.2971153
10. Chari, S., Jutla, C.S., Rao, J.R., Rohatgi, P.: Towards sound approaches to counteract power-analysis attacks. In: Wiener, M. (ed.) Advances in Cryptology – CRYPTO' 99, pp. 398–412. Springer, Berlin, Heidelberg (1999)
11. de Chérisey, E., Guilley, S., Rioul, O., Piantanida, P.: Best information is most successful: mutual information and success rate in side-channel analysis. IACR Trans. Cryptograph. Hardw. Embed. Syst. **2019**(2), 49–79 (2019). https://doi.org/10.13154/tches.v2019.i2.49-79
12. Coron, J.S.: Higher order masking of look-up tables. In: Nguyen, P.Q., Oswald, E. (eds.) Advances in Cryptology – EUROCRYPT 2014, pp. 441–458. Springer, Berlin, Heidelberg (2014). https://doi.org/10.1007/978-3-642-55220-5_25
13. Coron, J.S., Prouff, E., Rivain, M., Roche, T.: Higher-order side channel security and mask refreshing. Cryptology ePrint Archive, Paper 2015/359 (2015). https://eprint.iacr.org/2015/359
14. Dobraunig, C., Eichlseder, M., Mendel, F., Schläffer, M.: Ascon v1.2: lightweight authenticated encryption and hashing. J. Cryptol. **34**(3), 1–42 (2021). https://doi.org/10.1007/s00145-021-09398-9
15. Dobraunig, C., Eichlseder, M., Mendel, F., Schläffer, M.: Status update on Ascon v1.2 (2022). https://csrc.nist.gov/csrc/media/Projects/lightweight-cryptography/documents/finalist-round/status-updates/ascon-update.pdf
16. Duc, A., Faust, S., Standaert, F.X.: Making masking security proofs concrete or how to evaluate the security of any leaking device (extended version). Cryptology ePrint Archive, Paper 2015/119 (2015). https://eprint.iacr.org/2015/119
17. Durstenfeld, R.: Algorithm 235: random permutation. Commun. ACM **7**(7), 420 (1964). https://doi.org/10.1145/364520.364540
18. Gao, S., Marshall, B., Page, D., Oswald, E.: Share-slicing: friend or foe? IACR Trans. Cryptograph. Hardw. Embed. Syst. **2020**(1), 152–174 (2019). https://doi.org/10.13154/tches.v2020.i1.152-174
19. Gigerl, B., Mendel, F., Schläffer, M., Primas, R.: Efficient second-order masked software implementations of Ascon in theory and practice. In: Sixth NIST Lightweight Cryptography Workshop (2023). https://csrc.nist.gov/csrc/media/Events/2023/lightweight-cryptography-workshop-2023/documents/accepted-papers/04-efficient-second-order-masked-software.pdf
20. Herbst, C., Oswald, E., Mangard, S.: An AES smart card implementation resistant to power analysis attacks. In: Zhou, J., Yung, M., Bao, F. (eds.) Applied Cryptography and Network Security, pp. 239–252. Springer, Berlin, Heidelberg (2006)
21. Ishai, Y., Sahai, A., Wagner, D.: Private circuits: securing hardware against probing attacks. In: Boneh, D. (ed.) CRYPTO 2003. LNCS, vol. 2729, pp. 463–481. Springer, Heidelberg (2003). https://doi.org/10.1007/978-3-540-45146-4_27
22. Kocher, P., Jaffe, J., Jun, B.: Differential power analysis. In: Wiener, M. (ed.) Advances in Cryptology — CRYPTO' 99, pp. 388–397. Springer, Berlin, Heidelberg (1999). https://doi.org/10.1007/3-540-48405-1_25

23. Mangard, S., Oswald, E., Popp, T.: Power Analysis Attacks. Springer, Boston, MA (2007). https://doi.org/10.1007/978-0-387-38162-6
24. Mohajerani, K., Beckwith, L., Abdulgadir, A., Ferrufino, E., Kaps, J.P., Gaj, K.: SCA evaluation and benchmarking of finalists in the NIST lightweight cryptography standardization process. Cryptology ePrint Archive, Paper 2023/484 (2023). https://eprint.iacr.org/2023/484
25. Papagiannopoulos, K.: Low randomness masking and shuffling: an evaluation using mutual information. IACR Trans. Cryptograph. Hardw. Embedd. Syst. **2018**(3), 524–546 (2018). https://doi.org/10.13154/tches.v2018.i3.524-546
26. Papagiannopoulos, K., Veshchikov, N.: Mind the gap: towards secure 1st-order masking in software. Cryptology ePrint Archive, Paper 2017/345 (2017). https://eprint.iacr.org/2017/345
27. Prasad, S.H., Mendel, F., Schläffer, M., Nagpal, R.: Efficient low-latency masking of Ascon without fresh randomness. Cryptology ePrint Archive, Paper 2023/1914 (2023). https://eprint.iacr.org/2023/1914
28. Rivain, M., Prouff, E.: Provably secure higher-order masking of AES. Cryptology ePrint Archive, Paper 2010/441 (2010). https://eprint.iacr.org/2010/441
29. Rivain, M., Prouff, E., Doget, J.: Higher-order masking and shuffling for software implementations of block ciphers. Cryptology ePrint Archive, Paper 2009/420 (2009). https://eprint.iacr.org/2009/420
30. Standaert, F.X., Malkin, T.G., Yung, M.: A unified framework for the analysis of side-channel key recovery attacks (extended version). Cryptology ePrint Archive, Paper 2006/139 (2006). https://eprint.iacr.org/2006/139
31. Sönmez Turan, M., et al.: Status report on the final round of the NIST lightweight cryptography standardization process. NIST interagency or internal report (IR) 8454, National Institute of Standards and Technology (2023). https://doi.org/10.6028/NIST.IR.8454
32. Veyrat-Charvillon, N., Medwed, M., Kerckhof, S., Standaert, F.-X.: Shuffling against side-channel attacks: a comprehensive study with cautionary note. In: Wang, X., Sako, K. (eds.) ASIACRYPT 2012. LNCS, vol. 7658, pp. 740–757. Springer, Heidelberg (2012). https://doi.org/10.1007/978-3-642-34961-4_44
33. Weissbart, L., Picek, S.: Lightweight but not easy: side-channel analysis of the Ascon authenticated cipher on a 32-bit microcontroller. Cryptology ePrint Archive, Paper 2023/1598 (2023). https://eprint.iacr.org/2023/1598

A Hardware Design Methodology to Prevent Microarchitectural Transition Leakages

Mathieu Escouteloup[1]($^{\boxtimes}$) and Vincent Migliore[2]

[1] Université de Bordeaux, Bordeaux INP, Laboratoire IMS, UMR CNRS 5218, Bordeaux, France
mathieu.escouteloup@ims-bordeaux.fr
[2] LAAS-CNRS, Univ. Toulouse, CNRS, INSA, Toulouse, France
vincent.migliore@laas.fr

Abstract. Side-channel attacks allow information extraction from a system by analyzing indirect observations. For instance, power consumption is known to be correlated with sensitive data manipulated by digital components. Recent efforts have been put on securing the system at the software level with a formally proven method called masking. They rely on an abstract model of the target where automatic countermeasures can be efficiently applied. Recent work focused on microarchitecture, i.e., implementation details of the hardware, to deal with residual vulnerabilities which require strong knowledge of the system's hardware and have limited portability.

In this paper, we present a generic methodology to harden the processor's microarchitecture to allow straightforward software defense strategy implementation (like masking) with minimal knowledge of the hardware. Based on a fine-grained vulnerability diagnosis at the microarchitecture level and a generic design hardening strategy, our proposition can be applied to produce several processors with security, performance, and area tradeoffs. In addition, we provide two secured designs based on a customizable RISC-V processor and its memories, validated with real measurements on an FPGA.

Keywords: Power side-channels · Design method · Processor design · Microarchitecture · RISC-V

1 Introduction

Cyberphysical and connected objects have gained momentum recently due to their increasing adoption to address societal challenges (smart cities, connected cars, smart factories...). To support flexibility and updatability requirements, modern connected objects are generally processor-based. They have also gained in complexity, with the integration of more and more components into a single chip, such as System-on-Chip (SoC), making security assessment a serious challenge. Compared to usual computer systems, they also face a large range of physical attacks, which exploit some characteristics of the target system including both software and hardware. Among these, Side-Channel Attack (SCAs) can infer secret information from physical observations measured during the execution of sensitive computations. For instance, the AES encryption algorithm, considered as strongly secured, is highly vulnerable to SCAs.

For power observation, one of the well-known mitigation techniques is called masking [19]. The idea is to break down secret data into multiple values called *shares* that are individually statistically independent from the secret. For instance, to mask a secret s with boolean masking, a uniform value r is generated and XOR-ed with s, producing shares $(s \oplus r, r)$.

While theoretically unbreakable, masking suffers from weaknesses when implemented on a given target, especially when the system's model does not perfectly match the real hardware. For instance, in processor-based architecture, shares can be processed successively or simultaneously, leading to potential transitions between them, which can be directly exploited to reduce the global security level [5].

In practice, it has been proven that many registers or wires can generate transition between shares [5, 12, 23] meaning that processor's microarchitecture is a non-negligible source of leakage. Unfortunately, since they are deeply hidden in the microarchitecture, hardening software or hardware against power-based side-channel attacks is challenging. Several defense mechanisms have been proposed to increase the security level of masked implementations. Some of them try to patch the software directly by inserting basic instructions to clean internal hardware states, manually [26] or automatically [28, 29]. The Instruction Set Architecture (ISA) can also be directly modified [16] to integrate some instructions for hardware cleaning. However, in addition to impacting performance, they also need a precise understanding of the microarchitecture issue to know which transitions must be mitigated. This information is not always accessible in the gray-box system or in available models [17]. Finally, another approach is to directly harden the processor. Data obfuscation and hardware masking [4, 13, 33] are then used to build a new security layer at the hardware level. Hardening is also possible physically directly using Electronic Design Automation (EDA) tools [31]. However, all these strategies finally try to hide the transition leakages.

Contributions. Based on all these observations, we propose to address the transition leakage issue from its root cause: the microarchitecture. Instead of trying to modify existing software and hardware by target-specific countermeasures, we propose a generic design approach to mitigate transition leakages from microarchitecture's description. Using the properties of a high-level hardware description language (here Chisel), we develop a set of fundamental blocks where we apply most of our generic design strategies. They are then used to build a complete microarchitecture with security properties, limiting processor-specific changes. Finally, the whole strategy is analyzed using RTL simulations and then validated by performing real measurements on a Field-Programmable Gate Array (FPGA) target.

More generally, this works aims at addressing microarchitectural issues at that abstraction layer. It is part of a global security strategy where each layer of the system must be considered. In that way, other hardening strategies (masking for the software abstraction layer, or glitches for the physical layer) can be combined to achieve a given security level.

This approach offers new hardware designer directives to secure its design, allowing the removal of potential weaknesses before the fabrication. This methodology can be summarized in four steps, iterated to compare multiple hardened designs:

1. generate the associated Register Transfer Level (RTL) description from the target microarchitecture specification,
2. build a leakage model considering all data registers and signals are potential leakage sources,
3. evaluate in both the simulation and real target the security using a set of microbenchmarks to reproduce all the data transitions,
4. enrich the microarchitecture description using generic hardening strategies to remove the leaky transitions.

The rest of this paper is organized as follows. Section 2 provides a description of the threat model, the leakage model and a description of known hardware vulnerabilities. Section 3 presents our generic methodology in the design phase. Section 4, Sect. 5 and Sect. 6 provide a complete analysis and instantiation of the methodology to a processor-based microarchitecture, with a focus on microarchitecture description and RTL generation in Sect. 4, the required microbenchmarks for the security assessment in Sect. 5, and how to apply the generic countermeasures in Sect. 6. In Sect. 7, a validation of the hardened processor is proposed using both simulation and real measurements on an FPGA target.

2 Background

2.1 Threat Model

In this paper, we consider the side-channel scenario where the execution and manipulation of sensitive data impact its physical environment. Particularly, we are interested here in power consumption variations. Then, in our scenario, we consider that an attacker has physical access to its target (*e.g.* an Internet-of-Things (IoT) device with a processor). He also has the different necessary equipment to perform power consumption measurements. An attack is considered successful if a malicious person is able to observe variations which directly depend on sensitive data in the target. In the other way, an efficient defense strategy must ensure that an attacker will not be able to recover any information from sensitive data by analyzing power consumption traces. We will see in Subsect. 2.3 that it concerns the great majority of the potential leakages.

2.2 Transition Leakages

A transition is a value change in a wire or register from a data $d1$ to $d2$. Basically, at the circuit level, a bit flip ($0 \rightarrow 1$ or $1 \rightarrow 0$) in the system leads to a temporary consumption increase. Then, when a transition between two sensitive values occurs, it impacts the consumption proportionally to the Hamming Distance between $d1$ and $d2$. In the case of masking [15,19,20,22,26], consider a secret value s, a mask m and the masked value v, then: $v = m \oplus s$. Basically, only m and v are directly manipulated. This is what is done by some secure cryptographic implementations [10]. However, if a transition $m \rightarrow v$ occurs, the Hamming Weight will probably leak while it is directly correlated to s. By performing multiple measurements, it leads to a potential reduction of the global security level [11,26].

2.3 Hardware Sources

Transitions can occur in the hardware as soon as different data are successively manipulated. From a software point of view, the more visible case is one of the architectural registers or General Purpose Registers (GPRs). An executed application is directly able to know if it currently overwrites a destination register.

However, the issue is more important when it directly concerns the microarchitecture. Most of the potential transition leakage sources are completely abstract by the ISA: omit microarchitectural mechanisms can lead to security reduction [5]. By its structure, a processor pipeline unfortunately contributes to potential transitions: the same mechanisms process the different instructions cycle after cycle. Based on sets of microbenchmarks, different studies [12,23,27] expose the numerous potential leakage sources in current implementations. On both Arm [12,23] or RISC-V ISA [27] processors, multiple hardware mechanisms are then highlighted like pipeline registers, internal buffers or memory ports. By evaluating different boards, including SoCs and FPGAs with different ISAs, Marshall et al. have also highlighted that transition leakages really concern most of the systems [23]. Clearly, it appears that the microarchitecture has an important impact on leakage [3]. The issue is even deeper if we consider more complex microarchitectures like superscalar processors [7,19]. Indeed, the number of potential leaky mechanisms increases with the complexity, and the number of possible transitions is also higher due to simultaneous executions.

To deal with this complexity, an important part of the literature focused on building simulators to estimate power consumption efficiently for a given target [8,21,24,34,36] and then provide meaningful information for software developers about potential leakage. However, this type of simulator needs to be updated for each new microarchitecture to ensure that no source of leakage has been overlooked. An interesting approach is to automatically detect them at design time [4,6,18,30]. In this way, we ensure that results are automatically updated with any hardware changes.

2.4 Protection Strategies

Based on the detection of leakage sources, several strategies have been proposed to protect the system.

Pure software solutions try to catch the problem by only modifying the application itself. It leads to constraints for the software developer or compiler [19], which means they need information about the microarchitecture (*e.g.* pipeline stages). This is particularly useful to apply patches to existing hardware. However, it does not tackle the issue at its source and breaks the hardware abstraction from the ISA: the same program cannot be safely executed on different targets without changes. Because pure software solutions are difficult to efficiently implement, another approach is to directly modify the instruction set to add specific instructions. FENL [16] is a proposition of fencing to overwrite the different hardware registers and prevent transitions between the previous/next instructions. But this kind of approach involves modifying or recompiling the software and ensuring that the new instructions are efficiently introduced.

Another approach is a pure hardware solution where the microarchitecture is directly modified, allowing the code execution with transparent solutions. This principle is used in PARAM [4] to obfuscate direct value manipulation. However, they do not consider transition leakages. It can also be used to transparently add another layer of masking to increase the protection order [13]. But fundamentally, this approach does not remove the existence of transitions at their source. COCO [18] tackles this problem by splitting the hardening process between hardware and software. Deeply hidden transitions, such as unintended reads or switches in multiplexer trees, are effectively removed by modifying the hardware. But for a complete secured implementation, an important part is still delegated to the software, particularly to remove leakages due to successive instructions or architectural overwriting. This approach is interesting for simple processors like the IBEX core, whose data path is not pipelined. However, it is not enough when hidden microarchitectural buffers can keep sensitive data for multiple cycles.

For the rest of this paper, we propose a generic design methodology to tackle transition leakages by directly removing them from the microarchitecture. Our goal is to ensure that, independently of the software choices, the execution will not lead to a reduction in the security order due to the microarchitecture, even with pipelined or buffered mechanisms. Another kind of leakage targeting the hardware is glitches. However, they are due to physical phenomena considered at a lower abstraction level than the microarchitecture. In this paper, we only focus on the microarchitectural issue of transition leakages, trying to first eliminate this issue before integrating complementary protections during other design steps.

3 Methodology

To design a secure processor, one main challenge is to select a suitable abstraction level to make the hardening process efficient in terms of complexity and hardware overhead. While the ISA level does not allow a precise representation of the system, consider directly all the logic gates leads to numerous specific changes.

Hopefully, hardware description languages (HDLs) allow to efficiently describe a system from its microarchitecture specifications. Moreover, recent improvements now allow to efficiently produce RTL models while directly integrating generic strategies, such as hardening techniques.

In this work, we propose different hardening strategies at the microarchitecture level (described in Sect. 6). They allow different performance/security trade-offs, varying in the considered leakage sources (whole logic or registers only) and the execution throughput. In order to compare several processor configurations (number of pipeline stages, hardening strategies applied, *etc.*), we propose an iterative design methodology based on 4 steps. (a) From the target microarchitecture specifications, a RTL model of the target is produced. (b) Using a precise leakage model relying on the enumeration of all register and wire transitions, (c) leaky transitions are generated using a collection of software microbenchmarks suited for vulnerability assessment at the microarchitecture level. Then, with the help of a generic hardening approach, (d) the microarchitecture specifications are enriched to mitigate the diagnosed vulnerability depending on the performance overhead criteria.

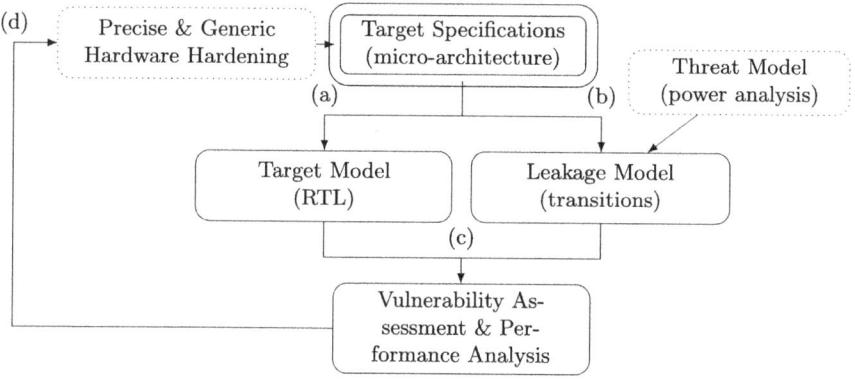

Fig. 1. Proposed methodology for generic and iterative microarchitecture hardening against power-based side-channel attacks.

In our case, to generalize the application of hardening strategies, we described in Sect. 4 how we increase this methodology by previously designing a set of fundamental blocks used to describe the microarchitectures. However, note that our methodology is still relevant for existing processors: the different hardening strategies must then be applied directly to each internal mechanism.

4 Targeted Design and Model Extraction

4.1 Generic Design Library

The goal of our methodology is to detail the needed steps to design a transition leakage-free processor. For that, some important changes in the whole microarchitecture will be needed to prevent these transitions. Instead of modifying each register or mechanism one by one, we decided to first design a generic design library. The idea is to define the fundamental modules before instantiating them to create the final design: register, buses with separated control and data parts, FIFO, *etc.* Then, to apply the design strategies described in the following Sect. 6, we only need to modify once the generic modules.

To push this strategy to the limit, we decided to use the Chisel language [2]. Based on the Scala language, it allows to efficiently generate Verilog/SystemVerilog descriptions and stay at the RTL level while benefiting from modern language features. Particularly, we use object-oriented programming and inheritance to design highly generic modules. For example, it is the same custom register module which will be used in the whole design, in the processor pipeline as well as in the memory controller. The whole code is available online [14].

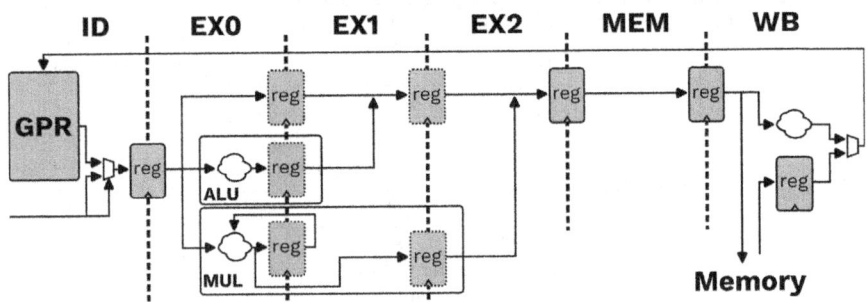

Fig. 2. Datapath of the targeted processor microarchitecture.

4.2 Microarchitecture Description

Using these generic modules, we designed the processor whose datapath is described in the Fig. 2. Based on the RV32I ISA [35], it also supports different extensions like M (multiply and divide) or ZiCsr.

Its microarchitecture is based on a configurable pipeline with four to seven stages. Each register (in gray), excepted GPRs, is based on the previously defined generic register module. The dotted ones on the Fig. 2 are registers which can be enabled or disabled during SystemVerilog generation. In the next sections, this will be useful to evaluate that our methodology can be applied on design with microarchitectural variations.

At the microarchitecture level, design choices can directly impact how the values in registers are modified. In our case, we have to notice that registers are updated only when a new valid instruction is in the corresponding stage/unit. This is a common practice to reduce consumption due to bit switches. However, it leads to the observation that a value is still in a register after many cycles, which can lead to hidden data transitions.

For the rest of this paper, we identify two different microarchitectures. C5U (*Core 5 Unprotected*) is the simple version with a five-stage pipeline: execution (EX) - memory (MEM) - write back (WB) stages are implemented. C7U (*Core 7 Unprotected*) is the most complex version with a seven-stage pipeline: EX is split into three stages and all the execution units are pipelined (one result register).

4.3 Simulation Analysis

The first step of the methodology involves generating an accurate simulation model from microarchitectural sources/description of our design to analyze potential leaky transitions. After generating the SystemVerilog description, this is done by compiling a fast executable to simulate our design using Verilator [32] able to generate .vcd file. This format is the standard to represent digital design waveforms by simply indicating value changes in each cycle. In our case, this is the perfect information to track potential transitions: this can simply be done by parsing files (*e.g.* with a Python 3 script). Moreover, it is fast applicable in any hardware design, independently of the internal changes.

5 Microbenchmark

After the extraction of the simulation model, the second step of our methodology is to try to generate transitions to detect microarchitectural leakage sources. A common strategy in the literature [12,23,27] is based on microbenchmarks using specific instruction patterns. If MicroPlumber [27] also uses the RISC-V ISA, it only targets a simple PicoRV32 core. Based on microbenchmarks available for the ARM ISA [12,23], we developed our own set for the RISC-V ISA. They are also available in an online repository [14].

5.1 Test Principle

Listing 1.1. Microbenchmark test structure

```
1  jal trigger_on
2  INSERT_NOP
3  instr0   # Handle op0
4  instr1   # Handle op1
5  instr2   # Handle op2
6  instr3   # Handle op3
7  INSERT_NOP
8  jal trigger_off
```

The idea behind microbenchmarking is to design a set of simple program patterns to test different parts of the microarchitecture. In our case, we want to reproduce transitions in any part of our processor. In a white-box scenario with a defined microarchitecture, this is possible with only a small set of microbenchmarks. Instructions could be considered in subsets using the same hardware mechanisms: ALU, multiply, branch and memories. It then considerably reduces the number of necessary tests.

All our microbenchmarks are designed following the structure described on Listing 1.1. First, a trigger is launched at the beginning (`jal trigger_on`) and stopped at the end (`jal trigger_off`) of each test. It allows synchronizing measurements and the different analyses. Then, `nop` instructions are inserted (here using a macro `INSERT_NOP`) to isolate the targeted pattern. Finally, a sequence of instructions is used to manipulate data and potentially generate transitions.

While two subsequent instructions are sufficient to produce a transition, microbenchmarks presented here are also adapted for complex microarchitectures with multiple buffers, FIFOs or superscalar execution. In these systems, additional instructions are needed to cover all the cases (fill the buffer, evaluate parallel operations, *etc.*). In the case of pipelined designs such as our target datapath presented in Fig. 2, two subsequent instructions are always enough to generate any transition. However, we decided to keep tracking of the four operands to highlight the detected leakage and their behaviors. It leads to 6 possible transitions which must be tracked.

5.2 Test Examples

We now describe some of the tests we used to generate transitions in our microarchitecture. Each time, the expected results have been verified by directly inspecting simulated execution traces: this is a benefit to directly have access to the RTL description. Another one is to be able to directly check if all the microarchitectural parts have been tested.

Listing 1.2. alu_alu_gpr

```
1 xor  t0,  zero,  op0
2 xor  t0,  op1,   zero
3 xor  t0,  zero,  op2
4 xor  t0,  op3,   zero
```

Listing 1.3. alu_alu_res

```
1 xor  t0,   zero,  op0
2 xor  t1,   op1,   zero
3 xor  zero, zero,  op2
4 xor  zero, op3,   zero
```

Listing 1.2 and Listing 1.3 are tests focusing on leakage due to arithmetic and logic sequences. In `alu_alu_gpr`, the goal is to generate transitions in all the microarchitectural registers and wires where the instruction results are stored, but also in an architectural register, here `t0`. In `alu_alu_res`, the goal is almost the same, excepting that no transition is expected in `t0`. Then, by executing both tests, we are supposed to distinguish the impact of architectural and microarchitectural registers.

Listing 1.4. mul_mul_s1

```
1  li    t4  , −1
2  mulhu t0  , op0 , t4
3  mulhu t1  , op1 , t4
4  mulhu zero, op2 , t4
5  mulhu zero, op3 , t4
```

Listing 1.5. mul_mul_res

```
1  li  t4  , 1
2  mul t0  , t4  , op0
3  mul t1  , op1 , t4
4  mul zero, t4  , op2
5  mul zero, op3 , t4
```

Listing 1.4 and Listing 1.5 focus on leakages due to multiplication support in the microarchitecture. Generally, multipliers are implemented in dedicated parts of the system. Then, the corresponding wires and registers are used only when multiplication instructions are executed. Here, mul_mul_s1 focuses on possible transitions between the first operand of the multiplication and mul_mul_res between the results.

Listing 1.6. leq_lw_lw

```
1  lw  t0 , 0(t4)
2  lw  t1 , 4(t4)
3  lw  t2 , 8(t4)
4  lw  t3 , 12(t4)
```

Listing 1.7. aeq_sw_sw

```
1  sw  t0 , 0(t4)
2  sw  t1 , 0(t4)
3  sw  t2 , 0(t4)
4  sw  t3 , 0(t4)
```

Transitions can occur in the whole processor pipeline, but also in any hardware mechanism where data are manipulated, such as memories. Some of our microbenchmarks try to evaluate them using load and store instructions. On Listing 1.6, leq_lw_lw allows to evaluate leakage when multiple sensitive operands are successively executed. On Listing 1.7, aeq_sw_sw is used to detect the impact of transition when sensitive values are overwriting each other in memory.

All the microbenchmarks previously described are not enough to test all the possible data transitions in the microarchitecture. Then, we also provide tests to target other mechanisms, such as the first instruction operand registers, the second operand registers, the resize buffer used by load instructions, the forwarding logic and the GPR read ports with immediate/register decoding.

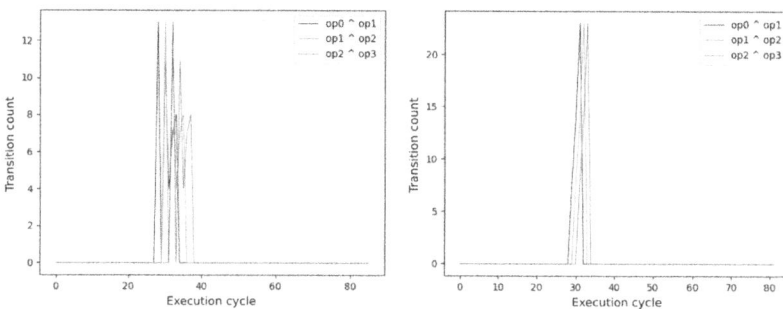

(a) Transition count for alu_alu_gpr (b) Transition count for alu_alu_res

Fig. 3. Analysis of ALU operations on C5U.

5.3 Model Analysis

After defining the different microbenchmarks, we can execute them, generate the representing .vcd files for each core and perform the analysis to detect the number of transitions and the responsible wires/registers. In our case, the execution of the microbenchmark on our cores is completely deterministic: only one execution of each test is enough to know in simulation if a transition occurs or not. Then, to perform the analysis, we simply fix the values of $op0$ to $op3$ and directly track them in the .vcd files. In our case, it only takes a few dozen minutes from the hardware generation to the analysis end on a desktop computer.

Figure 3a and Fig. 3b show the number of transitions occurring when executing respectively alu_alu_gpr and alu_alu_res on C5U. This analysis is simply performed by parsing the generated .vcd: for each cycle, we compare if a transition occurs between known operand values (from $op0$ to $op3$). Finally, we are able to know for each microbenchmark if a transition occurs, at which cycle and on which signal.

As expected, we see the transitions between the operands occurring successively during a few cycles. In the case of alu_alu_gpr, because these traces are completely noise-free, we are even able to distinguish subtle variations at the end of the curves, representing the last transition during the write-back.

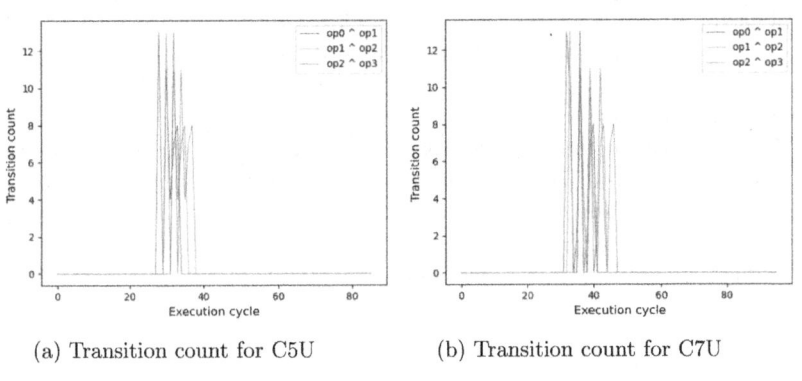

(a) Transition count for C5U   (b) Transition count for C7U

Fig. 4. Analysis of the mul_mul_s1 microbenchmark.

Figure 4a and Fig. 4b show the number of transitions occurring when executing mul_mul_s1 on both cores C5U and C7U. We can directly observe the impact of adding the microarchitecture by adding extra-registers in C7U.

Finally, for C5U and C7U, it is respectively 194 and 261 SystemVerilog wires or registers (logic) with transitions which have been detected in the pipeline and the internal RAM. If most of them are obviously directly dependent on this level, it highlights the importance of a generic approach to secure the system and ensure that no mechanism is missed.

6 Root Cause Protection Principles

After detecting leakage sources, secure the design involves modifying the microarchitecture. Particularly, we need a way to prevent all the possible leaky transitions. To keep our methodology as generic as possible, we need to define protection strategies, which can be applied to the whole system. For that purpose, we decided to generalize a principle called *data overwriting*.

6.1 Data Overwriting Principle

We saw in Sect. 2 that transitions occur when signal or register values directly change from a sensitive value to another. This type of event occurs regularly in processors where operations follow one another cycle by cycle. Some work [16] have shown that this can be prevented by overwriting hardware between two data manipulation. Fundamentally, the goal is to transform any possible $op0 \rightarrow op1$ transition (with $op1$ and $op2$ sensitive values) to $op0 \rightarrow tmp \rightarrow op1$ with tmp a temporary independent value.

Theoretically, data overwriting is possible at different levels. First at the software-level, we can possibly insert extra instructions to push some zero or random values into hardware mechanisms. However, due to the abstraction from the ISA, it becomes difficult to put into practice: any missed microarchitectural register can lead to a leakage. Then, another possibility is to directly enhance the ISA with dedicated instructions to clear the microarchitecture [16]. Called fencing, this strategy requires recompiling the executed programs to select when a clear is needed. Moreover, fencing has a major limitation: it cannot be similarly applied to architectural registers (*e.g.* GPRs) where data must not be modified. Finally, an ideal case would be to directly prevent the appearance of transitions in the microarchitecture at the hardware level. Then, any program can be safely executed, without necessary modifications during compilation. The challenge is then to ensure that no source of leakage is overlooked.

For that, we define five complementary strategies to systematically apply overwriting at the hardware-level. We then integrate them into our generic bricks defined with the Chisel language and described in Subsect. 4.1, allowing application to the entire design. Then, using iterations of our methodology, we ensure that there is no omitted leakage source.

6.2 Strategy 1.a: Complete Stage Overwriting

The first strategy called *complete stage overwriting* is described on the Fig. 5. It is the direct implementation of the overwriting principle.

Each cycle, a validity bit allows to indicate if the corresponding register holds a data (Fig. 5a). When the data is consumed by the following pipeline stage (indicated with a ready signal), an extra-cycle is used to overwrite the register with a zero (0x0) value. Finally, it is only after this operation that the register can be reused to hold a new data: it ensures that the transition $op0 \rightarrow op1$ is transformed into $op0 \rightarrow 0x0 \rightarrow op1$.

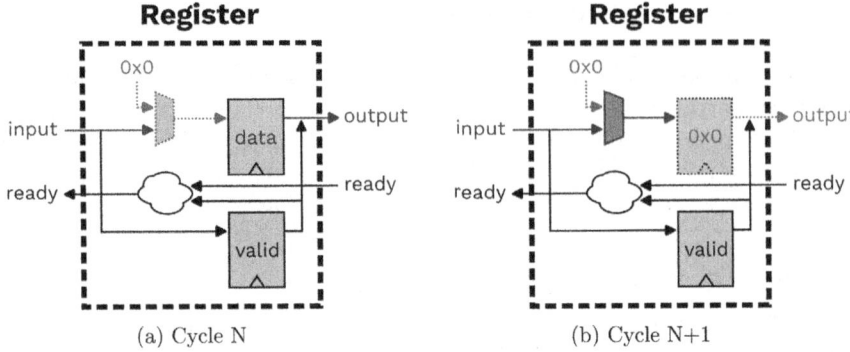

(a) Cycle N (b) Cycle N+1

Fig. 5. Register overwriting.

An essential point to note here is that for each overwriting operation performed in the register, the zero value is also propagated through the output signal. This behavior allows to also initialize all combinatorial signals which depend on this register. Finally, by adding this extra overwriting cycle, it is not only the registers which are initialized, but the complete pipeline stage including the combinatorial logic.

6.3 Strategy 1.b: Delayed Data Multiplexing

Execution in a complete system based on a processor is not always linear. For example, multiplexers in the microarchitecture allow to select data from multiple sources: register forwarding, skid buffers, *etc*. In these cases, complete stage overwriting is not sufficient for the multiplexer output if the sources are not always synchronized (overwritten at the same cycle).

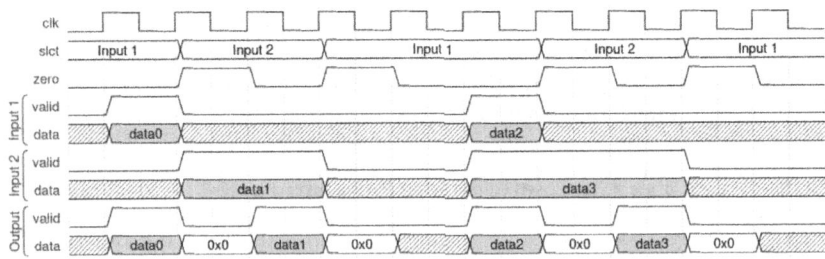

Fig. 6. Delayed data multiplexing description.

For these mechanisms, we implemented a complementary generic strategy called *delayed data multiplexing* described on the Fig. 6. The main idea is simply to introduce an overwrite cycle after each valid multiplexer output.

6.4 Strategy 2: Microarchitectural Register Duplication

Complete stage overwriting combined with delayed data multiplexing allow protecting all the transition sources in a pipelined structure. However, they have a major drawback for performances by inserting extra cycles. In the worst case, we can estimate that it can divide by two the execution rate: one extra overwriting cycle for each real operation cycle. Moreover, as shown in the Sect. 2, most of the leakages are caused by transitions directly occurring in registers. Depending on the constraints, the strategies 1.a and 1.b can be excessive.

For that purpose, we decided to evaluate another generic strategy called *microarchitectural register duplication*. The main idea is to parallelize the register overwriting and the real operation write to prevent the extra cycle. For that purpose, we implement the mechanism described on the Fig. 7.

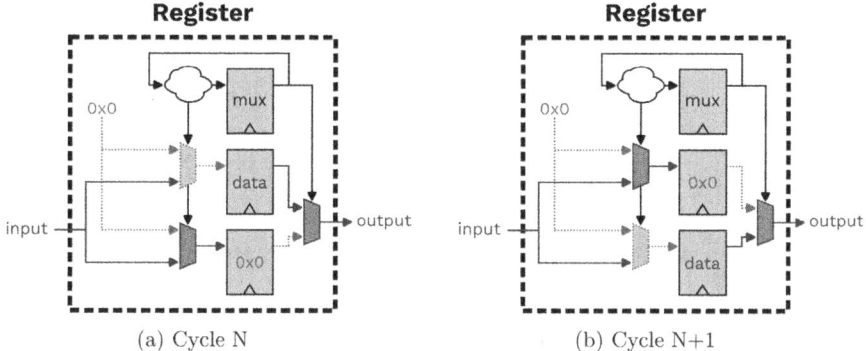

Fig. 7. Register duplication.

All the data registers are duplicated. In the cycle N described on the Fig. 7a, one part contains a real data and the other the zero value. A new multiplexer allows selecting them: the data register is selected for the output but the zero register is selected for the input. If the data is read and a new one is written, then the roles are reversed in the next cycle described on the Fig. 7b. Finally, the transition $op0 \to op1$ is split into two transitions $op0 \to$ 0x0 and 0x0 $\to op1$.

The initial idea here is similar to the principle of Secure Double Rate Registers [9]. However, we have two implementation differences. First, the registers are here parallelized (not pipelined): the latency is not impacted in our case. Introducing new stages like with Secure Double Rate Registers [9] can have a critical impact in the case of processor pipelines with data dependencies or branch management. Second, in our case, we do not need to double the whole frequency to have a similar rate: it is completely transparent as long as the critical path is not impacted.

6.5 Strategy 3.a: Architectural Register Pre-Writing

Previous strategies can be applied to any microarchitectural registers to prevent transitions. However, architectural registers (the ones defined by the ISA such as GPRs) must also be protected if we want to protect any software execution without specific changes. For that purpose, we defined another strategy called *register pre-writing*.

Unlike microarchitectural registers, an architectural register cannot simply be overwritten after usage: a data stored inside must remain as long as another valid data is written. This can lead to a leaky transition when the old and new data are both sensitive. Moreover, simply duplicate registers is here not a valid solution: the RV32I ISA considers 31 32-bit registers (x0 is hardwired to 0). Then, we implemented a new mechanism described on Fig. 8.

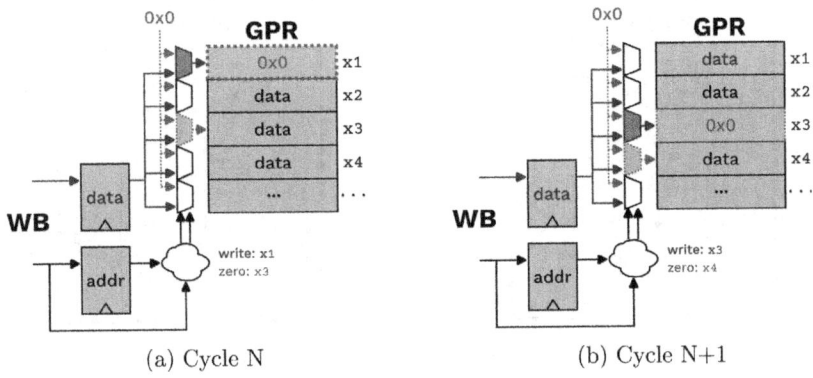

Fig. 8. GPR overwriting.

The main principle of this strategy is to ensure that each register is pre-written by an insensitive value (here 0x0) just before the new valid data. For that purpose, we add some logic and registers (where strategies 1 or 2 can be applied) to each write port of our GPRs. Their goal is to manage the pre-writing and hold the information to perform the real write in the next cycle. On the Fig. 8a, we can see that the previously pre-written register x1 is receiving a new data while x3 is not yet ready. In the next cycle on the Fig. 8b, it is finally another real data which is written in x3 when is pre-written.

Finally, for each write operation, there is only one cycle where no valid data is present on a GPR. However, during this time, the next data is available in the new write port register. Using a mechanism similar to a register forwarding, it is then still possible to transfer each time a valid data to a read port: if the read address is the same as the one in the write port register, the data is directly transferred, else the GPR is read. The architectural state is still preserved.

6.6 Strategy 3.b: Decoupled Memory Operations

Finally, the last hardware mechanism where data transitions can occur is memories. Basically, memories are part of the architectural state: the first three strategies cannot be strictly applied. Moreover, simultaneous write/pre-write of the fourth strategy needs two simultaneous write ports which are not always available for memories. In this case, we decided to establish a fifth strategy based on Finite State Machines (FSMs) to perform *decoupled memory operations*.

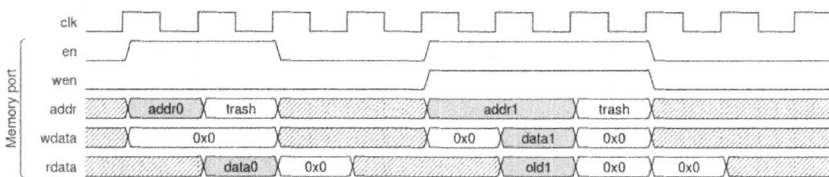

Fig. 9. New memory operation description with a real port.

In the case of read memory operations, transitions must be prevented between successive reads. For that, we decide to implement two-cycle read operations as described on the Fig. 9 (first transaction). Each real read is followed by an extra-cycle where a read to another address is performed. However, this other address must be carefully selected and ensure that no leaky data is inside. For that, we decided to lock the last four bytes of each memory for hardware operation: the software is not supposed to use them. Then, these memory locations can be used as the default trash addresses, like the x0 register in the GPRs. In this way, no transition is possible on the rdata signal and the wdata is set to 0 because it is unused.

The case of write operations is a bit trickier. First, like for an architectural register write, a pre-write is needed to ensure that no transition occurs between the old and the new data. This is the first part of the second transaction on the Fig. 9. Then, the real write can be performed. After that, we must ensure that no transaction can occur with a future operation on both wdata or rdata. Like for the read operation, an extra-cycle is then needed to perform a write to the trash address.

Finally, decoupled memory operations can also have an important impact on performance by slowing memory access. However, they must be considered when coupled with the other strategies presented here. With complete stage overwriting, extra-cycles are already introduced: the supplement impact will be here limited. In the case of register duplication, we only consider leakage occurring in the register. Then, transactions presented on the Fig. 9 can be simplified: only the pre-write is needed.

6.7 Implementations

For the evaluation in the next section, we have to compare the different strategies on different microarchitectures. It results in the implementations presented on the Table 1.

Table 1. List of the different processor configurations.

Configuration	Datapath stages	EX unit registers	S1.a	S1.b	S2	S3.a	S3.b
C5U	4	No	No	No	No	No	No
C5S1	4	No	Yes	Yes	No	Yes	Yes
C5S2	4	No	No	No	Yes	Yes	Partial
C7U	6	Yes	No	No	No	No	No
C7S1	6	Yes	Yes	Yes	No	Yes	Yes
C7S2	6	Yes	No	No	Yes	Yes	Partial

Each core is a different version of the configurable datapath presented on the Fig. 2. $C5^*$ cores use the simplest version of the datapath where no execution unit or intermediate EX registers are used. $C7^*$ cores use the complete version of the datapath, with all the registers enabled. $*U$ cores are the unprotected ones. $*S1$ and $*S2$ integrate respectively different strategies.

7 Evaluation

After implementing the different protection strategies, it is necessary to re-evaluate the targets to verify the efficiency: it is the last step of our methodology. For that, like in a classic design flow, we first perform verification in simulations using the same tools as previously. The results presented in this section were

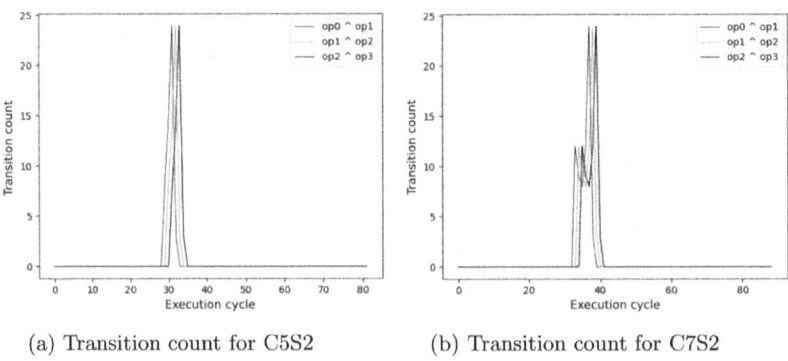

(a) Transition count for C5S2   (b) Transition count for C7S2

Fig. 10. Analysis of the alu_alu_gpr microbenchmark.

obtained after several iterations of our methodology, ensuring that no leakage source has been overlooked at the RTL level. Then, we validate the whole results by performing measurements and analysis on a real system.

7.1 Simulation Model

In the same way as in the Sect. 5, we execute once all the microbenchmarks on each target with fixed operands to allow direct transition detection with .*vcd* file analysis.

In the case of complete stage overwriting implementations, no more transitions were detected in the processor pipeline as well as in the memory controller. If it is the final expected result, a particular challenge was not to forget any leakage sources. Particularly, if the use of Chisel generic modules was enough for register modification (which are a very large proportion of the leakage sources), the implementations of delayed data multiplexing were done manually. It highlights the interest in a methodology with both a global approach combined with iterations to manage particular cases.

On the other side, register duplication is easier to implement: generic modules are enough because only the registers are considered here. Then, as expected, transitions can still be detected in wires, as described in the Fig. 10. As before, we can even see that the transitions are still implementation-dependent with differences between *C5S2* and *C7S2*.

7.2 Real Measurements

Simply analyzing transitions from .*vcd* is not enough to evaluate the efficiency of protection strategies in the real world. Some steps, such as logic synthesis or the place-and-route, can influence the behavior of mechanisms previously defined at the microarchitectural-level. Then, we perform a two-step security assessment, with evaluations on real FPGA targets to confirm the previous simulated results.

For that, we implemented our cores on the ChipWhisperer platform [25] with the CW305 FPGA target, integrating a Xilinx Artix-7. The processor is configured to run at 25 MHz when the sampling frequency is 100 MHz (4 samples by cycle). Each microbenchmark is then executed 50.000 times with random input operands, allowing to perform Correlation Power Analysis (CPA). For each execution on *U and *S2 cores, 300 samples are performed. Due to the insertion of extra cycles in *S1 cores, more cycles are needed to execute the different programs: we use for them 500 samples.

The Fig. 11 (right part) describes the CPA results for the aeq_sw_sw microbenchmark executed on the three versions of the C5 core. In each figure, the correlation for different transitions is calculated with valid operand values, but also with random values to estimate the noise range. With C5U, clear correlation peaks can be detected after 140 samples due to successive manipulation of the operands. On the other hand, no clear correlation is detected between the power consumption and data transitions with the C5S1 and C5S2 cores. Then, in this case, both secure implementations seem to offer the same protection.

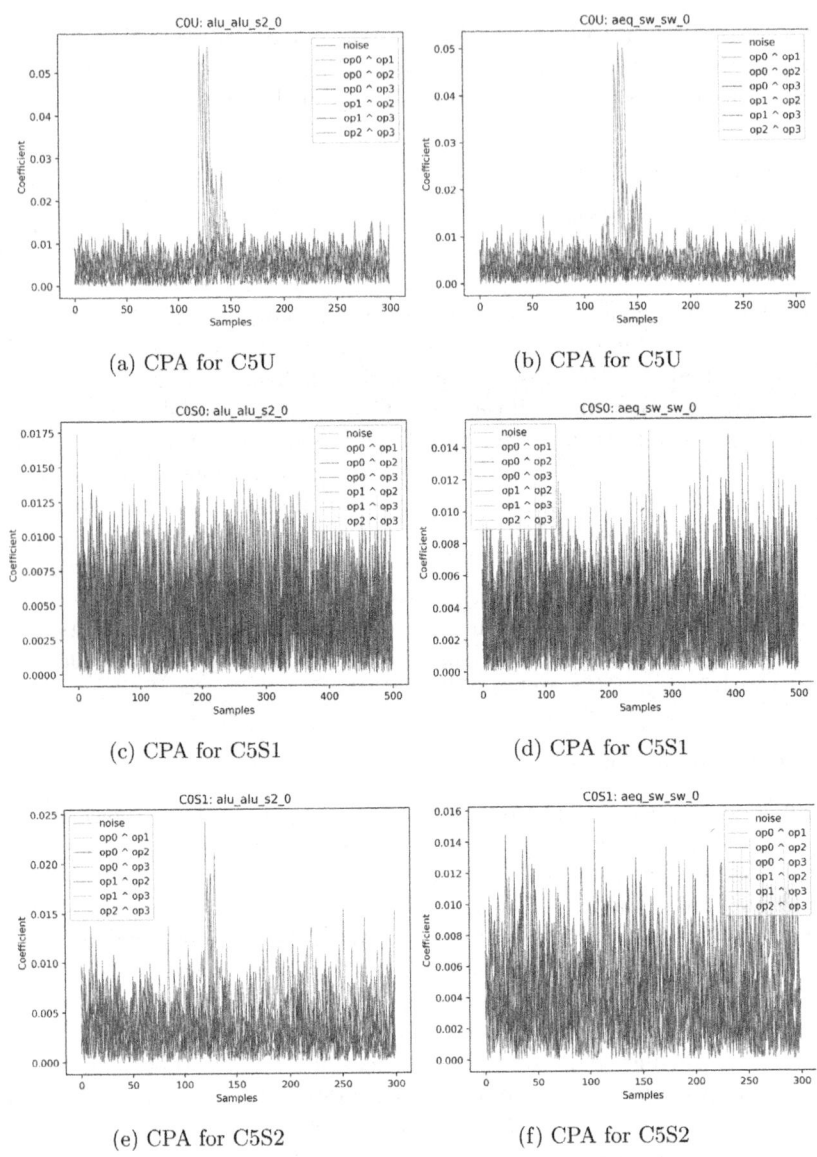

Fig. 11. CPA for the alu_alu_s2 (left) and aeq_sw_sw (right) microbenchmarks.

The Fig. 11 (left part) describes the CPA results for the alu_alu_s2 microbenchmark (leakages due to the second operand in arithmetic and logic operations). Like for the previous microbenchmark, we can see in Fig. 11a and Fig. 11c that C5U and C5S1 are still respectively leaky and non-leaky designs. The main information here is in Fig. 11e where we can observe weak correlation peaks. Then, for this microbenchmark, register duplication reduces the leakages (correlation decreases from 0.55 to 0.02), but it does not eliminate them completely.

Finally, considering that we obtained similar results with the other microbenchmarks (C5S2 is leaky depending on the targeted hardware mechanism), we can conclude that the observations on the FPGA target confirm our previous results in the simulations. As expected, completely removes transition at the RTL level allows to remove the root cause of transition leakage. On the other hand, only preventing transition in registers is not sufficient: leakages are deduced but still exist, and can be detected in some cases.

7.3 Overhead

The different strategies described in the Sect. 6 deeply impact the initial microarchitectures. However, in addition to security, processors must often satisfy other constraints like performance or resource utilization. The different results are summarized in the Table 2.

Table 2. Overhead of the different strategies.

Configuration	Embench (cycle)	Embench (ratio)	LUT (count)	LUT (ratio)	FF (count)	FF (ratio)
C5U	4 412 169	N/A	5 027	N/A	2 498	N/A
C5S1	8 222 197	+86.35%	5 295	+05.33%	2 520	+00.88%
C5S2	4 529 543	+02.66%	6 910	+37.46%	3 102	+24.18%
C7U	5 432 114	N/A	5 617	N/A	3 156	N/A
C7S1	8 051 161	+48.21%	6 244	+11.16%	3 224	+02.15%
C7S2	5 433 002	+00.02%	7.162	+27.51%	4.211	+33.43%

Performance. To evaluate performance, we executed the Embench [1] benchmark on all our microarchitectures and we averaged the number of cycles. Globally, the obtained results correspond to our expectations. Implementations with complete stage overwriting and associated strategies (*S1*) are highly impacted when changes to register duplication strategies (*S2*) are negligible. This is mostly due to the addition of the extra-cycle. However, we can see that this impact is highly reduced with the second core version (from +86.35% with C5S1 to +48.21% with C7S1). This is mainly due to the impact of false branch predictions, which already have an important impact on the reference version (C5U).

We choose here not to present the impact on the critical path (and the frequency) of our strategies due to not relevant results: the initial targeted microarchitectures have not been particularly optimized to increase the frequency. Then, the impact of simple changes (*e.g.* simply add a multiplexer) will not be as representative as for a state-of-the-art processor designed solely for performance.

Resource Utilization. To evaluate resource utilization, we decided to reuse results from Vivado 2023.1 during the implementation on the CW305 target. Each presented results are only for the processor pipeline, excluding the memories, the peripherals or the branch prediction mechanisms, which are major resource consumers in the initial designs. Both the number of used LUTs and registers (flip-flops) are presented. Here again, the obtained results correspond to our expectations. *$S2$ implementations use more resources due to register duplication. Depending on the implementations, the register increase is evaluated to +24.18% or +33.43%: it is more important for $C7S2$ due to the higher number of pipeline stages.

8 Conclusion

Power consumption measurements represent a threat to recover information from hardware systems. Particularly, data transitions are a burden to implement secure software algorithms.

In this paper, we establish a methodology to design transition leakage free processors. From a RTL model, we explained how we extract at simulation time information about wire and register states for each cycle. Combined with microbenchmarks, we use this step to precisely analyze and detect leakage sources in the microarchitecture. Then, we propose five generic strategies to tackle the root cause of these leakages: the transitions themselves. Using generic blocks defined with the Chisel language, we modify the microarchitecture of two variants of a custom RISC-V processor. Finally, we confirm the efficiency of our strategy by executing the microbenchmarks on an FPGA target and by performing real measurements. The different results highlight a clear trade-off between security and performances. If complete stage overwriting effectively removes all potential leakage sources, it has an important impact on performances (+86.35% number of cycles in the worst-case). On the other side, register duplication keeps transition in wires which can possibly be detected with better experimentation setup.

Future work will concern the other system layers to be able to consider security issues as a whole. Higher layers such as the ISA will be explored to allow a better adaptation of the system to the needs of the applications. Instead of fence instructions which need to be inserted at specific places depending on the microarchitecture to be effective, another promising strategy is contextualization to secure whole sensitive code blocks. Depending on the constraints of the targeted application, switching between the different strategies presented here can be an interesting trade-off. Lower layers will also be considered to ensure that no leakage sources are inserted later in the design process (during synthesis or place-and-route). This is directly linked to the management of glitches, which can be introduced in lower levels of the design: each security issue must be tackled at the corresponding system layer.

References

1. Embench: A Modern Embedded Benchmark Suite (2021). https://www.embench.org/
2. Chisel/FIRRTL Hardware Compiler Framework (2023). https://www.chisel-lang.org/
3. Arora, V., Buhan, I., Perin, G., Picek, S.: A tale of two boards: on the influence of microarchitecture on side-channel leakage. In: Grosso, V., Pöppelmann, T. (eds.) Smart Card Research and Advanced Applications, vol. 13173, pp. 80–96. Springer International Publishing, Cham (2022). https://doi.org/10.1007/978-3-030-97348-3_5
4. Arsath K F, M., Ganesan, V., Bodduna, R., Rebeiro, C.: PARAM: a microprocessor hardened for power side-channel attack resistance. In: 2020 IEEE International Symposium on Hardware Oriented Security and Trust (HOST), pp. 23–34 (2020). https://doi.org/10.1109/HOST45689.2020.9300263
5. Balasch, J., Gierlichs, B., Grosso, V., Reparaz, O., Standaert, F.-X.: On the cost of lazy engineering for masked software implementations. In: Joye, M., Moradi, A. (eds.) CARDIS 2014. LNCS, vol. 8968, pp. 64–81. Springer, Cham (2015). https://doi.org/10.1007/978-3-319-16763-3_5
6. Barenghi, A., Brevi, M., Fornaciari, W., Pelosi, G., Zoni, D.: Integrating side channel security in the FPGA hardware design flow. In: Bertoni, G.M., Regazzoni, F. (eds.) COSADE 2020. LNCS, vol. 12244, pp. 275–290. Springer, Cham (2021). https://doi.org/10.1007/978-3-030-68773-1_13
7. Barenghi, A., Pelosi, G.: Side-channel security of superscalar CPUs: evaluating the impact of micro-architectural features. In: Proceedings of the 55th Annual Design Automation Conference, pp. 1–6. ACM, San Francisco California (2018). https://doi.org/10.1145/3195970.3196112
8. Barthe, G., Gourjon, M., Grégoire, B., Orlt, M., Paglialonga, C., Porth, L.: Masking in fine-grained leakage models: construction, implementation and verification. IACR Trans. Cryptographic Hardware Embedded Syst. 189–228 (2021). https://doi.org/10.46586/tches.v2021.i2.189-228. https://tches.iacr.org/index.php/TCHES/article/view/8792
9. Bellizia, D., Bongiovanni, S., Monsurrò, P., Scotti, G., Trifiletti, A., Trotta, F.B.: Secure double rate registers as an RTL countermeasure against power analysis attacks. IEEE Trans. Very Large Scale Integr. (VLSI) Syst. **26**(7), 1368–1376 (2018). https://doi.org/10.1109/TVLSI.2018.2816914. https://ieeexplore.ieee.org/document/8327903
10. Bos, J.W., Gourjon, M., Renes, J., Schneider, T., van Vredendaal, C.: Masking Kyber: first- and higher-order implementations. IACR Trans. Cryptographic Hardware Embedded Syst. 173–214 (2021). https://doi.org/10.46586/tches.v2021.i4.173-214. https://tches.iacr.org/index.php/TCHES/article/view/9064
11. Coron, J.-S., Giraud, C., Prouff, E., Renner, S., Rivain, M., Vadnala, P.K.: Conversion of security proofs from one leakage model to another: a new issue. In: Schindler, W., Huss, S.A. (eds.) COSADE 2012. LNCS, vol. 7275, pp. 69–81. Springer, Heidelberg (2012). https://doi.org/10.1007/978-3-642-29912-4_6
12. Grandmaison, A., Heydemann, K., Meunier, Q.L.: ARMISTICE: microarchitectural leakage modelling for masked software formal verification. IEEE Trans. Comput. Aided Des. Integr. Circuits Syst. **41**(11), 3733–3744 (2022)
13. De Mulder, E., Gummalla, S., Hutter, M.: Protecting RISC-V against side-channel attacks. In: 2019 56th ACM/IEEE Design Automation Conference (DAC), pp. 1–4. ACM, Las Vegas NV USA (2019). https://doi.org/10.1145/3316781.3323485

14. Escouteloup, M., Migliore, V.: Design platform and microbenchmarks (2025). https://gitlab.com/herd-ware/root
15. Gao, S., Großschädl, J., Marshall, B., Page, D., Pham, T., Regazzoni, F.: An instruction set extension to support software-based masking. IACR Trans. Cryptographic Hardware Embedded Syst. 43 (2020)
16. Gao, S., Marshall, B., Page, D., Pham, T.: FENL: an ISE to mitigate analogue micro-architectural leakage. IACR Trans. Cryptographic Hardware Embedded Syst. 73–98 (2020). https://doi.org/10.13154/tches.v2020.i2.73-98. https://tches.iacr.org/index.php/TCHES/article/view/8545
17. Gao, S., Oswald, E., Page, D.: Reverse engineering the micro-architectural leakage features of a commercial processor. Cryptology ePrint Archive (2021)
18. Gigerl, B., Hadzic, V., Primas, R., Mangard, S., Bloem, R.: COCO: co-design and co-verification of masked software implementations on CPUs. In: 30th USENIX Security Symposium (USENIX Security 2021), p. 18 (2021)
19. Gigerl, B., Primas, R., Mangard, S.: Secure and efficient software masking on superscalar pipelined processors. In: Tibouchi, M., Wang, H. (eds.) ASIACRYPT 2021. LNCS, vol. 13091, pp. 3–32. Springer, Cham (2021). https://doi.org/10.1007/978-3-030-92075-3_1
20. Ishai, Y., Sahai, A., Wagner, D.: Private circuits: securing hardware against probing attacks. In: Boneh, D. (ed.) CRYPTO 2003. LNCS, vol. 2729, pp. 463–481. Springer, Heidelberg (2003). https://doi.org/10.1007/978-3-540-45146-4_27
21. Le Corre, Y., Großschädl, J., Dinu, D.: Micro-architectural power simulator for leakage assessment of cryptographic software on ARM cortex-M3 processors. In: Fan, J., Gierlichs, B. (eds.) COSADE 2018. LNCS, vol. 10815, pp. 82–98. Springer, Cham (2018). https://doi.org/10.1007/978-3-319-89641-0_5
22. Marshall, B., Page, D.: SME: Scalable Masking Extensions. Cryptology ePrint Archive p. 25 (2021)
23. Marshall, B., Page, D., Webb, J.: MIRACLE: MIcRo-ArChitectural leakage evaluation: a study of micro-architectural power leakage across many devices. IACR Trans. Cryptographic Hardware Embedded Syst. 175–220 (2021). https://doi.org/10.46586/tches.v2022.i1.175-220
24. McCann, D., Whitnall, C., Oswald, E.: ELMO: emulating leaks for the ARM Cortex-M0 without access to a side channel lab. IACR Cryptol. ePrint Arch. **2016**, 517 (2016)
25. O'Flynn, C., Chen, Z.: Chipwhisperer: an open-source platform for hardware embedded security research. In: Constructive Side-Channel Analysis and Secure Design (COSADE), pp. 243–260. Springer, Paris (2014)
26. Papagiannopoulos, K., Veshchikov, N.: Mind the gap: towards secure 1st-order masking in software. In: Guilley, S. (ed.) COSADE 2017. LNCS, vol. 10348, pp. 282–297. Springer, Cham (2017). https://doi.org/10.1007/978-3-319-64647-3_17
27. Roy, A., Schaumont, P.: Microplumber: Finding hidden sources of power-based SCL in microcontrollers. In: 2024 IEEE Computer Society Annual Symposium on VLSI (ISVLSI), pp. 762–765. IEEE, Knoxville (2024). https://doi.org/10.1109/ISVLSI61997.2024.00148. https://ieeexplore.ieee.org/document/10682629/
28. Shelton, M.A., Chmielewski, L., Samwel, N., Wagner, M., Batina, L., Yarom, Y.: Rosita++: automatic higher-order leakage elimination from cryptographic code. In: Proceedings of the 2021 ACM SIGSAC Conference on Computer and Communications Security, pp. 685–699. ACM, Virtual Event Republic of Korea (2021). https://doi.org/10.1145/3460120.3485380

29. Shelton, M.A., Samwel, N., Batina, L., Regazzoni, F., Wagner, M., Yarom, Y.: Rosita: towards automatic elimination of power-analysis leakage in ciphers. In: Proceedings 2021 Network and Distributed System Security Symposium. Internet Society, Virtual (2021). https://doi.org/10.14722/ndss.2021.23137
30. Šijačić, D., Balasch, J., Yang, B., Ghosh, S., Verbauwhede, I.: Towards efficient and automated side channel evaluations at design time. J. Cryptogr. Eng. **10**(4), 305–319 (2020)
31. Slpsk, P., Vairam, P.K., Rebeiro, C., Kamakoti, V.: Karna: a gate-sizing based security aware EDA flow for improved power side-channel attack protection. In: 2019 IEEE/ACM International Conference on Computer-Aided Design (ICCAD), pp. 1–8 (2019). https://doi.org/10.1109/ICCAD45719.2019.8942173
32. Snyder, W.: Verilator (2023). https://veripool.org/verilator/
33. Talaki, E.B., Savry, O., Bouvier Des Noes, M., Hely, D.: A memory hierarchy protected against side-channel attacks. Cryptography **6**(2), 19 (2022). https://doi.org/10.3390/cryptography6020019. https://www.mdpi.com/2410-387X/6/2/19
34. Veshchikov, N.: SILK: High level of abstraction leakage simulator for side channel analysis. In: 4th Program Protection and Reverse Engineering Workshop, pp. 1–11. New Orleans, Louisiana, USA (2014)
35. Waterman, A., Asanović, K., Hauser, J.: The RISC-V instruction set manual: volume I, version 20240411 (2024). https://github.com/riscv/riscv-isa-manual/releases/tag/20240411
36. Zeitschner, J., Müller, N., Moradi, A.: PROLEAD_SW: probing-based software leakage detection for ARM binaries. IACR Trans. Cryptographic Hardware Embedded Syst. 391–421 (2023). https://doi.org/10.46586/tches.v2023.i3.391-421. https://tches.iacr.org/index.php/TCHES/article/view/10968

Machine Learning

Taking AI-Based Side-Channel Attacks to a New Dimension

Lucas David Meier[✉][iD], Felipe Valencia[iD], Cristian-Alexandru Botocan[iD], and Damian Vizár[iD]

CSEM, Neuchâtel, Switzerland
{lucas.meier,andres.valencia,damian.vizAr}@csem.ch

Abstract. This paper revisits the Hamming Weight (HW) labelling function for machine learning assisted side channel attacks. Contrary to what has been suggested by pervious works, our investigation shows that, when paired with modern deep learning architectures, appropriate per-processing and normalization techniques; it can perform as well as the popular identity labelling functions and sometimes even beat it. In fact, we hereby introduce a new machine learning method, dubbed *dimension 0*, that helps solve the class imbalance problem associated to HW, while significantly improving the performance of unprofiled attacks. We additionally release our new, easy to use python package that we used in our experiments, implementing a broad variety of machine learning driven side channel attacks as open source, along with a new dataset AES_nRF, acquired on the nRF52840 SoC.

Keywords: Profiled and Unprofiled Side-Channel Attacks · Deep Learning · Softmax Function

1 Introduction

Cryptographic algorithms are designed to ensure that secret input arguments cannot be recovered given the knowledge of public data (such as ciphertexts of a blockcipher) or even given some inputs considered private (such as plaintexts of a block cipher). This is the purview of classical cryptanalysis, where the cryptographic algorithm of interest is treated as a black-box. However, in practical implementations on physical devices (software on microcontrollers or hardware accelerators), the execution of these algorithms involves physical processes. These processes can correlate with input values, making them observable through physical variables. For instance, the power consumption when loading a secret key correlates with its Hamming Weight, leaking key information. Side-Channel Attacks (SCA) exploit such physical channels to recover secret data, even from mathematically secure algorithms. Therefore, real-world security requires cryptographic robustness and secure implementation against SCA, especially in embedded systems that are often accessible to attackers.

The study of SCA began with Timing Attacks [18] and evolved to more complex methods such as Simple Power Analysis (SPA) and Differential Power Analysis (DPA) [19], Template Attacks [5], Welch's t-test [35], and Correlation Power Analysis (CPA) [4]. SCA techniques are classified based on adversarial control (passive or active), observed variables (i.e., power, electromagnetic radiation, timing, etc.), exploitation methods (i.e., statistical analysis, machine learning, etc.), and the use of the profiling phase. This paper focuses on passive power analysis attacks using machine learning, both profiled and unprofiled.

Artificial Intelligence (AI) proved to be very effective in SCA. The use of Machine Learning (ML) in SCA began in 2011 [13], and deep learning (DL) soon became popular for overcoming SCA countermeasures that resisted traditional statistical attacks, including template attacks [21]. While other ML methods like SVMs, decision trees, random forests, KNNs, and k-means were explored, deep neural networks (DNN) have shown the best performance [12]. Recent works have gained insights into the role of various NN components to in the efficacy of DNN-based SCA [42], optimized NN architectures for faster learning and better key recovery [39], and applied various deep learning techniques to enhance attack performance [11, 15, 28, 31, 40, 41].

The power of ML-SCA (ML) attacks based on NNs depends heavily on the selection of model hyperparameters, such as network topology, activation functions and learning rate. One of these critical hyperparameters is the choice of the leakage function. The two main options from the literature are either Hamming Weight (HW) labelling function or the identity (ID) labelling function.

The experiments of existing works investigating the use of HW labelling have suggested that models with ID labelling are capable of results that surpass what can be achieved with HW. For example, Picek et al. show that HW labeling suffers from the class imbalance problem [29], which can degrade model performance. In the study by Benadjila et al. [2], it was shown that during hyperparameter searching, no parameters result in a successful attack on an MLP model using HW labeling, whereas at least one successful attack is possible with ID. Following these finding, the popularity of ID labelling has exceeded that of HW, with works such as those by Wouters et al. [39] and Zaid et al. [42] focusing on attacks using only ID labeling. Recent works that used both labeling functions seemed to confirm the ID labeling superiority. For example, Rjisdijk et al. [31] reported superior results with ID labeling in an SCA study using RL techniques. Similarly, Kerkhof et al. [14] found that a new SCA loss function performed better with ID labeling than HW across multiple datasets. Finally, a recent study on the ASCAD datasets by Egger et al. [8] considered the HW leakage model for classical CPA attacks, but relied only on the Identity labelling for ML attacks.

All in all, the results published so far show HW labelling rather unfavorably, which resonates with the more frequent use of ID labeling in the more recent works. Yet, the existing evidence may not be sufficient to designate ID labeling as a generally superior option, as no works have experimentally verified efficacy of HW labelling on the modern DNN architectures, nor have there been any new attempts to overcome the class imbalance problem since 2019 [29]. At the same time, the interest in having a more up-to-date comparison between HW and ID labelling functions is not only purely academic. HW labeling allows to mount practical attacks targeting intermediate variables of 16, 32 or more bits, while the same using ID would incur impractical computational and storage complexities [1,22].

In this paper, we set out to close the gap between the amount of recent results ID and HW labelling, and seek to answer the question: *"Can HW labelling function match or out-perform ID with recent DNN models and suitable additional techniques?"* For that, we use state-of-the-art models and datasets from the ASCAD family [2], which have different levels of security (masked implementation and jittering). A major contribution of our work here is a new DL method, which allowed models with HW labelling to match, and sometimes outperform the same model using ID labelling. The new method consists of transposing the matrix containing a model's output logits for multiple input traces before the softmax function is evaluated.[1]

Contributions. Our contribution is threefold. First, we introduce a new DL method for SCA called *dim0*, which can outperform state-of-the-art balancing techniques on Hamming Weight labelled datasets, beat state-of-the-art using the easier identity labelling and has the potential to greatly improve unprofiled attacks as well. Second, we publish a new ML python-based package implementing a variety of the state-of-the-art ML-based SCA techniques that is easy to use and easy to extend.[2] Last, we release our home-made SCA dataset called AES_nRF acquired on the nRF52840 SoC for an unprotected implementation of AES. AES_nRF contains 47.5k profiling traces with random keys and 2.5k attack traces with fixed key.

2 Preliminaries

2.1 Notation

Throughout this document, we denote $\mathbf{v}_i$ or $\mathbf{v}[i]$ as being the i-th entry of a vector $\mathbf{v}$. Matrices are bold, capitalized and in italic, as $\boldsymbol{M}$. Let N_c denote the number of classes, N_p and N_a the number of profiling and attack traces, N_b the number of traces in a batch (batch size) and N_s the number of samples in a trace. Indexes t, c and e will refer to a trace, class and epoch number respectively.

2.2 Side-Channel Attacks

Side-Channels Attacks (SCA) are attacks that target the implementation instead of the mathematical structure of a security algorithm. They use side-channel information (timing, power, cache memories, etc.) that depends on secret values. To mount an attack the adversary 1) creates a model to estimate side-channel information as a function of secret values, 2) applies the function to multiple

---

[1] In other words, we change the *dimension*, along which the softmax is computed.
[2] The MLSCAlib is available on this link https://github.com/csem/MLSCAlib

secret values hypothesis, then 3) measures the side-channel information from the target device, and finally 4) discriminates incorrect secret values hypothesis comparing estimations with measurements [34]. The comparison can be made using means difference, correlation, mutual information, t-test [35], etc. The estimation model can be created with measurements of a controlled device, in this case it is a profiled attack, otherwise it is an unprofiled attack. In some profiled attacks the model is constrained to use most important time samples or Points Of Interest (POI). Machine learning can be used to find the POI, create the estimation model and/or to discriminate hypothesis [24].

2.3 AES

AES (Advanced Encryption Standard) [10] is a block cipher that, given a plaintext of 128 bits and a key of 128, 192, or 256 bits, produces a ciphertext of 128 bits. The decryption algorithm of AES recovers the plaintext given a ciphertext and a key. AES is an iterated block cipher that expands the key into several 128-bit round keys and iteratively applies a round function to the plaintext and a round key. The round function is composed of four transformations: addRoundKey (AK), subBytes (SB), shiftRows (SR) and mixColumns (MC), where the state is repersented as a matrix of 4×4 bytes. SubBytes transformation is an invertible non-linear byte substitution (substitution box or Sbox) applied bytewise on the AES state. The remaining transformations are linear. The last round does not have mixColumns and is followed by an xor of the final round key. The number of rounds depends on the key length.

2.4 Leakage Function

The attacker does not directly learn the key value from the traces. Instead, it targets an intermediate value of the AES encryption (i.e., typically, the 8-bit output or input of the Sbox operation) and uses a specific leakage function for evaluation. In SCA, the leakage function is the same as the labeling function in machine learning since both functions map data to a form that can be used for analysis. A common option for labelling is the identity function (ID) which repersents the actual byte value of the output, resulting in 256 different classes. Another option is the Hamming Weight (HW) of the output value. This usually works well since the power consumption of a computation is directly related to the number of bits set to one or zero. However, this gives rise to a class imbalance: the classes 0 and 8 are only reached through a single possible (Sbox) output value, whereas the class 4 is linked to 70 values. As a consequence, the rare classes are more informative than others (label 0 and 8 can only be produced by one key given a plaintext). Besides, physical observations of traces with a HW value 3,4 or 5 tend to look the same, while a trace with HW 0 and one with HW 8 are easily differentiable, as shown by Fan et al. [9] on their Fig. 5 plotting the HW-two-dimensional distribution of power consumption.

2.5 Machine Learning

Classification using machine learning (ML) is defined as training a model to learn from the input data features, such that it classifies the input and divides it into discrete classes. In the SCA context, we have as a training (profiling) dataset the side-channel traces from a device with known inputs and keys, each labeled with the associated intermediate value or key byte. After training, the model helps perdict secret keys by allocating probabilities to each class of traces in the testing dataset. This inference process is also called the attacking phase.

Multi-layer Perceptron. The MLP contains multiple layers of perceptrons. A perceptron is repersented as a function $f(\mathbf{x}) = \mathbf{w}^T\mathbf{x} + b$, where the trainable parameters $\mathbf{w}, b$ are called weight and bias term. The model is composed of an input layer, hidden layers in the middle of the network, and an output layer. An activation function (often RELU [25] or SELU [17]) is applied to the output of each perceptron to add non-linearity to the model.

Convolutional Neural Networks. Convolutional Neural Networks (CNN) combine data processing operations (e.g., convolutions, pooling, batch normalization, etc.) with a final Multi-Layer Perceptron layers (also called a fully Connected Layer in this context). Mathematically, the convolution is experssed as $\mathbf{x}^{i+1}[n] = \sum_k^{N_f} \mathbf{f}[k]\mathbf{x}^i[n-k]$, where $\mathbf{f}[n]$ repersents a filter with N_f elements and $\mathbf{x}^i$ the output of layer i (or the input trace for $i = 0$).

Logits. Logits are the raw, unnormalized output values produced by the last layer of a neural network, such as an MLP or CNN, before applying an activation function. These values repersent the model's confidence scores for each class. There is a one-to-one correspondence between the classes and the logits.

Softmax. In order to turn the logits into a probability distribution, the softmax function is used: $softmax_1(\mathbf{V}, t, c) = (e^{\mathbf{V}_{t,c}})/(\sum_{j=0}^{N_c-1} e^{\mathbf{V}_{t,j}})$, where $\mathbf{V}$ repersents a $N_b \times N_c$ matrix of logits, t the input number and c the class index. For each input, the sum of the probabilities over each class sums up to one.

Loss Functions. The loss function measures the discrepancy between perdicted classes and real classes. We use Negative Log-Likelihood (NLL) as loss function because it is asymptotically equivalent to maximizing the Perceived Information (PI), which at the same time is the lower bound of Mutual Information (MI). Training with NLL is an efficient estimation of MI [24].

Its definition is $\mathcal{L}_{nll} = \frac{1}{N_p} \sum_{i=1}^{N_p} -\log_2(\tilde{\mathbf{y}}_i) \mathbf{y}_i$, where $\mathbf{y}_i$ are the labels, $\tilde{\mathbf{y}}_i$ are the model's perdiction w.r.t the input vector $\mathbf{T}_i$ and the model parameters.

Batched Learning. In most of the cases, the training data is given in batches to the model in order to reduce the instantaneous memory consumption. The batch size is typically in the order of one hundred traces.

2.6 Confusion Matrix

The confusion matrix is a matrix whose vertical axis designates the ground truth, i.e. the real classes, and the horizontal axis is the actual perdiction for each class.

It shows which classes the model perdicts correctly. The value $M_{i,j}$ counts the samples from class i that were classified to class j by the model. When depicted graphically, we should see a diagonal shape (from top left to bottom right) in the confusion matrix if the model performs well. In case of imbalance, we may see vertical lines on common classes. Formally, the i-th row of the $N_c \times N_c$ confusion matrix M is defined by: $M_i = \sum_{j=0}^{N_a} \mathbb{1}\{y_j = i\} \cdot model(X_j) / \sum_{j=0}^{N_a} \mathbb{1}\{y_j = i\}$, where N_a is the number of traces in the attack dataset matrix X, y is the label vector for the attack traces and *model* the trained machine learning model.

2.7 Model Sensitivity and Unprofiled Attacks

Mainly used for unprofiled attacks, what we call the model sensitivity is the analysis of which part of an input trace is being used at which intensity by the model to make a perdiction. In ML-based unprofiled attacks, the correct key guess is distinguished from wrong key guesses using a metric. This metric may be the training or validation accuracy, or even the model sensitivity [23,33,38]. The underlying assumption of this method is that under a correct key guess, the model will be able to find the PoI of the traces and learn from that. In the other hand, a wrong key guess will lead to randomized labels, which will hinder the model from learning anything (inc. PoI) from the trace. In the current work, we'll use the model sensitivity [23,38] computed at each epoch and accumulated. At the end, we plot the absolute value and elect the key guess leading to a sensitivity with the highest peak as being the right key guess.

Formally, the model sensitivity is defined as $S_{input}[s] = \sum_{t=1}^{N_a} \frac{\partial \mathsf{L}_{T_t}}{\partial y_s} \times T_{t,s}$, for $s \in \{1, \ldots, N_s\}$. The first quantity in the sum is the partial derivative of the loss with regard to the s-th sample variable (y_s) for the t-th trace of the training set (T_t). $T_{t,i}$ corresponds to the value of the t-th trace at time sample s.

3 A New Dimension

A neural network's output layer consists of neurons, one per each possible perdicted class, outputting so-called *logits*. The higher a value of a logit, the more strongly is the associated class suggested by the NN for the given input sample. To normalize the output of the NN and make it consistently comparable across samples and between the individual logits, the softmax function is typically applied to the output logits of a NN for a single sample. Softmax transforms a vector of k real numbers into a distribution over k classes, i.e., a vector of k real numbers from the interval $[0, 1]$ that sum to 1, yielding pseudo-probabilities for each class given the sample. When the NN outputs are arranged into a matrix (a row holding the logits for a single sample), the softmax function is thus applied row by row. In a manner of speaking, the softmax is computed along the dimension 1 of the matrix (provided we index the dimensions from 0).[3] This section

---

[3] The naming comes directly from the PyTorch library. PyTorch's softmax function has a dimension argument, which can be set to either 0 or 1 for a 2D input.

describes our newly proposed method, based on applying the softmax function to the columns of the same matrix instead, computing a distribution over traces for each NN output class.

3.1 Definition

Throughout this paper, we refer to dimension 1 ($dim1$) or dimension 0 ($dim0$) as being the dimension argument of the softmax function applied on the output layer of a deep learning ML model, during the training and attacking phases. Formally, the softmax on dimension 0, denoted $softmax_0$, is defined by:

$$softmax_0(\boldsymbol{V}, t, c) = \frac{e^{V_{t,c}}}{\sum_{j=0}^{N_b} e^{V_{j,c}}} \quad (1)$$

where $\boldsymbol{V}$ repersents the $N_b \times N_c$ logits matrix, t the trace number, N_b the number of traces in the batch and c the class index. By definition, $dim0$ requires at least two input samples per batch to obtain a non-trivial output. The $softmax_0(\boldsymbol{V}, t, c)$ only depends on $\boldsymbol{V}_{i,c}$ for $i < N_b$ and a fixed class index c.

Proposition 1. *During inference, a model using $softmax_0$ will consider each class separately. During training, a model using $softmax_0$ can not increase the score of the same class for every input sample in a given batch between epochs. An increase of the normalized score for a given class input always results in the decrease of the normalized score for the same class in one or more other input samples of the same batch.*

Corollary 1. *During inference, the normalized scores for the different classes output by a model using $softmax_0$ for a given sample will not perserve the ratios between the raw class scores, mitigating the logits' inter-class bias. During training, a model using $softmax_0$ will elect best input repersentatives for every class, giving increased consideration to rare classes in imbalanced dataset scenarios.*

3.2 Outline

Section 3 will further explore and experimentally verify Proposition 1. Section 3.3 will show that these targeted classes have more impact in the mathematical key derivation itself. Section 3.4 will demonstrate that choosing an optimizer which allows to optimize each weight on its own maximizes the $dim0$ performance. Section 3.5 will elaborate on the rationale leading to the conclusion of Proposition 1. At last, we point to general limitations and recommendations for the $dim0$ approach.

3.3 Easily Classifiable Traces Have More Impact

Let's see why under $dim0$, the key ranking algorithm, combining each trace's perdiction by the ML model to deduce the most probable secret key, will give more importance to traces for which the model has a greater level of certainty.

First, it is important to make the observation that an inference done with $dim0$ will assign a probability distribution over the traces (in the batch) for each class. This means, for class 0, each trace will be assigned a probability of being of class 0, these probabilities summing to 1 over all traces. These probabilities could also be thought of as a measure of how well each of these traces "repersent" class 0. Consequently, when we sum such probabilities (we'll call it class-scores) over all classes for a given trace, the result will not be equal to 1. For example, a trivial perdiction assigning the same class-score for each class will lead to a sum of N_c/N_b for any trace, where N_c is the number of classes and N_b the batch size. As soon as the model starts to train on a particular class, the probability over the traces will diverge from $1/N_b$ for each trace, and consequently traces whose class the model choose to train on will have a higher expected sum of class scores than other traces. As we will see in Sect. 3.5, the model can chose to target easily classifiable traces (e.g. of label 0, 8 with HW labelling). Hence, we expect such traces to have a higher sum of class-scores. Classes which are difficult to train on will tend to keep their default $1/N_b$ probability assignment over each trace. We conducted an experiment on our AES_nRF dataset to confirm this claim. After a successful training using $dim0$ and a batch size of 50, we computed the sum of each trace class-scores for each batch grouped by their true label and computed the mean value. The expected sum of class-scores is hence $N_c/N_b = 0.18$. We experimentally obtained these class-scores means during inference, for traces of label 0 to 8: $[0.2622, 0.2245, 0.2038, 0.1871, 0.1721, 0.1712, 0.1707, 0.1732, 0.1792]$. As we see, traces whose true label value is 0,1,2 or 3 tend to have a higher class-score. The model had chosen to target on these classes. This means, traces of true label 0,1,2 and 3 will have a bigger impact during the secret key derivation, which blindly sums each of the potential key's class score (where the key is derived from the plaintext and the given class) for each trace-plaintext input.

3.4 Optimizers

In the context of machine learning, an optimizer is a mathematical algorithm used to adjust the parameters of a model in order to minimize the error in its perdictions. The optimizer iteratively updates the model's parameters based on the gradients of the loss function. How the updates are performed given the gradient values depends on the type of optimizer. In fact, $dim0$ allows a model to handle each class separately. But this effect is taken to its full potential if the optimizer in turn allows for a per-class (or per-weight) tuning.

We now compare five different optimizers and how their behavior adapts when confronted to a $dim0$ model.

Nesterov [27] is an optimizer that works like a Stochastic Gradient Descent (SGD) with momentum but additionally regulates the momentum by approximating the values of parameters in future updates. SGD, with momentum itself, computes the gradient of the loss function by considering only one (or a subset) of the input traces to compute the gradient to reduce the computational cost. The momentum adds memory to the learning process, meaning that we add a fraction of the perviously computed gradient to the current one.

Adagrad. [7] Its learning rate tends to vanish because it is inversely proportional to the sum of all the past squared gradients.

Adadelta. [43] It improves upon Adagrad by only considering a subset of the pervious squared gradients.

RMSprop. It improves upon Adagrad by dividing the learning rate by an exponentially decaying average of squared gradients, which should solve the learning rate vanishing problems.

Adam. [16] It improves upon Adagrad and RMSprop by storing an exponentially decaying average of past gradients in addition to the exponentially decaying average of past squared gradients.

Except for Nesterov, these optimizers are adaptive methods, meaning they have, for each batch, an adaptive learning rate for each parameter. As a result, parameters associated with low-frequency features tend to have larger learning rates than parameters associated with high-frequency features. For example, the gradient descent formula of Adam is:

$$\theta_e = \theta_{e-1} - \alpha \frac{\hat{m}_e}{\sqrt{\hat{v}_e} + \epsilon} \tag{2}$$

with $\hat{m}_e = \frac{m_e}{1-\beta_1^e}$, $m_e = \beta_1 m_{e-1} + (1-\beta_1)g_e$, $\hat{v}_e = \frac{v_e}{1-\beta_2^e}$, $v_e = \beta_2 v_{e-1} + (1-\beta_2)g_e^2$, and where e is the current epoch, θ_e the parameters at epoch e, g_e the gradient, α the learning rate, β_1 and β_2 the exponential decay rates for the moment estimates, ϵ a small constant, m_e the first moment estimate, v_e the second moment estimate, g_e the gradient of the loss function.

The division $\frac{\hat{m}_e}{\sqrt{\hat{v}_e}+\epsilon}$ from Eq. 2 ensures that each parameter has its own learning rate. Dividing by $\sqrt{\hat{v}_e} + \epsilon$ will make the optimizer adjust the learning rate for each parameter based on the historical gradient information. Parameters with smaller gradients (indicating more stable or low-frequency features) will have their updates scaled up, ensuring they receive sufficient updates (we use the term adaptive if the optmizer has this property). This is because the learning rate is scaled inversely with the square root of the sum of the squares of past gradients. Additionally, ϵ ensures that the learning rate does not vanish entirely for any parameter.

Some adaptive optimizers, such as Adam, additionally have an exponentially decay of the sum (or average) of past gradients (see β_1 and β_2), which helps in perventing the learning rate from becoming too small.

As a conclusion, we make the distinction between adaptive and non-adaptive optimizers (e.g. SGD or Nesterov). Adaptive optimizers might use exponential decay (as in Adam or RMSProp) or not (e.g. Adagrad, Adadelta).

Using *dim1* and HW Labelling. In this paragraph only, we'll use $softmax_1$ for training and try $softmax_0$ for attacking. Independently from the optimizer we choose to use on an imbalanced dataset, the *dim1* model will be biased towards the more common classes. The learning will stall or be slowed down

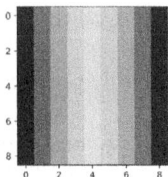 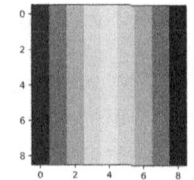 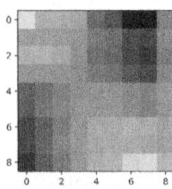

(a) Confusion matrix during training on *dim1*. (b) Confusion matrix on evaluating with *dim1*. (c) Confusion matrix on evaluating with *dim0*.

Fig. 1. Confusion matrices for training/evaluating on *dim1*/*dim0*. The training for the middle and the right-hand side figures have been done with *dim1*. Y-axis: true classes. X-axis: perdicted classes. Yellow/light: high probability. Dark/blue: low probability. (Color figure online)

for rare classes. Figure 1 confirms this claim experimentally. As we see, during training on *dim1*, the model is biased towards the common class (i.e. there is no diagonal to be seen, only a straight yellow line for class 4). During evaluation, this bias persisted. However, using *dim0* at inference, we observe that the model was able to train a bit on the rare classes with *dim1* during training. In fact, *dim0* during inference will remove the inter-class bias and consider each class separately. In this scenario, the model correctly picks the traces closest to class 0.

3.5 Per Class Optimization

A ML model chooses to adapt its weights following the steepest curve of the gradient of the loss function during the optimization. In other words, the model always use the easiest way to optimize itself. In the context of imbalanced datasets, a model with *dim1* will assign higher probabilities for common classes to reduce the loss. With *dim0*, this doesn't happen as for each class the probabilities over the traces in a batch must sum to one. The loss related to common classes is nonetheless high, but it can only be minimized effectively by training on other classes. In turn, if any of the less common class is easier to train on than others, it will focus on that particular class (following the steepest curve of the loss function gradient). In the SCA context, it is known that rare classes are easier to distinguish than common classes (as mentioned in Sect. 2.4). The model will hence focus on these rare classes to minimize the overall loss. What is more, in the SCA context, rare classes happen to be the most informative ones: a trace of class 0 can only be linked to *one* secret key. Traces of class 4 lead to 70 potential secret keys (refer to Sect. 2.4). Therefore, using *dim0* allows a model to train to recognize rare classes more successfully, which in turn significantly improve the narrowing-down of the candidate key pool. We experimentally tested this claim to see if our model indeed prioritizes the rare and easily classifiable classes over the common classes. To that end, consider Fig. 2. In this Figure, the y-axis repersents the mean value of each logit during training. The x-axis is the epoch number. Each class (logit) is repersented by a different line. The model used is

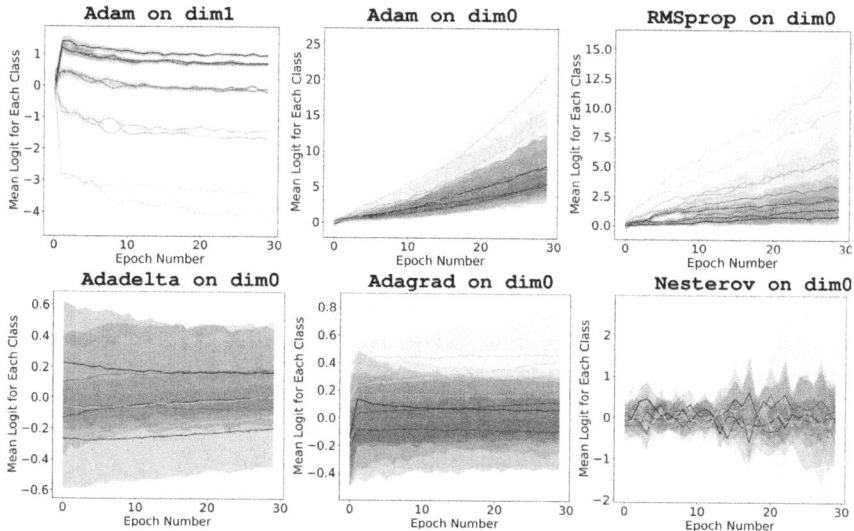

Fig. 2. Mean logit value for each class. Since we used the HW labelling, light green lines stand for rare classes. The darker the line, the more common is the underlying class (label 4 is the dark line, label 0 and 8 are the two lightest). We consider the logits of the first batch of each epoch, obtained with CNN_exp and our own AES_nRF dataset. (Color figure online)

the CNN_exp with AES_nRF dataset. The mean value of each logit has been calculated using the first batch (i.e., hundred traces) at each epoch. We averaged ten runs, plotting the mean and a 90% confidence interval.

In line with the expected behavior of a model trained with an imbalanced dataset, based on Fig. 2, we observe that a *dim1* models' logits are ranked in order of occurrence of the underlying class. This could be confirmed for all optimizers (not shown). The most common classes lie above the others, and the rare classes are in the bottom part. Though the figure only shows Adam on *dim1*, we noticed a slight difference in behavior for the Adam and RMSprop optimizers as compared to the others, in that one of the rare classes (actually class 0) keeps dropping. This aligns with what was observed in Fig. 1c: class 0 yielded a better perdiction than class 8. Apart from that, the logits do not seem to change much as the epoch increases: this confirms the expected behavior, the model seems to stall.

From Fig. 2, we observe that with a *dim0* model, the logit's behavior strongly depends on the optimizer:

Adagrad and Adadelta. They stabilize after a few epochs and change especially little afterward. But they are more or less located in the same amplitudes (the confidence intervals are large and interfere with each other). The model does not target a specific logit more than others across runs.

Adam and RMSprop. Logits related to rare classes increase faster than the other. This crucial observation confirms our claim that a per-class optimization is possible under *dim0*.

Nesterov. Using *dim0* does not yield interesting results. This non-adaptive optimizer was not able to take advantage of the *dim0* properties.

Mathematical Insights. The generic gradient descent algorithm, based on Equation (2), stipulates that the weight are adapted at each epoch as a function of the gradient of the loss function, a possible regularization, and the learning rate (which is set by the optimizer). The observation that logits related to rare classes increase faster than the others can be caused by either of these three ingredients. However, in our case no regularization is applied. Moreover, the gradient of the loss function is expected to be higher for common classes and not rare classes. This is a consequence of the $\mathcal{L}_{nll}$ (see Sect. 2.5): as each sample in the input dataset contributes for the same, the gradient for the common class will be higher.

As a conclusion, only the learning rate can be the root cause of privileging a rare class during training over a common class. Here, having adaptive learning rates in the optimizer, such as in Adam, RMSprop, Adagrad and Adadelta, seems to be necessary for the learning rate of rare classes.

3.6 Considerations

Choosing the Right Batch Size. A new hyperparameter has to be taken into account when doing ML-based SCA with *dim0*: the batch size. In fact, the new softmax Eq. (1) on *dim0* depends on the batch size.

If the batch size is too small, some classes may not have a trace related to it, or would be insufficiently repersented in certain batches and the model will mostly have to train on unrelated labels. This is because the model looks at each class separately. As a consequence, the model will overfit on the training dataset.

Using a reasonable batch sizes (at least 50) is recommend to mitigate the effects mentioned above. Section 5 proposes some countermeasures in case the number of attack traces is too small to form a complete batch.

Based on the pervious observations, we also verified the influence of the batch size on performance in *dim0* on a public dataset using 110'000 traces from ASCAD_variable with ID leakage model for profiling and 10'000 for attacking. The CNN_best model was employed for these experiments, trained for 250 epochs with the RMSprop optimizer at a learning rate of 10^{-5}. We tested the following batch sizes: $[50, 200, 700, 1000, 2000]$. Figure 3 indicates that the model performed best with a batch size of 1000. The next best performances were achieved with batch sizes of 2000 and 700, respectively. With a batch size of 1000, the model achieved a GE of 1 within the 250 epochs. No other batch size reached this level of performance within the same number of epochs.

However, we must point out that in this case *dim0* did not surpass the *dim1* state-of-the-art, which can successfully break ASCAD variable with only 1000 traces in 37 out of 60 cases [8]. This suggests that changing the batch size might not be the only variable to re-optimize when switching the dimension of the softmax function, and emphasizes the need to clarify dim0's needs and strengths in future research.

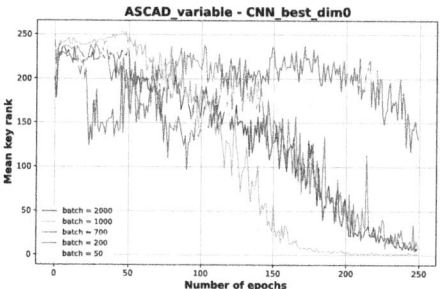

Fig. 3. Batch size influence on the dim 0 model.

Similarities with Bayesian MAP Approach. *Dim0* may be reminiscent of the Bayesian attack, as both compute overall class-scores by combining the class-scores from all leakage samples for every class. In the Bayesian attack, one does this using the Bayesian trick, necessitating to treat the distribution of samples (leakages) as statistically independent; the extended version of the paper by Standaert et al. [36,37] and its Theorem 1 for example assumes independence of leakages. This assumption is, however, not verified in practice as they all depend on the same hardware and software implementation of the cipher.

Using *dim0*, there is an additional step where class-sample-scores of the batch are normalized. The normalization is computed one class after another, using the non-normalized scores of all samples for the given class (i.e., logits). The normalized scores are then aggregated similarly as in the Bayesian attacks. No leakage-independence assumptions are made. Moreover, the class-wise normalization compensates the bias between the classes, which the a posteriori maximization alone does not involve. This treatment also has benefits that are specific to the ML-based approach. With conventional (i.e., *dim1*) training, the distributions of the output logits are forced to *"stay together"* (means not too far apart, with similar variances).

Discussion. As we saw, an adaptive optimizer will set the learning rate differently for each parameter; proportionally to the inverse of their gradient's variance. Using *dim0* lets an adaptive optimizer take advantage of the fact that the logits' individual values can increase with more liberty than with *dim1*. What is suggested by the experimental data from Adadelta and Adam plots from Fig. 2, is that an adaptive learning rate alone is not sufficient to achieve the logit's individual imbalance towards rare classes. Indeed, we additionally need them to follow an exponentially decay of the sum (or average) of past gradients (as for Adam or RMSprop). This exponential decay allows the learning rate not to vanish (or become small) on logits which have had a great change on pervious steps. As a consequence, the training will not stall.

Another point we observed when using *dim0* on an imbalanced dataset is that the model may choose one particular rare class to target (in our examples it is class 0). The model targets the easiest to train classes (arguably, as pointed in Fig. 5 of [9], class 0 or 8 are expected to be easier to distinguish than the other classes), and they happen to be the most informative ones. This fact is expected to also help the model perform better on balanced, ID-labeled datasets, where again some of the ID classes can be easier to distinguish than others. Last, the key-ranking algorithm itself will give more importance to easily classifiable traces, a paradigm shift from all former studies on the SCA topic.

4 Experiments

All the test cases for *dim0* persented in this Section will target a dataset using the Hamming Weight (HW) or Hamming Distance (HD) labelling function. To demonstrate its significance, *dim0* needs to outperform the current state-of-the-art class balancing technique, as well as models that use the easier Identity Labelling. According to work by Picek et al. [29], the best balancer in the SCA context is SMOTE [6].

We will hence compare *dim0* with a HW labelling against SMOTE and, for research purpose, also against state-of-the-art models with the identity labelling. At last, will show that *dim0* can also be used effectively on unprofiled attacks.

A detailed overview of the datasets and the ML models used for the experiments can be found in Appendix A. The experiments on the FPGA-based AES_HD [29] and ASIC-based DPAContestv4.2 [3] datasets showcase how our *dim0* model surpassed the same model with *dim1* on profiled and unprofiled attacks. To compete against the state-of-the-art, we target the ASIC-based ASCAD dataset and its variants [2], as multiple publications compared the HW performance on ASCAD.

4.1 Profiling Attacks and the Hamming Weight Labelling

In this section, experiments on the ASCAD datasets were run 10 times and all results reported with a 95% confidence interval.

AES_HD and DPAContestv4.2 Datasets. First, we show an attack of the AES_HD dataset ($N_p = 47'500, N_a = 2500$) with the HW leakage function. We used the CNNaeshd and the CNN_exp models. Figure 4a shows that *dim0* models worked much better in comparison with *dim1*, where the attacks are practically unfeasible. Additionally, we attack the DPAContestv4.2 ($N_p = 4500, N_a = 500$) dataset using the MLP_simple architecture. Figure 4b shows that the attack is easier for *dim0* than with *dim1*, as it converged within one epoch.

ASCAD_Fixed with MLP_Best. We attack the ASCAD_fixed dataset with the MLP_best architecture, as suggested in the work by Benadjila et al. [2]. We kept the proposed experiment setup, except for the softmax activation. As

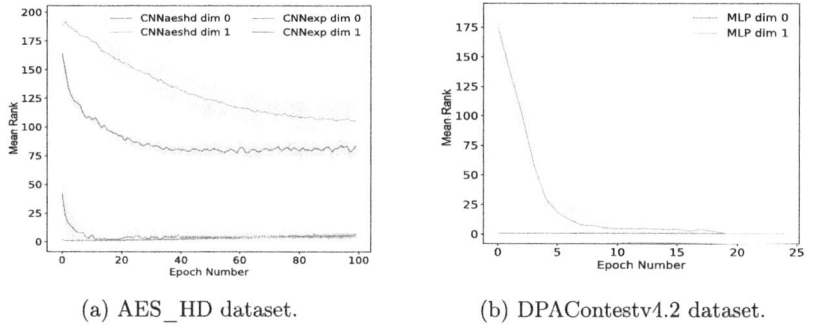

(a) AES_HD dataset.   (b) DPAContestv4.2 dataset.

Fig. 4. Attacking various HW-labelled datasets 50 times, comparing *dim0* and *dim1*.

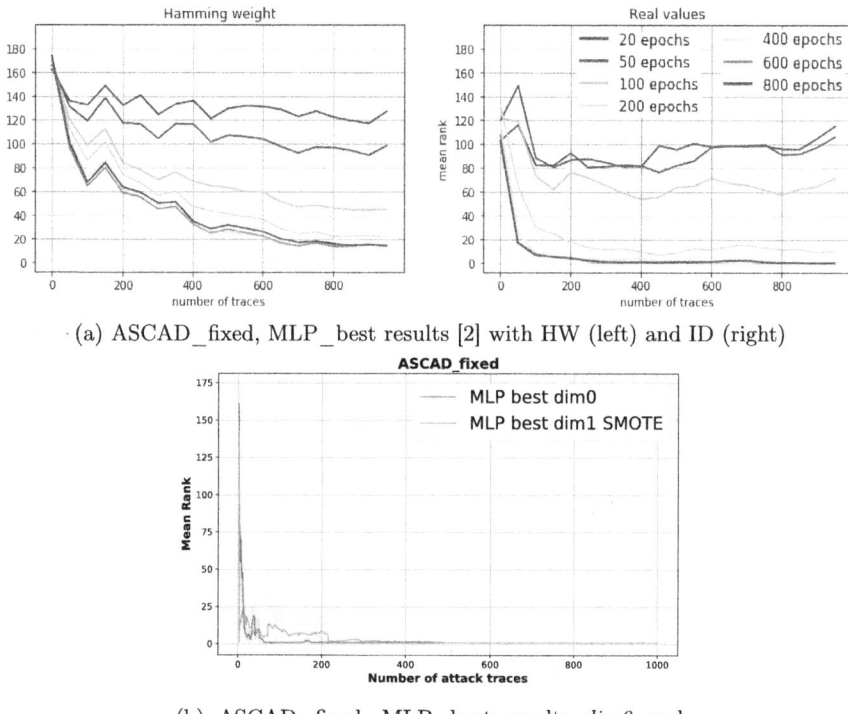

(a) ASCAD_fixed, MLP_best results [2] with HW (left) and ID (right)

(b) ASCAD_fixed, MLP_best results *dim0* and *dim1* with SMOTE with HW labelling

Fig. 5. Attacking ASCAD_fixed with the MLP_best model and $N_b = 100$.

such, 200 epochs will be used. Figure 5a shows the results reported in the original paper for HW labeling (left) and ID (right). The plot reports how the number of epochs affects the attack using the MLP_best architecture. In Fig. 5b, we report the performance of the MLP_best *dim0* vs the MLP_best *dim1* with SMOTE using the HW leakage model. In this scenario, the *dim0* approach with a HW labelling beats all its concurrents. We note that by flipping the dimension, the model is now able to converge within 200 traces, while the original attack (on the left hand-side of Fig. 5a) could not converge after 1000 traces. For SMOTE, more than 450 traces are required. And for the conventional technique, *dim1* with ID, at least 300.

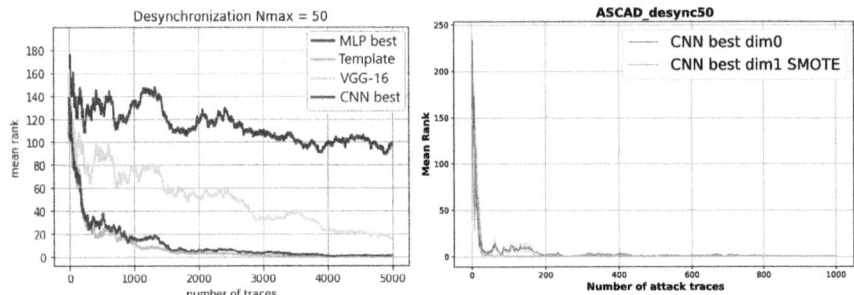

(a) ASCAD_desync50 results with ID labelling [30]

(b) ASCAD_desync50, CNN_best results with HW labelling

Fig. 6. Attacking ASCAD_desync50 with the CNN_best model and $N_b = 200$.

ASCAD_desync50 with CNN_Best. CNN_best is a ML model proposed in the work by Benadjila et al. [2] to attack the ASCAD_desync50 dataset. Figure 6a shows the best configurations' results on the ASCAD_desync50 dataset with the ID labeling on three ML models and a classical Template attack. In Fig. 6b, we observe that CNN_best *dim0* is better than any of the ASCAD_desync50 configurations since it needs less than 800 traces to reach $GE = 1$, against more than 4000 traces for *dim1*. However, *dim0* seems slightly less powerful than *dim1* with SMOTE. For the latter configuration, a successful attack is reached by using approximately 100 traces.

ASCAD_desync100 with CNN_Best. Fig. 7a illustrates the best configurations' results on the ASCAD_desync100 dataset using ID labeling for three ML models and one classical template attack. This plot was taken from the study by Benadjila et al. [2]. Figure 7b demonstrates that CNN_best *dim0* outperforms other ASCAD_desync100 configurations, requiring fewer than 550 traces to achieve $GE = 1$. In contrast, none of the configurations persented in the Benadjila et al. [2] is successful. Nonetheless, *dim0* is still marginally less effective than *dim1* with SMOTE—which required only a few traces (less than 30) to reach a key mean rank of 1.

In the following attacks, we report results from the work by Wouters et al. [39] for the CNN_zaid and No_conv architectures. We did not change the proposed parameters except the last layer (from *dim1* to *dim0*). We used the horizontal

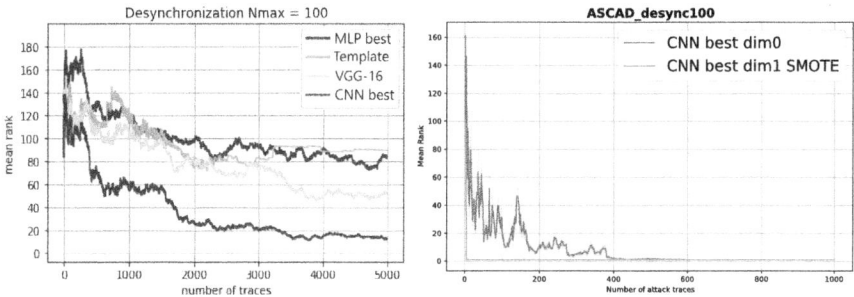

(a) ASCAD_desync100, results with ID labelling [2]

(b) ASCAD_desync100, CNN_best on $dim0$ and $dim1$ with SMOTE, HW labelling

Fig. 7. Attacking ASCAD_desync100 with the CNN_best model and $N_b = 200$.

standardization during perprocessing, as it offers the best results for $dim0$ and $dim1$ with SMOTE.

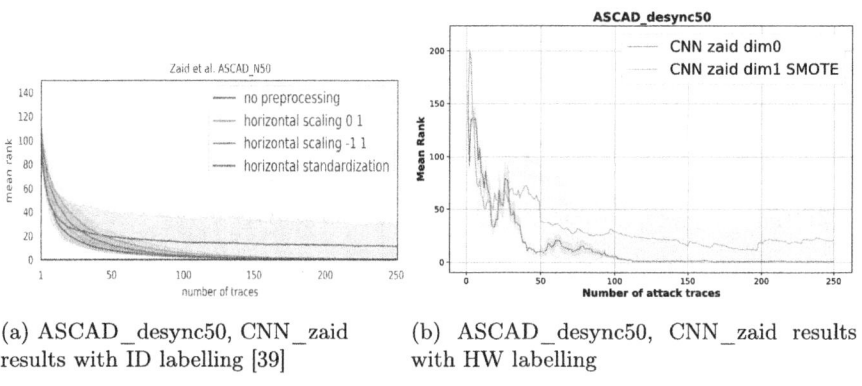

(a) ASCAD_desync50, CNN_zaid results with ID labelling [39]

(b) ASCAD_desync50, CNN_zaid results with HW labelling

Fig. 8. Attacking ASCAD_desync50 with the CNN_zaid model and $N_b = 50$.

ASCAD_desync50 with CNN_Zaid. In Fig. 8 we plot the results for the ASCAD_desync50 using the CNN_zaid architecture—comparing the original results of the ID leakage model with our runs in HW labelling. Figure 8b shows that $dim0$ outperforms $dim1$ with the SMOTE since it reached the $GE = 1$ with fewer than 175 traces. The HW-$dim0$ result is not that far from with the ID-$dim1$ result of the original paper, where approximately 140 traces are needed to reach a successful attack.

ASCAD_desync50 with No_Conv. Fig. 9 compares the state-of-the-art results with ID labelling against the HW labelling and $dim0$ or $dim1$ with SMOTE. The No_conv architecture is used to target the ASCAD_desync50

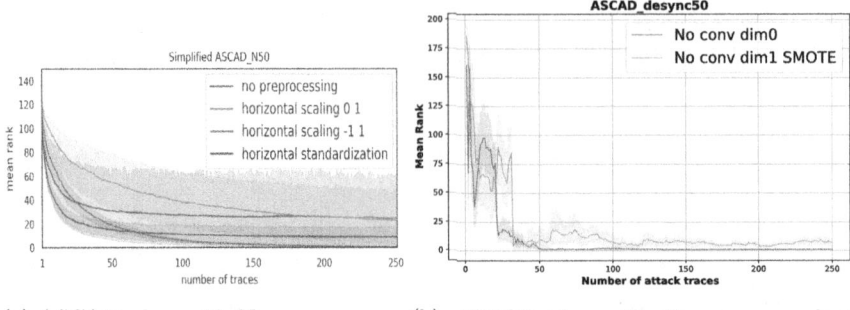

(a) ASCAD_desync50, No_conv results with ID labelling [39]

(b) ASCAD_desync50, No_conv on *dim0* and *dim1* with SMOTE, HW labelling

Fig. 9. Attacking ASCAD_desync50 with the No_conv model and $N_b = 50$.

dataset. Here again, the *dim0* technique beats all its opponents, requiring approximately 110 traces for a successful attack, while in the case of SMOTE, the performance fluctuates and does not reach a $GE = 1$. Moreover, the HW-*dim0* attack is better than any ID labeling attack by a 70 trace margin.

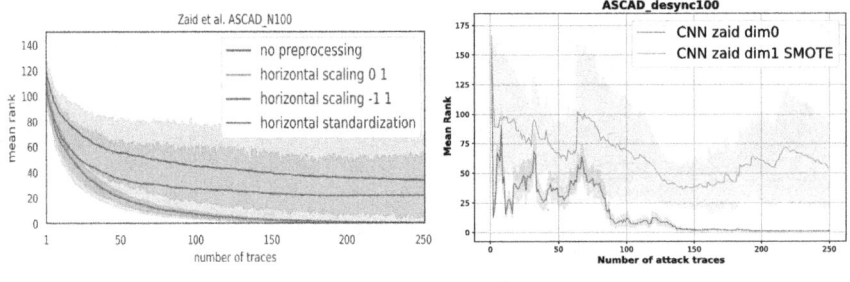

(a) ASCAD_desync100, CNN_zaid results with ID labelling [39]

(b) ASCAD_desync100, CNN_zaid on *dim0* and *dim1* with SMOTE, HW labelling

Fig. 10. Attacking ASCAD_desync100 with the CNN_zaid model, $N_b = 50$.

ASCAD_desync100 with CNN_Zaid. Fig 10 compares the performance of the CNN_zaid architecture on the ASCAD_desync100 dataset and our target scenarios. We see that the HW-*dim0* results are close to the Identity labelling results with *dim1*, while *dim0* definitely beats the HW-*dim1* with SMOTE which did not converge.

ASCAD_desync100 with No_Conv. Fig. 11 shows that for the No_conv models against the ASCAD_desync100, the ID labelling seems to perform better than any of the HW labelling attacks. We observe that in the original paper,

$GE = 1$ is reached after approximately 170 traces, while in Fig. 11b, none of the methods could achieve $GE = 1$ with the 250 traces.

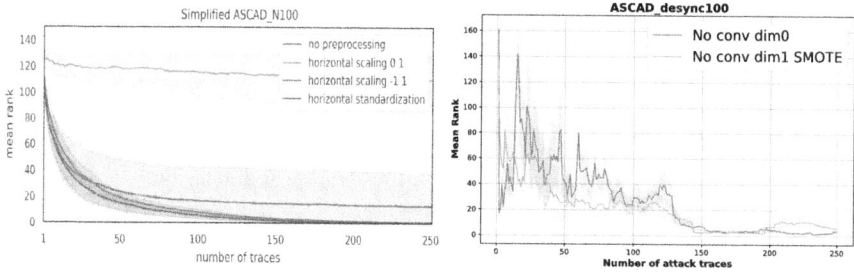

(a) ASCAD_desync100, No_conv results with ID labelling [39]

(b) ASCAD_desync100, No_conv on *dim0* and *dim1* with SMOTE, HW labelling

Fig. 11. Attacking ASCAD_desync100 with the No_conv model and $N_b = 50$.

4.2 Conclusion

An interesting pattern is emerging from the experiments, regarding *dim0*'s apparent performance's instability while the number of attack traces increases. This is a consequence of *dim0*'s nature: it seems to work best when the number of attack traces in a batch is close to a multiple of the training batch size. In fact the model was trained with a static batch size, while the plots shown in this section iteratively increase the number of attack traces fed to the model. Most notably, on Fig. 6b, we said that the model is successful after 800 traces (4 batches of 200 traces). However, after one batch, the model already achieved a key rank close to zero. The same at 600 traces (3 batches). Evaluating the traces for a non-batch size multiple (or close to it) seems to be the reason for the discrepancy between 600 and 800 traces as well.

Overall, we obtained good performance for profiling attacks by using *dim0* with HW labeling compared to the traditional ID leakage model in some cases. Moreover, we observed that the lightweight *dim0* method is more stable than the state-of-the-art computationaly expensive SMOTE solution for the imbalacing problems, especially for the desynchronized datasets, where we have smaller deviations from the mean over ten runs. The new method could however benefit from further specific model optimizations and is quite sensitive to the batch size. For a complete performance analysis overview, we refer the reader to Appendix B.

4.3 Unprofiled Attacks

We could successfully launch an unprofiled attack on the AES_HD dataset using the Hamming Distance labelling, 44'000 traces for training and 6000 for validation (used to compute the model sensitivity), using the CNNexp model with a classic regularization of 0.0008 applied on the Fully-Connected layer (weights & bias), and $N_b = 100$. As detailed in Sect. 2.7, we reuse Timon's strategy [38] exactly with *dim1* and only flip the softmax dimension for *dim0*. We launched ten attacks using *dim0* and *dim1* respectively. The results are shown in Table 1. The total duration of each attack was approximately 12 h for the 15 epochs using an i7-13700k Intel processor and no GPU.

Table 1. Unprofiled performance of the CNNexp model on the AES_HD dataset using a HD labelling with 15 epochs and over 10 attacks for each dimension.

Attack Number	1	2	3	4	5	6	7	8	9	10
dim0 Key Rank	1		1	2	10	6	2	1	1	14	1
dim1 Key Rank	126	2	80	3	18	168	1	66	5	58

5 Conclusion and Future Work

This paper persents a new technique for performing DL-based SCA, embedded in a new open-source toolbox for performing Side-Channel Attacks. This technique consists of transposing the logits matrix before applying the softmax function. It reduces the effect of imbalanced datasets, increases the convergence speed of some models (especially for adaptive optimizers) in the profiling phase, and can strongly improve the performance of unprofiled attacks as well. We compare our results with the state-of-the-art models used in ID labelling, and concluded that the *dim0* with the HW leakage model has the potential to match and beat the state-of-the-art in most scenarios. Additional model tuning seems to be necessary for the *dim0* to thrive and surpass the current results. While this publication focused on applying *dim0* on imbalanced datasets scenarios, Proposition 1 also applies to the Identity Labelling (ID) case. Preliminary experiments on our custom dataset showcased a faster convergence and a lowering of needed attack traces when using the ID labelling and *dim0*.

For future work, it would be interesting to see if an attack is possible with only a single attack trace using *dim0*. As a *dim0* model can only work with multiple traces (with one trace, the model outputs a 100% probability for each class), one possible avenue would be to compare the attack trace with some profiling traces and only consider the output probability of the attack trace.

Acknowledgments. This research was co-funded by the European Union's Chips Joint Undertaking (JU) under grant agreement No. 10111228.

A Experimental Setup

A.1 Datasets

AES_NRF is a home-made dataset taken from a software implementation of AES-128 without protection. Sbox is implemented as a look-up table. The target hardware was an nRF52840-DK board. We used a Chipwhisperer to capture the power consumption. The dataset contains 47'500 profiling traces with random keys and random plaintexts, as well as 2500 attack traces of random plaintexts and a constant key. We standardized the profiling and attack traces such that they have 0 mean and unit variance.

DPA Contest V4.2 [3] is an AES software implementation with a first-order masking technique [26].[4] Since the mask value is publicly known, we removed the masking and attack the key directly. We will use 4500 profiling traces and 500 attack traces. Each trace is 4000 samples long. We target the first S-Box output on the first byte.

AES_HD is a hardware implementation of AES with no protection introduced by Stjepan Picek et al. [29].[5] We used only a subset of 50'000 traces among the 100'000 ones available, with 1250 samples each. We target the last S-Box of the AES on byte 0. We either used the Hamming Weight labelling function on the last S-Box or the Hamming Distance labelling function, which yields the Hamming Weight value of the input of the last S-Box XOR its output.

ASCAD_Fixed is a second-order masked implementation of the AES128, introduced by Benadjila et al. [2]. The measurements collected repersent the power consumption of the first AES encryption round. Each measurement contains 700 samples, which denotes the usage of the third key byte (first masked byte) in the Sbox function. This dataset contains 50'000 traces for profiling and 10'000 for the attacking phase. All of them were created using the same key.

ASCAD_Desync50, ASCAD_desync100 are the traces from the **ASCAD_fixed**, with the same dimensionality (same number of traces, number of samples, and the same dataset split), but randomly desynchronized by artificially applying jittering on a range of 50 and 100 samples, respectively. Hence, those datasets introduced by Benadjila et al. [2] denote traces created by including two side-channel counter-measurements (masking and jitter).

ASCAD_Variable is the same second-order masked implementation of the AES128 as **ASCAD_fixed**. However, the difference between those two datasets consists of having a variable key for the profiling traces and a fixed key for the attacking ones—a scenario that is more plausible in real life. We have 200'000 traces for profiling and 100'000 for attacking. The traces contain 1400 samples

---

[4] https://cloud.telecom-paris.fr/s/JM2iaRZfwrNKtSp.
[5] https://github.com/AESHD/AES_HD_Dataset.

taken during the third Sbox transformation from the first encryption round. In our study, we will attack the third key byte (which is also masked).

A.2 Meta-Architectures

Our studies used different meta-architectures from state-of-the-art DL models, which performed well in pervious studies during the SCA. We use the same perprocessing techniques persented in their papers and sometimes hypertune some parameters (mainly the batch size). For all the models we use the *Negative-Log Likelihood (NLL)* loss function. The models are:

MLP_Simple. This model was used in the different studies [20,38] and consists only of 3 layers. The hyperparameters reported in the pervious works [20,38] were `batch_size` = 1000, `epochs` = 100, `optimizer` = Adam, and `learning_rate` = 10^{-3}. We mainly used them, with some exceptions persented in the experiments separately.

CNN_Exp. This model is taken from the work by Timon et al. [38] with the following default parameters:`batch_size` = 1000, `epochs` = 100, `optimizer` = Adam, and `learning_rate` = 10^{-3}. We'll mention any parameter change explicitly.

MLP_Best. This architecture was first proposed by Benadjila et al. [2] and performed well against the ASCAD_fixed dataset. We reutilized the parameter values proposed in their study: `batch_size` = 100, `epochs` = 200, `optimizer` = RMSprop, and `learning_rate` = 10^{-5}. The model was used in attacks against ASCAD_fixed, maintaining the same profiling-attacking setup with 50,000 traces for profiling and 10,000 traces for the attacking phase.

CNN_Best. This architecture was also introduced by Benadjila et al. [2] as an improvement over MLP_best for the ASCAD desynchronized datasets. We reused the parameter values from their paper: `batch_size` = 200, `epochs` = 100, `optimizer` = RMSprop, and `learning_rate` = 10^{-5}. This model was tested against ASCAD_desync50 and ASCAD_desync100, using the same profiling-attacking setup with 50,000 traces for profiling and 10,000 traces for the attacking phase.

CNN_Zaid. This architecture, initially proposed by Zaid et al. [42], performed well against the ASCAD datasets. We used the parameter values proposed by Wouters et al. [39], based on the paper and code, as they stated these parameters were more stable: `batch_size` = 50, `epochs` = 50, `optimizer` = Adam, and `learning_rate` = 0.005. Additionally, we employed the *One Cycle Policy* learning rate strategy [32]. The models `cnn_zaid50` and `cnn_zaid100` were used to attack ASCAD_desync50 and ASCAD_desync100, respectively, with the same profiling-attacking setup, and we compared our results with those persented by Wouters et al. [39].

No_conv. This architecture was proposed by Wouters et al. [39] as an improvement to the models by Zaid et al. [42]. We used the same parameter values proposed by Wouters et al. [39]: `batch_size` = 50, `epochs` = 50, `optimizer` = `Adam`, and `learning_rate` = 0.005. Since these models are derived from `cnn_zaid`, we also utilized the *One Cycle Policy* learning rate strategy [32]. The models `no_conv50` and `no_conv100` were used to attack ASCAD_desync50 and ASCAD_desync100, respectively, with the same profiling-attacking setup.

CNNaeshd. This model was proposed in the work by Zaid et al. [42] to attack the AES_HD dataset. We use in our attacks the proposed parameters: `batch_size` = 256, `epochs` = 20, `optimizer` = `Adam`, and `learning_rate` = 10^{-3}.

A.3 Preprocessing

On each of the attack mentioned in this paper, we did a standardization on the profiling and attack traces such that they have 0 mean and unit variance.

A.4 Evaluation Metric

In side-channel attacks, the effectiveness of the attack is evaluated using the average rank of the correct key candidate among all possible keys after analyzing a certain number of traces (attack traces). This metric is called the Guessing Entropy (GE). Lower GE values imply more effective attacks, with GE = 1 indicating the correct key is consistently the highest ranked. In our experiments, we measure the mean average key to compare different attacks, since the same metric is used in pervious studies.

B Dimension 0 Performance Overview

Table 2 gives a succinct overview of the *dim0* performance accros all the tested scenarios.

Table 2. Comparison of performance between model configurations from the literature and from this work, targeting different ASCAD [2] datasets, namely ASCAD_fixed ("fixed"), ASCAD_desync50 ("desync50"), ASCAD_desync100 ("desync100") and , ASCAD_variable ("variable"). To have a consistent comparison of several results that fits into a table, we report two metrics (whenever available): the average guessing entropy (GE) value achieved by the model when the number of attack traces (NT) is 200 ("GE at NT = 200") and the number of traces required to achieve a GE of 1 ("NT for GE = 1"). In this manner, we see both how many traces a model needs to perform optimally and how it perform when a limited number of traces is available. The * values are approximated based on the figures, since in some works, percise numerical values are not reported.

Paper	Configuration	fixed		desync50		desync100		variable	
		GE at NT=200	NT for GE=1	GE at NT=200	NT for GE=1	GE at NT=200	NT for GE=1	GE at NT=200	NT for GE=1
[2]	MLP_best + ID	1	250*	-	-	-	-	-	-
	MLP_best + HW	35*	>1000	-	-	-	-	-	-
	CNN_best + ID	-	-	60*	4000	95*	>5000	-	-
[8]	CNN_best + HW	-	-	-	-	-	-	19*	>1000
[39]	CNN_zaid + ID	-	-	1	140*	1	200*	-	-
	No_conv + ID	-	-	1	180*	1	170*	-	-
Our study, dim0	MLP_best + HW	1	195	-	-	-	-	-	-
	CNN_best + HW	-	-	5	780	10	570	240	>12'000
	CNN_zaid + HW	-	-	1	175	1	185	-	-
	No_conv + HW	-	-	1	110	5	>250	-	-
Our study, SMOTE	MLP_best + HW	10	450	-	-	-	-	-	-
	CNN_best + HW	-	-	1	100	1	26	200	12'000
	CNN_zaid + HW	-	-	25	>250	60	>250	-	-
	No_conv + HW	-	-	5	>250	7	>250	-	-

References

1. Azouaoui, M., Durvaux, F., Poussier, R., Standaert, F.-X., Papagiannopoulos, K., Verneuil, V.: On the worst-case side-channel security of ECC point randomization in embedded devices. In: Bhargavan, K., Oswald, E., Prabhakaran, M. (eds.) INDOCRYPT 2020. LNCS, vol. 12578, pp. 205–227. Springer, Cham (2020). https://doi.org/10.1007/978-3-030-65277-7_9
2. Benadjila, R., Prouff, E., Strullu, R., Cagli, E., Dumas, C.: Deep learning for side-channel analysis and introduction to ASCAD database. J. Crypt. Eng. **10**(2), 163–188 (2019). https://doi.org/10.1007/s13389-019-00220-8, https://doi.org/10.1007/s13389-019-00220-8
3. Bhasin, S., Bruneau, N., Danger, J.-L., Guilley, S., Najm, Z.: Analysis and improvements of the DPA contest V4 implementation. In: Chakraborty, R.S., Matyas, V., Schaumont, P. (eds.) SPACE 2014. LNCS, vol. 8804, pp. 201–218. Springer, Cham (2014). https://doi.org/10.1007/978-3-319-12060-7_14
4. Brier, E., Clavier, C., Olivier, F.: Correlation power analysis with a leakage model. In: International Workshop on Cryptographic Hardware and Embedded Systems, pp. 16–29. Springer (2004)

5. Chari, S., Rao, J.R., Rohatgi, P.: Template attacks. In: Cryptographic Hardware and Embedded Systems-CHES 2002: 4th International Workshop Redwood Shores, CA, USA, August 13–15, 2002 Revised Papers 4, pp. 13–28. Springer (2003)
6. Chawla, N.V., Bowyer, K.W., Hall, L.O., Kegelmeyer, W.P.: SMOTE: synthetic minority over-sampling technique. J. Artif. Intell .Res. **16**, 321–357 (2002)
7. Duchi, J., Hazan, E., Singer, Y.: Adaptive subgradient methods for online learning and stochastic optimization. J. Mach. Learn. Res. **12**(7) (2011)
8. Egger, M., Schamberger, T., Tebelmann, L., Lippert, F., Sigl, G.: A second look at the ASCAD databases. In: International Workshop on Constructive Side-Channel Analysis and Secure Design, pp. 75–99. Springer (2022)
9. Fan, X., Tong, J., Li, Y., Duan, X., Ren, Y.: Power analysis attack based on hamming weight model without brute force cracking. Secur. Commun. Netw. **2022**, 1–11 (2022). https://doi.org/10.1155/2022/7375097, https://doi.org/10.1155/2022/7375097
10. FIPS, P.: 197: Federal information processing standards publication 197. Announcing the Advanced Encryption Standard (AES) (2001)
11. Hettwer, B., Gehrer, S., Güneysu, T.: Profiled power analysis attacks using convolutional neural networks with domain knowledge. In: International Conference on Selected Areas in Cryptography, pp. 479–498. Springer (2018)
12. Hettwer, B., Gehrer, S., Güneysu, T.: Applications of machine learning techniques in side-channel attacks: a survey. J. Cryptograph. Eng. **10**(2), 135–162 (2019). https://doi.org/10.1007/s13389-019-00212-8, https://doi.org/10.1007/s13389-019-00212-8
13. Hospodar, G., Gierlichs, B., Mulder, E., Verbauwhede, I., Vandewalle, J.: Machine learning in side-channel analysis: a first study. J. Cryptogr. Eng. **1**, 293–302 (2011). https://doi.org/10.1007/s13389-011-0023-x
14. Kerkhof, M., Wu, L., Perin, G., Picek, S.: Focus is key to success: a focal loss function for deep learning-based side-channel analysis. In: International Workshop on Constructive Side-Channel Analysis and Secure Design, pp. 29–48. Springer (2022)
15. Kim, J., Picek, S., Heuser, A., Bhasin, S., Hanjalic, A.: Make some noise. unleashing the power of convolutional neural networks for profiled side-channel analysis. IACR Trans. Cryptogr. Hardw. Embed. Syst. **2019**(3), 148–179 (2019). https://doi.org/10.13154/tches.v2019.i3.148-179, https://tches.iacr.org/index.php/TCHES/article/view/8292
16. Kingma, D.P., Ba, J.: Adam: A Method for Stochastic Optimization (2014)
17. Klambauer, G., Unterthiner, T., Mayr, A., Hochreiter, S.: Self-normalizing neural networks. In: Advances in Neural Information Processing Systems 30 (NIPS 2017) (2017)
18. Kocher, P.C.: Timing attacks on implementations of Diffie-Hellman, RSA, DSS, and other systems. In: Advances in Cryptology - CRYPTO '96, 16th Annual International Cryptology Conference, Santa Barbara, California, USA, August 18-22, 1996, Proceedings. Lecture Notes in Computer Science, vol. 1109, pp. 104–113. Springer (1996). https://doi.org/10.1007/3-540-68697-5_9
19. Kocher, P.C., Jaffe, J., Jun, B.: Differential power analysis. In: Advances in Cryptology - CRYPTO '99, 19th Annual International Cryptology Conference, Santa Barbara, California, USA, August 15-19, 1999, Proceedings. Lecture Notes in Computer Science, vol. 1666, pp. 388–397. Springer (1999). https://doi.org/10.1007/3-540-48405-1_25

20. Kuroda, K., Fukuda, Y., Yoshida, K., Fujino, T.: Practical aspects on non-profiled deep-learning side-channel attacks against AES software implementation with two types of masking countermeasures including RSM. In: Proceedings of the 5th Workshop on Attacks and Solutions in Hardware Security, pp. 29–40. ASHES '21, Association for Computing Machinery, New York, NY, USA (2021). https://doi.org/10.1145/3474376.3487285, https://doi.org/10.1145/3474376.3487285
21. Maghrebi, H., Portigliatti, T., Prouff, E.: Breaking cryptographic implementations using deep learning techniques. In: Security, Privacy, and Applied Cryptography Engineering, pp. 3–26. Springer International Publishing (2016). https://doi.org/10.1007/978-3-319-49445-6_1, https://doi.org/10.1007/978-3-319-49445-6_1
22. Mangard, S., Oswald, E., Standaert, F.X.: One for all - all for one: unifying standard DPA attacks. Cryptology ePrint Archive, Paper 2009/449 (2009). https://eprint.iacr.org/2009/449, https://eprint.iacr.org/2009/449
23. Masure, L., Dumas, C., Prouff, E.: Gradient visualization for general characterization in profiling attacks. In: Constructive Side-Channel Analysis and Secure Design, pp. 145–167. Springer International Publishing (2019). https://doi.org/10.1007/978-3-030-16350-19, https://doi.org/10.1007/978-3-030-16350-1_9
24. Masure, L., Dumas, C., Prouff, E.: A comperhensive study of deep learning for side-channel analysis. Cryptology ePrint Archive, Report 2019/439 (2019), https://ia.cr/2019/439
25. Nair, V., Hinton, G.E.: Rectified linear units improve restricted Boltzmann machines. In: Proceedings of the 27th International Conference on Machine Learning (ICML-10), pp. 807–814 (2010)
26. Nassar, M., Souissi, Y., Guilley, S., Danger, J.: RSM: A small and fast countermeasure for AES, secure against 1st and 2nd-order zero-offset SCAs. In: Rosenstiel, W., Thiele, L. (eds.) 2012 Design, Automation & Test in Europe Conference & Exhibition, DATE 2012, Dresden, Germany, March 12-16, 2012, pp. 1173–1178. IEEE (2012). https://doi.org/10.1109/DATE.2012.6176671, https://doi.org/10.1109/DATE.2012.6176671
27. Nesterov, Y.E.: A method of solving a convex programming problem with convergence rate o\bigl(k^2\bigr). In: Doklady Akademii Nauk, vol. 269, pp. 543–547. Russian Academy of Sciences (1983)
28. Perin, G., Wu, L., Picek, S.: The need for speed: a fast guessing entropy calculation for deep learning-based SCA. Cryptology ePrint Archive, Report 2021/1592 (2021). https://ia.cr/2021/1592
29. Picek, S., Heuser, A., Jovic, A., Bhasin, S., Regazzoni, F.: The curse of class imbalance and conflicting metrics with machine learning for side-channel evaluations. IACR Trans. Crypto. Hardw. Emb. Syst. **2019**(1), 1–29 (2019). https://doi.org/10.13154/tches.v2019.i1.209-237, https://hal.inria.fr/hal-01935318
30. Prouff, E., Strullu, R., Benadjila, R., Cagli, E., Dumas, C.: Study of deep learning techniques for side-channel analysis and introduction to ASCAD database. Cryptology ePrint Archive, Paper 2018/053 (2018). https://doi.org/10.1007/s13389-019-00220-8, https://eprint.iacr.org/2018/053
31. Rijsdijk, J., Wu, L., Perin, G., Picek, S.: Reinforcement learning for hyperparameter tuning in deep learning-based side-channel analysis. IACR Trans. Cryptogr. Hardw. Emb. Syst., 677–707 (2021)
32. Smith, L.N.: Cyclical learning rates for training neural networks. In: 2017 IEEE Winter Conference on Applications of Computer Vision (WACV), pp. 464–472. IEEE (2017)
33. Sobol, I.M.: Global sensitivity indices for nonlinear mathematical models and their Monte Carlo estimates. Math. Comput. Simul. **55**(1–3), 271–280 (2001)

34. Socha, P., Miškovský, V., Novotný, M.: A comperhensive survey on the non-invasive passive side-channel analysis. Sensors **22**(21), 8096 (2022). https://doi.org/10.3390/s22218096, https://www.mdpi.com/1424-8220/22/21/8096, number: 21 Publisher: Multidisciplinary Digital Publishing Institute
35. Standaert, F.X.: How (not) to use Welch's T-test in side-channel security evaluations. In: Smart Card Research and Advanced Applications: 17th International Conference, CARDIS 2018, Montpellier, France, November 12–14, 2018, Revised Selected Papers 17. pp. 65–79. Springer (2019)
36. Standaert, F.X., Malkin, T.G., Yung, M.: A unified framework for the analysis of side-channel key recovery attacks (extended version). Cryptology ePrint Archive, Paper 2006/139 (2006). https://eprint.iacr.org/2006/139
37. Standaert, F.-X., Malkin, T.G., Yung, M.: A unified framework for the analysis of side-channel key recovery attacks. In: Joux, A. (ed.) EUROCRYPT 2009. LNCS, vol. 5479, pp. 443–461. Springer, Heidelberg (2009). https://doi.org/10.1007/978-3-642-01001-9_26
38. Timon, B.: Non-profiled deep learning-based side-channel attacks with sensitivity analysis. IACR Trans. Crypt. Hardw. Emb. Syst. **2019**(2), 107–131 (2019). https://doi.org/10.13154/tches.v2019.i2.107-131, https://tches.iacr.org/index.php/TCHES/article/view/7387
39. Wouters, L., Arribas, V., Gierlichs, B., Preneel, B.: Revisiting a methodology for efficient CNN architectures in profiling attacks. IACR Trans. Cryptogr. Hardw. Emb. Syst., 147–168 (2020)
40. Wu, L., Perin, G., Picek, S.: I Choose you: automated hyperparameter tuning for deep learning-based side-channel analysis. Cryptology ePrint Archive, Report 2020/1293 (2020), https://ia.cr/2020/1293
41. Wu, L., Picek, S.: Remove some noise: on per-processing of side-channel measurements with autoencoders. IACR Trans. Cryptogr. Hardw. Embed. Syst., 389–415 (2020)
42. Zaid, G., Bossuet, L., Habrard, A., Venelli, A.: Methodology for efficient CNN architectures in profiling attacks (2019). https://doi.org/10.13154/tches.v2020.i1.1-36, https://tches.iacr.org/index.php/TCHES/article/view/8391
43. Zeiler, M.D.: ADADELTA: An adaptive learning rate method (2012)

Avenger Ensemble: Genetic Algorithm-Driven Ensemble Selection for Deep Learning-Based Side-Channel Analysis

Zhao Minghui[1] and Trevor Yap[1,2,3](✉)

[1] School of Physical and Mathematical Sciences, Nanyang Technological University, Singapore, Singapore
minghui002@e.ntu.edu.sg, trevor.yap@ntu.edu.sg
[2] Temasek Laboratories, Nanyang Technological University, Singapore, Singapore
[3] National Integrated Centre of Evaluation, Nanyang Technological University, Singapore, Singapore

Abstract. Side-Channel Analysis (SCA) exploits physical vulnerabilities in systems to reveal secret keys. With the rise of Internet-of-Things, evaluating SCA attacks has become crucial. Profiling attacks, enhanced by Deep Learning-based Side-Channel Analysis (DLSCA), have shown significant improvements over classical techniques. Recent works demonstrate that ensemble methods outperform single neural networks. However, almost every existing ensemble selection method in SCA only picks the top few best-performing neural networks for the ensemble, which we coined as Greedily-Selected Method (GSM). This method of selecting DNN may not be optimal. In this work, we propose a new genetic algorithm-driven ensemble selection algorithm called Evolutionary Avenger Initiative (EAI) to create effective ensembles for DLSCA. We investigate two fitness functions and evaluate EAI across four datasets, including AES and ASCON implementations. We show that EAI outperforms GSM, recovering secrets with the least number of traces. Notably, EAI successfully recovers secret keys for ASCON datasets where GSM fails, demonstrating its effectiveness.

Keywords: Side-channel analysis · Deep learning · Ensemble learning · Genetic algorithm

1 Introduction

Side-channel analysis (SCA) exploits the physical vulnerabilities of a system like power consumption [8] and electromagnetic emanation [2] to reveal the secret key. Evaluating such attacks has become crucial, especially with the rise in the usage of Internet-of-Things (IoTs) in recent years [12]. One such side-channel attack is known as the profiling attack. In the profiling attack model, it is assumed that the attacker has access to a clone device that closely resembles the target device. Deep Learning-based Side-Channel Analysis (DLSCA) has been intensively explored in recent years [1,13,14,22], which demonstrated that Deep Neural Networks (DNNs) can significantly outperform classical SCA techniques like template attacks [13]. Furthermore, DLSCA has garnered significant interest because of its capability to recover the secret key of the protected implementations without needing to resynchronize traces.

Recent studies have demonstrated that ensembling multiple DNNs yields substantial performance gains compared to a single top-performing neural network [17,18,23]. DNNs of varying hyperparameters can extract different information from identical traces, yielding improved performance when combined together as an ensemble. Most of the works in DLSCA create an ensemble by greedily selecting the top few best-performing DNNs [17–19], herein referred to as the Greedily-Selected Method (GSM). However, the GSM may not be optimal as other combinations of DNNs could attain better results. Therefore, a natural question arises:

Can we develop a methodology to efficiently select neural networks for ensembles that outperform the traditional GSM?

To address this question, we focus on ensemble selection, which is defined as the process of selecting pre-trained DNNs to create an effective ensemble.

Our Contributions. Our contributions are stated as follows:

1. In this work, we proposed a new genetic algorithm-driven ensemble selection algorithm called Evolutionary Avenger Initiative (EAI) to generate a best-performing ensemble. To the best of our knowledge, this is the first work to investigate ensemble selection within the context of SCA. Furthermore, we investigate two fitness functions for EAI: ge_{+ntge} and validation loss.
2. We assess the efficiency of our methodology across four datasets, comprising three AES datasets (software and hardware implementations) of the widely recognized symmetric-key standard [5], and one ASCON dataset, NIST's lightweight cryptography standard winner, implemented in software [6]
3. By integrating EAI, we manage to recover the secret with the least number of traces across all datasets tested, outperforming traditional ensemble selection techniques, i.e., GSM. Furthermore, EAI with ge_{+ntge} has yielded significant performance gains across all tested settings and datasets. Notably, for the ASCON datasets (i.e., ASCON2 and ASCON4), EAI successfully recovered the secret key within 1000 attack traces, whereas the conventional GSM method failed to do so. This highlights the effectiveness of EAI.

We validate our approach on first-order masking traces, leaving higher-order masking for future work. The source code can be accessed at the following web link.[1]

---

[1] https://github.com/Sarahfbb/Avenger-Ensemble.

Paper Organization: The paper is organized as follows. We begin by reviewing some related works in Sect. 2. We then describe the background necessary for profiled SCA using an ensemble of DNN and a brief outline of Genetic Algorithm in Sect. 3. Next, Sect. 4 presents our proposed ensemble selection algorithm to generate the best-performing ensemble for profiling attacks. Section 5 discusses and analyzes our results on the four datasets tested. Finally, Sect. 6 concludes with some discussion and provides some future works.

2 Related Work

Ensemble within DLSCA. The introduction of ensemble methods in DLSCA is attributed to [17]. This pioneering work presented a methodology for computing the maximum log-likelihood of an ensemble for bagging and showcased its efficacy on AES-based datasets. However, they use GSM to build their ensemble, which may be suboptimal. Subsequently, [18] successfully apply GSM to ASCON implementations. Instead of considering GSM, the authors of [23] consider the "diversity" between the optimal DNNs and the non-optimal DNNs. Therefore, they proposed a loss function called Ensemble loss. The Ensemble loss helps to train a diverse ensemble to recover the secret. Nonetheless, the Ensemble loss has a drawback: it cannot scale for more than three classes. Consequently, its application is restricted, and it cannot be applied to block ciphers like AES (with 256 classes). The authors only tested it on an ECC dataset. Unlike [23], we do not take into account the training process but consider the same scenarios as [17]. Perin et al. [17] assume that a set of DNNs with randomly generated hyperparameters have already been trained. We highlight that the above methodologies considered are bagging [4]. In recent years, methods for stacking DNNs [11] and boosting DNNs [20] have been explored in SCA. For this work, we will focus on bagging ensembles. Furthermore, we exploit the capabilities of the genetic algorithm to find the optimal combination of pre-trained DNNs to produce the best-performing ensemble.

Ensemble Construction/Selection. The idea of constructing an ensemble is not new, as various works have considered [9,24]. Prior works use Bayesian optimization to generate well-performing ensembles. For instance, [9] propose using Bayesian optimization to tune the hyperparameters of one neural network while building the ensemble while [15] uses Bayesian optimization to form an ensemble through pre-trained DNNs. Other works like [24] model the ensemble construction as an optimization problem. The authors of [24] propose a method called Neural Ensemble Search to solve this optimization problem in order to attain a well-performing ensemble. For our work, we focus on ensemble selection. Recent advancements in ensemble selection have leveraged genetic algorithms to optimize ensemble composition. Notably, [25] proposed GASEN, which utilizes genetic algorithms to optimize weight coefficients that capture inter-DNN correlations. Specifically, GASEN selects DNNs for the ensemble based on their weight coefficients, including only those exceeding a predefined threshold. Ortiz et al.

propose EARN, a multi-objective evolutionary approach that generates efficient DNN ensembles [16] where they consider bagging, boosting, and stacking into the ensemble. Inspired by these, we develop a genetic algorithm for ensemble selection within SCA context.

3 Background

3.1 Profiling Attack Using Ensemble

One of the most common side-channel settings is known as the profiling attack. It assumes the worst-case scenario where the adversary has access to a clone device similar to the target device. The profiling attack is executed in two phases: profiling and attack phase.

In the profiling phase, the adversary either knows or can manipulate the key of the clone device. Then, distinguishers can be built from the profiling traces of a known set of random public variables (plaintext or ciphertext). During this phase, the adversary collects a set of traces t corresponding to known public variables to train distinguishers.

In the attack phase, the adversary performs the attack by collecting several attack traces from another set of known public variables of the target device. Typically, the traces are given to a single trained distinguisher for key recovery.

In [17] consider multiple distinguishers for key recovery. Formally, the traces are given to the trained distinguishers to obtain their output probability scores for each hypothetical sensitive value. These probabilities are combined together via:

$$\text{score}(k) = \sum_{j=1}^{N_{model}} \sum_{i=1}^{N_a} \log(Pr_j(Z = z_{i,k}|\mathbf{t}_i)) \quad (1)$$

where N_a represents the number of attack traces used, N_{model} is the number of models in the ensemble, $Pr_j(Z = z_{i,k}|\mathbf{t}_i)$ denotes the probability output by the jth distinguisher in the ensemble, and $z_{i,k}$ is the hypothetical sensitive value which depends on the key candidate k and the ith public variable that corresponds to the trace $\mathbf{t}_i$.

The $\text{score}(k)$ is computed for each key $k \in \mathcal{K}$, where $\mathcal{K}$ is the set of all possible key values. An attacker can sort the scores in descending order to create a guess vector $[G_0, \ldots, G_{|\mathcal{K}|}]$ where G_0 corresponds to the score for the most likely key candidate while the $G_{|\mathcal{K}|}$ represents the score for the least likely key candidate. Let the index of the guess vector be the rank of the key. Then, we define the Guessing Entropy (GE) as the rank of the correct key averaging over multiple experiments. In our analysis, we calculate this average over 100 separate experiments. When GE reaches zero, it indicates a completely successful attack - the correct key was consistently ranked first. To quantify attack performance, we denote the least number of traces for GE to reach zero as $NTGE$, which measures the minimum number of traces needed for key recovery.

3.2 Genetic Algorithm Framework

The genetic algorithm is a population-based optimization method inspired by natural evolution. Let $\mathcal{X}$ be the search space, and $f : \mathcal{X} \to \mathbb{R}$ be the fitness function that evaluates potential solutions. The population at generation t is denoted as
$$P^t = \{x_1^t, x_2^t, \ldots, x_n^t\},$$
where each individual chromosome $x_i^t \in \mathcal{X}$ represents a candidate solution, also referred to as a chromosome.

By evolving the population over successive generations, the genetic algorithm seeks to improve the overall fitness of the population, moving closer to the optimal solution. Each individual chromosome x_i^t is evaluated using the fitness function f, which assigns a numerical score to indicate its suitability or quality as a solution. The fitness scores guide the selection process, helping to determine which chromosomes will contribute genetic material to the next generation. The evolution process consists of the following phases:

1. **Initial Population:** The initial population P^0 is typically generated randomly across the search space $\mathcal{X}$.
2. **Elitism:** It preserves the best chromosomes from one generation to the next. The basic idea is to ensure that the fittest chromosomes are included in the next generation without any changes.
3. **Selection Method:** In genetic algorithms, several distinct selection methods exist for choosing chromosomes to generate subsequent generations. We shall recall the commonly used *Tournament Selection*. The Tournament Selection process in a genetic algorithm involves sampling multiple tournaments of size ℓ, where ℓ chromosomes are randomly chosen from the population. The fittest chromosome in each tournament is selected to generate new chromosomes for the next generation.
4. **Generic Operator:** Various genetic operators are proposed to generate new chromosomes; here, we will recall two such operators: Crossover and Mutation.
    - **Crossover:** The crossover operator is inspired by biological reproduction, where genetic material from two or more parent chromosomes is combined to produce one or more offspring. This process creates new chromosomes by exchanging segments between parents, thus propagating beneficial traits across generations. Crossover is typically applied with a high probability, denoted by Pr_{cross}, to enhance the convergence rate towards optimal solutions by exploiting existing genetic diversity.
    - **Mutation:** Mutation introduces variability and maintains diversity within a population. It involves making small, random changes to the values (or "genes") within an individual chromosome. These random tweaks help the algorithm explore new potential solutions, preventing premature convergence to suboptimal solutions. Mutation is typically applied with a low probability, denoted by $Pr_{\text{mut}} = 1 - Pr_{\text{cross}}$, to avoid drastic changes while enabling steady exploration of the solution space.

4 Evolutionary Avengers Initiative

In this section, we present our algorithm, called the Evolutionary Avengers Initiative (EAI). Each DNN can be viewed as a "superhero" endowed with distinct strengths. Drawing inspiration from the Avengers of the Marvel Studio, EAI aims to assemble a diverse group of "superheroes" called the Avenger Ensemble to recover the secret key.

The overview of the EAI Framework is described in Algorithm 1. EAI first initializes the population using a set of pre-trained DNNs from set $\mathcal{M}$. The population consists of N_{ens} ensembles, with each ensemble consisting of N_{model} DNNs. Subsequently, the steps described below are repeated over N_{gen} generations. Firstly, each ensemble within the population is evaluated using the fitness function (Line 4 of Algorithm 1). Next, the best-performing ensemble is then preserved for the next generation, a process known as elitism (Line 4 of Algorithm 1). Finally, generic operations such as crossover or mutation are applied to the whole previous population, generating a new population of ensembles (Line 5 of Algorithm 1). We shall describe each step in detail.

Algorithm 1. Evolutionary Avengers Initiative (EAI)

Input: $\mathcal{M}$: Set of all trained models, N_{ens}: Population size, N_{model}: Number of models per ensemble, Pr_{cross}: Crossover rate, Pr_{mut}: Mutation rate, ge_fitness_fn: Fitness function, N_{gen}: Number of generations

Output: E_{best}: Best-performing ensemble, s_{best}: Fitness value of E_{best}

1: Initialize Population of First Generation: $P = initialize\_pop(\mathcal{M}, N_{ens}, N_{model})$
2: $E_{best} = \emptyset, s_{best} = \infty$
3: **for** $t \leftarrow 1$ to N_{gen} **do**
4:     Evaluate population and apply Elitism:

$$P_{new}, S, E_{best}, s_{best} = Eval\_\&\_Elite(\texttt{ge\_fitness\_fn}, P, E_{best}, s_{best})$$

5:     Apply Crossover or Mutation:

$$P_{new} = GeneticOp(\mathcal{M}, P, P_{new}, S, Pr_{\text{cross}}, Pr_{\text{mut}})$$

6:     $P = P_{new}$
7: **end for**
8: **return** E_{best}, s_{best}

Initialize Population. Prior to the start of EAI, we train a set of DNNs, denoted as $\mathcal{M}$. We label each DNN with M_i for $0 \leq i \leq |\mathcal{M}|$. EAI will first initialize the population (Line 1 in Algorithm 1). Algorithm 2 describes how to initialize the population. The initial population P^0 is generated by picking N_{model} distinct models from $\mathcal{M}$ randomly to create a new ensemble E (Line 5 in Algorithm 2). Then, we check if ensemble E is in the initial population P^0

(Line 6 in Algorithm 2). If it is, then E is a duplicate ensemble, so we discarded the ensemble E; if not, the ensemble E is added into the initial population of ensembles (Line 6 to 8 in Algorithm 2). This process is repeated until there are N_{ens} ensembles within the population P^0.

Algorithm 2. Initialize Population

1: **procedure** $initialize\_pop(\mathcal{M}, N_{ens}, N_{model})$
2:     $P^0 \leftarrow \emptyset$ ▷ Population of unique ensembles
3:     $i = 0$
4:     **while** $i < N_{ens}$ **do**
5:        $E \leftarrow$ Randomly select N_{model} distinct models from $\mathcal{M}$.
6:        **if** E is not in P^0 **then**
7:           $P^0 \leftarrow P^0 \cup \{E\}$ ▷ Add ensemble to population
8:           $i = i + 1$
9:        **end if**
10:    **end while**
11:    **return** P^0
12: **end procedure**

Evaluate Population and Apply Elitism. In this step, all the ensembles' performances are evaluated using a fitness function. Furthermore, the top-performing ensemble is preserved for the next generation. Algorithm 3 provides the algorithm for *Eval_&_Elite*. Moreover, when evaluating the ensembles' performance, the best-performing ensemble throughout all the generations is recorded (line 6 to 8 of Algorithm 3).

Algorithm 3. Evaluate Population and Apply Elitism

Require:
1: **procedure** $Eval\_\&\_Elite(\texttt{ge\_fitness\_fn}, P, E_{best}, s_{best})$
2:     $S \leftarrow []$ ▷ Array of scores for current generation
3:     **for** each ensemble $E \in P$ **do**
4:        $s = \texttt{ge\_fitness\_fn}(E)$
5:        $S \leftarrow S + [s]$ ▷ Array Concatenation
6:        **if** $s < s_{best}$ **then**
7:           Set $s_{best} = s$ and $E_{best} = E$.
8:        **end if**
9:     **end for**
10:    $top\_pop\_ensemble \leftarrow \arg\min_{E \in P} S[E]$
11:    $P_{new} \leftarrow \{top\_pop\_ensemble\}$ ▷ Elitism: retain the best ensemble
12:    **return** $P_{new}, S, E_{best}, s_{best}$
13: **end procedure**

- **Elitism:** Next, when applying elitism to preserve the ensemble(s) for the next generation. EAI only considers the top-performing ensemble within this population to be preserved. It is possible to preserve more than one top-performing ensemble, but it requires sorting the performance of the ensembles, which is time-consuming. Therefore, we only select the top ensemble in the population. Furthermore, this enhances the search capability, allowing for more exploration of a diverse range of ensembles to identify the optimal combination.
- **Fitness Functions:** We investigate two fitness functions for EAI in the context of SCA. Namely, we explore ge_{+ntge} and validation loss (denoted as val_loss) as the fitness function for ensemble selection.
    1. **ge_{+ntge}** : The fitness function ge_{+ntge} is first proposed by [7]. The authors demonstrate that the metric yields consistently better results when combined with multifidelity hyperparameter tuning, called Bayesian Optimization HyperBand, to identify a single best-performing DNN. This composite metric combines GE with $NTGE$ to provide a comprehensive evaluation of side-channel analysis performance. The ge_{+ntge} function is defined as:

    $$ge_{+ntge}(\theta) = \begin{cases} NTGE & \text{if } GE = 0, \\ +N_a + c & \text{otherwise} \end{cases}$$

    where θ represents the model configuration/hyperparameters, N_a is the fixed number of attack traces for evaluation, and c is a small positive constant (set to 100 in our experiments). This metric considers both the ability to recover the key (GE) and the efficiency of the attack ($NTGE$). It also penalizes configurations that fail to recover the key within the given number of traces. This provides a single, comprehensive metric for optimizing SCA models.
    2. **val_loss:** Research has shown that minimizing categorical cross-entropy loss effectively maximizes the mutual information between the leakage model and the trace data, a concept referred to as perceived information in SCA [14]. Here, we investigate whether using the validation loss of attack traces as a fitness function, denoted as val_loss, can aid in ensemble selection.

Genetic Operators. The remaining ensembles in the population are generated using tournament selection, crossover, and mutation, which replace the non-elite ensembles. This configuration supports diversity within the population, which is critical for the effectiveness of subsequent generations.

Algorithm 4 outlines the methodology used to generate new offspring ensembles. To ensure diversity and effectiveness in the evolutionary process, we employ adaptive genetic operators [10], where the mutation and crossover probabilities/rates are dynamically adjusted based on population diversity (i.e., the proportion of unique ensembles in the population). This adaptive approach helps

Algorithm 4. Genetic Operators with Adaptive Rates

1: **procedure** $GeneticOp(\mathcal{M}, P, P_{new}, S, Pr_{cross}, Pr_{mut})$
2:     $\delta \leftarrow |set(tuple(ind) \text{ for } ind \text{ in } P)|/|P|$ ▷ Calculate population diversity
3:     $Pr_{cross}^{adaptive} \leftarrow Pr_{cross} \times \delta$ ▷ Adaptive crossover rate
4:     $Pr_{mut}^{adaptive} \leftarrow Pr_{mut} \times (1 + (1 - \delta))$ ▷ Adaptive mutation rate
5:     **while** $|P_{new}| < N_{ens}$ **do**
6:        **if** $\text{random}() < Pr_{cross}^{adaptive}$ **then**   ▷ Adaptive crossover operation
7:           $\text{parent}_1 \leftarrow \text{TournamentSelection}(P, S)$
8:           $\text{parent}_2 \leftarrow \text{TournamentSelection}(P, S)$
9:           $\text{offspring}_1, \text{offspring}_2 \leftarrow \text{Crossover}(\text{parent}_1, \text{parent}_2, N_{model})$
10:          $P_{new} \leftarrow P_{new} \cup \{\text{offspring}_1, \text{offspring}_2\}$
11:       **else**   ▷ Adaptive mutation operation
12:          $\text{parent} \leftarrow \text{TournamentSelection}(P, S)$
13:          $P_{new} \leftarrow P_{new} \cup \{\text{Mutation}(\text{parent}, \mathcal{M}, Pr_{mut}^{adaptive})\}$
14:       **end if**
15:    **end while**
16:    **return** P_{new}
17: **end procedure**

mitigate premature convergence and redundancy, which can arise from fixed probabilities/rates.

Let δ represent population diversity, calculated as the ratio of unique ensembles to the total population size. The adaptive mutation rate is defined as:

$$Pr_{mut}^{adaptive} = Pr_{mut} \times (1 + (1 - \delta)).$$

When δ is low, this formula increases the mutation rate since $(1 - \delta)$ is larger. A higher mutation rate potentially introduces new models from the set of all the pre-trained DNN, $\mathcal{M}$, into the population, encouraging exploration and generating novel ensembles. Conversely, when diversity is high, the mutation rate decreases to avoid disrupting the existing diversity.

Similarly, the adaptive crossover rate is defined as:

$$Pr_{cross}^{adaptive} = Pr_{cross} \times \delta.$$

This rate increases proportionally with δ, allowing for more frequent recombination within the population when the population contains a wide variety of ensembles. A high δ indicates ample genetic material, making crossover more effective in creating new and potentially superior ensembles. On the other hand, when δ is low, the reduced crossover rate prevents the overexploitation of similar ensembles. At the same time, increasing the probability of mutation allows the population to have more unique ensembles.

To implement these adaptive mechanisms, we set the base mutation probability to $Pr_{mut} = 0.1$ and the base crossover probability to $Pr_{cross} = 0.9$, following standard practice in genetic algorithms. By maintaining the diversity of ensembles within the population through adaptive mutation and crossover rates,

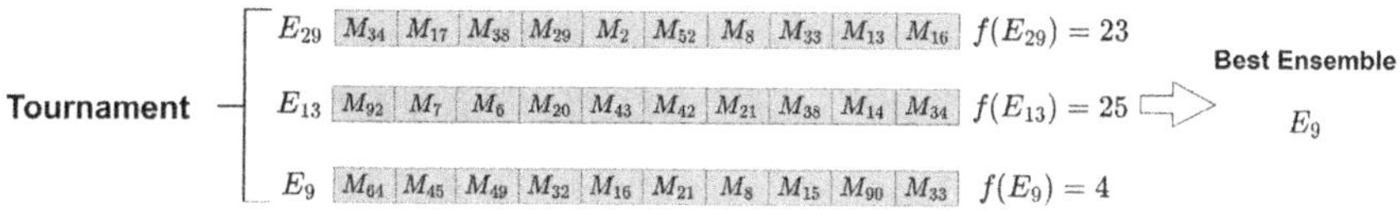

$$\text{Tournament} \longrightarrow \begin{bmatrix} E_{29} & M_{34} & M_{17} & M_{38} & M_{29} & M_2 & M_{52} & M_8 & M_{33} & M_{13} & M_{16} & f(E_{29}) = 23 \\ E_{13} & M_{92} & M_7 & M_6 & M_{20} & M_{43} & M_{42} & M_{21} & M_{38} & M_{14} & M_{34} & f(E_{13}) = 25 \\ E_9 & M_{64} & M_{45} & M_{49} & M_{32} & M_{16} & M_{21} & M_8 & M_{15} & M_{90} & M_{33} & f(E_9) = 4 \end{bmatrix} \Longrightarrow \begin{array}{c} \text{Best Ensemble} \\ E_9 \end{array}$$

Fig. 1. Illustration of a Tournament Selection within EAI when $\ell = 3$.

this approach promotes the generation of unique and high-performing ensembles throughout the evolutionary process.

1. **Tournament Selection:** The selection method that EAI uses would be the Tournaments Selection. For each tournament, ℓ ensembles are randomly selected from the population. Using the fitness value computed before, pick the best-performing ensemble out of the ℓ ensemble. This ensemble will be called a parent ensemble. Figure 1 provides an illustration of a Tournament Selection when $\ell = 3$.
2. **Crossover:** For Crossover, it uses two tournaments for creating two ensembles (aka offspring) as shown in Fig. 2. Assume that the ensembles $parent_1$ and $parent_2$ have the best fitness scores for two different tournaments. Then Crossover randomly generates two indexes c_1 and c_2. The two offspring ensembles are produced via:

$$\text{offspring}_1[j] = \begin{cases} \text{parent}_1[j] & \text{if } j < c_1 \text{ or } j > c_2 \\ \text{parent}_2[j] & \text{if } c_1 \leq j \leq c_2 \end{cases} \quad (2)$$

$$\text{offspring}_2[j] = \begin{cases} \text{parent}_2[j] & \text{if } j < c_1 \text{ or } j > c_2 \\ \text{parent}_1[j] & \text{if } c_1 \leq j \leq c_2 \end{cases} \quad (3)$$

Figure 2 provides an illustration of Crossover when $c_1 = 3$ and $c_2 = 6$ are chosen. This indicates that the segments from position 3 to 6 (inclusive) are swapped between the parents. We highlight that if crossover results in duplicate individuals within the population, the process is repeated to ensure uniqueness.
3. **Mutation:** As for Mutation, it only uses one tournament. During the Mutation process, one DNN from the selected ensemble is randomly replaced with a different pre-trained DNN from the set $\mathcal{M}$. Figure 3 depicts the Mutation process.

If the algorithm chooses Crossover when selecting the last ensemble for the next generation, we pick the first offspring produced.

Time Complexity Analysis: Recall that $|\mathcal{M}|$ is the total number of pre-trained models, N_{gen} is the number of generations, N_{ens} is the population size, and N_{model} is the number of models per ensemble. The time complexity of

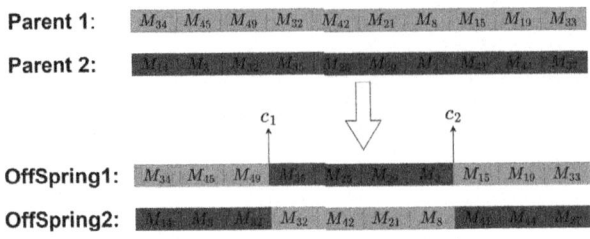

Fig. 2. Illustration of Crossover within EAI when $c_1 = 3$ and $c_2 = 6$.

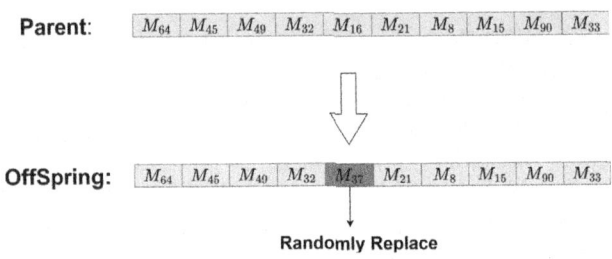

Fig. 3. Illustration of Mutation within EAI when taking a new model M_{37} from $\mathcal{M}$.

initialize_pop is $O(N_{ens} \times N_{model})$. For each generation, the time complexity is $O(N_{model})$ for *Eval_&_Elite* while $O(N_{ens} \times N_{model})$ for *GenericOp*. Since the time complexity mainly comes from *GenericOp*, the overall time complexity of the EAI algorithm is given by $O(N_{gen} \times N_{ens} \times N_{model})$.

5 Experiment Result and Setting

5.1 Datasets and Leakage Models

ASCADf & ASCADr: Both ASCADf and ASCADr are part of the commonly used ASCADv1 dataset [3]. It comprises of traces from first-order masked AES implementation on an 8-bit AVR microcontroller. ASCADf contains traces of the same fixed key for both profiling and attack. On the other hand, ASCADr considers the case where the profiling traces are generated from a random key setting while a fixed key is used to generate the attack traces. Both datasets contain 50000 profiling traces and 10000 attack traces. Each trace contains 700 sample points for ASCADf and 1400 sample points for ASCADr. We target the third byte of the first round sbox output, specifically $\text{Sbox}_{\text{AES}}(pt_3 \oplus k_3^*)$ where pt_3 represents the third plaintext byte and k_3^* denotes the third byte of the first round key.

Ascon:: We use the publicly available datasets by [21] for ASCON. The ASCON implementation is running on a ChipWhisperer Lite board on top of a STM32F4. The traces are collected using an 8-bit oscilloscope. We will only investigate the first-order protected implementation of ASCON-128. There are 50000 profiling traces from a random key setting and 10000 attack traces collected from a fixed key setting. We target the first round of permutation proposed by [21] and [18], where the sensitive variable is of the form:

$$y = k_1 \wedge (255 \oplus IV \oplus \mathfrak{n}_0) \oplus \mathfrak{n}_0 \oplus \mathfrak{n}_1,$$

where IV is the constant from the initialization value, while $\mathfrak{n}_0, \mathfrak{n}_1$ are 8-bits nonces values. Lastly, k_1 is the 8 bits key we are trying to recover. There are a total of 8 different bytes. We shall focus particularly on bytes 2 and 4, which have proven challenging for analysis as shown in [18] even with GSM ensemble. We denote ASCON2 and ASCON4 for byte 2 and byte 4 respectively.

AES_HD: The AES_HD dataset represents power leakage measurements from an unprotected AES hardware implementation running on an FPGA with a round-based architecture. Our analysis targets the side-channel leakage during the last round, specifically focusing on the Hamming Distance leakage model, i.e. $\text{Sbox}_{\text{AES}}^{-1}(ct_{15} \oplus k_{15}) \oplus ct_{11}$, where ct_i refers to the ith ciphertext byte and k_{15} corresponds to the 15th byte of the last round key. The dataset consists of 45000 profiling traces used for training and 3000 attack traces for evaluation.

Throughout this work, we use 1000 attack traces for each dataset.

Leakage Models: In this work, we consider three different leakage models.

- **Identity (ID):** The Identity leakage model assumes that the sensitive intermediate values, such as the AES S-box output $\text{Sbox}_{\text{AES}}(pt \oplus k)$, leak directly through side-channel emissions.
- **Hamming Weight (HW):** The HW leakage model corresponds to the Hamming weight of the sensitive variable. For example, for AES S-box output, we have $HW(\text{Sbox}_{\text{AES}}(pt \oplus k))$ as the leakage model. This model assumes that the amount of leakage is proportional to the number of 1-bits in the binary representation of the sensitive value.
- **Hamming Distance (HD):** The HD leakage model considers the side channel traces leaks the XOR of two sensitive variables.

For ASCADr and ASCADf datasets, we will investigate with ID and HW leakage models. As for ASCON datasets, we will present results for ID leakage model. On the other hand, we only use HD leakage model for AES_HD.

5.2 Hyperparameters Used for DNN and EAI

DNN's Hyperparameter Search Space. In this study, we consider the commonly used Multi-Layer Perceptron (MLP) and Convolutional Neural Network (CNN) in our study. We consider three different settings: solely MLPs, solely CNNs, and a Diverse DNN. For Diverse DNN, it consists of 25 MLPs and 25 CNNs. For solely MLPs (resp. solely CNNs), we randomly generate 50 MLPs (resp. CNNs). The 50 neural networks are randomly generated based on the hyperparameter search spaces defined in Tables 1.

Table 1. Hyperparameter Search Space

MLP	
Parameter	**Values**
Layers	1 to 7 (in step of 1)
Neurons	$10, 20, 50, 100, 200, 300, 400, or 500$
Activation Functions	ReLU, SELU, ELU, or Tanh
Batch Size	100 − 1000 (in steps of 100)
Learning Rate	$1e-3, 5e-4, 1e-4, 5e-5, or 1e-5$
Optimizer	RMSprop or Adam
Weight Initialization	Random uniform, Xavier uniform, or He uniform
CNN	
Parameter	**Values**
Convolutional Layers	$1-4$ (in step of 1)
Initial Filters	$4, 8, 12, 16$
Initial Kernel Size	$26-52$ (in step of 2)
Pooling Type	Max pooling, Average pooling
Pooling Size	$2, 4, 6, 8, 10$
Padding	$0, 4, 8, 12, 16$
Fully Connected Layers	$1-7$ (in step of 1)
Neurons	$10, 20, 50, 100, 200, 300, 400, 500$
Activation Functions	ReLU, SELU, ELU, Tanh
Batch Size	100 − 1000 (in steps of 100)
Learning Rate	$1e-3, 5e-4, 1e-4, 5e-5, 1e-5$
Optimizer	RMSprop, Adam
Weight Initialization	Random uniform, Xavier uniform, He uniform

Hyperparameters for EAI. The hyperparameters for EAI are shown in Table 2. All the hyperparameters listed are consistent across all datasets except for the number of generations. This is because both ASCON2 and ASCON4 require more time to run. Hence, we decrease the number of generations.

5.3 Experimental Results on Publicly Available Datasets

ASCADf. As shown in Table 3 and Fig. 4, we analyze the performance of different algorithms on the ASCADf dataset. The results demonstrate that our EAI with the ge_{+ntge} variant significantly outperforms both EAI with val_loss and GSM in terms of number of traces required to recover the key. Across different models, the ID leakage model consistently performs more effectively than the HW leakage model. Notably, the MLP model with ID leakage model achieves the best performance ($NTGE = 29$). We observed significant differences in performance between the use of fitness functions when applying EAI. Our results show

Table 2. Hyperparameters for EAI across all Datasets

Configuration for Each Dataset and Hyperparameters of EAI	ASCADf	ASCADr	Ascon2	Ascon4	AES_HD
Number of Generations, N_{gen}	50	50	5	5	50
Crossover Probability Pr_{cross}	0.9				
Mutation Probability, Pr_{mut}	0.1				
Models per Ensemble, N_{model}	10				
Number of Ensembles per Generation, N_{ens}	30				
Models per Tournament, ℓ	3				

that EAI using val_loss is ineffective in recovering the secret key in certain cases. Conversely, EAI with ge_{+ntge} consistently recovers the secret key across every scenario, surpassing GSM's performance. In addition, using EAI with ge_{+ntge} obtain below 100 attack traces (i.e., MLP (ID) has $NTGE = 29$ and Diverse DNN (ID) 58), outperforming the current state-of-the-art hyperparameter tuning techniques for single best-performing DNN (see Table 12 of [7]).

Table 3. NTGE for different algorithms and leakage models in ASCADf Dataset

Algorithm	MLP		CNN		Diverse DNN	
	HW	ID	HW	ID	HW	ID
GSM	785	365	825	385	817	329
EAI with ge_{+ntge}	615	29	727	140	590	58
EAI with val_loss	$(GE=19)$	98	$(GE=3)$	615	$(GE=66)$	113

However, it requires a longer time when executing EAI compared to GSM, as shown in Fig. 5. This is as expected since GSM only needs to select the top few models and execute the attack phase, but EAI will need to compute the fitness function for different ensembles over many different generations.

ASCADr. Similar to ASCADf, Table 4 and Fig. 6 demonstrates that EAI with ge_{+ntge} maintains superior performance on the ASCADr dataset, outperforming GSM for all scenarios. In contrast to the ASCADf dataset, the HW leakage model outperforms the ID leakage model. The EAI with val_loss shows particularly poor performance, failing to recover the encryption key across all model and leakage model combinations.

Ascon2. Our research investigated both ID and HW leakage models. Due to the unsuccessful recovery of the secret key using the HW leakage model across all tested methods, we will only present findings from the ID leakage model just like in [18]. We see that with GSM and EAI with val_loss, we are unable

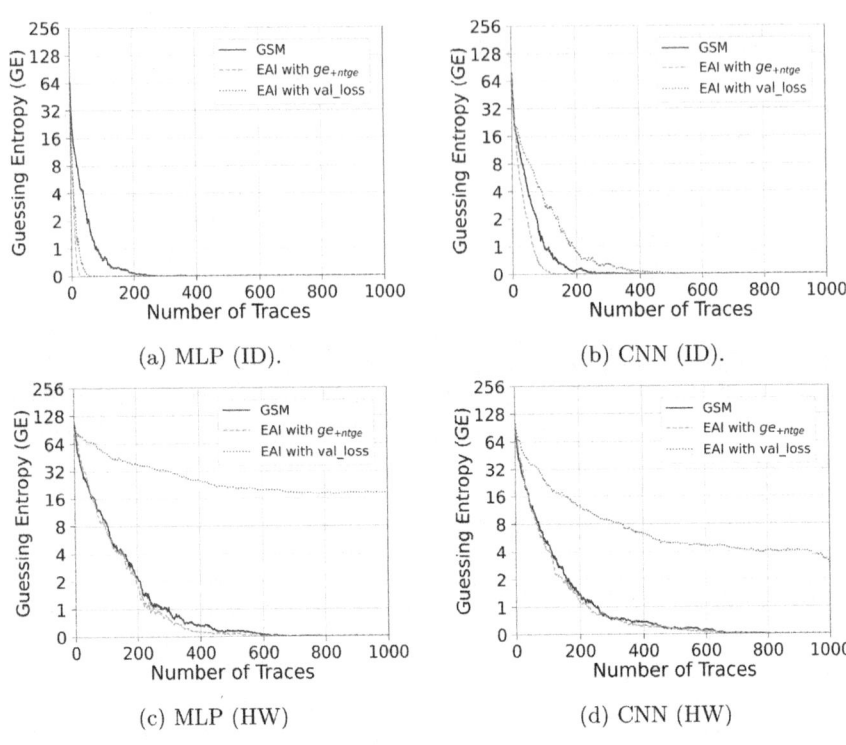

Fig. 4. Guessing entropy for ASCADf.

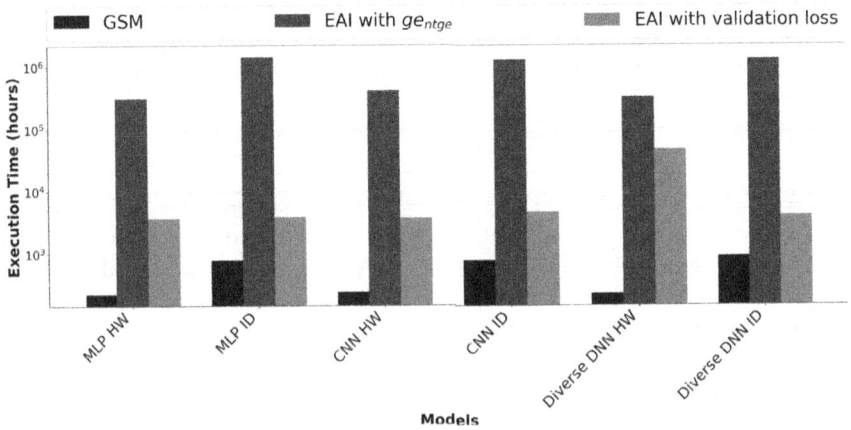

Fig. 5. Execution time comparisons for different algorithms and models in the ASCADf Dataset.

Table 4. NTGE for different algorithms and leakage models in ASCADr Dataset

Algorithm	MLP		CNN		Diverse DNN	
	HW	ID	HW	ID	HW	ID
GSM	548	976	810	$(GE = 126)$	445	$(GE = 14)$
EAI with ge_{+ntge}	296	523	619	$(GE = 3)$	257	923
EAI with val_loss	$(GE = 1)$	$(GE = 185)$	$(GE = 6)$	$(GE = 178)$	$(GE = 7)$	$(GE = 178)$

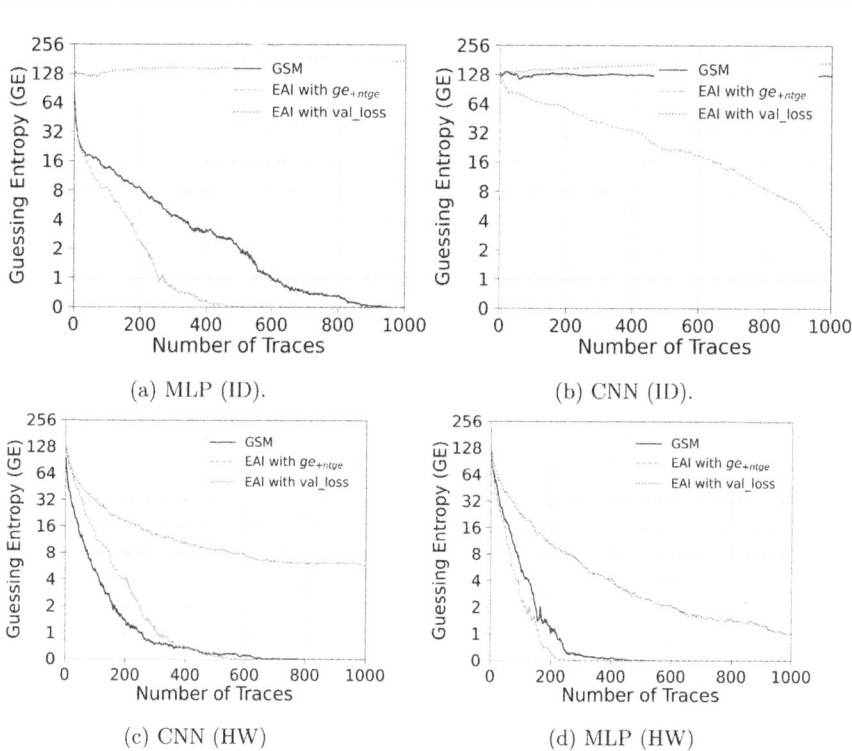

Fig. 6. Guessing entropy for ASCADr.

to successfully recover the secret key with $GE \geq 15$. However, using EAI with ge_{+ntge}, we manage to obtain the secret key with $NTGE = 977$ when building an ensemble of MLPs. Furthermore, we attain $GE \leq 3$ for having CNN ensembles and under the Diverse DNN setting. This overall shows the effectiveness of EAI with ge_{+ntge}.

Ascon4. Our findings show that ASCON4 yields similar results to ASCON2. Both GSM and EAI with val_loss attain high GE values, suggesting that these methods are unable to recover the secret key. However, under the Diverse DNN setting, EAI with ge_{+ntge} recovers the secret key with 914 attack traces. Further-

Table 5. NTGE for different algorithms and leakage models in the Ascon2 Dataset

Algorithm	MLP	CNN	Diverse DNN
GSM	$(GE = 15)$	$(GE = 54)$	$(GE = 40)$
EAI with ge_{+ntge}	977	$(GE = 1)$	$(GE = 3)$
EAI with val_loss	$(GE = 34)$	$(GE = 93)$	$(GE = 126)$

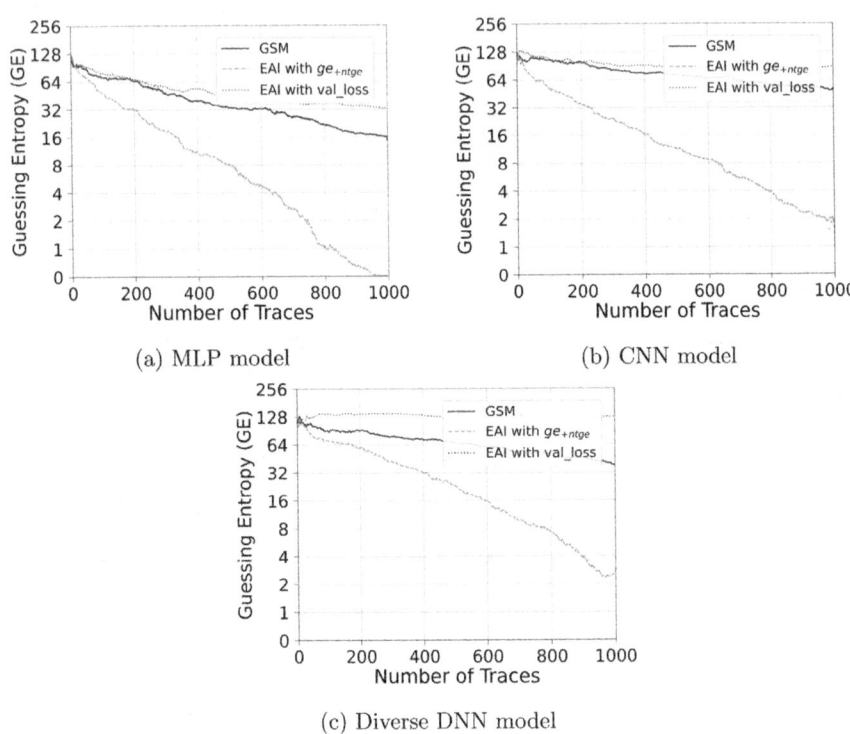

Fig. 7. Guessing entropy evaluation for different model architectures in Ascon2 Dataset.

more, when building a CNN-only ensemble, EAI with ge_{+ntge} attain $GE = 1$. These instances suggest the effectiveness of EAI with ge_{+ntge} in obtaining well-performing ensembles for successful key recovery in SCA.

AES_HD. Lastly, we also investigate the effectiveness of our methodology on hardware traces. Here, we only consider the HD leakage model as stated in Sect. 5.1. EAI with ge_{+ntge} manages to recover the secret for all the scenarios tested and outperform both GSM and EAI with val_loss in terms of the $NTGE$ needed for successful key recovery. In fact, the best $NTGE$ is almost half with 456 attack traces when using Diverse DNN compared to the traditional GSM,

Table 6. NTGE for different algorithms and leakage models in the Ascon4 Dataset.

Algorithm	MLP	CNN	Diverse DNN
GSM	$(GE = 140)$	$(GE = 135)$	$(GE = 136)$
EAI with ge_{+ntge}	$(GE = 34)$	$(GE = 1)$	914
EAI with val_loss	$(GE = 220)$	$(GE = 179)$	$(GE = 138)$

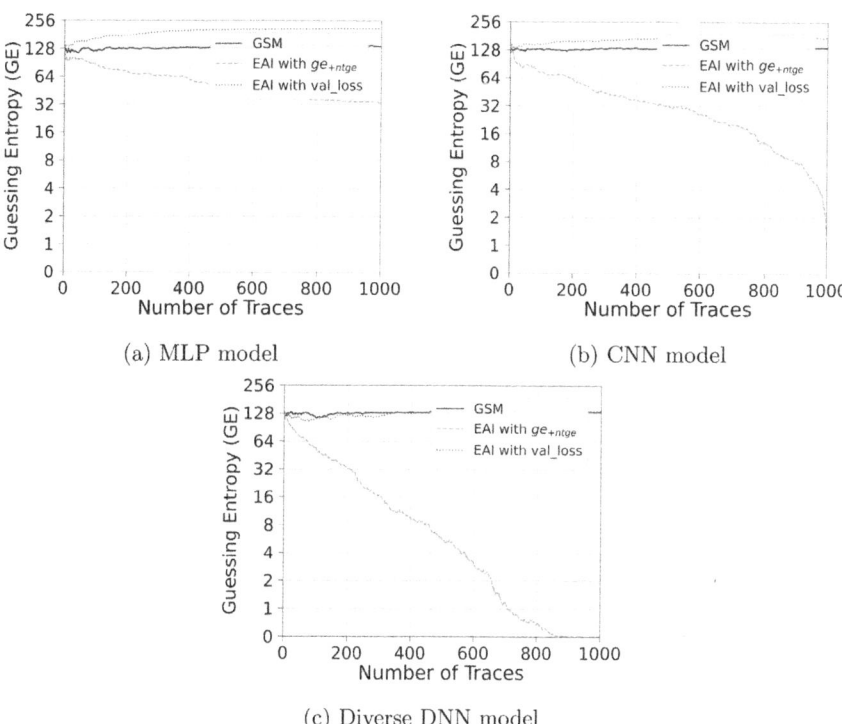

Fig. 8. Guessing entropy evaluation for different model architectures in Ascon4 Dataset.

which uses 840 attack traces when using CNN. These highlight once again that EAI with ge_{+ntge} is effective in finding well-performing neural networks.

6 Discussion and Future Work

In this work, we propose a novel ensemble selection methodology called EAI for generating well-performing ensembles from pre-trained neural networks. EAI significantly reduces the number of traces required for successful key recovery compared to traditional GSM when paired with an effective fitness function. We investigated two fitness functions, ge_{+ntge} and val_loss. We observe that with

Table 7. Number of traces for different algorithms and leakage models in the AES_HD Dataset

Algorithm	MLP	CNN	Diverse DNN
GSM	925	840	$(GE = 3)$
EAI with ge_{+ntge}	569	700	456
EAI with val_loss	998	$(GE = 12)$	662

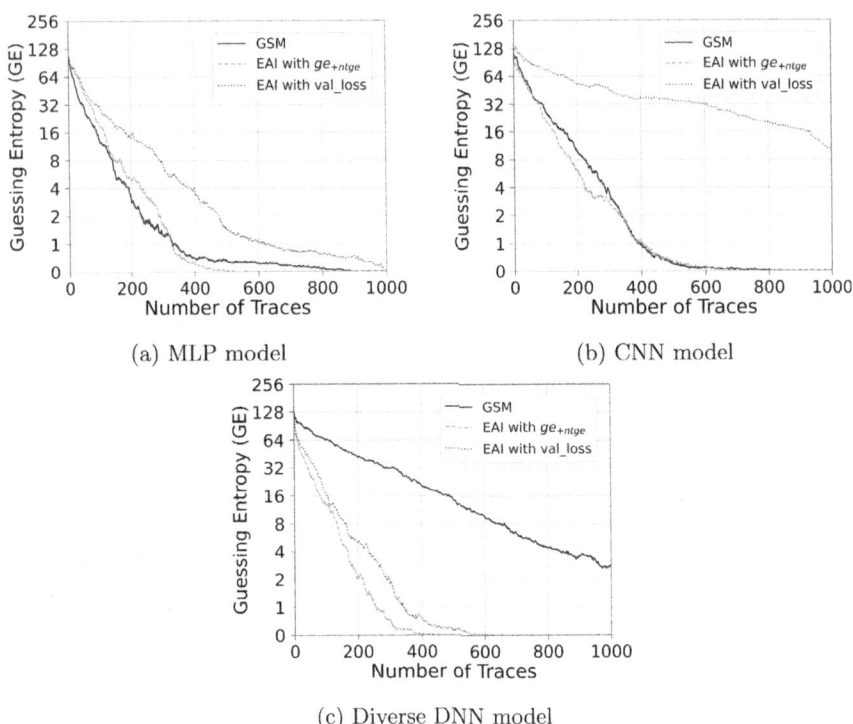

Fig. 9. Guessing entropy evaluation for different model architectures in AES_HD Dataset.

ge_{+ntge} as the fitness function, EAI consistently outperforms other methods across five different datasets. Furthermore, it managed to recover the secret key across all the datasets tested, showing the efficiency of the EAI with ge_{+ntge} as an ensemble selection algorithm. However, with val_loss, it can be observed that it did not find a well-performing ensemble, and in many instances, GSM has much better performances. This suggests that choosing the right fitness function is very important, therefore, we recommend to use ge_{+ntge} as the primary fitness function when employing EAI. However, EAI demands more computational resources, as evidenced by the longer execution times. Therefore, if resources are limited, GSM remains a preferable alternative.

We hope that this work opens up a new dimension of research into finding the optimal ensemble among pre-trained DNNs. Several directions offer potential for exploration. Firstly, as mentioned above, EAI requires lengthy execution times. One possible direction is to enhance this approach by leveraging multi-fidelity optimization methods [7]. Furthermore, ge_{+ntge} fitness function necessitates knowledge of the secret key for deployment. This limitation suggests that its application is restricted to white-box settings during evaluation, specifically for identifying worst-case scenarios. Developing a novel fitness function for EAI that does not require secret key knowledge and achieves comparable performance would be an intriguing area of study.

Acknowledgment. We would like to thank the anonymous reviewers for their insightful comments. We want to thank Azade Rezaeezade for providing the ASCON datasets and Shivam Bhasin for his valuable advice. This work received funding from Singapore NRF Investigatorship with project number NRF-NRFI08-2022-0013. This work is also supported in part by the Netherlands Organization for Scientific Research NWO project DISTANT (CS.019) and project PROACT (NWA.1215.18.014).

References

1. Acharya, R.Y., Ganji, F., Forte, D.: Information theory-based evolution of neural networks for side-channel analysis. IACR Trans. Cryptogr. Hardw. Embed. Syst. **2023**(1), 401–437 (2023). https://doi.org/10.46586/TCHES.V2023.I1.401-437
2. Agrawal, D., Archambeault, B., Rao, J.R., Rohatgi, P.: The EM Side-Channel(s). In: Jr., B.S.K., Koç, Ç.K., Paar, C. (eds.) Cryptographic Hardware and Embedded Systems - CHES 2002, 4th International Workshop, Redwood Shores, CA, USA, August 13-15, 2002, Revised Papers. Lecture Notes in Computer Science, vol. 2523, pp. 29–45. Springer (2002). https://doi.org/10.1007/3-540-36400-5_4
3. Benadjila, R., Prouff, E., Strullu, R., Cagli, E., Dumas, C.: Deep learning for side-channel analysis and introduction to ASCAD database. J. Cryptogr. Eng. **10**(2), 163–188 (2020)
4. Bishop, C.M.: Pattern recognition and machine learning, 5th Edition. Information science and statistics, Springer (2007). https://www.worldcat.org/oclc/71008143
5. Daemen, J., Rijmen, V.: The Design of Rijndael - The Advanced Encryption Standard (AES), Second Edition. Information Security and Cryptography, Springer (2020). https://doi.org/10.1007/978-3-662-60769-5
6. Dobraunig, C., Eichlseder, M., Mendel, F., Schläffer, M.: Ascon v1.2: lightweight authenticated encryption and hashing. J. Cryptol. **34**(3), 33 (2021). https://doi.org/10.1007/S00145-021-09398-9
7. Eng, T.Y.H., Bhasin, S., Weissbart, L.: Train Wisely: multifidelity bayesian optimization hyperparameter tuningin side-channel analysis. IACR Cryptol. ePrint Arch., 170 (2024). https://eprint.iacr.org/2024/170
8. Kocher, P.C., Jaffe, J., Jun, B.: Differential power analysis. In: Wiener, M.J. (ed.) Advances in Cryptology - CRYPTO '99, 19th Annual International Cryptology Conference, Santa Barbara, California, USA, August 15-19, 1999, Proceedings. Lecture Notes in Computer Science, vol. 1666, pp. 388–397. Springer (1999). https://doi.org/10.1007/3-540-48405-1_25

9. Levesque, J., Gagné, C., Sabourin, R.: Bayesian hyperparameter optimization for ensemble learning. In: Ihler, A., Janzing, D. (eds.) Proceedings of the Thirty-Second Conference on Uncertainty in Artificial Intelligence, UAI 2016, June 25-29, 2016, New York City, NY, USA. AUAI Press (2016). http://auai.org/uai2016/proceedings/papers/73.pdf
10. Lin, W., Lee, W., Hong, T.: Adapting crossover and mutation rates in genetic algorithms. J. Inf. Sci. Eng. **19**(5), 889–903 (2003). http://www.iis.sinica.edu.tw/page/jise/2003/200309_10.html
11. Llavata, D., Cagli, E., Eyraud, R., Grosso, V., Bossuet, L.: Deep stacking ensemble learning applied to profiling side-channel attacks. In: Bhasin, S., Roche, T. (eds.) Smart Card Research and Advanced Applications - 22nd International Conference, CARDIS 2023, Amsterdam, The Netherlands, November 14-16, 2023, Revised Selected Papers. Lecture Notes in Computer Science, vol. 14530, pp. 235–255. Springer (2023). https://doi.org/10.1007/978-3-031-54409-5_12
12. Lueth, K.L.: State of the IoT 2020: 12 billion IoT connections, surpassing non-IoT for the first time (2021)
13. Maghrebi, H., Portigliatti, T., Prouff, E.: Breaking cryptographic implementations using deep learning techniques. In: Carlet, C., Hasan, M.A., Saraswat, V. (eds.) Security, Privacy, and Applied Cryptography Engineering - 6th International Conference, SPACE 2016, Hyderabad, India, December 14-18, 2016, Proceedings. Lecture Notes in Computer Science, vol. 10076, pp. 3–26. Springer (2016). https://doi.org/10.1007/978-3-319-49445-6_1
14. Masure, L., Dumas, C., Prouff, E.: A comprehensive study of deep learning for side-channel analysis. IACR Trans. Cryptogr. Hardw. Embed. Syst. **2020**(1), 348–375 (2020). https://doi.org/10.13154/TCHES.V2020.I1.348-375
15. Mendoza, H., Klein, A., Feurer, M., Springenberg, J.T., Hutter, F.: Towards automatically-tuned neural networks. In: Hutter, F., Kotthoff, L., Vanschoren, J. (eds.) Proceedings of the 2016 Workshop on Automatic Machine Learning, AutoML 2016, co-located with 33rd International Conference on Machine Learning (ICML 2016), New York City, NY, USA, June 24, 2016. JMLR Workshop and Conference Proceedings, vol. 64, pp. 58–65. JMLR.org (2016). http://proceedings.mlr.press/v64/mendoza_towards_2016.html
16. Ortiz, M., Scheidegger, F., Casas, M., Malossi, A.C.I., Ayguadé, E.: Generating Efficient DNN-Ensembles with Evolutionary Computation. CoRR abs/2009.08698 (2020). https://arxiv.org/abs/2009.08698
17. Perin, G., Chmielewski, L., Picek, S.: Strength in Numbers: improving generalization with ensembles in machine learning-based profiled side-channel analysis. IACR Trans. Cryptogr. Hardw. Embed. Syst. **2020**(4), 337–364 (2020). https://doi.org/10.13154/tches.v2020.i4.337-364
18. Rezaeezade, A., Basurto-Becerra, A., Weissbart, L., Perin, G.: One for All, All for Ascon: ensemble-based deep learning side-channel analysis. In: Andreoni, M. (ed.) Applied Cryptography and Network Security Workshops - ACNS 2024 Satellite Workshops, AIBlock, AIHWS, AIoTS, SCI, AAC, SiMLA, LLE, and CIMSS, Abu Dhabi, United Arab Emirates, March 5-8, 2024, Proceedings, Part I. Lecture Notes in Computer Science, vol. 14586, pp. 139–157. Springer (2024). https://doi.org/10.1007/978-3-031-61486-6_9
19. Savu, I., Krcek, M., Perin, G., Wu, L., Picek, S.: The Need for MORE: unsupervised side-channel analysis with single network training and multi-output regression. In: Wacquez, R., Homma, N. (eds.) Constructive Side-Channel Analysis and Secure Design - 15th International Workshop, COSADE 2024, Gardanne, France, April 9-

10, 2024, Proceedings. Lecture Notes in Computer Science, vol. 14595, pp. 113–132. Springer (2024). https://doi.org/10.1007/978-3-031-57543-3_7
20. Wang, H., Dubrova, E.: Tandem deep learning side-channel attack on FPGA implementation of AES. SN Comput. Sci. **2**(5), 373 (2021)
21. Weissbart, L., Picek, S.: Lightweight but Not Easy: side-channel analysis of the ascon authenticated cipher on a 32-bit microcontroller. IACR Cryptol. ePrint Arch. p. 1598 (2023). https://eprint.iacr.org/2023/1598
22. Wu, L., Rezaeezade, A., Alipour, A., Perin, G., Picek, S.: Leakage model-flexible deep learning-based side-channel analysis. IACR Commun. Cryptol. **1**(3), 41 (2024). https://doi.org/10.62056/ay4c3txol7
23. Zaid, G., Bossuet, L., Habrard, A., Venelli, A.: Efficiency through diversity in ensemble models applied to side-channel attacks - a case study on public-key algorithms. IACR Trans. Cryptogr. Hardw. Embed. Syst. **2021**(3), 60–96 (2021). https://doi.org/10.46586/tches.v2021.i3.60-96
24. Zaidi, S., Zela, A., Elsken, T., Holmes, C.C., Hutter, F., Teh, Y.W.: Neural ensemble search for uncertainty estimation and dataset shift. In: Ranzato, M., Beygelzimer, A., Dauphin, Y.N., Liang, P., Vaughan, J.W. (eds.) Advances in Neural Information Processing Systems 34: Annual Conference on Neural Information Processing Systems 2021, NeurIPS 2021, December 6-14, 2021, virtual, pp. 7898–7911 (2021). https://proceedings.neurips.cc/paper/2021/hash/41a6fd31aa2e75c3c6d427db3d17ea80-Abstract.html
25. Zhou, Z., Wu, J., Jiang, Y., Chen, S.: Genetic algorithm based selective neural network ensemble. In: Nebel, B. (ed.) Proceedings of the Seventeenth International Joint Conference on Artificial Intelligence, IJCAI 2001, Seattle, Washington, USA, August 4-10, 2001, pp. 797–802. Morgan Kaufmann (2001)

Improving Leakage Exploitability in Horizontal Side Channel Attacks Through Anomaly Mitigation with Unsupervised Neural Networks

Gauthier Cler[1,2(✉)], Sebastien Ordas[2], and Philippe Maurine[1]

[1] University of Montpellier LIRMM, Montpellier, France
g.cler@serma.com
[2] SERMA Safety and Security ITSEF, Pessac, France

Abstract. The success of horizontal side-channel attacks depends heavily on the correct extraction of points of interest, which are expected to contain relevant leakages, and on the quality of the traces. If the latter is not sufficient, this will consequently degrade the identification of leakage candidates and often render attacks inapplicable. This work aims to assess the relevance of neural networks in the unsupervised context of horizontal attacks by proposing two methods with alternative objectives to mitigate noise artefacts from the input signal. Their application results in better traces exploitability when using clustering-based horizontal attacks.

Keywords: Horizontal Attacks · Side Channel Analysis · Neural Networks · Unsupervised Learning

1 Introduction

Horizontal side-channel attacks are a family of attacks which rely on the use of a single acquired trace for exploitation. As the presence of masking or randomization makes the use of multiple traces irrelevant, they are often sought as the last attack vector. However, their applicability and success capability heavily relies on the quality of the provided patterns (processed trace). As no profiling phase nor leakage assessment is available in this attack scenario, it can often be hard to improve the patterns quality by reducing noise or digital filtering, without the risk of leakage degradation.

On the other side, neural networks are widely used for profiled side channel attacks [3,6,15,17,24]. They aim at building a model that characterizes the leakage manifestation on an open device, which can then be applied to a target device during the attack phase. While this approach has been shown to be efficient, it requires knowledge of the labels associated with the traces/patterns to be applied. In fact, this is mandatory for network training based on an error objective, since their weights are updated based on the error between predicted and ground truth labels.

This rise of neural network architectures in the supervised side-channel analysis domain leads to the question of their applicability in an unsupervised context, and more precisely for horizontal attacks. While proposed supervised methods have shown competitive performance against more traditional methods for profiled attacks (such as template attacks [7]), their applicability in an unsupervised context is far from straightforward. In fact, training objective such as error-based optimization cannot be considered since no training data (thus no true labels) is available. Instead, alternative training mechanisms that are applicable in this context should be explored.

Within this context, this work provides several contributions to improve the quality of side-channel traces and thus their exploitability. Among them are:

- the identification and quantification of abnormal values in the input data and their impact on the selection of points of interest (PoI). This includes the presence of outliers or extreme values. These latter values result in truncated statistical distributions at the end of traces capture because of a specific setting, intentional or unintentional, of the digital sampling oscilloscope.
- the correction of anomalies through the application of a robust autoencoder (RAE) framework [14,25], in a completely unsupervised manner.
- their mitigation in a self-supervised manner using anomalies models, based on generative networks (GAN) [12].

Correcting outliers and extreme values can be beneficial for many side-channel analyses. However, it is expected to be of particular interest in the context of horizontal attacks. In fact, due to the randomization of the scalar or secret exponent, only a single trace can be analyzed at a time to try to recover the secret. Thus, any outlier can cause the loss of a scalar or exponent bit to be recovered. This explains why focus is made on this context in the rest of the paper, and more particularly on clustering-based horizontal attacks.

To that aim, the remaining of the paper is organized as follows. Section 2 recalls the context of clustering-based horizontal attacks and derives the way adopted to check the soundness of the proposals. Section 3 deals with the identification of abnormal values, which include outliers and extreme (truncated) values. Section 4 illustrates the effect of such values on univariate PoI selection. Section 5 highlights the limits of traditionally used anomalies mitigation, while Sects. 6.1 and 6.2 propose two correction methods using either a Robust Auto-Encoder (RAE) or a specific Cycle-Generative Adversarial Network (Cycle-GAN), respectively. Section 7 presents and discusses the results obtained on the publicly available datasets considered. Finally, the 8 section concludes the paper.

2 Clustering-Based Horizontal Attacks and Figures of Merit

This section describes the working foreground that have been adopted for the development and evaluation of the proposed contributions. It first recalls the backbone of clustering-based horizontal attacks. Then, the figures of merit considered to evaluate the benefits of the proposed solutions to mitigate outliers and extremes values are given and discussed. Finally, it ends by presenting the two publicly available datasets that have been selected to evaluate the soundness of the proposals.

2.1 Clustering-Based Horizontal Attacks

Horizontal attacks based on unsupervised clustering are typically carried out in two or three steps, with the third step being optional. Considering, for example, the proposals of Perin *et al.* in [20,21], these steps are:

- **Step 1 : Selecting points of interest (PoI)**: Usually, the selection of the PoI is done thanks to a univariate analysis of each time sample of aligned patterns (traces). There are several ways to analyze each time sample. Some proposals recommend analyzing their statistical distribution, assuming that PoIs are expected to be a balanced Gaussian mixture of two normal distributions [9,19]. Others like [21] suggest to cluster each time sample and to compute the DoM (Difference of Means), or extended but related figures of merit [20] between each cluster to identify PoI.
- **Step 2 : Guessing the scalar or exponent bits**: After identifying and ranking the PoIs, a clustering algorithm (e.g., k-means or expectation maximization) is applied to a subset of the PoIs to obtain an estimate of the secret scalar or exponent.
- **Step 3 : Correcting the guess**: As a possible last step, one could apply a correction phase to the estimation of the scalar or exponent bits, using a neural network as described in [4,20]. However, the efficiency of these networks depends significantly on the percentage of bits that are already correct in the estimate provided by the previous step.

Of course, in a supervised context, the first step could be performed in a guided manner thanks to the knowledge of the secret scalar or exponent bits. In this way, one could use the t-value as a leakage metric.

2.2 Figures of Merit

As described above, clustering-based horizontal attacks are performed in two or three successive steps. The effect of outliers and extreme values is not expected to be known on each of this step, and furthermore could be cumulative. It is probably the case, since it is showed that the quality of traces can drastically affect the quality and efficiency of such attacks [4].

The evaluation of the soundness of techniques that allow to mitigate the effects of outliers and extremes could thus be performed according to different points of view.

From the point of view of the end application, the success rate of an attack could be a good measure of the efficiency of such techniques. In this paper, it makes use of the Bit Recovery Rate (BRR) [9], which corresponds to the percentage of secret bits successfully recovered through the clustering partitioning process. This metric is obviously not available during the attack but is used here in a study purpose.

From a pure leakage point of view, considering leakage assessment metrics such as t-values, either applied in a supervised or unsupervised manner, might be a more meaningful solution.

Global indicators are also considered for measuring the global changes in the patterns, namely the Signal to Noise ratio (SNR) and the Mutual Information (MI) between the patterns and associated labels.

As a last criterion for evaluation, the evolution of the number of values identified as outliers or extremes has been considered as a natural indicator to characterize the efficiency of the proposed mitigation process. As the mitigation is conducted in an entirely unsupervised manner, it is important to ascertain the extent to which the proposed approaches can correctly identify such values.

In the remainder of this paper, these three criteria will therefore be considered in turn. First, the capability of a technique to identify and correct outliers and extremes will be assessed by considering the percentage of outliers before and after mitigation. Second, the proposed method will be evaluated to determine whether it emphasizes the leakage manifestation by computing the t-values in a supervised manner. Third, the bit recovery rate (BRR) obtained with the attacks described in [9,21] is considered.

2.3 Considered Targets

Two public datasets that target Curve25519 curve from μNaCl library on a STM32F4 are used for this study, namely Cswap Pointer and Arith from Nascimento and Chmielewski work [19]. These datasets are known to be at the same time leaky but very noisy as depicted by Fig. 1. It shows random patterns from both datasets. The presence of outliers and extreme observable values (-128 or 127) at many time points is clearly visible and supports the choice of these

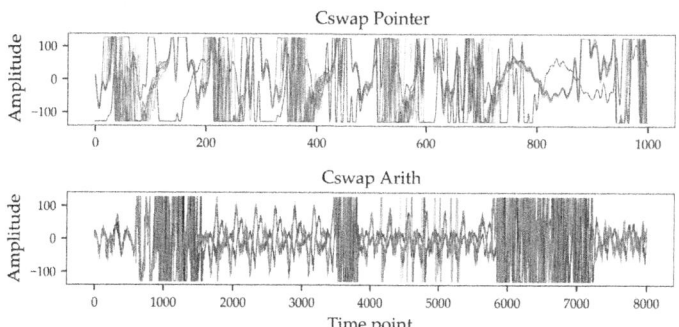

Fig. 1. Random patterns from Cswap Pointer and Cswap Arith datasets. [19]

datasets as a suitable target to demonstrate the soundness of this work proposals.

The choice of these datasets is also sustained by the fact that several papers have reported the success rates of different horizontal attacks applied to these datasets [4,9,20] . This is interesting for a comparison purpose. For reference, Fig. 2 shows the supervised t-value for the two considered datasets.

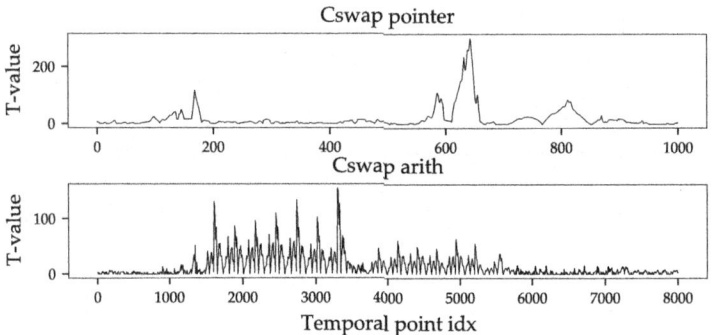

Fig. 2. t-value on each temporal point accross all patterns, for the two considered datasets.

3 Identification and Quantification of Outliers

The identification of outliers and extreme values is an old statistical topic that could potentially be revisited depending on the end application. In this paper, two methods have been considered to identify such abnormal values.

Extreme Values. During traces acquisition, the oscilloscope's vertical resolution during digital sampling determines the number of values a signal can take. For example, a high-end oscilloscope with an 8-bit resolution can produce waveforms with a very large number of points, but all with values between -128 and 127. In case of a misconfiguration (intentional or not) of the acquisition hardware, the statistical distribution of some points could be truncated. This results in a large number of extreme values in the measurement of these points, which do not contain any valuable information. In this work, such values are called extremes. Considering signed values, saturated values for 8-bit and 12-bit resolution would respectively correspond to $\xi(8) = \{-128, 127\}$ and $\xi(12) = \{-2048, 2047\}$. For the rest of this work, only $\xi(8)$ is considered as the studied datasets are encoded on 8-bit. Thus a sample x would be flagged as saturated if $x \in \xi(8)$.

Interquartile Range Outliers. Some noisy behaviors generated by the target or measurement environment can also introduce additional components into the distribution of time samples that can span the entire oscilloscope range up or down to extreme values. Values associated with these parasitic components are referred to as outliers in the remainder of this paper.

In the analysis of distributions, an outlier is defined as a value that is statistically significantly different from the others. If the interquartile range is considered (as in [19]), this corresponds to samples outside of the range $R = [Q_1 - \alpha \operatorname{IQR}, Q_3 + \alpha \operatorname{IQR}]$, where the $\operatorname{IQR} = Q_3 - Q_1$. Usually one considers $\alpha = 1.5$. Thus, all samples x with a high deviation from the quartiles such that $x \notin R$ are usually considered as outliers.

These definitions of extremes and outlier's models are interesting because they can be applied in an unsupervised context. Their application to the two datasets considered is thus straightforward. Figure 3 shows the percentage of such values for each time point. As expected from a first glance at the traces, a significant number of time points show a high number of anomalies for both datasets. Some time points even show a percentage of detected anomalies (extreme values) close to 100%. This means that in the current state of trace quality, there is almost no exploitable leakage at these time points. Hence, the choice of these datasets to estimate the efficiency of any solution that allows to reduce outliers and extremes seems reasonable.

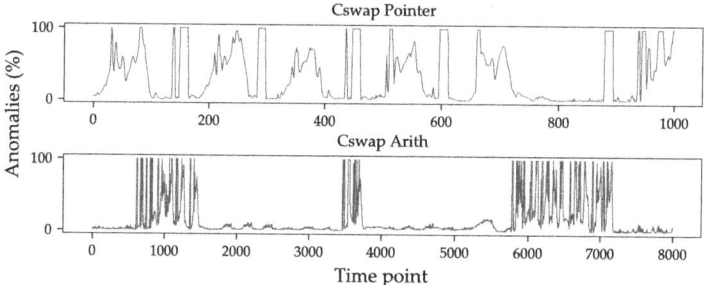

Fig. 3. Percentages of anomalies (outliers + saturated values) in Cswap Pointer and Arith datasets.

4 Impact of Anomalies on the PoI Selection Process

When performing a clustering-based horizontal attack, the selection of the PoI (step 1) is done by applying a clustering algorithm to each time point of the aligned patterns and selecting some points highlighted by a distinguisher such as the DoM or the t-value. The relevance of the selected point is, of course, related to the quality of the traces. Indeed, the Gaussian noise, outliers and extreme values of the measurement could affect the efficiency of both the clustering algorithm and the distinguisher. Regarding outliers and extreme values, the impact could be huge, especially on the result provided by the clustering algorithm. Indeed, few outliers or extreme values could be sufficient to significantly shift the centroids and as a results bias the values provided by the distinguisher.

By way of illustration, Fig. 4 shows the effect of the extreme values on clustering results obtained with the k-means applied to sampled data from an univariate Gaussian mixture $p(x) = \pi_1 \mathcal{N}(\mu_1, \sigma_1) + \pi_1 \mathcal{N}(\mu_2, \sigma_2)$, with parameters $\pi_1 = \pi_2 = 0.5$, $\mu_1 = 1$, $\mu_2 = 4$, $\sigma_1 = \sigma_1 = 0.5$. The x-axis indicates the percentage of values drawn from the underlying mixture that have been replaced by extreme values equal to 10. This process has been averaged over 10 experiments. As shown, the effect first remains moderated up to a certain value, in that case only 10%, above which there is a sudden and significant shift of the centroid values and of the associated DoM. Above this threshold, distance value involved in the k-means is mostly dominated by the presence of sufficient extreme values. In turn, this induced shift causes a rapid decrease in the bit recovery rate, i.e. the correctness of the guessed scalar or exponent bits. This trend (and more precisely the suddenness of the shift) clearly suggests that even correcting extreme values could be beneficial in some cases to exploit the leakage or bring back some time samples of traces in the exploitable domain.

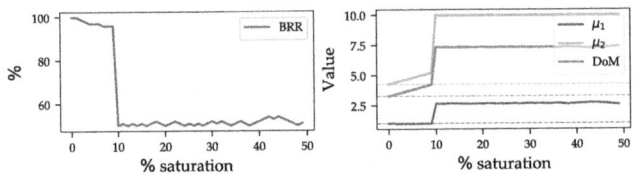

Fig. 4. Effect of extreme values on (Left): The BRR, (Right): the clustering centroid values and DoM.

In a similar fashion, the impact of outliers on the clustering capability has been studied. Considering the same data as before drawn from an univariate mixture distribution with same parameters, a percentage of random values from the distribution is replaced with $Q_3 + \alpha \, \mathrm{IQR}$. This is done with increasingly percentage and various α values. Results are showed on Fig. 5.

Ones can notice the same behavior as in the previous experiment. Indeed, the BRR falls down towards 50% abruptly given a sufficient percentage of data on the right tail or alpha value. This shows that a sufficiently low α value should be used. In this work, $\alpha = 1.5$ is used.

Still, one may wonder if the presence of outliers and saturated values can negatively impact the PoI selection process on real data. Thus, some leaking points (in terms of high t-values) of the Cswap Pointer dataset have been corrupted. More precisely, some values of time samples with a significant leakage have been progressively replaced with extreme values the evolution of the BRR and centroids with respect to the percentage of corrupted values has been observed.

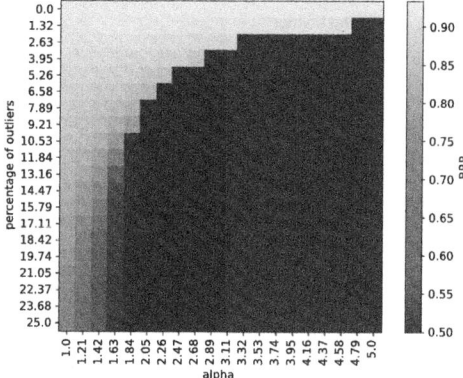

Fig. 5. Resulting BRR when replacing random values by right tail of the global distribution, with different percentage and alpha value.

Figure 6 shows the results obtained considering only the first 5000 patterns of Cswap Pointer, for time points 640 and 168.

A supervised leakage analysis using the t-test gave t-values of 300 (the highest value obtained across all points) and 116 respectively. The number of extreme values (either -128 or 127) before corruption was counted as 2 for both points that differs mainly by their mean and standard deviation. The figure clearly shows that a few extreme values (7% and 2% respectively) are sufficient to completely deceive the k-means and cause a drastic reduction of the BRR from 92% and 70% respectively to values close to 50%. It seems that these few extreme values are indeed sufficient to significantly attract the centroids (at least one of the two) found by the k-means close to them. Hence, it is straightforward to see that noisy sets of traces as the ones considered for this study would be harder to exploit using a clustering based strategy. However, ones can wonder if the mitigation of such abnormal values would be beneficial for the exploitation.

5 Anomalies Mitigation Through Ablation

As seen in the previous section, clustering process in the presence of saturated values or outliers can results in incorrect clusters estimation. From this, it would be necessary to take action to mitigate such values. Outliers mitigation is a well-studied topic in various statistical domains [1, 10].

One proposal can be to replace identified anomalies values based on the values of other samples. For side channel analysis purpose in [19], considering the outliers model described above, authors proposed the following mitigation strategy. For each time point, it consists in replacing the value of identified outliers with the median of non-outliers on this time point. This could be applied as well for saturated values $x \in \xi(8)$. This can be a relevant approach if the percentage of anomalies is really low, but it has however no (or very low) beneficial effect

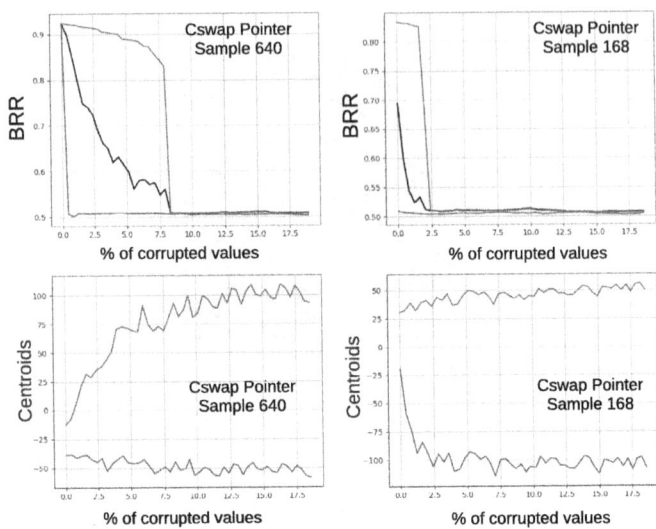

Fig. 6. Top: $Q_{0.99}$ (red), mean (black) and $Q_{0.01}$ (blue) of the BRR obtained by applying 100 times the k-means to time samples 640 and 168 from Cswap Pointer patterns. Bottom: Evolution of the centroid's values provided by the k-means applied to time samples 640 and 168. (Color figure online)

on the quality of the PoI selection procedure in case of highly noisy context. Furthermore, this can have the consequence to degrade the classes discrimination through clustering, as the formed distribution tends towards an unimodal Gaussian distribution as the number of outliers increases.

Another straightforward approach can be to remove time points if the percentage of anomalies across all patterns is higher than a defined threshold. This, however, can has a doubled-edged effect. Firstly, this can result in the removal of leaking time points depending on the arbitrary chosen threshold, thus in a decrease of leakage information in the patterns. Furthermore, in cases with high amount of anomalies (as seen on considered datasets in this work), this would have the effect of removing the majority of time points. For reference on Cswap Pointer and Arith datasets, a threshold above 5% of anomalies, would result in 34.8% and 53.65% respectively of time points removed.

From this status, the motivation behind this work lies as follow. Using a neural network unsupervised approach, it hopes to significantly increase the exploitability of the leakage present in some time samples by correcting outliers or extremes they may contain. Additionally, as the correction process is unsupervised, it should not have a degradation effect on the leakage.

6 Neural Based Anomalies Mitigation

This sections aims at studying neural architectures candidate that could be relevant for anomalies mitigation in a horizontal attack context. To do so, said architecture would require to be trained in an unsupervised manner (or semi-supervised), without knowing the associated value to each pattern. For this work, two architectures have been studied, which training is based on alternative objective, applicable in the context of horizontal attacks. These methods are applied on the whole patterns, without discarding any time points.

6.1 Unsupervised Mitigation with RAE

The first approach considered in this work to mitigate (or correct) outliers and extremes is an unsupervised approach. It consists of a variation of the autoencoder architecture. While the use of autoencoders for multivariate leakage extraction can give relevant results in noiseless (or low noise) contexts (as well as projections methods such as the Principal Component Analysis), it often fails in noisy ones [8]. Instead, a variant of the vanilla autoencoder, known as the robust autoencoder (RAE) [14,25] is considered in this paper. The RAE can be seen as non-linear generalization of the Robust Principal Component Analysis (RPCA) [5], trained using gradient descent. The idea behind the RPCA/RAE is to recover a low rank matrix L from corrupted matrix X and extract artifacts into an sparse noise matrix S. It can be described by the following decomposition:

$$X = L + S \qquad (1)$$

where each term in this study context corresponds to:

- X, the input matrix, containing noisy artefacts, corresponding to the patterns obtained after the traces acquisition and pre-processing (verticalization and alignment procedure).
- L, the clean matrix, which should be free of abnormal values after the anomalies mitigation process,
- S, the noise matrix, from the difference $S = X - L$, which is a sparse matrix containing the positions of the extracted noise artefacts.

Rather than attempting to project relevant information into a low-dimensional subspace and thus focusing on its compression capability as traditional autoencoder would do, the RAE is used to mitigate anomalies in their reconstruction phase with an objective function consisting in two terms:

$$\mathcal{L}(\theta, \phi) = ||L - \mathcal{F}_\theta(\mathcal{E}_\phi(L))||_2 + \tau||S||_1 \qquad (2)$$

where the left term is the autoencoder reconstruction error optimized by gradient descent (with $\mathcal{E}_\theta$ and $\mathcal{F}_\phi$ the encoder and decoder networks respectively) and the right term is the proximal optimization of S. The proximal optimization of the ℓ_1 norm corresponds to the shrinkage operator:

$$\text{prox}_{\ell_1}(x, \tau) = \begin{cases} x - \tau & \text{if } x > \tau \\ x + \tau & \text{if } x < -\tau \\ x & \text{if } x \in [-\tau, \tau] \end{cases} \qquad (3)$$

where the parameter τ defines the level of sparsity of S such that small τ will encourage more data to be identified as noise or outliers.

Since the combined objective of Eq. 2 cannot be optimized as a whole, it should be split into two sub-objectives that can be optimized by the alternating direction method of multipliers (ADMM) algorithm. It consists of alternately optimizing one sub-objective while keeping the other fixed. This leads to the following ADMM optimization procedure for the RAE.

1. Train the autoencoder to minimize the reconstruction error of $L = X - S$ using gradient descent (left term of Eq. 1).
2. Derive the noisy matrix $S = X - L$.
3. Minimize S by proximal optimization (right term of Eq. 1).

These three steps are repeated until convergence is reached, which is defined as the point at which no change is observed in the matrices. Details about network architecture and parameters are described in Appendix A. It is important to note that the mitigation process can have an impact on non-abnormal points. Indeed, as the RAE produces synthetic patterns during the reconstruction process, which are then used as new patterns, it can affect all values of all time points. In a side channel context, this could thus affect the observed leakage levels. This method was applied to the patterns of the two datasets considered. An identical network architecture was used for both datasets. The analysis of results that were obtained considering the cleaned matrix L are presented in Sect. 7.

6.2 Self-Supervised Mitigation with CycleGAN

As an alternative approach to mitigate outliers and extremes values, the application of a self-supervised framework may be a more interesting and controllable solution. Indeed, as described in Sect. 3, it is possible to identify abnormal values in a completely unsupervised manner. Thus, it allows to control the learning process of the neural network used for anomalies mitigation to ensure that only the identified abnormal values are corrected, while the remaining data points remain unchanged. This approach thus differs from the one considered by the use of the RAE described previously. To that aim, an approach based on the CycleGAN architecture that trains on pairwise sets of data is therefore proposed. Such architecture is made up from a pair of two GAN, [12], that is two generators G_A, G_B and two discriminators D_A, D_B. GAN models are optimized through adversarial training, where a discriminator D aims at distinguish training samples as real or fake, while a generator G tries to fool the discriminator by generating convincing examples. The CycleGAN architecture has been widely applied for cross domains images translation [26]. The objective function of the CycleGAN is the following:

$$\begin{aligned}\mathcal{L}(G_A, G_B, D_A, D_B) = &\mathcal{L}_{\text{GAN}}(G_A, D_B, B, A) \\ &+ \mathcal{L}_{\text{GAN}}(G_B, D_A, A, B) \\ &+ \lambda \mathcal{L}_{\text{cyc}}(G_A, G_B)\end{aligned} \quad (4)$$

where each GAN objective, $\mathcal{L}_{\text{GAN}}$, is defined by:

$$\min_G \max_D \mathcal{L}_{\text{GAN}}(G, D, X, Z) = \mathbb{E}_{x \sim X} \log D(x) \\ + \mathbb{E}_{z \sim Z} \log[1 - D(G(z))] \quad (5)$$

In addition, a consistency loss, $\mathcal{L}_{\text{cyc}}(G_A, G_B)$, is added to ensure mapping bijections between domains:

$$\mathcal{L}_{\text{cyc}}(G_A, G_B) = \mathbb{E}_{a \sim A} ||G_B(G_A(a)) - a||_1 \\ + \mathbb{E}_{b \sim B} ||G_A(G_B(b)) - b||_1 \quad (6)$$

with λ used to balance terms in Eq. 4. The proposed architecture for mitigating abnormal values differs from existing approaches in several ways. First, as a single dataset $X \in \mathcal{M}_{n,p}(\mathbb{R})$, ($n$ patterns of p time points) is available for horizontal attacks, it thus should be split into two subsets, designated as A and B. These subsets are constructed to contain samples with the greatest disparity in abnormal values. This is done by first computing the binary anomalies matrix $M \in \mathcal{M}_{n,p}(\{0,1\})$ such that each matrix element is:

$$m_{i,j} = \begin{cases} 1, & \text{if } x_{i,j} \in \xi(8) \vee x_{i,j} \notin R(x_{:,j}) \\ 0, & \text{otherwise} \end{cases} \quad (7)$$

To recall, R corresponds to the interquantile range as defined in Sect. 3. Then, each pattern pair (a_i, b_i) is built such that it maximizes the Hamming distance between their abnormal values:

$$\underset{i,j \in \{1,\ldots,n\}}{\arg\max} \ \text{HW}(m_{i,:} \oplus m_{j,:}), \quad i \neq j \quad (8)$$

Second, multiplexers (mux) are added between the output of generators and the input of discriminators. Multiplexers are defined as follows:

$$A'' = \text{mux}(A, G_B(B), M_A) = (M_A \wedge G_B(B)) \vee (\neg M_A \wedge A) \\ B'' = \text{mux}(B, G_A(A), M_B) = (M_B \wedge G_A(A)) \vee (\neg M_B \wedge B) \quad (9)$$

where matrices M_A and M_B contains the positions of the anomalies (both outliers and saturated values) for subsets A and B. This does not affect the gradients propagation during the backward phase. The idea behind the application of the CycleGAN to outliers mitigation is to correct identified abnormal values in A from non outliers elements from B. This results in the fact that only samples in the original patterns flagged as abnormal are modified during training. For the optimization, this ensures that the discriminators D_A and D_B can train and backward propagate on the multiplexer outputs (rather than the whole synthetic patterns from the generators) to provide better judging capabilities. In parallel, the generators are specifically trained to generate convincing synthetic corrected points inplace of the anormal ones. The complete proposed architecture for the CycleGAN framework is shown in Fig. 7. A cycle of the mitigation process is then given as follows:

1. Calculate the anomalies matrix M (Eq. 7).
2. Split the original input data into two subsets A and B with highest Hamming distance between pairs of rows of M (Eq. 8).
3. Train the CycleGAN until convergence (Eq. 4).
4. Replace anomalies in initial patterns with generated points through the multiplexers (A'' and B'').

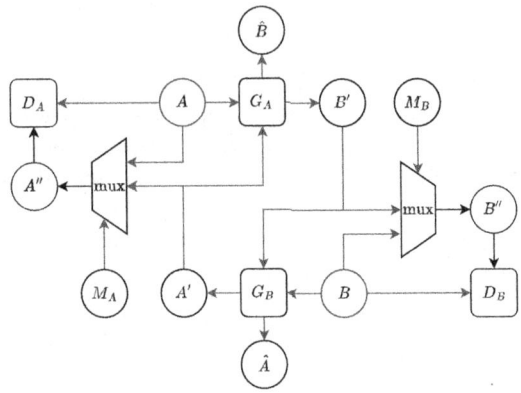

Fig. 7. Proposed CycleGAN architecture with multiplexers. Blue and red colors show data paths through the architecture. (Color figure online)

These steps are repeated until $||M||_0$ converges, that is when the number of anomalies reach zero or no changes are observed. Details of the CycleGAN architecture and optimization process are given in Appendix B. The results of application of this framework are given in the next section, where its performance is compared to the RAE correction capability.

7 Results and Discussion

In order to assess the efficiency of the proposed neural methods in mitigating outliers, several metrics were discussed and described in Sect. 2. This section presents the results obtained for the two proposed methods, applied on the considered datasets.

7.1 Percentage of Corrected Outliers and Extremes

Table 1 presents the percentage of anomalies identified using the IQR and extreme values methods before and after the application of the two proposed mitigation approaches.

On the two datasets examined, the CycleGAN shows better outlier mitigation, while the RAE performs better at correcting extremes. Overall, the RAE

Table 1. Percentage of outliers and extremes obtained on original patterns, after applying the RAE and the CycleGAN. Best results are highlighted in bold.

	Cswap Pointer			Cswap Arith		
	Before	RAE	GAN	Before	RAE	GAN
Outliers (%)	4.32	5.36	**1.67**	5.15	4.73	**1.35**
Extreme (%)	30.27	**1.19**	10.22	12.88	**0.01**	5.19
Total (%)	33.39	**6.55**	11.85	16.54	**4.75**	6.49

shows slightly better results for total anomaly correction. However, the latter has a greater impact on the extreme than on the outliers in the mitigation process and changes all values of the patterns, which could be risky and alter the leakage.

7.2 Leakage Assessment on Time Samples

Successful mitigation can be translated to no degradation in the observed leakage levels. In order to assess the capability of the considered approaches using RAE and CycleGAN, the Supervised t-test, as well as clustering using k-means and computing the BRR percentage is done. Figure 8 displays the difference values obtained for each time point before and after application of the CycleGAN and RAE, in a *after minus before* fashion. In other words, positive values translates to improvement of the t-values (respectively BRR), while negative values means that the time point leakage exploitability has been degraded.

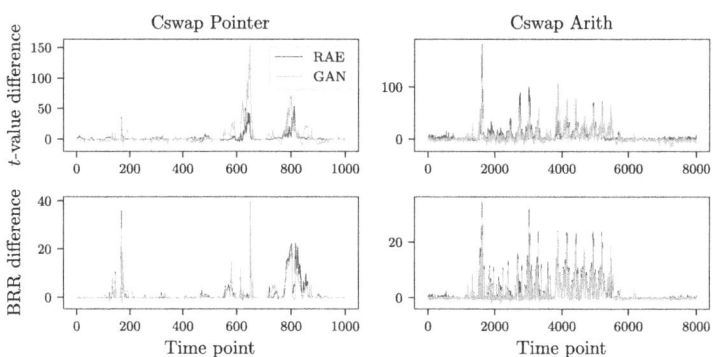

Fig. 8. Metrics difference before and after application of the RAE and CycleGAN. Top: t-values. Bottom: BRR. Positive values correspond to improvement, negative values to degradation.

For many time points, the mitigation process produces an improvement, which means that the correction of anomalies allows a better partitioning of classes by the clustering process. Additionally, some new areas show high BRR values while they were close to 50% before the mitigation process. This is especially visible for the area between samples 3500 and 5500 of the Arith dataset. However, these observations do not allow us to conclude that the information contained in these time points has increased or is simply more exploitable, which is more likely. This point is discussed at the end of this section.

It also interesting to observe the distributions of time samples whose BRR has been drastically increased by the mitigation process. Figure 9 shows the empirical p.d.f before and after application of the RAE and CycleGAN of time samples 650 and 168 of Pointer dataset and for time samples 1617 and 3028 of Arith dataset.

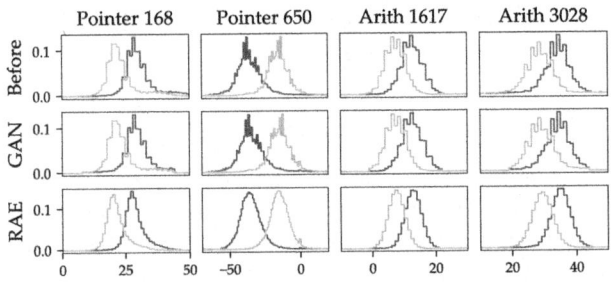

Fig. 9. Empirical p.d.f of four samples before and after application of the RAE and CycleGAN to mitigate abnormal values. Blue p.d.f corresponds to class $c = 0$ (resp. red $c = 1$). (Color figure online)

The changes in the distribution caused by the application of the CycleGAN is not visible to the eye. This is to be expected, since only a few percentages of the points (outliers and extremes values) are corrected by the CycleGAN because of the multiplexers. Other points are left unchanged, thus preserving the overall shape and moments of the distributions.

On the other hand, generated samples from the RAE seems to produce smoother mixture of normal distributions. This is an expected behavior as the RAE decomposition produces a completely new and thus changed patterns without any guarantee that the moments and the shape of the distributions (and thus the leakage) are preserved.

Overall, both methods allow for leakage exploitation through the clustering process without significant degradation of the input patterns. While unsupervised, these approaches seem to preserve the leakage and seem thus applicable in the context of unsupervised horizontal attacks.

7.3 Success Rate of Attacks

To estimate the effect on the end application, the success rates of different attacks have been compared.

The first attacks applied, before and after outlier and extreme reduction, consisted of *supervised* selection and ranking of PoIs with the *t*-test and then applying the *k*-means. Thus, the set of selected PoIs can be assumed to be close to the optimal one. Figure 10 shows the BRR versus the number of selected PoIs ranked according to the *t*-values. The application of RAE and GAN led to a slight increase in the BRR obtained on Cswap Pointer and Arith when the number of selected PoIs is below 50 and 100 respectively, because these points are only slightly affected by outliers. Above these numbers, the gain in BRR becomes more significant and is around 30% when the number of selected PoI remains below 150 and 200 respectively. This is an indication of the soundness of the proposed mitigation techniques, which delay the fall of the BRR by including more noisy and leaking points in the exploitable domain.

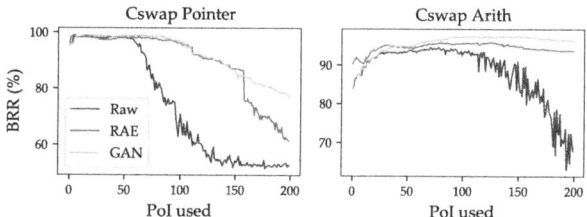

Fig. 10. BRR vs number of PoI considered when the mitigation of outliers is applied before PoIs selection and the selection and ranking of PoIs are done in a supervised manner.

The second attack considered is the unsupervised one proposed in [21]. The mitigation of outliers and extremes with the RAE and CycleGAN was applied either before the PoI selection (step 1) or immediately afterwards. In both cases, no improvement in the success rate of the attack was observed, regardless of the number of selected PoIs. It remained around 52%. Further analysis of the results showed that the effects of the mitigations were insufficient to significantly change the set of selected PoIs, which is not correct when using the DoM as a distinguisher on these trace sets. This was not a surprising result, as the number of points corrected with the RAE or CycleGAN is too limited to significantly change the DoM values.

Finally, the attack proposed in [9] has been considered. Similarly to what have been done for the attack reported in [21], the RAE or CycleGAN have been applied either before or after the selection of PoIs, thus considering a new set of PoI or the same than those found on raw traces.

Figure 11 shows the success rate of the attack when the mitigation is done before the selection of PoIs thus with a new set of PoI. The effect of the mitigation of outliers obtained on Pointer dataset is limited, in average, to a slight increase of the success rate. For Arith, the same conclusion can be drawn except that the BRR values falls down to values close to 50% when more than 80 PoI, instead of 40, are considered. This indicates that some points that were unexploitable are now exploitable. The effect of mitigation would have been more valuable on a dataset where the first 40 PoIs were not present. This is not the case here but one could concede this could happen.

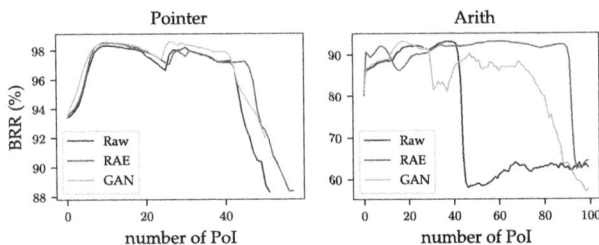

Fig. 11. BRR vs number of PoI considered when the mitigation of outliers is applied before PoIs selection and ranking with the method described in [9].

Figure 12 shows the success rate when the mitigation is applied after the selection of PoIs, i.e. considering the set of PoI found before mitigation.

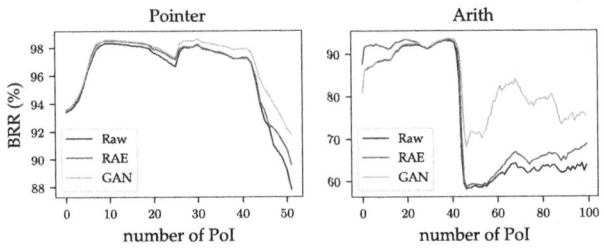

Fig. 12. BRR vs number of PoI considered when the mitigation of outliers is applied after PoIs selection and ranking with the method described in [9].

For Pointer datasets, there is no significant change in the results. Only a slight increase of the BRR is observed. For Cswap Arith, a similar trend can be observed, where PoIs with indexes 50 to 100 are more exploitable than before. However, these points are not the same than in previous the figure. This gives an indication that the mitigation of outliers and extremes was not sufficient to converge toward the best set of PoI which can be assumed to be one found in a supervised way.

Overall, the effects of mitigating outliers and extremes on the BRR of the supervised attack considered are significant, but are limited once PoI selection is done in an unsupervised manner (at least with the methods considered). This suggests that the proposed methods for reducing outliers are sound and that there is significant room for improvement in the way PoIs are selected, which appears to be the main limiting factor in the success rate of the attacks.

When comparing both approaches, it appears that mitigation before the PoI selection can produce more unreliable results during the PoI selection than applying the mitigation after a prior PoI selection. While identified PoI on raw patterns and after mitigation are almost the same (the overlap of their indexes is big), in some cases, new PoI which carry leakage are also identified if the selection is applied after the mitigation, especially matching indexes from Fig. 8. These side-effects from the unsupervised mitigation can affect the attack (positively or negatively) as showed on Fig. 11. Hence for these datasets a more robust strategy would be to firstly identify relevant PoI (even they are noisy) and then apply the cleaning process while keeping these PoI for the attack phase. Another possible strategy could also be for example to perform two attacks on both cases (mitigation before or after PoI selection) and combine the results. It is however necessary to apply the mitigation process on the whole patterns (and not only selected PoI) as relevant information can be also extracted from non identified PoI and neighboring points.

Finally, the overall attack complexity and remaining necessary exhaust after classes partitioning will depend on the used attack strategy. In this work, effort is put at showing the benefit of anomalies correction on the resulting leakage and exploitability rather than complete attack scheme. Furthermore, based on the successfully recovered part of the scalar, the effort for complete recovery will also depends on the exhaust strategy (see [18,23]). That is why only the BRR is considered as an indicator of the overall attack success. This allows to assess the relevance of proposed methods and is easily comparable between approaches.

Still, at this stage, one may wonder whether the mitigation preserves or restores the leakage, or simply limits the effect of outliers on the clustering process, thus allowing a more accurate estimation of centroids. This point is addressed in the next paragraphs.

7.4 Leakage Recovery Discussion

In order to obtain evidence on the ability of CycleGAN and RAE to restore (or preserve) the leakage when correcting an anomaly, the BRR values considering only the modified points by the networks have been extracted. This is depicted on 13. Using CycleGAN, only a few ($\leq 10\%$) of the points are corrected, while for RAE most of the points are modified, even if the changes are small.

As can be seen for Cswap Arith, in the leaky part of the patterns (time samples 1500 to 6000), many (between 55% and 80%) of the corrected time samples are classified in the correct cluster by the k-means after applying the RAE. The same can be observed with the CycleGAN, although the percentage of correctly classified bits is lower (between 55% and 70%). There are two reasons that could explain these results. Firstly, it is surprising but possible that both RAE and CycleGAN are able to recover some of the leakage thanks to the multidimensional treatment of the patterns. Secondly, the reduction of outliers and extremes limits their impact on the values of the centroids, allowing a better classification of all points.

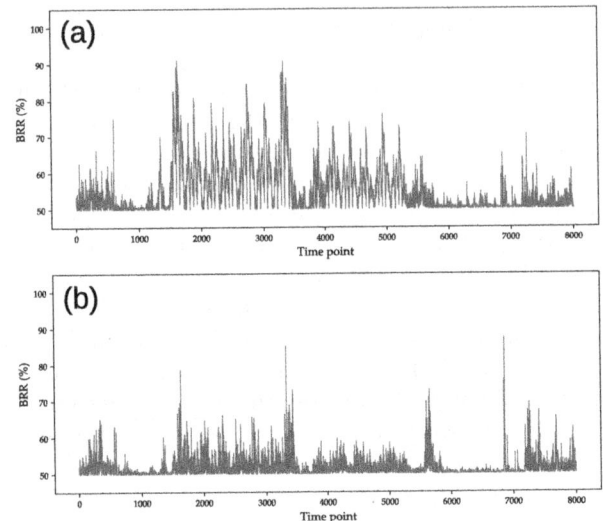

Fig. 13. BRR obtained for points of Cswap Arith whose values have been changed by the RAE or CycleGAN, on the two considered datasets.

The values of the two centroids before and after mitigation were therefore checked. Figure 14 shows the absolute differences between the centroids provided by the k-means applied to the raw patterns and after mitigation of the outliers with the RAE and the CycleGAN.

Results are given only for Cswap Arith dataset, since the results for Cswap Pointer are similar. From the analysis of Fig. 8, it appears that the time samples where the BRR has significantly increased (time samples indexes 1500 to 6000) due to the reduction of outliers and extremes coincide with the time samples where the centroids have been significantly shifted (corrected) by the RAE or CycleGAN. Thus, the BRR improvements appear to be at least partially, perhaps entirely, due to centroid correction, i.e., limiting the impact of outliers on centroid estimates. If the gains in BRR were entirely due to the correction of centroids, this would suggest that there is no recovery of leakage.

7.5 Denoising and Information Recovery

Still, one would wonder what is the impact of the proposed mitigation processes on the patterns noise levels and underlying information. It is crucial to know if the proposed framework globally reduces the leakage information or not. To this aim, the global Signal-to-noise ratio (SNR) [22] has been computed before and after application of the considered methods. Results are showed in Table 2.

An improvement over the measured SNR can be observed through the mitigation process. Indeed, the proposed methods allows to increase the SNR on Cswap Pointer by a factor of 1.7 using the CycleGAN, and by a factor of 2.3 on

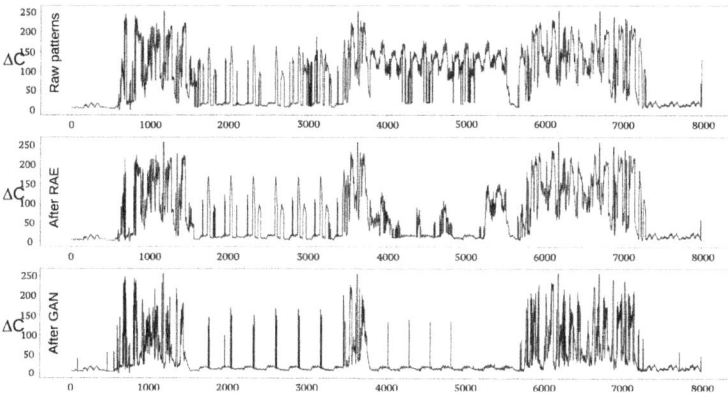

Fig. 14. Absolute differences between the centroids provided by the k-means without any mitigation of outliers and after application of the RAE or the CycleGAN, on the Cswap Arith dataset.

Table 2. Signal to noise ratio. Best results are highlighted in bold.

Dataset	Method		
	Raw patterns	After RAE	After GAN
Cswap Pointer	0.030	0.037	**0.052**
Cswap Arith	0.009	**0.021**	0.020

Cswap Arith using the RAE. This supports that the anomalies mitigation has a denoising effect on the treated patterns.

Finally, to decide on whether information was recovered or not, the mutual information (MI) between the correct scalar labels and the complete patterns was computed using MINE, a linearly scalable neural mutual information estimator [2,11] for high dimensionality estimation. Before the anomalies correction, the information contained in Cswap Arith (resp. Pointer) was estimated to be close to 0.923 bits (resp. 0.933 bits). After correction with the RAE and CycleGAN, the information contained in Cswap Arith is now estimated to be 0.943 bits and 0.949 bits, respectively. For Pointer, it is about 0.922 bits and 0.936 bits. The MI values between the *complete* patterns and the secret bits were thus very little changed by the anomalies reduction process. This supports the claim that no information has been recovered, but that the better estimation of the centroids allows more information (that was already present in the raw patterns) to be correctly exploited.

However, MINE was also used to estimate the MI between labels and sub-parts of the patterns. The sub-parts of the patterns consisted in 100 bins, thus blocks of 10 and 80 consecutive time points for Cswap Pointer and Cswap Arith, respectively. Figure 15 shows the difference in *local* MI before and after application of RAE or CycleGAN. Increases (or decreases) in MI are depicted in green (or red). Several increases in local MI of up to 0.3 bits for Arith and up to 0.2 bits for Cswap Pointer can be observed when applying the RAE. This corresponds to increases of about 20% of the *local* MI. The absolute MI gains are lower when the CycleGAN is used.

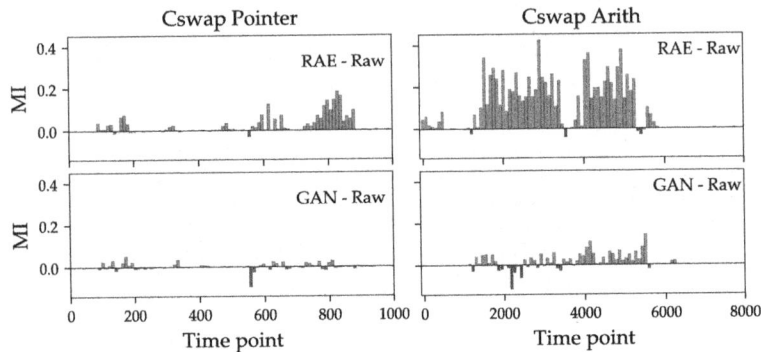

Fig. 15. Differences between local MI obtained after and before application of the RAE and CycleGAN to Pointer and Arith datasets.

Given that no *global* increase in MI was induced by the application of either RAE or CycleGAN, and that significant increases in *local* MI were observed, it is suggested through this observation that both RAE and CycleGAN transpose some of the information contained in outlier-free parts of the patterns into altered subparts during the anomalies correction process, and that this transposition brings back some time points with too many outliers or extremes values into the exploitable domain for the attacks. This helps the k-means to provide better estimates of centroids and thus slight increases of the BRR obtained through the clustering process.

8 Conclusion

The presence of outliers and extremes values in side-channel datasets can seriously reduce the efficiency of attacks, especially horizontal attacks, as well as leakage assessment methods. Classical methods are often used to mitigate the impact of outliers in an unsupervised way, although they are insufficient in high noise contexts.

In this paper, the potential of deep learning based (and thus multidimensional) methods have been investigated to mitigate the effects of anomalous values. To this aim, two candidates has showed to be efficient architectures for unsupervised anomalies mitigation. The first relevant candidate is a robust autoencoder (RAE) that can be applied in a fully unsupervised manner. The only a prior required is the percentage of abnormal values, which can be easily estimated. The second candidate is a modified generative model (CycleGAN), which can also be applied in a fully unsupervised way, as its multiplexers only requires the positioning of anomalies values. These methods have been applied to two noisy public datasets considered for horizontal attacks. It has been found that some time samples that were not exploitable for attacks before mitigation became exploitable after application of RAE and CycleGAN, probably caused by a transposition of leakage from outlier-free parts of patterns to corrected parts of patterns. Furthermore, their application showed improvement over the Signal-to-noise ratio and no degradation of the underlying leakage information, quite the opposite. While it is possible that the process of applying the two methods subsequently could be beneficial in some cases, on the considered datasets, the mitigation using either the RAE or CycleGAN impact the same leakage areas and thus would not be seen as an added value if combined. Furthermore, If done, it would result in overly complexity for choosing appropriate architecture and parameters tuning of both methods for the application in the context of horizontal attack. Furthermore, some side-effect could arise from application of the two methods together. Instead, some benefit could be seen if the two methods would be applied separately on the same data and their results used for further analysis.

Finally, It should also be noted that no special effort has been made to optimize the network architectures used or to tune their parameters. Therefore, there is still room for improvement.

Finally, one should note that although the application of these techniques led to an increase in the exploitability of the leakage for the datasets studied, the result could vary and dependent on the used datasets, the considered outliers or noise model as well as their associated quantities. Indeed, it would be relevant for future work to consider alternative anomalies models than the ones used in this work.

A Robust Autoencoder Architecture

The complete optimization procedure for the RAE, based on [14] work, is described in Algorithm 1.

Parameter ϵ corresponds to the stopping criterion for the optimization. The value of τ was chosen such that it reflects the amount of observed anomalies (see [14] for details). For the considered datasets, this parameter was set to $\tau = 0.04$ for Cswap Pointer and $\tau = 0.05$ for Cswap Arith respectively.

The network architecture was identical for the two datasets. The encoder network was built using four fully connected layers such that each layer size (the number of neurons) is the half of the previous one. The opposite was done for the decoder network. Each layer uses the ReLU activation, except the decoder last layer wich uses a hyperbolic tangent activation. The Adam optimizer was used with learning rate $\alpha = 10^{-4}$. The model forward/backward propagation is performed for 10 epochs at each optimization step using a batch size of 64 samples. Overall, no extensive architecture search nor parameter tuning has been performed, as the described configuration already exhibited sufficient efficiency.

Algorithm 1. Robust autoencoder optimization procedure

Require: X, τ, ϵ
Ensure: $X = L + S$
   $L \leftarrow 0$
   $S \leftarrow 0$
   $X^* \leftarrow X$
   repeat
      $L \leftarrow X - S$
      $\theta, \phi = \text{backprop}(L, \mathcal{F}_\theta, \mathcal{E}_\phi)$ ▷ optimize left term of Eq. 2 using gradient descent
      $L \leftarrow \mathcal{F}_\theta(\mathcal{E}_\phi(L))$
      $S \leftarrow X - L$
      $S \leftarrow \text{prox}(S, \tau)$ ▷ update S by minimizing $\tau\|S\|_1$ using Eq. 3
      $\epsilon_1 \leftarrow \frac{\|X - L - S\|_2}{\|X\|_2}$
      $\epsilon_2 \leftarrow \frac{\|X^* - L - S\|_2}{\|X\|_2}$
      $X^* \leftarrow L + S$
   until $\epsilon_1 \leq \epsilon$ or $\epsilon_2 \leq \epsilon$
   return L, S

Indeed, a simple architecture allowed to produce satisfactory results. It is thus important to keep in mind that the aforedescribed architecture and tuning should not be treated as optimal for the given task.

B CycleGAN with Multiplexers Architecture

The following network structures and parameters tuning has been chosen in the application of the proposed framework on the two considered datasets. Hereafter, one dimensional convolution of a filters, b kernel size and c stride is denoted as $C(a, b, c)$. Similarly, the one dimensional convolution transpose is noted $C'(a, b, c)$. Bath normalization layers is noted as B and non linear activation as $\underset{d}{A}$ with d the activation function.

Firstly, the GANs generator use the LSGAN architecture [16], to prevent vanishing gradient that could occurs during training. G_A, G_B are built from convolutional autoencoders, composed of three downsampling blocks for the encoders

$$C(64, 7, 1) \rightarrow B \rightarrow \underset{ReLU}{A} \rightarrow C(128, 3, 2) \rightarrow B \rightarrow \underset{ReLU}{A} \rightarrow C(256, 3, 2) \rightarrow B \rightarrow \underset{ReLU}{A}$$

and the three upsampling ones for the decoders. ReLU activation are used on all layers, except for last layer of the decoder where tanh is used instead.

$$C'(256, 3, 2) \rightarrow B \rightarrow \underset{ReLU}{A} \rightarrow C'(128, 3, 2) \rightarrow B \rightarrow \underset{ReLU}{A} \rightarrow C'(64, 7, 1) \rightarrow B \rightarrow \underset{tanh}{A}$$

GANs dicriminators D_A, D_B are pixel discriminators [13], where each point is classified as fake or real instead of the whole pattern. They are built from three convolutional blocks:

$$C(64, 1, 1) \rightarrow \underset{ReLU}{A} \rightarrow C(128, 1, 1) \rightarrow \underset{ReLU}{A} \rightarrow C(1, 1, 1)$$

The discriminator loss is computed using the mean squared error between the output of last convolutional block and ground truth, which corresponds to the vector $\mathbf{1}_h$ if the input is real or $\mathbf{0}_h$ if it has been generated, where h match the size of the discriminators output. The architecture is trained for 10 epochs at each optimization step, with a learning rate $\alpha = 10^{-5}$ and a batch size of 16 samples.

C Details on Implementation

The experimentations have been performed using Python 3.9. Implementation of the neural networks models has been done using the Pytorch library. For the proposed multiplexer CycleGAN, the implementation of the GAN networks is highly inspired from [27]. Based on this resource, implementation of the described multiplexer CycleGAN should be more straightforward.

For both methods, the complete optimization procedure is performed under 30 min using a Nvidia RTX 3080 GPU and Intel i9-10900k CPU.

Data scaling is applied globally (not featurewise) on the input raw matrices so that points lie in the range $(-1, 1)$ before training through the networks. This is computed as follow:

$$X' = 2 \cdot \frac{X - \min(X)}{\max(X) - \min(X)} - 1 \tag{10}$$

This is mandatory since tanh activations are used for networks output (RAE and CycleGAN generators).

References

1. Bakker, M., Wicherts, J.M.: Outlier removal, sum scores, and the inflation of the type i error rate in independent samples t tests: the power of alternatives and recommendations. Psychol. Methods **19**(3), 409–427 (2014). https://doi.org/10.1037/met0000014
2. Belghazi, I., Rajeswar, S., Baratin, A., Hjelm, R.D., Courville, A.C.: MINE: mutual information neural estimation. arXiv preprint arXiv:1801.04062 (2018)
3. Benadjila, R., Prouff, E., Strullu, R., Cagli, E., Dumas, C.: Deep learning for side-channel analysis and introduction to ASCAD database. J. Cryptogr. Eng. **10**(2), 163–188 (2020)
4. Boussam, S., Albillos, N.C.: Keep it unsupervised: horizontal attacks meet simple classifiers. In: Bhasin, S., Roche, T. (eds.) Smart Card Research and Advanced Applications, pp. 213–234. Springer, Cham (2024). https://doi.org/10.1007/978-3-031-54409-5_11
5. Candès, E.J., Li, X., Ma, Y., Wright, J.: Robust principal component analysis? J. ACM **58**(3) (2011). https://doi.org/10.1145/1970392.1970395
6. Carbone, M., et al.: Deep learning to evaluate secure RSA implementations. IACR Trans. Cryptograph. Hardw. Embedded Syst. **2019**(2), 132–161 (2019). https://doi.org/10.13154/tches.v2019.i2.132-161 https://doi.org/10.13154/tches.v2019.i2.132-161 https://doi.org/10.13154/tches.v2019.i2.132-161

7. Chari, S., Rao, J.R., Rohatgi, P.: Template attacks. In: Kaliski, B.S., Koç, C.K., Paar, C. (eds.) Cryptographic Hardware and Embedded Systems - CHES 2002, pp. 13–28. LNCS, Springer, Berlin, Heidelberg (2003). https://doi.org/10.1007/3-540-36400-5_3
8. Cler, G.: Horizontal side channel attacks on noisy traces, Theses, Université de Montpellier (2024). https://theses.hal.science/tel-04730413
9. Cler, G., Ordas, S., Maurine, P.: Bernoulli at the root of horizontal side channel attacks. In: Bhasin, S., Roche, T. (eds.) Smart Card Research and Advanced Applications, pp. 107–126. Springer, Cham (2024). https://doi.org/10.1007/978-3-031-54409-5_6
10. Cowell, F.A., Victoria-Feser, M.P.: Robustness properties of inequality measures. Econometrica **64**(1), 77–101 (1996)
11. Cristiani, V., Lecomte, M., Maurine, P.: Leakage assessment through neural estimation of the mutual information. In: Zhou, J., et al. (eds.) ACNS 2020. LNCS, vol. 12418, pp. 144–162. Springer, Cham (2020). https://doi.org/10.1007/978-3-030-61638-0_9
12. Goodfellow, I.J., et al.: Generative adversarial networks. arXiv preprint arXiv: 1406.2661 (2014)
13. Isola, P., Zhu, J.Y., Zhou, T., Efros, A.A.: Image-to-image translation with conditional adversarial networks. arXiv preprint arXiv:1611.07004 (2018)
14. Kieu, T., et al.: Robust and explainable autoencoders for unsupervised time series outlier detection—extended version. arXiv preprint arXiv:2204.03341 (2022)
15. Kim, J., Picek, S., Heuser, A., Bhasin, S., Hanjalic, A.: Make some noise. unleashing the power of convolutional neural networks for profiled side-channel analysis. IACR Trans. Cryptograph. Hardw. Embedded Syst. **2019**, 148–179 (2019). https://doi.org/10.13154/tches.v2019.i3.148-179
16. Mao, X., Li, Q., Xie, H., Lau, R.Y.K., Wang, Z., Smolley, S.P.: Least squares generative adversarial networks. arXiv preprint arXiv:1611.04076 (2017)
17. Masure, L., Dumas, C., Prouff, E.: Gradient visualization for general characterization in profiling attacks. In: Polian, I., Stöttinger, M. (eds.) Constructive Side-Channel Analysis and Secure Design, pp. 145–167. Springer, Cham (2019). https://doi.org/10.1007/978-3-030-16350-1_9
18. Micheli, G.D., Heninger, N.: Recovering cryptographic keys from partial information, by example. Cryptology ePrint Archive, Paper 2020/1506 (2020). https://eprint.iacr.org/2020/1506
19. Nascimento, E., Chmielewski, L.: Applying horizontal clustering side-channel attacks on embedded ECC implementations (extended version), p. 23
20. Perin, G., Chmielewski, L., Batina, L., Picek, S.: Keep it unsupervised: horizontal attacks meet deep learning. IACR Trans. Cryptogr. Hardw. Embed. Syst. **2021**(1), 343–372 (2021)
21. Perin, G., Imbert, L., Torres, L., Maurine, P.: Attacking randomized exponentiations using unsupervised learning. In: Prouff, E. (ed.) COSADE 2014. LNCS, vol. 8622, pp. 144–160. Springer, Cham (2014). https://doi.org/10.1007/978-3-319-10175-0_11
22. Prouff, E., Strullu, R., Benadjila, R., Cagli, E., Dumas, C.: Study of deep learning techniques for side-channel analysis and introduction to ASCAD database. Cryptology ePrint Archive, Paper 2018/053 (2018). https://doi.org/10.1007/s13389-019-00220-8
23. Schindler, W., Walter, C.D.: Optimal recovery of secret keys from weak side channel traces. In: Parker, M.G. (ed.) IMACC 2009. LNCS, vol. 5921, pp. 446–468. Springer, Heidelberg (2009). https://doi.org/10.1007/978-3-642-10868-6_27

24. Zaid, G., Bossuet, L., Habrard, A., Venelli, A.: Methodology for efficient CNN architectures in profiling attacks. IACR Trans. Cryptograph. Hardw. Embedd. Syst. **2020**, 1–36 (2020). https://doi.org/10.13154/tches.v2020.i1.1-36
25. Zhou, C., Paffenroth, R.C.: Anomaly detection with robust deep autoencoders. In: Proceedings of the 23rd ACM SIGKDD International Conference on Knowledge Discovery and Data Mining, pp. 665–674. KDD '17, Association for Computing Machinery, New York, NY, USA (2017). https://doi.org/10.1145/3097983.3098052
26. Zhu, J.Y., Park, T., Isola, P., Efros, A.A.: Unpaired image-to-image translation using cycle-consistent adversarial networks. arXiv preprint arXiv:1703.10593 (2020)
27. Zhu, J.Y., Park, T., Wang, T.: CycleGANandpix2pixinPyTorch. https://github.com/aitorzip/PyTorch-CycleGAN

Profiling Side-Channel Attack on HQC Polynomial Multiplication Using Machine Learning Methods

Tomáš Rabas[1](✉)[iD], Jiří Buček[1][iD], Vincent Grosso[3][iD], Karolína Zenknerová[2][iD], and Róbert Lórencz[1][iD]

[1] Faculty of Information Technology, Czech Technical University in Prague, Prague, Czech Republic
{tomas.rabas,jiri.bucek,robert.lorencz}@fit.cvut.cz
[2] National Cyber and Information Security Agency, Prague, Czech Republic
[3] Université Jean Monnet Saint-Etienne, CNRS, Institut d'Optique Graduate School, Laboratoire Hubert Curien UMR 5516, 42023 Saint-Etienne, France
vincent.grosso@cnrs.fr

Abstract. The Hamming Quasi-Cyclic (HQC) cryptosystem was selected for standardization in the 4th round of the NIST post-quantum standardization competition targeting Public-key Encryption and Key-establishment algorithms. In this paper, we propose a profiling power side-channel attack on a HQC cryptosystem exploiting power consumption leakage during polynomial multiplication in the beginning of the decryption. The new attack scheme is based on generic methods such as Welch's ANOVA test or multilayer perceptron with a grid-search algorithm used for the hyperparameter tuning. Consequently, it is easily extendable also to other side-channel attacks. Results of the practical evaluation are presented, using a 32-bit STM32F303 Arm Cortex-M4 processor as a target. We show that a trained model is able to recover the correct key bit from large majority of tests – in the practical evaluation, maximum 6 out of 20 000 tests failed in recovering the correct key bit. For the testing, we follow a single-trace scenario, which assumes that only one decryption power trace is available.

Keywords: Side-Channel Attack · Polynomial Multiplication · HQC · Post-Quantum Cryptography · Machine Learning

1 Introduction

Recent advances in quantum computer design have given rise to one of the greatest security threats in modern cryptography. Indeed, in 1994, Peter Shor published algorithms dedicated to quantum computers, which were able to efficiently solve problems associated with discrete logarithms and factorization of big integers [Sho94] – two mathematical operations on which the classical public-key cryptography is based. This has started a new era of the so-called post-quantum cryptography (PQC) [NSB+23].

In 2016, the National Institute of Standards and Technology (NIST) has started a new public-key algorithm contest aiming to select new quantum-resistant public-key algorithms. In July 2022, NIST closed the 3rd selection round [AAC+22], in which the CRYSTALS-Kyber algorithm has been selected as a new standard for the Public-key Encryption and Key-establishment algorithms, under the name of ML-KEM in the Federal Information Processing Standard (FIPS) 203. At the same time, NIST has started the 4th selection round aiming to find an alternative algorithm. Four candidates were included in the 4th round: BIKE, Classic McEliece, HQC and SIKE. While SIKE was later found to be critically vulnerable [CD23], the HQC algorithm was later on 11th March 2025 from the remaining candidates chosen as the new standard.

Besides the algorithmic aspects, also the implementation aspects including possible side-channel attacks have to be evaluated in the framework of the selection process. This remains an open task.

Related Works. The first published power side-channel attack on HQC [SRSWZ21] presents how to build an oracle that specifies whether the BCH decoder in HQC's decryption algorithm corrects an error for a chosen ciphertext with 10 000 measurements (traces).

Goy et al. [GLG22] show that it is possible to retrieve a static secret key targeting the Hadamard transform in the Reed-Muller (RM) decoding step with an electromagnetic attack using 20 000 traces (Table 1).

Table 1. Known side-channel attacks on the HQC cryptosystem

Article	Attacked part	# traces	Method	Targeted secret
[SRSWZ21]	BCH decoder	$4^a/10\,000^b$	PC Oracle (templates)	private key
[GLG22]	Hadamard transf. (RM dec.)	20 000	PC Oracle (LDA^c)	private key
[SHR+22]	RSRM decoder	$1\,000^1/100\,000^2$	PC Oracle (templates)	private key
[GMGL24]	RS decoder	1	PC Oracle (SASCA)	shared secret key
[DG24]	RM decoder	< 1 000	PC Oracle (CNN^d)	private key
This paper	base_mul	1	MLP^e	private key

^{a} number of template traces for initialization of the oracle
^{b} number of correctly classified traces necessary for oracle calls for full-key recovery
^{c} Linear Discriminant Analysis (LDA)
^{d} Convolutional Neural Network (CNN)
^{e} Multilayer Perceptron (MLP)

The attack proposed by Schamberger et al. [SHR+22] targets the Reed-Muller Reed-Solomon (RMRS) version of HQC from the 3rd round of the NIST competition by adapting the idea of the attack from [UXT+22]. The attack exploits side-channel information from the execution of a pseudorandom function (PRF) or pseudorandom number generator (PRG) in the re-encryption of the KEM decapsulation. The attack in [SHR+22] creates a Plaintext-Checking

(PC) oracle using SCA. The oracle is then exploited to recover the private key block by block.

Moving to more recent results, the study by Dong and Guo [DG24] presents plaintext-checking oracle based attack using templates constructed from offline access to the publicly available decoding function of Reed-Muller codes. This attack significantly reduces the number of oracle calls.

The first Soft Analytical Side-Channel Attack (SASCA) on code-based cryptography and HQC was presented by Goy et al. [GMGL24]. They targeted mainly the Reed-Solomon (RS) decoder and achieved to recover a shared secret key using a single power trace. As part of the attack, they also target a polynomial multiplication inside the RS decoder, which computes a multiplication of an 8-bit polynomial representing part of a codeword as the first input and an 8-bit polynomial representing part of the parity check matrix as the second input. In comparison with this paper, we target a polynomial multiplication that occurs before the RS decoder itself and where the private key and ciphertext are the inputs for the multiplication. Also, we focus on recovering the private key (not shared secret key), as the attacker with its possession can simply decode the shared secret key from transmitted data.

It can be observed that all attacks designed to recover the private key necessitate a minimum of one thousand traces. Conversely, the sole single trace attack is capable of recovering the shared secret key.

Regarding HQC implementation protected by a countermeasure, Spyropoulos et al. [SVP+24] presented a masked NIST submission specification-compliant vector generation function. It provides a secure implementation of one part of the whole HQC KEM.

Contributions. In this paper, we perform a simple yet efficient profiled side-channel attack against the additional implementation of HQC. It is the first attack targeting the polynomial multiplication in the beginning of the HQC decryption (i.e. before decoding), and also the first single-trace SCA attack against HQC cryptosystem which targets the private key.

As described in Sect. 4.3, practical evaluation suggests that we can recover the full private key with 51.1% probability from a single trace. The complexity of further brute-forcing the potentially incorrect bits is $2^{14.11}$ following the strategy presented by Zaid et al. [ZBHV21], making the attack highly feasible. We also propose two countermeasures based on masking [GP99,ISW03]. The first countermeasure is a low-entropy approach that leverages the sliding window technique utilized in the base_mul operation. The second countermeasure is a classical Boolean masking implementation of the base_mul sensitive function with two shares. Security evaluation of these countermeasures is provided using our proposed attack, showing that both of them prevent the recovery of the private key in the attack.

Our attack consists of a profiling phase and an attacking phase. In the profiling phase, we:

- measure the training dataset of 40 000 traces and validation dataset of 10 000 traces, both with a unique random key and ciphertext for each trace;

- select points of interest using the Welch's ANOVA statistical tests on the training dataset;
- train the multi-layer perceptron models for each bit using the datasets for training and validation.

In the attacking phase, we test the ability of the models to recover the private key bits using an independently measured dataset of 20 000 traces. At the last step, classical post-processing may be needed to correct a few incorrectly predicted bits.

Paper Organization. In Sect. 2, we begin by presenting the targeted Hamming Quasi-Cyclic (HQC) cryptosystem, providing details of the concrete target implementation and explaining algorithms that we use for the attack. In Sect. 3, we present a profiling side-channel analysis (SCA) process on the polynomial multiplication at the beginning of the HQC decryption. In Sect. 4, we describe two possible mitigations with different cost and security efficiencies and show the results of our attack with a comparison to the original implementation. In the end, we summarize the results of this paper in Sect. 5.

2 Background

In this section, we provide overview of the HQC algorithm and describe the hardware and software which was used to validate the attack principle, and briefly describe generic attack methods which have been used.

We denote by GF(2) the binary finite field consisting of the elements 0 and 1, and we denote by $\mathcal{R}$ the polynomial ring $GF(2)[X]/(X^n-1)$, where n is a positive integer. For a polynomial $h \in \mathcal{R}$, the Hamming weight w_h refers to the number of non-zero coefficients in the vector representation of h. The notation sample($\mathcal{R}$) indicates that we uniformly sample an element from $\mathcal{R}$, while sample($\mathcal{R}, w_h$) specifies that the Hamming weight of the sampled element must be equal to w_h.

2.1 Overview of the Hamming Quasi-Cyclic (HQC) Cryptosystem

Hamming Quasi-Cyclic (HQC) algorithm [MAB+18] is an IND-CCA2 secure post-quantum cryptographic scheme for Key Encapsulation Mechanisms (KEM) based on HQC Public-Key Encryption (PKE) which is only CPA secure. The HQC PKE relies on the hardness of problems related to codes, specifically leveraging the hardness of the Quasi-Cyclic Syndrom Decoding (QCSD) problem. QCSD is a restriction of the Syndrom Decoding (SD) problem to quasi-cyclic codes. The SD problem can be described as follows: Given a matrix H, a syndrome s, and a weight w, find a vector e of weight w such that $He = s$. The SD problem has been proved to be NP-complete in 1978 by Berlekamp, McEliece and van Tilborg [BMvT78].

Although we only focus our attack on the decryption operation described in Algorithm 3, for the sake of completeness, we also include a concise description of the rest of the cryptosystem.

HQC Public Key Encryption. Following the description from [HSC+23], HQC PKE consists of three algorithms – key generation, encryption and decryption. HQC uses two codes. The first one is a public $[n, k]$-code $\mathcal{C}$, generated by G, which can correct at least Δ errors efficiently. The second one is a random double-circulant $[2n, n]$-code, where the parity check matrix can be expressed as $(1, h)$, exploiting the double-circulant property. The code $\mathcal{C}$ has been originally proposed as a concatenated code of BCH and Repetition code. Later on, it was superseded by a concatenation of Reed-Muller and Reed-Solomon code (RMRS) that was found to be strictly better than the BCH-Repetition version [HQCa].

In key generation, polynomials h, x and y are first randomly sampled, where the Hamming weight of x and y is w. Then, the private and public key are set to be $sk = (x, y)$ and $pk = (h, s)$ respectively, where $s = x + h \cdot y$. The process is described in Algorithm 1.

Algorithm 1. The key-generation algorithm of the HQC PKE.

Require: HQC security parameters
Ensure: private key $sk = (x, y)$ and public key $pk = (h, s)$
1: $h \leftarrow \texttt{sample}(\mathcal{R})$
2: $x \leftarrow \texttt{sample}(\mathcal{R}, w)$
3: $y \leftarrow \texttt{sample}(\mathcal{R}, w)$
4: $s \leftarrow x + h \cdot y$
5: **return** $sk = (x, y)$ and $pk = (h, s)$

In encryption, first a pseudo-random number generator is initialized by θ. Polynomials r_1 and r_2 with Hamming weight w_r and polynomial e with Hamming weight w_e are (deterministically) sampled. Then, a ciphertext $c = (u, v)$ is formed, where polynomials u and v are computed as follows: $u = r_1 + h \cdot r_2$ and $v = m\mathbf{G} + s \cdot r_2 + e$. The matrix $\mathbf{G}$ is defined by the code $\mathcal{C}$ being used. The process is described in Algorithm 2.

Algorithm 2. The encryption algorithm of the HQC PKE.

Require: public key $pk = (h, s)$, plaintext m, seed θ
Ensure: ciphertext $c = (u, v)$
1: $r_1 \leftarrow \texttt{sample}(\mathcal{R}, w_r)$
2: $r_2 \leftarrow \texttt{sample}(\mathcal{R}, w_r)$
3: $e \leftarrow \texttt{sample}(\mathcal{R}, w_e)$
4: $u = r_1 + h \cdot r_2$
5: $v = m\mathbf{G} + s \cdot r_2 + e$
6: **return** $c = (u, v)$

Decryption only consists of decoding $v - u \cdot y$, where

$$\begin{aligned} v - u \cdot y &= m\mathbf{G} + s \cdot r_2 + e - (r_1 + h \cdot r_2) \cdot y \\ &= m\mathbf{G} + (x + h \cdot y) \cdot r_2 + e - r_1 \cdot y - h \cdot y \cdot r_2 \\ &= m\mathbf{G} + \underbrace{x \cdot r_2 - r_1 \cdot y + e}_{\text{denoted } e'} \end{aligned}$$

The decoding will be successful if the Hamming weight of the error term e' is sufficiently small so that the code $\mathcal{C}$ can correct it. In this paper, we focus on the side-channel leakage of the polynomial multiplication $u \cdot y$ computed during the decryption process. The process is described in Algorithm 3, where the target operation is highlighted on line 1. More specifically, our attack focuses on recovering the bits in operand y.

Notice that the polynomial multiplication is computed before the decoding even starts. This makes our attack independent of the choice of the concatenated code $\mathcal{C}$. Also, it allows us to focus on the side-channel leakage during the first operations that manipulate the private key bits in the decryption process.

Algorithm 3. The decryption algorithm of the HQC PKE.

Require: private key $sk = (x, y)$, ciphertext $c = (u, v)$
Ensure: plaintext m
1: $m = \mathcal{C}.\text{Decode}(v - \boxed{u \cdot y})$
2: **return** m

2.2 Attacked Target Implementation

As side-channel attacks are in general device dependent and their validation is greatly affected by the hardware and software used, in this subsection we will describe our choice of both for our experiments.

Software. The authors of HQC submitted several implementations of this algorithm to the NIST PQC competition. In October 2022 they added a pure constant-time (not optimized) implementation in C referred as "additional implementation". From the implementation of the whole HQC cryptosystem [HQCb], we extracted our target gf2x.c which implements the multiplication of two polynomials, together with the necessary dependency files. Note that the additional implementation remained the same also in the latest updated submission package for round 4 [HQCc].

The multiplication is implemented by the Karatsuba algorithm followed by a modular reduction of the resulting polynomial. Once the input into recursive calls of Karatsuba reaches a size of only 64 bits, the implementation computes the algorithm mul1 from [BGTZ08] in the function called base_mul.

The high-level description of `base_mul` multiplication for polynomials over GF(2) is as follows. Each polynomial such as $a = \sum_{i=0}^{63} a_i X^i$ is stored as a sequence of its coefficients $(a_{63}, a_{62}, \ldots, a_0) = a_{63..0}$, and $b = b_{63..0}$, resulting in a 128-bit polynomial $c = a \cdot b = c_{127..0}$.

Important to note is that the polynomial multiplication function takes the private key as its first operand and the ciphertext as its second operand. This holds true also for the call of the `base_mul` function. Therefore, in the rest of the paper we focus on extracting the bits from the first input operand a, which in fact stores the bits of the private key.

The first step (see Listing 1) is precomputing the table u of sixteen 64-bit words with the partial products of the lower 60 bits of b with all possible 4-bit polynomials (lines 8–13). The first partial product $g = a_{3..0} \cdot b_{59..0}$ is prepared using the table u (lines 14–19), which in effect is $g = u[a_{3..0}]$. This way, the lower 64-bit word l of the result is obtained, and the higher word h is zeroed (lines 20–21).

Step 2: The other bits, $a_{63..4}$ are scanned (in increments of 4), and each partial product $g = u[a_{i+3..i}] = a_{i+3..i} \cdot b_{59..0}$ is computed (lines 24–29). Then it is shifted and added by xoring at the appropriate position in the pair of low and high words l, h (lines 30–31). By the end of Step 2, the intermediate product is $(h, l) = a \cdot b_{59..0}$.

Step 3: The remaining top 4 bits of b are now multiplied bit by bit with a by logical "and" masking and added to the result at the top 4 positions (lines 34–45). The result is $c_{127..0} = (h, l) = a \cdot b$.

In the additional implementation, the algorithm `mul1` from [BGTZ08] is adapted to be time-constant and resistant to cache timing attacks. To protect against cache timing attacks, each time a tabulated pre-calculated value needs to be used, *all* pre-calculated values are accessed so that the attacker cannot determine which value was accessed by cache measurement. This protection measure corresponds to the for loops in lines 16-19 and 26-29.

The processing of the a operand described above is reflected in the power consumption dependency on the values of individual bits of a. This will be visible in the heat map we present in Fig. 3 as part of our attack description below.

```
1  void base_mul(uint64_t *c, uint64_t a, uint64_t b) {
2      uint64_t h = 0;
3      uint64_t l = 0;
4      uint64_t g;
5      uint64_t u[16] = {0};
6      uint64_t mask_tab[4] = {0};
7      // Step 1
8      u[0] = 0;
9      u[1] = b & ((1ULL << (64 - 4)) - 1ULL);
10     for(int i=2;i<16;i+=2){
11         u[i] = u[i/2] << 1;
12         u[i+1] = u[i] ^ u[1];
13     }
14     g=0;
15     uint64_t tmp1 = a &15;
16     for(int i = 0; i < 16; i++) {
17         uint64_t tmp2 = tmp1 - i;
18         g ^= (u[i] & -(1 - ((tmp2 | -tmp2) >> 63)));
19     }
20     l = g;
```

```
h = 0;
// Step 2
for (uint8_t i = 4; i < 64; i += 4) {
    g = 0;
    uint64_t tmp1 = (a >> i) &15;
    for (int j = 0; j < 16; ++j) {
        uint64_t tmp2 = tmp1 - j;
        g ^= (u[j] & -(1 - ((tmp2 | -tmp2) >> 63)));
    }
    l ^= g << i;
    h ^= g >> (64 - i);
}
// Step 3
mask_tab [0] = - ((b >> 60) & 1);
mask_tab [1] = - ((b >> 61) & 1);
mask_tab [2] = - ((b >> 62) & 1);
mask_tab [3] = - ((b >> 63) & 1);
l ^= ((a << 60) & mask_tab[0]);
h ^= ((a >> 4) & mask_tab[0]);
l ^= ((a << 61) & mask_tab[1]);
h ^= ((a >> 3) & mask_tab[1]);
l ^= ((a << 62) & mask_tab[2]);
h ^= ((a >> 2) & mask_tab[2]);
l ^= ((a << 63) & mask_tab[3]);
h ^= ((a >> 1) & mask_tab[3]);
c[0] = l;
c[1] = h;
}
```

Listing 1. The base_mul function from gf2x.c from the "additional implementation" in the HQC submission packages (rounds 3 and 4)

The objective of the proposed attack is to recover the bits of the polynomial a while it is being used in the aforementioned base_mul function. The proposed countermeasures are based on a modification of the core of the base_mul function.

Target Hardware and Measurement Platform. Target hardware was a 32-bit STM32F303RBT6 Arm Cortex-M4 microcontroller with 128 KB Flash and 40 KB SRAM. The target is integrated in a single-board version of NewAE ChipWhisperer-Lite connected through a micro USB cable to a standard PC workstation. A simplified schematic is depicted in Fig. 1. For capturing the traces, we used the in-built capturing solution (oscilloscope that is integrated into ChipWhisperer-Lite) synchronized with the target with a limited trace length of around 25k samples per trace.

We capture the power consumption corresponding to the beginning of the polynomial multiplication involved in decryption of the ciphertext with the private key. In the available trace length, we observe samples influenced by the first approx. 100 bits of the private key. This limitation could be overcome by using an external oscilloscope or capturing device with a streaming mode for long captures like CW1200 ChipWhisperer-Pro or ChipWhisperer-Husky.

Due to the small SRAM memory of the target microcontroller, the parameter n defining the length of the private key had to be reduced for the experiment in this paper and the original size proposed in the NIST submission (for any level of security) unfortunately could not be used.

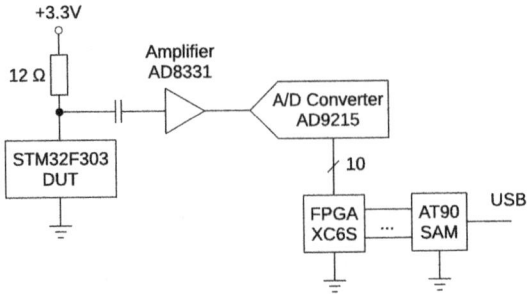

Fig. 1. Simplified block diagram of the ChipWhisperer-Lite power side channel analysis platform. The Device Under Test (DUT) is the microcontroller that runs the attacked cryptosystem. The measured signal is filtered, amplified, sampled and converted by the integrated capture circuitry of ChipWhisperer-Lite. It is then transferred over USB to the PC (not depicted).

2.3 Overview of Attack Algorithms

In the side-channel analysis presented in this paper, we used two generic techniques: the Welch's ANOVA test and the multilayer perceptron machine-learning algorithm with grid search hyperparameter tuning.

Welch's ANOVA Test. This statistical test was introduced in 1951 by Bernard Lewis Welch in [Wel51]. The test was used to decide whether two or more population means are equal. Compared to the classical analysis of the variance (as it is done in the ANOVA test), the Welch's ANOVA test does not assume equal variances, but it still requires normal distributions of the tested populations and independence of individual samples.

Later, the Welch's ANOVA test started to be used also as a tool for side-channel leakage assessment [YJ21]. The idea is to divide side-channel samples into multiple classes and test the difference among these classes using the test. The leakage points and points which do not leak can be distinguished by determining whether the null hypothesis is accepted or not. The leakage points selected by the tests are commonly called Points of Interest (POIs).

For implementation of the Welch's ANOVA test, we used the `welch_anova()` function from the Pingouin library [Val18] written for the Python programming language.

MLP. Multilayer perceptron (MLP) is a simple supervised feed-froward neural network with an input layer, one or more hidden layers and an output layer. We have chosen this model since it is commonly used for classification tasks.

In this paragraph we briefly describe MLP and provide some details about our training. For more information about MLP and backpropagation we refer to the Pattern Recognition and Machine Learning by Christopher Bishop [Bis06].

The i-th output of neuron y_i from a hidden layer in MLP can be described as follows: let $x_1, \ldots x_n$ be outputs from the previous layer, let $w_1, \ldots w_n$ be weights, β_i is a bias and f is an activation function. Then

$$y_i = f\left(\left(\sum_{j=1}^{n} x_j \cdot w_j\right) + \beta_i\right),$$

where f is applied to every neuron in the hidden layer. We use two types of activation functions, ReLU and tanh, which are defined as follows:

$$\text{ReLU}(x) = \begin{cases} x & \text{if } x > 0 \\ 0 & \text{otherwise,} \end{cases}$$

$$\tanh(x) = \frac{e^x - e^{-x}}{e^x + e^{-x}}.$$

Our input layer consists of POIs of one trace. The output layer is a single neuron with the sigmoid activation function that performs classification of the chosen bit of the key. The sigmoid function is defined as follows:

$$\text{sigmoid}(x) = \frac{1}{1 + e^{-x}}.$$

Sometimes we also add a batch normalization layer that normalizes a mini-batch of samples. The batch normalization is described in the paper [IS15] by S. Ioffe and Ch. Szegedy.

The goal of model training is to obtain parameters, weights and biases which minimize the loss function. We use the binary cross-entropy loss function and we evaluate the result using the binary accuracy metric. The corresponding functions are described in The Basics of Machine Learning [Cer23].

The training algorithm automatically minimizes the loss function and finds parameters using backpropagation. We use the AdamW optimizer algorithm for the training. AdamW was introduced in 2017 as a modification of the Adam optimizer [LH17].

For the implementation of MLP model and for training we used the Keras [C+15] and PyTorch [AYH+24] libraries written in Python.

Hyperparameter Tuning and Grid Search. Hyperparameters are parameters that cannot be trained and they have to be set manually, e.g., the number of neurons in one layer. Searching for hyperparameters which optimize the training procedure and give us the best model can be automated. Grid search exhaustively searches through all chosen values of hyperparameters, trains a model for every setting and returns the model with the best accuracy on validation data.

We combined the grid search with an early stopping. The early stopping is used to stop the training when the loss on the validation data stops improving. We used EarlyStopping from Keras library. We implemented grid search and early stopping using the Keras [C+15], KerasTuner [OBL+19] and PyTorch [AYH+24] libraries.

3 Profiling SCA on Polynomial Multiplication in HQC Multiplication

In this section, we describe our attack and experimental results against polynomial multiplication in HQC decryption implemented by gf2x.c function in the additional implementation submitted to the NIST PQC competition. It is a side-channel attack with the assumption of the attacker's ability to get access to the device and measure side-channel leakage physically – in our case, power consumption of the device while running the target operation. We also use a profiling phase in our attack scheme, which assumes the ability of the attacker to have the same kind of device in hand together with the ability to measure the side-channel leakage of the target operation with known inputs (including private keys) on this device.

Due to the limitations of the utilised hardware, we present in this paper experimental validation of our attack scheme only on the HQC polynomial multiplication with reduced parameter $n = 1234$, which is shorter than the size of the private key $n = 17\,669$ for level 1 according to NIST security categories, and would make the cryptosystem practically insecure against classical cryptanalysis. We argue that the shortening does not conflict with the main idea of exploiting power leakage from the implemented algorithm to gain knowledge about the private key, since we did not take any advantage of the shortening of the private key in our attack scheme and it does not alter the implementation in any significant way other than in number of recursive calls of the Karatsuba algorithm.

3.1 Attack Scheme

For implementing the attack we measured three datasets: 40 000 traces for training, 10 000 traces for validation in hyperparameter tuning, and 20 000 traces for testing.

For each bit of the private key, we selected POIs using Welch's ANOVA test on the training dataset, trained machine-learning multilayer perceptron model with grid search hyperparameter tuning using POIs from the training and validation datasets, and then tested the best model on 20 000 traces from the testing dataset.

Note that following this scheme we get one multilayer perceptron model for each bit of the private key.

The POI selection is done by dividing all training traces into two groups according to the possible values of the key-bit 0 or 1. For each sample of traces (where each trace consists of around 24 000 samples), we run the Welch's ANOVA test and store the resulting F-statistics. We select 480 points with the highest F-statistics and those are the POIs (features) used for machine-learning training, validation and testing.

The grid-search for MLP hyperparameter tuning was run through the following parameters: First layer: 512 or 1024 nodes, second layer: 128 or 256 nodes, activation function: ReLU or tanh, batch size: 200, 500 or 800. The last parameter run through 3 selected ways how to construct MLP: two layers with the same chosen activation function and batch normalization between them, two layers with the same chosen activation function but without batch normalization, and MLP just from one layer.

3.2 Attack Complexity

For training, validation and testing of MLP models, we used hardware with the following parameters: Memory – 96 GiB; Processor – Intel® Xeon(R) Gold 6136 CPU @ 3.00 GHz × 48; Disk Capacity – 3TB; OS – Ubuntu 22.04.5 LTS. Note that we did not use hardware with a GPU.

The most time-consuming part of the attack scheme is the grid search for the MLP hyperparameter tuning, which uses 40 000 samples for training and independent 10 000 samples for validation, both with 480 features (i.e. chosen POIs). If 24 cores (as a parameter for the PyTorch library) are used with the hardware specified above, we get the following times:

For one bit of the private key, it takes 4 234 seconds (1 h 10 min 34 s) to do the grid search hyperparameter tuning. For all the bits of the private key with parameter $N = 17\,669$, that would be 74 810 546 s (865d 20 h 42 min 26 s).

Such an effort would probably not be justifiable by an actual attacker, so further optimizations of the attack would need to occur despite achieving slightly worse results in total. Such optimizations could be to 1) avoid tuning MLP models for each bit and instead re-use the hyperparameters trained on a smaller subset of selected bits for the others or 2) train the MLP models on several bits at once.

Our results from the grid search show that from the first 25 bits, almost all winning models had the following structure: two hidden layers with ReLU activation function with 512 and 128 nodes, respectively, with batch normalization layer between them and batch size 200. The only exceptions have been winning models for the 4th and 21st bit, where for the 4th bit, better results had a model with 256 nodes in the second layer and batch size 800; for the 21st bit, the only difference was in batch size to be 500. As we described earlier, in all cases, the output layer consists of 1 node with a sigmoid activation function.

To see how difficult the classification problem we are facing in terms of SCA, we provide Signal-to-Noise Ratio (SNR) [Man04] for our data in Table 2. More specifically, a maximum, mean and min of SNR from 480 POIs for each bit.

3.3 Attack Results

Trained models after hyper-parameter tuning are tested on 20 000 samples, each with 480 features (selected POIs), corresponding to 20 000 independently measured traces, each with unique random ciphertext and private key. In Fig. 2, we see each model's number of misclassifications on the corresponding key-bit it was trained for. From 20 000 traces, trained models made very few wrong guesses for

Table 2. Max, mean and min of SNR from POIs for individual bits of the private key (restricted just to the first 24 bits as an example).

private key bit	0	1	2	3	4	5	6	7	8	9	10	11
max SNR	12.38	10.93	11.04	21.91	9.70	8.60	10.83	14.80	9.06	6.89	9.97	14.32
mean SNR	0.49	0.47	0.54	0.97	0.88	0.85	0.87	1.18	0.83	0.80	0.83	1.16
min SNR	0.02	0.03	0.02	0.02	0.14	0.08	0.08	0.11	0.13	0.07	0.10	0.11

private key bit	12	13	14	15	16	17	18	19	20	21	22	23
max SNR	9.17	7.02	10.32	15.18	9.00	7.00	10.21	14.61	9.04	6.68	10.32	14.46
mean SNR	0.86	0.80	0.83	1.14	0.87	0.81	0.84	1.15	0.84	0.79	0.83	1.13
min SNR	0.14	0.07	0.10	0.11	0.08	0.07	0.10	0.08	0.13	0.07	0.07	0.09

the key-bit. Note that each testing trace is independent (with a unique random private key), and we do not exploit information from other traces from the testing dataset to find the key bits that correspond to the trace we test at the moment. Therefore, we are in the single-trace attack scenario. That is important for us because HQC, as other KEMs from NIST PQC competition, is expected to be used in an ephemeral way so that for each shared key which results from the KEM, a new pair of private and public keys is generated and used. When HQC is used in an ephemeral way, the attacker can effectively run only single-trace attacks.

Taking in mind that the length of the private key according to the NIST submission parameters would in practice be 17 669, 35 851, or 57 637, depending on the security level, for full recovery of the private key it would be necessary to do some further processing using classical cryptanalytical techniques or brute-force through residual entropy in the private key.

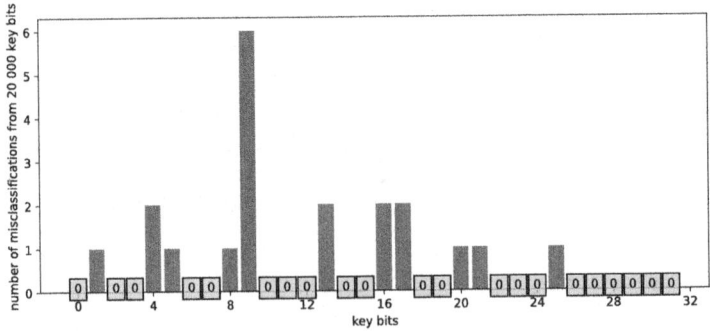

Fig. 2. Results of the attack phase for recovering the individual bits from the private key. The height of the columns corresponds to the misclassifications of individual bits. Most of the bits have been recovered with perfect accuracy. The worst result was for the 9th bit with 6 errors of 20 000, i.e. with the accuracy of 0.9997.

4 Proposed Countermeasures

In this section, we present and evaluate two countermeasures implemented at the base_mul level. The first one, presented in Sect. 4.1, exploits the windows technique used in Brent et al. [BGTZ08] to introduce some randomness but can protect only one out of three bits. The second countermeasure corresponds to a classical masking technique [GP99,ISW03]. Due to the high linearity of the polynomial multiplication over GF(2), Boolean masking presented in Sect. 4.2 is highly competitive.

Both countermeasures are based on Boolean secret sharing. The idea of such countermeasure is to split the sensitive value s into several shares s_i such that $\bigoplus_i s_i = s$.

4.1 Windowing the Self-unmasking

The idea of this countermeasure is to exploit the linearity of polynomial multiplication and the windows technique. Instead of scanning the bits of the first input a in groups of 4 bits independently through the loop described in Line 23

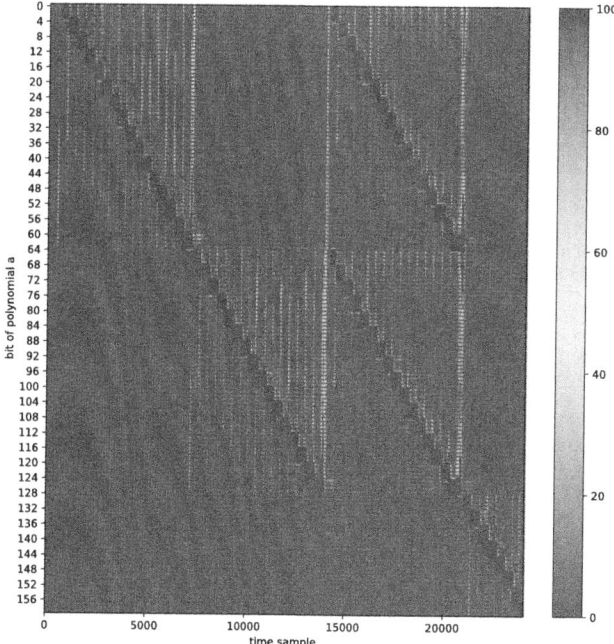

Fig. 3. Heat map of F-statistics from the Welch's ANOVA test for the first 160 bits of the "additional implementation" polynomial multiplication. Three whole calls to base_mul are visible; Dependence on $a_{63..0}$, then $a_{127..64}$, and then $a_{63..0} + a_{127..64}$ corresponds to the base case of a recursive Karatsuba multiplication.

of Listing 1, we use Line 28 of Listing 2, i.e. we overlap the scanning of one bit. If we look at two consecutive iterations of the loop, we can see that the value of the MSB of the ith iteration $MSB(a, i) = a[i \times 3 + 3]$ and the LSB of the $(i + 1)$th iteration $LSB(a, i + 1) = a[(i + 1) \times 3]$ are the same value. So we can mask only this bit, and thus unmask on the fly.

Example 1. With the overlapping window, we scan the bits of a by groups of 4 bits but shift the windows of three. For $a = a_0 + a_1 X + a_2 X^2 + a_3 X^3 + a_4 X^4 + a_5 X^5 + a_6 X^6 + a_7 X^7$, we first consider $a_0 + a_1 X + a_2 X^2 + a_3 X^3$ and next $a_3 X^3 + a_4 X^4 + a_5 X^5 + a_6 X^6$, which means by using bit operation we can choose to perform the multiplication by $a_3 X^3$ either in the first iteration or the second iteration.

```
void base_mul_prot(uint64_t *c, uint64_t a, uint64_t b) {
    uint64_t h = 0;
    uint64_t l = 0;
    uint64_t g;
    uint64_t u[16] = {0};
    uint64_t mask_tab[4] = {0};
    // Step 1
    u[0] = 0;
    u[1] = b & ((1ULL << (64 - 4)) - 1ULL);
    for(int i=2;i<16;i+=2){
        u[i] = u[i/2] << 1;
        u[i+1] = u[i] ^ u[1];
    }
    g=0;
    uint64_t tmp1 = a &15;
    uint64_t at=a;
    uint64_t bit=rand()%2;
    tmp1^= (bit<<3);
    for(int i = 0; i < 16; i++) {
        uint64_t tmp2 = tmp1 - i;
        g ^= (u[i] & -(1 - ((tmp2 | -tmp2) >> 63)));
    }
    at&=((-1ull)^(1ull<<(3)));
    at|=(bit<<(3));
    l = g;
    h = 0;
    // Step 2
    for (uint8_t i = 3; i < 60; i += 3) {
        g = 0;
        uint64_t bit=rand()%2;
        uint64_t tmp1 = (at >> i) & 15 ;
        tmp1^= (bit<<3);
        for (int j = 0; j < 16; ++j) {
            uint64_t tmp2 = tmp1 - j;
            g ^= (u[j] & -(1 - ((tmp2 | -tmp2) >> 63)));
        }
        at&=((-1ull)^(1ull<<(i+3)));
        at|=(bit<<(i+3));
        l ^= g << i;
        h ^= g >> (64 - i);
    }
    uint8_t i=60;
    g = 0;
    tmp1 = (at >> i) & 15 ;
    for (int j = 0; j < 16; ++j) {
        uint64_t tmp2 = tmp1 - j;
        g ^= (u[j] & -(1 - ((tmp2 | -tmp2) >> 63)));
    }
    l ^= g << i;
```

```
    h ^= g >> (64 - i);
    // Step 3
    mask_tab [0] = - ((b >> 60) & 1);
    mask_tab [1] = - ((b >> 61) & 1);
    mask_tab [2] = - ((b >> 62) & 1);
    mask_tab [3] = - ((b >> 63) & 1);
    l ^= ((a << 60) & mask_tab[0]);
    h ^= ((a >> 4) & mask_tab[0]);
    l ^= ((a << 61) & mask_tab[1]);
    h ^= ((a >> 3) & mask_tab[1]);
    l ^= ((a << 62) & mask_tab[2]);
    h ^= ((a >> 2) & mask_tab[2]);
    l ^= ((a << 63) & mask_tab[3]);
    h ^= ((a >> 1) & mask_tab[3]);
    c[0] = l;
    c[1] = h;
}
```

Listing 2. Windowing the self-unmasking implementation of base_mul.

The introduction of this low entropy masking helps us to reduce the effectiveness of the attack, as shown by the heat map in Fig. 4a. Compared with the heat map of the additional implementation, we can notice that instead of having a vertical block of 4 bits, we have a block of 2 bits plus a third one with less information. The two effects can be explained by the fact that 2 bits remain unmasked so it is natural to have information about them, the third one is masked so we have no information, and this third bit appears in two consecutive multiplications, once as the MSB and then as the LSB.

We can still see the thin vertical line for each bit before each computation, confirming that this leakage is due to the selection of the window of a.

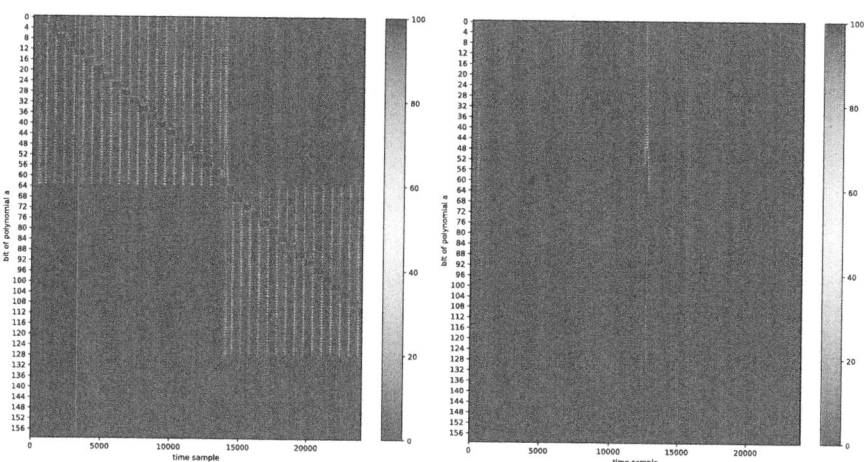

(a) Self-unmasking base_mul_prot function

(b) Masked implementation with 2 shares, base_mul_mask

Fig. 4. Heat map of F-statistics from the Welch's ANOVA test for the first 160 bits of the two variants of the protected implementation of base_mul.

It is obvious that the execution time of a single base multiplication is considerably longer than that of the additional implementation. In the additional implementation, this corresponds to 6 500 points in the trace, while with the window self-unmasking, the multiplication corresponds to slightly less than 14 000 points. The observed increase in execution time is unexpected given the number of iterations of the loop, which is 15 in the additional implementation and 20 in the proposed approach. A 33% increase was anticipated. However, the proposed approach involves a significant amount of bit manipulation of 64-bit words in a 32-bit microcontroller, which results in a considerable increase in the number of instructions.

4.2 Full Mask Implementation

In this section, we evaluate the security of the classical Boolean masking at the base_mul level. The inputs, designated as a and b, are passed to the function unmasked. In our case study, only the value a is sensitive; consequently, we only mask this value. This is illustrated by Lines 10-11 in Listing 3. Subsequently, a random mask, designated as $mask$, is generated and xored with the sensitive value, $a = a \oplus mask$. The subsequent step involves the exploitation of the linearity of polynomial multiplication to perform operations on the two shares independently. This is then followed by the unmasking of the result, as illustrated in lines 77 and 78.

Of course, since the inputs are unmasked, we expect some leakage, but we wanted to evaluate if some security could be achieved even in a lazy engineering way by a first order masking with only two shares for long computation in between the shares, this may indicate that the results of [BGG+14] are pessimistic.

```
void base_mul_mask(uint64_t *c, uint64_t a, uint64_t b) {
    uint64_t h = 0;
    uint64_t l = 0;
    uint64_t hm = 0;
    uint64_t lm = 0;
    uint64_t g;
    uint64_t u[16] = {0};
    uint64_t mask_tab[4] = {0};
    uint64_t mask = rand();
    mask=(mask*(1ull<<31)+rand())*(1ull<<33)+(rand()%4);
    a=a^mask;
    // Step 1
    u[0] = 0;
    u[1] = b & ((1ULL << (64 - 4)) - 1ULL);
    for(int i=2;i<16;i+=2){
        u[i] = u[i/2] << 1;
        u[i+1] = u[i] ^ u[1];
    }
    g=0;
    uint64_t tmp1 = (a) &15;
    for(int i = 0; i < 16; i++) {
        uint64_t tmp2 = tmp1 - i;
        g ^= (u[i] & -(1 - ((tmp2 | -tmp2) >> 63)));
    }
    l = g;
    h = 0;
    g=0;
```

```
    tmp1 = (mask) &15;
    for(int i = 0; i < 16; i++) {
     uint64_t tmp2 = tmp1 - i;
     g ^= (u[i] & -(1 - ((tmp2 | -tmp2) >> 63)));
    }
    lm = g;
    hm = 0;
    // Step 2
    for (uint8_t i = 4; i < 64; i += 4) {
     g = 0;
     uint64_t tmp1 = ((a) >> i) &15;
     for (int j = 0; j < 16; ++j) {
      uint64_t tmp2 = tmp1 - j;
      g ^= (u[j] & -(1 - ((tmp2 | -tmp2) >> 63)));
     }
     l ^= g << i;
     h ^= g >> (64 - i);
    }
    for (uint8_t i = 4; i < 64; i += 4) {
     g = 0;
     uint64_t tmp1 = ((mask) >> i) &15;
     for (int j = 0; j < 16; ++j) {
      uint64_t tmp2 = tmp1 - j;
      g ^= (u[j] & -(1 - ((tmp2 | -tmp2) >> 63)));
     }
     l ^= g << i;
     h ^= g >> (64 - i);
    }
    // Step 3
    mask_tab [0] = - ((b >> 60) & 1);
    mask_tab [1] = - ((b >> 61) & 1);
    mask_tab [2] = - ((b >> 62) & 1);
    mask_tab [3] = - ((b >> 63) & 1);
    l ^= (((a) << 60) & mask_tab[0]);
    h ^= (((a) >> 4) & mask_tab[0]);
    l ^= (((a) << 61) & mask_tab[1]);
    h ^= (((a) >> 3) & mask_tab[1]);
    l ^= (((a) << 62) & mask_tab[2]);
    h ^= (((a) >> 2) & mask_tab[2]);
    l ^= (((a) << 63) & mask_tab[3]);
    h ^= (((a) >> 1) & mask_tab[3]);
    lm ^= (((mask) << 60) & mask_tab[0]);
    hm ^= (((mask) >> 4) & mask_tab[0]);
    lm ^= (((mask) << 61) & mask_tab[1]);
    hm ^= (((mask) >> 3) & mask_tab[1]);
    lm ^= (((mask) << 62) & mask_tab[2]);
    hm ^= (((mask) >> 2) & mask_tab[2]);
    lm ^= (((mask) << 63) & mask_tab[3]);
    hm ^= (((mask) >> 1) & mask_tab[3]);
    c[0] = l^lm;
    c[1] = h^hm;
}
```

Listing 3. Masked implementation of base_mul.

As demonstrated by the heat map in Fig. 4b, the computation demonstrates minimal leakage of the value of a. However, the emergence of such leakage is discernible when computing the final two lines, specifically in the unmasking segment. Additionally, a minor leakage was initially observed during the execution of the computation, which is anticipated given that the data loaded into the function is unprotected. It is also worth mentioning that the highest and lowest bits of a are more susceptible to leakage. This phenomenon can be attributed to the fact that, in the context of multiplication, the output monomials of the highest and lowest degrees are more dependent on a single bit, as a result of the inherent nature of the multiplication operation. Furthermore, as we are utilizing sparse polynomials, this may be valid for several monomials.

It is somewhat unexpected that the computation does not exhibit significant leakage when manipulating the share. This suggests that in the case of long linear operations, where shares are manipulated that are longer than the word considered in the result of reference [BGG+14], the aforementioned security estimate may be overly pessimistic.

It can be observed that the computation time of the full masked implementation is comparable to that of the windowing self-unmasked implementation and is approximately twice that of the unprotected base_mul. This is to be expected, given that the operations are GF(2)-linear and Boolean secret sharing is employed.

4.3 Comparison of Implementations

We compare the three different implementations in terms of efficiency and security improvement for the attack. Because of the hardware memory limitations (see Sect. 2.2), we did not perform the attack on all bits of the private key, but we restricted our practical evaluation to the first 25 bits. In Table 3, we provide the mean of bit error ϵ_{bit} for this subset and compute extrapolated values of naive complexity [ZBHV21] and success rate for $n = 1234$ and $n = 17669$. The success rate is calculated simply as $(1 - \epsilon_{bit})^n$, which gives us a probability of perfect recovery of the private key from a single trace. For estimating the remaining entropy for the attacker to brute-force potentially wrongly predicted bits, we use naive complexity $\mathcal{C}_{NC}$ computed as

$$\mathcal{C}_{NC}(n, \epsilon_{bit}) = \log_2 \left(\sum_{i=0}^{\lceil n \cdot \epsilon_{bit} \rceil} \binom{n}{i} \right).$$

We can see that for NIST security level 1 with parameter $n = 17669$ we get 51.1% probability for the additional implementation with base_mul from

Table 3. Comparison of the different approaches

	Additional implementation	Self-unmasking	Full-mask
# clock cycles	6.5k	14k	14k
random bits	0	20	64
Max F-statistic	198 607	41 226	4 381
Mean bit-error ϵ_{bit}	3.8e-05	0.008	0.048
Naive complexity ($n = 1234$)	10.27	80.86	337.69
Success rate ($n = 1234$)	0.954	4.5e-05	8.22e-27
Naive complexity ($n = 17669$)	14.11	1194.30	4868.05
Success rate ($n = 17669$)	0.511	7.4e-63	3.2e-374

the NIST submission. The naive complexity is only 14.11, which shows that the key recovery attack is highly practical. For the proposed mitigation described in Sect. 4.1, we get the naive complexity of 80.86, putting the attack on the border of feasibility. For the full mask implementation described in Sect. 4.2, we get the naive complexity of 337.69, making this particular SCA attack worse than the state-of-the-art cryptanalytic attacks on code-based cryptosystems.

5 Conclusion

In this paper, we presented a new attack on HQC post-quantum cryptosystem targeting only polynomial multiplication used in the decryption operation. We have shown and verified that a significant part of the private key can be extracted using a power side-channel attack on the Karatsuba algorithm with base_mul function. This function is used by the additional implementation of HQC in the NIST submission, a pure C constant-time implementation of the cryptosystem provided by the submitters into the NIST PQC competition. This implementation is of high relevance because it is imported also by the PQClean library [KSSW22,PQC] from the Open Quantum Safe (OQS) project, and the algorithm itself is used by BouncyCastle libraries for Java [Boub] and C# [Boua].

The proposed attack is the first attack targeting the polynomial multiplication in the beginning of the HQC decryption and the first single-trace SCA attack against HQC cryptosystem which targets the private key. In our attack, we assume that the attacker can acquire power traces during the profiling/training phase on the same or similar device. During the attacking/testing phase we use only one trace for the private key extraction. We used the Welch's ANOVA test for POI selection and multi-layer perceptron models for classification of the private-key bits.

We presented experimental results of the attack, which has been realized on the ChipWhisperer-Lite platform featuring the 32-bit STM32F303RBT6 Arm Cortex-M4 target processor. For the practical evaluation, we used 40 000 traces for training, 10 000 traces for validation and independent 20 000 traces for the attack itself, with reduced size of the private key because of the hardware limitations. We used a unique random ciphertext and private key for each trace with the intention to get as close to the real scenario as possible. The results show that we can recover the private key with 51.1% probability for NIST security level 1, threatening the security of the cryptosystem if such implementation is used in practice to protect sensitive data.

We also implemented two possible mitigations with different performance and randomness costs and evaluated our attack on them. Our results show that both mitigations protect the private key to a sufficient level, making the attack unfeasible in practice.

5.1 Future Work

There are several directions for future work that we consider beneficial. The first is an evaluation of the attack scheme on a more powerful processor that would be able to run HQC with full parameters. The second is to implement more machine learning methods and classical template attacks with a comparison of their effectiveness. The third would be a more granular study of specific assembler operations inside Karatsuba and `base_mul` functions with respect to the compiling process and target processor together with evaluation of their differences in leakage and possible more precise targeting of these operations during the attack. The fourth is relaxing the attacker's abilities by exploring distant electromagnetic leakage in contrast to power analysis.

Acknowledgements. This work was supported by the Grant Agency of the Czech Technical University in Prague, grant No. SGS23/211/OHK3/3T/18 funded by the MEYS of the Czech Republic, and also by the Project Barrande No.8J23FR012, funded by the MEYS of the Czech Republic.

References

AAC+22. Alagic, G., et al.: Status report on the third round of the NIST post-quantum cryptography standardization process. Technical report, US Department of Commerce, National Institute of Standards and Technology (2022)

AYH+24. Ansel, J., et al.: PyTorch 2: faster machine learning through dynamic python bytecode transformation and graph compilation. In: 29th ACM International Conference on Architectural Support for Programming Languages and Operating Systems, Volume 2 (ASPLOS 2024). ACM (2024)

BGG+14. Balasch, J., Gierlichs, B., Grosso, V., Reparaz, O., Standaert, F.X.: On the cost of lazy engineering for masked software implementations. In: Joye, M., Moradi, A. (eds.) Smart Card Research and Advanced Applications - 13th International Conference, CARDIS 2014, Paris, France, November 5–7, 2014. Revised Selected Papers, volume 8968 of Lecture Notes in Computer Science, pp. 64–81. Springer (2014). https://doi.org/10.1007/978-3-319-16763-3_5

BGTZ08. Brent, R.P., Gaudry, P., Thomé, E., Zimmermann, P.: Faster Multiplication in GF(2)[x]. In: van der Poorten, A.J., Stein, A. (eds.) ANTS 2008. LNCS, vol. 5011, pp. 153–166. Springer, Heidelberg (2008). https://doi.org/10.1007/978-3-540-79456-1_10

Bis06. Bishop, C.: Pattern recognition and machine learning. Springer (2006). https://doi.org/10.1007/978-3-319-16763-3_5

BMvT78. Berlekamp, E., McEliece, R., van Tilborg, H.: On the inherent intractability of certain coding problems (coresp.). IEEE Trans. Inf. Theory **24**(3), 384–386 (1978)

Boua. Bouncy Castle. Bouncy Castle – C#, HQC implementation, GF2PolynomialCalculator. https://github.com/bcgit/bc-csharp/blob/master/crypto/src/pqc/crypto/hqc/GF2PolynomialCalculator.cs. Accessed 17 Dec 2024

Boub. Bouncy Castle. Bouncy Castle – Java, HQC implementation, GF2PolynomialCalculator. https://github.com/bcgit/bc-java/blob/main/core/src/main/java/org/bouncycastle/pqc/crypto/hqc/GF2PolynomialCalculator.java. Accessed 17 Dec 2024

C+15. Chollet, F., et al.: Keras (2015). https://keras.io

CD23. Castryck, W., Decru, T.: An efficient key recovery attack on SIDH. In: Annual International Conference on the Theory and Applications of Cryptographic Techniques, pp. 423–447. Springer (2023). https://doi.org/10.1007/978-3-031-30589-4_15

Cer23. Cerulli, G.: The Basics of Machine Learning, pp. 30–33. Springer International Publishing, Cham (2023)

DG24. Dong, H., Guo, Q.: OT-PCA: new key-recovery plaintext-checking oracle based side-channel attacks on HQC with offline templates. Cryptology ePrint Archive (2024)

GLG22. Goy, G., Loiseau, A., Gaborit, P.: A new key recovery side-channel attack on HQC with chosen ciphertext. In: International Conference on Post-Quantum Cryptography, pp. 353–371. Springer (2022). https://doi.org/10.1007/978-3-031-17234-2_17

GMGL24. Goy, G., Maillard, J., Gaborit, P., Loiseau, A.: Single trace HQC shared key recovery with SASCA. IACR Trans. Cryptographic Hardware Embed. Syst. **2024**(2), 64–87 (2024)

GP99. Goubin, L., Patarin, J.: DES and differential power analysis the "duplication" method. In: Koç, Ç.K., Paar, C. (eds.) CHES 1999. LNCS, vol. 1717, pp. 158–172. Springer, Heidelberg (1999). https://doi.org/10.1007/3-540-48059-5_15

HQCa. HQC authors: HQC specification. https://pqc-hqc.org/doc/hqc-specification_2025-02-19.pdf. Accessed 8 Mar 2025

HQCb. HQC Authors: Submission of HQC – round 3 – with additional implementation. https://pqc-hqc.org/doc/hqc-submission_2023-04-30.zip. Accessed 27 Feb 2024

HQCc. HQC Authors: Submission of HQC – round 4 – latest – February 2025. https://pqc-hqc.org/doc/hqc-submission_2025-02-19.zip. Accessed 27 Feb 2024

HSC+23. Huang, S., Sim, R.Q., Chuengsatiansup, C., Guo, Q., Johansson, T.: Cache-timing attack against HQC. Cryptology ePrint Archive (2023)

IS15. Ioffe, S., Szegedy, C.: Batch normalization: accelerating deep network training by reducing internal covariate shift. *arXiv preprint*arXiv:1502.03167 (2015)

ISW03. Ishai, Y., Sahai, A., Wagner, D.: Private circuits: securing hardware against probing attacks. In: Boneh, D. (ed.) CRYPTO 2003. LNCS, vol. 2729, pp. 463–481. Springer, Heidelberg (2003). https://doi.org/10.1007/978-3-540-45146-4_27

KSSW22. Kannwischer, M.J., Schwabe, P., Stebila, D., Wiggers, T.: Improving software quality in cryptography standardization projects. In: IEEE European Symposium on Security and Privacy, EuroS&P 2022 - Workshops, Genoa, Italy, June 6–10, 2022, pp. 19–30. IEEE Computer Society, Los Alamitos (2022)

LH17. Loshchilov, I., Hutter, F.: Decoupled weight decay regularization. arXiv preprint arXiv:1711.05101 (2017)

MAB+18. Melchor, C.A., et al.: Hamming quasi-cyclic (HQC). NIST PQC Round **2**(4), 13 (2018)

Man04. Mangard, S.: Hardware countermeasures against DPA – A statistical analysis of their effectiveness. In: Okamoto, T. (ed.) CT-RSA 2004. LNCS, vol. 2964, pp. 222–235. Springer, Heidelberg (2004). https://doi.org/10.1007/978-3-540-24660-2_18

NSB+23. Newhouse, W., et al.: Migration to post-quantum cryptography quantum readiness: testing draft standards. Technical Report NIST Special Publication 1800-38C, US Department of Commerce, National Institute of Standards and Technology (2023)

OBL+19. O'Malley, T., et al.: Kerastuner (2019). https://github.com/keras-team/keras-tuner

PQC. PQClean: PQClean, HQC implementation, gf2x.c. https://github.com/PQClean/PQClean/blob/master/crypto_kem/hqc-128/clean/gf2x.c. Accessed 16 Dec 2024

Sho94. Shor, P.W.: Algorithms for quantum computation: discrete logarithms and factoring. In: Proceedings 35th Annual Symposium on Foundations of Computer Science, pp. 124–134. IEEE (1994)

SHR+22. Schamberger, T., Holzbaur, L., Renner, J., Wachter-Zeh, A., Sigl, G.: A power side-channel attack on the reed-muller reed-solomon version of the HQC cryptosystem. In: International Conference on Post-Quantum Cryptography, pp. 327–352. Springer (2022). https://doi.org/10.1007/978-3-031-17234-2_16

SRSWZ21. Schamberger, T., Renner, J., Sigl, G., Wachter-Zeh, A.: A power side-channel attack on the CCA2-secure HQC KEM. In: Liardet, P.-Y., Mentens, N. (eds.) CARDIS 2020. LNCS, vol. 12609, pp. 119–134. Springer, Cham (2021). https://doi.org/10.1007/978-3-030-68487-7_8

SVP+24. Spyropoulos, M., Vigilant, D., Perion, F., Pacalet, R., Sauvage, L.: Masked vector sampling for HQC. Cryptology ePrint Archive (2024)

UXT+22. Ueno, R., Xagawa, K., Tanaka, Y., Ito, A., Takahashi, J., Homma, N.: Curse of re-encryption: a generic power/EM analysis on post-quantum KEMs. In: IACR Transactions on Cryptographic Hardware and Embedded Systems, pp. 296–322 (2022)

Val18. Vallat, R.: Pingouin: statistics in Python. J. Open Source Softw. **3**(31), 1026 (2018)

Wel51. Bernard Lewis Welch: On the comparison of several mean values: an alternative approach. Biometrika **38**(3/4), 330–336 (1951)

YJ21. Yang, W., Jia, A.: Side-channel leakage detection with one-way analysis of variance. Secur. Commun. Netw. **2021**(1), 6614702 (2021)

ZBHV21. Zaid, G., Bossuet, L., Habrard, A., Venelli, A.: Efficiency through diversity in ensemble models applied to side-channel attacks:–a case study on public-key algorithms–. In: IACR Transactions on Cryptographic Hardware and Embedded Systems, pp. 60–96 (2021)

Author Index

A
Abdelmonem, Mohamed 185
Aghaie, Anita 211

B
Bauer, Sven 211
Béguinot, Julien 387
Berzati, Alexandre 3
Botocan, Cristian-Alexandru 505
Buček, Jiří 580

C
Cayrel, Pierre-Louis 67, 311
Chancel, Geoffrey 410
Chartouny, Maya 3
Cheng, Wei 387
Cler, Gauthier 554
Colombier, Brice 67

D
D'Anvers, Jan-Pieter 119
Danger, Jean-Luc 387
Debande, Nicolas 45
Devevey, Julien 93
Drăgoi, Vlad-Florin 67

E
Escouteloup, Mathieu 478
Eynard, Julien 343

G
Galissant, Pierre 261
Gierlichs, Benedikt 429
Goubin, Louis 261
Grosso, Vincent 67, 311, 580
Guerreau, Morgane 93

H
Hiltenbrand, Aymeric 343
Holzbaur, Lukas 185
Husum, Stian 367

K
Kamel, Dina 159
Koleci, Kristjane 211
Kühne, Ulrich 387
Kundu, Suparna 119

L
Legavre, Thomas 93
Lórencz, Róbert 580

M
Mailly, Frédérick 410
Mainka, Linus 451
Marçais, David 291
Martinelli, Ange 93
Maurine, Philippe 410
Maurine, Philippe 554
Meier, Lucas David 505
Migliore, Vincent 478
Minghui, Zhao 532

N
Nasir, Neelam 387
Nguyen, Viet Sang 311
Norga, Quinten 119
Nouet, Pascal 410

O
Ordas, Sebastien 554

P
Pace, Pierugo 235
Papagiannopoulos, Kostas 451
Pelletier, Hervé 235
Poussier, Romain 343

R
Rabas, Tomáš 580
Raddum, Håvard 185, 367
Ricosset, Thomas 93

S
Santis, Fabrizio De 211
Sarde, Vladimir 45
Schupp, Jonas 27
Sigl, Georg 27
Sluys, Pcy 429
Stam, Martijn 367
Standaert, François-Xavier 159

T
Toulemont, Julien 410

V
Valencia, Felipe 505
Vaudenay, Serge 235
Verbauwhede, Ingrid 119, 429
Viera, Andersson Calle 3
Vigilant, David 3
Vizár, Damian 505

W
Wouters, Lennert 429
Wurcker, Antoine 291

Y
Yap, Trevor 532

Z
Zeh, Alexander 185
Zenknerová, Karolína 580

Made in the USA
Monee, IL
03 May 2026

49438652R00339